A NEW VARIORUM EDITION OF

SHAKESPEARE

Othello

Edited by

HORACE HOWARD FURNESS

Dover Publications, Inc.
New York   New York

This new Dover edition, first published in 1963, is an unabridged republication of the work first published by J. B. Lippincott & Company in 1886, to which has been added a detailed Table of Contents.

Manufactured in the United States of America

Dover Publications, Inc.
180 Varick Street
New York 14, N. Y.

3-1303-00033-2511

IN MEMORIAM

— NEITHER PRESENT TIME, NOR YEARS UNBORN
CAN TO MY SIGHT THAT HEAVENLY FACE RESTORE.

CONTENTS

Preface v
THE TRAGEDIE OF OTHELLO, THE MOORE OF
VENICE 1
   Act I, Scene i 1
     Scene ii 29
     Scene iii 43
   Act II, Scene i 91
     Scene ii 124
   Act III, Scene i 154
     Scene ii 158
     Scene iii 159
     Scene iv 215
   Act IV, Scene i 232
     Scene ii 254
     Scene iii 274
   Act V, Scene i 283
     Scene ii 291
   The Names of the Actors 335
Appendix 339
   The Text 339
   The Date of Composition 344
   Date of the Action 357
   Duration of the Action 358
   The Source of the Plot 372
   Othello's Colour 389
   Actors 396
   Costume 404
   English Criticisms 407
   German Criticisms 431
   French Criticisms 447
   Can Shakespeare be Translated? 453
   List of Editions Collated in the Textual Notes . . 459
   List of Books from which Extracts have been Made . . 463
Index 467

PREFACE

THE SHAKESPEARE Club,—'many millions strong' as CHRISTOPHER NORTH says,—is made up of readers of Shakespeare and students of Shakespeare. All are readers, and some at times students. When reading Shakespeare, we resign ourselves to the mighty current, and let it bear us along whithersoever it will; we see no shoals, heed no rocks, need no pilot. Whether spoken from rude boards or printed in homely form, the words are Shakespeare's, the hour is his, and a thought of texts is an impertinence.

But when we study Shakespeare, then our mood changes; no longer are we 'sitting at a play,' the passive recipients of impressions through the eye and ear, but we weigh every word, analyse every expression, sift every phrase, that no grain of art or beauty which we can assimilate shall escape. To do this to our best advantage we must have Shakespeare's own words before us. No other words will avail, even though they be those of the wisest and most inspired of our day and generation. We must have Shakespeare's own text; or, failing this, the nearest possible approach to it. We shall be duly grateful to the wise and learned, who, where phrases are obscure, give us the words which they believe to have been Shakespeare's; but, as students, we must have under our eyes the original text, which, however stubborn it may seem at times, may yet open its treasures to our importunity, and reveal charms before undreamed of.

This original text is to be found in the First edition of his Works, published in 1623, and usually known as the FIRST FOLIO, which was presumably printed from the words written by Shakespeare's own hand, or from Stage copies adapted from his manuscripts. Be it that the pages of this First Folio are little better than proof-sheets, lacking supervision of the author or of any other, yet 'those who had Shakespeare's manuscript before them were more likely to read it right than we who read it only in imagination,' as Dr JOHNSON said.   Even grant that the First Folio is, as has been asserted, one of the most carelessly printed books ever issued from the press, it is, nevertheless, the only text that we have for at least sixteen of the plays, and condemn it as we may, 'still is its name in great account, it still hath power to charm' for all of them.   Can any good reason be urged why, in this present play at least, we should not, in the hours devoted to study, be it remembered, have the text of the First Folio as our guide?   Is there not every reason why we should?   If misspellings occur here and there, surely our common-school education is not so uncommon that we cannot silently correct them.   If the punctuation be deficient, surely it can be supplied without an exorbitant demand upon our intelligence.   And in lines incurably maimed by the printers, of what avail is the voice of a solitary editor amid the Babel that vociferates around, each voice proclaiming the virtues of its own specific?   Who am I that I should thrust myself in between the student and the text, as though in me resided the power to restore Shakespeare's own words?   Even if a remedy be proposed which is by all acknowledged to be efficacious, it is not enough for the student that he should know the remedy; he must see the ailment.   Let the ailment, therefore, appear in all its severity in the text, and let the remedies be exhibited in the notes; by this means we may make a text for ourselves, and thus made, it will become a part of ourselves, and speak to us with more power than were it made for us by the wisest editor of them all—it may be 'an ill-favoured thing, sir,' but—it will be 'our own.'

Impressed with this belief, I have in this volume abandoned the plan, heretofore followed in this edition, and instead of giving a modernised text, have reproduced the First Folio, reprinting it from my own copy with all the exactitude in my power, scanning it letter by letter, and have recorded in the Notes the various readings of all other critical editions.   For a fuller exposition of what I have done, o· left undone, in this regard, and in regard to the text in general, I must refer to p. 460 of the Appendix.

I have long been of the opinion that in the interpretation of Shakespeare's plays, our first appeal, and perhaps our last, should be made
to the dramatic instinct, as it has been termed, with which eminent
Actors are especially endowed. To see KEAN, it has been said, was
to read Shakespeare by 'flashes of lightning.' Yet how seldom do
we find in Shakespearian Commentaries any reference to the dramatic
rendering of a character, or of a passage, by an eminent Actor. This
is, however, not altogether the fault of the Commentators. All who
have read much of the Biographies of Actors will, I think, agree with
me in the regret that explicit, specific descriptions of their acting are
so meagre. Of vague generalisations, conveying no definite ideas, we
have a superfluity; but of the tones, or looks, or emphasis on particular words or lines there is a plentiful lack. What help is given
to us by the information that nothing could surpass the fervour of
GARRICK's wooing as Romeo, or that MRS SIDDONS was wonderfully
tragic as Lady Macbeth? What we require is the report like that
of an eye-witness whose record is taken on the spot; then we shall
know Romeo's every tone and look when rich music's tongue unfolds
imagined happiness. There are, however, scattered here and there,
explicit definite descriptions of the treatment by eminent Actors of
various passages; those which I deemed worthy of preservation I
have recorded in the Commentary. At my solicitation my friend,
MR EDWIN BOOTH, wrote out for me, in an interleaved copy of this
play, much of his 'business;' I cannot but think that to others his
notes will be as interesting and as valuable as I have found them.
It is to be borne in mind for his sake that the notes were made
with no view to their being printed.

It cannot be but that, in the selection of notes for an edition like
the present, an editor, working single-handed, must be influenced
by his own tastes and predilections. I can honestly say, however,
that if I have been single-handed I have been also single-eyed,—
single-eyed to the one object of elucidating the text. We do not
go to Shakespeare to study grammar or scanning, but we study his
grammar that we may understand him, and arrange the scansion,
that every charm which rhythm can yield may be his, as of right.

Hence the prominence which I have given to all grammatical and verbal criticism; which is to be regarded solely as a means to an end. Without a complete understanding of the words the meaning of the whole sentence will be lost,—and is not the meaning of Shakespeare the very butt and sea-mark of our utmost sail? It is as contributors towards this object that I regard Actors, and have, therefore, recorded their interpretations. Herein the selection of notes for this volume has been influenced by my own preference. 'It is impossible,' says DR JOHNSON, 'for an expositor not to write too little for some, 'and too much for others. He can judge what is necessary only by 'his own experience; and how long soever he may deliberate, will at 'last explain many lines which the learned will think impossible to be 'mistaken, and omit many for which the ignorant will want his help. 'These are censures merely relative, and must be quietly endured.'

Since these words were written, a hundred and twenty years ago, what numberless busy 'expositors,' high and low, wise and simple, learned and ignorant, clerk and lay, at home and abroad, have been, down to this hour, poring over every Act, and Scene, over every line, and syllable! Is there anything left for us to explore or to discover? 'Gentlemen,' said DR BARCLAY in one of his Edinburgh Lectures, 'Anatomy may be likened to a harvest-field. First come the reapers, 'who, entering upon untrodden ground, cut down great store of corn 'from all sides of them. These are the early anatomists of modern 'Europe. Then come the gleaners, who gather up ears enough from 'the bare ridges to make a few loaves of bread. Such were the anat-'omists of the last century. Last of all come the geese, who still 'continue to pick up a few grains scattered here and there among the 'stubble, and waddle home in the evening, poor things, cackling 'with joy because of their success. Gentlemen, we are the geese'

The next play in this edition, if there ever be one, will be, probably, *The Merchant of Venice*.

To my Father, the REV. DR FURNESS, be my thanks pressed down and running over for all that he has done for me, especially for his translation of my selections from the German in the Appendix.

H. H. F.

MARCH, 1886

THE TRAGEDIE OF

Othello, the Moore of Venice.

Actus Primus. Scœna Prima.

[310 *a*]   *Enter Rodorigo, and Iago.*

Rodorigo.

Euer tell me, I take it much vnkindly

That thou (*Iago*) who haſt had my purſe,   5

---

1. Actus...Prima.] Om. Qq. Act. I, Scene I. Rowe.

2. [Scene Venice. Rowe.   Scene, a Street in Venice. Theob.

     Enter...] Enter *Iago* and *Roderigo.* Qq. Enter...Iago. Q'81, Rowe, Pope (so spelled throughout).

     4. *Neuer*] *Tuſh, neuer* Qq. Warb. Jen. Steev. Var. Coll. Sta. Wh. Glo. Cam. Dyce iii, Rlfe, Huds.

     4. *me,*] *me.* Johns. Steev.'73. *me ;* Jen. Dyce, Sta. Glo. Cam. Ktly, Rlfe, Huds Wh. ii.

     much] *very* Ff, Rowe.

     5. *thou*] *you* Q₁.

     Iago] Om. Q₂Q₃.

     haſt] *has* Q₁.

     had] *held* Cap. conj (p. 26 *α*).

---

1. SCENE.] FECHTER : A street in Venice—on the right a house with practicable door and window. Night. BOOTH : Venice. A dark street. Full stage.

2. The bracketed numbers and letters [310 *a*, etc.] indicate the page and column in F₁.

4. **Neuer**] COLERIDGE (*Notes*, &c., p. 247) : Admirable is the preparation, so truly and peculiarly Shakespearian, in the introduction of Roderigo, as the dupe on whom Iago shall first exercise his art, and in so doing display his own character. Roderigo, without any fixed principle, but not without the moral notions and sympathies with honour, which his rank and connections had hung upon him, is already well fitted and predisposed for the purpose; for very want of character and strength of passion, like wind loudest in an empty house, constitute his character. The first three lines happily state the nature and foundation of the friendship between him and Iago,—the purse,—as also the contrast of Roderigo's intemperance of mind with Iago's coolness,—the coolness of a preconceiving experimenter. The mere language of protestation,—' If ever I did dream of such a matter, abhor me,'—which, falling in with the associative link, determines Roderigo's continuation of complaint,—' Thou told'st me, thou didst hold him in thy hate,'—elicits at length a true feeling of Iago's mind, the dread of contempt habitual to those who encourage in themselves, and have their keenest pleasure in, the expression of contempt for others. Observe Iago's high self-opinion, and the moral, that a wicked man will employ real feelings, as well as assume those most alien from his own, as instruments of his purposes :—' And, by the faith of man, I know my

As if ỹ ſtrings were thine, ſhould'ſt know of this.   6
Ia. But you'l not heare me.   If euer I did dream

6. Two lines, F₄, Rowe.
this.] *this*— Han. Warb. Dyce, Sta.
this ; Cap.
7. *But*] *S'blood, but* Q₁. *'Sblood, but*
Jen. Steev. Var. Coll. Dyce, Sta. Wh. Glo.
Cam. Ktly, Clarke, Rlfe, Huds. *'Sdeath,*
but Fechter.
＇ *But...me.*] One line, QqF₄, Rowe +,
Cap. Jen. Steev. Var. Coll. Dyce, Sta.

Wh. Glo. Rlfe, Huds. *But...euer* One
line, Mal.
7. *you'l*] *you will* Q₁, Jen. Steev. Var.
Coll. Dyce, Wh. Glo. Cam. Rlfe, Huds.
you'le Q₂. *you'll* F₃F₄ et cet.
7, 8. *If...me.*] One line, Qq, Rowe +,
Jen. Var. Coll. Wh. i. *If...matter,* One
line, Han. Cap. Steev. Dyce, Sta. Wh. ii,
Glo. Cam. Rlfe, Huds.

price, I am worth no less a place.' [I am afraid that Collier 'frolicked in conjecture' when he suggests (ed. iii) that 'the interjection *Tush* may have been formed from
hush ; while *Tut* (often used) was probably an abbreviation of *Tell you what.*' SKEAT
cites *Prompt. Parv.*, where WAY (in a note s. v. *Ptrot*) says that ' Palsgrave observes, in
his enumeration of interjections, "Some be interiections of indignacion, *trut,* as *trut
auant, trut !*" "*Trut,* an interjection importing indignation, tush, tut, fy man. *Trut
avant,* a fig's end, no such matter, you are much deceived; also, on afore for shame."
Cotgrave.'—ED.]

4. me] KNIGHT believes that by the emphasis falling on 'me,' as here in the F, the
expression is somewhat more in Roderigo's vein, and that the omission of *Tush* was
not accidental.

6. this] HUDSON: The intended elopement. Roderigo has been suing for Desdemona's hand, employing Iago to aid him in his suit, and paying his service in advance.
The play opens pat upon her elopement with the Moor, and Roderigo presumes Iago
to have been in the secret of their intention.

7. But] KNIGHT, the first editor to proclaim an absolute trust in the First Folio,
and to give a reason for the faith that was in him, here at the very outset offers
battle. STEEVENS, following the Qq, had said that, 'the Folio suppresses the
oath *'sblood.*' The use of the word *suppresses* seems to cast a slur; and KNIGHT
is instantly on hand, 'but Steevens does not tell us,' he says, 'what the Folio does
besides. It accommodates the rhythmical arrangement of the sentence to the suppression of the oath. This is certainly not the work of some botcher coming after the
author. Such instances of right feeling and good taste, in the omission of offensive
expressions, constantly occur throughout this play in F₁. In the Qto such offensive
expressions are as constantly found. The modern editions cling to the Qto in this
particular, upon the supposition that in the Folio the passages were struck out by the
Master of the Revels. The Master of the Revels must have been an exceedingly
capricious person if he thus exercised his office in 1623, and thus neglected it in 1622.
We have not a doubt, seeing that the structure of the verse is always accommodated to
the alteration, that every such change was made by the author of the play. It was not
that the Master of the Revels was scrupulous in the use of his authority with F₂, and
negligent with Q₁, but that both Qto and Folio were printed at a period when the Statute of 1604 [*Qu.* 1605 ?] for restraining the profane use of the sacred name in stage-
plays, had fallen into neglect. But the Qto was printed from an early copy of the play
which existed before the Statute came into operation. The Folio contains the author's
additions and corrections. This would be a sufficient reason, if there were no other,
for preferring the text of the Folio in this as well as in other matters.' COLLIER (ed. i)

Of fuch a matter, abhorre me.   8
  Rodo. Thou told'ft me,
Thou did'ft hold him in thy hate.   10
  Iago. Defpife me
If I do not. Three Great-ones of the Cittie,
(In perfonall fuite to make me his Lieutenant)
Off-capt to him : and by the faith of man   14

8. *matter, abhorre me.*] *matter,*— Cap. *me.*] *me then.* Han.

9, 10. *Thou...hate.*] One line, Qq, Rowe+, Cap. Jen. Steev. Var. Knt, Coll. Sing. Dyce, Sta. Wh. Glo. Cam. Ktly, Rlfe, Huds. *Thou...hold* One line, Han.

11, 12. *Defpife...Cittie*] One line, Qq, Cap. Jen. Steev.Var. Knt, Coll. Sing. Dyce, Sta. Wh. Glo. Cam. Ktly, Rlfe, Huds.

11–18. Lines end *not...fuit...him... price...loving...with...ftufft...conclusion* (following Q₁) Han.

12. *Great-ones*] *great ones* Qq et cet.

13. *Lieutenant*] *Leiutenant* Q₁. *Lievetenant* F₂.

14. *Off-capt*] *Oft capt* Qq. *Oft capp'd* (subs.) Rowe, Pope, Han. Steev.Var. Coll. Sing. Ktly, Dyce iii, Huds.

---

is thoroughly conservative, observing that if the Master of the Revels expunged ''Sblood,' he certainly did not erase 'Tush,' and since both were probably written by Shakespeare, both had better be retained.

14. **Off-capt**] That is, says THEOBALD, stood cap in hand, soliciting him. So in *Ant. & Cleo.* II, vii, 64 : 'I have ever held my cap off to thy fortunes,' and in *Tim.* IV, iii, 212 : 'And let his very breath, whom thou'lt observe, Blow off thy cap.' JENNENS suggests that we are not to suppose that the Great ones *often* begged Othello, cap in hand, to promote Iago, and adds, ''tis very likely the original reading was *Off'd cap.*' The reading of the Qq, says RITSON (p. 225) is 'nonsense;' whereas an 'intimate knowledge of the Qq' convinces MALONE that 'they ought not without very strong reason to be departed from.' No such strong reason appears to him here, probably because to him as well as to all who adopt *oft capped*, MASON'S explanation seems conclusive, namely that 'to *cap* is to salute by taking off the cap. It is still an academic phrase.' KNIGHT comes to the defence of F₁, and, admitting that *to cap* in ancient academical phrase meant to take the cap off, and that it is so used by other early English authors, as in Drant's *Horace*, 1567, yet, asks Knight, 'is *oft capp'd* supported by the context? As we read the whole passage, three great ones of the city wait upon Othello; they "off-capp'd,"—they took cap-in-hand,—in personal suit that he should make Iago his lieutenant; but he evades them, &c. He has already chosen his officer. Here is a scene painted in a manner well befitting both the dignity of the great ones of the city and of Othello himself. The audience was given, the solicitation was humbly made, the reasons for refusing it courteously assigned. But take the other reading, *oft* capp'd; and then we have Othello perpetually haunted by the three great ones of the city, capping to him and repeating to him the same prayer, and he perpetually denying them with the same bombast circumstance. Surely this is not what Shakespeare meant to represent.' WHITE (ed. i) suggests that 'capped' seems 'to have meant to keep the cap on, not to take it off. For example: "And this of Paull, that a man should neither pray nor preach capped, or with his head covered, is also cleane abolished."—Cranmer's *Confutation of Unwritten Verities*, 1582, p. 62.' But DYCE (ed. iii) is not convinced, and after quoting Malone, opposes White with a definition from Coles's *Latin Dict.:* 'To cap a person, *coram aliquo caput aperire, nudare.*' [I

I know my price, I am worth no worſſe a place.   15
But he (as louing his owne pride, and purpoſes)
Euades them, with a bumbaſt Circumſtance,
Horribly ſtufft with Epithites of warre,
Non-ſuites my Mediators.   For certes, ſaies he,   19

15. *I am*] *I'm* Pope +, Dyce iii, Huds.
worſſe] *woſe* F₂.
16. *his owne*] *His* Han.
purpoſes] *purpoſe* Theob. Warb.
Johns.
17. *bumbaſt*] QqFf, Rowe, Pope, Han.
bombaſt Theob.
18. *Epithites*] *Epithets* F₃F₄.
18, 19. *warre, Non-ſuits*] Ff, Knt, Sing
ii. *warre: Non-ſuits* Q₂Q₃, Rowe. *warre:
And in concluſion, Nonſuits* Q₁ et cet.
18–21. Ending lines, *warre...conclu-*

ſion...ſayes he...was he?...Arithmetition
Q₁,Jen. Coll. *war...conclusion...says he...
officer...was he?...arithmetician* Pope +,
Cap. Rann, Dyce, Sta. Wh. Glo. Cam.
Rlfe. *war...mediators...already...was he?
...arithmetician* Mal. *war...nonsuits...
says he...officer...was he?...arithmetician*
Steev. Var. *war...mediators...officer.
arithmetician* Ktly. *war...mediators..
chose...was he?...arithmetician* (reading
I've) Huds.
19. *For certes*] *Certes* Pope +.

prefer F₂, which presents no difficulty. To Theobald's citations add *Tim*. II, i, 18, where the posture of importunity is represented as when 'the cap plays in the right hand.'—ED.]

17. **bumbast**] NARES: Originally cotton. Hence, because cotton was commonly used to stuff out quilting, &c., *bombast* also meant the stuffing of clothes, &c. Hence applied to tumid and inflated language. [Cotgrave gives: Cottoner. *To bumbast, or stuffe with cotton.*—ED.]

17. **Circumstance**] REED: That is, circumlocution. See *Greene's Tu Quoque* [p. 93, Dodsley] 'a needless labour, sir, To run and wind about for circumstance; When the plain word, "I thank you," would have serv'd.' Also in Massinger's *Picture* [I, i.] 'therefore, without circumstance, to the point.' [The editor of *Greene's Tu Quoque* calls attention to the great similarity between the line there cited and 'To wind about my love with circumstance' in *Mer. of Ven*. I, i, 154; conf. *Ham*. I, v, 127.—ED.] KNIGHT: *Iago* does not mean to say that Othello made a long rigmarole speech to the three great ones, and then in conclusion nonsuited the mediators by telling them that he had already chosen his officer. But, in the spirit of calumny, he imputes to Othello that, having chosen his officer before the personal suit was made to him for Iago, he suppressed the fact; evaded the mediators; and nonsuited them with a bombast circumstance. F₁ distinctly separates, *for, certes, says he*, from *nonsuits my mediators*. Othello, according to *Iago's* calumnious assertion, says the truth only to himself.

19. **Non-suites**] LORD CAMPBELL (p. 112): Here is a striking instance of Shakespeare's proneness to legal phraseology. *Nonsuiting* is known to the learned to be the most disreputable and mortifying mode of being beaten; it indicates that the action is wholly unfounded on the plaintiff's own showing, or that there is a fatal defect in the manner in which his case has been got up; insomuch that Mr. Chitty, the great special pleader, used to give this advice to young barristers practising at *nisi prius*:—'Always avoid your attorney when nonsuited, for till he has a little time for reflection, however much you may abuse the Judge, he will think that the nonsuit was all your fault.'

19. DYCE (ed. iii): 'F₁ and Q₂ wrongly omit "And, in conclusion;" but probably something has been lost before them.'—W. N. LETTSOM.

I haue already chofe my Officer. And what was he?   20
For-footh, a great Arithmatician, *Caſsio*
One *Michaell Caſſio*, a *Florentine*,
(A Fellow almoft damn'd in a faire Wife)   23

chofe] *chofen* Q₂, Jen. Steev.'78,'85,   *Arithmetician* Ff.
          22, 23. *a... Wife*](*a* Florentine's...*wife*)
Warb.

'*d*] *dambd* Qq.
wife QqF₂F₄.   *face* Cap.   *life*

PE in the omission of *For*, was
the edd. who follow the QqFf,
Rolfe, Huds. Wh. ii, mark the
For can be no part of Othello's
the quotation.—ED.

SCHMIDT (*Lex.* s. v.) says that
yllable, an assertion which I am
ich that admirable lexicographer
present line with *certes* as a dis-
promises no element,' is scanned
of which WALKER (*Vers.* p. 62)
es of 'certes' as a dissyllable in
espeare, almost any other word in
agree with Schmidt. 1887.]—ED.
& Jul. Mercutio says: 'one that
means to represent Cassio not as a
hird in your bosom,' but as a man
ew no more of a squadron than the
Iago refers to Cassio as a man whose
rely from books on tactics, wherein
'the movements requisit...   column, &c. are worked out numeri-
cally on the base of a tactical unit.'   C. A. .WN (*Sh.'s Autobiog. Poems*, p. 110),
in his essay to prove that Shakespeare had visited Italy, says that there was good
reason why Cassio, the Florentine, should be derisively termed by Iago 'a great arithmetician,' 'a counter-caster' with his 'debtor and creditor.' 'A soldier from Florence,
famous for its bankers throughout Europe, and for its invention of bills of exchange,
book-keeping, and everything connected with a counting-house, might well be ridiculed
for his promotion, by an Iago, in this manner.'

22. **Cassio**] BODENSTEDT (p. ix) says that Othello chose Cassio because he preferred him personally as a go-between in his wooing of Desdemona, and moreover it
ministered to Othello's pride to refuse the personal suit of the great ones of the city.

22, 23. **Florentine, . . . Wife**] THEOBALD maintains that Iago, not Cassio, was
the Florentine; and that 'wife' could not apply to Cassio, who was unmarried, but that
it does apply to Iago, whose 'fair wife' attends on Desdemona, and whose marriage
and possible subjection to his wife was one reason, probably, why Othello himself, an
unmarried man, rejected him as an officer. Iago is therefore the 'fellow almost damn'd
in a fair wife,' whereby Shakespeare 'means Iago had so beautiful a Wife that she was

[22, 23. 'Florentine, (A Fellow almost damn'd in a faire Wife).']

his Heaven on Earth, that he idoliz'd her, and that he forgot to think of Happiness in an After-state, as placing all his Views of Bliss in the single Enjoyment of her. In this sense, Beauty, when it can so seduce and engross a Man's Thoughts, may be said "almost to damn him." A somewhat similar thought is in *Mer. of Ven.* III, v, 80–83.' Theobald therefore puts these words in parenthesis, reading: (the Florentine's A fellow almost damn'd in a fair wife,). HANMER was the first to point out that 'from many passages of this play (rightly understood) Cassio was a Florentine, and Iago a Venetian,' and that as Cassio was unmarried, there must be some mistake in giving him a wife; but Cassio's beauty is often hinted at—an attribute which rough soldiers, naturally enough, would treat with scorn and ridicule. Wherefore Hanmer reads 'a fellow almost damn'd in a fair *phyz.*' JOHNSON resigns the lines to 'corruption and obscurity,' adding, 'I cannot think it very plain from III, i, 44, that Cassio was or was not a Florentine.' TYRWHITT (p. 2): The great difficulty is to understand in what sense any man can be said to be 'almost damn'd in a fair wife' or 'a fair phyz.' I cannot find any ground for supposing that either the one or the other has ever been reputed to be damnable sins in any religion. There is the same expression in *Mer. of Ven.* I, i, 98: 'If they should speak, would almost damn those ears, Which, hearing them, would call their brothers fools.' And there the allusion is evident to the Gospel-judgment against those who call their brothers fools. I am inclined, therefore, to believe that the true reading here is: 'A fellow almost damn'd in a fair *life*,' and that Shakespeare alludes to the judgment denounced in the Gospel against those *of whom all men speak well.* The character of Cassio is such as would be very likely to draw upon him all the peril of this denunciation, literally understood. Well-bred, easy, sociable, good-natured, with abilities enough to make him agreeable and useful, but not sufficient to excite the envy of his equals or to alarm the jealousy of his superiors. In several other passages Iago bears his testimony to the amiable qualities of his rival. Conf. 'the daily beauty of his life,' V, i, 22. I will only add that however hard or far-fetch'd this allusion (whether Shakespeare's or only mine) may seem to be, Archbishop Sheldon had exactly the same conceit when he made that singular compliment to a nephew of Sir William Temple, that 'he had the curse of the Gospel, because all men spoke well of him.' HEATH (p. 551) adopts Theobald's 'Florentine's,' and 'apprehends the meaning to be that, notwithstanding Iago had a fair wife, he had little chance for going to heaven, as by the watchfulness of his jealousy he made it extremely difficult for her to do her part toward sending him thither.' JENNENS in his text marks the line as an *Aside*, and, retaining the parenthesis, reads 'A fellow's almost damn'd in a fair wife!' In his note, after condemning Theobald's emendation, and asserting that Hanmer's is simply equivalent to saying that 'Cassio's a damn'd handsome fellow,' he upholds his own text by pleading that he has 'only supplied an *s* after "fellow;"' and by supposing that 'Shakespeare meant the line to be spoke apart, expressing a sudden motion of jealousy in Iago on naming Othello and Cassio, of both of which that he was jealous appears from II, iii. And Iago's meaning is, "To be married to a handsome woman (as I am) is almost as bad as being damn'd; as the number of her admirers will doom the husband to a state of perpetual jealousy."' TOLLET (*Var.*'78): Some might have no objection to read 'a *false* wife;' as the jealous Ford says, 'see the *hell* of having a false woman.'—*Merry Wives*, II, ii; but the original text may mean a fellow almost as unhappy as the damned, with jealousy of a fair wife. STEEVENS: That Cassio was *married* is not sufficiently implied in the words 'a fellow almost damn'd in a fair wife,' since they mean, according to Iago's licentious manner

[22, 23. 'Florentine, (A Fellow almost damn'd in a faire Wife).']

of expressing himself, no more than a man 'very near being married.' This seems to have been the case with Cassio; see IV, i, 142. Had Shakespeare, consistently with Iago's character, meant to make him say that Cassio was 'actually damn'd in being married to a handsome woman,' he would have made him say it *outright*, and not have interposed the palliative *almost*. Whereas, what he says at present amounts to no more than that (however near his marriage) he is not yet *completely damned*, because he is not *absolutely married*. The succeeding parts of Iago's conversation sufficiently evince that Shakespeare thought no mode of conception or expression too brutal for that character. This note of Steevens, MALONE thinks, clearly explains the line, and has therefore 'no doubt that the text is right.' M. MASON denies the correctness of Tyrwhitt's emendation, because Iago would never have given to Cassio the highest commendation while wishing to depreciate him to Roderigo; though afterward in speaking to himself in V, i, he gives him his just character. HENLEY: Iago is enumerating Cassio's disqualifications; surely his *being well spoken of by all men* could not be one of them. It was in regard to the reported marriage of Cassio to the 'customer,' the 'most *fair* Bianca,' that Iago called the new lieutenant *a fellow almost damn'd*. COLERIDGE (*Notes*, &c., 248) prefers *life* 'as fitting to Iago's contempt for whatever did not display power, and that intellectual power.' MARTINUS SCRIBLERUS (p. 16) proposes to include 'almost damn'd in a fair wife' in parenthesis, as thus uttered by Iago in the rapidity of his thoughts, and thus paraphrases: 'That is, "a fellow that never set a squadron in the field (a circumstance, which, in the estimation of a soldier, almost throws contempt even upon a beautiful woman, is *almost damn'd in a fair wife*)". He then carries on the same idea, and adds, "nor the division of a battle knows *more than a spinster*."' BECKET (i, 179): For 'wife' read *wise*, i. e. *manner*. The construction is: A fellow, in a fair wise, almost damn'd,' i. e. a fellow of whom it may be *fairly said*, or *to use a fair manner of speaking*, that he is almost damned (*a worthless fellow*). JACKSON (p. 402): Why should Cassio be *almost damned* by marrying a *fair* woman? Beauty, in the softer sex, detracts not from virtue. We should certainly read: 'almost damn'd in a *frail* wife;' which at once announces the licentious character of Bianca, and that odium designed by the speaker is thus cast on the spirit of Cassio. I make no doubt the compositor mistook the word, and am inclined to think that for 'damn'd' we should read *bann'd;* meaning, that they were as near being married as though the *bans* were published. TIECK (viii, 357) assumes, and it is mere assumption, that Florence in Shakespeare's time was noted for its immorality—as noted, indeed, as Bulgaria was from earlier times; and that Iago calls the Veronese Cassio 'a Florentine,' in order to cast on him the imputation of extreme immodesty. KNIGHT finds no such mystical meaning in these words as Tieck imputes to them, but that Iago distinctly refers to Bianca. As to whether Cassio was, or was not, a Florentine, Knight maintains that we can gather no trustworthy intimation from anything which Iago may say on this or on any other subject (wherein the present editor agrees with him). 'It is not to be forgotten that Iago, throughout the whole course of his extraordinary character, is represented as utterly regardless of the differences between truth and falsehood. The most absolute lie,—the half lie,—the truth in the way of telling it distorted into a lie, are the instruments with which Iago constantly works. This ought to be borne in mind with reference to his assertion that Cassio was a Florentine.' But whether Iago was lying or not in this instance, Knight thinks emphatically that Iago meant to speak 'disparagingly of Cassio when he called him a Florentine. He was an "arithmetician," a "counter-caster," a native of a state whose inhabitants, pursuing the peaceful and

[22, 23. 'Florentine, (A Fellow almost damn'd in a faire Wife).']
gainful occupations of commerce, had armies of mercenaries. Cassio, for this reason,
upon the showing of Iago, was one that "never set a squadron in the field."' COL-
LIER thinks that the unaltered text is most likely right, but records as a not very probable conjecture the substitution of *guise* for 'wife' by Mr Petrie of Edinburgh. DYCE
(*Remarks*, p. 233): The text may be right, though I doubt it; but I cannot help wondering greatly that Mr Petrie, when he conjectured *guise*, should not have stumbled
upon *wise* (way). [Wherein Dyce is anticipated by Becket.] MAGINN (p. 264): The
word 'damn'd' is, I think, a corruption of some word which signified *delicate, soft,
dainty,* or something of the kind; and that for 'in,' we should read *as.* 'A fellow
almost as soft and delicate as a fair wife,' as dainty as a woman. I am not fortunate
to supply it, but I have somewhat thought it was 'almost *trimmed as* a fair wife.' Such
a fellow as the 'neat *trimly*-dressed' courtier, 'perfumed as a milliner,' who excited the
impatience of Hotspur. I throw out my hint for the leading, or misleading, of future
editors. WHITE (ed. i) reads 'almost damn'd in a fair *wise,*' that is, 'a fellow almost
damned if the judgment had been given in a fair manner, a use of *damn* still common
as applied to plays and operas.' The difference between 'wife' and *wife,* with the long
s, is so slight that White wonders at any difficulty to be found in the passage. 'Besides, if Cassio *had* been betrothed to "a customer," "a fitchew," what had that to do
with his soldierly qualifications?' In his (ed. ii) White abandons the passage as incomprehensible, if the difficulty have not arisen in this mistake of the long *s* for an *f.*
CARTWRIGHT (p. 38): Read *other wise.* COWDEN-CLARKE says that 'wife' is here
used in the sense of *woman,* and that of the several interpretations proposed the true
one is: 'A fellow who would almost go to perdition for a handsome woman,' or 'a
fellow who is almost lost in his fondness for a fine woman;' and to it Cassio's conduct
with respect to Bianca adds probability. STAUNTON shrewdly asks: 'Are we quite
assured that when Iago calls Cassio a Florentine, he means merely that Cassio was a
native of that town? The system of book-keeping called *Italian Book-keeping* came,
as is well known, originally from Florence; and he may not improbably use "Florentine," as he employs "arithmetician," "counter-caster," and "debtor-and-creditor," in
a derogatory sense, to denote the mercantile origin and training which he chooses to
attribute to his rival.' As to the belief that Iago in 'a fair wife' refers to the report
that Cassio was about to marry Bianca, Staunton thinks that the 'objection is unanswerable that there is no reason for supposing that Cassio had ever seen Bianca until they
met in Cyprus.' And in despair of eliciting a satisfactory meaning from the line,
Staunton says that he has sometimes thought Shakespeare must have written 'almost
damn'd in a *fair-wife.*' That is, 'a fellow by habit of reckoning debased almost *into*
a *market-woman. In* of old was commonly used for *into;* we still say *fall in love.*'
F. A. LEO (*N. & Qu.* 1865, 3d, vii, 453): Iago intends to say that Othello has made
a bad choice in his lieutenant, a man who is a mere theorizer, never exposed to a
shower of bullets, and knowing no more of the division of a battle than a spinster,
in short, 'a fellow almost damn'd in a *faint* wife.' J. J. B. WORKARD (*N. & Qu.*
1865, 3d, viii, 80): Read 'almost damn'd in a fair *strife.*' Here the unity of the
idea is preserved throughout. *Str,* in sixteenth-century writing, might easily be mistaken for *w.* Δ (*Ibid,* p. 126): No, do not alter Shakespeare, and make him more
obscure when unnecessary. I have never had a doubt about his meaning in this passage, which really seems clear enough. Iago wishes to show that Cassio's weakness
goes beyond even that of a woman—'A fellow' of so soft a character that a similar
disposition would be 'almost damned in a fair wife.' In fine, Cassio is so weak a

[22, 23. 'Florentine, (A Fellow almost damn'd in a faire Wife).']
creature that had you a fair wife of that sort you would condemn her.   BIBLIOTHECAR.
CHETHAM (*Ibid.*): Your second correspondent [Workard] in this passage is undoubtedly
right in his emendation, but not, I think, in insisting on unity of idea.   The strife is not
that of the battlefield, but of the election.   'A fellow [who would have been] almost
damn'd In a fair strife.'   ARROWSMITH (p. 38) [whose interpretation will be found,
I think, to have been foreshadowed by Martinus Scriblerus, and by Δ.—ED.] : Hard
above all has been the fate of 'in;' let but Iago say that for soldiership his com-
rade Cassio is 'a fellow almost damned in a fair wife'—that his qualifications for
the post of lieutenant would be almost discreditable in a woman; let him add
withal, as though on set purpose to preclude every chance of being misunderstood,
that Cassio possesses no more strategic knowledge than a 'spinster,' when lo! a
goodly troop of commentators, clerk and lay, bishop and bookseller, lawyer and anti-
quary, critic professional and critic amateur, home-born and outlandish, men who have
read much and men who have read nothing, swarm forth to bury this simple remark
under a pile of notes, that from first to last contain not an inkling of its purport. . . . .
The words are to be taken circumscriptly, not sent gadding after Bianca, or no one
knows who; their meaning must be sought and found within the compass of the line
in which they stand.   Had Shakespeare written 'a fellow almost damned in a raw
lad,' the dullest brain could scarcely have missed the imputation that Cassio's military
abilities would be almost disallowed, condemned as hardly up to the mark in an inexperienced boy; or had the words run, 'a fellow almost damned in an old maid,' then,
though it might not be understood how an officer, after Iago's report, of Cassio's incapacity, should be almost damnèd in one of her sex and condition, she at any rate
could not, like the 'fair wife,' have been discovered at Cyprus in a young courtesan.
Or not altering a syllable, with only a slight change in their order, let us place the
words thus : 'a fellow in a fair wife almost damned;' by this disposition of them the
reader is pinned to their true construction; the alliance between Cassio and the fair
wife is closer than the commentators suspected; they harp upon conjugal union, Iago
speaks of virtual identity; they seek the coupling of two persons in wedlock, he con-
templates an embodiment of the soldiership of the one in the condition of the other,
and so incorporated he pronounces it to be 'in a fair wife' almost reproveable; adding,
in the same vein, that it was no better than might be found in 'a spinster.'   To dwell
on this point longer would be to upbraid the reader's understanding.   [Of Arrowsmith's
explanation DYCE (ed. iii) says : 'Though it may appear to some to be rather forced and
obscure, I am far from asserting it to be wrong.']   FORSYTH (*Shakspere*, &c., p. 107) :
As contrasted with Staunton's and similar glosses, our proposal is simplicity itself.   It
consists in throwing out the word 'wife' as a misprint very easily made, and by a difference in pointing (to which, as all know, neither the early Qq nor the Ff paid much
attention) to read thus : 'A fellow almost damned; in a fair *strife* That never,' &c. . . . .
The greatest deficiency of the expositors, in our humble view, has been their inability
to compare the author with himself, and if this is intelligently done in the present case,
there can be small doubt of the result.   EARL OF SOUTHESK (*Saskatchewan*, p. 413) :
May it not mean simply—'A man almost degraded into a woman' (through feminine
tastes and habits)? as when one says : 'A soldier wasted in a parson,' 'A farmer spoilt
in a king.'   This sense might seem clearer were the definite article employed—*the* fellow, *the* fair wife.   DR SCHMIDT avails himself of a translator's privilege, and finding
no emendation that at all meets the requirements of the case he strikes out the line
altogether, 'confident that no reader will perceive the gap.'   HERR thinks that '*fram'd*

That neuer fet a Squadron in the Field,
Nor the deuifion of a Battaile knowes   25

25. *Battaile*] Battell QqF$_3$F$_4$.

---

or damn'd in a *form o' wax*' is harmonious with the context, and agrees with Iago's contemptuous references to Cassio. HUDSON (ed. iii) reads *wight* in his text instead of 'wife,' which, he thinks, 'cannot be explained to any fitting sense but by methods too subtile and recondite.' Of all the readings hitherto offered he prefers Capell's *face*. 'It suits the occasion and the speaker very well; for Iago dwells much on Cassio's handsomeness of person; recurs to it again and again; and builds his scheme partly on that circumstance, as if he longed to make it the ruin of Cassio, sure enough. On the other hand, however, Iago's thought may well have been that Cassio was badly damaged by the fascinations of a handsome mistress; thus referring to the amorous intrigue with Bianca, which comes out so strongly in the course of the play. So I am satisfied we ought to read *wight*. It seems to me a very natural and fitting word for the place; and, if spelled phonographically, *wite*, might easily be misprinted "wife;" and Iago seems rather fond of using it scoffingly in reference to women. It may not be amiss to note that Iago's talk about Cassio is full of contempt. Surely a reading that requires an explanation so forced as Arrowsmith's may well be distrusted. It has set me more than ever against the old text.' JOHN HUNTER: Cassio is here regarded as about to marry his mistress, Bianca, whose charms, it would seem, were such as to make this world a paradise for him, and thus put him in danger of forfeiting the happiness of the world to come. The notion is founded on the parable of Dives and Lazarus: 'Son, remember that *thou in thy life-time receivedst thy good things*, and likewise Lazarus evil things; but now he is comforted, and thou art tormented.'—Luke xvi, 25. Cf. *Mer. of Ven.* III, v, 78–83. BULLOCH (*Studies*, p. 248): The line is a concentrated essence of Iago's opinion of Cassio's soldiership. It is, as it were, spoken by the bye, and amplified in the speech. I therefore propose 'almost damn'd in *warfare life.*' *Warfare* does not occur in Shakespeare, though it does in our English Bible. CROSBY (*Robinson's Epit. of Lit.*, 15 Mar. 1879) justifies F$_1$ by interpreting 'in' as equivalent to *on account of*, and 'wife' as *woman in general*. Thus: 'a fellow who is willing to go to perdition—almost sell himself to the devil—for a beautiful woman.' R. M. SPENCE (*N. & Qu.* 1879, 5th, xi, 383): I offer: 'A fellow all must damn in affairs wise.' Iago says, that all who are wise in military affairs must condemn the appointment of a man who knows nothing of war, but 'bookish theorie.' F. A. LEO (*Shakespeare-Notes*, p. 116, 1885) finds, as far as the sound is concerned, that 'damn'd in' could have been 'very easily misunderstood for *tempting*,' and that the *ductus literarum* would readily explain 'almost' as *at most;* and therefore proposes, as suiting the requirements of sound, of sense, and of letters: 'A fellow, *almost tempting* a fair wife.' [In conclusion I merely re-echo Dr Johnson's words: 'This is one of the passages which must, for the present, be resigned to corruption and obscurity. I have nothing that I can, with any approach to confidence, propose.'—ED.]

22–27. COLERIDGE (*Notes*, &c., 248): Let the reader feel how by and through the glass of two passions,—disappointed vanity and envy,—the very vices of which he is complaining are made to act upon him as if they were so many excellences; and the more appropriately, because cunning is always admired and wished for by minds conscious of inward weakness; but they act only by half, like music on an inattentive auditor, swelling the thoughts which prevent him from listening to it.

25. **Battaile**] Cotgrave: *Battaile:* f. A batell, or fight, betweene two armies;

More then a Spinſter.   Vnleſſe the Bookiſh Theoricke: 26
Wherein the Tongued Conſuls can propoſe
As Maſterly as he.   Meere pratle (without praȼtiſe)
Is all his Souldierſhip.   But he (Sir) had th'eleȼtion;   29

26. *Spinſter.   Vnleſſe*] *Spinſter, vnleſſe*
Qq, Rowe.   *Spinſter; but* Pope+.   *Spin-*
ſter: Vnleſſe Ff, Cap. et cet.

　　Bookiſh Theoricke] *bookiſh Theor-*
ique Qq (*blockiſh* Q₃).

27. *Tongued*] Q₂Q₃Ff, Rowe, Pope,
Han. Knt, Sta. Wh. i.   *togèd* Dyce, Huds.
toged Q₁ et cet.

28. *he.   Meere*] Johns.   *he, Meere* F₂.

he, meer F₃F₄.   *he; meere* Qq, Rowe et
cet.

29. *Is all*] *In all* F₃F₄.
　　Souldierſhip...had] *soldiership--*
he had Pope+.
　　th'election] Ff, Rowe+, Jen. Coll.
Wh. Huds.   *the election* Qq, Han. Cap.
et cet.

---

also a battell, or maine battell; the middle battallion, or squadron of an army, wherein
the Prince, or Generall, most commonly marcheth; also the whole army; and sometimes also, any squadron, battalion, or part thereof.   NARES refers to Strutt (*Manners
and Customs*, &c., iii, 2), where is an account from an old MS. of the method of regu-
lating these divisions.   See *Macb.* V, vi, 4, and notes on 'Lead our first battle,' where
also is a reference to Holinshed: 'when his whole power was come togither, he divided
the same into three battels.'

26. **Theoricke**]: For the two other instances of the use of this word, see Mrs
Cowden-Clarke's *Concordance*.

27. **Tongued**]: The First Qto gave THEOBALD the hint for his emendation, viz.:
'that the Senators assisted the Duke in Council in their proper *gowns*.'   Where,
farther on, Iago bids Brabantio 'put on his gown,' Theobald does not think that
night-gown is meant, but gown of office, the Senatorial Gown; adding that there is
not that contrast of terms betwixt 'tongued,' that there is betwixt *toged* and *soldiership;* and thereupon cites six or seven instances from Latin authors (among them, of
course, Cicero's 'cedant arma togæ'), showing that 'the same opposition is for ever
made' between *toga* and *arma*.   BOSWELL says wisely, that 'tongued' agrees better
with the words which follow: 'mere *prattle* without practice,' a remark which DYCE
cites, but does not uphold, believing 'tongued' to be a misprint for *togèd*, since the
Folio has a similar error in *Cor.* II, iii, 122: 'Why in this Wooluish *tongue* should I
stand heere,' &c.

27. **Consuls**]: THEOBALD reads *couns'lors*, because the Venetian nobility constituted the great *Council* of the Senate; and we know that Brabantio was summoned to
the Council as a Senator, for 'Consul' he certainly was not; and lastly, because the
offices of Consuls and Tribunes were abolished when the government was entrusted to
Doges.   But STEEVENS says, that 'consuls' seems to have been commonly used for
counsellors, as in the second scene of this act.   'Geoffrey of Monmouth, and Matthew
Paris after him, call both dukes and earls "consuls."'   MALONE: The *rulers of the
state* or civil governors.   The word is used by Marlowe, in the same sense, in *Tambur-
laine*, 1590 [*First Part*, I, ii]: 'Both we will raigne as *consuls* of the earth.'   [But
Marlowe's very next line: 'And mighty kings shall be our Senators,' may be with
equal propriety cited as a proof that 'senators' also meant 'civil governors.'—ED.]

28. **Masterly**]: For other instances where *-ly* represents *like*, of which it is a cor-
rupᵗᵎᵒn, see ABBOTT, § 447.

And I (of whom his eies had feene the proofe   30
At Rhodes, at Ciprus, and on others grounds
Chriften'd, and Heathen)muft be be-leed, and calm'd
By Debitor, and Creditor.   This Counter-cafter,   33

31. *Ciprus,*] *Cipres,* Qq. *Cyprus ;* Cap.
Steev. Var. Sing. ii.
others] Ff. *other* Qq et cet.
32. *Chriften'd*] F₂, Knt. *Chriftn'd*
Q₂Q₃. *Chriftian* Q₁F₃F₄ et cet.
be be-leed] *be led* Q₁, Pope. *be let*
Warb.

33. *Debitor*] *Debtor* Han.
Debitor, and Creditor] *debitor-and-*
creditor Sta.
Creditor. This Counter-cafter,] Ff,
Rowe, Johns. Jen. Knt, Sta. Glo. Cam.
Creditor, this counter-cafter : Qq, Pope
et cet.

30. **his**] WHITE : That is, Othello's.

31. **others**] WALKER (*Crit.* i, 233) notices the remarkable frequency in F₁ of the interpolation of an *s* at the end of a word, and adds that 'those who are conversant with the MSS. of the Elizabethan Age, may, perhaps, be able to explain its origin. Were it not for the different degrees of frequency with which it occurs in different parts of the F,—being comparatively rare in the *Comedies* (except, perhaps, in *Wint. Tale*), appearing more frequently in the *Histories,* and becoming quite common in the *Trage-dies,*—I should be inclined to think it originated in some peculiarity of Shakespeare's handwriting.' [See *Lear,* V, iii, 258. Walker gives the following nine instances, in this play, of this interpolation as he considers it, viz : the present passage, where 'others' appears as *other* in Qq; 'eares' in F₁ as *eare* in QqFf, I, iii, 245; 'likings,' QqFf, III, i, 53; 'disproportions,' Ff as *disproportion* in Qq, III, iii, 274; 'Horrors,' QqFf, III, iii, 427; 'sorrowes,' QqFf, III, iv, 136; 'workes' in Ff as *worke* in Qq, IV, i, 54; 'scuses' in Ff as *scuse* in Qq, IV, i, 93; 'behauiors,' Ff as *behauior* in Qq, IV, i, 119. To these nine instances a tenth may be added : 'Thicks-lips,' F₁, as *thick lips* in Qq, I, i, 72, and perhaps we might include an eleventh : 'warres' in III, iii, 77. Now if from this list we eliminate the three words wherein the Ff and the Qq agree, and wherein no critic but Walker has found the *s* superfluous, viz : *likings, horrors,* and *sorrowes,* and add the fourth, *warres,* which only Capell changed to *war,* we shall have seven instances remaining where this *s* is found in the Ff, but not in the Qq. If then Walker's adumbration of the cause of this *s* be accepted, viz : that it originates in some peculiarity of the writing of that hand which left 'scarse a blot in his papers,' this manifest distinction between the two copies adds a vindication, by no means insignificant, of the superior authority of the First Folio.—ED.]

32. **Christen'd**] I can see no excellent reason why we should not retain this word.—ED.

32. **be-leed**] STEEVENS : One vessel is said to be in the *lee* of another, when it is ·o placed that the wind is intercepted from it. Iago's meaning, therefore, is, that Cassio had got the wind of him and be-calmed him from going on. HEATH and STAUNTON conjectured 'must be *lee'd*,' led to it by Q₁ and the imperfect measure of the line.

33. **Debitor, and Creditor**] JOHNSON (*Cym.* V, iv, 171) : That is, an accounting-book. DYCE (*Gloss.*) : Compare the title-page of a very early work on book-keeping : 'A Profitable Treatyce, called the Instrument or Boke to learne to knowe the good order of the kepyng of the famouse reconynge, called in Latyn, Dare and Habere; and in Englyshe, *Debitor and Creditor,*' &c., 1543.

33. **Counter-caster**] WAY (*Foot-note* in *Prompt. Parv.* s. v. Awgrym. *Algaris-*

He (in good time) muſt his Lieutenant be,
And I (bleſſe the marke) his Mooreſhips Auntient.   35

34. *Lieutenant*] *Leiutenant* Qq. Q_1 et cet.
35. *I* (*bleſſe*] Ff, Knt. *I Sir* (*bleſſe*   35. *Mooreſhips Auntient*] *Worſhips*
Q_2Q_3, Rowe, Johns. Jen.   *I, God bleſſe*   *Ancient* Q_1.

---

mus): 'Augrym, *algorisme*. To counte, reken by cyfers of agryme, *enchifrer*. To cast an accomptes in aulgorisme with a penne, *enchifrer*. To cast an accomptes with counters after the aulgorisme maner, *calculer*. To cast an accomptes after the comen maner, with counters, *compter par iect*. I shall reken it syxe times by aulgorisme, or you can caste it ones by counters.'—PALSG. It would hence appear that towards the commencement of the XVIth century the use of the Arabic numerals had in some degree superseded the ancient mode of calculating by the abacus; and counters, which at the period when the Promptorium was compiled, were generally used. Hereafter we find the word 'Countinge Borde' as an evidence. They were not, indeed, wholly disused at a time long subsequent; an allusion to calculation by counters occurs in Shakespeare, and later authors prove that they had not been entirely discarded. Algorithm or algorism, a term universally used in the XIVth and XVth centuries to denote the science of calculation by 9 figures and zero, is of Arabic derivation. DYCE (*Gloss.*) says that pieces of false coin were used for counters. See *Cym.* V, iv, 173.

35. **marke**] STEEVENS: Kelly, in his comments on Scots proverbs, observes that the Scots, when they compare person to person, use this exclamation. DYCE (*Gloss.*) quotes this note of Steevens, adding, 'but the origin and the meaning of the exclamation are alike obscure.'

35. **Auntient**] J. D. (*N. & Qu.* 1879, 5th, xii, 4): The common interpretation of this word is that it means an ensign, in the double sense of standard and standard-bearer. So our older Dictionaries explain it; Cotgrave has: '*Enseigne*, an ensigne, auncient, standard-bearer.' The explanation is correct as far as it goes, but is not sufficiently precise. The ancient was a banner bearing an heraldic device, the token of ancient or noble descent, borne by a gentleman or leader in war. 'Lord Westmorland his ancyent rais'd, The dun bull he rais'd on hie.'—*The Rising in the North*. 'Master, master, see you yon faire ancyent, Yonder is the serpent and the serpent's head.'—Percy's *Rel.* (ed. 1867) i, 303. The servant recognized by this device that the ship belonged to Duke John of Austria. The word was, however, used to denote one who was connected with some blazon of this kind, whether as an attendant to a standard or to some gentleman who had armorial bearings. In the English edition of the *Janua Linguarum Trilinguis*, by J. Comenius, 1662, it is said, that 'the standard-bearers carrie the standards in the midst of the troops, whom the ancients march before with hangers;' the Latin is, 'quos præcedunt antesignani cum romphæis' (p. 245). The word *antesignanus* is explained by Ducange as one 'qui præibat vexillo ad illius custodiam.' In Anchoran's *Gate of Tongues Unlocked* (ed. 1639), which is based on the work of Comenius, the passage runs thus: 'whom the lieutenants precede or go before with long two-handed swords' (p. 143). From these instances it is easy to see how the word came to mean a personal attendant or body-squire, who, says Fosbrooke (*Ant.* ii, 752), 'had the care of the things relating to the person of the knight, carried his master's standard, and gave the catchword in battle,' an office often borne by men of honourable descent. This is the meaning of the word in *Othello*. Iago was the personal attendant of the Moor in a military capacity, in modern language, his aide-de-

Rod. By heauen, I rather would haue bin his hangman.   36
Iago. Why, there's no remedie.
'Tis the curffe of Seruice;
Preferment goes by Letter, and affection,
And not by old gradation, where each fecond   40
Stood Heire to'th'firft.   Now Sir, be iudge your felfe,
Whether I in any iuft terme am Affin'd
To loue the *Moore*?
   Rod. I would not follow him then.
   Iago. O Sir content you.   45
I follow him, to ferue my turne vpon him.
We cannot all be Mafters, nor all Mafters
Cannot be truely follow'd.   You fhall marke   [310 *b*]

37, 38. One line, Qq et cet.
37. *Why*] *But* Qq, Pope+, Cap. Jen.
Steev. Var. Coll. Ktly.
38. *Seruice;*] *feruice*, Qq.
39. *Letter*] *favour* Coll. (MS).
40. *And...old*] *Not by the olde* Qq, Jen.
Steev. Var. Coll.   *Not (as of old)* Warb.
41. *to'th'*] *to th'* F₃F₄, Huds.   *t'the*

Coll. *to the* Qq, Cap. et seq.
41. Two lines, Qq.
42. *Whether*] *If* Pope+.
   Affin'd] *affign'd* Q₁, Pope, Theob.
Han. Warb.   *Affirm'd* F₂.
45. *you.*] *you*, Q₂Q₃.   *you;* Rowe.
46. *him, to*] *him to* Q₁ et cet.
48. *follow'd.   You*] *followed, you* Qq.

---

camp, receiving orders from his superior, especially, but not exclusively, about military
movements.   It was in accordance with his duties that he received, through Cassio,
Othello's lieutenant, directions about the watch that guarded the camp, in II, iii
WHITE: *'Ancient:* a mere phonetic corruption of "ensign," consequent upon the pronunciation of *e* as short *a*, and of *s* before a vowel as *sh ; ancient* was pronounced not
ane-shent, but *an-shent* until a late period.

39. **Letter**] JOHNSON : By recommendation from powerful friends.   COWDEN-
CLARKE : May it not mean 'according to the letter of his promise,' or 'in accordance
with theoretical knowledge and pretensions'? in reference either to Othello's answer,
'I have chose my officer,' or to Cassio's 'bookish theoric.'

40. **old gradation**] JOHNSON : That is, gradation established by *ancient* practice.

41. **Stood**] ABBOTT (§ 361) : The subjunctive (a consequence of the old inflection)
was frequently used, not as now with *would, should*, &c., but in a form identical with
the indicative, where nothing but the context (in the case of past tenses) shows that it
is the subjunctive.   In the present instance, if it be asked, what is the difference between 'stood' here and 'would have stood' I should say that the simple form of the
subjunctive, coinciding in sound with the indicative, implied to an Elizabethan more
of *inevitability* (subject, of course, to a condition which is not fulfilled).   'Stood'
means 'would certainly have stood.'   The possibility is regarded as *an unfulfilled fact*,
to speak paradoxically.   Compare the Greek idiom of *ἵνα* with the indicative.

42. **Affin'd**] JOHNSON : Do I stand *within* any such *terms* of propinquity, *or* relation
to the Moor, as that it is my duty to love him?   STAUNTON : By any moral obligation
am *bound*, &c.   [See II, ii, 243.]

48. **shall**] ABBOTT (§ 315) : 'You shall' is especially common in the meaning of

Many a dutious and knee-crooking knaue;
That (doting on his owne obfequious bondage)   50
Weares out his time, much like his Mafters Affe,
For naught but Prouender, & when he's old Cafheer'd.
Whip me fuch honeft knaues. Others there are
Who trym'd in Formes, and vifages of Dutie,
Keepe yet their hearts attending on themfelues,   55
And throwing but fhowes of Seruice on their Lords
Doe well thriue by them.
And when they haue lin'd their Coates
Doe themfelues Homage.
Thefe Fellowes haue fome foule,   60
And fuch a one do I profeffe my felfe. For (Sir)

49. *dutious*] *duteous* Rowe ii.
52. *naught*] *noughe* Q$_1$. *nought* Qq
et cet.
        &^ when he's old] *and when old,'s*
Han. *when old,* Steev.
when] Om. Q$_3$.
Cafheer'd] *cafhierd* Qq.
Two lines, Q$_2$Q$_3$.
53–56. *Whip...Lords*] Five lines, ending *knaues:...formes,...hearts,...throw-
ing...Lords* Q$_1$. Ending, *knaues:...are,
...duty,...themfelues...Lords* Q$_2$Q$_3$.
54. *trym'd*] *trimd* Q$_1$. *trimm'd* Rowe.

56. *but*] *out* Quincy (MS.).
57–60. *Doe...foule*] Two lines, Rowe
et cet.
57. *Doe well*] *Well* Pope+, Huds.
them.] *'em,* Qq, Jen.
58. *they haue*] *they've* Pope+, Dyce.
59. *themfelues*] *themfelmes* F$_2$.
60. *Thefe*] *Thofe* Qq.
Fellowes] *folks* Pope+.
61. *For (Sir)*] Om. Pope+. Separate
line, Cap. Steev. Var. Sing. Coll. Wn. i,
Dyce, Hal. Glo.

---

you may, you will, applied to that which is of common occurrence, or so evident that
it *cannot but be* seen.

49. **knaue**] STAUNTON thinks that it carries no opprobrious meaning here, but is
simply *servitor*. In line 53, JOHNSON says that it is used for *servant,* but with a sly
mixture of contempt.

50. **obsequious**] STAUNTON: That is, *obedient, submissive* thraldom.

53. **me**] The ethical dative, adding emphasis or vivacity to the expressi>?. For
instances see ABBOTT, § 220.

54. **trym'd**] COLLIER (ed. ii) notes that his (MS.) amends this line to '*learn'd* in
forms and *usages* of duty,' and adds: 'If alteration were necessary we might read,
"*train'd* in forms and *usages;*" but change is inexpedient, since the meaning is clear,
and "visages" may be intended as an antithesis to "hearts" in the next line.' STAUN-
TON paraphrases the line: 'dress'd in shapes and masks of duty.' WHITE pronounces
Collier's emendation not improbable.

56. **throwing**] WALKER (*Vers.* p. 120) cites this among many other instances as
the contraction frequent in participles, where a short vowel is preceded by a long one
or a diphthong. Conf. *Ham.* V, ii, 'That on the view and knowing of these contents.'

57. **Doe**] HUDSON thinks this was probably caught by the transcriber's or printer's
eye from 'Doe' in line 59.

It is as fure as you are *Rodorigo*,   62
Were I the Moore, I would not be *Iago*:
In following him, I follow but my felfe.
Heauen is my Iudge, not I for loue and dutie,   65
But feeming fo, for my peculiar end:
For when my outward Action doth demonftrate
The natiue act, and figure of my heart
In Complement externe, 'tis not long after
But I will weare my heart vpon my fleeue   70
For Dawes to pecke at ; I am not what I am.

65.   *Heauen*] *Heav'n* Rowe +.
Heauen...I] One line, Qq.
is my] *be my* Jen.
not I] *not I*, QqFf, Rowe, Pope,
Theob. Warb. Johns. Jen.
65, 66. *for...fo*] One line, Q₁.
for...end] One line, Q₂Q₃.
66. *peculiar*] *pecular* Q₃.

67. *doth*] *does* Q₁.
69. *Complement*] QqFf, Han. Knt,
Sing. ii, Ktly, Del. Huds. *compliment*
Rowe ii, et cet.
71. Two lines, Qq.
Dawes] *Doues* Q₁, Mal.
I am...am] *I'm...seem* Pope +.
I'm...am Johns.

---

61. For (Sir)]: For instances of placing ejaculations, appellations, &c. (as in Greek φεῦ, &c.) out of the regular verse, as Capell placed these words, see ABBOTT, § 512.

63. I would] HUDSON: Perhaps for *should;* and if so the meaning may be, 'Were I in the Moor's place, I should be quite another man than I am.' Or, 'if I had the Moor's nature, if I were such an honest dunce as he is, I should be just a fit subject for men that "have some soul" to practise upon.' Perhaps, Iago is purposely mixing some obscurity in his talk in order to mystify the gull.

69. Complement externe] JOHNSON: 'In that which I do only for an outward show of civility.' 'Surely,' says KNIGHT, 'this interpretation [of Johnson], by adopting the secondary meaning of "Complement" (*compliment*), destroys Iago's bold avowal, which is, that when his actions exhibit the real intention and motives of his heart *in outward completeness*, he might as well wear it on his sleeve.' WALKER (*Crit.* iii, 285) cites Tourneur, *Revenger's Tragedy*, III, i (Dodsley, vol. iv, p. 329): 'The old duke, Thinking my outward shape and inward heart Are cut out of one piece (for he that prates his secrets, His heart stands o'th'outside), hires me by price To greet,' &c.

71. Dawes] MALONE (1790) adopts *doves* of Q₁, and justifies it in a note which I should have thought scarcely worth the quoting, were it not that HALLIWELL, in his Folio edition, has reprinted it. Malone suspects that Shakespeare had in his thoughts the following passage from Lyly's *Euphues and his England*, 1580, [p. 322, Arber's Reprint]: 'For as al coynes are not good yat haue the Image of *Cæfar*, nor al golde that are coyned with the kinges stampe, so all is not trueth that beareth the shew of godlines, nor all friends that beare a faire face, if thou pretende such loue to *Euphues*, carrye *thy heart on the backe of thy hand*, and thy tongue in the palme, that I may see what is in thy minde, and thou with thy fingers claspe thy mouth. . . . . I can better take a blister of a Nettle, then a prick of a Rose; more willing that a Rauen should pecke out mine eyes, then a *Turtle pecke at them.*' STEEVENS thought it worth while to defend F₁, saying that Iago means that he would expose his heart as a prey to the most

Rod. What a fall Fortune do's the Thicks-lips owe   72
If he can carry't thus?
Iago. Call vp her Father:
Rowſe him, make after him, poyſon his delight,   75

72. *fall*] Ff, Knt.   *full* Qq et cet.
  do's] *does* Qq.
  Thicks-lips] *thicklips* Qq.   *thicke-*
lips F$_2$.   *thick-lips* F$_3$F$_4$ et cet.
  73. *carry't*] *carry'et* Q$_1$.   *carry her*
Pope, Theob. Han. Warb. Jen.

74, 75. *Father: Rowſe him*,] Ff, Theob.
Ktly.   *father, Rowſe him*, Qq, Rowe ii,
Pope, Han. Warb. Jen.   *Father.   Rouse
him*, Rowe i.   *father, Rouse him*. Johns.
et cet. (subs.).

---

worthless of birds,—*daws*, which are treated with universal contempt. 'Shakespeare would scarcely have degraded the amiable tribe of *doves* to such an office, nor is the mention of them at all suitable to the harsh turn of Iago's speech.' MALONE rejoins that Iago meant to say, that 'not only birds of prey, but gentle and timid doves might peck at him with safety.' ['Daws' are the only carnivorous birds, I think, that could be here referred to with contempt, or without dignifying the allusion.—ED.] HARTING (p. 119): The Jackdaw (*Corvus monedula*) has not been so frequently noticed by Shakespeare as many other birds, and in the half-dozen instances where it is mentioned it is termed 'daw.'

71. **am**] JENNENS: This signifies I am not that inwardly which I am outwardly, or, I am not what I seem to appear to be. Pope has here turned poetry into prose. HUDSON: Iago probably means 'I am not what I *seem*,' but to speak thus would not smack so much of the peculiar dialect with which he loves to practise on the dupe. MAGINN (p. 268): Can these last words be intended as a somewhat profane allusion to the title by which the Almighty reveals himself to Moses? *Exod.* iii, 14. I AM THAT I AM is the name of the God of truth. *I am not what I am* is, therefore, a fitting description of a premeditated liar.

72. **fall**] I can recall no instance in this play where KNIGHT ('Good Knight,' as Douglas Jerrold said his epitaph should be) displays more ingenuity in extracting a meaning from a misprint in F$_1$, than in this word, and not only a meaning, but a hidden beauty thoroughly Shakespearian. '*Full* fortune,' says Knight, 'means simply *how fortunate he is*. But the F$_1$ conveys a much more Shakespearian idea. If the Moor can carry it thus,—appoint his own officer, in spite of the great ones of the city who capp'd to him, and, moreover, can secure Desdemona as his prize,—he is so puff'd up with his own pride and purposes, and is so successful, that *fortune owes him a heavy fall*. To *owe* is used by Shakespeare not only in the ancient sense of to *own*, but in the modern sense of *to be indebted to, to hold* or *possess for another*. Fortune here owes the thick-lips a fall, in the same way that we say, " He owes him a good or an evil turn." This reading is very much in Shakespeare's manner of throwing out a hint of coming calamities.' STEEVENS cites 'full fortune' as used in *Cymb.* V, iv, 110, and MALONE adds another instance in *Ant. & Cleo.* IV, xv, 24.

72. **Thicks-lips**] For the spelling, see note on 'others,' line 31.

72. **owe**] 'To *owe* in ancient language is to *own*,' says STEEVENS; 'very true,' says PYE, 'but do not explain it so often.'

73. **carry't**] JENNENS interprets the Qto as a 'mistake of the printer, who put *t* for *r*, and it might originally be written *carry 'er*, a contraction for *carry her*.'

75. **him . . . him**] ROLFE says, that 'the first "him" refers to Brabantio, the

Proclaime him in the Streets.   Incenfe her kinfmen,   76
And though he in a fertile Clymate dwell,
Plague him with Flies : though that his Ioy be Ioy,
Yet throw fuch chances of vexation on't,
As it may loofe fome colour.   80
  Rodo. Heere is her Fathers houfe, Ile call aloud.
  Iago. Doe, with like timerous accent, and dire yell,
As when (by Night and Negligence) the Fire
Is fpied in populus Citties.   84

76. *Streets.*] *ftreete,* Q₁. *ftreet,* Q₂Q₃,
Jen. *ftreets,* F₄.
  77, 78. *though*] *tho* Qq.
  79. *Yet throw*] *Yet : throw* Fechter.
    chances] Ff, Rowe, Knt, Sta. Del.
changes Qq et cet.
    on't] *out* Qq.
  80. *loofe*] *lofe* Q₃.

81. *houfe, Ile*] *houfr, ile* Q₃.
    [going towards the door. Ca .
  82. *Doe,*] QqFf, Rowe+,Wh. ii.   *Do ;*
Cap. et cet.
    with like] *with* Jen.
    timerous] Qq, *timorous* Ff.
  83. *the Fire*] *a fire* Han.

---

second to Othello;' which is true if we follow Dr Johnson's punctuation. But I prefer to follow F₂, where clearly Othello alone is referred to in both cases. Of course
we know that Brabantio is 'roused,' and we, therefore, suppose that reference is here
made to that fact; but ' Call up her father ' is uttered in the same hurried, parenthetical
way that ' Incense her kinsmen ' is immediately afterward; the main idea is to rouse, and
disturb Othello, and poison his delight. But I am not countenanced by Booth, whose
notes were made for me after the foregoing was written. Booth says, ' make this clear
to the audience by pointing off toward the Sagittary at the second "him;" the first,
of course, refers to Brabantio, but gesture must explain this to the " quantity of barren
spectators." '—Ed.

  77. **And though**] WALKER (*Crit.* ii, 156): 'And' is clearly out of place; read,
' Incense her kinsmen : An though he,' &c.

  78. **though that**] See ABBOTT, § 287; *Macb.* IV, iii, 106, *Lear*, IV, vi, 214.

  78. **be Ioy**] KEIGHTLEY (*Exp.*, p. 299): Perhaps this second 'joy' was suggested
by the first, instead of *high, bright,* or some other adjective.

  79. **chances**] KNIGHT defends the F₂, and rightly, I think. ' When Roderigo,' he
says, 'suggests that fortune owes Othello a fall, Iago eagerly jumps at the *chances of
vexation,* which the alarm of Desdemona's father may bring on him.' It seems hardly
necessary to define ' chances,' as STAUNTON does, by *crosses* or *casualties,* a *cross of
vexation* is almost tautological; I think ' chances ' mean here simply *possibilities* of
vexation, which might discolour Othello's joy. To read *changes of vexation* (with
the Qq) renders the contingency of ' may lose ' superfluous. A *change of vexation*
could scarcely fail to make his joy lose colour.—ED.

  80. **As**] There is but one instance given in ABBOTT, § 109, of *as* in the sense, as
here, of *that* or *as the result of which,* after *such ;* it is from the *Sonn.,* but no number
is given and I cannot verify it.

  82–84. GOULD (p. 83): J. B. Booth uttered these words, without heat, with a devilish unconcern, as if pleased with the fancy of terror and dismay; and playing, meanwhile with his sword-hilt or pulling at his gauntlets. He then strikes on the door

Rodo.   What hoa : *Brabantio*, Siginor *Brabantio*, hoa.   85

Iago.   Awake : what hoa, *Brabantio* : Theeues, Theeues.

Looke to your houfe, your daughter, and your Bags,

Theeues, Theeues.

Bra. Aboue.   What is the reafon of this terrible

Summons ? What is the matter there ?   90

Rodo.   Signior is all your Familie within ?

Iago.   Are your Doores lock'd *?*

Bra.   Why ? Wherefore ask you this ?

Iago.   Sir, y'are rob'd, for fhame put on your Gowne,   94

85, 86. *hoa*] *ho* QqF₄.

85. *Siginor*] *Seignior* Qq.   *Signior* Ff.

86. *Awake...Brabantio*] One line, Qq.

Theeues, Theeues] Ff, Knt, Sta.   *ho !*
thieves, thieves ! Pope +.   *Theeues, theeues,*
theeues (sep. line) Qq. (in same line), Cap.
et cet.

87. *your daughter*] *you Daughter* Q₁.

89. Aboue.] at a window. Qq.   within.
Cap.   Scene II. Pope +, Jen.

89, 90. *What...Summons ?*] Ff.   One
line, Qq et cet.

92. *your Doores lock'd*] *all doore lockts*
Q₁.   *all doors lock'd* Pope +.

94. *Sir*] Q₂Q₃Ff, Rowe, Johns. Cap.
Knt.   *Zounds fir* Q₁, Pope et cet.
y'are] *you are* Qq, Johns. Cap. Jen.
Steev. Var. Knt, Coll. Del.   *you're* Rowe.
rob'd] *robb'd* Q₃Ff.   *robd* Q₁Q₂.

---

of Brabantio's house, and speaking through the key-hole, sounds the resonant alarm,
'What ho, Brabantio !' Yet in saying this, we felt his mind was 'playing with some
inward bait.' The duplicity, the double nature, the devil in him, was subtly manifest.

83, 84. WARBURTON : This is not sense, take it which way you will. If 'night and
negligence' relate to 'spied,' it is absurd to say, 'the fire was spied by negligence.' If
'night' and 'negligence' refer only to the time and occasion, it should then be *by night*
and *thro' negligence.* Otherwise the particle *by* would be made to signify *time* applied
to one word, and *cause* applied to the other. We should read, therefore, ' Is *spred*,' by
which all these faults are avoided. [STAUNTON queries if Warburton be not right.]
EDWARDS (p. 144) : The plain meaning is,—not the fire was spied by negligence, but
—the fire, which came by night and negligence, was spied. And this double meaning
to the same word is common to Shakespeare with all other writers, especially where the
word is so familiar a one, as this in question. Ovid seems even to have thought it a
beauty, instead of a defect. JOHNSON : The particle *by* is used equivocally; the same
liberty is taken by writers more correct : ' The wonderful creature ! a woman of reason !
Never grave *out of* pride, never gay *out of* season.' M. MASON : This means 'during
the time of night and negligence.' KNIGHT thinks that had the parenthesis of F₁ been
adopted, all discussion might have been saved. DELIUS interprets it, 'according tc
Shakespeare's use of the copulas, as equivalent to *nightly negligence* or *negligence by
night*, and qualifying 'fire.' [Surely night is the cause that a fire takes place without
being observed ; it is because of night that the fire is neglected. Could we not here
use *from* quite as well as *by ?*—ED.]

89. **Bra. Aboue**] BOOTH : Brabantio should be seen through the open window at
his book or papers ; this would account for his appearance, instead of his servants, at
this 'terrible summons.' Iago should keep in shadow during this.

94. **rob'd**] GÉRARD here detects a pun, decidedly clearer in French than in Eng-

Your heart is burſt, you haue loſt halfe your ſoule   [311 *a*]
Euen now, now, very now, an old blacke Ram   96
Is tupping your white Ewe.   Ariſe, ariſe,
Awake the ſnorting Cittizens with the Bell,
Or elſe the deuill will make a Grand-ſire of you.
Ariſe I ſay.   100

    Bra.   What, haue you loſt your wits *?*
    Rod.   Moſt reuerend Signior, do you know my voice?
    Bra.   Not I : what are you ?
    Rod.   My name is *Rodorigo.*
    Bra.   The worſſer welcome :   105
I haue charg'd thee not to haunt about my doores :
In honeſt plaineneſſe thou haſt heard me ſay,
My Daughter is not for thee.   And now in madneſſe
(Being full of Supper, and diſtempring draughtes)
Vpon malitious knauerie, doſt thou come   110
To ſtart my quiet.
    Rod.   Sir, Sir, Sir.
    Bra.   But thou muſt needs be ſure,   113

---

95. *ſoule*] *ſoule ;* Qq, Rowe et seq.
96. *Euen now, now*] *Euen now* Qq,
F₃F₄, Rowe, Jen. Steev. Rann. Sing. *Ev'n
now, ev'n* Pope +.
99, 100. One line, Qq.
99. *deuill*] *Diuell* Q₁Q₂.   *Deuill* Q₃.
Diuell F₂.   *Devil* F₃F₄.
    you.] *you,* Qq.
100. *ſay*] *ſad* Q₃.
101. [appearing above, at a Window.
Cap.
104. *is*] *is—* Cap. Steev. Rann. Var.

Sing.
105. *worſer*] *worſe* Qq, Pope, Theob.
Han. Warb. Cap. Jen. Steev. Rann. Var.
Coll.
106. *I haue*] *I've* Pope +, Dyce iii,
Huds.
108. *Daughter is*] *daughter's* Pope +.
110. *knauerie*] Ff, Rowe, Knt, Del.
brauery Qq et cet.
111. *quiet.*] *quiet ?* Qq.   *quiet :* Cap.
112. *Sir.*] *sir, sir—* Steev. Var.   *Sir—*
Rowe et cet.

---

lish : Il y a peut-être un jeu de mots entre le mot *robb'd* et *robed* 'revêtu d'une robe.
Vous êtes un robin, par pudeur mettez votre robe.'

94. **for shame**] KNIGHT : This is not used as a reproach, but means—*for decency*
put on your gown.   [See note on 'tongued,' line 27, where Theobald thinks that this
refers to his Senatorial gown.]

95. **burst**] For many instances where this means *break*, see SCHMIDT s. v.

105. **worsser**] For many instances of double comparatives and superlatives, see
ABBOTT, § 11.

109. **distempring**] MALONE : To be distempered with liquor was, in Shakespeare's
time, the phrase for intoxication. Conf. *Ham.* III, ii, 288.

110. **Vpon**] See ABBOTT, § 191, or *Lear*, V, iii, 166.

112. **Sir**] GOULD (p. 84) : Why cannot some actor who represents the silly gentleman,' make him interrupt the old man at intervals in order to get a hearing, instead of
repeating 'Sir, sir, sir' all at once, as is invariably done upon the stage ? and which

My ſpirits and my place haue in their power
To make this bitter to thee. 115
   Rodo. Patience good Sir.
   Bra. What tell'ſt thou me of Robbing?
This is Venice : my houſe is not a Grange.
   Rodo. Moſt graue *Brabantio,*
In ſimple and pure ſoule, I come to you. 120
   Ia. Sir : you are one of thoſe that will not ſerue God,
ıf the deuill bid you. Becauſe we come to do you ſeruice,
and you thinke we are Ruffians, you'le haue your Daugh-
ter couer'd with a Barbary horſe, you'le haue your Ne- 124

---

114. *ſpirits*] Ff, Rowe. *ſpirit* Qq et cet.
   their] Ff, Rowe+, Cap. Knt. *them*
Qq et cet.
117. *What*] What, Qq.
117, 118. *What... Venice*] Ff. One line,
Qq et cet.
118. *Grange*] *graunge* Qq.

121. *Sir :*] Sir, Q₂Q₃Ff, Rowe, Pope,
Han. Johns. Knt. *Zouns Sir*, Q₁ et cet.
   you are] *you are not* Han. (misprint?)
122. *deuill*] *Divell* F₂.
123. *and you*] *you* Qq, Pope+, Cap.
Jen. Steev. Rann. Var. Sing. Ktly.

---

indeed is in the text so set down? BOOTH: This should indeed be so spoken, impatiently, but without interrupting Brabantio.

114. In this line KNIGHT silently adopts *spirit* of Qq, and retains 'their' of the Ff. I think it would have been better had the change been reversed; 'spirits' in the plural, thus used, is quite Shakespearian.—ED.

118. **Grange**] WARTON: That is, you are in a populous city, not in a lone house, where a robbery might be easily committed. 'Grange' is properly the farm of a monastery, where corn (Lat. *granum*) is reposited. But in Lincolnshire, and in other Northern counties, every lone house, or farm which stands solitary, is called a *grange*. STEEVENS: Conf. *Meas. for Meas.* III, i, 278, 'at the moated grange resides this dejected Mariana.' KNIGHT refers to the picture of neglected loneliness, which this 'moated grange' in *Meas. for Meas.* suggested to Tennyson, in those verses which are familiar to us all.

122. **deuill**] GOULD (p. 84): Actors usually commit the ludicrous mistake of bring ing down the emphasis plump on 'devil,' as if the highest motive for serving God were the devil's bidding! J. B. BOOTH said: 'that will not serve *God*, if the devil *bid* you,' giving the plain meaning, that the devil's bidding was no argument *against* serving God.

123. **Ruffians**] STAUNTON: Here employed in its secondary sense of *roisterer, swash-buckler,* and the like, though its primary meaning was, undoubtedly, *pander;* Latin 'leno,' the Italian 'roffiano.'

124. **Nephewes**] STEEVENS: Here, like Lat. *nepos,* it signifies a grandson, or any lineal descendant, however remote. BOSWELL: The word *grandson* never occurs in Shakespeare. DYCE (*Gloss.*): 'Nephew,' like cousin, was formerly used with great laxity. See *1 Hen. VI:* II, v, 64, where *nephew* ought to mean *cousin.* HALLIWELL appositely cites the fact that Shakespeare in his Will speaks of his grand-daughter, Elizabeth Hall, as his *niece.* [See Richardson's *Dict.* for manifold citations, from Robert of Gloucester down, where *nephew* is used for grandson or lineal descendant. Cooper's *Thes.* 'Nepos: the sonne or daughters sonne, a nephew.'—ED.]

phewes neigh to you, you'le haue Courfers for Cozens: 125
and Gennets for Germaines.

Bra.   What prophane wretch art thou?

Ia.   I am one Sir, that comes to tell you, your Daughter and the Moore, are making the Beaſt with two backs.

Bra.   Thou art a Villaine.   130

Iago.   You are a Senator.

Bra.   This thou ſhalt anſwere. I know thee *Rodorigo.*

Rod.   Sir, I will anſwere any thing. But I befeech you
If't be your pleaſure, and moſt wiſe confent,

(As partly I find it is) that your faire Daughter,   135
At this odde Euen and dull watch o'th'night

125. *neigh*] *ney* Q₁.
   Cozens] *coufens* Qq. *Coufins* F₃F₄.
126. *Germaines*] Iermans Q₁. Germans Q₂Q₃F₃F₄. *Germans* F₂.
128. *that comes*] *that come* Qq.
129. *are*] Ff, Rowe, Knt. *are now*
Qq et cet.
131. *are a*] QqFf, Rowe+, Knt. *are*

—*a* Cap. et cet.
132. *know*] *kow* F₂.
   Rodorigo] *Roderigo* Q₁Q₃.
134–150. Om. Q₁.
136. *odde Euen*] *od euen* Q₂Q₃. *odd-
even* Mal. et seq. *odd season* Rann. conj.
odd hour Cartwright.

126. **Gennets**] WEDGWOOD: Genet, a small-sized Spanish horse. Sp. *gineto*, a
light horseman, named from the Berber tribe of Zeneta, who supplied the Moorish
sultans of Grenada with a body of horse on which they placed great reliance. [While
the alliteration is here evident of *gennets* and *germans*, it is not impossible that, in
addition, in Shakespeare's time, the Berber or Moorish origin of the gennet was suggested to an auditor quite as much as the Spanish.—ED.]

126. **Germaines**] DYCE (*Gloss.*): Relations.

127. **prophane**] JOHNSON: That is, what wretch of gross and licentious language?
In that sense Shakespeare often uses this word. STEEVENS: Howell, in a dialogue
prefixed to his edition of Cotgrave, 1673, has the following: 'J' aimerois mieux estre
trop ceremonieux, que trop prophane,' which he thus anglicizes: 'I had rather be too
ceremonious, than too prophane.' [See II, i, 188.]

129. See Rabelais, liv. I, cap. iii.

131. **You are**] It was UPTON who suggested the dash after these words, which is
found in all editions since Capell's time, except Knight's. 'A senator,' says Upton (p.
176), 'is added beyond expectation; any one would think Iago was going to call him
as bad names as he himself was called by the senator Brabantio.'

132. **thou**] DELIUS: This is to be emphasized. Brabantio does not know Iago, and
therefore Roderigo, whom he does know, must answer for Iago's insulting remarks.

136. **odde Euen**] JOHNSON: The *even* of *night* is *midnight*, the time when night
is divided into *even* parts. HENLEY: This 'odd even' is simply the interval between
twelve at night and one in the morning. STEEVENS, in his earlier editions, suggested
'odd *steven*,' a Chaucerian word signifying *time;* but he wisely withdrew the suggestion
in his Var. '93, although not before M. MASON said that he 'should chuse to read *dull
season* as an expression that would more naturally occur either to Shakespeare or to
Roderigo.' MALONE thinks that 'this *odd-even* of the night' appears to mean that it

Tranſported with no worſe nor better guard,   137
But with a knaue of common hire, a Gundelier,
To the groſſe claſpes of a Laſciuious Moore :
If this be knowne to you, and your Allowance,   140
We then haue done you bold, and ſaucie wrongs.
But if you know not this, my Manners tell me,
We haue your wrong rebuke.   Do not beleeue
That from the ſence of all Ciuilitie,
I thus would play and trifle with your Reuerence.   145
Your Daughter (if you haue not giuen her leaue)
I ſay againe, hath made a groſſe reuolt,
Tying her Dutie, Beautie, Wit, and Fortunes
In an extrauagant, and wheeling Stranger,   149

137. *nor*] *or* F₃F₄, Rowe.
138. *common*] Om. Pope+.
    Gundelier] FfQ₂Q₃.   *Gundalier*
Rowe+.   *Gondelier* Johns. Jen.   *Gondolier*
Cap.
139. *Moore :*] *Moor,*— Mal.
140. *and*] *and to* Q₃.

141. *wrongs.*] *wrongs ?* Q₂Q₃.
146, 147. (*if...againe,*] In parenthesis,
Q₃.
148. *Tying*] *Laying* Coll. ii (MS).
149. *In an*] *To an* Pope+, Rann.   *On
an* Cap. Coll. ii (MS).

---

was just approaching to, or just past, that it was doubtful whether at that moment it
stood at the point of midnight, or at some other less equal division of the twenty-four
hours; which a few minutes either before, or after, midnight would be.   So in *Macb.*
III, iv, 126 : ‘What is the night? *Lady M.* Almost at odds with morning, which is
which.’   ABBOTT, § 435 : *And* is omitted.   Cicero says, that the extreme test of a
man’s honesty is that you can play at odd and even with him in the dark.   And perhaps ‘odd-(and-)even’ here means, a time when there is no distinguishing between
odd and *even.*

137. **Transported**] To mend this incomplete sentence HANMER, followed by CA-
PELL, added *Be* before line 136 : ‘Be at this odd-even,’ &c.   MASON added it before
line 137.   STAUNTON says, that ‘transported’ is equivalent to *transported herself*
[which I doubt], and KNIGHT says that he must leave the sentence as he finds it.

138. **But**] See ABBOTT, § 127, for instances of *but* used in the sense of *except*, following negative comparatives, where we should use *than.*

138. **Gundelier**] WALKER (*Vers.* p. 218) shows that, just as *pioneer, engineer,
muleteer*, &c. should be written *pioner, enginer, muleter*, &c., so here the verse requires
gundeler.   DYCE (ed. iii) yields to Walker’s authority, and asserts that ‘if the author
did not write “gundeler” (“gondoler”), he certainly intended the word to be so pronounced.’   ABBOTT does not include this word in the list which he gives (§ 492) of the
class referred to by Walker, but places it under ‘apparent Alexandrines’ (§ 497), and
contracts it *gond(o)lier.*   Walker’s treatment is, I think, the better.—ED.

141. **saucie**] That is, insolent, outrageous, used in a stronger sense than merely
malapert.   Conf. *Macb.* III, iv, 25 : ‘I am . . . . bound in To saucy doubts and fears.’

144. **from**] For instances where ‘from’ means ‘apart from,’ ‘away from,’ see AB-
BOTT, § 158.   Also *Macb.* III, i, 131, ‘something from the palace.’

149. **In**] It is scarcely necessary, I think, to suppose that ‘In’ is here used for *on* or

Of here, and euery where : ftraight fatisfie your felfe.   150
If fhe be in her Chamber, or your houfe,
Let loofe on me the Iuftice of the State
For thus deluding you.

   Bra.   Strike on the Tinder, hoa :
Giue me a Taper : call vp all my people,   155
This Accident is not vnlike my dreame,
Beleefe of it oppreffes me alreadie.
Light, I fay, light.   *Exit.*

   Iag.   Farewell: for I muft leaue you.
It feemes not meete, nor wholefome to my place   160
To be producted, (as if I ftay, I fhall,)   [311 *b*]
Againft the Moore.   For I do know the State,
(How euer this may gall him with fome checke)   163

---

151. *her*] *your* Ff, Rowe, Jen.
153. *thus deluding you*] *this delufion* Q₁.
158. *Exit.*] Om. QqFf. Exit Bra. from above. Han.
160. *place*] *pate* Q₁.

161. *producted*] Ff. *produc'd* Qq et cet.
163. *How euer*] *Now euer* Q₁ [thus noted by Jen. and Camb. edd. *How euer* in Ashbee.]
   may] *my* Q₃.

---

to. The idea of the entire surrender of Desdemona to Othello is intended, which 'in' certainly conveys, even better than *on.* There are, assuredly, instances where *in* is used where we should now use *on,* as in Gen. i, 22; Matt. vi, 10, also *1 Hen. VI*: I, ii, 2 (all cited in *Bible Word-Book*), where, however, the phrase 'in the earth,' is immediately connected with 'in the heavens,' and is not, therefore, exactly parallel with the present instance. See 'in your owne part,' I, iii, 91, *post.*—ED.

   149. **extrauagant**] Used by Shakespeare three times and uniformly in its classical sense of *wandering, vagrant.*

   149. **wheeling**] COLLIER (ed. ii) adopts *wheedling* from his (MS), as it is 'just the epithet that would be applied by Roderigo to Othello, who had cajoled and cheated Brabantio out of his daughter.' SINGER (*Sh. Vind.* p. 279): Even could Collier adduce an instance of *wheedling* before the reign of Charles II., it would be difficult to perfuade us to displace 'wheeling;' for, connected, as it is, with 'extravagant,' it is ro doubt used like the Italian 'girevole,' with its secondary meaning of *inconstant, un steady.* That *wheedling* should have been suggested, makes it certain that Collier's (MS) in this instance lived not earlier than the last century. STAUNTON says, that he would prefer *whirling.* SCHMIDT (*Lex.*) thinks that from meaning 'to fetch a compass,' as in *Cor.* I, vi, 19, it came to mean 'to err about,' as here and in *Tro. & Cress.* V, vii, 2.

   156. **dream**] COLERIDGE (*Notes*, &c. 249): The old careful senator, being caught careless, transfers his caution to his dreaming power at least. BOOTH: This dream is to the superstitious Italian convincing proof of what he is told, and accounts for his sudden belief in his friend's treachery.

   163. **checke**] JOHNSON: Some rebuke.

Cannot with fafetie caft-him. For he's embark'd
With fuch loud reafon to the Cyprus Warres,   165
(Which euen now ftands in Act)that for their foules
Another of his Fadome, they haue none,
To lead their Bufineffe. In which regard,
Though I do hate him as I do hell apines,
Yet, for neceffitie of prefent life,   170
I muft fhow out a Flag, and figne of Loue,
(Which is indeed but figne)that you fhal furely find him
Lead to the Sagitary the raifed Search: 173

164. *caft-him*] Hyphen, only in F₁.
embark'd] *imbark'd* QqF₂.
165. *Cyprus*] *Cipres* Qq. *Cyprus'*
Theob. Warb. Johns. Cap. Jen. Steev. Var.
Knt, Sing. Sta. Ktly.
Warres] *war* Cap. Rann.
166. *ftands*] QqFf, Rowe, Cap. Rann.
Del. *stand* Pope et cet.
167. *Fadome*] *fathome* Qq. *fadom* F₄,
Rowe+, Wh. *fathom* Cap. et cet.
none] *not* Q₁, Cap. Jen. Steev.
Rann. Sing. Ktly.
168. *Bufineffe*] *business on* Cap.

169. *Though*] *Tho* Qq.
hell apines] *hell* Ff. *hells paines*
Qq, Rowe+, Jen. Sing. *hell pains* Cap.
Steev. Var. Knt, Coll. *hell-pains* Dyce et
cet.
172. *figne*)] Ff. *figne*, Qq. *sign :* Rowe
i. *sign*.) or *sign*. Rowe ii et cet.
fhall furely find] *may surely find*
Pope+. *may find* Han.
172, 173. *find...Search*] One line, Q₁.
173. *Sagitary*] *Sagittar* Q₁, Cap. Mal.
Sagittary Q₂Q₃F₄.

164. **cast**] JOHNSON: That is, dismiss him. [See II, ii, 31; II, ii, 302; V, ii, 400.]
PURNELL: Cf. 'castaway,' and Anglo-Indian 'a caster,' 'a horse sold out of a regiment
as useless.'

165. **Cyprus**] See ABBOTT, § 22, for instances of the conversion of proper names
into adjectives, for which license, Abbott says, the reason is to be found in an increasing
dislike and disuse of the inflection in 's. Conf. 'Verona walls,' *Rom. & Jul.* III, iii,
17 [and 'hell pains,' line 169 below, where, by the way, in F₁, the *a* and *p* have simply
changed places.—ED.]

167. **Fadome**] BOOTH: Touch your head to indicate *judgement*, not your breast to
imply *courage*.

168. **Businesse**] COLERIDGE (*Notes*, &c. 250): The forced praise of Othello, followed by the bitter hatred of him in this speech! And observe how Brabantio's dream
prepares for his recurrence (l. 188) to the notion of philtres, and how both prepare for
carrying on the plot of the arraignment of Othello on this ground.

173. **Sagitary**] STEEVENS: This means the sign of the fictitious creature so-called,
i. e. an animal compounded of man and horse, and armed with a bow and quiver.
KNIGHT: This is generally taken to be an inn. It was the residence at the Arsenal
of the commanding officers of the navy and army of the republic. The figure of an
archer with his drawn bow, over the gates, still indicates the place. Probably Shakespeare had looked upon that sculpture. SINGER: Yet Cassio's inquiry, 'Ancient, what
makes he here?' seems to imply that to Shakespeare the sign, whencesoever he derived
it, was that of a private house or inn; and that it was a representation of the centaur
of the zodiac, or of the Tale of Troy, and not a mere bowman. TH. ELZE (*Shake-*

And there will I be with him. So farewell.   *Exit.*

Enter Brabantio, with Seruants and Torches.   175
Bra. It is too true an euill. Gone ſhe is,
And what's to come of my deſpiſed time,   177

175. Scene III. Pope+, Jen.
Enter...] Enter *Brabantio* (*Bar-
bantio* Q₁) in his night gowne, and Seruants with Torches Qq, Rowe, Pope,
Theob. Jen.

speare *Jahrbuch*, 1879, xiv, 174) gives a curious list of the Inns of Venice in Othello's day, of which history has preserved the names, as follows: '*al Selvadego, allo Sturione, al Cavaletto, al Capello, alle do (due) Spade, alla Campana, al S. Giorgio* or *al Flauto, al Lion bianco, al Gambaro, alla Luna, all' Aquila nera, alla Corona, all' Angelo, alla Torre,*—but *al Sagittario* has not yet been discovered. The most probable supposition is,' continues Th. Elze, 'that it was an imaginary name devised by Shakespeare, which we should be as little likely to discover as *The Pegasus* in Genoa, where the Pedant lodged with Baptista in *Tam. of Shr.* IV, iv, 5. A certain appropriateness in the names and characters is not lacking: the soldier lives in the *Sagittary*, the Pedant in the *Pegasus.*' ROLFE disposes of Knight's assertion, that this was the Arsenal. 'It appears,' he says, in his Notes ad loc. 'from I, ii, 53, below, that Othello was not at his usual lodging, and the messengers of the Senate had not known where to find him. Cassio also asks "What makes he here?" which implies that he was in an unfamiliar place. Note also what Othello says, in I, iii, 143. If the Arsenal had been the "place," no guide to it would have been necessary.' In an *Addendum* on p. 210, Rolfe still more emphatically disproves Knight's remark: 'We cannot find any evidence that the Arsenal at Venice was ever called "the Sagittary;" probably this is a mere conjecture of Knight's. The figure mentioned by Knight is not "over the gates," but is one of four statues standing in front of the structure. It represents a man holding a bow (not "drawn") in his hand, but is in no respect more conspicuous than its three companions. If Shakespeare was ever in Venice he probably saw the statue (if it is as old as the gateway, which was built in 1460), but we cannot imagine why it should suggest to him to call the place *the Sagittary.* That word means not an ordinary archer, but a *Centaur* with a bow, as in the familiar representations of the zodiacal sign Sagittarius. This is its sense in the only other passage in which Shakespeare uses it, *Tro. & Cress.* V, v, 14: "the dreadful Sagittary Appals our numbers." That *the Sagittary* in the present passage cannot be the Arsenal is, however, sufficiently clear from I, iii, 143, 144. The Arsenal was by far the largest and most prominent public building, or collection of buildings, in all Venice, its outer walls being nearly two miles in circuit. To suppose that anybody in the employ of the government would need the help of Iago in finding the place is absurd.'

177. **despised**] WARBURTON: We should read *despited*, i. e. vexatious. HEATH: Brabantio very properly calls the remaining part of his life a 'despised time,' since the ill-conduct of his only daughter, in matching herself to an adventurer so much beneath her birth and rank, could not, in his apprehension, but draw great contempt on himself. JOHNSON: 'Despised time' is *time of no value;* time in which 'There's nothing serious in mortality, The wine of life is drawn, And the mere dregs Are left this vault to brag of,' *Macb* II, iii, 89. STEEVENS: Again, in *Rom. & Jul.* I, iv, 110: 'a despised life closed in my breast.'

Is naught but bitterneſſe. Now *Rodorigo*,   178
Where didſt thou ſee her? (Oh vnhappie Girle)
With the Moore faiſt thou? (Who would be a Father?)   180
How didſt thou know 'twas ſhe? (Oh ſhe deceaues me
Paſt thought:) what ſaid ſhe to you? Get moe Tapers:
Raiſe all my Kindred.   Are they married thinke you?

    Rodo.   Truely I thinke they are.

    Bra.   Oh Heauen: how got ſhe out?   185
Oh treaſon of the blood.
Fathers, from hence truſt not your Daughters minds
By what you ſee them act.   Is there not Charmes,
By which the propertie of Youth, and Maidhood
May be abus'd? Haue you not read *Rodorigo*,   190
Of ſome ſuch thing?

---

178. *Is*] *I* Q₃.
    naught] Ff, Rowe i.   *nought* Qq
et cet.
    bitterneſſe.   Now] *bitterneſſe now*
Qq.
    180. *ſaiſt*] *saidst* Theob. ii, Han. Warb.
Johns.
    181. *ſhe deceaues*] *thou deceiueſt* Q₁,
Johns. Jen. Steev. Rann. Var. Coll. (No
parentheses in this speech in Q₁.)

182. *moe*] Ff, Ktly.   *more* Qq et cet.
183. *kindred*] *kinred* F₂F₃.
185, 186. One line, Qq, Cap. et cet.
185. *got*] *gat* Rowe ii+.
186. *of the*] *of my* Ff, Rowe+.
188. *Is there*] Qq, Var. Sing. Dyce,
Ktly, Glo. Cam.   *Are there* Ff et cet.
189. *Maidhood*] *manhood* Qq.
191. *thing?*] *thing.* Q₁Q₂.   *things?* Q₃.

---

181. **deceaues**] May it not be permitted here to 'frolic in conjecture,' and suggest
that the printer has accidentally substituted an *s* for a *d*, and that we should read *deceaued*? Even if we adopt the reading of Q₁, I should prefer *they deceaued* to 'thou
deceiuest.'   In both cases a certain symmetry of the sentence is preserved in the alter-
nation of thought, which is first fixed on the daughter, and then on the Moor, then
recurring to the daughter, then to the Moor and the daughter both together, then to
the daughter, and then to them both together again.—ED.

186. **blood**] BOOTH: With emotion, as with Shylock: 'my own flesh and blood to
rebel!'

188. **Is**] See ABBOTT, § 335, for instances where the quasi-singular verb *precedes*
the plural subject.   This usage Abbott explains on the ground, that when the subject is
as yet future, and, as it were, unsettled, the third person singular might be regarded as
the normal inflection.   Such passages are very common, particularly in the case of
'There is.'

188. **charmes**] BOOTH: In your study of this play bear in mind the superstition
that pervades it.   Even Othello, while sneering at it, humours it when Desdemona is
brought before the Duke as a witness against him; and he has faith in the 'antique
token' and the sword of 'ice-brook's temper.'   Reflections like these help the actor to
feel the character he assumes.

189, 190. **By . . . abus'd**] JOHNSON: By which the faculties of a young virgin
may be infatuated and made subject to illusions and false imagination.

Rod.   Yes Sir : I haue indeed.   192
Bra.   Call vp my Brother : oh would you had had her.
Some one way,ſome another.   Doe you know
Where we may apprehend her,and the Moore ?   195
Rod.   I thinke I can diſcouer him, if you pleaſe
To get good Guard, and go along with me.
Bra.   Pray you lead on.   At euery houſe Ile call,
(I may command at moſt)get Weapons (hoa)
And raiſe ſome ſpeciall Officers of might :   200
On good *Rodorigo,* I will deſerue your paines.   *Exeunt.*

192. *Yes...indeed*] *I haue ſir* Q₁.
193. *Brother*] *brothers* F₃F₄, Rowe,
Pope, Han.
    oh would] *O that* Q₁, Mal. Steev.
Coll.   *Oh, 'would* Theob. ii, Warb. Johns.
Rann. Ktly.
194. *you*] *yon* Q₁.
195. *her, and*] *her and* Theob. ii et seq.
198. *you lead*] *leade me* Q₁.

198. *Ile*] *ile* Q₃.   *I'le* F₃.   *I'll* F₄.
199. *moſt*)] *moſt :* or *most.* Qq et cet.
    Weapons (hoa)] *weapons ho,* Qq.
200. *might*] FfQ₂Q₃, Rowe+, Cap.
Jen. Del.   *night* Q₁ et cet.
201. *On good*] *On, good* F₄.
    I will] Ff, Rowe, Knt.   *Ile* Q₁Q₂.
ile Q₃.   *I'll* Pope et cet.

193. **Brother**] SINGER : Gratiano was in the poet's mind, though he is not wanted
or called upon the stage till the Fifth Act.

197. **go**] ABBOTT, § 30, notes that here, as in *Mid. N. D.* I, i, 123, *Tam. of Shr.*
IV, v, 7; *2 Hen. IV:* II, i, 191, 'go' is used where we should use *come.*

199. **at most**] JOURDAIN (*Philol. Soc. Trans.,* 1860, p. 141): It here means, 'in
the *greatest degree,*' Brabantio being one of the council of three.   See note on I, ii, 16.
[It was not until I had read Jourdain's note, and the following in the excellent edition
of M. D'HUGUES : 'Nous n'avons trouvé dans aucun lexique l'explication de cette locution *at most,*' that any obscurity appeared to me here.   Notwithstanding Jourdain's explanation, I still think that ' at most ' is simply elliptical for *at most of them.*   Brabantio
says, in effect, ' I'll call at all the houses of my kindred ; at most of them my call will
be obeyed.'—ED.]

200. **might**] MALONE : I have no doubt that Shakespeare, before he wrote this
play, read *The Commonwealth and Government of Venice,* translated from the Italian
by Lewes Lewkenor, and printed in Qto, 1599; a book prefixed to which we find a
copy of verses by Spenser.   This treatise furnished our poet with the knowledge of
those *officers* of night whom Brabantio here desires to be called to his assistance.   ' For
the greater expedition thereof of these kinds of judgements, the heades or chieftaines
of the *officers by night* do obtaine the authority of which the advocators are deprived.
These *officers of the night* are six, and six likewise are those meane officers, that have
only power to correct base vagabonds and trifling offenses.   Those that do execute this
office are called heades of the tribes of the city, because out of every tribe (for the city
is divided into six tribes,) there is elected an *officer of the night,* and a head of the
tribe.—The duty of eyther of these officers is, to keepe a watch every other night by
turn, within their tribes ; and, now the one, and then the other, to make rounds about
his quarter, till the dawning of the day, being always guarded and attended on with
wearoned officers and serjeants, and to see that there be not any disorder done in the

Scena Secunda.

Enter Othello, Iago, Attendants, with Torches.

Ia. Though in the trade of Warre I haue ſlaine men,
Yet do I hold it very ſtuffe o'th'conſcience
To do no contriu'd Murder : I lacke Iniquitie   5
S ometime to do me ſeruice.   Nine, or ten times
I had thought t'haue yerk'd him here vnder the Ribbes.
Othello. 'Tis better as it is.   8

---

1. Scene IV. Pope+, Jen.
2. Attendants] and attendants Qq.
    with Torches] Om. Cap. Steev. Mal.
Var. Sing.
    [The Street. Rowe.   Another Street,
before the Sagittary. Theob.
    4. *ſtuffe o'th'conſcience*] *ſtuft of conſcience* Q₁.
    5. *Murder*] *murrher* Q₁. *murther* Q₃,
Pope, Theob. ii, Han. Warb. Cap. Knt, Wh.
i, Rlfe.
        lacke] *lack* Q₃. *lake* F₂F₃. *take* F₄.

Rowe.
    6. *Sometime*] Ff, Rowe, Knt, Sta.
Sometimes Qq et cet.
        Nine,] *nine* QqF₃F₄.
    7. *I had*] *I* Pope+.   *I'd* Wh. ii.
        t'haue] Dyce ii, Huds. Wh. ii.   *to've*
Pope+.   *to haue* QqFf et cet.
        yerk'd] *ierk'd* Q₁.   *jerk'd* Q₂Q₃,
Pope+, Jen. Rann. Wh. ii.
        vnder the Ribbes] Separate line, Qq.
        Ribbes] *Rib* F₄, Rowe.
    8. *'Tis*] *It's* Pope+.

---

darkness of the night, which alwaies emboldeneth men to naughtinesse; and that there
be not any houses broken up, nor thieves nor rogues lurking in corners with intent to
do violence.'—*Commonwealth of Venice*, pp. 97, 99. [This note of Malone seems to
have satisfied, with the exception of DELIUS, all modern editors, even KNIGHT, who
has, in many another passage, maintained the F₁ on grounds less substantial than he
might have stood on here. If Brabantio had wished to summon to his aid the customary guardians of the night, the epithet 'special' is needless, whereas it is not only
expressed, but it is emphasized; it is transposed from the noun it particularly qualifies
in order to give it importance. The logical order is 'officers of special might,' just as
'the whole ear of Denmark' in *Ham.* I, v, 36, means 'the ear of all Denmark,' or as
'course of direct session,' *Oth.* I, ii, 105, means the 'direct course of session.' I am
afraid that here the zeal of Malone's learning hath eaten him up, and that 'night' of
Q₁ is a misprint.—ED.]

    2. **Torches**] DELIUS: To Shakespeare's public this conveyed the idea not only
that the time was night, but also that the scene was in the street.

    4. **it very**] Is not this a case of the absorption of the definite article in the *t* sound
of 'it'?—ED.

    4. **stuff**] JOHNSON: That is, substance or essence of the conscience. LLOYD: Iago
gains the confidence of Roderigo by the proper force of his will, and by plain exposition
of politic hypocrisy; this is his course with a fool destitute of principles; his pretensions
to honesty [as in this line] gain him the confidence of Othello, whose credulousness in
this respect would, in truth, appear to us as gross as that of Roderigo, but that it is not
associated with the same circumstances of disgracefulness.

    7. **yerk'd**] DYCE: To strike with a quick, smart blow. WHITE (ed. ii): A mere
phonetic spelling of *jerked*.

    8. COLERIDGE: How well these few words impress at the outset the truth of Othello's

Iago.   Nay but he prated,
And fpoke fuch fcuruy, and prouoking termes   10
Againft your Honor, that with the little godlineffe I haue
I did full hard forbeare him. But I pray you Sir,
Are you faft married ? Be affur'd of this,
That the Magnifico is much belou'd,
And hath in his effect a voice potentiall   15
As double as the Dukes : He will diuorce you.

---

11. *Againft your Honor*] Separate line, Pope et seq.

12. *pray you*] Ff, Rowe, Knt, Dyce, Sta.Wh. Glo. Cam. Del. Rlfe, Huds. *pray* Qq et cet.

13. *Be affur'd*] Ff, Rowe, Cap. Knt,

Dyce, Sta.Wh. Glo. Cam. Del. Rlfe, Huds. *For be fure* Qq et cet.

15. *his*] *its* Quincy (MS).

16. *double*] *noble* Quincy (MS). *capable* Cartwright. *indubitable* Bulloch.

Dukes] *Duke* Q_3.

---

own character of himself at the end—'that he was not easily wrought'! His self-government contradistinguishes him throughout from Leontes. GOULD (p. 94): J. B. Booth gave this with a gravity, a weighty distinctness on the last three words, 'better—as—it is,' which conveyed a reproof, and was intended to dismiss the subject.

9. **he prated**] STEEVENS asks, 'of whom is this said? Of Roderigo?' KNIGHT answers: 'Iago is preparing Othello for the appearance of Roderigo with Brabantio, which he does by representing that Roderigo has communicated to him his intention to apprise Desdemona's father of her flight, and that he resented his expressions toward Othello.'

12. **forbeare**] SCHMIDT (*Lex.*): To spare, to let alone. Conf. *Ham.* V, i, 261: 'For love of God, forbear him.'

12. **But**] BOOTH: Now let your manner be more serious.

12. **you**] A mere enclitic in pronunciation, absorbed in the final sound of 'pray.'— ED.

14. **Magnifico**] TOLLET: 'The chiefe men of Venice are by a peculiar name called *Magnifici*, i. e. Magnificoes.'—Minsheu [s. v. *Magnificent*. Minsheu adds: Et Academiarum Rectores in Germania, eodem titulo insigniuntur.—ED.]

15. **his**] STAUNTON: Here employed for the then scarce known *its*, and refers to 'voice.'

16. **double**] WARBURTON, followed by THEOBALD (not CAPELL, as KNIGHT says), interpreted this as signifying *as large, as extensive*, equivalent to the Greek διπλοῦς, and cited Dioscorides and Theocritus. Whereupon Dr JOHNSON thus improved the occasion : All this learning, if it had even been what it endeavors to be thought, is, in this place, superfluous. There is no ground for supposing, that our author copied or knew the Greek phrase ; nor does it follow, that, because a word has two senses in one language, the word which in another answers to one sense should answer to both. *Manus*, in Latin, signifies both a *hand* and *troop of soldiers*, but we cannot say, that 'the captain marched at the head of his hand;' or, 'that he laid his troop upon his sword.' It is not always in books that the meaning is to be sought of this writer, who was much more acquainted with naked reason and with living manners. 'Double' has here its natural sense. The president of every deliberative assembly has a *double* voice. In our courts the chief justice and one of the inferior judges prevail over the other two.

[16. 'As double as the Dukes.']

because the chief justice has a *double* voice. Brabantio had in his effect, tho' not by law yet by *weight* and *influence*, a voice not *actual* and *formal*, but *potential* and operative, as *double*, that is, a voice that when a question was suspended would turn the balance as effectually *as the Duke's*. 'Potential' is used in the sense of science; a caustic is called a potential fire.   MALONE'S studies in early Venetian polity played him false here; so far from the Duke's having a '*double* voice,' it appears from Thomas's *History of Italy*, 1560, that it was exactly what he had not: 'Whereas,' says Thomas, 'many have reported, the duke in ballotyng should have *two voices;* it is nothinge so, for in giving his voice he hath but one ballot, as all others have.'   Nothing discouraged, Malone at once surmises that 'Shakespeare might have gone on this received opinion, which he might have found in some other book.   Supposing, however, that he had learned from this very passage that the Duke had *not* a double voice in the Council of Seven, yet as he had a vote in each of the various Councils of the Venetian State (a privilege which no other person enjoys,) our poet might have thought himself justified in the epithet which he has here used; and this circumstance, which he might have found in a book already quoted, Contareno's *Commonwealth and Government of Venice*, 1599, was, I believe, here in his thoughts : " So great is the prince's authoritie, that he may, in whatsoever court, adjoine himselfe to the magistrate therein, being president, as his colleague and companion, and have equal power with the other presidents," &c., p. 41.   Again, p. 42 : " Besides this, the prince hath in *every Councell* equal authoritie with any of them, for one suffrage or lotte."   Thus we see, continues Malone, though he had not a double voice in any one assembly, yet as he had a vote in all the various assemblies, his voice, thus *added* to the voice of each of the presidents of those assemblies, might with strict propriety be called *double* and *potential*.'   STEEVENS : *Double* and *single* anciently signified *strong* and *weak* when applied to liquors, and perhaps to other objects.   In this sense the former epithet may be employed by Brabantio, and the latter by the chief justice speaking to Falstaff : ' Is not your wit single ?'   Here the phrase may, therefore, only signify that Brabantio's voice, as a magnifico, was as forcible as that of the Duke.   HENLEY : 'The double voice' of Brabantio refers to the opinion, (which, as being a magnifico, he was no less entitled to, than the duke himself), *either*, of nullifying the marriage of his daughter contracted without his consent; *or*, of subjecting Othello to fine and imprisonment for having seduced an heiress.   PYE [does one reader in a thousand know or remember, that Pye is a predecessor of Tennyson as Poet-Laureate ?—ED.] : Surely the obvious purport of the passage is that Brabantio, from his popularity and wealth, has effectually such a weight in the Senate as gives him a power equal to the double vote conferred by the constitution on the duke.   KNIGHT : It is clear that Shakespeare did not take the phrase in a literal sense; for, if he had supposed that the duke had a double voice as duke, he would not have assigned the same privilege to the senator Brabantio.   DELIUS : If what Brabantio says has as much weight as what the duke says, his voice must be twice as potential as that of the other nobles, i. e. as double as the duke's.   HUDSON : 'A voice potential or powerful *as much so as* the Duke's.'   JOURDAIN (*Philol. Soc. Trans.*, 1860, p. 142) : This is an historical mistake made by a typographical error; the 'as' should be *of*. The Duke had not a double voice, but the members of the Council of Three had very nearly such, as the following will show :—' Next vnto the Duke are three called the Signori Capi or Cai, whiche outwardly seeme inferioure to the Duke, and yet are of more auctoritee than he.   For theyr power is so absolute that if there happen cause why, they maie arrest the Duke.'—*The historie of Italie*, by William Thomas, 1549.

Or put vpon you, what reftraint or greeuance,   17
The Law (with all his might, to enforce it on)   [312 *a*]
Will giue him Cable.

Othel.   Let him do his fpight;   20
My Seruices, which I haue done the Signorie
Shall out-tongue his Complaints.   'Tis yet to know,
Which when I know, that boafting is an Honour,
I fhall promulgate.   I fetch my life and being,
From Men of Royall Seige.   And my demerites   25
May fpeake (vnbonnetted)to as proud a Fortune

17. *or greeuance*] Ff, Rowe+, Cap. Coll. Sing. Wh. i, Ktly, Del. *and greiv-ances* Q₃. *and greeuance* Q₁Q₂ et cet.
18. *The*] *That* Q₁.
    enforce] *inforce* Qq.
19. *Will*] *Weele* Qq.
21. *Seruices*] *feruice* Q₃.
22. *out-tongue*] *out tongue* Q₁.
    Complaints.] *complaints,* Qq.
23. *Which...know*] Om. Q₁.
24. *promulgate.*] *provulgate,* Q₁. *pro-*

mulgate) or *promulgate,* Pope et seq. *pro-mulge* Cap. conj. (p. 21, *a*).
25. *Seige.*] F₂. *height,*Q₁Q₂,]Jen. *hight,* Q₃. *Siege* F₃F₄ et cet.
    demerites] *demerrits,* Q₁.
26. *(vnbonnetted)*] *vnbonnited* Q₁. *un-bonneting* Pope, Warb. *and bonneted* Theob. Johns. Cap. Jen. *e'en bonneted* Han.
    to] Om. Q₂Q₃.

Therefore I read, 'as double *of* the Duke's.' [In note on I, i, 199, Jourdain asserts that Brabantio belonged to this Council of Three.—ED.] WHITE (ed. ii): A doubtful reading, but it may possibly mean merely as potential. [If Johnson's interpretation be not the obvious one, then I agree with White that the reading is doubtful, and am inclined to think that we might read 'as double *of.*' It is Iago's aim to poison Othello's delight and plague him with flies, therefore he exaggerates Brabantio's power in the State, even to saying that the effect of Brabantio's voice is as potential as double that of the Duke. But it is hardly worth the time and labour expended on it. We have the 'double,' and surely in the notes the 'toil and trouble,' needing but the 'fire and chauldron' to complete the round.—ED.]

21. To smooth away this Alexandrine, ABBOTT (§ 471) scans: My seru | ices which | I've done | the Sign | iorie. See also WALKER, *Vers.*, p. 243.

23, 24. BOOTH: The keynote of his nature, a modest, simple-hearted *gentleman,* not a braggart as Iago would make him out.

25. **Seige**] JOHNSON: Men who have sat upon royal *thrones.* CLARENDON: Seat, thence *rank,* because people sat at table and elsewhere in order of precedence. See *Ham.* IV, vii, 77.

25. **demerites**] STEEVENS: This has the same meaning, among Elizabethan writers, as *merits.* [Both Bullokar, 1621, and Minsheu, 1617, give *Demerit:* A desert.] STAUNTON: 'Demerit' now signifies only *ill* desert; in Shakespeare's day it was used indiscriminately for good or ill deserving. In the present instance it is apparently employed in the good sense, for Othello could hardly mean that his blemishes might stand without concealment beside the dignity he had achieved.

26. **vnbonnetted**] POPE: It should be *unbonneting,* i. e. without putting off the bonnet. THEOBALD: To speak 'unbonnetted' is to speak *with the cap off,* which is

As this that I haue reach'd.　For know *Iago*,　　27
But that I loue the gentle *Defdemona*,
I would not my vnhoufed free condition　　29

---

29. *not my...condition*] *not, my...condition*, Qq.

directly opposite to the poet's meaning.　So in *Lear*, III, i, 14, 'unbonneted he runs.'
Othello means to say, that his birth and services set him upon such a rank that he may
speak to a Senator of Venice with his hat *on*, i. e. without showing any marks of deference or inequality.　I, therefore, am inclined to think Shakespeare wrote : ' May speak,
and bonnetted,' &c.　Or, if any like better the change of the negative *un*, in the corrupted reading, into the epitatic *im*, we may thus reform it : ' May speak *imbonnetted*,'
&c.　[This last conjecture was withdrawn by Theobald (ed. ii), but proposed anew by
Steevens, without credit.]　JOHNSON : Pope's emendation may as well be *not putting
on* as *not putting off*, the bonnet.　STEEVENS : *Bonneter*, says Cotgrave, is to put off
one's cap.　So in *Cor.* II, ii, 30.　Mr Fuseli explains this passage as follows : ' I am
his equal or superior in rank; and were it not so, such are my demerits, that, unbonneted, without the addition of patrician or senatorial dignity, they may speak to as
proud a fortune,' &c.　' At Venice the *bonnet*, as well as the toge, is a badge of aristocratic honours to this day.'　A. C. (in *Var.'21*) : ' Unbonneted ' is uncovered, revealed, made known.　See a similar expression in II, iii, ' you *unlace* your reputation.'
COLERIDGE (*Notes*, &c., p. 250) : Theobald's argument goes on the assumption that
Shakespeare could not use the same word differently in different places; whereas I
should conclude, that as in the passage in *Lear* the word is employed in its direct
meaning, so here it is used metaphorically; and this is confirmed by what has escaped
the editors, that it is not ' I ' but ' my demerits ' that may speak ' unbonneted,'—without
the symbol of a petitioning inferior.　STAUNTON : The import we take to be,—my services when revealed (*unbonneted*) may *aspire* or *lay claim to* (*may speak to*) as proud
a fortune as this which I have attained.　Even with Fuseli's interpretation it is indispensable for the integrity of the passage that 'speak to' be understood in the sense
just mentioned of *aspire* or *lay claim to*.　SCHMIDT (*Lex.*) : Perhaps the meaning is
simply : I may say so with all courtesy and humility, and Othello's words must, perhaps, be accompanied by a corresponding gesture, as the writing of F_1 seems to imply,
by placing the word ' unbonnetted ' in a parenthesis.　WHITE (ed. ii) : The question
of manners in Shakespeare's time as to the hat seems very difficult.　The remembering
courtesy, the off-capping, and the unbonneting are quite incongruous.　No attempt to
reconcile these expressions has been at all successful.

29. **vnhoused**] JOHNSON : Free from *domestic* cares.　A thought natural to an adventurer.　WHALLEY : To Othello, talking as a soldier, ' unhoused ' may signify the having no settled house or habitation.　HUNTER (*New Illust.*, ii, 282) : This passage affords
one of the best proofs of Shakespeare's acquaintance with the Italian language.　' Un
housed ' conveys to English ears no idea of anything which any one would be unwilling to resign; and, in fact, it is only by recollecting the way in which the Italians use
cassare that we arrive at its true meaning, which is *unmarried*.　A soldier was as
much ' unhoused,' in the ordinary meaning of the term, after marriage as before.
Othello would not resign the freedom of his *bachelor estate*.　KNIGHT : Othello expresses no satisfaction at having been houseless, but he simply uses ' unhoused ' for
unmarried.　The *husband* is the head or *band* of the *house*,—the unmarried is ᴜhe
unhouse-banded—the ' unhoused.'

Put into Circumſcription,and Confine,   30
For the Seas worth. But looke, what Lights come yond?

Enter Caſſio, with Torches.

Iago. Thoſe are the raiſed Father, and his Friends :
You were beſt go in.
Othel. Not I : I muſt be found.   35
My Parts, my Title, and my perfeᶜt Soule
Shall manifeſt me rightly. Is it they ?   37

31. *Seas*] *sea's* Theob. et seq. *seas'*
Anon. (ap. Cam.)
   worth.] *worth,* Qq.
   Lights come] *light comes* Johns.
   yond] *yonder* Qq, Pope+, Jen.
Steev. Var. Coll. Sing. Wh. i, Ktly. *yond'*
Cap.
   Scene V. Pope+, Jen.
   32. *Enter...*] Enter *Caſſio* with lights,
Officers, and Torches (after *worth,* line 31)

Qq. Enter, at a Distance...Cap. After *no,*
line 38, Coll.
   33. *Thoſe*] *Theſe* Qq, Jen. Steev. Var.
Coll. Sing. Wh. i, Ktly.
   34. *in.*] *in :* Q₁.
   35. *found.*] *found,* Qq.
   36. *Parts*] *part* Han.
   37. *manifeſt*] *manifeſtly* F₂.
      me rightly.] *my right by :* Q₂Q₃.
      Is it they ?] *it is they.* Q₁.

31. **the Seas worth**] JOHNSON : I would not marry her, though she were as rich
as the Adriatic, which the Doge annually marries. STEEVENS : As the gold ring annually thrown by the Doge into the Adriatic cannot be said to have much enriched it,
I believe the common and obvious meaning of this passage is the true one. PYE : I
think Steevens indubitably right, but not for the reason he gives. I believe Johnson
thought no more of the Adriatic being enriched by the annual wedding-ring, than
Shakespeare did of the Adriatic at all. [Steevens refers to the occurrence of the same
phrase in D'Avenant's *Cruel Brother* (p. 131, ed. Maidment), and adds, 'perhaps the
phrase is proverbial.' A citation from D'Avenant, in a case like this, carries but little
weight. I doubt if there be an Act in all D'Avenant's plays, wherein Shakespearian
phrases may not be found. For instance, the sixth line of this very play of *The Cruel
Brother* reads : 'This way to madness leads,' and 'excellent wretch,' occurs more than
once farther on. With more propriety Steevens refers to *Wint. Tale,* IV, iv, 501, and
Hen. V : I, ii, 164 ; but is again far afield in referring to Pliny's Chapter (IX, 34) on
The Riches of the Sea, which alludes to the high prices paid by luxury 'in furnishing
the table with such varietie of dishes, in pleasing and contenting the taste with so
many dainty and delicate fishes.' Conf. *Rich. III :* I, iv, 26 : 'Wedges of gold, great
anchors, heaps of pearls, Inestimable stones, unvalued jewels, All scatter'd in the bottom of the sea.'—ED.] BOOTH : Note the frequent reference to the sea ;—for the same
reason, that I gave anent the 'superstition' in the play.

34. **You were**] WALKER (*Crit.* ii, 202) : *Thou wert* (sometimes written in the old
poets *Th'wert*), *you were, I was,* &c., occur frequently, both in Shakespeare and contemporary dramatists, in places where it is clear they must have been pronounced as
one syllable, in whatever manner the contraction was effected. [See *Ham.* IV, v, 14,
and ABBOTT, § 461.]

36. **Parts**] SCHMIDT and ROLFE agree in interpreting this as *merits.* It seems to
me that it is rather the endowments of nature, his natural gifts, like 'your sum of parts'
in *Ham.* IV, vii, 74.—ED.

Iago.   By *Ianus,* I thinke no.   38
Othel.   The Seruants of the Dukes?
And my Lieutenant?   40
The goodneffe of the Night vpon you (Friends)
What is the Newes?
Caffio.   The Duke do's greet you (Generall)
And he requires your hafte, Poft-hafte appearance,
Enen on the inftant.   45
Othello.   What is the matter, thinke you?
Caffio.   Something from Cyprus, as I may diuine:
It is a bufineffe of fome heate.   The Gallies
Haue fent a dozen fequent Meffengers
This very night, at one anothers heeles: 50
And many of the Confuls, rais'd and met,

39, 40. One line, Qq, Rowe et seq.
  39. *Dukes ?*] *Duke,* Qq, Rowe et seq.
  40. *Lieutenant ?*] *Leiutenant,* Q$_1$.
Leiutenant ? Q$_2$Q$_3$. *lieutenant :* or *lieutenant.* Rowe et cet.
  41. *you*] *your* Q$_1$.
  42. *Newes ?*] *newes.* Q$_1$.
  44. *hafte, Poft-hafte*] Ff, Rowe+, Cap.
Var. Coll. Sing.Wh. i, Ktly.   *haft, poft haft*
Q$_1$.   *haft, poft-haft* Q$_2$Q$_3$.   *haste-post-haste*

Steev.'93 et cet.
  46. *What is*] *What's* Qq, Jen.
  you ?] *you :* Q$_1$.
  47. *Cyprus*] *Cipres* Qq.
  48. *Gallies*] *Galleyes* Qq.
  49. *dozen*] *dozzen* F$_2$.
  fequent] *frequent* Q$_1$
  50. *at one*] *one at* Q$_2$Q$_3$.
  51. *Confuls*] *Counsel* Han.   *Council*
Johns.

38. Ianus] WARBURTON: There is great propriety in making the double Iago
swear by Janus, who had two faces.   The address of it likewise is as remarkable; for
as the people coming up appeared at different distances to have different shapes, he
might swear by Janus without suspicion of any other emblematic meaning.

  39, 40. Is it not better, as more dramatic, to retain the two separate questions of the
Folio than to combine them as in the Qto?   KNIGHT separates them by a semicolon,
and STAUNTON by an exclamation-mark.—ED.

  41. goodness] DELIUS: May night, usually unfriendly to everybody, show only its
good side to you.   [Is it not simply the ordinary salutation 'good day,' or 'Godgigoden'
adapted to the hour?—ED.]

  43. BOOTH: Cassio alone knew where Othello was to be found.   Othello says, that
he knew from first to last of the secret love, &c.   Remember this when Iago tells you.
'he's married,' &c.

  44. haste, Post-haste] RITSON: The comma, hitherto placed after 'haste,' should
be a hyphen.   'Your haste-post-haste appearance' is *your immediate appearance.*   The
words 'Haste, post, haste,' were, in our author's time, usually written on the cover of
packets or letters sent express.

  51. Consuls] THEOBALD changed this to *Couns'lers,* for the reasons given at I,
i, 27.   KNIGHT says, that in both cases *senators* were probably meant.   TH. ELZE
(*Sh. Jahrbuch,* xiv, 179): Shakespeare has not clearly distinguished between the *Collegio* and the *Senate.*   Brabantio's accusation of Othello could not have been brought

Are at the Dukes already.   You haue bin hotly call'd for,   52
When being not at your Lodging to be found,
The Senate hath fent about three feuerall Quefts,
To fearch you out.   55
  Othel.   'Tis well I am found by you :
I will but fpend a word here in the houfe,
And goe with you.
  Caffio.   Aunciant, what makes he heere?
  Iago.   Faith, he to night hath boarded a Land Carract,   60

---

54. *hath fent*] *fent* Qq, Pope, Theob.
Han. Warb. Dyce iii, Coll. iii, Huds.
    about] *aboue* Q₁Q₂. *aboue* Q₃,
Pope+, Coll. i, Wh. i. *out* Johns.
    57, 58. One line, Qq.
    57. *I will but fpend*] *Ile fpend* Q₁. *I
will fpend but* F₃F₄.

58. *And goe*] *And then go* Ktly.
    [Exit Othello. Rowe et seq.
59. *Aunciant*] *Ancient* Q₂Q₃Ff.
60. *boarded*] *boorded* QqFf, Rowe 1.
    Carract] *Carrick* Q₁. *Carriact*
Q₂Q₃. *Carrac* Ff.

---

before the Senate, but before the Ministerial Council—the *Collegio.* The Third Scene of the First Act is correctly laid in the 'Council Chamber,' not in the 'Hall of the Senate.' Properly also, Shakespeare speaks of 'the Council' and the 'Consuls,' that is, the *Counsellors;* but improperly in the same speech of the 'Senate' and [line 255] of the 'Senators.' But, perhaps, Shakespeare purposely avoided the use of the word *College*, because of its ambiguity to English ears.

52. **You haue**] LETTSOM (ap. DYCE, ed. iii) would read 'you *had* been,' &c. HUDSON adopted the emendation.

54. **about**] JOHNSON : That is, *about* the city. COLLIER (ed. i) preferred *above* of the Qq, because a ' "quest" necessarily searches in various directions; and the word "about" may, therefore, be considered surplusage. Cassio means that more than "three several quests" have been sent in search of Othello.' But as his (MS) retained 'about,' Collier, in his subsequent editions, followed it.

54. **Quests**] STEEVENS : That is, *searches.* So in Heywood's *Brazen Age*, 1613 : 'Now, if in all his quests, he be withheld.' An ancient MS. entitled *The Boke of Huntyng that is cleped Mayster of Game,* has the following explanation of the word 'quest' : 'This word quest is a terme of herte hunters of beyonde the see; and is thus moche to say as whan the hunter goth to fynde the hert and to herborow him.' HALLIWELL cites Cotgrave, s. v. 'Queste : f. A quest, inquirie, search, inquisition, seeking,' &c.

57. **spend**] GÉRARD : Les expressions *to spend* et *to pay* sont à tout moment employées par les Anglais, peuple commerçant et pratique par excellence. Ils ne rendent pas, ils *paient* une visite; ils ne passent pas, ils *dépensent* leur temps. En Amérique la première question que l'on fait sur quelqu'un, c'est : Combien vaut-il ? [When Mons. Gérard enacts the 'Pow'r,' and 'wad the giftie gie us,' shall not we Americans accept it, however startling the revelation ?—ED.]

59. BOOTH : Speak this with curiosity, as if to learn what Iago knows of the marriage.

60. **Carract**] SKEAT (*Etym. Dict.*, s. v.) : A ship of burden. (We also find *carrick*, which comes nearer to Low Lat. *carrica*, a ship of burden.) Low Lat. *carracare*, better *carricare,* to lade a car.—Lat. *carrus*, a car. STAUNTON : A ship of large

If it proue lawfull prize, he' made for euer.   61
   Caſſio.   I do not vnderſtand.
   Iago.   He's married.
   Caſſio.   To who?
   Iago.   Marry to————Come Captaine, will you go.?   65
   Othel.   Haue with you.
   Caſſio.   Here come sanother Troope to ſeeke for you.

   Enter Brabantio, Rodorigo, with Officers, and Torches.

   Iago.   It.is *Brabantio:*Generall be aduis'd,   69

---

63. *married*] *marri'd* F$_2$.
64. *who*] *whom* Q$_2$Q$_3$Ff, Rowe+, Jen.
Coll. Ktly.

   [Enters *Brabantio, Roderigo,* and others with lights, and weapons. Qq. (Enter... Q$_2$Q$_3$). Re-enter. Oth. Cap.
   65. *go ?*] *go ?* Enter Oth. Rowe+.

66. *Haue with you.*] *Ha, with who ?* Q$_1$. *Ha' with you.* Q$_2$Q$_3$.
68. Scene VI. Pope+, Jen.
   Enter...] After line 64, Qq. After *intent* line 70, Coll. Dyce, Wh. Glo. Cam. Sta. Del. Rlfe, Huds.

---

burden, like the Spanish galleon; but the compound in the text appears to have been a dissolute expression.

   61. lawfull prize] LORD CAMPBELL (p. 114): A very distinct proof that Shakespeare was acquainted with Admiralty law, as well as with the procedure of Westminster Hall, the trope indicating, that there would be a suit in the High Court of Admiralty to determine the validity of the capture.

   61. he'] This should be 'he's,' as it is in every other text, but in the copy of F$_1$, from which this is reprinted, the *s* has fallen out.—ED.

   62. BOOTH: But show the audience that you do.

   64. To who] THEOBALD (Nichols's *Illust. of Lit.*, ii, 586): Surely, this is a terrible forgetfulness in our author. How came Cassio such a stranger to this affair, when it afterward appears he went a-wooing with Othello and took his part in the suit? [Cf. III, iii, 82.] RITSON (p. 227): It is very easy to imagine, that Cassio might wish to know if Iago were acquainted with the lady, to prevent the latter's suspecting that *he* was. BLACKSTONE: Cassio's seeming ignorance might only be affected, in order to keep his friend's secret till it became publicly known. MALONE: Or he might fear that Othello had proved false to the gentle Desdemona, and married another. STEEVENS: How far this suspicious apprehension would have become the benevolent Cassio, the intimate friend of Othello, let the reader judge. SINGER: It was probably a mere oversight of the poet. ABBOTT, § 274, gives many instances where the inflection of *who* is neglected. See IV, ii, 115; *Macb.* III, iv, 42; *Ham.* II, ii, 193; *Lear*, IV, iii, 7 and V, iii, 249. BOOTH: Feign much surprise, but do it carefully.

   65. Captaine] ABBOTT, § 506: It is obvious that a syllable or foot may be supplied by a gesture, a beckoning, a movement of the head to listen, or of the hand to demand attention, as here: 'Márry | to—(*Enter O'thello.*) | Come, cáp | tain, wíll | you gó ?' However, we may scan, 'Marry | to—Come | Cap(i) | tain will | you go,' but very harshly and improbably.

   66. you] STEEVENS: This expression denotes readiness.

   69. aduised] JOHNSON: That is, be *cool*, be *cautious*, be *discreet*.

He comes to bad intent.   70
   Othello.   Holla, ſtand there.
   Rodo.   Signior, it is the Moore.
   Bra.   Downe with him, Theefe.
   Iago.   You, *Rodorigoe?* Cme Sir, I am for you.
   Othe.   Keepe vp your bright Swords, for the dew will   75
ruſt them.   Good Signior, you ſhall more command with
yeares, then with your Weapons.
   Bra.   Oh thou foule Theefe,
Where haſt thou ſtow'd my Daughter?
Damn'd as thou art, thou haſt enchaunted her   80
For Ile referre me to all things o f ſenſe,   [312 *b*]
(If ſhe in Chaines of Magick we re not bound)
Whether a Maid, ſo tender, Faire, and Happie,
So oppoſite to Marriage, that ſhe ſhun'd
The wealthy curled Deareling of our Nation,   85

---

71. *Holla,*] *Ho la,* Q$_3$.
73. [They draw on both sides. Rowe.
74. *Rodorigoe? Cme*] *Rodorigo? Come*
Ff.   *Rodorigo, come* Booth's Rep.
75-77. Verse ending *them...years...
Weapons* Qq, Rowe et seq.
76. *ruſt them*] *ruſt em* Qq. *rust 'em*
Rowe+, Jen.
78, 79. One line, Qq, Rowe et seq.
79. *ſtow'd*] *ſtowed* Qq. *'stow'd* Wh. i,

Coll. iii.
80. *Damn'd*] *Dambd* Qq.
81. *Ile*] *ile* Q$_x$.
  things] *thing* Q$_x$.
82. Om. Q$_x$.
85. *wealthy curled*] *wealthy culled*
Warb. Theob. ii. *wealthiest cull'd* Han.
  Deareling] *Dearling* F$_2$F$_3$, Knt.
Darling F$_4$. *dearlings* Wh. i. *darlings*
Qq et cet.

---

72. BOOTH: This is spoken 'within.'

74. BOOTH: This is to prevent harm to Roderigo, for whose purse Iago has a tender
regard.   Make the audience understand this by your manner of singling him out,—a
look will do it.   [See Textual Notes for another instance of the difference between the
copy of F$_x$, from which Lionel Booth reprinted, and that from which this edition is
reprinted.—ED.]

75. BOOTH: Othello's party—Cassio, Iago, and others—should 'motion' to draw,
when these words restrain them.   Brabantio's friends enter with swords drawn.   Be
very respectful to Brabantio, resent his abuse, merely with a look of momentary anger.

75. **for**] See WALKER (*Crit.* ii, 321), for an Article, with many examples, on the
confusion in the Folio of *or* and *for.*   Walker would here read *or,* which may be
correct, but of the instances of this confusion, cited by Walker, the present is, perhaps,
the least manifest.—ED.

75. HUDSON: If I mistake not there is a sort of playful, good-humoured irony expressed in the very rhythm of this line.

85. **curled**] WARBURTON: I read *culled,* i. e. select, chosen.   Shakespeare uses
the word frequently.   Cf. *Hen. V:* III, cho. 24.   'Curled' was an improper mark
of diffe ence between a Venetian and a Moor, which latter people are remarkably

Would euer haue (t'encurre a generall mocke)   86
Run from her Guardageto the footie bofome,
Of fuch a thing as thou: to feare, not to delight?
Iudge me the world, if'tis not groffe in fenfe,
That thou haft practis'd on her with foule Charmes   90
Abus'd her delicate Youth, with Drugs or Minerals,

86. *t'encurre*] F_2F_3.   *t'incurr* F_4,   88. *as thou:*] *as thou?* Qq.
Rowe+, Dyce iii, Huds.   *to incurre* Qq   *delight?*] *delight*, Q_1. *delight:* Q_2Q_3.
et cet.   89-94. Om. Q_1.
87. *Guardage*] *gardage* Qq.   89. *not*] *no* Q_3.

---

curl'd by nature. JOHNSON: 'Curled' is *elegantly and ostentatiously dressed.* He had not the hair particularly in his thoughts. STEEVENS: Shakespeare evidently alludes to the hair in 'the curled Anthony,' *Ant. & Cleo.* V, ii, 304. D'Avenant uses the same expression in his *Just Italian* [but as was said before, parallel expressions in D'Avenant are of small avail.—ED.] MALONE: In *R. of L.*, 981, the hair is expressly mentioned, and the epithet 'curled' is added as characteristic of a person of the highest rank: 'Let him have time to tear his curled hair.' [See notes in *Lear*, III, iv, 84, 'A Serving-man, proud in heart and mind; that curled my hair.'—ED.]

85. **Deareling**] KNIGHT: This Saxon word is used in a plural sense. DYCE (*Remarks*, p. 233): The fact is, the *s* has been omitted in the Folio by a mistake of the compositor. In Shakespeare's time *dearling* could never have been used as a plural. That even Spenser (who antiquated his language more than any of his contemporaries) did not venture to employ such an archaism, is proved by the following from his *Hymne in honour of Love :*—'in a Paradize Of all delight, and ioyous happie rest, Where they doe feede on Nectar heauenly wize, With *Hercules* and *Hebe*, and the rest Of *Venus* dearlings, through her bountie blest.'

87. **Guardage**] ROLFE: Guardianship, used by Shakespeare nowhere else.

88. **to feare**] STEEVENS: To terrify, as in *3 Hen. VI:* V, ii, 2, 'a bug that fear'd us all.' The line is redundant in measure. It might originally have ran, 'Of such as thou: to fear, not to delight.' MALONE takes 'fear' to be a substantive, and used for the object of fear; but ABBOTT, § 405, more correctly explains the phrase as an ellipsis, common among Elizabethans, after *will* and *is*, e. g. 'I will to the weird sisters.' 'I must to Coventry.' 'I am to thank you for it,' i. e. I am *bound* to thank you for it; so here 'such a thing as thou (a thing *fit*) to fear (*act.*), not to delight.'

89. **Judge me**] ABBOTT, § 365, Let the world judge for me. This optative use of the subjunctive, dispensing with 'let,' 'may,' &c., gives great vigour to the Shakespearian line. [It is doubtful if 'me' be here the Ethical Dative, as in I, i, 53 : 'Whip me such honest knaues,' or 'He plucked me ope his doublet,' *Jul. Cæs.* Brabantio calls upon the world really to judge him and his position, which he immediately proceeds to state.—ED.]

90. **practis'd**] Very frequently used, as here, in the sense of plotting, with arts or magic. See *Lear*, III, ii, 57 : 'Has practis'd on man's life.'

91. **Minerals**] In *Ham.* IV, i, 26, 'a mineral' means a *mine*, but in *Cymb.* V, v, 50, in the present passage, and in II, i, 330, it is used in the sense of a drug or mortal poison.

That weakens Motion.   Ile haue't difputed on,   92

92. *weakens Motion*] *weaken motion* Rowe, Pope i, Knt, Coll. Dyce, Glo. Cam. Del. Rlfe. *weaken notion* Theob. Pope ii, Warb. Johns. Cap. Jen. Rann. *waken*

motion Han. Steev. Var. Sing. Wh. Sts. Huds. *wakens motion* Ktly. *wake emotion* Anon.

---

92. **weakens Motion**] THEOBALD suggested and adopted *weaken notion*. 'That is, her *apprehension*, right *conception* and *idea* of things, *understanding, judgment;* and supported the change by the apposite passage, 'his notion weakens,' *Lear*, I, iv, 221. CAPELL thought Theobald's change was 'open to no objections.' MALONE and STEEVENS approved of Hanmer's text, seeing that *motion* is used afterward in I, iii, 364, in the same sense, and also in *Cymb.* II, v, 20; *Ham.* III, iv, 72; *Meas. for Meas.* I, iv, 59; and because, as Malone said, there was 'good reason to believe that the words *weaken* and *waken* were in Shakespeare's time pronounced alike.' 'The objection to Theobald's "notion,"' continues Malone, 'is that no opiates or intoxicating potions or powders of any sort can distort or pervert the *intellects*, but by destroying them for a time; nor was it ever, at any time, believed by the most credulous that *love-powders*, as they were called, could *weaken the understanding*, though it was formerly believed that they could *fascinate* the *affections;* or, in other words, *waken* motion. Brabantio afterward asserts, "That with some mixtures powerful o'er the *blood* He wrought upon her." Shakespeare, in almost all his plays, uses *blood* for passion. And one of the Senators asks Othello, not whether he had *weakened* Desdemona's *understanding*, but whether he did "by indirect and forced courses subdue and *poison* this young maid's *affections*."' RITSON (p. 227), however, satisfactorily vindicates the Folio, thus: To 'weaken motion' is to *impair the faculties.* It was till very lately, and may be still an opinion, that philtres or love potions have the power of perverting, and of course weakening or impairing, both the sight and judgement, and of procuring fondness or dotage toward any unworthy object who administers them. And by *motion* Shakespeare means the senses which are depraved and weakened by these fascinating mixtures. STAUNTON thinks that this view is expressly contradicted by what Brabantio has just said: that Desdemona was 'so opposite to marriage,' and he 'therefore readily accepts the easy emendation Hanmer offers. Brabantio's grievance, it is plain, was not that Othello had, by charms and medicines, abated the motions of Desdemona's sense, but that he had aroused and stimulated them.' R. M. SPENCE (*N. & Qu.*, 1879, 5th, xi, 383): Twice elsewhere in this Act 'motion' means *emotion;* the *usus loquendi* thus warrants me to regard *emotion* as the meaning of the word in this passage also; if so, then Hanmer's *waken* must indubitably be adopted. [Truly does KNIGHT say of this passage that the notes, here very much abridged, of the Commentators are neither satisfactory in a critical point of view, nor edifying in a moral one.—ED.]

92. **disputed on**] STAUNTON: This is an allusion to the manner in which causes were debated by the judges according to the custom of Venice formerly, aud it affords one of many proofs that before writing *Othello* Shakespeare had attentively perused Lewkenor's translation of *The Commonwealth and Government of Venice*, written by the Cardinall Gasper Contareno, &c., 1599. From this work he obtained his information concerning those 'officers of night,' whom Brabantio directs to be summoned; his knowledge of the *Arsenal;* as well as several particular expressions, such as Mine *eares enclined;* doe *their countrie service; experience the mistresse of all things; serve 'he turne;* their *countrie customs*, and others which he has modified and transplanted

'Tis probable, and palpable to thinking ;   93
I therefore apprehend and do attach thee,
For an abuſer of the World, a practiſer   95
Of Arts inhibited, and out of warrant;
Lay hold vpon him, if he do reſiſt
Subdue him, at his perill.
   Othe.   Hold your hands
Both you of my inclining, and the reſt.   100
Were it my Cue to fight, I ſhould haue knowne it
Without a Prompter.   Whether will you that I goe
To anſwere this your charge ?
   Bra.   To Priſon, till fit time
Of Law, and courſe of direct Seſſion   105

---

93. *probable*] *portable* Q₂Q₃, Jen.	102. *Whether*] *Whither* Ff, Rowe.
95. *For*] *Such* Q₁.	*where* Qq et cet.
96. *warrant ;*] *warrant ?* Q₁.	*that*] Om. Pope+.
99. *hands*] *hand.* F₄.	103. *To anſwere*] *And anſwer* Q₁.
101. *Cue*] *Qu.* Q₁.	104, 105. *fit...Seſſion*] Sep. line, Han.

* * *

into the piece. [Staunton then gives a long extract from Contareno, minutely setting forth the way in which criminal questions were *disputed on* in the ancient legal courts of Venice, which I do not reprint. I cannot detect a trace of any influence which this legal method had upon Shakespeare's mind, either while writing *Othello* or anything else, other than that, perhaps, he might have found there the two uncommon words *disputed* and *of*, which Staunton italicizes.—ED.]

95, 96. BOOTH: Othello and Cassio exchange smiles of pity for the old man's credulity.

99. BOOTH: Now Othello's friends draw. Othello stands between the two parties with sheathed scimetar held up; its crescent shape lends a little Oriental atmosphere to the picture. 'Tis harmless.

101. **Cue**] In *Ham.* II, ii, 534, WEDGWOOD'S definition is quoted : 'The last words of the preceding speech, prefixed to the speech of an actor in order to let him know when he is to come on the stage. From the letter Q by which it was marked, "because," says Butler, *Eng. Gram.*, 1634, "it is the first letter of *quando*, when, showing when to enter and speak."' [Note Q₁ in Textual Notes.] SKEAT now gives a different derivation; he says, 'that an actor's *cue* seems to be the same word as *queue*, as signifying the last words or tail-end of the speech of the preceding speaker. Oddly enough, it was, in this sense, sometimes denoted by Q; owing to the similarity of the sound.'

102. **Whether**] This passage is cited by WALKER (*Vers.* 106) as one of the many instances in which *hither, whether,* &c. are printed as dissyllables, where the verse indicates that they are monosyllables. Cf. *Macb.* I, iii, 111; *Ham.* III, ii, 193; *Lear,* II, i, 53, also in ABBOTT, § 466.

105. **direct Session**] HUDSON: The language is rather odd, and, perhaps, somewhat obscure; but the meaning probably is, till the time prescribed by law and by the regular course of judicial procedure.

Call thee to anfwer.   106

 Othe.   What if do obey?
How may the Duke be therewith fatisfi'd,
Whofe Meffengers are heere about my fide,
Vpon fome prefent bufineffe of the State,   110
To bring me to him.

 Officer.   'Tis true moft worthy Signior,
The Dukes in Counfell, and your Noble felfe,
I am fure is fent for.

 Bra.   How? The Duke in Counfell?   115
In this time of the night? Bring him away;
Mine's not an idle Caufe.   The Duke himfelfe,
Or any of my Brothers of the State,
Cannot but feele this wrong, as 'twere their owne :
For if fuch Actions may haue paffage free,   120
Bond-flaues, and Pagans fhall our Statefmen be.   *Exeunt*

---

107. *if do*] *if I* Pope, Han.   *if I doe*
QqFf et cet.
 111. *bring*] *beare* Qq, Coll. i, ii.
 112. Officer] I. O. Cap.
  '*Tis*] Om. Pope+.

114. *I am*] *I'm* Pope+, Dyce iii, Huds.
116. *night*] *nigh* F$_2$.
117. *Caufe.*] *caufe*, Q$_x$.   *caufe :* Q$_2$Q$_3$
121. *Bond-flaues*] *Bondflaues* QqF$_3$.
Bond flaues F$_4$.

---

116. **In**] For other instances of the use of 'in' for *during* or *at*, see ABBOTT, § 161.
 121. **Pagans**] THEOBALD : Would Brabantio infer, if his private injury were not
redressed, the Senate should no longer pretend to call themselves Christians? But
pagans are as strict and moral as the most regular Christians in the preservation of pri
vate property.   Difference of faith is not concerned, but mere human policy.   I therefore read *pageants*, i. e. if we let such injurious actions go unpunished our statesmen
must be slaves, ciphers in office, and have no power of redressing, be things of mere
show and gaudy appearance only.   STEEVENS : I believe the morality of either Chris
tians or pagans was not in our author's thoughts.   He alludes to the common condition of all blacks, who come from their own country both *slaves* and *pagans ;* and
uses the word in contempt of Othello and his complexion.   If this Moor is now
suffered to escape with impunity, it will be such an encouragment to his black countrymen, that we may expect to see all the first offices of our state filled up by the *pagans*
and *bondslaves* of Africa.   HEATH (p. 534).   It is certain from this very play that the
Moor had been both a *bondslave* and a *pagan*, though at that time he was neither.
MALONE : In Shakespeare's time *pagan* was a very common expression of contempt

Scæna Tertia.

Enter Duke, Senators, and Officers.

Duke. There's no compofition in this Newes,
That giues them Credite.

1. *Sen.* Indeed, they are difproportioned;   5
My Letters fay, a Hundred and feuen Gallies.

Duke. And mine a Hundred fortie.

2. *Sena.* And mine two Hundred :
But though they iumpe not on a iuft accompt,
(As in thefe Cafes where the ayme reports,   10

---

1. Scene VII. Pope+, Jen.
The Senate House. Rowe. A Council
Chamber. Cap.

2. Enter...] Enter Duke, and Senators
fet at a Table, with lights and Attendants.
Qq.

3. *There's*] *There is* QqFf et cet.
   this] Ff, Rowe. *his* Q₃. *thefe* Q₁Q₂
et cet.

5. *they are*] *they're* Pope, Theob. Han.

Johns. Dyce iii, Huds.

5. *difproportioned*] QqFf, Rowe, Jen.
Sta. *difproportion'd* Pope et cet.

7. *And mine*] *and mine* Q₂.
   a Hundred fortie] F₂F₃, Knt, Sta.
an hundred and forty Q₂Q₃. *a hundred
and forty* Q₁F₄ et cet.

10. *the ayme*] *they aym'd* Q₁. *they ayme*
Q₂Q₃. *they aim* Pope, Theob. Johns. Jen.
Rann. Sing. Hal.

---

2. LLOYD: Central in the First Act is the scene in the Council Chamber; and the
consideration, by the Duke and Senators, of the news from Cyprus is no mere surplusage; it strikes a tone of dispassionate appreciation of evidence and opinion that domi-
nates all the succeeding scenes of agitation and disorders. From inconsistent intelligence, the main point of agreement is carefully adopted for further examination,
notwithstanding predisposition to underrate it; intelligence, otherwise of good authority, is condemned as fallacious from collateral indications; and lastly, thus prepared for,
the last courier has full credence, and the critical circumstances once understood action
follows at once. Othello is dispatched that very night. The same solid perspicacity
distinguishes the reception of the complaint of Brabantio.

3. **composition**] WARBURTON: That is, consistency, concordancy.

3. **this Newes**] SKEAT (*Dict.* s. v.): The form *newes* does not seem to be older
than about A. D. 1500. It is nothing but a plural formed from *new* treated as a subs.,
so also *tidings*. It is a translation of F. *nouvelles*, plural of *nouvelle*, new (Cotgrave);
so also Lat. *nova* = new things, i. e. news. [From a rough calculation by means of Mrs
Cowden-Clarke's *Concordance*, I find that Shakespeare uses this word in the singular
more than three times as often as in the plural.—ED.]

7. **Hundred fortie**] WHITE (ed. i): I think it not improbable that this passage
stood, as the rhythm requires : ' My letters say a hundred seven galleys. *Duke.* And
mine a hundred forty. *2 Sen.* Mine, two hundred.' PURNELL: The occasional omission of the conjunction in numerals may be a relic of the French usage (cent-quarante).

10. **the ayme**] WARBURTON: Where there is no better ground for information
than conjecture. JOHNSON: The reading of Q₂ has a sense sufficiently easy and commodious. Where men *report* not by certain knowledge, but by *aim* and conjecture.
[For *ther* instances of its use in the sense of *guess, conjecture,* see SCHMIDT, *Lex.*

'Tis oft with difference)yet do they all confirme   11
A Turkiſh Fleete, and bearing vp to Cyprus.
    Duke.   Nay, it is poſſible enough to iudgement:
I do not ſo ſecure me in the Error,
But the maine Article I do approue   15
In fearefull ſenſe.
    Saylor within.   What hoa, what hoa, what hoa.

Enter Saylor.

    Officer.   A Meſſen g er from the Gallies.   [313 *a*]
    Duke.   Now? What's the buſineſſe?   20
    Sailor.   The Turkiſh Preparation makes for Rhodes,
So was I bid report here to the State,
By Signior *Angelo.*
    Duke.   How ſay you by this change?
    1. Sen.   This cannot be   25
By no aſſay of reaſon. 'Tis a Pageant

---

11. *do*] Om. Pope, Han.
12. *Cyprus*] *Cipreſſe* Q₁. *Cipres* Q₂Q₃.
14. *in the*] *to the* Qq.
15. *Article*] *Articles* Q₁.
17. Saylor within] One within Qq.
   hoa] *ho* Qq.
18. Enter Saylor.] Enter a Meſſenger.
(after *ſenſe*, line 16), Qq. Enter an Officer
bringing in a Sailor. Cap. After *Gallies*,
line 19, Dyce.

19. Officer] Sailor Q₁. First Off. Dyce.
   Gallies] *Galley* Q₁.
20. *Now? What's the*] *Now, the* Qq,
Coll. Wh. Ktly. *Now? the* Cap. Steev.
Mal. Knt, Sing.
23. *By Signior* Angelo] Om. Q₁,
Pope+. Ending line 22, Q₂Q₃.
   [they withdraw. Cap.
25, 26. *This...reaſon*] One line, Qq.
26. *reaſon*] *reaſon—* Qq.

---

s. v.] COLLIER (ed. ii) adopts from his (MS) '*with the same* reports,' with the note
that 'the clear meaning being, that even when reports of such occurrences are mainly
the same, it is often with difference. It appears highly probable that the passage was
misheard, as well as misprinted, and that the true text is what we have adopted.'
[Nevertheless, Collier returned to F₁ in the text of his ed. iii. The Cam. Ed. records
'aim besorts' and 'main accords' as anonymous conjectures.—ED.]

   14. secure] STAUNTON paraphrases, 'I do not so *over-confidently* build on the discrepancy;' but PURNELL, with more fidelity to the derivation of the word, 'I do not
lay aside anxiety on account of the discrepancy.'

   21. Rhodes] See Appendix, 'Date of the Action.'

   24. by] For other instances where 'by' means *about, concerning*, see ABBOTT, § 145.
PURNELL refers [as does also Abbott] to '1 Corinth. iv, 4, "I know nothing by myself"
(the Greek being, "I am conscious of nothing against myself"), where Alford quotes,
"I know no harm by him," as a midland-county current expression.'

   25, 26. cannot . . . no] For instances of double negatives, see ABBOTT, § 406.

   26. assay] JOHNSON: Bring it to the *test*, examine it by reason as we examine
metals by the *assay*, it will be found counterfeit by all trials.

To keepe vs in falſe gaze, when we conſider   27
Th'importancie of Cyprus to the Turke;
And let our ſelues againe but vnderſtand,
That as it more concernes the Turke then Rhodes,   30
So may he with more facile queſtion beare it,
For that it ſtands not in ſuch Warrelike brace,
But altogether lackes th'abilities
That Rhodes is dreſs'd in.   If we make thought of this,
We muſt not thinke the Turke is ſo vnskillfull,   35
To leaue that lateſt, which concernes him firſt,
Neglecting an attempt of eaſe, and gaine
To wake, and wage a danger profitleſſe.

Duke.   Nay, in all confidence he's not for Rhodes.

Officer.   Here is more Newes.   40

Enter a Meſſenger.

Meſſen.   The *Ottamites*, Reueren'd, and Gracious,   42

27. *gaze,*] *gaze:* or *gaze.* Qq et cet.
31. *facile*] *fertile* Pope.
32–38. Om. Q₁.
33. *But*] *Who* Q₂Q₃.
34. *thought*] *nought* Q₂ (ap. Steevens's reprint).
37, 38. *eaſe, and gaine To wake,*] F₂.

eaſe and gaine, To wake Q₂Q₃F₃F₄ et cet.
39. *Nay,*] *And* Q₁.
all] Om. Rowe ii.
41. a Meſſenger.] a 2. Meſſenger. Q₁. a 2 Meſſenger Q₂Q₃.
42. *Reueren'd*] *reverend* QqF₃F₄.

28. **importancie**] ROLFE: Used by Shakespeare nowhere else.

31. **facile question**] JOHNSON: 'Question' is for the *act of seeking*, with more *easy endeavour.*   MASON: May carry it with less dispute, with less opposition. SCHMIDT (*Lex.*) from the use of 'question' in the sense of a *judicial* trial, deduces the meaning here of 'a trial and decision by the force of arms as the ultima ratio regum.'

32. **brace**] JOHNSON: State of defence.   WHITE (ed. ii): Warlike strain, military necessity or compulsion.   [I cannot understand how White deduces this interpretation. The very point of the speech is, that Cyprus is of greater 'military necessity' to the Turk than Rhodes.   'Brace' is, I think, here equivalent to *readiness;* when a knight had braced on his armour he was ready.—ED.]

38. **wage**] STEEVENS gives as the meaning here, to *fight,* to *combat,* and cites in proof, 'To wage against the enmity o'th'air.'—*Lear,* II, iv, 206; but 'wage' is transitive here; accordingly, SCHMIDT gives the better interpretation: to *hazard,* to *attempt.*

42. BOOTH here begins his Scene IV, in the Council Chamber.   The Duke and the Senators are discovered R. with a Messenger who is kneeling before them.   Enter as the scene opens, Gra. Rod. and others.   The advantage of placing the Duke at the side instead of at the back as in the old 'set' is, that the characters need not turn their backs on the audience when addressing the Duke.

Steering with due courfe toward the Ile of Rhodes,   43
Haue there inioynted them with an after Fleete.
    1.Sen.   I, fo I thought : how many, as you gueffe ?   45
    Meff.   Of thirtie Saile : and now they do re-ftem
Their backward courfe, bearing with frank appearance
Their purpofes toward Cyprus.   Signior *Montano,*
Your truftie and moft Valiant Seruitour,
With his free dutie, recommends you thus,   50
And prayes you to beleeue him.
    Duke.   'Tis certaine then for Cyprus :
Marcus Luccicos is not he in Towne ?
    1. Sen.   He's now in Florence.   54

---

44. *inioynted*] *injoin'd* Rowe, Pope,
Theob. Han. Warb.
    them] Om. Q$_1$, Huds. iii.
    Fleete.] *fleete* Q$_1$. *fleet,* Q$_2$Q$_3$. *fleet—*
Rowe+, Jen.
45. Om. Q$_1$.
46. *thirtie*] 30. Qq.
    re-ftem] *refterine* Q$_1$.   *refterne*
Q$_2$Q$_3$.
48. *toward*] *towards* Q$_1$Q$_3$. *towarcs* Q$_2$.
50. *his*] *this* Cap. (misprint).

50. *thus*] *this* Lettsom (ap. Dyce iii).
51. *beleeue*] *relieve* (T. Clark, Cap.
conj.), Sing. ii, Ktly.
52, 53.' *Tis...Luccicos*] One line, Theob.
Warb. Johns.
53. *Luccicos*] *Lucchese,* Cap. Steev.
Var. Rann.   Luccicos, Booth's Rep.
    not he] *not here* Q$_1$. *he not* Ff, Rowe,
Pope, Han. Steev. Var.   *he not here* Theob.
Warb. Johns.
    Towne ?] *Towne.* Q$_1$.

---

44. **inioynted**] WALKER (*Crit.* iii, 285): *Injoint ? Ham.* I, ii, 20 : 'Our state to
be disjoint, and out of frame.' Yet I doubt whether the cases are parallel. [For
other instances of the omission, in participles, of *ed* after *d* or *t*, see WALKER (*Crit.* ii,
324), and ABBOTT, § 342.]

    51. beleeue] JOHNSON: The late learned and ingenious Mr Thomas Clark, of Lin-
coln's Inn, read the passage, '*relieve* him.' But the present reading may stand. He
entreats you not to doubt the truth of this intelligence. CAPELL: Montano's message
to the Senate is worded with great politeness in all the parts of it; in this last *relief,*
the thing he stood in want of and wish'd, is only insinuated; knowing it would follow
from them, was *belief* accorded him. [This emendation of *relieve* for 'believe,' COL-
LIER attributed to Rev. Mr Barry; White pro-
nounces it 'plausible;' DYCE (ed. iii) quotes LETTSOM as follows : 'Believe,' I think
right as Johnson takes it. *Relieve* would mean '*send a successor.*']

    53. Luccicos] CAPELL changed this to *Lucchese,* and justified the change in a
note in his usual style : 'The corruptions of "Veronese" may induce belief, that this
which we are come to is no strain'd one.; and the Italian will call it necessary, terminations like that below being unknown in his language.' 'But,' asks KNIGHT, with
more shrewdness than grammar, 'who is the Duke inquiring after ? Most probably a
Greek soldier of Cyprus, an Estradiot, one who from his local knowledge was enabled
to give him information. Is it necessary that the Greek should bear an Italian name ?
And does not the termination in *cos* better convey the notion which we believe the poet
to have had ?'

Duke. Write from vs, 55
To him, Poft, Poft-hafte, difpatch.
  1. *Sen.* Here comes *Brabantio*, and the Valiant Moore.

*Enter Brabantio, Othello, Caffio, Iago, Rodorigo,
and Officers.*

Duke. Valiant *Othello*, we muft ftraight employ you, 60
Againft the generall Enemy *Ottoman.*
I did not fee you : welcome gentle Signior,
We lack't your Counfaile, and your helpe to night.
  Bra. So did I yours : Good your Grace pardon me.
Neither my place, hor ought I heard of bufineffe 65
Hath rais'd me from my bed ; nor doth the generall care

55, 56. Two lines, Ff, Rowe, Pope, Han. Cap. One line, Qq et cet.
  Write...Poft,] One line, Cap.
  Write...him] One line, Pope, Han.
  56. *To him,*] *wifh him* Q$_1$, Cap. Steev, Var. Rann. Sing. *to him* Q$_2$Q$_3$.
  Poft, Poft-hafte] *poft, poft haft* Qq. *Post-haste* Pope, Han. *post-post-haste* Steev. Var. Sing. Dyce, Sta. Del. Glo. Cam. Huds. Rlfe, Wh. ii.
  Poft-hafte, dispatch] *Post-haste: dispatch* Cap. Steev. Var. Sing.

57. *Valiant*] Om. Ff, Rowe. Scene VIII. Pope+, Jen.
  59. and Officers] Defdemona, and Officers Qq (after line 56).
  60. *employ*] *imploy* Qq.
  61. Ottoman] Ottaman Q$_1$.
  62. [To Braban. Theob.
  63. *lack't*] *lacke* Q$_1$.
  65. *hor*] *nor* Qq. *for* Ff. *ought*] *aught* Theob. ii.
  66. *nor*] *not* Q$_2$. *care*] Om. Pope, Theob. Han. Warb.

56. To] MALONE interprets the text of the Qq, for those who adopt it, as meaning : 'tell him we wish him to make *all possible haste*;' and adds that all messengers in the time of Shakespeare were enjoined, 'Haste, haste; for thy life, post haste.'

61. Ottoman] MALONE: It is part of the policy of the Venetian state never to entrust the command of an army to a native. 'To exclude, therefore, (says Contareno, trans. by Lewkenor, 1599) out of our estate the danger or occasion of any such ambitious enterprises, our ancestors held it a better course to defend the dominions on the continent with foreign mercenary soldiers, than with their home-bred citizens.' Again : 'alwaies they do entertain in honourable sort with great provision a *captaine generall*, who alwaies is a *stranger borne*.' REED: So in Thomas's *Hist. of Italy*, p. 82 : 'By lande they are served of straungers, both for generalls, for capitaines, and for all other men of warre; because theyr lawe permitteth not any Venetian to be capitaine over an armie by lande : Fearing, I thinke, Cæsar's example.' SCHMIDT (*Lex.*) queries whether this be used here as an adjective or substantive; ROLFE inclines to think it is the former.

62. BOOTH : The Duke should be busy with papers or conferring with the Senators, while Brabantio takes his seat; which will account for his 'I did not see you.'

64. Good your] ABBOTT, §13 : The possessive adjectives when unemphatic are sometimes transposed, being really combined with nouns (like the French *monsieur, milord*).

Take hold on me.   For my perticular griefe   67
Is of ſo flood-gate, and ore-bearing Nature,
That it engluts, ſnd ſwallowes other ſorrowes,
And it is ſtill it ſelfe.   70
    Duke.   Why ? What's the matter ?
    Bra.   My Daughter : oh my Daughter !
    Sen.   Dead ?
    Bra.   I, to me.
She is abus'd, ſtolne from me, and corrupted   75
By Spels, and Medicines, bought of Mountebanks;
For Nature, ſo prepoſtrouſly to erre,   77

67. *hold on*] *any hold of* Q₁. *hold of*
Q₂Q₃, Coll. Wh. i.   *any hold on* Rann.
   griefe] *griefes* Q₁.
69. *engluts*] *ingluts* Ff, Rowe+, Jen.
   ſnd] F₁.
70. *And it*] *And yet* Rowe, Pope,

Theob. Han. Warb. Jen. Rann.
73. Sen.] All. Qq.
74. *I,*] *I* Qq. *Ay*, Rowe. Om. Pope+.
75. *ſtolne*] *stollen* Rowe ii, Pope.
76. *Medicines*] *medicions* Q₃. *med'-
cines* Cap. (Errata).

66. To eliminate the two extra syllables in this line, JOHNSON proposes to omit
'care' at the end; and STEEVENS, 'Hath' at the beginning, and 'my' before 'bed.'

68. **so**] See ABBOTT, § 67, for instances where 'so' is used before an adjective,
where now-a-days we use the adverbial *such* or *so* with *a*. But note, says Abbott, that
in these instances the 'so' follows a preposition. After prepositions the article (see
§ 90) is frequently omitted. Shakespeare could have written, 'My grief is of nature
so floodgate,' &c.

69. **engluts**] PURNELL; French 'engloutir,' to swallow.

76. **Spels**] GREY (ii, 312) cites a law of 1 Jac. cap. xii, to the effect : 'That if any
person or persons should take upon him or them, by witchcraft, inchantment, charm or
sorcery, to the intent to provoke any person to unlawful love; and being thereof law-
fully convicted, should, for the first offence, suffer imprisonment for the space of one
whole year,' &c. WARBURTON says that Rymer ridicules this accusation of charms
and medicines, but the passage in Rymer has escaped me, and small wonder, in that
headlong torrent of amusing abuse of Shakespeare. Warburton, however, avails himself of the chance to cite a Venetian law, *Dei maleficii et herbarie*, cap. xvii, of the
code, entitled 'Della promission del maleficio.' Whereupon STEEVENS remarks :
'Though I believe Shakespeare knew no more of this Venetian law than I do, yet
he was well acquainted with the edicts of that sapient prince King James the First.'
'But,' says RITSON (p. 228), 'there is no doubt that Shakespeare had the substance of
Brabantio's speech from Cinthio's novel, however he might come by it; and Cinthio, it
may be supposed, knew something of the Venetian Statute.' At this line and at line
80, BOOTH says, Cassio and Othello should exchange smiles, as at I, ii, 95.

77–79. **to erre . . . could not**] ABBOTT cites this passage under § 350, where examples are given of the use of 'to' when the finite principal verb is an auxiliary or
like an auxiliary, as in *Ham.* I, v, 18 and 178, and thus explains : 'Here either (1)
" *to* err " depends on " could," *i. e.* " Nature was not able *to* err ;" or (2) " could not "
might perhaps stand for " could not be," " was impossible," having for its subject

(Being not deficient, blind, or lame of fenfe,)   78
Sans witch-craft could not.
   Duke.   Who ere he be, that in this foule proceeding   80
Hath thus beguil'd your Daughter of her felfe,
And you of her; the bloodie Booke of Law,   [313 *b*]
You fhall your felfe read, in the bitter letter,
After your owne fenfe : yea, though our proper Son
Stood in your Action.   85
   Bra.   Humbly I thanke your Grace,
Here is the man; this Moore, whom now it feemes
Your fpeciall Mandate, for the State affaires
Hath hither brought.
   All.   We are verieforry for't.   90
   Duke.   What in yonr owne part, can you fay to this?
   Bra.   Nothing, but this is fo.
   Othe.   Moft Potent, Graue, and Reueren'd Signiors,   93

78. Om. Q$_1$.
   not] Om. Q$_3$.
   or] *nor* Johns.
79. *Sans*] *Saunce* Q$_1$.
   not.] *not—* Rowe+, Jen. Steev.
Rann. Var. Knt, Sing. *not be* Cap. Ktly.
82. *her;*] *her,* Qq.
84. *your owne*] *its owne* Qq, Coll. i.
   fenfe : yea, though] *fenfe, tho* Q$_1$.

fenfe, yea tho Q$_2$Q$_3$. *sense; though* Pope.
90. All.] Duke and Sen. Mal.
   We are] *We're* Pope+, Dyce iii,
Huds.
   verieforry] *very forry* F$_2$.
   for't] *for it* Steev. Var. Rann. Coll.
Sing. Wh. Ktly, Del.
91. [To Othel. Theob. et seq.
   yonr] F$_1$.

"Nature to err." In (2) "for" may be either (*a*) a conjunction, or (*b*) a preposition: "It was not possible for Nature thus to err." I prefer (1).'

77. **prepostrously**] MOREL : Worcester donne comme étymologie directe un adjectif français 'prépostère,' dont nous n'avons pu trouver trace.

84. **your**] DYCE (*Remarks*, p. 234): 'Your' of the Folio is manifestly the true reading, *i. e.* 'According to your own interpretation.'

84. **proper**] That is *own*, *very*. Is there not a survival, in the copious vocabulary of old English phrases still to be found in New England, of this word in this sense? I have frequently heard the phrases there, 'proper good,' 'proper nice,' in the sense of '*very* good,' '*very* nice.' Webster marks it, in this sense, as 'colloquial and vulgar,' which is in favour of its antiquity. GÉRARD calls attention to it, as having 'la même valeur que *propre* en français: "notre propre fils." '—ED.

85. **action**] JOHNSON : Were the man exposed to your *charge* or *accusation.* MOREL : C'est là un sens tout français du mot.

91. **in**] ABBOTT, § 160, gives instances of 'in' used for *on*. See note on I, i, 149.

93, &c. RYMER (p. 100): We find the Duke of Venice with his Senators in Councel at Midnight, upon advice that the Turks or Ottamites, or both together, were ready in transport Ships, put to sea, in order to make a Descent upon Cyprus. This is the posture, when we see Brabantio and Othello join them. By their Conduct and manner of talk, a body must strain hard to fancy the Scene at Venice; And not rather in some

My very Noble, and approu'd good Masters;
That I haue tane away this old mans Daughter,   95
It is most true : true I haue married her;
The verie head, and front of my offending,
Hath this extent; no more.   Rude am I, in my speech,
And little bless'd with the soft phrase of Peace;
For since these Armes of mine, had seuen yeares pith,   100
Till now, some nine Moones wasted, they haue vs'd
Their deerest action, in the Tented Field :
And little of this great world can I speake,
More then pertaines to Feats of Broiles, and Battaile,
And therefore little shall I grace my cause,   105
In speaking for my selfe.   Yet, (by your gratious patience)

98. *am I*] *I am* Q₂Q₃.
my] Om. Johns.
99. *soft*] *set* Qq,Warb. Jen. Steev. Var.
Coll.
101. *now, some*] *now some* Qq.
Moones] *more* Jourdain.
102. *deerest*] *dearst* F₄.

104. *Feats of Broiles*] Ff, Rowe +, Jen.
Knt, Sta. *feate of broyle* Q₁. *feates of broyles* Q₂Q₃. *feats of broil* Cap. et cet.
105. *grace*] *grac* Q₂.
106. *for*] *of* Q₃.
gratious] Om. Pope, Theob. Han.
Warb.

of our Cinque-ports, where the Baily and his Fisher-men are knocking their heads together on account of some Whale, or some terrible broil upon the Coast.   But to show them true Venetians, the maritime affairs stick not long on their hand; the public may sink or swim.   They will sit up all night to hear a Doctors Commons, Matrimonial, Cause. And have the Merits of the Cause at large laid open to 'em, that they may decide it before they stir.   What can be pleaded to keep awake their attention so wonderfully? Never, sure, was *form of pleading* so tedious and so heavy, as this whole scene and midnight entertainment.

96. **her**] FECHTER : To Brabantio with tender courtesy.

98. FECHTER'S version : ' Hath this—(*to the Senate*) this extent! (*with passion on the mute denial of* Brabantio) no more! (Brabantio *rises in anger : They regard each other with menace.   Several members rise simultaneously;* Othello *is at once calm, and submits to the* Council.)

99. **soft**] WARBURTON : This apology, if addressed to his mistress, had been well expressed.   But what he wanted, in speaking before a Venetian Senate, was not the *soft* blandishments of speech, but the art and method of masculine eloquence.   I am persuaded, therefore, that *set* of the Qq is right.

101. **wasted**] KNIGHT : He had been unemployed during nine months.

102. **deerest**] JOHNSON : That is, *dear*, for which much is paid, whether money or labour; *dear action* is action performed at great expense, either of ease or safety. MALONE thinks it here means *most important;* STEEVENS that in modern language we should say, their *best exertion;* and M. MASON that it means their *favourite* action. [To me, Dr W. ALDIS WRIGHT'S definition seems exact : ' *dear* is used of whatever touches us nearly, either in love or hate, joy or sorrow.'   See *Ham.* I, ii, 182.—ED.]

106. **speaking**] Forrest emphasized this word, and not 'myself.'—Rees's *Life* p. 140.

I will a round vn-varnifh'd u Tale deliuer,　　107
Of my whole courfe of Loue.
What Drugges, what Charmes,
What Coniuration, and what mighty Magicke,　　110
(For fuch proceeding I am charg'd withall)
I won his Daughter.
　　Bra.　A Maiden, neuer bold :
Of Spirit fo ftill, and quiet, that her Motion　　114

107. *I will*] *I would* Q₂Q₃.
vn-varnifh'd] *vnrauifh'd* Q₂. *un-
ravifh'd* Q₃.
108, 109. One line, Qq et cet.
109, 110. *Drugges,...Charmes,...Con-
iuration,*] *Drugs ?...Charmes ?...conju-
ration ?* F₃F₄, Rowe i.

111. *proceeding*] *proceedings* Qq.
I am] *am I* Qq, Jen.
112. *Daughter.*] *Daughter with.* Ff,
Rowe+, Cap. Jen. Steev. Rann. Coll. Sing.
Ktly, Huds.
113, 114. *A...Spirit*] One line, Q₁
(reading *bold of fpirit,*).

107. **vn-varnish'd u**] This is a noteworthy and praiseworthy attempt at correcting a typographical error : ' vn-varnifh'd ' should be spelled *vn-uarnifk'd*. In aiming at correcting it by the substitution of the *u* for the *v*, the compositor forgot to remove the *v*, and put *u*, with unusual accuracy, within seven letters of its true place.—ED.

108. **my . . . Loue**] That is, 'the whole course of my love.' This construction, plain enough here, sometimes gives rise to difficulty : see ' your sovereignty of reason,' *Ham.* I, iv, 73; ' his means of death,' *Ib.* IV, v, 207; ' my better part of man,' *Macb.* V, viii, 18, and many other examples in ABBOTT, § 423.

109. **What**] The preposition *with*, which is here omitted, as in so many other instances of adverbial expressions of time, or of manner (see ABBOTT, § 202), the F₂ supplied after ' daughter,' line 112, ' The editor of that edition,' says Dyce (ed. iii), ' not knowing that, according to the earlier phraseology, such an addition was unnecessary for the sense.' Doubtless through inadvertence, GRANT WHITE (ed. ii) says that *with* was ' recklessly omitted.' Cf. ' The interim having weighed it,' *Macb.* I, iii, 154; ' shall . . . . More suffer and more sundry ways,' *Ib.* IV, iii, 48; ' Which time she chaated,' *Ham.* IV, vii, 179. DELIUS thinks that *with* was omitted, because the preceding line in the parenthesis ended in ' withal.'

112. RYMER (p. 101) : All this is but *Preamble*, to tell the Court that He wants words. This was the Eloquence which kept them up all night, and drew their attention in the midst of their alarms. One might rather think the novelty and strangeness of the case prevail'd upon them : no, the Senators do not reckon it strange at all. Instead of starting at the Prodigy, every one is familiar with *Desdemona*, as he were her own natural Father, rejoice in her good fortune, and wish their own several Daughters as hopefully married. Should the Poet have provided such a Husband for an only daughter of any noble Peer in *England*, the Black-amoor must have chang'd his Skin, to look our House of Lords in the face.

114. **Motion**] This may mean, undoubtedly, as GRANT WHITE (ed. ii) interprets it : ' her natural desires,' but I prefer to interpret it with SCHMIDT (*Lex.*), ' movement of the soul, tendency of the mind, impulse; German, *Regung*,' especially since ' herself,' in the next line, refers to it. Shakespeare frequently refers to the soul as feminine. Cf. ' Since my dear soul was mistress of her choice,' *Ham.* III, ii, 58; ' Could force his soul . . . . That from her working,' *Ib.* II, ii, 526.—ED.

Blufh'd at her felfe, and fhe, in fpight of Nature,   115
Of Yeares, of Country, Credite, euery thing
To fall in Loue, with what fhe fear'd to looke on;
It is a iudgement main'd, and moft imperfe&.
That will confeffe Perfe&ion fo could erre
Againft all rules of Nature, and muft be driuen   120
To find out pra&tifes of cunning hell
Why this fhould be.   I therefore vouch againe,
That with fome Mixtures, powrefull o're the blood,
Or with fome Dram,(coniur'd to this effe&)
He wtought vp on her.   125
To vouch this, is no proofe,
Without more wider, and more ouer Teft
Then thefe thin habits, and poore likely-hoods   128

115. *her felfe*] *it selfe* Pope+, Jen.
117. *on ;*] Ff. *on*—Rowe+, Jen. *on ?*
or *on !* Qq et cet.
118. *main'd*] *maimd* Q₁Q₂. *maim'd*
F₂ et cet.
      imperfect.] *imperfect,* Qq.
119. *Perfection*] *Affection* Theob. Han.
Jen.
      could] *would* Qq, Jen.
122. *be.*] *be,* Qq.
125. *wtought*] F₁.

125. *vp on*] F₁.
126. *To*] Du. *To* Q₁ et cet.
      vouch] *youth* Q₁.
127. *wider*] *certaine* Qq, Pope+, Cap.
Jen. Steev. Var. Rann. Coll. Sing. Cam.
Huds. *evidence* Coll. (MS).
      ouer Teft] *over-Teft* Ff. *over teft*
Q₃, Rowe. *ouert teft* Q₁Q₂ et cet.
128. *Then thefe*] *Thefe are* Qq, Coll.
Sing. Wh. i, Huds.

118. **main'd**] In reference to this misprint DYCE says, that he does not mean to
defend it when he observes that in *2 Hen. VI:* IV, ii, 172, we have the provincialism
in Cade's speech: 'mained,' *i. e.* lamed.

119. **Perfection**] To THEOBALD the expression *perfection erring* seemed a contradiction. 'I have ventured,' he says, 'to imagine that our author wrote *"Affection* so
could err."' DR JOHNSON: The objection is childish; 'perfection' is used here, as
almost everywhere else, for a high degree of excellence.

121. **practises**] That is, *stratagems, treacherous plots,* very frequently thus used.
Cf. 'a pass of practice,' *Ham.* IV, vii, 139; 'my practices ride easy,' *Lear,* I,
ii, 172.

127. **more wider**] Is not this to be preferred to 'more certain' of the Qq? A wide
and open proof seems to stand in clear contrast to thin, narrow shows and trivial conjectures. JOHNSON defines 'overt test,' *open proofs, external evidence;* and the phrase
'thin . . . . seeming,' *weak show of slight appearance.* For the double comparative
'more wider,' see Shakespeare *passim.*—ED.

128. **habits**] SINGER: 'Thin habits' may be a metaphor from dress, but it may also
be a Latinism from *habita,* things considered, reckoned, as in the phrase *habit* and
repute, *i. e.* held and esteemed. JOHN HUNTER: Than the thin garb with which you
invest the matter, and vour slender probabilities as to the aspect in which it must be
generally regarded.

Of moderne feeming, do prefer againft him.

    Sen. But *Othello*, fpeake,   **130**

Did you, by indireƈt, and forced courfes

Subdue, and poyfon this yong Maides affeƈtions?

Or came it by requeft, and fuch faire queftion

As foule, to foule affordeth?

    Othel. I do befeech you,   **135**

Send for the Lady to the Sagitary.

And let her fpeake of me before her Father;

If you do finde me foule, in herreport,

The Truft, the Office, I do hold of you,

Not onely take away, but let your Sentence   **140**

Euen fall vpon my life.

    Duke. Fetch *Defdemona* hither.

    Othe. Aunciant, conduƈt them:

You beft know the place.

And tell fhe come, as truely as to heauen,   **145**

I do confeffe the vices of my blood,

So iuftly to your Graue eares, Ile prefent

How I did thriue in this faire Ladies loue,   **[314 a]**

And fhe in mine.

    Duke. Say it *Othello*.   **150**

    Othe. Her Father lou'd me, oft inuited me:

129. *feeming*] *feemings* Q₁Q₂.
   do] *you* Qq, Coll. Sing. Wh. i, Huds. *doe* F₂.
130. **Sen.**] 1 Sena. Qq, Rowe et cet.
   But] Om. Han.
   fpeake,] *speak;* Theob.
135. *do*] Om. Pope +.
136. *Sagitary*] *Sagittar* Q₁, Cap. *Sagittary* Q₂Q₃F₄ et cet.
139. Om. Q₁.
142. [Exit two or three. Qq. (Exeunt...

Q₂Q₃).
143, 144. One line, Qq, Rowe et cet.
144. [Exit Iago. Rowe. Exeunt Attendants and Iago. Cap.
145. *tell*] F₁.
   truely] *faithfull* Q₁.
   heauen,] *Heav'n* or *Heaven* Rowe et cet.
146. Om. Q₁.
151–154. Lines end *father...queftion'd me...to year...pafs'd.* Mal.

129. **moderne**] Always, I believe, used by Shakespeare in the sense of trite, ordinary, commonplace.—ED. MOREL: On comprend quelle association d'idées a pu donner au mot cette valeur. Il y a là un corollaire de l'idée qui a inspiré l'adage célèbre: major a longinquo reverentia.

133. **question**] That is, conversation, discourse, as in 'made she no verbal queftion,' *Lear*, IV, iii, 24.

136. **Sagitary**] See I, i, 173.

147. **iuftly**] That is, truthfully. Among the Four Cardinal Virtues: Temperance, Juftice, Prudence, and Fortitude, the second includes or implies Truth.—ED.

151. FECHTER: (*Regarding Brabantio with regret.*) Her father lov'd me!—(*check-*

Still queſtion'd me the Storie of my life,   152
From yeare to yeare : the Battaile, Sieges, Fortune,
That I haue paſt.
I ran it through, euen from my boyiſh daies,   155
Toth'very moment that he bad me tell it.
Wherein I ſpoke of moſt disaſtrous chances :
Of mouing Accidents by Flood and Field,
Of haire-breadth ſcapes i'th'imminent deadly breach ;
Of being taken by the Inſolent Foe,   160
And ſold to ſlauery.   Of my redemption thence,

152. *queſtion'd*] *queſtioned* Qq.
    Storie] *ſtoryes* Q₃.
153. *yeare :*] *yeare*, Qq.
    Battaile] *battailes* Qq.   *Battails*
F₂.   *Battells* F₃F₄, Rowe.   *battles* Warb.
et seq.
    Fortune] Ff, Knt.   *fortunes* Qq et
cet.
154. *haue paſt.*] *haue paſt :* Qq.   *had
past.* Coll. (MS).   *have passed.* With his
demands complying, Ktly conj.

155. *from*] *to* Q₃.
156. *bad*] *bade* Q₁Q₂, Johns. et seq.
157. *ſpoke*] Ff, Rowe+, Jen.Var. Ktly.
ſpake Qq, Cap. et cet.
158. *Accidents by*] *accident of* Q₁.
159. *imminent deadly*] Hyphened by
Sta. Del. Pur.
160. *Foe,*] *foe :* Q₁.
161. *ſlauery.*] *ſlauery*, Q₁.   *ſlauery ;*
Q₂Q₃, Rowe et cet.
    Of my] *and my* Q₁.

ing his emotion, and continuing calmly).   BOOTH : Brabantio may, perhaps, manifest
denial of Othello's assertion ; and Othello's tone, after a slight pause, may imply that
he had at least had reason to think so.   But *Love* often meant merely *liking*, and since
certainly Brabantio did *like* the Moor, it may not be proper for him to express any disapprobation here.

153. **Fortune**] MOREL : *Aventures* ou *accidents*.   Comparez le sens du mot chez
Froissard : ' Leurs vaisseaux eurent si grand *fortune* sur mer . . . . que plusieurs de
leurs nefs furent peries.'

154. **PURNELL** : The hemistich adds to the effect of the enumeration by giving the
actor time to think over the list.

157 et seq. **BOOTH** : All this as modestly as possible,—not a breath of bluster, and
not declamatory ; *very* difficult to render naturally.   The Duke and Senators, indeed
all present, should listen with rapt attention.

161–168. In some early Acting Copies these lines are omitted, and in their place the
following inserted :

> ' Of battles bravely, hardly, fought ; of victories
> For which the conqueror mourn'd, so many fell :
> Sometimes I told the story of a siege,
> Wherein I had to combat plagues and famine ;
> Soldiers unpaid ; fearful to fight,
> Yet bold in dangerous mutiny.'

The earliest trace of them that I can find is in the Acting Copy for the ' Theatres Royal
ın Drury-Lane and Covent-Garden ' in 1770.   As Garrick did not retire from Drury-
Lane until June, 1776, it is not improbable that these lines were written by him ; it is
hard to see why he felt any necessity for the substitution, unless he were infected with
Iago's ſcor for ' fantastical lies.'   WOOD (*Personal Recollections*, &c., p. 265) says

And portance in my Trauellours hiftorie.   162
Wherein of Antars vaft, and Defarts idle,

162. *portance in my*] *with it all my* Q₁,
Pope, Han. Warb.
Trauellours] *trauells* Qq, Rowe.
Travellers F₂F₃. *Traveller's* F₄, Knt,
Sing. Ktly. *travels'* Glo. Cam. Dyce iii,
Huds. Wh. ii. *travel's* Pope et cet.

163. *Antars*] QqFf, Rowe. *Antrees*
Q₁. *antrées* Pope. *antres* Theob. et cet.
Defarts] *Deferts* Q₁, Sing. i, Coll.
et seq.

idle] *wilde* F₂F₃. *wild* F₄, Pope,
Han. Sing. i.

that he 'distinctly remembers finding these lines in an old Covent-Garden Prompt-book of our early library, not in the printed text, but interwritten upon a blank leaf. [Edmund] Kean, like every other actor or reader to whom I have applied, had never met with them, but acknowledged their great beauty and power.'—ED.

162. **portance**] RYMER (p. 90) in quoting this line reads *portents*. JOHNSON reads 'portance *in't ;*' and explains : ' my redemption from slavery, and my behaviour in it.' STEEVENS : Perhaps Shakespeare meant—my behaviour in my travels *as described in my history of them.* ' Portance ' is used in *Cor.* II, iii, 232. DYCE (*Gloss.*) : That is, bearing, carriage, deportment, behaviour. KNIGHT puts a full stop after ' portance,' and includes ' Wherein . . . . speake,' 163-165, in parenthesis, with only a comma after ' speake.' MOREL : Montaigne l'emploie comme synonyme de ' façon d'agir.'

162. **Trauellours**] I cannot but think the Qq are right here. KNIGHT thus upholds the Ff : Othello modestly, and somewhat jocosely, calls his wonderful relations *a traveller's history,*—a term by which the marvellous stories of the Lithgows and Coryats were wont to be designated in Shakespeare's day. DYCE : A personage less inclined to *joceseness* than Othello cannot well be conceived. Dr Richardson suggests to me that ' Trauellours ' is a misprint for *travellous* (or *travailous*), and adds that Wiclif has ' Jobs *trauailous* nights ' and ' the *traveilous* presoun of the Egiptians ;' but though the epithet is very properly applied to ' nights ' or to a ' prison,' can we speak of a ' *travailous* history ' ?

163. **Antars**] POPE : French, grottoes. JOHNSON : Caves and dens. CHALMERS, (*Supp. Apol.*, 464), whose learning was rather tickle o' the sere, has on this line a good specimen note : ' Shakespeare by no very uncommon quibble has used the expressions "anters vast " and " desarts idle " in one sense, when he meant another. The progress of the word "anters" seems to be this : anters, aunters, aventers, adventures ; and hence the word "anters" came to signify, in the language of Yorkshire, *strange things* or *strange stories.* So in a disputation *bytwene a Chrystens mon and a Jew,* written before the year 1300 : " Hur schull we longe abyde Auntres [adventures] to hear." The play on " desarts idle " consists in confounding " desart " for a *wilderness* with *desert* for merit ; and *deserts idle,* or unworthy desert, might be deemed desert, *sine pulvere.*'

163. **idle**] JOHNSON : Every mind is liable to absence and inadverdency, else Pope could never have rejected a word like this so poetically beautiful. ' Idle ' is an epithet used to express the infertility of the chaotic state in the Saxon translation of the Pentateuch. GIFFORD (*Sejanus,* I, i) : It does not seem to have occurred to the commentators that *wild* might add a feature of some import, even to a desert ; whereas, *sterile* leaves it j.st as it found it, and is (without a pun) the *idlest* epithet which could be applied.])pe, too, had an ear for rhythm ; and as his reading has some touch of Shakespeare, which the other has not, and is besides better poetry, I should hope that it will one day resume its proper place in the text.

Rough Quarries, Rocks, Hills, whofe head touch heauen,
It was my hint to fpeake.   Such was my Proceffe,   165
And of the Canibals that each others eate,
The *Antropophague*, and men whofe heads   167

164. *Hills*] *and hils* QqFf, Rowe et cet.
   head] Rowe ii.   *heads* QqFf etcet.
165. *hint*] *hent* Q₁, Warb.
   fpeake.] *fpeake*, Qq, Knt.
   my] Q₂Q₃Ff, Rowe, Knt.   *the* Q₁

et cet.
166. *others*] F₂.   *other* QqF₃F₄ et cet.
   eate,] *eate;* Qq.
167. Antropophague] Anthropophagie
   Qq.   Anthropophagi Ff, Rowe et cet.

165. **hint**] WARBURTON adopted *hent*, interpreting it as meaning *use, custom*, a meaning which JOHNSON said *hent* did not have either in Shakespeare or in any other author, adding: 'hint' or *cue* is commonly used for occasion of speech, which is explained by *such is the process*, that is, the course of the tale required it.   SKEAT (*Etym. Dict.*, s. v.): Only the substantive occurs in Shakespeare . . . . *Hint* properly signifies 'a thing taken,' i. e. a thing caught or apprehended; being a contraction of Middle English *hinted*, taken; or rather a variant of the old past participle *hent*, with the same sense, ... which occurs in *Meas. for Meas.* IV, vi, 14.

167. **Antropophague**] WHALLEY (p. 73) says, that the origin of all these fables is to be found in Sir John Mandeville's Travels.—'Aftreward men gon be many Yles be See, unto an Yle that men clepen *Milke:* and there is a fulle cursed peple: for thei delyten in ne thing more, than for to fighten and to sle men.   And thei drynken gladlyest mannes Blood, the whiche thei clepen Dieu' [p. 195, ed. Halliwell].   'And in another Yle, toward the Southe duellen folk of foule Stature and of cursed kynde, than have no Hedes; and here Eyen ben in here Scholdres' [p. 203, *Ib*.].   THEOBALD: Sir Walter Raleigh in his Travels [*The Discoverie of Gviana*, 1596, p. 85, ed. Hakluyt Soc.] has given the following account: 'Next vnto these there are two riuers *Atoica* and *Caora*, and on that braunch which is called *Caora* are a nation of people, whose heades appeare not aboue their shoulders, which though it may be thought a meere fable, yet for mine owne parte I am resolued it is true, because euery child in the prouinces of *Arromaia* and *Canuri* affirme the same: they are called *Ewaipanoma:* they are reported to haue their eyes in their shoulders, and their mouths in the middle of their breasts, and that a long train of haire groweth backward betwen their shoulders . . . . It was not my chaunce to heare of them til I was come away, and if I had but spoken one word of it while I was there, I might haue brought one of them with me to put the matter out of doubt.   Such a nation was written of by *Maundeuile*, whose reportes were held for fables many yeares, and yet since the East *Indies* were discouered, wee finde his relations true of such thinges as heeretofore were held incredible: whether it be true or no the matter is not great, neither can there be any profit in the imagination, for mine owne part I saw them not, but I am resolued that so many people did not all combine, or forethinke to make the report.' . . . . 'To the west of *Caroli* are diuers nations of *Canibals*, and of those *Ewaipanoma* without heades' [p. 108, *Ib*.   In a footnote the editor, Sir R. H. Schomburgk, calls attention to Humboldt's mention of an old Indian whom he met, who boasted of having seen these Acephali with his own eyes.—ED.]   This passage in Othello, continues Theobald, and the same allusion in *Temp.* III, iii, 46, help us in fixing the date of these plays; neither of them could have been written before 1596.   The mystery of these headless People is accounted for by Olearius, who, speaking of the Samojeds, a people of Northern Muscovy, says: 'Their

Grew beneath their fhoulders.   Thefe things to heare,   168

168. *Grew*] Ff. *Did grow* Rowe. *Doe*   Rowe, Jen. *All these* Pope+. *this* Q,,
grow Qq et cet.   Coll. Dyce, Wh. Glo. Sta. Cam. Del. Rlfe,
   Thefe things] Ff. *thefe* Q₂Q₃,   Huds.

garments are made like those that are call'd *Cosaques,* open only at the Necks. When
the Cold is extraordinary, they put their *Cosaques* over their Heads, and let the Sleeves
hang down; their Faces being not to be seen, but at the Cleft which is at the Neck.
Whence Some have taken Occasion to write, that in these Northern Countries there
are People without Heads, having their Faces in their Breasts.' STAUNTON thinks
that possibly Shakespeare had in mind the 2d chap. of the Seventh Book of *Plinies
Naturall History,* wherein the Anthropophagi and these headless men are mentioned;
but I am inclined to think that if Shakespeare had ever read this chapter in Pliny,
brimming over as it is with monstrosities, he would not have selected as a striking
item in Othello's 'trauels history' such a trifling distortion as a man with his face in
his breast. Within a few pages of the account of the Anthropophagi in Sir Walter's
Discouerie, mention is made of a very high hill, and of digging out crystals with daggers and fingers,—rough quarrying certainly.—ED.

168. RYMER (p. 90): This was the Charm, this was the philtre, the love-powder
that took the Daughter of this Noble Venetian. This was sufficient to make the
Black-amoor White, and reconcile all, tho' there had been a Cloven-foot into the bargain. A meaner woman might be as soon taken by *Aqua Tetrachymagogon.* Shakespeare in this Play calls 'em the supersubtle Venetians. Yet examine throughout the
Tragedy, there is nothing on the noble *Desdemona,* that is not below any Country
Chambermaid with us. And the account of their Noblemen and Senate can only be
calculated for the latitude of *Gotham.* SHAFTESBURY (*Advice to an Author,* 1710,
Part III, sect. 3): Tho *Christian* Miracles may not so well satisfy 'em [i. e. Atheists];
they dwell with the highest Contentment on the Prodigys of *Moorish* and *Pagan*
Countrys. They have far more Pleasure in hearing the monstrous Accounts of monstrous Men and Manners, than the politest and best Narrations of the Affairs, the Gov-
ernments, and Lives of the wisest and most polish'd People. . . . . This Humour our
old Tragick Poet seems to have discover'd. He hit our *Taste* in giving us a *Moorish*
Hero, full fraught with Prodigy: a wondrous *Story-teller!* But for the attentive Part,
the Poet chose to give it to Woman-kind. What passionate Reader of *Travels,* or
Student in the prodigious Sciences, can refuse to pity that fair Lady, who fell in Love
with the *miraculous* Moor? especially considering with what sutable grace such a
Lover cou'd relate the most monstrous Adventures, and satisfy the wondering Appetite
with the most wondrous Tales; [lines 163-169 are here quoted]. Seriously, 'twas a
woful Tale! unfit, one wou'd think, to win a tender Fair-one. It's true, the Poet sufficiently condemns her Fancy; and makes her (poor Lady!) pay dearly for it in the
end. But why, amongst his *Greek* names, he shou'd have chosen one which denoted
the Lady *Superstitious,* I can't imagine: unless, as Poets are sometimes Prophets too,
he shou'd figuratively under this dark *Type* have represented to us, That about a hundred Years after his Time, the Fair sex of this Island shou'd, by other monstrous *Tales,*
be so seduc'd as to turn their Favour chiefly on the persons of the *Tale-tellers;* and
change their natural Inclination for fair, candid, and courteous Knights into a Passion
for a mysterious Race of black Enchanters: such as of old were said to *creep into
Houses,* and *lead captive silly Women.* . . . . But whatever monstrous Zeal or superstitious Passion the Poet might foretel, either in the Gentlemen, Ladys, or common

Would *Desdemona* serioufly incline :
But ftill the houfe Affaires would draw her hence :   170
Which euer as fhe could with hafte difpatch,
She'l'd come againe, and with a greedie eare   172

170. *houfe Affairs*] *house-affairs* Pope.   171. *Which*] *And* Q₁.
     hence] Ff, Rowe, Del. *thence*   172. *She'l'd*] *Shee'd* Qq. *She'ld* Ff.
Qq et cet.

People, of an after Age; 'tis certain that as to Books, the same *Moorish* Fancy, in its plain and literal sense, prevails strongly at the present time.   Monsters and Monsterlands were never more in request : And we may often see a Philosopher, or a Wit, run a Tale-gathering in those *idle Desarts*, as familiarly as the silliest Woman or the merest Boy.   WARBURTON : Discourses of this nature made the subject of the politest conversation, when voyages into, and discoveries of, the new world were all in vogue.   So, when the Bastard Faulconbridge in *King John*, describes the behaviour of upstart greatness, he makes one of the essential circumstances of it to be this kind of table-talk. The *fashion* then running altogether this way, it is no wonder a young lady of quality should be struck with the history of an adventurer.   JOHNSON : Whoever ridicules this account of the progress of love, shows his ignorance not only of history, but also of nature and manners.   It is no wonder that, in any age or in any nation, a lady— recluse, timorous, and delicate—should desire to hear of events and scenes which she could never see ; and should admire the man who had endured dangers and performed actions, which, however great, were yet magnified by her timidity.

170. **still**] That is, constantly.   Very frequent in Shakespeare thus used, see *Rom. & Jul.* V, iii, 106; *Macb.* V, viii, 14; *Lear*, II, iv, 102; *Ham.* II, ii, 42.

170. **would**] ABBOTT, § 330: 'Would' often means 'liked,' 'was accustomed.' Compare ἐφίλει.

170. **hence**] Is there any necessity for deserting the Ff here?   Is not 'hence' somewhat more vivid than 'thence,' just as *here* is nearer than *there?*—ED.

172. **greedie eare**] MALONE cites, 'Hang both your greedy ears upon my lips; Let them devour my speech,' as a parallel passage from *Lust's Dominion*, which he says was written by Marlowe, and before 1593.   If Marlowe were the author, it was, of course, written before that year, the year in which Marlowe was killed.   Collier, however, has shown (Dodsley's *Old Plays*, vol. ii, p. 311, ed. 1825) by internal evidence that this tragedy was written after 1598, the year in which Philip II. of Spain died, whose death is represented in the First Act; furthermore, that a tract was printed in London in 1599, called 'A briefe and true Declaration of the Sicknesse, last words, and Death of the King of Spain, Philip Second,' from which various passages of the play were clearly borrowed; Collier cites three or four of them, which reveal not 'similarity, but identity.'   In Henslowe's *Diary* (p. 165, ed. Shaks. Soc.), an item refers to the payment on 'the 13 of febrearye, 1599,' of three pounds 'for a boocke called the Spanesche Mores tragedie, unto Thomas Deckers, Wm. Harton, John Daye;' this tragedy Collier conjectured (*Hist. of Dram. Poetry*, vol. ii, p. 477, ed. 1879), with 'great probability,' says Dyce (Marlowe's *Works*, i, p. lviii), to be the same as *Lust's Dominion.*   I have thought it worth while to be thus particular about this miserable stuff, quite as wretched as portions of *Titus Andronicus*, which it somewhat resembles, because Malone finds in it another parallelism with *Othello*, in II, i, 229, and Steevens goes so far as to suggest that possibly Shakespeare may have acted in it.   Collier men-

Deuoure vp my difcourfe.   Which I obferuing,   173
Tooke once a pliant houre, and found good meanes
To draw from her a prayer of earneft heart,   175
That I would all my Pilgrimage dilate,
Whereof by parcels fhe had fomething heard,
But not inftinctiuely : I did confent,
And often did beguile her of her teares,
When I did fpeake of fome diftreffefull ftroke   180
That my youth fuffer'd : My Storie being done,
She gaue me for my paines a world of kiffes: 182

173. *difcourfe.*] *difcourfe;* Qq. *Dif-*
courfe, F₄.
176. *dilate*] *relate* Quincy (MS).
177. *parcels*] *parcell* Q₁.
178. *not*] *nought* Cap. conj.
inftinctiuely] *diftinctively* Ff,

Rowe+, Cap. Rann. *intentively* Qq,
Johns. et cet.
180. *diftreffefull*] *diftreffed* Q₁, Morel.
181. *fuffer'd*] *fuffered* Qq.
182. *kiffes*] Ff, Rowe. *thanks* Southern (MS). *fighes* Qq et cet.

---

tions no earlier printed copy of it than 1657. Malone also cites from the *Faerie Queene*,
VI, ix (231, ed. Grosart), 'Whylest thus he talkt, the knight with greedy eare Hung still
upon,' &c. And STEEVENS shows that *aures avidæ* may be found in Cicero.

174. **good**] Forrest emphasized this word—Rees's *Life*, p. 141.

176. **dilate**] That is, relate at length. Conf. *Ham.* I, ii, 38, 'these dilated articles.

178. **instinctiuely**] KNIGHT: A decided typographical error. This, and a few
other errors of the same sort which are corrected by a reference to the Qto, prove that
the Folio was printed from MS., and most probably before the publication of the Qto;
had it been consulted, these errors would not have been committed. STEEVENS : *Intention* and *attention* were once synonymous. Desdemona, who was often called out
of the room on house-affairs, could not have heard Othello's tale *intentively*, i. e. with
attention to all its parts. DYCE (*Remarks*, p. 234): *Intentively* was always used as
equivalent to *attentively*, not only by the writers of Shakespeare's time, but by those
of a much earlier date. Palsgrave has '*Intentyfe*, hedefull.'—'*Ententyfe*, busy to do a
thynge or to take hede to a thyng.' SINGER quotes Bullokar's *Expositor:* '*Intentiue* ·
Which listeneth well, and is earnestly bent to a thing.' LETTSOM (Walker's *Crit.* i,
181, Foot-note): 'Distinctiuely' seems a mere sophistication of F₂ for *instinctiuely*, the
nonsensical reading of F₁. In this particular passage *intentively* seems to mean either
all at a stretch, or *so as to comprehend the story as a whole.* R. M. SPENCE (*N. &
Qu.*, 5th, xi, 383) upholds *distinctively*, which means, he alleges, *in detail.* [*Enten-
tivement:* Jntentiuely, busily, earnestly; attentiuely, carefully, heedfully.—Cotgrave
But it is needless to multiply proofs that *intentiue* meant *attentiue.* Lettsom seems to
me to have rightly interpreted the requirements of the meaning here.—ED.]

180. **distresseful**] MOREL, whose thoughtful edition enlists respect for his opinion,
prefers the Qto, as an instance where the past participle in -*ed* is equivalent to the adjective in -*full*, as *delighted* for delightful, &c.

182. **kisses**] POPE : *Sighs* is evidently the true reading. The lady had been forward indeed, to give him a world of *kisses* upon the bare recital of his story, nor does it
agree with the following lines. [And yet we must remember that kissing in Eliza-

She fwore in faith 'twas ftrange : 'twas paffing ftrange,   183
'Twas pittifull : 'twas wondrous pittifull.
She wifh'd fhe had not heard it, yet fhe wifh'd   185
That Heauen had made her fuch a man.   She thank'd me,

183. *in faith*] *I faith* Qq.   *ful,...pitiful.* F₄, Ktly. *pitiful,...pitiful—*
       ftrange : ...ftrange,] *ftrange,...*   Rowe+, Jen. *pittifull,...pittifull;* Qq et
ftrange, F₂, Rowe+, Jen. Glo. Rlfe, Wh.   cet.
ii. *ftrange,...ftrange.* F₃F₄. *ftrange,...*   185. *wifh'd*] *wifht* Qq.
ftrange; Qq et cet.   186. *thank'd*] *thanked* Qq.
     184. *pittifull :...pittifull.*] F₂F₃. *piti-*

beth's time was not as significant as it is now.   See the openness with which, in II, i,
Cassio kisses Emilia.—ED.]

   183. **swore**] STEEVENS quotes Whitaker's *Vindication of Mary Queen of Scots*, ii,
487 : ' Let not the modern reader be hurt here and in paragraph X. at a Lady, a
Queen, and a Mary, *swearing*.   To aver upon faith and honour was then called swearing, equally with a solemn appeal to God, and considered the same with it. . . . . And
thus Shakespeare makes Othello to represent Desdemona as acting, in a passage [the
present one] that I have often condemned, before I saw this easy explanation of it, as
one among many proofs of Shakespeare's inability to exhibit the delicate graces of
female conversation.'   ' This remark,' adds Steevens, ' serves at once to justify Desdemona and Queen Mary, and to show what kind of swearing was done by both; not
a bold and masculine oath put into the mouth of Desdemona, such as Elizabeth frequently used, but a more earnest affirmation upon her faith and honour, which she considered as the same with a solemn appeal to God.'   Whitaker's confession that he had
once condemned this passage as one of the many proofs of Shakespeare's inability to
exhibit the delicate graces of female conversation, KNIGHT quotes, but attributes it to
Steevens, and upon Steevens lets fall his bitter indignation.   ' Perhaps,' he says, ' the
remainder of his many proofs would, in the same way, have been destroyed, if he had
possessed the slightest capacity for distinguishing between the true and the meretricious
in sentiment and style; but what could be expected of a man who, writing Notes upon
the Sonnets, laments his " piteous constraint to read such stuff at all" ?'
   183, 184. The punctuation of F₁ (discarded by almost every modern editor) in these
two lines is noteworthy, and, in my opinion, should be retained.   ' It was strange; nay,
it was much more than strange, it was pitifull : it was wondrous pitifull.'   Staunton
says, at V, ii, 236, that ' strange ' here means more than it now means, it is equivalent
to ' incredible.'—ED.
   185, 186. **She . . . man**] In this wish of Desdemona is ' her ' the accusative or
the dative ?   Our German brothers, in their translations, are forced to decide this question; we can smiling put it by.   TIECK (or, probably, BAUDISSIN, to whose share fell
the translation of *Othello*) notes that Eschenburg in 1779 translated ' her ' as an accusative, and rightly, as Tieck thinks : ' der Himmel hätte solch einen Mann aus ihr
gemacht,' but that in his translation of 1805 he had gone astray on the dative : ' der
Himmel hätte ihr solch einen Mann bestimmt.'   Tieck did not notice that the error,
f such it be, lay farther back than Eschenburg.   In 1766 Wieland translated the line :
 der Himmel hätte einen solchen Mann für sie gemacht.'   Among English editors
KNIGHT is not sure that the dative is wrong; COWDEN-CLARKE (surely a good authority on matters of womanly delicacy,—if not the court of last resort therein) decides for

And bad me, if I had a Friend that lou'd her,   187
I fhould but teach him how to tell my Story,
And that would wooe her.   Vpon this hint I fpake,
She lou'd me for the dangers I had paft,   190
And I lou'd her, that fhe did pitty them.
This onely is the witch-craft I haue vs'd.   192

187. *had*] *hat* Q$_3$.   189. *hint*] *heate* Qq.
    lou'd] *loued* Qq.   190. *lou'd*] *loued* Q$_3$.
189. *wooe*] *woe* Q$_2$Q$_3$.   *had*] *have* Ff, Rowe.
    Vpon] *On* Pope+.

the dative, and even thinks it strange that it should be questioned; HUDSON also is emphatically in favour of the dative, and exclaims at those who, 'lest the lady's delicacy should be impeached!' insist on the accusative; ROLFE pronounces in favour of the dative: 'That is, *for* her,' and adds that what follows 'favours this explanation.' PURNELL thinks it is the dative, but gives it a shade of softness by calling it the ethical dative.   And yet in spite of all this array, I cannot bring myself to believe that the young girl's thoughts had so quickly turned to marriage,—she was still lost in the wondrous, pitiful story, which, although she had with earnest heart prayed for it, she now wished she hadn't heard; '*yet* she wished' she could herself have seen these wondrous sights, and have been herself the hero of these distressful strokes.   Is it not a most natural wish, to be the very hero himself before whose feet smooth success is strewed, as it had been before Othello's?   Is it unusual to hear a girl express the wish that she were a man?   It was not in this wish that Othello detected the 'hint,' but in the 'Friend that loved her.'   If Desdemona had expressed the wish to Othello's face, that Heaven had made a husband for her just like Othello himself, I doubt if the latter, or any one else, would have softened the expression into a '*hint*.'—ED.

192. LEWES (*On Actors*, &c., p. 5): Even in earlier and better days there was much in [Kean's] performance of Othello which was spasmodic, slovenly, false.   The address to the Senate was very bad.   He had little power of elocution, unless when sustained by a strong emotion; and this long, simple narrative was the kind of speech he could not manage at all.   He gabbled over it, impatient to arrive at the phrase: 'And this was all the witchcraft I have used.   Here comes the lady, let her witness it.'   His delivery of this 'point,' always startled the audience into applause by its incisive tone and its abrupt transition; yet nothing could be more out of keeping with the Shakespearian character.   Othello might smile with lofty disdain at the accusation of witchcraft, or rebut it calmly, but not make it the climax of a withering sarcasm,— attacking the word 'witchcraft' with high and sudden emphasis, and dropping into an almost disrespectful colloquialism as the lady appeared.   Indeed, throughout the First and Second Acts, with the exception of occasional flashes (as in the passionate fervour with which he greets Desdemona on landing at Cyprus), Kean's Othello was rather irritating and disappointing,—arresting the mind, but not satisfying it.   From the Third Act onwards, all was wrought out with a mastery over the resources of expression such as has been seldom approached.   In the successive unfolding of these great scenes he represented with incomparable effect the lion-like fury, the deep and haggard pathos, the forlorn sense of desolation alternating with gusts of stormy cries for vengeance, the misgivings and sudden reassurances, the calm and deadly resolution of one not easily moved, but who, being moved, was stirred to the very depths.

Here comes the Ladie : Let her witneffe it.   193

> *Enter Defdemona, Iago, Attendants.*

Duke. I thinke this tale would win my Daughter too,   195
Good *Brabantio*, take vp this mangled matter at the beft :
Men do their broken Weapons rather vfe,
Then their bare hands.
  Bra. I pray you heare her fpeake ?
If fhe confeffe that fhe was halfe the wooer,   200
Deftruction on my head, if my bad blame
Light on the man. Come hither gentle Miftris,
Do you perceiue in all this Noble Companie,
Where moft you owe obedience?
  Def. My Noble Father,   205
I do perceiue heere a diuided dutie.

193. Two lines, Qq.
    Ladie :] *Lady*, QqF₃F₄.
194. Attendants.] and the reft. Qq.
Scene IX. Pope+, Jen.
195. *too*,] *to*,— Q₁. *to ;*— Q₂Q₃. *too*—
Pope+. *too.* Rowe, Johns. et seq.
196. *Good* Brabantio] Separate line,

Pope et seq.
201. *on my head*] *lite on me* Qq. (*light
... Q₂Q₃*).
203. *this*] *his* F₂.
204. *moft you*] *you moft* Pope+. *you
must* Warb.
205. *My Noble*] *Noble* Pope, Han.

BOOTH : Let this line be the climax, not 'she did pity them.' After 192 : Re-enter
Roderigo and others. Their return announces the lady's coming. FECHTER'S Stage
direction here is : 'Goes to lead in Desdemona.'

195. BOOTH : Othello should playfully acknowledge this compliment. LLOYD :
This round, unvarnished tale carries conviction to all,—even to Brabantio himself; for
though he professes to reserve his belief till his daughter shall confess whether she
were half the wooer, he never asks her that question, but another instead, which she
could not have answered otherwise than she did, had the accusation of witchcraft been
well founded.

202. **Come hither**] FECHTER directs Othello to conduct Desdemona to the place
he (Othello) occupied, and then retire among his followers. BOOTH : The 'evil eye'
is dreaded, even now, by superstitious Italians, more than other charms; it is strange
that Shakespeare did not refer to it. Othello must not 'give a loop to hang a doubt
on' touching his influence over Desdemona; he must not even *look* at her, nor, worse
still, go to meet her, which the Court would not permit. But he must turn his back
towards her until she announces him as her husband, then let him turn and face her
and the whole Court.

206–210. BOADEN (*Life of John Kemble*, i, 258) : I question whether equal dis-
crimination was ever before given [as by Mrs Siddons] to these lines : 'My noble
father, I do perceive HERE, a *divided* duty; To YOU, I am bound, &c. But *here's* my
husband.' MOBERLY (*Rom. & Jul.* II, vi, 25, in that most exquisite of all love-scenes
where Romeo begs Juliet to 'let rich music's tongue unfold the imagined happiness') :
Compare 'he admirable way in which Desdemona, when called upon to say whether

To you I am bound for life, and education :   207
My life and education both do learne me,
How to refpect you.   You are the Lord of duty,
I am hitherto your Daughter.   But heere's my Husband;   210
And fo much dutie, as my Mother fhew'd
To you, preferring you before her Father :   [314 *b*]
So much I challenge, that I may profeffe
Due to the Moore my Lord.

    Bra.   God be with you : I haue done.   215
Pleafe it your Grace, on to the State Affaires;
I had rather to adopt a Child, then get it.
Come hither Moore;
I here do giue thee that with all my heart,
Which but thou haft already, with all my heart   220

207, 210, 222. *I am*] *I'm* Pope +, Dyce
iii, Huds.
  209. *you.*] *you*, Qq.
    You are] *You're* Pope +, Dyce iii,
Huds.
    the Lord of] *Lord of all my* Q₁.
  211. *fhew'd*] *fhewed* Qq.
  213. *much*] *much muſt* Q₃.
  215. *God...you :*] *God bu'y*, Qq.   *God*

b'w'ye, Jen.   *God be wi'you;* Cap. Glo.
Ktly.   *God b'wi'you!* Sing. ii, Wh. i,
Dyce iii, Huds.
    haue] *ha* Qq.   *ha'* Jen.
  219. *with all*] *withall* Q₂Q₃.
  220. Om. Q₁.
    Which] *Which*, F₄, Rowe et seq.
    all] Om. Pope, Han.

---

her love for Othello grew up as he had said, confines herself, with perfect dignity, to a
declaration that her duty is now to the Moor, her lord, in the same sense in which her
mother's duty had been to her father. The same point is prettily brought out in the
Galilée of Ponsard, in which two lovers, Taddeo and Antonia, are imagining a conversation between two like themselves in the moon : '*Ant.* Et comment répond elle ?
Tadd. Ah, je l'ignore ! *Ant.* Eh, bien, Je le sais, moi. *Tadd.* (ardemment) Parlez !
que dit elle ? *Ant.* Rien. *Tadd.* Rien ? *Ant.* Mais elle sourit, sur son bras s'appuie
Et se sent tout émue et tout épanouie.'

    208. **learne**] See SCHMIDT (*Lex.*) for eight or ten instances, besides the present,
where we should now use *teach*.

    214, 215. WALKER (*Vers.*, 227): 'God be with you is, in fact, *God b' wi' you :*
sometimes a trisyllable, sometimes contracted into a disyllable; now *Good-bye*. Accordingly write : '*Due to the Moor, my lord.   God b' wi' you! I've done*' [one line.
See III, iii, 433.]

    214. FECHTER: Othello advances, and kisses her hand. Brabantio, overpowered,
resumes his seat.

    217. SCHMIDT (*Trans.*) refers to a similar thought, amplified, in *Much Ado*, IV,
i, 129.

    217. **get**] That is, beget. For other instances of dropped prefixes, see ABBOTT, § 460.

    220. WHITE : The omission of this line in the Qto is doubtless due to an oversight
of the compositor, caused by the recurrence of the same words at the end both of this
and of the previous line.

I would keepe from thee.   For your fake (Iewell)   221
I am glad at foule, I haue no other Child,
For thy efcape would teach me Tirranie
To hang clogges on them.   I haue done my Lord.
    Duke.   Let me fpeake like your felfe :   225
And lay a Sentence,
Which as a grife, or ftep may helpe thefe Louers.   227

---

221. *For your*] *And for your* Han.
Cap.

222. *foule, I*] *foule. I* Q₁.

224. *them.*] *em*, Qq.
    my Lord] *lord* Q₁ (Steevens's
Rep.).

225, 226. One line, Qq, Rowe et seq.

225. *your felfe*] *our self* Warb.

227. *as a*] *like a* Ff, Rowe, Pope, Han.
Cap.
    grife] *greefe* Qq.
    Louers.] Ff, Rowe, Knt.   *louers
Into your fauour* (reading *Into...fauour*
as a separate line) Qq et cet.

---

219 et seq. BOOTH : Let the actor speak these lines with anguish, and he'll find
out why the ' First Old Man ' is generally cast for so small a part ; the audience will
tell him.

220. **hast**] Equivalent to ' hast *it* ;' the *it* has been absorbed in the final *t* of ' hast.'
Compare ' That' worthied him,' *Lear,* II, ii, 116.—ED.

221. **your**] LETTSOM : The sense, as well as the metre, requires ' For *my own* sake,
jewel.' [Although HUDSON, in his ed. iii, adopts this reading of Lettsom, yet in his
note he gives what is, to my thinking, a sufficient reason for adhering to the Folio :
' For *your* sake ' can nowise be made to tally with the context, except by taking the
phrase as equivalent to *on your account,*—a sense which, to be sure, it sometimes
bears,' and which I cannot but think is the very meaning here : ' It is on account of
your example, jewel, that I am glad,' &c., is what I think Brabantio says in effect.—
ED.]

223. **escape**] COWDEN-CLARKE : Besides its meaning of ' getting forth,' ' flight,'
' elopement,' we think it probable that ' escape ' here includes the sense of ' sally,'
' prank,' as shown to be derived from the French, *escapade.*

224. **To hang**] That is, *in hanging clogs,* &c.   For instances of the infinitive thus
indefinitely used, see ABBOTT, § 356.

225–227. HANMER reads and divides thus : · Let me now speak more like yourself ;
and lay ‖ A sentence in, which, like a grise or step ‖ May help these lovers here into your
favour.'

225. **your selfe**] WARBURTON : It should be ' *our* self,' i. e. let me mediate between
you as becomes a prince and common father of his people.   The prince's opinion, here
delivered, was quite contrary to Brabantio's sentiment.   JOHNSON : The duke seems to
mean, when he says he will speak like Brabantio, that he will speak sententiously.
HEATH (p. 557) : That is, Let me add my own judgement in confirmation of what
you yourself have just said.   For in effect, what Brabantio had just said, implying an
acquiescence in what was done, merely because it was done and could not be undone,
is the very purport of the duke's speech.   SIR JOSHUA REYNOLDS : That is, let me
speak as yourself would speak were you not too much heated with passion.

227. **grise**] DYCE (*Gloss.*) : A step.   ' She gan anone by greces to assende Of a
Touret in to an hye pynacle.'—Lydgate's *Warres of Troy,* B. i, ed. 1555.   See *Twelfth
Night,* III, i, 135 ; *Tim.* IV, iii, 16.

When remedies are paſt, the griefes are ended   228
By ſeeing the worſt, which late on hopes depended.
To mourne a Miſcheefe that is paſt and gon,   230
Is the next way to draw new miſchiefe on.
What cannot be preſern'd, when Fortune takes :
Patience , her Iniury a mock'ry makes.
The rob'd that ſmiles, ſteales ſomething from the Thiefe,
He robs himſelfe, that ſpends a booteleſſe griefe.   235
　　Bra.   So let the Turke of Cyprus vs beguile,
We looſe it not ſo long as we can ſmile :
He beares the Sentence well, that nothing beares,
But the free comfort which from thence he heares.
But he beares both the Sentence, and the ſorrow,   240
That to pay griefe, muſt of poore Patience borrow.
Theſe Sentences, to Sugar, or to Gall,
Being ſtrong on both ſides, are Equiuocall.
But words are words, I neuer yet did heare :
That the bruized heart was pierc'd through the eares.   245

---

228. *ended*] *ended,* Qq, Cap. *ended ;* Han.

229. *the worſt*] *worſt* F$_3$F$_4$.

230. *gon*] F$_1$.

231. *new*] *more* Qq, Coll. Wh. i.

232. *preſern'd*] *preſeru'd* QqFf. *takes :*] *takes,* Qq.

233. *mock'ry*] *mockery* Q$_1$Q$_2$Ff. *mocker* Q$_3$.

234. *the Thiefe*] *a thiefe* Q$_3$.

236. *So let*] *So, let* Theob.+, Jen. *Cyprus*] *Cipres* Q$_1$.

237. *looſe*] *loſe* QqFf.

238, 239. *beares…comfort*] *cares For the false comforts* Han.

240. *beares*] *heares* F$_3$. *hears* F$_4$, Rowe Pope. *heaps* Han.

244. *words,…heare :*] *words,…heare,* Qq. *words :…hear,* F$_3$F$_4$.

245. *bruized…pierc'd*]*bruis'd…pierced* QqFf et cet.

pierc'd] *pieced* Theob.+, Cap.

eares] F$_1$.

---

227. **louers**] The addition of the Qq : 'Into your favour' is not needed; does it not, in fact, sound a little weak after the Duke has said, ' Let me speak like *yourself*' ? —Ed.

228. Compare ' Past cure is still past care,' *Love's Lab.* V, ii, 28; ' What's gone and what's past help Should be past grief,' *Wint. Tale*, III, ii, 223; ' Things without all remedy Should be without regard,' *Macb.* III, ii, 11.—Ed.

238. **nothing beares**] RANN : Who is no further interested therein than barely to admire the moral beauties it contains.

239. **free comfort**] JOHNSON : But the moral precepts of consolation, which are liberally bestowed on occasion of the sentence.

245. **pierc'd**] THEOBALD : It is obvious that the text must be restored, as Mr Warburton acutely observed to me : *pieced*, i. e. That the wounds of sorrow were ever cured or a man made *heart-whole* merely by words of consolation. JENNENS : Theobald and all after, read *pieced* (i. e. cured), because ' pierced ' (it seems) signifies

[245. the bruized heart was pierc'd through the eares].

wounded.   True, so it does sometimes; but it is also used in a good sense, as here, for touching, affecting, comforting, as with music, the 'bruised heart'—'the ear-piercing fife.'—*Pierc'd* is a wretched emendation; who ever talked of *piecing* a bruise?   SIR JOSHUA REYNOLDS: Shakespeare was continually changing his first expression for another, either stronger or more uncommon; so that very often the reader, who has not the same continuity or succession of ideas, is at a loss for its meaning.   Many of Shakespeare's uncouth, strained epithets may be explained by going back to the obvious and simple expression, which is most likely to occur to the mind in that state. I can imagine that the first mode of expression that occurred to the poet was this: ' The *troubled* heart was never cured by words.'   To give it poetical force, he altered the phrase: ' The wounded heart was never reached through the ear.'   *Wounded* heart he changed to *broken,* and that to ' bruised,' as a more common expression.   *Reached* he altered to *touched,* and the transition is then easy to ' pierced,' i. e. thoroughly *touched.* When the sentiment is brought to this state, the commentator, without this unravelling clue, expounds *piercing the heart* in its common acceptation *wounding the heart,* which, making in this place nonsense, is corrected to *pieced the heart,* which is very stiff, and, as Polonius says, *is a vile phrase.*   STEEVENS's thoughts turn to surgery, and he suggests that as inflammation sometimes results from a *bruise,* a cure can be effected only by ' piercing' or lancing.   MALONE: ' Pierced' is merely a figurative expression, and means not *wounded,* but *penetrated in a metaphorical sense;* thoroughly affected. [Malone here gives a dozen citations from Shakespeare, Spenser, Marlowe, and *The Mirrour for Magistrates,* which merely show that what is *pierced* is *penetrated;* while the need is, in this instance, of examples in proof that *piercing* can mean, what Jennens rightly says it means, viz.: penetrating with a soothing or consoling power.   Of Malone's many quotations only four are in this sense quite germane, viz.: ' Honest plain words best pierce the ear of grief,' *Love's Lab.* V, ii, 763; ' With sweetest touches pierce your mistress' ear,' *Mer. of Ven.* V, i, 67; ' Nor thee, nor them, thrice noble Tamburlane, Shall want my heart to be with gladness pierc'd,' Marlowe's *Tamburlane,* Part First, I, ii; ' Whose [Melibœe's] sensefull words empierst his hart so neare That he was rapt with double rauishment,' *Faerie Queene,* Bk VI, ix, 233 (ed. Grosart). Another example Malone gives from Spenser, where, as he says, ' we have the very words of the text,' with the implication that the drift is parallel, which I do not think is the case.   It is in the description of *Sclaunder,* Bk IV, viii, 231: ' *Her words . . . . Which passing through the eares, would pierce the hart* And wound the soule it selfe with grief vnkind: For like the stings of Aspes, that kill with smart, Her spightfull words did pricke, and wound the inner part.'   Malone quoted only the words which are italicized, probably in all honesty, and the trifling matter would not have deserved attention had not Knight, and Staunton, and even Dyce, been misled into citing the passage, assuredly without looking it up; the two former, unfortunately, without acknowledgement to Malone.   Hudson cites it, but had verified it.   PURNELL says, that we must ' take the word here as meaning merely reached.'   BAILEY (ii, 107), whose notes life (or at least, my life) is, alas, too short to cite in full, and whereof the felicity is not always in direct ratio to their length, proposed as an emendation, which he is ' quite sure is far more likely to have been Shakespeare's language' than either ' pierced' or ' pieced': ' That the bruis'd heart was *plaster'd* through the ear.'— ED.]

245. **eares**] See I, i, 31.

I humbly befeech you proceed to th'Affaires of State.   246

  Duke. The Turke with a moſt mighty Preparation
makes for Cyprus : *Othello*, the Fortitude of the place is
beſt knowne to you.   And though we haue there a Subſti-
tute of moſt allowed fufficiencie; yet opinion, a more   250
ioueraigne Miſtris of Effeĉts, throwes a more ſafer
voice on you : you muſt therefore be content to ſlubber   252

---

246. *I...proceed*] *Befeech you now* Qq,
Theob. Warb. Johns. Jen. Coll. Wh. i,
Ktly, Huds. Rlfe. *I humbly befeech you
to proceed* F₃F₄ (*Humbly* F₄).
    to th'...of State] *to the...of the
ſtate* Qq. *to the...o'th' State* Theob. Warb.
Johns. Jen.
247. *a moſt*] *moſt* Qq. *a* Johns.

249. *you.*] *you,* Qq.
    there] *here* Q₃.
250. *sufficiencie ;*] Ff, Rowe+, Jen.
fufficiency, Qq, Cap. et cet.
    a more] Ff, Rowe, Pope, Han.
Knt. *a* Qq et cet.
251. *ſafer*] *ſafe* Ff, Rowe+, Cap.
Rann.

---

246. I] As a trifling instance of the way in which typographical errors are perpetu-
ated in the early editions, it may, perhaps, be worth noting that in one of my two copies
of F₃ this letter is exceedingly faint, in the other copy it has failed to leave any impression whatever, although the type has not fallen out; the space that it should occupy
is still there and the line begins 'humbly,' &c.   The compositor of F₄, using F₃ as his
copy, failing to note the omission of this 'I,' leaves a space at the beginning of the line
and boldly starts with a capital letter : 'Humbly,' &c.—ED.

247-254. COLLIER : As this speech is the only one in this part of the scene printed
as prose, it may be doubted, especially from the rhythm of some of the passages, whether
it was not originally verse.   It would not be difficult to render it metrical.   DELIUS :
This sudden change from verse to prose indicates a transition, correspondingly sudden,
from theoretical moralizing and epigrammatic banter to the practical demands of the
moment.   For this reason in the Ff the prose begins even in the last words of Brabantio's speech, whereas the Qq continue the rhythm : 'Beseech you now to the affairs
of state.'

248. Fortitude] MOREL : C'est un vieux mot français que Montaigne employait
encore ; mais il n'a jamais eu dans notre langue que le sens du latin *fortitudo*, force
morale.

248. BOOTH : Othello leaves Desdemona with Cassio, who regards her with tender,
yet respectful admiration.   Iago, at back, watches them curiously, but let him not be
obtrusive ; he must keep in the background and assume this expression, and feel the
curiousness, even if only one person in the whole audience sees or understands it ; the
'censure,' as Hamlet calls it, of that one is worth all the rest.

250. more] COLLIER : The printer caught 'more' from the line below, and inserted
it also before 'sovereign ;' it is altered to *most* in the (MS).   [Is there any good reascn
why we should not retain the 'more' of the Ff here ?—ED.]

251. Mistris] D'HUGUES : Il est naturel que l'opinion soit regardée comme souve-
raine dans une république.   Cependant en France, dans le courant du XVIIe siècle,
Pascal lui rendait le même témoignage à propos d'un livre italien intitulé, *Della opinione, regina del mondo.*

252. slubber] STEEVENS : That is, *obscure.* So in the *First Part of Jeronimo,*
1605 : 'The evening, too, begins to slubber day' [p. 74, ed. Dodsley].   ROLFE : This

the glofſe of your new Fortunes, with this more ſtub-   253
borne, and boyſtrous expedition.

Othe.   The Tirant Cuſtome, moſt Graue Senators,   255
Hath made the flinty and Steele Coach of Warre
My thrice-driuen bed of Downe.   I do agnize
A Naturall and prompt Alacartie,
I finde in hardneſſe : and do vndertake
This preſent Warres againſt the *Ottamites*.   260
Moſt humbly therefore bending to your State,
I craue fit diſpoſition for my Wife,
Due reference of Place, and Exhibition,   263

---

253. *gloſſe*] *groſſe* F$_2$. *groſs* F$_3$F$_4$,
Rowe.

    more] *most* Rowe ii.

255. *Graue*] *great* Q$_1$.
256. *Coach*] Ff, Rowe.   *Cooch* Qq.
couch Pope et cet.

257. *thrice-driuen*] *thrice driuen* Q$_1$.
258. *Alacartie*] F$_1$.
259. *in*] *it* Theob. i, Steev.'85.
hardneſſe] *harness* Mason.

259. *do*] *would* Q$_1$.
260. *This... Warres*] *This...warre* Q$_2$
F$_2$.   *This...war* Q$_3$F$_3$F$_4$, Rowe+, Cap.
Jen. Rann. Sing. Ktly, Dyce iii, Huds.
These...wars Mal. et cet.

    Ottamites] *Ottomites* Q$_2$Q$_3$Ff et
seq.

263. *reference*] *reuerence* Q$_1$. *reverence* F$_3$F$_4$, Rowe, Pope, Han.

---

word occurs in Shakespeare only here, and, in the sense of slighting, slurring over, in
Mer. of Ven. II, viii, 39 : 'slubber not business for my sake.'

253. **glosse**] STEEVENS : See *Macb.* I, vii, 34 : 'golden opinions Which would be
worn now in their newest gloss.'   ROLFE adds from *Much Ado*, III, ii, 6 : 'that would
be as great a soil in the new gloss of your marriage.'

257. **thrice-driuen**] JOHNSON : A *driven* bed is a bed for which the feathers are
selected by *driving* with a fan, which separates the light from the heavy.   BOOTH says
that he has heard his mother say that this *driving* of the feathers was for the purpose
of drying them, and that not until they had been *thrice driven* were they considered fit
for use.   'A suggestive movement of the hands,' he adds, 'might explain this.'

257. **agnize**] MURRAY (*New Eng. Dict.*, s. v.) : To recognize the existence of, to
acknowledge, to confess (with examples from Becon, *Policy of War*, 1543 ; Woolton,
Chr. Manual, 1576.   In Shakespeare only here).   MOREL : C'est du vieux français
agniser.

259. **hardness**] SCHMIDT (*Lex.*) : Hardship.   Also in *Cymb.* III, vi, 21 : 'hardness ever Of hardiness is mother.'   [In the Quincy (MS) it is corrected to *hardiness*.]
POTWIN (*Bibliotheca Sacra*, July, 1862) : Compare 'endure *hardness* as a good soldier
of Jesus Christ.'—*2 Tim.* ii, 3.

260. **This . . . Warres**] DYCE (ed. iii) : No doubt formerly the plural of *war*
was sometimes used as equivalent to the singular ; but in the next page Desdemona,
speaking of the same expedition, calls it 'the war.'   [See I, i, 31 ; also *Lear*, V, iii,
258.   'This present war' seems to be preferable to 'These present wars.'—ED.]

263. **reference**] JOHNSON : I desire that proper *disposition* be made for my wife,
that she may have *precedency* and *revenue*, *accommodation* and *company*, suitable to
her rank.   I should read *preference*.

With fuch Accomodation and befort
As leuels with her breeding.   265
    Duke.   Why at her Fathers ?
    Bra.   I will not haue it fo.
    Othe.   Nor I.
    Def.   Nor would I there recide,
To put my Father in impatient thoughts   270
By being in his eye.   Moft Grcaious Duke,
To my vnfolding, lend your profperous eare,
And let me finde a Charter in your voice
T'affift my fimpleneffe.
    Duke.   What would you *Defdemona* ?   275
    Def.   That I loue the Moore, to liue with him,

---

264. *With*] *Which* Q$_x$.
    Accomodation] *accomodation ?* Q$_x$.
266. *Why...Fathers*] Ff, Rowe+, Knt, Del. *If you pleafe, bee't at her fathers* (One line) Qq, Jen. (Beginning new line with *Bee't*) Cap. et cet.
267. *I will*] Ff, Rowe+, Rann, Knt. *Ile* Qq, Cap. et cet.
269. *Nor...there*] Ff, Rowe+. *I would not there* Knt i. *Nor I, I would not there* Qq, Cap. et cet.

272. *your profperous*] *a gracious* Qq, Cap. Jen. Steev. Mal. Rann. Var. *your gracious* Pope, Theob. Han. Warb.
273. *Charter*] *character* Ff, Rowe.
274. *T'affift*] *And if* Q$_x$. *To assist* Cap.
    fimpleneffe.] *fimpleneffe.—* Qq.
275. *you* Defdemona ?] *you—fpeake.* Q$_x$.
276. *I loue*] Ff, Knt. *I did loue* Qq et cet.

---

263. **Exhibition**] STEEVENS : Allowance. The word is at present used only at the Universities. [See ' The king . . . . Confined to exhibition,' *Lear,* I, ii, 25 and notes.]

264. **besort**] COWDEN-CLARKE : Befitting attendance, proper retinue. Compare ' such men as may besort your age,' *Lear,* I, iv, 244.

268. **Nor I**] BOOTH : Not harshly, but firmly.

272. **prosperous**] STEEVENS : Propitious. MOREL : Le mot n'a plus en anglais le sens que nous trouvons ici et que le français a longtemps conservé. ' S'il révère les dieux, ils lui seront *prospères* '—Desmarets, cité par Littré.

273. **Charter**] JOHNSON : Let your favour *privilege* me. HUDSON : About the same as *pledge* or *guaranty.* The word is used in a considerable variety of senses by Shakespeare, and seems to have been rather a favourite with him, as with other Englishmen, probably from the effect of *Magna Charta* and other like instruments in securing and preserving the liberties of England.

276. **I loue**] KNIGHT : Desdemona's love remains, and though the *did* of the Qq assists the rhythm, it enfeebles the sense. COWDEN-CLARKE : Desdemona is gentle even to timidity ; but, like many women whose gentleness has been wrought into timidity by a too rigid strictness of their elders, she is capable of singularly bold action and of self-assertion on occasion. Her independent act in leaving her father's house, and in marrying the man of her choice, is precisely characteristic of the one, and her present speech is an eminent specimen of the other. Encouraged by loving treatment, she is capable of moral strength ; chilled by severity, she is a moral coward.

My downe-right violence, and ſtorme of Fortunes,   277
May trumpet to the world.   My heart's ſubdu'd   [315 a]
Euen to the very quality of my Lord;   279

277. and...Fortunes] and ſcorne of   278. heart's ſubdu'd] hearts ſubdued
Fortunes Q₁.   to forms, my fortunes Warb.   Qq.
   Fortunes] Fortune Ktly.   279. very quality] vtmoſt pleaſure Q₁.

---

277. EDWARDS (Canons, &c., p. 144): 'Downright violence,' means the unbridled
impetuosity with which her passion hurried her on to this unlawful marriage; and
'storm of fortunes' may signify the hazard she thereby ran of making shipwreck of
her worldly interest.   Both very agreeable to what she afterwards says: 'to his honours and his valiant parts Did I my soul and fortunes consecrate.'   HEATH (p. 557):
That is, my entrance upon the fortunes I have chosen in that violent manner of proceeding as if I had taken them by storm.   JOHNSON: 'Violence' is not violence suffered, but violence acted.   Breach of common rules and obligations.   Perhaps the Qto
has the true reading.   M. MASON cannot understand the 'storm of fortunes' with 'fortunes' in the plural, and asserts that we should read either 'scorn of fortunes,' or
'storm of Fortune,' the latter meaning 'not the injuries of Fortune, but Desdemona's
own high-spirited braving of her.'   STEEVENS: The same mistake of scorn for 'storm'
occurs in the old copies of Tro. & Cress. I, i, 35: 'as when the sun doth light a
scorn.'   DYCE (Remarks, &c., p. 234) believes that scorn of the Qto was 'no doubt
right;' but as an editor he preferred 'storm.'   He cites a passage, which Mason had
cited before him, from B. and Fl.'s Honest Man's Fortune, IV, i: 'where we find,' says
Dyce, 'according to the old eds., "He'll laugh and storm you," &c., while the excellent MS. of that play in my possession affords the true reading: "He'll laugh and
scorn you," &c.'   SINGER: 'Storm' seems to be used intensively of violence, 'the
stormy violence I have used against my fortunes.'   HUDSON: The meaning, probably,
is the state or course of life which the speaker has boldly ventured upon in forsaking
the peaceful home of her father to share the storms and perils, the violences and
hardships, of a warrior's career.   Scorn will not cohere with violence, unless by making
it express a quality of Desdemona herself, not of her fortunes.   She evidently means
the violence and storm of fortunes which she has braved or encountered in marrying
the Moor, and not any thing of a violent or scornful temper in herself.   ROLFE: The
bold action I have taken, and the stormy fortunes I have voluntarily encountered, in
order to marry him.

279. quality] MALONE: That is, profession.   'I am so much enamoured of Othello,
that I am even willing to endure all the inconveniences incident to a military life and
to attend him to the wars.'   That this is the meaning appears not only from the reading of the Qto: 'even to the utmost pleasure of my lord, i. e. so as to prompt me to go
with him wherever he wishes I should go,' but also from the whole tenour of Desdemona's speech, viz: that as she had married a soldier, so she was ready to accompany
him to the wars, and to consecrate her soul and fortunes to his honours and his valiant
parts; i. e. to attend him wherever his military character and his love of fame should
call him.   COWDEN-CLARKE says 'quality' here means 'individual nature,' 'moral and
mental identity.'   ROLFE interprets it 'very nature.'   HUDSON: 'Quality' is here put
for nature, idiom, distinctive grain, or personal propriety.   Desdemona means that her
heart is tamed and tuned into perfect harmony with the heroic manhood that has spoken
out to her from Othello's person, that her soul gravitates towards him as its pre-estab-

I faw *Othello's* vifage in his mind,   280
And to his Honours and his valiant parts,
Did I my foule and Fortunes confecrate.
So that (deere Lords)if I be left behind
A Moth of Peace, and he go to the Warre,
The Rites for why I loue him, are bereft me :   285
And I a heauie interim fhall fupport
By his deere abfence.   Let me go with him,   287

---

280. Othello's] Othelloes Qq.   Ktly.
283. deere] my dear Q₃.   285. for why] Ff, Rowe, Knt, Del.
285. Rites] rights Warb. Knt. parts   for which Qq et cet.

---

lished centre and home.   So that the sense of the passage may be fitly illustrated from
the 111th *Sonn.* : 'And almost thence my nature is subdued To what it works in, like
the dyer's hand.'   [MALONE's interpretation of 'quality' has been followed by DYCE,
SINGER, DELIUS, and STAUNTON, and unquestionably it is a technical interpretation
which 'quality' frequently bears; see a striking instance of it in *Ham.* II, ii, 333 :
'Will they pursue the quality no longer than they can sing?' and *Ib.* 411, 'give us a
taste of your quality,' but I cannot think that the word has this technical sense here.
Desdemona is vindicating her indifference to the storm of fortunes, and, glorying in
that as a virtue which others would impute to her as a fault, proclaims that the 'quality' in Othello which might be supposed to be most abhorrent to her, '*even to that very
quality*' her heart is subdued.   What that quality is, the connection of thought shows :
'I saw Othello's *visage* in his mind;' and as she had fallen in love with his mind, his
honours, and his valour, without a taint of passion, so had she fallen in love with the
very colour of his face.   HENLEY says, that 'quality' means 'the *Moorish complexion*
of Othello and his *military profession*,' but I do not think that the passage appeared to
Henley as it appears to me, for he goes on to say that the 'virtues of Othello had subdued her heart in spite of his visage;' whereas the 'very quality' distinctive of Othello
was the colour of his visage, and to that, even to that, Desdemona would trumpet to
the world, her heart was subdued.—ED.]

280. ROFFE (*Ghost Belief of Sh.*, p. 4) finds included in these words 'the all-im-
portant facts' that we are all ghosts clad in gross dimensions and muddy vestures of
decay; that the ghost, which is truly the man, is *in a human form* as much as the
body is; and that the body is in that form simply because the ghost or soul is so.
'The common expression that *we see the mind in the countenance*, of course conveys a
truth, or rather a part of the truth; but Desdemona's words are fuller, for they give the
fact that *the mind has a visage of its own.*'

285. Rites] WARBURTON: Without question Shakespeare wrote *rights*, i. e. the
right of sharing his dangers with him.   Othello tells the Senate: 'She lov'd me for
the dangers I had passed,' and she was now desirous of sharing with him what were
to come.   KEIGHTLEY (*Exp.*, 299): Is not this, whether we read 'rites' or *rights*,
rather indelicate coming from the lips of Desdemona?   Juliet (*Rom. & Jul.* III, ii, 8)
might, to herself, speak of the 'amorous rites,' but for Desdemona to do so before the
Senate of Venice! impossible.   Would it not, then, be better to read *parts?*   She had
just said, that it was 'for his honours and his valiant parts' she loved him.

287. deere] See WRIGHT's definition, line 102.

Othe.   Let her haue your voice.   288
Vouch with me Heauen, I therefore beg it not
To pleaſe the pallate of my Appetite: 290
Nor to comply with heat the yong affeċts
In my defunċt, and proper ſatisfaċtion.   292

288, 289. *Let...I*] *Your voyces Lords:
beſeech you let her will, Haue a free way,
I* Q₁, Pope +, Cap.   *Your voyces Lords:
beſeech you let her will Haue a free way:
Vouch with me heauen, I* (reading *Haue
a free way* as a separate line) Q₂Q₃, Rowe,
Jen. Steev. Mal. Rann. Var. Sing. Ktly,
Coll. iii, Dyce iii, Huds.   (*I do beſeech you
let Her will* Rann.   As a separate line,
Your voices, lords Ktly, Coll. iii, Dyce iii,
Huds.)
288. *haue your voice*] Ff, Knt, Sta.
Del.   *have your voices* Dyce i, Wh. Glo.
Cam. Rlfe.
291, 292. *heat...defunċt,*] F₁, Rowe,
Wh. i.   *heate, the young affeċts In my
defunċt,* Qq.   *heat the young effeċts In my
defunċt,* Ff (*yong* F₂).   *heat the young*

affects, In my defunct Pope, Knt.   *heat
the young affects In my defunct* Warb.
heat, the young Affects, In my distinct
Theob. Steev.'93.   *heat affects the young,
In my distinct* Han.   *heat, the young Affects, In my defunct* Johns. Coll. i, Del.
heat, (the young affects In me defunct)
Upton, Cap. Jen. Sing. Dyce, Glo. Sta.
Cam. Coll. iii, Rlfe, Wh. ii.   *heat, (the
young effects In me defunct)* Steev.'85.
heat, the young affects, In my disjunct
Mal. Var.   *heat, (the young affect's In
me defunct)* Rann.   *heat of the young
affects In my distinct* Ktly.   *wi' th' heat
of young affects,—In me defunct,*— Huds.
iii.   *heat, and young affects, In my distinct* Steev. conj.   *heat, and young affects,
In my disjunct* Rann. conj.

288, 289. I do not think that the Qq here give us a reading which is of essential
importance. There is a tone of humble, almost servile, entreaty in 'beseech you,'
which jars a little on the dignified, 'unbonneted' bearing of Othello throughout this
⊷cene.—ED.

291, 292. **heat . . . defunċt**] THEOBALD was the first to note the obscurity of this
passage, which, as it had been theretofore printed, he pronounced a 'period of as stubborn nonsense as the editors have obtruded upon poor Shakespeare throughout his
whole works;' the difficulty lay, he thought, in the word 'defunct,' which 'signifies
nothing else either primitively or metaphorically' than *dead;* and Othello could not
mean to say that 'appetite was dead in him,' because he afterwards says, 'I am declined Into the vale of years; yet *that's not much.*' Wherefore Theobald changed
'defunct' to *distinct,* and paraphrased the passage thus: 'I do not beg her company
with me, merely to please myself; nor to indulge the heat and affects (i. e. affections)
of a new-married man, in my own distinct and proper satisfaction, but to comply with
her in her request and desire of accompanying me.' Shakespeare, he adds, uses
'affects' for *affections* in several other passages which are cited. UPTON (p. 183),
reading 'the young affects' in parenthesis, says that 'defunct' is 'not to be taken
strictly here as signifying absolutely dead, but almost so; or from the Latin *defunctus,*
it might mean, discharged from youthful appetite, and proper to his age and character.
So afterwards (II, i, 262), Iago says, "there should be loveliness in favour, sympathy
in years, manners, beauties, all which the Moor is *defective* in." Now, if any alteration be proposed, instead of "defunct" the properest word seems *defect:* "In my
defect and proper satisfaction," in whic. sense the Latins use *defectus.* Or what if,
with a slighter variation still, we read: "Nor to comply with heat (the young affects
In *me* defunct) and proper"? &c.' WARBURTON paraphrases thus: 'with that heat and

[291, 292. **heat the yong affe&ts In my defun&t**].

new affections which the indulgence of my appetite has raised and created;' and then dogmatically adds: 'this is the meaning of "defunct," which has made all the diffi culty of the passage.' JOHNSON, whose note, wherein he follows Upton's 'in *me* de- funct,' does not agree with his text, says: 'I do not think Theobald's emendation clears the text from embarrassment, though it is, with a little imaginary improvement, received by Hanmer. Warburton's explanation is not more satisfactory: what made the difficulty will continue to make it. "Affects" here stands not for *love*, but for *quality*, for that by which anything is affected. "I ask it not," says he, "to please appetite, or satisfy loose desires, the passions of youth which I have now outlived, or for any particular gratification of myself, but merely that I may indulge the wishes of my wife."' STEEVENS: In *The Bondman* (I, iii, p. 29, ed. Gifford) by Massinger is a passage which seems to countenance and explain 'the young affects In me *defunct*.' Timoleon is the speaker, and says to Cleon, 'youthful heats, That look no further than your outward form, Are long since *buried* in me.' TYRWHITT (p. 5): If I could per- suade the reader, as I am almost persuaded myself, that lines 292 and 293 have by some accident changed places, and that the passage ought to read: 'Nor to comply with heat, the young affects; But to be free and bounteous to her mind, In my defunct and proper satisfaction,' I would then recommend it to consideration, whether the word 'defunct' (which would be the only remaining difficulty) is not capable of a sig- nification drawn from the primitive sense of its Latin original, which would very well agree with the context. TOLLET: I would propose: 'In my *defenc't*, or *defenc'd*,' &c., i. e. I do not beg her company merely to please the palate of my appetite, nor to comply with the heat of lust which the *young* man *affects*, i. e. loves and is fond of, in a gratification which I have by marriage *defenc'd*, or inclosed and guarded, and made my own property. . . . . I am persuaded that the word 'defunct' must be at all events ejected. HENLEY: Othello here supposes that his petition for the attendance of his bride might be ascribed to one of these two motives: either solicitude for the enjoy- ment of an unconsummated and honourable marriage, or the mere gratification of a sensual and selfish passion. But as neither was the true one, he abjures them both: 'I therefore beg it *not* To please the palate of my appetite; *Nor* to comply with heat (———— ————) and proper satisfaction.' The former, having nothing in it unbecoming, he *simply* disclaims; but the latter, ill-according with his season of life, he assigns a reason for renouncing: 'the young affects In me *defunct*.' As if he had said, 'I have out- lived *that* wayward impulse of passion by which younger men are stimulated.' By 'young affects' the poet clearly means those 'youthful lusts' which St. Paul admon- ishes Timothy to flee from and the Romans to mortify. MALONE: For the emendation *disjunct* I am responsible. Some emendation is absolutely necessary, and this appears to me the least objectionable of those which have been proposed. . To the reading of Upton '(the young affects In me defunct),' there are three strong objections. The first is, the suppression of the word *being* before *defunct*, which is absolutely necessary to the sense, and of which the omission is so harsh that it affords an argument against the probability of the proposed emendation. The second and the grand objection is, that it is highly improbable that Othello should declare on the day of his marriage that the youthful affections were dead in him. He himself (as Theobald has observed) informs us afterwards that he is 'declined into the vale of years;' but adds at the same time, 'yet that's *not much*.' This surely is a decisive proof that the text is corrupt. My third objection to Upton's regulation is, that by the introduction of a parenthesis, which is not found in the old copies, the words 'and proper satisfaction' are so unnaturally

[291, 292. heat the yong affects In my defunct].

disjoined from those with which they are connected in sense, as to form a most lame and impotent conclusion; to say nothing of the awkwardness of using the word 'proper' without any possessive pronoun prefixed to it. All these difficulties are done away by retaining the original word 'my,' and reading *disjunct,* instead of 'defunct;' and the meaning will be, 'I ask it not for the sake of my *separate* and private enjoyment, by the gratification of appetite, but that I may indulge the wishes of my wife.' RANN (reading 'the young affect's In me defunct'): 'The tumult of such young desires is at my time of life considerably abated.' Rann here anticipates GIFFORD, who in his note on the passage in Massinger's *Bondman,* cited by Steevens, says: '"Affects" occurs incessantly in the sense of *passions, affections:* "young affects" are, therefore, perfectly synonymous with *youthful heats.* Othello was not an old man, though he had lost the fire of youth; the critics might, therefore, have dismissed that concern for the lady, which they have so delicately communicated for the edification of the rising generation. . . . . I would wish the future editors of Shakespeare to consider whether he might not have given *affect* in the singular (this also is used for *passion*) to correspond with *heat.*' KNIGHT: 'Comply' may be used in the sense of *supply,* 'affects' are *affections,* and 'defunct' does not necessarily mean *dead.* Tyrwhitt considers that 'defunct' may be used in the Latin sense of *performed.* As *function* has the same Latin root, we would suggest that Shakespeare used 'defunct' for *functional,* and then the meaning is clear: 'nor to gratify the young affections in my *official* and *individual* satisfaction.' COLLIER (ed. i): 'In my *defunct* and *proper* satisfaction' is merely 'in my *own dead* satisfaction' or gratification, the youthful passions or 'young affects' being comparatively 'defunct' in him. For the sense, though not for the harmony of the verse, it ought to have run 'for my proper and defunct satisfaction;' and had it so run, we doubt if so much ink would have been spilt and wasted upon it. It requires no proof that 'proper' was often used for *own.* DYCE (*Remarks,* p. 235) apprehends that 'few persons will be satisfied with Collier's explanation; nobody, assuredly, with Knight's,' and then cites the passage already given from Massinger's *Bondman,* together with one from Fletcher's *Fair Maid of the Inn,* I, i, first cited by Gifford, to show, as Gifford had already observed, how these lines of Shakespeare were understood by his contemporaries. 'They also show,' adds Dyce, 'that Upton's alteration of "my" to *me* is absolutely necessary.' Both Dyce and Gifford approve of Johnson's explanation. COLLIER (ed. ii) gives the lines as they are made to stand in his (MS), thus: 'Nor to comply wi' the young affects of heat (In me defunct) and proper satisfaction.' JOURDAIN (*Trans. Philolog. Soc.,* 1860, p. 139) is anticipated by Tyrwhitt in suggesting that the lines should be transposed, but asserts as 'his firm persuasion' that 'defunct' is a misprint for *default,* meaning 'in my want of appearance, in my absence, and for my own satisfaction.' For the use of *default* in this sense Jourdain cites several examples. WHITE (ed. i): Utterly unable either to explain this passage or to suggest in what particular it may be corrupted, I leave it exactly as it appears in the old copies. Of the page after page of comment which has been written upon it, and the several conjectural attempts which have been made to modify it into intelligibility, only Johnson's appears worthy of notice. . . . . That Shakespeare, although he may very probably have written 'comply with heat,' wrote 'comply with proper satisfaction,' I think almost impossible. BAILEY (ii, 102) is dissatisfied with all that has been said about this passage, and asserts that nothing can be less felicitous than Johnson's text, wherein the parenthesis and the change of 'my' to *me* combine 'to ruin the meaning of the speaker, which yet seems plain enough.' 'The epithet "young" does

[291, 292. **heat the yong affects In my defunct**].

not refer, as is generally supposed, to young people or the young, but to the recency of his marriage.' [Wherefore Bailey proposes to read:] 'Nor to comply with heat *of young affects.*' 'Instead of merely "heat," *th'heat* might be put with advantage and with the probability that it was the original reading. This slight emendation gives to the line clearness, precision, and propriety.' '"Defunct" is used in its etymological sense *to have done with*, like "defunctus laboribus" of Horace, and by its use here Othello refers to the gratification of his moments of leisure and privacy, when he would be free from the duties of his office. Perhaps, to comprise the same meaning in another single epithet, we could not select a better than *unofficial:* "In my unofficial and proper or personal satisfaction."' KEIGHTLEY (*Expositor*, p. 300) after citing Upton's reading, asks: 'But can any one produce a single instance of Shakespeare's thus interposing a parenthesis between two substantives connected by a *copula*, or forming a sentence like that in the parenthesis? and what can be more rugged and disjointed than the whole passage as thus arranged? Would not the following not very violent corrections make the whole more Shakespearian and more harmonious? [See Textual Notes.] "*Distinct* and proper" means separate and peculiar. *Distinct*, the correction of "defunct," I regard as nearly certain. Its meaning here is *separate*. "Sheds stuff'd with lambs and goats, distinctly kept, Distinct the biggest, the more mean distinct, Distinct the youngest."—Chapman, *Odyss.*, ix, 34.' DANIEL (*Notes*, &c., p. 77): Read: 'heat the young affects—In *me* defunct—*but for her* satisfaction *And* to be,' &c. Hudson adopts this reading with the remark that it seems to him 'one of the happiest emendations ever made of the Poet's text. Nor can the changes be justly termed violent; as *forher* might easily get misprinted "proper;" and such transpositions as *and* and *but* are among the commonest of typographical errors.' Daniel interprets 'the young affects' as that 'which affects the young,' in which interpretation he follows DELIUS, who conceived himself justified therein by Malone, but over which Dyce lifts his hands in wonder at 'what Gifford would have thought if he had lived to read it. ROLFE: Othello only means that the early impetuosity of youthful passions is past —that he can control them, and is no longer controlled by them. WHITE (ed. ii): The parenthetic passage is in a very doubtful condition. The confession put into Othello's mouth is the last that a lover would make, and on this occasion, especially after Desdemona's foregoing speech. HUDSON: '"Defunct" properly goes with "heat," not with "affects." Othello means simply that the heat of youthful impulse has cooled down, that his passions have become tempered to the rule of judgement.' Hudson agrees with Bailey in thinking that 'with' should be *with the*, regarding it as a case of absorption, as in 'Bring her to Try *with* Maine-course,' *Temp.* I, i; 'Let's all sink *with*' King,' *Ib.* [Cf. also 'Holds such an enmity with' blood of man,' *Ham.* I, v, 65, and ALLEN's note in *Rom. & Jul.*, p. 429.] Hudson adds, 'that to "comply with one's own satisfaction" is not and never was English, as it seems to me.' [Is not this the speech to be expected from Othello after what Desdemona had just said? As there was no alloy of passion in her love for him whose visage she saw in his mind, and to whose honours she had consecrated her soul, so Othello proclaimed that it was for the nobler intercourse of marriage that he wanted Desdemona to accompany him, to be free and bounteous to her *mind*, not to please the palate of his appetite; and in saying this, he wishes as delicately as possible to intimate that the 'compulsive ardour' of 'flaming youth,' as Hamlet calls it, was over for him. This, I think, is the idea which, if we heard the speech on the stage only, we should all gather from it, nor do the various emendations and changes convey any very different meaning. Here then,

But to be free, and bounteous to her minde :   293
And Heauen defend your good foules, that you thinke
I will your ferious and great bufineffe fcant   295
When fhe is with me.   No, when light wing'd Toyes
Of feather'd *Cupid,* feele with wanton dulneffe   297

293. *to her*] *of her* Q,.
295. *great*] *good* Qq.
296. *When*] Ff, Rowe, Pope, Knt. *For*
Qq et cet.
    me.] *me ;—* Qq. *me—* Rowe,
Pope, Han.

297. *Of*] *And* Qq.
    feele] F₂F₃. *foyles* Qq. *feel* Rowe
ii. *fail* Pope+, Jen. Coll. Ktly. *feel* F₄ et
cet.
    dulneffe] *dalliance* Theob. conj.
(withdrawn).

I think, we may rest. The object of the speaker is attained; he has given us his
meaning. As a mere intellectual amusement we may inquire into the passage more
curiously, and rearrange the puzzle while retaining the sense; the pleasure and the
profit will, by the exercise, accrue to ourselves alone, with but little likelihood of ever
heading, except in imagination, a band of converts. Moreover, in the inexplicable passages in Shakespeare, like 'the runaway's eyes,' 'the dram of eale,' 'Vllorxa,' the
present passage, and others, after the printers have borne all the obloquy which we can
heap upon them, might we not frown a little at Shakespeare himself? He must have
written rapidly. Would his fame be seriously impaired or stabbed to the centre, if we
cautiously whispered among ourselves that he now and then wrote carelessly ?—ED.]

294. **defend . . . soules**] STEEVENS says, and he has been followed by all editors
who have noticed the word, that 'defend' here means to *forbid,* a meaning which it
undoubtedly bears in many passages; but it may be doubted if it be worth while to
reject here its ordinary meaning; if it has a military flavour it is certainly not inappropriate to Othello. ABBOTT gives *prevent* as its equivalent, which to me is scarcely better
than *forbid.*—ED. COLLIER (*Notes,* &c., p. 451): 'Good souls' become *counsels* in
the (MS). Othello would hardly apply 'good souls' to the Duke and Senators of
Venice. [Certainly a plausible emendation, which evidently gave DYCE pause; he ad-
vises (*Few Notes,* p. 149) 'an editor of Shakespeare to weigh it well before he adopts
it.' 'What is the meaning,' he asks, 'of "Heaven *defend* your *counsels*"?' adding in
parenthesis: 'If "defend" be equivalent here, as Steevens supposes, to *forbid,* the
alteration [*counsels*] must be decidedly wrong.'—ED.]

294. **that . . . think**] ABBOTT, § 368: 'Think' seems used subjunctively, and
'that' as a conjunction, in this passage, i. e. 'that you (should) think.'

296. **When**] Is there any urgent reason for deserting the Ff here ? For those, however, who prefer the Qq, ABBOTT, § 151, gives many examples where *For* is equivalent
to *because.*—ED.

297. **seele**] HARTING (p. 69): 'Seeling,' consisted in sewing a thread through the
upper and under eyelids of a newly-caught hawk to obscure the sight for a time, and
accustom her to the hood. Turbervile, in his *Book of Falconrie,* 1575, gives the following directions 'how to seele a hawke': 'Take a needle threeded with untwisted
thread, and (casting your Hawke) take her by the beake and put the needle through
her eye-lidde, not right against the sight of the eye, but somewhat nearer to the beake,
because she may see backwards. And you must take good heede that you hurt not
the webbe, which is under the eye-lidde, or on the inside thereof. Then put your
needle also through that other eye-lidde, drawing the endes of the thread together, tye

My fpeculatiue, and offic'd Inftrument :   298
That my Difports corrupt, and taint my bufineffe :
Let Houfe-wiues make a Skillet of my Helme,   300

298. *offic'd*] *actiue* Qq, Johns. Jen.   299. *my busineffe*] *by business* Steev
Steev. Mal. Var. Coll. Wh. i, Ktly, Huds.   '85.
    Inftrument] Ff, Rowe, Cap. Knt,   300. *Houfe-wiues*] *hufwiues* Qq.
Sing. Del. *inftruments* Qq et cet.   *Skillet*] *skellet* Qq.

them over the beake not with a straight knotte, but cut off the threedes endes neare to
the knotte and twist them together in such sorte, that the eye-liddes may be raysed so
upwards, that the Hawke may not see at all, and when the threed shall ware loose or
untyed, then the Hawke may see somewhat backwardes, which is the cause that the
threed is put nearer to the beake.   For a Sparrow-hawke should see somewhat backwardes, and a Falcon forwardes.   The reasõ is that if the Sparrow-hawke should see
forwardes, shee would beat off her feathers or break them when she bateth upon the
fist, and seeing the companie of men, or such like, she would bate too much.'   Sir
Emerson Tennant (*Sketches of the Nat. Hist. of Ceylon*, p. 246), says : ' Where it [the
goshawk] is trained for hawking, it is usual, in lieu of a hood, to darken its eyes by
means of a silken thread passed through holes in the eyelids.'   This practice of 'seeling,' has happily given way to a great extent to the more merciful use of the hood.
[See *post*, III, iii, 242; also notes on 'seeling night,' *Macb.* III, ii, 46.—ED.]   WRIGHT
(*Bible Word-Book*, s. v. *Cieled*) : The etymology of this word is obscured by the spelling, which seems to connect it with the Fr. *ciel*, It. *cielo*, 'a canopy.'   To *seel* or *seele*
a room was to cover it with boards, or wainscotting, like Fr. *plancher*.   To *seel* the eyes
of a hawk or dove (Fr. *siller* les yeux) was to sew up their eyelids.   'What we now call
the *ceiling* was formerly called the upper-*seeling*, Fr. sus-lambris, to distinguish it from
the *seeling* or wainscotting on the walls.'—Wedgwood, *Dict.*

298. MALONE : 'Speculative instruments,' in Shakespeare's language, are the *eyes*,
and 'active instruments,' the *hands and feet*.   As 'seel' is here metaphorically used,
it applies very properly to the '*speculative* instruments ;' but *foils*, of the Qq, agrees
better with '*active* instruments.'   KNIGHT : The modern editors have made up a text
between the Qto and Ff.   They reject the *foils* of the Qto, and adopt the 'seel' of
the Ff, while they substitute the *active* of the Qto for the 'offic'd' of the Ff.   Having
accomplished this hocus-pocus, they tell us that speculative instruments are the eyes,
and active instruments the hands and feet; that to 'seel' is to close the eyelids of a
bird, which applies very properly to the speculative instruments, but that *foils* better
suits the active.   It is their own work they are quarrelling with, and not that of the
author.   Either reading is good, if they had let it alone.   The speculative and *active
instruments*, which are *foiled*, are the thoughts and the senses; the speculative and
offic'd instrument, which is *seeled*, is *the whole man* in meditation and in action.   When
the poet adopted the more expressive word *seel*, he did not leave the ugly anomaly
which the commentators have made.   He took the whole man as an instrument, spiritual and material, and metaphorically seeled the perceptions of that instrument.   [Cf.
'no speculation in those eyes,' *Macb.* III, iv, 95.]

300. **Skillet**] HALLIWELL : It is unlikely that the poet had any substantial image
in his mind when penning this line; but, nevertheless, the following note, communicated by Mr Fairholt, is an exceedingly curious one : 'The Museum of London Antiquities, formed by C. Roach Smith, F. S. A., furnishes a curious illustration of this
passage, proving the custom of so turning an old helmet to use.   In this instance a

And all indigne, and bafe aduerfities,   301
Make head againft my Eftimation.

    Duke.   Be it as you fhall priuately determine,
Either for her ftay, or going : th'Affaire cries haft:
And fpeed muft anfwer it.   305
    Sen.   You muft away to night.
    Othe.   With all my heart.
    Duke.   At nine i'th'morning, here wee'l meete againe.
Othello, leaue fome Officer behind
And he fhall our Commiffion bring to you :   310
And fuch things elfe of qualitie and refpect
As doth import you.
    Othe.   So pleafe your Grace, my Ancient,   313

302. *Eftimation*] *reputation* Qq, Coll. Ktly.

304. *Either*] *Or* Pope +.
    her] Om. Q₁.
    th'Affaire cries] *the affaires cry* Q₁.

305. *anfwer it.*] *anfwer, you muft hence to night.* Qq. *anfwer. You muft hence to-night.* Pope+, Jen. Coll. iii. *anfwer it. You must hence to-night.* Johns. Cap. Steev. Mal. Rann. Var. Coll. ii, Kfly. *answer't; you must hence to-night.* Cam.

306. Sen. *You...night*] Defd. *To night*

my Lord? Du. *This night.* Qq, Theob. Warb. Johns. Cap. Jen. Steev. Mal. Rann. Var. Coll. Cam. Ktly. Des. *To-night, my lord, to-night?* Pope, Han. I. Sen. *You... night.* Duke. *This night.* Wh. i.

308. *nine*] *ten* Q₁.

311. *And fuch*] Ff, Rowe +. Cap. Jen. Rann. Knt. *With fuch* Qq et cet.
    and refpect] *or refpect* Q₁.

312. *import*] *concerne* Q₁. *import to* F₃F₄, Rowe.

313. *So*] Om. Qq, Pope +, Cap. Jen. Steev. Mal. Rann. Var. Coll. Wh. i.

---

crested Morion of the sixteenth century has been fitted with a hook and chain, and formed into a camp-kettle. It was found in dredging the Thames near the Tower of London.'

301. **indigne**] DYCE (*Gloss.*): Unworthy, disgraceful.

303. BOOTH : After consultation with the Senators.

306. BOOTH : Roderigo shows alarm at this, but Iago quiets him. This must not interfere with the action of the scene, but merely be suggested.

306. In reference to the reading of the Qq, KNIGHT says : It appears to us that the careful rejection of the speech of Desdemona was a great improvement in the Folio. COLLIER (ed. ii) : It is surely very natural that Desdemona should express surprise at the suddenness of the command, and our persuasion is, that the words were left out in the Folio by accident. WHITE (ed. i) : In my judgement Shakespeare probably wrote the passage originally as in the Qq, but modified it from a consciousness that Desdemona had already expressed with sufficient candour the nature of her feelings towards Othello, and that both delicacy and truth of characterization would be gained by suppressing her exclamation.

308. **nine**] BOOTH : Probably the hour of rehearsal in Shakespeare's time.

312. **As doth**] For other instances of singular verbs in relative sentences where the antecedents are plural, see ABBOTT, § 247 ; also, 'it is not words that shakes me thus,' IV, i, 5?; 'they laugh, that winnes,' IV, i, 141 ; 'you [gods] that stirs,' *Lear*, II, iv, 271.

A man he is of honefty and truft:
To his conueyance I affigne my wife,   315
With what elfe needfull, your good Grace fhall think
To be fent after me.
   Duke.   Let it be fo:
Good night to euery one.   And Noble Signior,
If Vertue no delighted Beautie lacke,   320
Your Son-in-law is farre more Faire then Blacke.
   Sen.   Adieu braue Moore, vfe *Defdemona* well.
   Bra.   Looke to her(Moore)if thou haft eies to fee:
She ha's deceiu'd her Father, and may thee.   *Exit.*   324

---

316. *good*] Om. Q₃.

319. [*to Bra.* Cap.

320. *delighted*] *delighting* Han. Cap.

322. *Sen.*] 1 Sena. Qq.

323. *if…eies*] *haue a quicke eye* Q₁,
Johns. Jen. Steev. Mal. Rann. Var. Sing.

Ktly.·

324. *deceiu'd*] *deceiud'd* Q₂. *deceivd'd*
Q₃.

and may thee] *may doe thee* Q₁.

Exit.] Exeunt. Qq.

313–315. *So . . . wife*] COLERIDGE (*Notes*, &c., 250): Compare this with the behaviour of Leontes to his true friend Camillo.

316. **needfull**] ROLFE: That is, whatever else your grace shall think needful, &c.
For many similar transpositions, see ABBOTT, §419 *a*.   Cf. 'whiter skin of hers then
snow,' V, ii, 6.

320. **delighted**] WARBURTON: This is a senseless epithet. We should read *be-
lighted*, i. e. white and fair.   JOHNSON: I should rather read *delight or*.   *Delight* for
delectation or *power of pleasing*, as it is frequently used.   STEEVENS: The meaning is,
if virtue comprehends everything in itself, then your virtuous son-in-law is, of course,
beautiful; he has that beauty which delights every one.   'Delighted' for *delighting*,
Shakespeare often uses the active and passive participles indiscriminately.   The same
sentiment occurs in *Twelfth Night*, III, iv, 403.   TYRWHITT: 'Delighted' is used for
delighting or *delightful* in *Cymb.* V, iv, 102.   [In illustration of 'the delighted spirit'
in *Meas. for Meas.* III, i, RITSON cites from Sir Thos. Herbert's *Relation of Some
Years Travels*, &c., 1634, p. 104: 'Mirza . . . . gave a period to his miseries in this
world by supping a delighted cup of extreame poyson,' which WALKER (*Crit.*, ii, 11)
interprets as meaning *rendered delicious* by the admixture of certain ingredients.
Thereupon Walker queries if 'delighted' be not used here in *Othello* nearly as in Herbert—that is, *endowed with delights, deliciis exornata.*   DELIUS adopts this interpretation, and it is to me also eminently satisfactory both here and in *Meas. for Meas.*: 'If
virtue lacks not beauty that is endowed with every delightsome quality, Then,' &c.—ED.]

323–325. **Looke . . . faith**] COLERIDGE (*Notes*, &c., 251): In real life, how do
we look back to little speeches as presentimental of, or contrasted with, an affecting
event?   Even so, Shakespeare, as secure of being read over and over, of becoming a
family friend, provides this passage for his readers and leaves it to them.

324. LLOYD: Thus it is that the Venetian Senate comes to the truth of a matter,
and the impression thus gained of its judiciousness gives great emphasis to the parting
words of the Senator as he goes out.   The words fall on the heart like an omen; it is
true, then, that the Senator recognizes as no improbability the ill-treatment of Desde-

Othe.   My life vpon her faith.   Honeſt *Iago*,   325
My *Deſdemona* muſt I leaue to thee :
I prythee let thy wife attend on her,
And bring them after in the beſt aduantage.
Come *Deſdemona*, I haue but an houre
Of Loue, of wordly matter, and direction   330
To ſpend with thee.   We muſt obey the the time.   *Exit.*
   Rod.   Iago.
   Iago.   What ſaiſt thou Noble heart ?
   Rod.   What will I do, think'ſt thou ?   334

325. *faith.*] *faith ;* Q₁. *faith* Q₃.
327. *prythee*] *preethee* Q₁. *prethee* Q₂
Q₃F₃F₄.
328. *them*] *her* Qq, Pope +, Jen. Coll.
Wh. i.
   the] *their* Ff, Rowe.
330. *wordly*] F₄.
   matter] Ff, Rowe +, Cap. Jen.
Knt, Sta. *matters* Qq, Mal. et cet.
331. *ſpend*] *ſpeake* F₂. *ſpeak* F₃F₄,
Rowe +.
   thee.] *thee,* Qq.

331. *the the*] F₁.
   Exit.] Exit Moore and *Deſde-*
mona. Qq. Exeunt. Manent Rodorigo
and Iago. Pope.
   Scene X. Pope +, Jen.   Scene V. A
dark Street. Booth.
332. *Iago.*] *Iago*— Johns. Cap. Sta. Glo.
Dyce iii, Huds. Rlfe, Wh. ii.
333. *ſaiſt*] *sayest* Rowe +, Jen.
334. *think'ſt*] *thinkeſt* Q₁, Rowe +, Var.
Coll. Sing. Dyce, Glo. Cam. Ktly, Rlfe.

mona by the gallant husband she has chosen for herself at such a sacrifice.   Even so,
and the words strengthen the sense of separation between the Moorish and the Venetian noble ; for addressed by one equal to another, they would justify an answer with
the hand at the sword-hilt.

324. FECHTER : Brabantio goes out last, disengaging himself from his daughter, who
attempts to kiss his hand ; and addressing Othello with threatening irony.   BOOTH :
Exeunt Duke and Senators.   All bow to them as they pass.   Desdemona appeals, in
action, to her father.

326. LLOYD : Some critics moralize the fate of Desdemona as punishment for un
dutiful and ill-assorted marriage, yet the punishment falls quite as severely on the
severity of Brabantio,—on his cruelty, we may say, for he is the first,—and out of unnatural pique,—to belie his own daughter's chastity.   MOREL : Ce premier acte nous a
donné jusqu'ici une exposition complète du sujet.   Othello, Desdémone, Iago, Cassio,
les caractères de tous les personnages principaux nous sont déjà parfaitement connus ;
tous les faits dont le jeu et les conséquences amèneront les péripéties diverses de l'action sont indiqués, toutes les données du problème dramatiques sont fixées.—Les deux
vers dits par Brabantio sont le prélude d'une phase nouvelle de l'intrigue : ils nous font
pressentir les suites tragiques de ces amour sur lesquilles pèse dès la première heure la
malédiction d'un père.

328. *aduantage*] JOHNSON : Fairest opportunity.

329. GUIZOT : C'est justement le contraire de ce que Voltaire a fait dire à Orosmane.
cet autre jaloux, dans *Zaïre :* ' Je vais donner une heure aux soins de mon empire Et le
reste du jour sera tout à Zaïre.'

334. *will*] The despairing emphasis laid on this word shows, I think, why it is used,
and n ʳ *shall.*—ED.

Iago.   Why go to bed and fleepe.   335

Rod.   I will incontinently drowne my felfe.

Iago.   If thou do'ft, I fhall neuer loue thee after.   Why
thou filly Gentleman?

Rod.   It is fillyneffe to liue, when to liue is torment:
and then haue we a prefcription to dye, when death is   340
our Phyfition.

Iago.   Oh villanous : I haue look'd vpon the world
for foure times feuen yeares, and fince I could diftinguifh   343

---

337. *If thou do'ft*] Ff, Rowe, Pope,
Han. Knt, Dyce, Glo. Sta. Cam. Huds.
Rlfe, Wh. ii.   *Well, if thou doeft* Qq et cet.
after.] *after it*, Qq, Jen. Steev.
Mal. Var. Coll. Wh. i, Del.

337, 338. *Why...Gentleman*] Separate
line, Qq, Theob. Warb.

338. *Gentleman?*] Ff. *Gentleman.* Q₁
Q₂. *Gentleman,* Q₃. *Gentleman!* Rowe

339. *torment*] Ff, Knt, Dyce, Glo. Sta.
Cam. Huds. Rlfe, Wh. ii.   *a torment* Qq
et cet.

340. *haue we*] *we haue* Qq.
prefcription to dye] *prefcription,
to dye* Qq.

342. *Oh villanous*] Om. Q₁.
I haue] *I ha* Qq.   *I ha'* Jen.

---

336. **incontinently**] ROLFE: Immediately; used by Shakespeare here only; see
'incontinent,' IV, iii, 16, in the same sense. MOREL: Le mot, employé par Montaigne et Amyot, a été introduit en anglais par les écrivains du XVIe siècle, mais ne
s'est pas imposé à l'usage.

338. **Gentleman**] BOOTH: Tapping him playfully on the forehead.   Roderigo is a
gentleman, though a silly one, not a 'stage-idiot.'

343. **yeares**] MALONE: From this, Iago's age may be ascertained; and it corresponds
with the account in the novel on which *Othello* is founded, where he is described as a
young, handsome man.   [LE TOURNEUR having said in his translation : Jago pouvoit
avoir environ quarante ans; les années qu'il compte sont celles de l'expérience, Malone
replies:] that Iago meant to say he was but twenty-eight years old is clearly ascertained
by his marking particularly, though indefinitely, a period *within that time* ['and *since*
I could distinguish,' &c.] when he began to make observations on the characters of
men.   VERPLANCK: The actors who have been most celebrated in the part, from Quin
to Cooke, are understood to have represented Iago as at least a middle-aged man.   Yet
the incident of Iago's youth seems to add much to the individuality and intensity of the
character.   An old soldier of acknowledged merit, who, after years of service, sees a
young man like Cassio placed over his head, has not a little to plead in justification of
deep resentment, and in excuse, though not in defence, of his revenge; such a man
may well brood over imaginary wrongs.   The caustic sarcasm and contemptuous estimate of mankind are, at least, pardonable in a soured and disappointed veteran.   But
in a young man the revenge is more purely gratuitous, the hypocrisy, the knowledge,
and dexterous management of the worst and weakest parts of human nature, the recklessness of moral feeling,—even the stern, bitter wit, intellectual and contemptuous,
without any of the gayety of youth,—are all precocious and peculiar; separating Iago
from the ordinary sympathies of our nature, and investing him with higher talent and
blacker guilt. COWDEN-CLARKE: It is remarkable that Shakespeare has here taken
pains to specify the exact age of Iago, as he has specified that of Hamlet.   They are,

betwixt a Benefit, and an Iniurie : I neuer found man that [315 b]
knew how to loue himſelfe.   Ere I would ſay, I would   345
drowne my ſelfe for the loue of a Gynney Hen, I would
change my Humanity with a Baboone.

    Rod. What ſhould I do ? I confeſſe it is my ſhame
to be ſo fond, but it is not in my vertue to amend it.

    Iago. Vertue ?   A figge, 'tis in our ſelues that we are   350
thus, or thus.   Our Bodies are our Gardens, to the which,
our Wills are Gardiners.   So that if we will plant Net-   352

---

344. *betwixt*] *betweene* Qq, Jen. Mal.
Var. Sing. Ktly.   Om. Steev.'93.
    Iniurie :] *iniury*, QqFf.
    man] *a man* Qq, Mal. Steev. Var.
Coll. Sing. Wh. i, Ktly, Del.
346. *Gynney Hen*] *Ginny Hen* Qq.

Guinney-*Hen* F₄, Rowe+.   Guinea-*hen*
Johns.
    348. *do ?*] *doe*, Ff, Rowe.
    349. *in my*] *in* Mal. Steev.'93, Var.
    551. *our Gardens*] *gardens* Qq, Jen.
Coll. Wh. i, Dyce, Cam.
    352. *Gardiners.*] *Gardiners*, Qq.

---

perhaps, the two most intellectual characters that our poet has drawn; and he has made
them nearly of the same age, as if at that period of life a man's intellect were at the
culminating point of activity and energy. . . . . Iago is a hard, cold-blooded, almost
vivacious scoundrel from inherent disposition, who uses his keen intellect with the
same fierce joy in its skill and power to destroy that he uses his sharp dagger or sword.
HUDSON (*Introd.*, p. 22) : Moreover Iago's youth goes far to explain the trust which
others repose in him; they cannot suspect one so young of being either skilled in villainous craft or soured by hard experience of the world; while his polished manners
and winning address gain him the credit of superior parts, without breeding any question of his truth.

    346. **Gynney Hen**] STEEVENS : Anciently the cant term for a prostitute.

    350. **Vertue**] COLERIDGE (*Notes*, 251) : This speech comprises the passionless
character of Iago.   It is all will in intellect; and therefore he is here a bold partisan
of a truth, but yet of a truth converted into a falsehood by the absence of all the necessary modifications caused by the frail nature of man.   And then comes the last sentiment : 'Our raging motions, our carnal stings, our unbitted lusts, whereof I take this
that you call—love to be a sect or scion !'   Here is the true Iagoism of, alas ! how
many !   Note Iago's pride of mastery in the repetition of 'Go, make money !' to his
anticipated dupe, even stronger than his love of lucre; and when Roderigo is completely won—'I am chang'd.   I'll go sell all my land,' when the effect has been fully
produced, the repetition of triumph—'Go to; farewell; put money enough in your
purse !'

    351. **thus, or thus**] BOOTH : Qy. Point up and down, to signify good or bad ?

    351. **our Gardens**] In his first ed. WHITE considered 'our' an interpolation of the
printers, due to the recurrence of the same word twice elsewhere in this clause of the
sentence.

    352, 353. **Nettels**] ELLACOMBE (p. 136) : We have two native species (*Urtica
urens* and *U. dioica*).   'Nettle,' etymologically, is the same word as needle, and the
plant is so named not for its stinging properties, but because at one time it supplied the
chief aid to sewing; not in the little familiar instrument, but in the thread, and very

tels, or fowe Lettice : Set Hifope, and weede vp Time: 353
Supplie it with one gender of Hearbes, or diftract it with

353. *Lettice :*] *Lettice,* Qq.   *kttuce;*   353. *Hifope*] *Ifop* Qq. *Hyfop* F₃. *Hyf-*
Theob.   *fop* F₄.
                                                  Time] *thyme* Pope.

---

good linen it made.   In many parts of England the young shoots are boiled and much
relished as food, and M. Soyer tried hard, but almost in vain, to introduce it as a most
dainty dish.   In other points the nettle is a most interesting plant.   Microscopists find
in it most beautiful objects; entomologists value it as a favourite of butterflies and other
insects, of which in Britain alone upwards of thirty varieties feed solely on the nettle-
plant, and it marks the progress of civilization by following man wherever he goes.
But as a garden plant the only advice to be given is to keep it out of the garden by
every means, where, if allowed, it would soon become a sad weed.

353. **Lettice**] ELLACOMBE (p. 106): This excellent vegetable with its Latin name
came to us, probably, from the Romans.   It was cultivated by the Anglo-Saxons, who,
in recognition of its narcotic qualities, called it 'Sleepwort.'   In Shakespeare's time the
sorts cultivated were very similar to ours, and probably as good.

353. **Hisope**] ELLACOMBE (p. 97): The *Hyssopus officinalis* is not a British plant,
but it was held in high esteem in Shakespeare's time.   It is now very little cultivated;
it has not much beauty, and its medicinal properties are not much esteemed; yet it will
always have an interest to readers of the Bible, though whether or not the hyssop of
Scripture is the *Hyssopus offic.* is still a question.   It seems likely from the following
passage in Lyly's *Euphues,* that the plants were not named at random by Iago : 'Good
gardeiners, in their curious knots, mixe Hisoppe with Time, as ayders the one to the
growth of the other; the one beeing drye, the other moyst' [p. 37, ed. Arber].

353. **Time**] ELLACOMBE (p. 233): It is one of the most curious of the curiosities
of English plant names that the Wild Thyme,—a plant so common and so widely distributed, and that makes itself so easily known by its fine, aromatic, pungent scent that
it is almost impossible to pass it by without notice,—has yet no English name, and
never seems to have had one.   Thyme is the Anglicized form of the Greek and Latin
Thymum, which it probably received from its use as incense in sacrifices; while its
other name, *serpyllum,* refers to its creeping habit.   It is another curious point connected with the name that *thymum* does not occur in the old English vocabularies.
Nor is even its Latin form found, except in the *Prompt. Parv.,* where it is 'Tyme,
herbe, *Tima, timum*—Tyme, flowre, *Timus.*'   It is thus a puzzle to know how it can
have got naturalized among us, for in Shakespeare's time it was completely naturalized.
It is as a bee-plant especially that the thyme has always been celebrated.   See Ovid's
Fasti, v; Vergil, *Ecl.* vii.   The wild thyme can be scarcely considered a garden plant,
except in its variegated and golden varieties; but if it ever should come naturally in the
turf, it should be welcomed and cherished for its sweet scent.

354. **gender**] BUCKNILL (*The Medical Knowledge of Shakespeare,* p. 270): This
word, which with a degree of probability not more overstrained than that which attributes to Shakespeare the knowledge of Harvey's great discovery, by a literal reading
would lead to the conclusion that he had anticipated Linnæus's theory of the sexes of
plants.   No other author I know of uses the word 'gender' in any other sense than
to mark the attributes of sex; while he himself uses it in this sense in several passages :
'the ιumbers of the genders,' *Merry Wives,* IV, i, 73.   But he also uses it to desig-

many : either to haue it ſterrill with idleneſſe, or manu-   355
red with Induſtry, why the power, and Corrigeable authoritie of this lies in our Wills.   If the braine of our liues
had not one Scale of Reaſon, to poize another of Senſu-
alitie, the blood, and baſeneſſe of our Natures would
conduct vs to moſt prepoſtrous Concluſions.   But we   360
haue Reaſon to coole our raging Motions, our carnall
Stings, or vnbitted Luſts : whereof I take this, that you
call Loue, to be a Sect, or Seyen.

    Rod.   It cannot be,

    Iago.   It is meerly a Luſt of the blood, and a permiſſion   365
of the will.   Come, be a man : drowne thy ſelfe ?   Drown

---

355. *to haue*] *haue* Ff, Rowe+, Cap.
Jen. Rann.

355, 356. *manured*] *manur'd* Qq.

357. *Wills*] *will* Rowe ii +.

    braine] F₂. *Ballence* Q₃. *brain*
F₃F₄. *beam* Theob. Cap. Rann. *ballance*
Q₁Q₂, Rowe et cet.

361. *our carnall*] *or carnall* Ff (*car-*

nal F₄).

362. *or*] Ff. *our* Qq, Rowe et cet.

363. *Sect*] *slip* Han. *set* Johns.

    Seyen] *ſyen* Qq, Rowe+. *scyon*
Han. Cap. Steev. Mal. *scien* Johns. *scyen*
Jen. *scion* Steev.'93.

365. *of the blood*] *of blood* Q₃.

    permiſſion] *primiſſion* Q₃.

---

nate a kind or species, as 'the great love the general gender bear him,' *Ham.* IV, vii,
18.   It is probable, therefore, that it is in this sense the word is used by Iago, and that
Shakespeare had not necessarily any idea of the sexual physiology of plants which the
great Swedish naturalist developed into a system; and thus also when he refers, in
other places, to the sex of plants, that it is merely a poetical metaphor.

356. **Corrigeable**] For many instances of the use of adjectives in *able* and *ible* in
an *active* sense, see WALKER, *Crit.*, i, 183; ABBOTT, § 3; also *Ham.* I, i, 57; *Lear*,
I, iv, 300.   PURNELL refers to Milton's use of *deceivable* in both an active and a passive sense, 'what not in man Deceivable and vain,' *Sams. Agon.* [349]; 'blind, and
thereby Deceivable,' *Ib.* [941].

357. **braine**] THEOBALD rejected *ballance* of the Qto as 'certainly wrong,' because
it is equivalent to saying, 'if the *scale* of our lives had not one *scale*,' &c.; wherefore he
believed that the true word is *beame*, inasmuch as Shakespeare 'generally distinguishes
betwixt the Beam and Balance; using the latter to signify the scales, and the former
the steel bar to which they are hung and which poises them.'   [Theobald's argument
and the examples which he cited in support, especially one from *Rich. II:* III, iv, 87,
where *balance* signifies *scale* and nothing else, quite converted CAPELL, who 'yerked'
out the following note]: Were *beam* spelt as of old with an (*e*) final, it's corruption
into the word below is very easy and natural: consider'd then as a true Folio reading,
the word *beam* or *beame* merits preference that way; and if consider'd another way, as
a word absolutely unequivocal, and used often by Shakespeare in the sense that belongs
to it, we shall not greatly applaud the gentlemen who discard it for *balance*.   [Theo-
bald overlooked, I think, a notable instance where 'balance' is used for both scales
and beam in *Mer. of Ven.* IV, i, 255 : 'Are there balance here to weigh the flesh ?'—
ED.]

363. **Sect**] STEEVENS: By modern gardeners calle' a *cutting.*

Cats, and blind Puppies. I haue profeſt me thy Friend,   367
and I confeſſe me knit to thy deſeruing, with Cables of
perdurable toughneſſe. I could neuer better ſteed thee
then now. Put Money in thy purſe : follow thou the   370
Warres, defeate thy fauour, with an vſurp'd Beard. I ſay
put Money in thy purſe. It cannot be long that *Deſdemona*
ſhould continue her loue to the Moore. Put Money in
thy purſe : nor he his to her. It was a violent Commencement in her, and thou ſhalt ſee an anſwerable Seque-   375
ſtration, put but Money in thy purſe. Theſe Moores

---

367. *haue profeſt*] *profeſſe* Qq, Coll. i.
369. *toughneſſe*] *toughnheſſe* Q₃.
ſteed] *ſteede* Q₁Q₂. *stead* Han.
et seq.
370. *thou the*] Ff, Knt, Dyce, Glo. Sta.
Cam. Huds. Wh. ii. *thou these* Rowe+,
Jen. Rann. *theſe* Qq et cet.
371. *defeate*] *disseat* Warb.
vſurp'd] *uſurped* Ff.
372, 373. *be...continue*] Ff, Rowe, Knt,
Wh. i. *be, that* Deſdemona *ſhould long
continue* Qq. (*be, the* Q₃) et cet.
373. *to the*] *vnto the* Qq, Cap. Coll. i.

373, 374. *Moore. Put...purſe : nor*]
Moore,—put...purſe,—nor Qq et cet.
(subs.).
374. *he his*] *he* Q₁.
375. *in her*] Ff, Rowe+, Cap. Knt,
Del. Om. Qq et cet.
Sequeſtration] *ſequeſteration* Q₃.
376. *put but*] *but put* F₃F₄, Rowe,
Pope, Han.
376, 377. *purſe. Theſe...wils : fill*] Ff,
Rowe+. *purſe.—Theſe...wills :—fill* Qq
et cet. (subs.).

---

368. **deseruing**] SCHMIDT (*Lex*, s. v.) interprets this as 'that which is due to thee,
viz. : Desdemona's love ;' I rather think that it has here no special reference, but refers
to *deserts* or *merits* in general, quite equivalent to *worthiness* as used by Shakespeare
elsewhere.—ED.

369. **perdurable**] Simply *durable* with the Latin prefix *per-*, equivalent to *througn*,
thorough.—ED.

371. **defeate**] MALONE : Florio, *A Worlde of Wordes*, 1598, gives Disfare, *to vnaoe,
to ſpoile, to waſte, to marre, to vnmake, to defeate.* [Cotgrave, Desfaire. To vndoe,
breake, defeat.]

371. **fauour**] HENLEY : It here means that combination of features which gives tne
face its distinguishing character. WRIGHT (*Bible Word-Book*) : From Fr. *faveur;* it
is the rendering of a word meaning 'face, countenance, or appearance,' in which sense
it constantly occurs in old writers, and is retained in the adjectives ill-*favoured*, well-
favoured.

375, 376. **Sequestration**] JOHNSON : There seems to be an opposition of terms
here intended, which has been lost in transcription, We may read, 'It was a violent
conjunction, and thou,' &c. ; or, what seems to me preferable, ' It was a violent commencement, and thou shalt see an answerable *sequel*.' STEEVENS : I believe 'sequestration' is here used for *sequel*. Shakespeare might conclude that it was immediately
derived from *sequor;* it may, however, mean no more than *separation*. We have ' a
sequestor from liberty,' III, iv, 48. MALONE : Surely 'sequestration' was used in the
sense of *separation* only, or, in modern language, of *parting*. It is explained in Bullokar [*Expositor*] : *a putting apart*. DYCE (*Gloss.*) : No doubt it means *separation*.

are changeable in their wils : fill thy purſe with Money.   377
The Food that to him now is as luſhious as Locuſts,
ſhalbe to him ſhortly, as bitter as Coloquintida.   She
muſt change for youth : when ſhe is ſated with his body   380
ſhe will find the errors of her choice.   Therefore, put Money in thy purſe.   If thou wilt needs damne thy ſelfe, do
it a more delicate way then drowning.   Make all the Money thou canſt : If Sanctimonie, and a fraile vow, be-   384

378. *Locuſts*] *Locuſt* Q₃.   *loches* Warb.
lohocks Johns.

379. *ſhalbe...ſhortly*] *ſhall to him ſhortly bee* Ff, Rowe.   *shall shortly be* Pope +.
     as bitter as] *as acerbe as the* Q₁.
as bitter as a Warb. Johns.

379, 380. *She...youth*] Om. Q₁, Theob.
Warb. Johns.

381. *errors*] Ff, Rowe+, Knt.   *error*
Qq et cet.

     choice. Therefore] Ff, Rowe, Pope,
Han. Cap. Knt.   *choyce : ſhee muſt haue
change, ſhe muſt. Therefore* Qq et cet.

---

378. **Locusts**] WARBURTON : Whether you understand by this the insect or the
fruit, it cannot be given as an instance of a delicious morsel, notwithstanding the exag-
gerations of lying travellers.   The true reading is *loches*, a very pleasant confection
introduced into medicine by the Arabian physicians ; and so very fitly opposed both to
the bitterness and use of Coloquintida.   [Warburton's ' very pleasant confection ' becomes a.' sirop très-doux ' in Le Tourneur's translation, which he poetically converts in
his text into ' la manne des roseaux.'—ED.]   BEISLY (p. 163) : These ' locusts ' are
the fruit of the Carob tree (*Siliqua dulcis*).   Gerarde in his *Herball* says : ' The carob
groweth in Apulia, a province of Naples, and other countries eastward, where the cods
are so full of sweet juice that it is used to preserve ginger.   It groweth also in sundry
places in Palestine, where there is such plenty of it that it is left unto swine and other
wild beasts to feed on.   Moreover, both young and old feed thereon for pleasure, and
some have eaten thereof to supply and keep the necessary nutriment of their bodies.
This is of some called St. John's bread, and thought to be that which is translated
locusts whereon St. John did feed when he was in the wilderness.   The fruit or cod is
called *Siliqua dulcis*.'   ELLACOMBE (p. 113) says it is the fruit of 'the *Ceratonia siliqua*,
a native of Southern Europe and the Levant.   Its fruit contains a sweet pulp, and in
Spain and elsewhere it is fed to cattle.   The Carob was cultivated in England before
Shakespeare's time.   Its name survives in the *carat* of the jewellers, who in trading in
the East used the Carob beans for weighing small objects.   Though the Carob tree did
not produce the locusts on which St. John fed, there is little doubt that the " husks
which the swine did eat," and the prodigal son longed for, were the produce of the
Carob tree.'

379. **Coloquintida**] REED : This, says Bullein (*Bulwarke of Defence*, 1579), ' is
most bitter, white like a baule, full of seedes, leaves like to cucummers, hoat in the
second, dry in the third degree.'   He then gives directions for the application of it,
and concludes, ' and thus do I end of coloquyntida, which is most bitter and must be
taken with discretion.'

381. PURNELL : The repeated reference to ' money ' is equivalent to ' This is your
game.   But you must be prepared to pay for it.'

383. **delicate way**] DELIUS : That is, by adultery with Desdemona.

twixt an erring Barbarian, and fuper-fubtle Venetian be   385
not too hard for my wits, and all the Tribe of hell, thou
fhalt enioy her : therefore make Money : a pox of drowning thy felfe, it is cleane out of the way.   Seeke thou rather to be hang'd in Compaffing thy ioy, then to be
drown'd, and go without her.   39c

   Rodo.   Wilt thou be faft to my hopes, if I depend on
the iffue ?

   Iago.   Thou art fure of me: Go make Money : I haue
told thee often, and I re-tell thee againe, and againe, I
hate the Moore.   My caufe is hearted; thine hath no leffe   395
reafon.   Let vs be coniunctiue in our reuenge, againft
him.   If thou canft Cuckold him, thou doft thy felfe a
pleafure, me a fport.   There are many Euents in the
Wombe of Time, which wilbe deliuered.   Trauerfe go,   399

---

385. *erring*] *arrant* Han.   *errant*
Warb.
    and] Ff, Knt.   *and a* Qq, Pope
et cet.
    fuper-fubtle] *super-supple* Coll.
(MS).
387. *Money : a*] *money,—a* Qq.
387, 388. *of drowning thy felfe*] *a
drowning* Qq.   *of drowning* Jen.
388. *it is*] *tis* Qq, Jen.
390. *drown'd*] *drowned* Qq.
391, 392. *if...iffue*] Om. Q₁.

393. *me : Go...Money : I*] *me—goe...
Money—I* Qq.
    haue] *had* Wh. ii (misprint ?)
394. *re-tell*] *tell* Qq.
    thee] *the* Q₃.
395. *hath*] *has* Qq.
396. *coniunctiue*] *communicatiue* Q₁.
397. *Cuckold*] *cuckole* Q₃.
398. *me*] *and me* Q₁Q₂, Theob. Warb.
Johns. Jen. Steev. Mal. Rann. Var. Sing.
Ktly.
399. *Trauerfe*] *Trauerce* Q₁.

---

385. **erring**] WARBURTON : We should read *errant*, that is, a *vagabond*, one that has
no house nor country.   STEEVENS : So in *Ham.* I, i, 154, ' Th' extravagant and erring
ipirit.'   MALONE : Perhaps he means a *rover* from *Barbary.*   M. MASON : ' Erring '
is explained by ' extravagant and wheeling stranger,' I, i, 149.   RITSON (p. 229) : Here
is a collection of quibbles.   By an ' erring Barbarian ' is meant not only a *roving Moor,*
but a *shallow, blundering brute ;* and this character is set in opposition to that of a
supersubtle Venetian woman.   The vow, he concluded, must needs be frail that was
made between two such unnatural extremes as brutal folly and the most refined female
cunning.   WHITE (ed. ii) considers Hanmer's text ' plausible.'

389. **hang'd**] See Cotgrave, s. v. *Couillatris.*—ED.

399. **Trauerse**] STEEVENS, who has, I think, been uniformly followed, says this is
an ' ancient military word of command,' and cites in proof, from *2 Hen. IV :* III, ii,
291, Falstaff's command to Wart after a caliver has been put in Wart's hand, ' Hold,
Wart, traverse,' which is clearly the ordinary fencing or musket-drill phrase, and is
scarcely parallel with the present passage.   MALONE cites BULLOKAR (*Eng. Exp.*, s.
v.) : ' *Trauerse.* To march vp and downe, or to moue the feete with proportion as in
dancing,' which seems somewhat more appropriate here, but is not altogether satisfactory.   L. Booth's Reprint gives a comma after ' Trauerfe.'—ED.

prouide thy Money.   We will haue more of this to mor-   400
row.   Adieu.

Rod.   Where fhall we meete i'th'morning ?

Iago.   At my Lodging.

Rod.   Ile be with thee betimes.

Iago.   Go too, farewell.   Do you heare *Rodorigo* ?   405

Rod.   Ile fell all my Land.   *Exit.*

Iago.   Thus do I euer make my Foole, my purfe :
For I mine owne gain'd knowledge fhould prophane
I fI would time expend with fuch Snpe,   409
But for my Sport, and Profit : I hate the Moore,   [316 *a*]
And it is thought abroad, that 'twixt my fheets
She ha's done my Office.   I know not if't be true,
But I, for meere fufpition in that kinde,
Will do, as if for Surety.   He holds me well,   414

---

401. *Adieu*] *Adiue* Q$_1$.

405. *Do*...Rodorigo?*] Om. Cap.
heare] *here* F$_2$F$_3$.

405–407. *Rodorigo?*... *Thus*] Ff, Rowe,
Pope.   Roderigo? Rod. *what fay you ?*
Iag. *No more of drowning, doe you heare ?*
Rod. *I am chang'd.* Exit Roderigo. Iag.
*Goe to, farewell, put money enough in your
purfe :* Thus Q$_1$; followed subs. (except
that after *chang'd* they add merely *Ile goe
fell all my land.* Exit Roderigo. Iag.
Thus) Q$_2$Q$_3$, Rann, Dyce, Glo. Cam. Rlfe,
Wh. ii. Q$_1$ is also followed (including *Ile...
land* from Q$_2$) by Theob. Warb. Johns.
Jen. Steev. Mal. Var. Knt, Coll. Sing. Wh.

i, Ktly, Sta. Del. Huds.   *Roderigo? No
more drowning.* Rod. *I'll sell all my
land.*   Iago. *Thus* Han.

406. *Ile fell*] *Ile goe fell* Q$_2$Q$_3$, Theob.
Warb. Johns. Jen. Rann, Dyce, Glo. Sta.
Cam. Wh. ii.

Exit.] Exit Roderigo. Qq.

Scene XI. Pope+, Jen.

408. *would*] *fhould* Q$_3$, Pope+, Jen.

409. *Snpe*] *a fnipe* Qq.   *a Swaine* F$_2$.
a Swain F$_3$F$_4$, Rowe, Pope, Han.

412. *She ha's*] *Ha's* Qq.   *He ha's* F$_2$.
'Has Dyce iii.   *He has* F$_3$F$_4$ et cet.

true,] *true*— Qq.   *true ;* Johns.

413. *But I*] *Yet I* Qq, Jen. Coll. Del.

---

409. **would**] See ABBOTT, § 331, for passages where 'would' is not used for *should.*
Here 'would' is equivalent, says Abbott, to 'If I *were willing* to expend,' &c., and
should would take from the sense.

409. **Snpe**] STEEVENS : *Woodcock* is the term generally used by Shakespeare to
denote an insignificant fellow; but Iago is more sarcastic, and compares his dupe to a
smaller and meaner bird.   HALLIWELL cites Cotgrave : 'a snipe-knave, so called because two of them are worth but one snipe.'

410. COLERIDGE (p. 251) : Iago's soliloquy—the motive-hunting of a motiveless
malignity—how awful it is !   Yea, whilst he is still allowed to bear the divine image,
it is too fiendish for his own steady view,—for the lonely gaze of a being next to devil
and only not quite devil,—and yet a character which Shakespeare has attempted and
executed, without disgust and without scandal !   FECHTER : Roderigo runs out at the
door at back.   Iago, who has followed him so far, and, leaning against the door-post,
watches him as he goes ; then breaks out into a loud laugh.

414, 415. HERAUD (p. 268) : Iago is the really jealous person, and suspecting

The better fhall my purpofe worke on him : 415
Caffio's a proper man : Let me fee now,
To get his Place, and to plume vp my will
In double Knauery.   How? How? Let's fee.
After fome time, to abufe *Othello's* eares,
That he is too familiar with his wife : 420
He hath a perfon, and a fmooth difpofe

417. *his*] *this* QqFf, Rowe, Pope.
    to plume] *to make* Q$_1$. *plume* F$_3$F$_4$.
418. *In*] *A* Qq, Pope+, Jen. Steev.
Mal. Var. Sta.
    Knauery...fee] *knauery—how,
how,—let me fee* Qq.

418. *Let's*] *let me* Qq, Jen. Steev. Mal,
Var. Sing. Ktly.
419. *eares*] Ff, Rowe, Pope, Han. *eare*
Qq et cet.
420. *his*] *my* Q$_3$.
421. *hath*] *has* Qq.

Othello with his own wife hates him accordingly, and determines on revenge. SNIDER
(vol. i, p. 100) : The true motive for Iago's hate is given here in this and in his succeeding soliloquies, since he would not be likely to announce his own shame or herald
his self-degrading suspicions. He considers that Othello has destroyed the chastity of
his wife. . . . . It is often taken for granted that his suspicions are wholly groundless,—
in fact, that he does not believe them himself. [In the Appendix will be found Sni
der's theory that Othello's guilt in this regard is one of the hinges of the tragedy.—
ED.] But that Iago is sincere in his belief cannot be consistently questioned. . . . .
With this interpretation there is a motive quite adequate for the subsequent vindictive
conduct of Iago ; otherwise, he is an unnatural character,—a monstrosity. His slight
in regard to promotion would doubtless excite his enmity, but not an enmity sufficient
to involve Desdemona in destruction, or even Othello. To inflict worse than death
upon a man because he did not advance a subordinate when he could have done so is
altogether disproportionate to the offence, but to cause his wife to perish also is merely
horrible. Thus Iago is a monster, a wild beast, and needs no motive at all,—not even
neglect of promotion,—to bring on a rabid fit of cruelty. And what then becomes of
the artistic merit and beauty of this drama ? . . . . The second motive is therefore the
true one, and at the same time is adequate. The family of Iago has been ruined by
Othello ; now Iago, in his turn, will ruin the family of the destroyer of his domestic
life. Hence Desdemona is included in his retaliation. He thus requites the Moor
with like for like. His conduct is logical, and his revenge only equals the offence.
But there is absolutely no proportion between motive and deed if he involved Othello's
family in destruction merely because the latter would not promote him.

  414. Surety] M. MASON : That is, ' I will act as if I were certain of the fact.'
  414. holds] REED : That is, ' esteems me.' So in *Matt.* xxi, 26 : ' All hold John
as a prophet.'
  416. proper] BOOTH : Not only *handsome*, but a *refined* and *dignified gentleman ;*
so ' proper ' that his conduct when tipsy is the more surprising.
  417. plume vp] COWDEN-CLARKE : As if any project that involved reduplication
of knavery were a feather in the cap of his depraved will, a thing to plume himself
upon as a feat of intellectual volition.
  421. dispose] KEIGHTLEY (*Expositor*, p. 301) : I do not see clearly the sense of
' dispose ' here ; perhaps we should read *discourse*. ABBOTT, § 451, cites this in a list

To be fufpected : fram'd to make women falfe.   422

The Moore is of a free, and open Nature,

That thinkes men honeft, that but feeme to be fo,

And will as tenderly be lead by'th'Nofe   425

As Affes are :

I haue't : it is engendred : Hell, and Night,

Muft bring this monftrous Birth, to the worlds light.   428

---

423. *is...Nature*] *a free and open na-ture too,* Q₁.

424. *feeme*] *feemes* Q₁Q₂. *feems* Q₃.

425, 426. One line, Qq.

425. *lead*] *led* QqF₃F₄.

425. *by'th'Nofe*] *bit'h nofe*— Q₁. *bith' nofe*— Q₂Q₃.

427. *haue't*] *ha't* Qq.

engendred] *ingender'd* Q₁Q₂. *in-gendr'd* Q₃.

[*Exit.* Qq.

---

of words used by Shakespeare as nouns, to which we should append *-ation* or *-ition*, *-ure* or *-ing*. [See also 'every gale and *vary*,' *Lear*, II, ii, 74.]

427. **Night**] WARBURTON changed this to *spite*, 'i. e. love of mischief and love of revenge,' an emendation which HEATH (p. 559) properly called 'insipid,' and inter-preted the original as meaning 'Hellish practices working in impenetrable darkness.'

428. FECHTER'S Iago, while meditating revenge, 'sits on the angle of the table,' 'leaning his forehead on his hands, his face hidden,' but at 'How? how? Let's see,' he 'slowly raises his head and shows his face, which gradually brightens with a diabol-ical smile.' At the last word of the scene he 'breaks into a savage, ringing laugh, stops suddenly, turning quickly round, and looking on all sides, in fear that he has been overheard.' BOOTH says: Be not too flippant with Roderigo, nor too eager to show the audience your villainy. Change your manner at Roderigo's exit from 'bonhomie' to seriousness.

428. 'Menar per il naso, *to leade by the nose, to make a foole of one.*' Florio, *A Worlde of Wordes*, 1598—New Sh. Soc.

428. W. N. (*Memorials of Sh.*, p. 356): Shakespeare has shown great judgement in the darkness which he makes to prevail in the first counsels of Iago. To the poet himself all the succeeding events must have been clear and determined; but to bring himself again into the situation of one who sees them in embryo, to draw a mist over that which he had already cleared, must have required an exertion of genius peculiar to this author alone. In so lively a manner does he make Iago show his perplexity about the future management of his conduct, that one is almost tempted to think that the poet had determined as little himself about some of the particulars of Iago's de-struct on.

Actus Secundus. Scena Prima.

Enter Montano, and two Gentlemen.

Mon.   What from the Cape, can you diſcerne at Sea?

1.*Gent.*   Nothing at all, it is a high wrought Flood:
I cannot 'twixt the Heauen, and the Maine,   5
Deſcry a Saile.

Mon.   Me thinks, the wind hath ſpoke aloud at Land,
A fuller blaſt ne're ſhooke our Battlements:
If it hath ruffiand ſo vpon the Sea,   9

---

1. Actus...] Actus 2. Scæna 1. Qq.
The Capital City of Cyprus. Rowe. A
plat-form. Cap. A Sea-port town in Cyprus. A Platform. Mal. ...An open place
near the quay. Glo.

2. Enter...] Enter *Montanio*, Gouernor
of *Cypres*, with two other Gentlemen. Qq
(*Cyprus* Q₂Q₃). Enter Montano, and Gentlemen. Ff.

4. *high wrought*] *high-wrought* F₄,
Pope et seq.

5. *Heauen*] *hauen* Q₁, Mal.Var. *heav'ns*
Rowe ii, Pope, Han.

7. *hath ſpoke*] *does ſpeake* Q₁Q₂. *doth
ſpeake* Q₃.

Land] *hand* Q₃.

9. *hath*] *ha* Qq.

RYMER: For the Second Act, our Poet having dispatcht his affairs at Venice shews
the Action next (I know not how many leagues off) in the Island of Cyprus. The
Audience must be there too; And yet our Bays had it never in his head to make any
provision of Transport Ships for them. In the days that the Old Testament was Acted
in Clerkenwell by the Parish Clerks of London, the Israelites might pass through the
Red Sea; but alas, at this time we have no Moses to bid the Waters *make way*, and to
Usher us along. Well, the absurdities of this kind break no Bones. They may make
Fools of us, but do not hurt our Morals. FECHTER: Cyprus: A Platform before the
Town looking upon the Harbour. At the back of the Scene a large Arcade. Gate
on the right. Left corner a Capstan, around it bales of merchandise. In the distance
a storm which is gradually abating. BOOTH: Famagusta, a fortified seaport Town in
the island of Cyprus. Castle on Platform R. Sea-view C. Stone seat C. Platform
and Steps at back. Arch L. The Scene is a front of the Castle at Sunset. Cassio,
Montano, and several gentlemen discovered. [For the notes of Malone, Reed, and
others on the locality, see Appendix, ' Date of the Action.']

3. COLERIDGE (*Notes*, 253): Observe in how many ways Othello is made, first, our
acquaintance, then our friend, then the object of our anxiety, before the deeper interest
is to be approached!

5. **Heauen**] MALONE is the only editor who prefers the *haven* of Q₁; we should
not have had his note in defence of it had he not read in Knolles's *History of the
Turks*, 1570, that there was a ' *haven* of Famagusta, which was defended from the
main by two great rocks ' forty paces apart.

What ribbes of Oake, when Mountaines melt on them,   10
Can hold the Morties.   What ſhall we heare of this?
2 A Segregation of the Turkiſh Fleet :
For do but ſtand vpon the Foaming Shore,
The chidden Billow ſeemes to pelt the Clowds,   14

10. *Mountaines...them,*] *the huge mountaine mes lt,* Q_1. *mountaine...them,* Q_2. *Mountains...them* F_3F_4. *the huge mountains melt* Pope, Rann. *the huge mountain melts* Jen.

11. *Morties.*] Ff, Rowe. *morties,—* Qq. *morties ?* Pope, Theob. i. *mortise ? or mortice ?* Theob. ii et cet.

12. 2] 2 Gent. Qq.

13. *Foaming*] *banning* Q_1.

14. *chidden*] Ff, Rowe, Knt, Coll. Dyce i, Wh. Glo. Sta. Cam. Del. Rlfe. *chiding* Qq et cet.

Billow] *billowes* Q_2Q_3, Pope +, Jen. *ſeemes*] *ſeem* Q_3, Pope +, Jen.

10. **Mountaines**] In adopting the Qq, POPE evidently supposed that 'mountains' here referred, not to water but, to land; THEOBALD showed that Shakespeare refers to 'hills of seas' in this very Scene, line 215, and 'liquid mountains' in *Tro. & Cress.*, and that he had abundance of classical authority for the simile, in Homer, and Vergil, and Ovid; and that therefore 'mountains' here refers to *waves.* Despite this clear exposition, JENNENS, the sturdy follower of Q_1, thinks that 'the sense seems to require' either Pope's text or his own, both founded on the Qto. In the *mes lt* of Q_1 he sees, correctly, a typographical error for *melts*, and thus interprets the passage: 'If it hath ruffian'd so upon the sea as here at land, where the huge mountain melts away before the storm, what ribs of oak can hold the mortise? Theobald did not consider the impropriety of *waves melting; clouds* have been said to melt indeed, but never *waves* that I remember. I don't doubt that Shakespeare had the following passage of Scripture in his eye, " The mountains melt at the presence of the Lord," &c.'

12. **Segregation**] DYCE (*Gloss.*): A separation, or dispersion. WHITE (ed. ii): The opposite of congregation; an extraordinary use of the word.

13. **Foaming**] STEEVENS: The Qto offers the bolder image, i. e. the shore that execrates the ravage of the waves. DELIUS: Even if *banning* were erased by Shakespeare and 'foaming' substituted, the former justifies 'chidden' rather than *chiding.*

14. **chidden**] KNIGHT: How weak is the *chiding* billow *pelting* the clouds ! but the billow 'chidden' by the blast is full of beauty. [Both DYCE and SCHMIDT give to this word in this passage the meaning of 'to sound, to resound, to echo' and 'to be noisy about,' and they refer in support to the Qto. But this definition contains, it seems to me, but a small share of the full definition of 'chidden.' I have searched in vain for a passage in Shakespeare where 'to chide' has the meaning *to sound,* and that meaning alone; in every instance there is, it seems to me, the essential idea of *scolding, brawling, contention* in all degrees, from 'chiding as loud as thunder' to 'the sweet chiding' of well-tuned sounds.' The 'gallant chiding' which Hippolyta (*Mid. N. D.* IV, i, 120) heard when Hercules and Cadmus bayed the bear in a wood in Crete, applies, I think, to the hunters scolding, urging on, the hounds; which Hippolyta afterward calls a 'musical discord;' the 'discord' was the brawling of the hunters, the hounds, their followers, and the bear; the 'music' was the softened echoes of it all from 'the skies, the fountains, every region near.' The essential idea of 'chiding' is there not merely 'sound.' The 'chiding nativity' of Marina (*Per.* III, i, 32) was the rude, brawling welcome to the world given to her by the contest of 'fire, air, water, earth, and Heaven.'—ED.]

The winde-ſhak'd-Surge, with high & monſtrous Maine   15
Seemes to caſt water on the burning Beare,
And quench the Guards of th'euer-fixed Pole: 17

15. *winde-ſhak'd-Surge*] F₁F₂. *winde
ſhak'd ſurge* Qq. *wind-ſhak'd Surge* F₃F₄
et cet.

    Maine] F₂. *mayne* Qq. *Main* F₃

F₄, Rowe+, Cap Jen. Steev. Mal. Var.
mane Knt et cet.

    17. *euer-fixed*] *euer fired* Qq, Pope+,
Jen. *euer fixed* F₄, Rowe, Johns.

15. **Maine**] To KNIGHT belongs the credit of giving the modern spelling and interpretation of this word; his note is: What is 'high and monstrous main'? We use the word *main* elliptically; for the main sea, the great sea, as Shakespeare uses it, in ''twixt the heaven and the main.' The main is the *ocean*. Substitute that word, and what can we make of the passage before us? 'the wind-shak'd surge with high and monstrous *ocean*.' But adopt the word *mane*, and it appears to us we have as fine an image as any in Shakespeare. It is more striking even than the passage in *Hen. IV.*: '—the winds, Who take the ruffian billows by the top, *Curling* their monstrous heads.' In the *high and monstrous mane* we have a picture which was probably suggested by the noble passage in Job: 'Hast thou given the horse strength? Hast thou clothed his *neck* with thunder?' One of the biblical commentators upon this passage remarks, that Homer and Vergil mention the mane of the horse; but that the sacred author, by the bold figure of thunder, expresses the *shaking of the mane*, and the *flakes of hair* which suggest the idea of lightning. The horse of Job is the war-horse, 'who swalloweth the ground with fierceness and rage;' and when Shakespeare pictured to himself his *mane* wildly streaming, 'when the quiver rattleth against him, the glittering spear and the shield,' he saw an image of the fury of the 'wind-shak'd surge,' and of its very form; and he painted it with 'high and monstrous mane.'

17. **Guards**] JOHNSON: Alluding to the star *Arctophylax*. STEEVENS: I wonder that none of the advocates of Shakespeare's learning have observed that *Arctophylax* literally signifies 'the guard of the Bear.' J. F. MARSH (*N. & Qu.*, 1877, 5th, viii, 83): Both Johnson and Steevens are in error; and Shakespeare knew better than his commentators what he was talking about when he spoke of the guards of the pole, and not of the guard of the Bear. Arctophylax is not a synonym for the star Arcturus, but for the constellation Boötes; and the Bear, of which he is the guard, or rather keeper, is not the Little Bear, of which Polaris is the lucida, but the Great Bear, as will be evident in the most cursory glance at a celestial globe. Arctophylax, whether it mean the star or the constellation, has no connection with the Polar guards. They are the two stars β and γ Ursæ Minoris, on the shoulder and foreleg of the Little Bear, as usually depicted, or sometimes on the ear and shoulder. They were more observed in Shakespeare's time than now for the purposes of navigation. Norman's *Safeguard of Sailers*, 1587, has a chapter, 'Howe to knowe the houre of the night by the Guards,' &c. They were even made the subject of mechanical contrivances for facilitating calculation, one of which is described in *The Arte of Navigation*, trans. by Richard Eden from the Spanish of Martin Curtis (or Cortez), 1561, consisting of fixed and movable concentric circles with holes, through which to observe 'the two starres called the Guardians, or the mouth of the horne.' Further details will be found in Admiral Smyth's *Cycle of Celestial Objects*, ii, 331, where is also cited Tap's *Seaman's Grammar*, 1609, 'containing still more upon the Guards;' and Hood's *Use of the Celestial Globe*, 1590, deriving the name 'from the Spanish word *guardare*, which is to beholde,

I neuer did like molleſtation view   18
On the enchafed Flood.

    Men.   If that the Turkiſh Fleete   20
Be not enſhelter'd, and embay'd, they are drown'd,
It is impoſſible to beare it out.

Enter a Gentleman.

3 Newes Laddes : our warres are done :
The deſperate Tempeſt hath ſo bang'd the Turkes,   25
That their deſignement halts.   A Noble ſhip of Venice,
Hath ſeene a greeuous wracke and ſufferance   27

---

19. *On the enchafed*] *On the inchafed*
Qq. *On'th'enchaf'd* Han. *On th'en-chaf'd* Steev.'93.
  20. *that the*] *that be the* F₄.
  21. *enſhelter'd*] *inſhelter'd* QqFf,
Rowe+, Cap. Jen. Coll. Wh.
    embay'd] *embayed* Qq.
    they are] *they're* Pope+, Jen. Sta.
Dyce iii, Huds.
  22. *to beare*] Ff, Q₂Q₃, Rowe+, Knt,
Coll. Sing. Dyce i, Wh. i, Cam. Del. *they
beare* Q₁ et cet.
    [Scene II. Pope+, Jen.

23. Enter...] Enter a third Gentleman.
Qq.
  24 and throughout. 3.] 3 Gent. Qq.
    Laddes :] F₂. *Lords,* Q₁, Pope+,
Jen. *Lords !* Steev. Mal.Var. Rann. *Lads,*
or *Lads :* Q₂Q₃F₃F₄, Rowe, Johns. et cet.
our] *your* Qq.
  25. *Turkes*] *Turke* Qq.
  26. Two lines, Q₂Q₃.
  26, 27. *That...ſeene*] One line, Q₁.
  26. *A Noble*] *Another* Q₁, Pope. *A*
Han.
  27. *wracke*] QqFf, Rowe, Pope, Knt,
Sing. Del. *wreck* Theob. ii et cet.

---

because they are diligently to be looked unto, in regard of the singular use which they
have in navigation.' Shakespeare probably meant to include in the Guards all the
three stars [i. e. β and γ Ursæ Minoris, and Polaris] required for the observations
above noticed. Otherwise in describing a tempest which seemed to cast water on one
constellation, and quench two of the principal stars of another, he could scarcely have
avoided mentioning the third star, the brightest and most important of the three.

  19. **enchafed**] There is an unusual number, in this Scene, of words with the prefix
en : *enshelter'd, embay'd, ensteep'd, enclogge, enwheele.* In Scene iii, *enfetter'd, en-mesh* ; in IV, i, *encave.* For this usage elsewhere, see ABBOTT, § 440.

  22. **to beare**] For those who prefer *they bear* of Q₁, ABBOTT, § 368, explains that
it is probably a subjunctive, and 'that' is omitted.

  27. **wracke**] HUNTER (*Disq. on The Tempest*, p. 134) condemns the substitution
of the modern spelling in this word as a loss in melody in the lines he cites from *The
Tempest*, and implies that we should throughout the plays retain the old word. 'These
are but niceties (he says), but poetry is a luxury, and should therefore be as refined and
perfect as possible.' 'The reason for the substitution is evident. "Wrack" has in a
great measure gone out of use, though we still use the familiar phrase "wrack and
ruin." But "wrack" continued in use long after Shakespeare, and cannot have been,
by any means, extinct in the days of Rowe.' [For four instances from *V. & A., R. of
L.,* and the *Sonn.,* where the rhyme will not permit the substitution of *wreck,* see Mrs
Furness's *Concordance,* s. v.—ED.]

On moſt part of their Fleet. 28

Mon. How? Is this true?

3 The Ship is heere put in.· A *Verenneſſa, Michael Caſſio* 30

28. On] *Of* Johns.
their] *the* Q₁Q₃, Pope ii, Theob.
Warb. Johns.
30. Two lines, Qq, Pope et seq.
is heere] *is* F₄, Rowe.
in : A Verenneſſa,] *in : A Veroneſſa,*
ϙq, Sta. *in : A* Veroneſſo, Ff, Rowe, Pope.
in, A Veronessa; Theob. Warb. Jen. Knt,

Sing. Dyce i, Del. *in ; A Veronessa ;* Han.
in, A Veronese ; Johns. Cap. Steev.'85. *in,*
A Veronesè : Mal. Rann, Steev.'93, Var.
Coll. iii. *in : A Veronesè,* Coll. i, Wh. i,
in ; A Florentine, Coll. (MS). *in, A*
Veronesa ; Glo. Cam. Dyce iii. *in. A*
Veronesè, Ktly. *in ; A Veronese,* Rlfe,
Wh. ii.

28. most] For many other instances of the omission of *the*, see ABBOTT, § 89.

30. **Verennessa**] THEOBALD, by simply altering the punctuation, was the first to make this refer to the ship and not to Cassio, 'who was no Veronese,' says Theobald in his ed. i; 'but we find from other passages in the play he was of Rome' (withdrawn in ed. ii). 'The vessel properly belonged to Verona, but was in the service of Venice.' HEATH: Shakespeare had no ship in his thoughts, but intended to inform us that Cassio was of Verona, an inland city of the Venetian State. The word Veronese should be pronounced after the Italian manner as a quadrisyllable. T. WARTON: It was common to introduce Italian words, and in their proper pronunciation then familiar; see *Faerie Queene*, III, xii, 90: 'And sleeues dependant *Albanese*-wyse.' The ship was a Veronesé, just as we now say a Hamburgher. Cassio was a Florentine. In this speech the Third Gentleman, who brings the news of the wreck of the Turkish fleet, returns to the tale, and tells the circumstances more distinctly. In his former speech he speaks of 'a noble ship of Venice,' and now he adds: 'The very ship is just now put into port, and she is a Veronesé.' That is, a ship fitted out or furnished by the people of Verona, a city of the Venetian State. STEEVENS: I believe we are all wrong. Verona is an inland city. Every inconsistency may, however, be avoided if we read *The* Veronessa, i. e. the name of the ship is the Veronessa. [While all the critics thus far had stated that Verona was tributary to Venice, yet, having cited no authority, they had apparently drawn the fact from the depths of their consciousness; it was reserved for MALONE to justify the assertion in a note, which is the only one from the mass that DYCE quotes, as follows :] 'Besides many other towns (says Contareno), castles, and villages, they [the Venetians] possess seven faire cities; as Trevigi, Padoua, Vicenza, *Verona*, Brescia, Bergamo, and Crema.'—*Commonwealth of Venice*, 1599. KNIGHT retains the *Veronessa*, because 'as a feminine it is applicable to a ship.' COLLIER: The Third Gentleman has already said that the ship was 'of Venice,' and it is not likely that he would assert just afterwards that she was a 'Veronesé;' it seems much more probable that he would by mistake call Cassio, whom he did not know, a 'Veronesé.' SINGER: Whether a *Veronessa* signified a ship fitted out by Verona, or designated some particular kind of vessel, is not yet fully established. But as it has not hitherto been met with elsewhere, the former is most probably the true explanation. WHITE (ed. i): There is difficulty in either reading; but of the two errors, one of which it is necessary to suppose on Shakespeare's part, a momentary forgetfulness appears the more probable. KEIGHTLEY (*Exp.*, 301): Another instance of the poet's negligence or forgetfulness. . . . . Though the metre is perfect, it might be better to insert *nam'd* or *one*. It is not likely that the ship was called 'the *Veronessa*.' DANIEL (p. 78): Read : 'The ship is here put in, | "La Veronesa:" Michael Cassio, |

Lieutenant to the warlike Moore, *Othello*,   31
Is come on Shore . the Moore himfelfe at Sea,
And is in full Commiffion heere for Cyprus.
　Mon.   I am glad on't :
'Tis a worthy Gouernour.   35
　3 But this fame *Caffio*, though he fpeake of comfort,
Touching the Turkifh loffe, yet he lookes fadly,
And praye the Moore be fafe ; for they were parted
With fowle and violent Tempeft.
　Mon.   Pray Heauens he be :   40
For I haue feru'd him, and the man commands   [316 *b*]

---

31. *Lieutenant*] *Leiutenant* Q₁Q₂.
　to] *of* F₄, Rowe+.
32. *on Shore*] *afhore* Q₁. *a fhore* Q₂Q₃.
　Moore] *Moor's* Dyce conj.
　himfelfe] QqFf, Dyce, Glo. Sta.
Cam. Del. Rlfe, Wh. ii. *himfelf's* Rowe
et cet.

33. *heere*] *bound* Daniel.
34, 35. One line, Qq, Rowe et seq.
34. *I am*] *I'm* Pope+, Dyce iii, Huds.
38. *praye*] *prayes* QqF₂F₃. *prays* F₄
et cet.
40. *Heauens*] *Heauen* Qq, Cap. Jen.
Steev. Mal. Var. Knt, Coll. Sing. Ktly.

Lieutenant,' &c. HUDSON adopts Daniel's suggestion. ROLFE agrees with White that the confusion is perhaps due to a momentary forgetfulness on Shakespeare's part. TH. ELZE (*Sh. Jahrbuch*, xiv, 176): The word is clearly corrupt, but F₁ puts us on the right track. Let the true word be 'verrinessa,' and the changes, due to editorial lack of knowledge, through 'verennessa' and 'Veronessa' to 'Veronese' are easily understood. Now although I cannot at the moment give an Italian authority for the noun 'verinessa,' yet there is the word 'verrina' and the verb 'verrinare,' which is an old nautical term and still in use, equivalent in meaning to *tenebrare, perforare, traforare,* that is, to 'cut through,' to 'cleave,' like the French *percer*. Wherefore the 'noble ship of Venice' was a *verrinessa*, 'un perceflot.' [Is not this the exact equivalent of the nautical term 'cutter'? If only an instance of the use of the Italian word could be produced, this vexed question would be settled for ever. As it is, Th. Elze's explanation seems far more satisfactory than any other; but if a supersubtle compositor forces us to choose between a lack of memory on Shakespeare's part and a lack of geographical information, I prefer the latter. The nationality of a chance ship, mentioned once and never again, is of less moment than the nationality of an important character; the same wind that can blow a ship to Aleppo can waft one from Verona. Furthermore, how in the wild excitement of the moment could the Third Gentleman find out from what city of Italy Cassio came? That he was the lieutenant to the warlike Moor might be revealed at a glance by some distinctive decoration of his dress, such as the scarf of company, which always bore the Captain's colours.—ED.

33. heere for Cyprus] Unless this means 'for Cyprus, here,' it is not easy to explain it. Daniel's emendation perfects the sense, but the *ductus literarum* is against it.—ED.

34. JOHN HUNTER: Montano would be well pleased to resign the post in a time of so great peril to such a man as Othello, under whom he had served.

34. on't] See ABBOTT, § 181.

Like a full Soldier.   Let's to the Sea-fide (hoa)   42
As well to fee the Veffell that's come in,
As to throw-out our eyes for braue *Othello*,
Euen till we make the Maine, and th'Eriall blew,   45
An indiftinct regard.
    Gent.   Come, let's do fo ;
For euery Minute is expectancie
Of more Arriuancie.

               Enter Caffio.   50

    Caffi.   Thankes you, the valiant of the warlike Ifle,
That fo approoue the Moore : Oh let the Heauens
Giue him defence againft the Elements,
For I haue loft him on a dangerous Sea.
    Mon.   Is he well fhip'd ?   55
    Caffio.   His Barke is ftoutly Timber'd, and his Pylot
Of verie expert, and approu'd Allowance ;   57

---

42. Two lines, Qq.
   hoa] *ho* Qq. Om. Pope+.
44. *throw-out*] F$_2$. *throw out* QqF$_3$F$_4$
et cet.
45, 46. Om. Q$_1$.
   th' Eriall blew] F$_2$F$_3$. *th' Ayre all
blue* Q$_2$Q$_3$. *th' Erial blue* F$_4$, Rowe. *th'*
or *the aerial blue* Pope et cet.
46. *An*] *And* FfQ$_3$.
47. Gent.] 3 Gent. Qq.
49. *more*] *our* F$_4$.
   Arriuancie] *Arrivancy* Ff, Knt.
arriuance Qq et cet.
   Scene III. Pope+, Jen.
51. *Thankes you,*] Ff, Rowe, Coll. i,
Dyce,Wh.i. *Thankes to* Qq, Pope+, Cap.

Jen. Steev. Mal.Var. Coll. iii. *Thanks you*
Ktly. *Thanks, you* Knt et cet.
51. *the*] Ff, Knt, Coll. iii. *this* Qq et
cet.
   warlike] *worthy* Q$_1$, Jen. Rann.
Om. Q$_2$Q$_3$.
52. *Moore : Oh let*] *Moore, and let* Qq.
Moor ! O, let Knt.
53. *againft*] *from* F$_4$.
   the] *their* Qq.
54. *a*] *the* Q$_3$.
56. *his*] *is* Q'81.
   Pylot] *Pilate* Q$_1$. *Pilote* Q$_2$Q$_3$.
Pilot F$_3$F$_4$.
57. *Of...and*] *Very expert, and of*
Johns. conj.

---

44. **to throw**] A typographical error, in the omission of 'to,' begun in Reed's *Var.*
of 1803, was continued in the *Var.* of 1813, of 1821, and in Singer's ed. i.   The line
thus mutilated, and almost painfully prosaic, was accepted as complete by GUEST (i,
239), and thus bravely scanned : ' As | throw out | our eyes | : for braue | Othel | lo.'
ED.

49. **Arriuancie**] DYCE: A manifest error caught from the 'expectan*cie*' of the preceding line.   COWDEN-CLARKE: There is a marked prevalence of words ending in *ce*
in this play.

57. **expert, and approu'd Allowance**] STEEVENS: This is put for 'allow'd and
approv'd expertness.' [For a list of similar expressions where the relations of adjectives and their nouns seem inverted, like 'paly ashes,' 'shady stealth,' &c. see the excellent *Grammatical Obs.* on p. 1417 of SCHMIDT'S *Lex.*—ED.]

Therefore my hope's (not furfetted to death)   58
Stand in bold Cure.
Within.   A Saile, a Saile, a Saile.   60

58. *hope's*] F₂Qq. *hopes* F₃F₄ et cet.   60. Within.] Meff. Qq. 4 G. Cap.
59. [Enter a Meffenger. Qq. Enter an-   Without. Sta.
other Gentleman. Cap.   Within...*Saile.*] In margin as Stage
                                                                         Direction Glo. Cam. Rlfe, Wh. ii.

58, 59. JOHNSON: I do not understand these lines. I know not how *hope* can be *surfeited to death*, that is, *can be increased, till it be destroyed;* nor what it is, 'to stand in bold cure;' or why *hope* should be considered a disease. Shall we read : 'Therefore my *fears*, not surfeited to death'? &c. This is better, but it is not well. Shall we strike a bolder stroke, and read thus : 'Therefore my hopes, not *forfeited* to death, Stand *bold, not sure*'? JENNENS : Wishes may be called the food upon which hope is very apt to surfeit; and to surfeit to death too, when there is no ground or foundation to expect the thing hoped for. Hope is in perfect health where the grounds for it are equal to the wish; but if the wish preponderate the grounds of expectation, hope is in a sickly state. This was the case with Cassio; his wishes for Othello's safety were greater than the probability of it, for he had left him on a dangerous sea; so his hope was sick; but not sick to death, because the ship had a good pilot; this thought *phys-ick'd* hope, and put it in a bold state of cure. STEEVENS : Presumptuous hopes, which have no foundation in probability, may poetically be said to surfeit themselves to death, or forward their own dissolution. 'In bold cure' means in confidence of being cured. MALONE : It is not *hope* which is here described as the disease; those misgiving appre-hensions which diminish hope are, in fact, the disease, and hope itself is the patient. HENLEY : I believe that Solomon upon this occasion will be found the best interpreter : 'Hope deferred maketh the heart sick.' KNIGHT : Hope upon hope, without reali-zation, is a surfeit of hope and extinguishes hope. Cassio had some reasonable facts to prevent his hope being 'surfeited to death.' COLLIER : The meaning seems to be, that Cassio's hopes are not destroyed by constant repetition and disappointment. SINGER : Therefore my hopes, not surfeited to death *by excess of apprehension,* stand in *confi-dence of being cured.* STAUNTON (Note on *Ant. & Cleo.* II, i, 38) : As in our early language to *expect* most commonly meant to *stay* or *wait,* so to *hope* on some occasions was used where we should now adopt *to expect.* (Note on present passage) : 'Hopes' here are *expectations* or *presentiments.* COWDEN-CLARKE : My hopes, not having been utterly destroyed by reiterated false excitement and successive defeat, remain in confident expectation of being fulfilled. HUDSON : Cassio, though anxious, does not despair; and the meaning of 'stand in bold cure' seems to be, 'my hopes, though near dying, stay themselves upon, or are kept alive by, *bold* conjecture;' or, it may be, 'are confident of being cured.' I was for a while in doubt whether to read 'not *suffocate* to death' or 'not *sick yet unto* death;' but on the whole preferred the former as involv-ing somewhat less of change, and as being perhaps rather more in Shakespeare's man-ner. D'HUGUES : Il est clair cependant que les espérances s'ajoutant aux espérances, sans être jamais réalisées, constituent un trop plein (surfeit) d'espérances, qui fait éva-nouir toute espérance. C'est la même chose que Molière a voulu dire dans le fameux sonnet d'Oronte : Belle Philis, on désespère Alors qu'on espère toujours. [These para-phrases are all of them intelligible, and would be entirely satisfactory could we only forget the text, which as it now stands is unintelligible to me, and I am willing to 'say ditto to' Dʳ Johnson.—ED.]

Caʃʃio.   What noiʃe ?   61

Gent.   The Towne is empty ; on the brow o'th'Sea
Stand rankes of People, and they cry, a Saile.

Caʃʃio.   My hopes do ʃhape him for the Gouernor.

Gent.   They do diʃcharge their Shot of Courteʃie,   65
Our Friends, at leaʃt.

Caʃʃio.   I pray you Sir, go forth,
And giue vs truth who 'tis that is arriu'd.

Gent.   I ʃhall.   *Exit.*

Mon.   But good Lieutenant, is your Generall wiu'd?   70

Caʃʃio.   Moʃt fortunately : he hath atchieu'd a Maid
That paragons deʃcription, and wilde Fame :
One that excels the quirkes of Blazoning pens,
And in th'eʃʃentiall Veʃture of Creation,
Do's tyre the Ingeniuer.   75

61. *noiʃe*] *news* Cap.

62. Gent.] Meʃʃ. Qq.   4 G. Cap.
empty ; on] *epmty, one* Q₃.

63. *Stand*] *otand* Q₁.   *Stands* Q₂Q₃.

64. *Gouernor*] *guernement* Q₁.   *gou-ernment* Q₂.   *government* Q₃.
[Guns heard. Cap.

65, 69, 78, 112. Gent.] 2 Gen. Qq.
their] *the* Qq.

66. *Friends*] *friend* Qq.
[A ʃhot. Qq.   Sound of cannon. Johns.

70. *Lieutenant*] *Leiutenant* Q₁Q₂.

71. *fortunately :*]   *fortunately,*   Qq, Rowe, Pope, Theob. Han. Warb.

73. *quirkes of*] Om. Q₁.

74. *th'eʃʃentiall*] *the eʃʃentiall* Qq.

75-77. *Do's...in ?*] One line, Qq et cet.

75. *tyre the Ingeniuer.*] *beare all excel-lency :—* Q₁, Pope +, Jen. Steev. Mal.Var. Coll. Wh. i, Ktly.   *beare an excellency :—* Q₂Q₃, Rowe.   *tire the Ingeniver* Ff.   *tire the inventer.* Cap. Rann.   *tire the ingener.* Knt, Dyce, Glo. Sta. Cam. Del. Huds Rlfe.   *tire the ingenier* Sing. ii.   *bear all excellence* Wh. ii.   *tire the imaginer* Jervis.

73. **excels**] MALONE : See 103d *Sonn.: '* a face That over-goes my blunt invention quite, Dulling my lines, and doing me disgrace.'

74, 75. WARBURTON : It is plain that something very hyperbolical was here in-tended.   But what is there as it stands ?   Why this, that in the essence of creation she bore all excellency.   The expression is intolerable, and could never come from one who so well understood the force of words as our Poet.   The *essential vesture* is the same as *essential form.*   So that the expression is nonsense.   For the *vesture of crea-tion* signifies the *forms* in which created beings are cast.   And *essence* relates not to the *form,* but to the *matter.*   Shakespeare certainly wrote : ' And in *terrestrial* vesture,' &c.   And in this lay the wonder, that all created excellence should be contained within an earthly mortal form.   HEATH (p. 559) : I entirely agree with Warburton that the common reading is indefensible. . . . . I should rather suspect that the poet wrote : And in *the sensual* vesture,' &c.   The sense is, And within that vesture of the human senses with which she is clothed by the Creator she is endued with every excellency. JOHNSON : I do not think ' essential inexplicable ; it seems to be used for *existent, real.* She excels the praises of invention says he, and in *real* qualities with which *creation* has *invested* her *bears all excellency.*   [Line 75 in the Folio] I explain thus : Does tire

[74, 75. **essentiall Vesture of Creation, Do's tyre the Ingeniuer.**]

the *ingenious verse.* This is the best reading, and that which the author substituted in his revisal. STEEVENS: I believe the word 'tire' was not introduced to signify to *fatigue*, but to *attire*, to *dress*. The verb to *attire* is often so abbreviated. Thus in Holland's *Leaguer*, 1633: 'Cupid's a boy, And would you *tire* him like a Senator?' Again in *Com. of Err.* II, ii, 99: 'To save the money he spends in tiring' ['trim ming.'—Glo.] 'The essential vesture of Creation' tempts me to believe that it was so used here. I would read something like this: Does tire the *ingenuous virtue*, i. e. invests her artless virtue in the fairest form of earthly substance. In *Mer. of Ven.* V, i, 64, Lorenzo calls the body 'the muddy vesture of decay.' It may be observed that *ingener* did not anciently signify one who manages the *engines* or *artillery* of an army, but any *ingenious person*, any *master of liberal science.* Cf. Jonson's *Sejanus*, I, i: 'No, Silius, we are no good *ingeners*, We want the fine arts,' &c. *Ingener*, therefore, may be the true reading of this passage; a similar thought occurs in *Temp.* IV, i, 10: 'For thou shalt find she will outstrip all praise, And make it halt behind her.' In the Argument of *Sejanus*, Jonson likewise says that his hero 'worketh with all his *ingene*,' apparently from the Latin, *ingenium.* MALONE: Perhaps we should read: 'Does tire the *ingene* ever.' *Ingene* is used for *ingenium* by Puttenham, *Arte of Poesie*, 1589: 'Such also as made most of their workes by translation out of the Latin and French tongue, and few or none of their own *engine*;' *engine* is here without doubt a misprint for *ingene*. I believe, however, the reading of the Qto is the true one. If 'tire' was used in the sense of *weary*, then 'ingener' must have been used for the ingenious person who should attempt to enumerate the merits of Desdemona. We have in Fleckno's *Discourse of the English Stage*, 1664: 'We in England . . . . having pro ceeded no further than to bare painting, and not arrived to the stupendous wonders of your great *ingeniers*.' For a similar imagery to that in the first of these lines, see one of Daniel's *Sonnets:* 'Though time doth spoil her of her fairest vaile That ever yet mortalitie did cover.' M. MASON: The reading of the Folio appears to have been, 'Does *tire* the *engineer*,' that is, 'One whose real perfections were so excellent that to blazon them would exceed the abilities of the ablest masters.' HENLEY: 'Ingenieur' is no doubt of the same import with *ingener* or *ingeneer*, though perhaps differently written by Shakespeare in reference to *ingenious*, and to distinguish it from *ingeneer*, which he has elsewhere used in a military sense. Daniel uses *ingeniate:* 'Th' adulterate beauty of a falsèd cheek Did Nature (for this good) ingeniate,' &c. KNIGHT: The text of the Folio presents no difficulty when we understand the word *ingener*. The word *engine* is so called 'because not made without great effort (*ingenii*) of *genius*, of ingenuity, of contrivance.'—Richardson. The *ingener*, then, is the contriver by ingenuity, the designer, and, here applied to a poet, is almost literally the Greek ποιητής, *maker.* COLLIER (ed. i): 'Ingeniuer' has been taken for *inginer*, though if that were the true word, we cannot tell why the compositor should have put so many letters into it. JERVIS (p. 25): Read: 'doth tire the *imaginer*.' Cf. 'And still he did it by first telling the imaginer, and after bidding the actor think.'—Bacon's *Nat. Hist.* [Century X, p. 205, ed. 1677.—Dyce]. STAUNTON: By *ingener* is meant, perhaps, the *painter* or *artist*, as in the extract from Fleckno [quoted by Malone]. Ingenier, or ingener, was, however, a term for any ingenious person; and from a passage in *Certain Edicts from a Parliament in Eutopia*, by Lady Southwell: 'Item, that no Lady shall court her looking-glasse, past one houre in a day, unlesse she professe to be *an Ingenir*,' it might be thought in the present instance to signify what is now called a *mociste*, or deviser of new fashions in female apparel. WHITE (ed. i): The tame

[74, 75. **essentiall Vesture of Creation, Do's tyre the Ingeniuer.**]
reading of the Qto is given [in the text] with the full consciousness that it does not represent the passage as Shakespeare left it, and in the belief that very probably he did not write it at all. The attempt to make something of the Folio text by regarding the last word as a misprint of *ingener*, i. e. artist, writer, ingenious person, I cannot but regard as utterly futile. Possibly 'tire' here means attire, and refers to 'vesture;' it may also mean weary, and have for its subject the word or phrase which is incorrectly, or both incorrectly and imperfectly, represented by 'ingeniuer.' For in *V. & A.*, Venus's tongue is called 'the engine of her thoughts;' and in *Tit. And.* III, i, Marcus styles Lavinia's tongue 'that delightful engine of her thoughts.' Here Shakespeare may have meant Cassio to say, that Desdemona's charms were beyond description either by pen or tongue. I am inclined to believe that the reading of the text [i. e. the Qto] was substituted for the true, but illegible or incomprehensible, reading by the transcriber of the passage who prepared the copy. BR. NICHOLSON (*N. & Qu.*, 1865, 3d, viii, 43): The Qto text lacks a sufficient rise in hyperbole to conclude fitly the previous hyperbolic praises, and a poetical conclusion to the simile commenced in 'vesture.' In the Folio 'tire' cannot mean *weary;* but as a verb suggested by 'vesture,' and having reference to it, it must be either the shortened form of *attire*, or formed (perhaps for the nonce, as is not unfrequent in writers of that day) from *tire*, a head-dress; and this either transitively or agentially in the sense of 'arrange a head-dress,' or reflectively in the sense of 'to act as.' But if creation be represented as a vesture, it follows that Desdemona, as a part of creation, should (agreeably to the last given meaning of 'tire') be part of the dress; and giving the word this sense, we obtain the plain meaning corresponding with the reading of the Qto,—that creation being the vesture, she, Desdemona, is the tire, tiara, or crown of it, one who 'tops all.' Again, if all creation be represented as a vesture, it can only be as the regal robe of God its ingener or artificer; hence we may consider ingeniver as the representative of some form of ingener; the exact form is unimportant, but I would prefer the French, *ingenieur*, as this, printed *ingenievr*, might easily have been changed by an ignorant compositor into *ingeniver*. As to the probable origin of the phrase, I cannot but think that these two lines were formed on the remembrance of Psalm cii, 25, 26: 'Thou hast laid the foundation of the earth, and the heavens are the work of Thine hands, ... they all shall wax old as doth a garment, and as a vesture shalt Thou change them, and they shall be changed.' This being combined with the thought of Desdemona as a pure daughter of Eve, the last and therefore, according to the previous gradation of creation, the crowning work of God. Combined, perhaps, with these, and assisting the association of the two, may have been the remembrance of the ray, circlet, or 'glory,' which surrounds the head of sacred images or pictures, and the phrase 'forasmuch as man is the glory of God.' Possibly the reader who has not paid attention to the frequency with which Shakespeare draws from Scriptural sources, and to the frequency with which these form his phrases, may consider my remarks more subtle than sound; but the addition of the word 'essential' strongly corroborates them, and illustrates how fully and perfectly Shakespeare elaborated a thought, and how comprehensively and succinctly he expressed it. Desdemona is represented as a being of purity and love, a female Abdiel 'mong Italian women; and hence Cassio is made to break out into such expression-seeking praise as to call her the top of creation, as creation is 'essentially' and without 'the accident' of sin, or as it was when it was beautiful before God and pronounced to be very good. KEIGHTLEY (*Exp.*, p. 301): It seems almost impossible to make any good sense out of the Folio. 'The essential,' &c. means person, body, form.

Enter Gentleman.   76

How now? Who ha's put in?

Gent. 'Tis one *Iago*, Auncient to the Generall.

Caffio. Ha's had moft fauourable, and happie fpeed :

Tempefts themfelues, high Seas, and howling windes,   80

The gutter'd-Rockes, and Congregated Sands,

Traitors enfteep'd, to enclogge the guiltleffe Keele,   82

Scene IV. Pope+, Jen.
76. Enter...] Enter 2 Gentleman (after line 77) Qq. Re-enter Sec. Gent. Cap.
77. *How now ?*] *now*, Qq. *Now ?* Cap. Rann.
    ha's] *has* QqFf.
79. Caffio.] Om. (continuing speech to 2 Gent.) Qq.
    Ha's] *H'as* Rowe+. *Has* Dyce i,

Glo.Wh. ii. *He's* Wh. i, Huds. Rlfe. *'Has*
Dyce iii. *He has* Qq et cet.
80. *high*] *by* Q₁.
81. *gutter'd-Rockes*] *guttered rocks* Qq.
    gutter'd Rocks Ff.
82. *enfteep'd*,] *enfcerped;* Q₁. *enur'd*
    Pope conj.
    enclogge] F₂F₃. *enclog* F₄, Cap.
    Knt, Del. *clog* Qq et cet.

HUDSON : This seems to mean, she is one who surpasses all description, and in real beauty or outward form goes beyond the power of the artist's inventive or expressive pencil. ROLFE : The reading of the Folio is doubtful, but it is preferable to the tame phrase of the Qto. WHITE (ed. ii) : From the text of the Folio no tolerable reading or sense has yet been extracted. [It is to be feared that Steevens's remark on I, iii, 291, is equally applicable here, and that it is 'highly probable that this passage will prove a lasting source of doubt and controversy.'—ED.]

79. **Ha's**] An instance of the absorption of the personal pronoun, similar to that of 'it' in I, iii, 220. DYCE in his last edition has indicated this. SCHMIDT in his admirable translation thus renders this line : 'Er stand in eines guten Engels Schutz,' and pleads for it thus : If we consider the meaning of this line in connection with what follows it is evident that there must be some reference to Desdemona. 'Speed' in Shakespeare means not only *swiftness, haste*, but *success, fortune*, and also *that propitious power*, or *exalted guardianship, which brings success*, especially in the expression of good wishes. 'Saint Nicholas be thy speed !' *Two Gent.* III, i, 301 ; 'Hercules be thy speed,' *As You Like It*, I, ii, 222, and elsewhere ; and with a comic turn in 'good manners be your speed,' *1 Hen. IV :* III, i, 190. Hence, therefore, Desdemona is here the guardian angel who saves Iago's ship, and at the conclusion of the speech she is styled not without a purpose, 'the divine Desdemona.'

82. **ensteep'd**] THEOBALD (*Sh. Rest.*, p. 143) : That is, That Rocks and Shoals lurk under, and lye covered by the Deep, treacherously to destroy Vessels which happen to be thrown upon them. STEEVENS : Perhaps *escerped* was an old English word borrowed from the French, *escarpé*, which Shakespeare, not finding congruous to the image of clogging the keel, afterwards changed. I once thought it might be Traitors *enscarf'd*, i. e. muffled in their robes, as in *Jul. Cæs.* or *Ham.*, 'My sea-gown *scarf'd* about me.' HENLEY : Steevens's difficulty would, perhaps, have been removed had he recollected Othello's· speech in IV, ii, 60 : 'Steep'd me in poverty to the very lips.' BOSWELL : Traitors ensteep'd are merely traitors concealed under the water. KNIGHT : Rocks and sand are beneath the water, and what is beneath the water is *steep'd* in the water. The identical word thus applied is in the *Faerie Queene*, I, xi, 276 : 'Now gan the golden Phœbus for to steepe His fierie face in billowes of the west.' WHITE (ed

As hauing fence of Beautie, do omit   83
Their mortall Natures, letting go fafely by
The Diuine *Defdemona*.   85
   Mon. What is fhe?
   Caffio. She that I fpake of:
Our great Captains Captaine,
Left in the conduct of the bold *Iago*,
Whofe footing heere anticipates our thoughts,   90
A Senights fpeed. Great Ioue, *Othello* guard,
And fwell his Saile with thine owne powrefull breath,
That he may bleffe this Bay with his tall Ship,
Make loues quicke pants in *Defdemonaes* Armes,
Giue renew'd fire to our extincted Spirits.   95

     Enter Defdemona, Iago, Rodorigo, and Æmilia.
Oh behold,   97

84. *mortall*] *common* Qq.
  go fafely] *fafe go* Pope+, Cap.
87, 88. One line, Qq, Rowe et seq.
87. *fpake*] *fpoke* Q₁. *fpeak* Q'81.
88. *great*] Om. Q₃.
94. *Make...in*] *And fwiftly come to*
Qq, Jen.
95. Two lines, Qq.

95. *extincted*] *extinctef* F₃F₄. *extin-*
guifh'd Rowe, Pope, Theob. Han. Warb.
Spirits.] Ff. *fpirits : And bring*
all Cypreffe comfort,— (subs.) Qq et cet.
(*And give* Rowe).
96. Enter...] After *armes*, line 94 Qq.
Scene V. Pope+, Jen.

---

i) reads *enscarp'd* and upholds the word : because Shakespeare never uses 'steep' in
the sense of 'plunge' or 'submerge,' but always in that of 'lave' or 'soak,' which is
almost ridiculously inappropriate here; because 'scarp' in Shakespeare's day meant
the inner slope of a ditch or intrenchment, then as now descriptive of shelving rocks:
and because *enscarped* might be easily mistaken for 'enseeped,' owing to the likeness
between *c* and *t* in the MS. of the early seventeenth century. DYCE in his ed. ii reminded White of Henley's reference to IV, ii, 60, and White adopted 'enfteep'd' in
his ed. ii, and *enscarp'd* was heard of no more.

84. *mortall*] REED: That is, deadly, destructive.

88. *Captaine*] MALONE: Cf. 'And she shall be sole victress, Cæsar's Cæsar,' *Rich*
III: IV, iv, 336.

91. *Ioue*] MALONE: For this absurdity I have not the smallest doubt that the Master of the Revels, and not our poet, is answerable. [Malone made the same remark
on *2 Hen. VI:* IV, x, 56, where the Ff have 'Jove,' and the Qq *God.* The inference is that Malone deemed *God* the true word here; Hudson has adopted it.—ED.]
COWDEN-CLARKE : We believe it to have been the author's own word characteristically put into Cassio's mouth here. To this day Italians use mythological adjurations
in common with Christian appeals; and in Shakespeare's time the custom was almost
universal.

95. The omission in the Folio of the phrase found in the Qto, WHITE (ed. i) pronounces due to 'manifest accident;' as well as *me* in line 104.

The Riches of the Ship is come on fhore :   98
You men of Cyprus, let her haue your knees.
Haile to thee Ladie : and the grace of Heauen,   100
Before, behinde thee, and on euery hand
Enwheele thee round.

    Def.   I thanke you, Valiant *Caffio,*
What tydings can you tell of my Lord ?

    Caf.   He is not yet arriu'd, nor know I ought   [317 *a*]
But that he's well, and will be fhortly heere.   106

    Def.   Oh, but I feare :
How loft you company ?

    Caffio.   The great Contention of Sea, and Skies
Parted our fellowfhip. But hearke, a Saile.   110

    Within.   A Saile, a Saile.

    Gent.   They giue this greeting to the Cittadell :
This likewife is a Friend.   113

98. *on fhore*] *afhore* Q₁.
99. *You*] Ff, Rowe, Pope, Theob. Han.
Warb. Cap. Knt, Wh. i. *Ye* Qq et cet.
100. *thee Ladie*] *the Lady* Q'81.
104. *tell*] *tell me* QqFf et cet.
105. *yet*] Om. Ff.
    arriu'd] *arriued* Q₁Q₂. *arived* Q₃.
    ought] QqFf, Rowe, Pope, Han.
Warb. *aught* Theob. et cet.
107, 108. One line, Qq et cet.
107. *feare : How*] Ff. *feare :—how*
Qq, Cap. Steev. Mal. Sing. *fear.—How*
Coll. i, Wh. i, Ktly. *fear—how* Rowe et
cet.

109. *Sea*] *the fea* QqFf et cet.
110. *fellowfhip.*] Ff, Rowe+, Jen. Del.
Huds. *fellowship—* Glo. Cam. Rlfe, Wh.
ii. *fellowfhip :* Qq et cet.
111. *Within....Saile*] [within] *A faile,
a faile* (Stage direct. after line 108) Qq.
Sound of Cannon. Johns. Cry within of—
A sail ! a sail : afterwards, Guns (Stage
direct.) Cap. After *fellowfhip* Coll.
112. *this*] Ff, Rowe+, Steev.'85. *their*
Qq et cet.
    greeting] *geerting* Q₃.
    to the] *to this* Rowe ii.

---

98. **Riches**] For instances of its use, according to its derivation as a singular noun,
see SCHMIDT, s. v.

100–102. WALKER (*Crit.*, iii, 286): *Wheel* for *circle* is not altogether unfrequent in
the old dramatists. Cf. 'Heaven's grace in-wheel you, And all good thoughts and
prayers dwell about you.'—B. and F. *The Pilgrim*, I, ii, p. 17, ed. Dyce. PECK (*Memoirs of Milton*, p. 164) : These lines are almost directly copied in *Il Penseroso*, 151 :
'And, as I wake, sweet music breathe Above, about, and underneath.'

103. BOOTH : Desdemona gives her hand to Cassio, who kisses it, and rises from
his knee.

107. **fear**] D'HUGUES : Est-ce un pressentiment vague et mystérieux de la destinée
qui l'attend dans cette tle ? Ce mot n'est évidemment pas placé au hasard : tout a un
sens dans Shakespeare.

112. **this**] WHITE (ed. i) : This seems a misprint, due to the occurrence cf 'this
in the next line. [It hardly can be called a misprint. To me, it is doubtful if it be
not a little better than *their*.—ED.]

Caſſio. See for the Newes:

Good Ancient, you are welcome.   Welcome Miſtris: 115

Let it not gaule your patience (good *Iago*)

That I extend my Manners.   'Tis my breeding,

That giues me this bold ſhew of Curteſie.

Iago. Sir, would ſhe giue you ſomuch of her lippes,

As of her tongue ſhe oft beſtowes on me,   120

You would haue enough.

Deſ.   Alas : ſhe ha's no ſpeech.

Iago.   Infaith too much :   123

---

114. *See...Newes*] *So ſpeakes this voyce* Q₁.

[Exit Gentleman. Cap. et seq.

115. [To Æmilia. Rowe et seq.

117. [Kisses her. Johns.

119. *Sir,*] *For* Q₁.

120. *oft beſtowes*] *has beſtowed* Qq. *on*] *of* Ff, Rowe i.

121. *You would*] Ff, Rowe. *You'd* Qq et cet.

123. *Infaith*] F₂F₃. *I know* Q₁. *In faith* Q₂ et cet.

---

118. **Courtesy**] COLERIDGE (*Notes*, &c., 254): Here is Cassio's warm-hearted, yet perfectly disengaged, praise of Desdemona, and sympathy with the 'most fortunately' wived Othello; and yet Cassio is an enthusiastic admirer, almost a worshipper, of Desdemona.   Oh, that detestable code that excellence cannot be loved in any form that is female, but it must needs be selfish!   Observe Othello's 'honest,' and Cassio's 'bold Iago, and Cassio's full guileless-hearted wishes for the safety and love-raptures of Othello and 'the divine Desdemona.'   And also note the exquisite circumstance of Cassio's kissing Iago's wife, as if it ought to be impossible that the dullest auditor should not feel Cassio's religious love of Desdemona's purity.   Iago's answers are the sneers which a proud, bad intellect feels towards women, and expresses to a wife. Surely it ought to be considered a very exalted compliment to women, that all the sarcasms on them in Shakespeare are put in the mouths of villains.   BOOTH: Kiss her face; not, as is frequently done, her hand.   Iago winces slightly, for he 'suspects Cassio with his nightcap.'   I was once so irritated by Cassio's kissing the hand of Emilia, despite directions at rehearsal, that I said 'If she would give you so much of her *hand*,' &c., which staggered Cassio and set all the actors giggling.

123 et seq. RYMER (p. 110): Now follows a long rabble of Jack-pudding farce betwixt Jago and Desdemona, that runs on with all the little plays, jingle, and trash below the patience of any Country Kitchenmaid with her Sweetheart.   The Venetian Donna is hard put to 't for pastime!   And this is all, when they are newly got on shore, from a dismal Tempest, and when every moment she might expect to hear her Lord (as she calls him) that she runs so mad after, is arrived or lost.   And moreover 'in a town of war, the people's hearts brimful of fear.'   Never in the World had any Pagan Poet his Brains turned at this Monstrous rate.   But the ground of all this Bedlam-Buffoonery we saw in the case of the French Strollers, the company for acting *Christ's Passion*, or the *Old Testament*, were Carpenters, Cobblers, and illiterate fellows; who found that the Drolls, and Fooleries interlarded by them, brought in the rabble, and lengthened their time, so they got money by the bargain.   Our Shakespeare, doubtless, was a great Master in this craft.   These Carpenters and Cobblers were the guides he followed.   And it is then· no wonder that we find so much farce and Apocryphal matter in his Tragedies.

I finde it ftill, when I haue leaue to fleepe.

Marry before your Ladyfhip, I grant,   125

She puts het tongue a little in her heart,

And chides with thinking.

Æmil. You haue little caufe to fay fo.

Iago. Come on, come on : you are Pictures out of

doore : Bells in your Parlours : Wilde-Cats in your Kit-   130

chens : Saints in your Iniuries : Diuels being offended :

124. *it ftill, when*] *it, I; for when* Q₁.
it ftill, for when Q₂Q₃.
   haue] *ha* Qq.
   leaue] Q₂Q₃Ff, Coll. i,Wh. i. *luft*
Coll. ii (MS). *lift* Q₁ et cet.
126. *het*] *her* QqFf.
   in her] *in* Q₃.
128. *haue*] *ha* Q₁Q₂.

129–133. Verse, ending *doore :...kitch*
ens :...offended :...beds. Qq, Rowe et seq.
129. *you are*] *you're* Pope+, Dyce iii,
Huds.
129, 130. *of doore*] Knt. *adores* Q₁.
of dores Q₂F₂Q₃. *of doores* F₃. *o'door*
Cap. *of doors* F₄ et cet.

Thereby un-hallowing the Theatre, profaning the name of Tragedy ; And instead of representing Men and Manners, turning all Morality, good sense, and humanity into mockery and derision.

124. **Leaue**] DYCE (*Remarks*, &c., p. 237) : When Collier adopted 'leave' of the Folio, what meaning did he attach to it ? did he suppose it to be only another form of 'leve,' 'leef,' or 'lief' (a word which, I apprehend, was never used as a substantive) ? *List* is clearly the true reading. COLLIER (ed. ii) : *Luft* is from the (MS.). 'Leave' merely means 'when I have *permiffion* to sleep,' and has nothing to do with 'leef,' 'leve,' or 'lief.' DYCE (*Strictures*, p. 197) : Collier's present explanation of 'leave' makes Iago talk sheer nonsense.

129. **Pictures**] GÉRARD : Nous avons en français la même expression : 'Sage comme des images.' [This refers to the 'paintings' with which Hamlet taxes women, III, i, 142 : 'I have heard of your paintings too, well enough ; God has given you one face, and you make yourselves another.'—ED.]

129–133. STEEVENS : Almost the same thoughts are to be found in Puttenham's *Arte of Poesie*, 1589 : 'We limit the comely parts of a woman to consist in foure points, that is to be a shrewe in the kitchin, a saint in the Church, an Angell at the bourd, and an Ape in the bed' [p. 299, ed. Arber]. See also Middleton's *Blurt, Mas ter-Constable*, 1602 [III, iii], and *The Miseries of Inforced Marriage*, 1607 [I, i, p. 10, ed. Collier]. Puttenham, who mentions all other contemporary writers, has not once spoken of Shakespeare ; so that it is probable that he had not produced anything of so early a date. The truth is, that this book appears to have been written several years before its publication. See p. 115 [p. 152, ed. Arber], where the author refers to Sir Nicholas Bacon, who died in 1579, and recounts a circumstance, from his own knowledge, that happened in 1553. MALONE : How does it appear that this book was written several years before its publication, from the circumstances mentioned ? Puttenham does not speak of Sir Nicholas Bacon as living ; but speaks of those that *knew* him ; from which we might rather infer that it could not be written before 1578, when that lord keeper died.

131. **Saints**] JOHNSON : When you have a mind to do injuries, you put on an au of sanctity

Players in your Hufwiferie, and Hufwiues **in your**   132
Beds.

Def.   Oh, fie vpon thee, Slanderer.

Iago.   Nay, it is true : or elfe I am a Turke,   135
You rife to play, and go to bed to worke.

Æmil.   You fhall not write my praife.

Iago.   No, let me not.

Defde.   What would'ft write of me, if thou should'ft
praife me ?   140

Iago.   Oh, gentle Lady, do not put me too,t,
For I am nothing, if not Criticall.

Def.   Come on, affay.
There's one gone to the Harbour ?

Iago.   I Madam.   145

Def.   I am not merry : but I do beguile

---

132. *Hufwiferie*] *houfwifery* Q₁. *Huf-*
wifery Ff, Rowe, Pope, Knt. *huswifry*
Cap.   *houfewifery* Q₂Q₃ et cet.
     and] Om. Han.
     Hufwiues] Ff, Rowe, Cap. Knt.
houfwiues Q₁, Pope. *houfewiues* Q₂Q₃
et cet.
     134. Def.] Om. Q₁.
     139. Two lines, Qq.   One line, as verse,
Rowe et seq.

139. *would'ft*] Ff, Rowe, Knt. *wouldft*
thou Qq et cet.
140. *me ?*] *me.* F₂F₃.
141. *too,t*] *toot* F₂.   *to't* QqF₃F₄.
143. *Come on, affay*] *Come, one assay*
Pope +.
143, 144. One line, Qq, Rowe et seq.
     affay. There's] *affay—there's* Qq.
144. *Harbour ?*] *Harbour—* Rowe,
Pope, Theob. Han. Warb.
145. *I*] *I,* F₃F₄.   *Ay,* Rowe et seq.

---

132. **Huswiues**] WHITE (ed. ii) : In Shakespeare's day, and in some parts of England still, *housewife* is pronounced *husif*, which has passed into *hussy*, with a half joc-
ular, half serious, implication of wantonness, which seems not to have been lacking
three hundred years ago.   Indeed, perhaps, we should read here ' hussies in your beds.'

134. JENNENS : Perhaps this speech should be Æmilia's ; Iago's next speech seems
to require it.   COLLIER : In a handwriting of the time it is given to Emilia in the
Duke of Devonshire's copy of Q₁.

138. **No**] BOOTH : Linger on ' no,' with a significant side glance at her.   All that
he says till he speaks ' Aside' should be delivered humorously, to conceal his bitterness, which his features occasionally reveal.

140. **praise me ?**] HORN (i, 340) : Many a poet, heaping up tragic devices for
tragic ends, would have probably represented Desdemona as feeling an involuntary,
foreboding aversion to Iago; but even her very freedom from all forebodings is in
itself deeply tragic, and devised with a rare insight into character.

142. **Criticall**] JOHNSON : That is, censorious.   MALONE : Cf. *Sonn.*, 122, ' my
adder's sense To *critic* and to flatterer stopped are.'

145. BOOTH : Cassio should make this reply.   He has been awaiting their arrival,
Iago has just landed with Desdemona.

146. COLERIDGE (*Notes*, &c., 254) : The struggle of courtesy in Desdemona to

The thing I am, by feeming otherwife.   147
Come, how would'ft thou praife me?

Iago. I am about it, but indeed my inuention comes
from my pate, as Birdlyme do's from Freeze, it pluckes   150
out Braines and all. But my Mufe labours, and thus fhe
is deliuer'd.

If fhe be faire, and wife : faireneffe, and wit,
The ones for vfe, the other vfeth it.

Def. Well prais'd: 155
How if fhe be Blacke and Witty?

Iago. If fhe be blacke, and thereto haue a wit,
She'le find a white, that fhall her blackneffe fit.

Def. Worfe, and worfe.

Æmil. How if Faire, and Foolifh?   160

Iago. She neuer yet was foolifh that was faire,
For euen her folly helpt her to an heire.

Defde. Thefe are old fond Paradoxes, to make Fooles
laugh i'th'Alehoufe. What miferable praife haft thou
for her that's Foule, and Foolifh.   165

149–152. Prose Ff, Rowe, Pope, Theob.
Han. Warb. Four lines of verse, ending
inuention...freeze...labors...deliuer'd Qq
et cet.

   149. *indeed*] Om. Q₃.
      my] Om. Johns.

   150. *Freeze*] FfQq, Rowe+, Cap. Jen.
frieze Huds. Wh. ii. *frize* Steev. et cet.

   151. *Braines*] *braine* Qq.

   152. *deliuer'd*] *deliuered* Q₂FfQ₃,
Rowe+, Jen.

   153, 154, 157, &c. Printed in Roman, Q₁.

153. *wife:*] *wife,* Qq. *wise,*— Cap.
154. *vfeth*] *vfing* Q₁.
155, 156. One line, Qq, Rowe et seq.
158. *fit*] *hit* Q₁.
160, 165. *Foolifh?*] *foolifh.* F₂F₃.
162. *her to an heire*] *her, to a haire* Q₁.
163–165. Three lines, ending *Alehoufe,*
...her,...foolifh? Qq.
163. *old fond*] *old* Qq.
164. *i'th'Alehoufe.*] *i'the Alehoufe,* Q₁.
i'th Alehoufe: Q₂. *i'th Alehoufe* Q₃.
      haft] *hafte* F₂.

---

abstract her attention. DELIUS: Perhaps lines 146, 147 should be considered as an
aside.

   158. **fit**] STEEVENS: I believe Q₁ has the true reading here, as in *Love's Lab.* IV, i,
127. [To the same effect, STAUNTON. See *Bishop Percy's Folio MS.*, vol. iv.—ED.]

   161, 162. JOHNSON: We may read: 'She *ne'er* was yet *so* foolish that was fair, *But*
even,' &c. Yet I believe the common reading to be right; the law makes the power
of cohabitation a proof that a man is not a *natural;* therefore, since the foolishest
woman, if *pretty,* may have a child, no *pretty* woman is ever foolish. HALLIWELL:
To elucidate this sentence, the reader may remember, that 'if one have so much knowledge as to measure a yard of cloth; number twenty pence rightly; name the days of
the week; or become the parent of a child; he shall not be accounted an idiot by the
laws of the realm.' A statement of which may be seen in *The Student's Companion,*
or the Reason of the Law, 2d ed. 1734.—*Anon.*

   163. **fond**] DYCE (*Lex.*): Foolish, simple, silly.

Iago.   There's none ſo foule and fooliſh thereunto,   166
But do's foule pranks, which faire, and wiſe-ones do.

Deſde.   Oh heauy ignorance : thou praiſeſt the worſt
beſt.   But what praiſe could'ſt thou beſtow on a deſeruing woman indeed ?   One, that in the authorithy of her   170
merit, did iuſtly put on the vouch of very malice it [*317 b*]
ſelfe.

Iago.   She that was euer faire, and neuer proud,
Had Tongue at will, and yet was neuer loud :
Neuer lackt Gold, and yet went neuer gay,   175
Fled from her wiſh , and yet ſaid now I may.

167. *wiſe-ones*] Hyphen, F₁.
168. *thou praiſeſt*] *that praiſes* Qq.
170. *indeed ?*] *indeed !* Sing. *indeed,*—
Dyce, Sta. *indeed,* Glo. Cam. Rlfe, Wh.
ii. *indeed;* Huds.

170. *authorithy*] F₁.
171. *merit*] *merrits* Q₁. *merits* Q₂Q₃.
171, 172. *it ſelfe.*]Ff, Ktly. *it ſelfe ?*
Qq et cet.
175. *went neuer*] *never went* Theob. ii.

170. STEEVENS : The hint for this question, and the metrical reply of Iago, is taken
from a strange pamphlet, called *Choice, Chance, and Change, or Conceits in their Colours,* 1606 ; when after Tidero has described many ridiculous characters in verse, Arno-
filo asks him, 'But, I pray thee, didst thou write none in commendation of some worthy
creature ?' Tidero then proceeds, like Iago, to repeat more verses. [It would not have
been worth while to cite this note of Steevens, had not SINGER repeated it, without
acknowledgement, in both his First and Second editions. I never saw the pamphlet,
and dislike to depart from the safe rule of verifying all Steevens's citations, especially
those wherefrom Steevens asserts that Shakespeare 'took hints,' assertions always doubtful, frequently absurd, and here especially uncertain, in view of the date 1606.—ED.]

171. **put on**] THEOBALD could not understand how merit could put *on* the vouch
of malice. ' I should rather think,' he says, 'that merit was so safe in itself, as to repel
and put off all that malice and envy could advance to its prejudice.' He therefore
changed his text to ' put *down*.' WARBURTON : The sense is, one that was so conscious of her own merit, and of the authority her character had with every one, that
she durst venture to call upon malice itself to vouch for her. This was some commendation. And the character only of the clearest virtue ; which could force malice, even
against its nature, to do justice. JOHNSON : To *put on* the vouch of malice, is to
assume a character vouched by the testimony of malice itself. CAPELL (p. 142) : ' Put
on ' is—push on, push forward the unwilling ; so that the sense is—push malice on to
vouch, dare it to give its testimony, say what it knows of her ; this is the very force
of ' put on ' and ' vouch,' and their explanation combin'd ; and other comment than
this the passage does not require.

173 &c. BOOTH : These lines should be spoken as though composed on the spur of
the moment ; not glibly, as though studied beforehand.

173. **She that**] ABBOTT, § 268 : Generally it will be found that *which* is more defi
nite than *that*. *Which* follows a name, *that* a pronoun. Sometimes *which* is used in
this sense to denote an individual or a defined class, while *that* denotes a hypothetical
person or an indefinite class, as here.

She that being angred, her reuenge being nie,   177
Bad her wrong stay, and her displeasure flie:
She that in wisedome neuer was so fraile,
To change the Cods-head for the Salmons taile: 180
She that could thinke, and neu'r disclose her mind,
See Suitors following, and not looke behind:
She was a wight, (if euer such wightes were)
    Des. To do what?
    Iago. To suckle Fooles, and chronicle small Beere.   185

177. being] *when* Pope+.
181. neu'r] *ne're* QqF₃F₄. *nev'r* F₂. *ne'er* Rowe.
182. Om. Q₁.
    not] *ne'er* Johns.

183. such wightes] Ff, Knt, Sta. Del. *such wight* Qq et cet.
were)] F₂F₃, Rowe ii+, Jen. *were.* Q₁. *were,*) Q₂, Rowe i. *were.*) F₄. *were,—* Johns.

180. To] For the omission of *as* in relative constructions, see *Lear,* I, iv, 36, or ABBOTT, § 281.

180. Cods-head] STEEVENS: That is, to exchange a delicacy for coarser fare. See Queen Elizabeth's Household Book for the 43d year of her Reign: 'Item, the Master Cookes have to fee all the salmons' tailes,' &c., p. 296. WHITE (ed. ii): That is, to give up the best part of a homely thing for the worst part of something very fine. LÜDERS (p. 43) detects herein another, and für feinere Ohren weniger schmackhafte Bedeutung. PURNELL: By the despised salmon's tail he means Othello, whom she had chosen in preference to the wealthy, curled darlings of Venice.

182. BOOTH: A glance at Roderigo would imply that Desdemona is the 'wight' particularly referred to. Roderigo has long been an unnoticed follower. [Qu. Ought not Roderigo to be disguised? Did not Iago tell him to defeat his favour with a usurped beard? It seems almost impossible to suppose that Cassio had never met in Venice, Desdemona's assiduous wooer, Roderigo, and yet see line 297 of this scene, where Iago tells Roderigo that Cassio does not know him. Can this refer to anything else than to his 'defeated favour'?—ED.]

183, 185. were . . . Beere] This rhyme is recorded merely in Ellis's *Early-Eng. Pron.,* p. 965. It is hazardous to deny that a perfect rhyme is here intended, and yet it seems to me that Iago pauses so long in search of one that Desdemona breaks in with her question; and that Iago, thus spurred, rushes to his lame and impotent conclusion, where a defective rhyme would indicate its off-hand character, and supply a dash of humour to counteract the bitterness. There is, however, authority elsewhere for rhyming *were* and *beer.* In *Com. of Err.* IV, ii, 9–10, we have *were* and *here;* in *R. of L.* 631, *were* and *appear;* in *Sonn.* 140, 5, *were* and *near;* but *were* rhymes with *bear* in *Sonn.* 13, 6. Chapman frequently rhymes *here, were, there, cheer,* and *dear.*—ED.

185. Chronicle] In this word JOHNSON discerned an allusion 'to the Roman practice of marking the jars with the name of the Consul. The appearance of such a woman would make an era, but as the merit of the best woman is but small, that era might be properly applied to the distinction of the different ages of small beer.' This note was not repeated in either of the two editions which Dr Johnson and Steevens afterwards edited. In its stead appeared the interpretation by STEEVENS, which has been since then generally accepted, 'of keeping the accounts of a household.'

Defde. Oh moft lame and impotent conclufion. Do   186
not learne of him *Æmilia*, though he be thy husband.
How fay you (*Caffio*) is he not a moft prophane, and liberall Counfailor ?

Caffio. He fpeakes home (Madam) you may rellifh   190
him more in the Souldier, then in the Scholler.

Iago. He takes her by the palme : I, well faid, whifper. With as little a web as this, will I enfnare as great
a Fly as *Caffio*. I fmile vpon her, do : I will giue thee
in thine owne Courtfhip. You fay true, 'tis fo indeed.   195
If fuch tricks as thefe ftrip you out of your Lieutenantrie, it had beene better you had not kifs'd your three fingers fo oft, which now againe you are moft apt to play
the Sir, in. Very good : well kifs'd, and excellent Curt-   199

186–189. Four lines, ending *conclufion :*
...*husband ;*...*liberall*...*Counfellour.* Qq.
187. *learne*] *larne* Q₃.
188. *liberall*] *illiberal* Han.
189. *Counfailor*] *censurer* Theob. Han.
Cap. Coll. iii (MS), Huds.
190, 191. *He...him*] One line, Qq.
191. *the Scholler*] *Scholler* F₂.
[They converse apart. Cap.
192. Iago.] Iago. Aside. Rowe.
I,] *I* Qq. Ay, Rowe et seq.
faid,] *fed,* Qq. said— Rowe.
whifper] *whisper*— Rowe.
193. *With as...will I*] *as...will* Q₁.
194. *Fly*] *Flee* Q₁. *Flie* Q₂Q₃.
I fmile] *I, fmile* Q₂Q₃Ff. Ay,
smile Rowe.
do :] *do*— Rowe.

194. *giue*] F₃F₄. *catch* Qq, Jen. *gyve*
F₂, Rowe et cet. *glue* Daniel.
thee] *you* Qq, Jen.
195. *thine*] *your* Qq, Jen.
Courtfhip] *courtefies* Q₁, Jen.
indeed.] *indeed*— Rowe.
196, 197. *Lieutenantrie*] *Lieutenancy*
Rowe+, Jen.
197. *kifs'd*] *rift* Qq.
198. *againe*] *againe*, Qq.
199. *Very good*] *good* Q₁. *Very good*—
Rowe.
kifs'd,] *kiss'd !* Steev. et seq.
(Johns. conj.).
and] Q₂Q₃Ff, Rowe+, Cap. Knt.
an Q₁ et cet.
Curtfie] *courtefie* Qq. *Curtefie*
F₄.

188. **prophane**] JOHNSON : Gross of language, of expression broad and brutal. See
'profane wretch,' I, i, 127.

188. **liberall**] WARBURTON : Licentious.

189. **Counsailor**] JOHNSON : This seems to mean not so much a man that *gives*
counsel, as one that discourses fearlessly and volubly. A talker.

192. COLERIDGE (*Notes*, &c., 254) calls attention in this speech to the importance
given to trifles, and made fertile by the villainy of the observer.

192. **palme**] BOOTH : The hands of both should be ungloved. They seldom are so.

192. **well said**] SCHMIDT (s. v. 4, 2) : That is, *well done.* So also IV, i, 133, and
V, i, 124.

194. **giue**] POPE : Catch, shackle.

195. **Courtship**] KNIGHT : This is used for paying courtesies.

195. **You . . . indeed**] DELIUS : This is in answer to Cassio's last speech.

197. **three fingers**] BOOTH : Cassio kisses his three fingers as though describing
some pleasing act or scene, not as though complimenting Desdemona.

fie : 'tis fo indeed.   Yet againe, your fingers to your   200
lippes ? Would they were Clufter-pipes for your
fake.

The Moore I know his Trumpet.

Caffio.   'Tis truely fo.

Def.   Let's meete him, and recieue him.   205

Caffio.   Loe, where he comes.

Enter Othello, and Attendants.

Oth.   O, my faire Warriour.

Def.   My deere *Othello*.

Othe.   It giues me wonder great, as my content   210
To fee you heere before me.

Oh my Soules Ioy :

If after euery Tempeft, come fuch Calmes,

May the windes blow, till they haue waken'd death :   214

---

200. *'tis fo] tis* Q₃.
    againe,] againe Q₂Q₃.   *again—*
Rowe.
    to] at Qq, Jen.
  201. *Clufter-pipes] Clifterpipes* Qq.
Clifter-pipes F₂F₃.   *Clyfter-pipes* F₄.
  202. *fake.] fake.—* Q₁Q₃.
    [*Trumpet.* Rowe.
  203. *Moore] Moore,* Qq.   *Moor—*
Theob.   *Moor.* Johns.   *Moor !* Coll.
  206. *comes] come* F₃F₄.

207. Enter...] Trumpets within. Enter
...(after line 203) Qq.   (Trumpet Q₂Q₃).
Scene VI. Pope+, Jen.
  211, 212. One line, Qq, Rowe et seq.
  212. *Oh*] Om. Pope, Han.
  213. *come] came* Q₃.
    Calmes] calmeneffe Qq, Steev.'85,
Mal. Rann.   *calms* F₄.
  214. *waken'd] wakened* Q₁Q₂.   *wakned*
Q₃.

---

199. **the Sir**] HENLEY : That is, to show your good breeding and gallantry. STAUN-
TON : The courtier, or gallant.

199. **Curtsie**] JOHNSON : Spoken when Cassio kisses his hand, and Desdemona
courtesies.   MALONE : We have just had 'I will catch you in your own courtesies'
[Q₁].   Here, therefore, he probably meant only to speak of Cassio, while kissing his
hand.   'Well kissed ! an excellent courtesy !' i. e. an excellent salute.   *Courtesy,* in
the sense of *obeisance* or *salute,* was applied to men as well as to women.   'The
homely villain court'sies to her low,' *R. of L.* 1338.   ROLFE : It is doubtful whether
this refers to Cassio or Desdemona.

208. **Warriour**] STEEVENS : In III, iv, 173, Desdemona calls herself an 'unhand-
some Warrior.'   This phrase was introduced by our copiers of the French Sonneteers.
Ronsard frequently calls his mistresses *guerrières;* and Southern, his imitator, is not
less prodigal of the same appellation.   Had I not met with the word thus fantastically
applied, I should have concluded that Othello called his wife a 'warrior' because she had
embarked with him on a warlike expedition, and not in consequence of Ovid's observation : 'Militat omnis amans, et habet sua castra Cupido.'   [Southern was not born until
nigh a half century after Shakespeare's death. Steevens's reading was so extensive,
his memory so tenacious, and his wit so ready, that we shall always owe him gratitude

And let the labouring Barke climbe hills of Seas   215
Olympus high : and duck againe as low,
As hell's from Heauen.   If it were now to dye,
'Twere now to be moſt happy.   For I feare,
My Soule hath her content ſo abſolute,
That not another comfort like to this,   220
Succeedes in vnknowne Fate.
   Deſ.   The Heauens forbid
But that our Loues
And Comforts ſhould encreaſe
Euen as our dayes do grow.   225
   Othe.   Amen to rhat (ſweet Powers)
I cannot ſpeake enough of this content,
It ſtoppes me heere : it is too much of ioy.
And this, and this the greateſt diſcords be
That ere our hearts ſhall make.   230

215. *climbe*] *clime* Qq.
216. Olympus *high*] *Olympus-high*
Steev.'93 et seq.
   high :] *high,* Qq.
217. *from*] *for* Q₃.
   it] *I* Rowe ii+.
223, 224. One line, Qq, Rowe et seq.
224. *encreaſe*] *increaſe* QqF₄.

225. *do grow*] Om. Steev. conj.
226. *rhat (ſweet Powers)*] *that ſweett*
power, Q₁.   *that ſweet Prayer!* Warb.
that.—Sweet powers! Sing.   *that, ſweet*
Powers! Rowe et cet.
229. *And*] *Let* Quincy (MS).
   diſcords] *diſcord* Qq.
   [they kiſſe. Q₁.   kiſſe. Q₂Q₃.

for his labours, and ought not to 'mock his useful toil' if now and then he wanders
far, very far, afield.   Desdemona had protested that she could not stay at home a
'moth of peace,' but must go to 'the War' with Othello; and to that, I think, is the
allusion here.—ED.].   WALKER (*Vers.* p. 175) notes this as pronounced *dissolutè*.
BOOTH : They embrace, with delicacy.   There is nothing of the animal in this 'noble
savage.'

   215. **climbe**] STEEVENS : Cf. 'The sea making *mountaines* of itself, over which
the tossed and tottering ship should *climbe*, to be straight carried downe againe to a *pit
of hellish darknesse*.'—Sidney's *Arcadia*, b. i.

   217. WHALLEY (p. 71): Thus in Terence's *Eunuchus* [III, v, 2; ed. Weise],
Chærea in an ecstasy of joy breaks out in a like exclamation: 'Pro Juppiter!   Nunc
est profecto, interfici quum perpeti me possum, Ne hoc gaudium contaminet vita aegri-
tudine aliqua.'   BOOTH : To be uttered in low, foreboding tones.

   229. **and this**] MALONE : So in Marlowe's *Lust's Dominion :* 'I pri'thee chide,
if I have done amiss, But let my punishment be *this and this* [*Kissing the Moor.*'
STEEVENS : Marlowe's play was written before that of Shakespeare, who might possibly have acted in it [see I, iii, 172].   BOOTH : I think their *heart-throbs* are better
than kisses.   Holding Desdemona clasped to his breast, Othello feels the quick beating
of her heart against his own.   [However much more refined than kissing this interpretation may seem to us to be, the stage direction in the Qq leaves us in no doubt as
to the practice in Shakespeare's day.—ED.]

Iago. Oh you are well tun'd now : But Ile fet downe   231
the peggs that make this Muficke, as honeft as I am.
    Othe. Come : let vs to the Caftle.   [318 *a*]
Newes (Friends) our Warres are done :
The Turkes are drown'd.   235
How do's my old Acquaintance of this Ifle ?
(Hony) you fhall be well defir'd in Cyprus,
I haue found great loue among'ft them.   Oh my Sweet,
I prattle out of fafhion, and I doate   239

231, 232. Prose, Ff, Rowe, Pope, Theob.
Warb.   Verse, ending *now,...mufique,...*
am. Qq et cet.
    231. [Aside. Rowe et seq.
        Oh] Om. Han.
        fet] *let* Pope+, Cap. Jen. Steev.'85.
    232. *make*] *makes* Q_2Q_3.
    233. *let vs*] *lees* Q_3.   *let's* Rowe ii+,
Cap. Mal. Steev.'93, Var. Sing.
    234, 235. One line, Qq, Rowe et seq.

234. *Newes*] *Now* Rowe ii+.
235. *drown'd*] *dro* Q_2.
236. *do's my*] *doe our* Q_1, Pope+, Jen.
Steev. Mal. Var. Sing. Ktly.
        of this] *of the* Q_1.   *in this* Rowe ii.
        [To Montano. Cap.
237. *Hony*] *Honny* Qq.   *Honey* F_4.
238. *I haue*] *I've* Pope+, Dyce iii,
Huds.

---

231. **set downe**] MALONE: Who can prove that *set down* [in opposition to *let down*] was not the language of Shakespeare's time, when a viol was spoken of? To *set* formerly signified to *tune*, though it is no longer used in that sense. STEEVENS: To 'set down' has this meaning in no other part of our author's works. However, *virtus post nummos;* we have secured the phrase, and the exemplification of it may follow when it will. BOSWELL: To 'set down' has the same meaning as to *put down*, to *lower*. Yet, as the phrase to *let down* is the usual phrase, and might be easily corrupted, it was probably the true one. COWDEN-CLARKE: It is possible that '*set* down' was formerly as much a technical musical phrase as '*let* down' is now. HUDSON: It is worth noting that Milton's Satan relents at the prospect of ruining the happiness before him, and prefaces the deed with a gush of pity for the victims; whereas the same thought puts Iago in a transport of jubilant ferocity. Is our idea of Satan's wickedness enhanced by his thus indulging such feelings, and then acting in defiance of them, or as if he had them not? or is Iago more devilish than he? BOOTH: This should be spoken with calm assurance; not too pointedly. He knows he will make the discord,—so does the audience.

236. **Acquaintance**] CAPELL supposed that this was addressed to Montano only, but both JENNENS and KNIGHT assume that it is here a noun of multitude.

237. **well desir'd**] STEEVENS: That is, much solicited by invitations. So in the *Paston Letters :* 'at the whych weddyng I was with myn hostes, and also desyryd by the jentylman hym selfe' [i, 296, ed. Fenn; iii, 241, ed. Gairdner]. DELIUS doubts this interpretation, and prefers the simpler and more obvious meaning of *welcome, well beloved*, like 'a well-wish'd king' in *Meas. for Meas.*, II, iv, 27; in which both ROLFE and the present editor agree with him.

239. **fashion**] JOHNSON: Out of method, without any settled order of discourse.

239. **dote**] SCHMIDT: Talk irrationally. GÉRARD: Comparez le mot **français** *radote·*

In mine owne comforts. I prythee, good *Iago*,   240
Go to the Bay, and difimbarke my Coffers :
Bring thou the Mafter to the Cittadell ,
He is a good one, and his worthyneffe
Do's challenge much refpeĉt. Come *Defdemona*,
Once more well met at Cyprus.   245

Exit Othello and Defdemona.

Iago. Do thou meet me prefently at the Harbour.
Come thither, if thou be'ft Valiant, (as they fay bafe men
being in Loue, haue then a Nobilitie in their Natures,
more then is natiue to them) lift-me; the Lieutenant to   250

---

240. *comforts*] *comfort* Pope+.
   I] Om. Pope+.
   prythee] *preethee* Q$_1$. *prethee* Q$_2$Q$_3$
F$_3$F$_4$.
241. *difimbarke*] *difembarke* F$_3$F$_4$.
   my] *thy* Ff.
244. *Do's*] *Doe's* F$_2$.
   Defdemona.] Defdemoda Q$_3$.
246. Exit...] Exit. Q$_1$. Exeunt. Q$_2$Q$_3$.
Exeunt. F$_4$.
   Scene VII. Pope+, Jen.

247. *thou*] *you* Ff, Rowe+, Cap.
   Harbour] *Habour* Q$_1$.
248. *thither*] Ff, Rowe+, Knt. *hither*
Qq, Cap. et cet.
   [Calling him back. Cap.
248, 250. (*as...them*)] *as...them*— Q$_1$.
(*as*—*them*)— Q$_2$Q$_3$. *as...them*. Johns.
250. *lift-me*.] *lift me.* QqF$_4$, Rowe et
seq. *List me*, Johns.
   Lieutenant] *Leiutenant* Q$_1$Q$_2$.

---

242. **Master**] Johnson says this is the Pilot, but Malone says that the 'Master' is a
distinct person, and has the principal command and care of the navigation of the ship,
under the captain; Steevens quotes from Smith's *Sea-Grammar*, 1627, 'The Master
and his Mates are to direct the course, command all the sailors, for steering, trimming,
and sailing the ship,' &c.

245. **well met**] John Hunter : This generally means *you* (not *we*) are well met,
that is, I am glad to meet you.

247. This dialogue, Coleridge (*Notes*, &c., 255) says, is the rehearsal on the dupe
of the traitor's intentions on Othello.

247. Collier (ed. i): Roderigo, in his foolish haste, was probably starting off to
meet Iago before Iago was himself gone, when he was impatiently recalled by 'Come
hither.' Iago had already told him to meet him at the harbour, so that the repetition
'Come hither' was needless. Afterwards Iago changes his mind and tells Roderigo
to meet him at the citadel. Delius supposes that line 242 was addressed to a servant.
[To me, the simplest explanation of 'Come hither' is that Iago wishes Roderigo to
come nearer to him that he may talk more confidentially.—Ed.].

248. **they say**] Where is this reference to be found ? To this question, with the
suggestion that it might be in Plato's *Symposium*, where love is discussed, Prof. J. D.
Butler (*Shakespeariana*, p. 444, Sept., 1885) replied that the original was to be found
in the following passage: οὐδεὶς οὕτω κακός, ὅντινα οὐκ ἂν αὐτὸς ὁ Ἔρως ἔνθεον ποιήσειε
πρὸς ἀρετήν, ὥσθ᾽ ὅμοιον εἶναι τῷ ἀρίστῳ φύσει.—*Symposium*, p. 179 *a*, ed. Hermann.
'No man is such a coward that love would not so inspire him to valor [or virtue in
the classical sense that he would become like him who is bravest [best] by
nature.

night watches on the Court of Guard.   Firſt, I muſt tell   251
thee this : *Deſdemona*, is directly in loue with him.

    Rod.   With him ?   Why, 'tis not poſſible.

    Iago.   Lay thy finger thus : and let thy ſoule be in-
ſtructed.   Marke me with what violence ſhe firſt lou'd   255
the Moore, but for bragging, and telling her fantaſticall
lies.   To loue him ſtill for prating, let not thy diſcreet
heart thinke it.   Her eye muſt be fed.   And what delight
ſhall ſhe haue to looke on the diuell ?   When the Blood
is made dull with the Act of Sport, there ſhould be a   260
game to enflame it, and to giue Satiety a freſh appetite.

---

251. *Court of Guard*] *Court-of-Guard*
Dyce, Ktly.
    of] Om. Rowe ii.
    muſt] *will* Qq, Jen.
    252. *thee this :* Deſdemona,] *thee, this*
Deſdemona Q₁, Theob. Warb. Johns. *thee
this :* Deſdemona F₃F₄, Rowe, Pope,
Han. Cam.   *thee this,* Deſdemona Q₂Q₃
et cet.
    254. *finger*] *fingers* F₄, Rowe, Pope,
Theob. Han. Warb.
    255. *firſt*] Om. Ff, Rowe.
    257. *To*] Ff, Rowe, Cap. Knt. *and
will ſhe* Qq et cet.

257. *prating,*] Ff, Rowe, Knt. *prating !*
Cap.   *prating ?* Qq et cet.
    thy] *the* Qq.
    258. *thinke it*] *thinke ſo* Q₁.
    260. *be a game*] Ff, Rowe, Pope. *be
againe* Q₁, Theob.+, Del. *be,—again*
Cap. et cet.
    261. *enflame*] *influence* Wh. ii (mis-
print ?).
    to giue] *giue* Qq.
    Satiety] *ſaciety* Q₁Q₂. *ſatity* Q₃.
    appetite.] FfQq. *appetite ;* Rowe,
Pope. *appetite,* or *appetite,—* Theob. Cap.
et cet.

---

    251. **Court of Guard**] STEEVENS : The place where the Guard musters.

    253. BOOTH : Express by a slight pause and by a reflective tone, after ' him,' that
you believe her to be incapable of loving any man but Othello.   In the dialogue that
follows, Iago sees that Roderigo is losing hope, and shows his anxiety by rapid utterance and nervous manner.

    254. **thus**] JOHNSON : On thy mouth, to stop it while thou art listening to a wiser
man.   D'HUGUES : Ces parolles sont accompagnées d'une pantomime, dans laquelle
Iago saisi: la main de Roderigo, et porte l'un de ses doigts sur ses lèvres, comme pour
lui recommander le silence le plus absolu.

    257. The Qq have the better text here, albeit the infinitive in the Ff might be used
as indicating supreme incredulity.—ED.

    259. **diuell**] HUDSON : Another characteristic fling at Othello's color.

    261. **Satiety**] The spelling in Q₁Q₂ is not accidental, but is the same as that in the
only other three instances where the word occurs in Shakespeare.   ' And yet not cloy
thy lips with loth'd sacietie,' *V. & A.*, 1593 ; ' A mere sacietie of commendations,' F₁,
Tim. I, i.   ' And with sacietie seeks to quench his thirst,' F₁, *Tam. of Shr.*, I, i.   I am
inclined to think that occasionally it must be pronounced as a trisyllable—certainly in
the lines from *Tam. of Shr.* and *V. & A.*, where a trisyllabic termination is wholly
out of place.   WALKER (*Vers.* 206) goes so far as to suggest that the Elizabethan poets
dropped the syllable before *-ty* in ' all substantives, such as *honesty, liberty, purity.*   Hence
majesty is almost uniformly a disyllable.'   BOADEN (*Life of Kemble*, i, 252), speaking

Louelineſſe in fauour, ſimpathy in yeares, Manners,   262
and Beauties : all which the Moore is defeƈtiue in.   Now
for want of theſe requir'd Conueniences, her delicate
tenderneſſe wil finde it ſelfe abus'd, begiu to heaue the,   265
gorge, diſrelliſh and abhorre the Moore, very Nature wil
inſtruƈt her in it, and compell her to ſome ſecond choice.
Now Sir, this granted (as it is a moſt pregnant and vnforc'd poſition) who ſtands ſo eminent in the degree of
this Forune, as *Caſſio* do's : a knaue very voluble : no   270
further conſcionable, then in putting on the meere forme
of Ciuill, and Humaine ſeeming, for the better compaſſe
of his falt, and moſt hidden looſe Affeƈtion ?   Why none,
why none : A ſlipper, and ſubtle knaue, a finder of occa-   274

262. *Louelineſſe*] *Loue lines* Q₁. *Loue-lynes*, Q₃.

265, 266. *the, gorge*] *the gorge* QqFf.

266. *abhorre*] *arbhore* Q₃.

267. *in it*] *to it* Qq.

268. *a moſt*] *moſt* Q₂Q₃.

268, 269. *vnforc'd*] *vnforced* Qq.

269. *eminent*] *eminently* Qq, Cap. Jen. Steev. Mal. Var. Coll. Sing. Wh. i, Cam. Ktly.

270. *Forune*] F₁.

271. *further*] *farder* Qq. *farther* Jen. Coll.

272. *Humaine ſeeming*] *hand-ſeeming* Q₁. *human ſeeming* Rowe, Pope. *humane ſeeming* Q₂Q₃Ff et cet.

compaſſe] Ff, Rowe. *compaſſing*

Qq et cet.

273. *moſt hidden looſe*] *hidden* Q₁. *most hidden-loose* Walker, Sta. Del. Huds.

Affection ?] *affections :* Qq, Jen.

273, 274. *Why none, why none :*] Om. Qq, Pope+, Jen.

274. *ſlipper, and ſubtle*] *ſubtle ſlippery* Qq, Jen. Coll. *ſlippery, and ſubtle* F₂F₃. *ſlippery and ſubtle* F₄, Rowe+,Cap. Steev. Mal. Var. Sing. Ktly.

274, 275. *finder of occaſion*] Ff. *finder out of occaſions* Qq, Cap. Jen. Steev. Mal. Var. Coll. Sing. Cam. Ktly, Del. Huds. (*finder-out,* Cap. Del. Huds.). *finder of warm occasions* Johns. *finder out of occaſion* Wh. i. *finder of occasions* Rowe et cet.

of Sheridan's Readings, says : ' The word *satiety* is commonly pronounced, I think, with the full power given to all the letters as they stand, and the accent on the letter *i* in the second syllable.   Mr. Sheridan pronounced it as if written *sassiety*.'   Although Boaden goes on to say that Chapman in his *Homer* always spells and accents this word *saciety*, he does not make it any clearer whether Sheridan pronounced it as of three syllables or of four.   It is scarcely likely that Sheridan pronounced it *sas-si-e-ty;* it would bear too strong a similarity in sound to *society*.   In Sheridan's Dictionary, 1797, the pronunciation is given, sa-ti'-e-ty.—ED.

262. **simpathy in yeares**] PURNELL: Perhaps here, as in *Mid. N. D.* I, i, 137, Shakespeare is thinking of his own marriage.

266. **very**] As in Latin.

268. **pregnant**] NARES: Full of force or conviction, or full of proof in itself. [See *Lear,* II, i, 76, and note.—ED.]

270. **voluble**] STAUNTON: Not fluent in speech, as the word now imports, but *fickle, inconstant.*

274. **slipper**] KNIGHT: Why, when the editors followed the Ff in the arrangement of the words, could they not have retained this fine old adjective ?

fion : that he's an eye can ftampe, and counterfeit Ad-   275
uantages, though true Aduantage neuer prefent it felfe.
A diuelifh knaue : befides, the knaue is handfome, young:
and hath all thofe requifites in him, that folly and greene
mindes looke after.   A peftilent compleat knaue, and the
woman hath found him already.   280

Rodo.   I cannot beleeue that in her, fhe's full of moft
blefs'd condition.

Iago.   Blefs'd figges-end .   The Wine fhe drinkes is
made of grapes.   If fhee had beene blefs'd, fhee would
neuer haue lou'd the Moore : Blefs'd pudding.   Didft thou   285
not fee her paddle with the palme of his hand?   Didft not
marke that ?

Rod.   Yes, that I did : but that was but curtefie.

Iago.   Leacherie by this hand : an Index, and obfcure
prologue to the Hiftory of Luft and foule Thoughts.   290
They met fo neere with their lippes, that their breathes
embrac'd together.   Villanous thoughts *Rodorigo*, when
thefe mutabilities fo marfhall the way, hard at hand
comes the Mafter, and maine exercife, th'incorporate
conclufion : Pifh.   But Sir, be you rul'd by me.   I haue   295

275. *he's*] has QqFf.
  eye] *eye*, Qq.
  275, 276. *counterfeit...it felfe*] *counterfeit the true aduantages neuer prefent
themfelues* Q$_1$.
  277. *A diuelifh knaue*] Om. Qq.
  279. *peftilent compleat*] *pestilent-com-
plete* Walker, Sta. Dyce iii, Huds.
  280. *hath*] *has* Qq.
  281. *in her*] *of her* Pope+.
  282, 283, 284. *blefs'd*] *bleft* Qq, Cap.
Jen. Cam.   *blessed* Var. Coll. Dyce, Sta.
Glo. Ktly, Del. Huds. Rlfe.
  282. *condition*] *conditions* Q$_3$,Cap.conj.
Wh. i.
  283. *drinkes*] *drinke* F$_2$.
  285. *Blefs'd pudding*] Om. Qq. *blessed
pudding* Dyce, Sta. Glo. Ktly, Coll. iii,
Rlfe, Huds.

  286. *fee her*] *fe her* Q$_3$.
  286, 287. *Didft...that*] Om. Q$_1$.   *ded'.fi
...that* Q$_3$.
  288. *that I did*] Om. Qq, Cap.
  289. *Leacherie*] *Lechery* Qq.
  obfcure] Om. Q$_1$.   *obscene* Sta
conj.
  291. *met*] *meet* Warb.
  292. *Villanous thoughts*] Om. Q$_1$.
  Rodorigo] Om. Qq.
  293. *mutabilities*] Ff, Rowe.   *mutuxi
ities* Qq et cet.
  hard] *hand* Qq.
  294. *comes...and*] *comes the* Q$_1$, Johns.
comes Roderigo, *the mafter and the* Q$_2$Q$_3$.
  th'incorporate] *the incorporate* Q$_1$
Q$_2$.   *the incorrupt* Q$_3$.
  295. *Pifh*] Om. Qq.

---

278. **greene mindes**] Johnson : Minds unripe, not yet fully formed.
282. **condition**] Johnson : Qualities, disposition of mind.   [See IV, i, 210.]
286. **paddle**] Pufnell : Corruption of *pattle*, to pat gently.
289. **Index**] Edwards (*Canons*, p. 156) : The index was formerly placed at the
beginning of a book.   [See *Ham.* III, iv, 52.]

brought you from Venice. Watch you to night : for   296
the Command, Ile lay't vpon you.   *Caſſio* knowes you
not : Ile not be farre from you.   Do you finde ſome occaſion to anger *Caſſio*, either by ſpeaking too loud, or [318 *b*]
tainting his diſcipline, or from what other courſe   300
you pleaſe, which the time ſhall more fauorably mi-
niſter.

Rod. Well.

Iago. Sir, he's raſh, and very ſodaine in Choller : and
happely may ſtrike at you, prouoke him that he may : for   305
euen out of that will I cauſe theſe of Cyprus to Mutiny.
Whoſe qualification ſhall come into no true taſte a-
gaine, but by the diſplanting of *Caſſio*. So ſhall you
haue a ſhorter iourney to your deſires, by the meanes I
ſhall then haue to preferre them.   And the impediment   310
moſt profitably remoued, without the which there were
no expectation of our proſperitie.   312

296, 297. *for the*] *for your* Q₁. *for* Q₂Q₃.

300. *tainting*] *taunting* Cap. conj. (p. 26 a).

    courſe] *cauſe* Q₁, Coll. iii.

304. *he's*] Ff, Rowe+, Knt. *he is* Qq et cet.

305. *happely*] *haply with his Trunchen* Qq, Jen. Steev. Mal. Coll. Sing. Wh. i, Ktly. (*hoply* Q₃. *happely* Wh. i). *happily* Ff, Rowe+. *haply* Johns. et cet.

306. *theſe*] *those* Rowe ii+.

    Cyprus] ·Cypres Q₁.

306. *Mutiny*.] *mutiny*, Qq.   *mutiny* . Pope et seq.

307. *qualification*] *qualifications* Jen. *taſte*] *truſt* Q₁.   *taſt* Q₃.

307, 308. *againe*] *again't* Qq.

308. *by the*] *by* F₃F₄, Rowe+.

    diſplanting] *diſplaying* Q₃. *transplanting* Theob. ii, Warb.

310. *impediment*] *impediments* Rowe ii+.

311. *profitably*] *profitable* Q₃.

    the which] *which* Qq, Pope+, Jen.

    were] *was* Pope, Theob. Han. Warb.

297. **knowes you not**] See note, line 182.

300. **tainting**] JOHNSON : Throwing a slur upon his discipline.

307. **qualification**] JOHNSON : Whose resentment shall not be so *qualified* or *tempered* as to be *well tasted*, as not to *retain some bitterness*.   The phrase is harsh, at least to our ears.   SINGER : ' Qualification,' in our old writers, signifies appeasement, pacification, assuagement of anger.   ' To appease and *qualifie* one that is angry ; tranquillum facere ex irato.'—Baret.   STAUNTON : Whose *temperament, crasis.* [In Baret, 1580, I do not find the definition literally as cited by Singer.   Under ' Appease ' (to which the word ' qualifie ' is referred) is given, ' To asswage, appease or qualifie.   Iracundias restinguere et cupiditates.—Cic.'   I do not think that Dr. Johnson's paraphrase is happy, although it is adopted by both DYCE and ROLFE.   HALLIWELL, HUDSON, COWDEN-CLARKE, and PURNELL follow Singer.—ED.]

310. **preferre**] MALONE : That is, advance, promote.

Rodo.   I will do this, if you can bring it to any oppor-   313
tunity.

Iago.   I warrant thee.   Meete me by and by at the   315
Cittadell.   I muſt fetch his Neceſſaries a Shore.   Farewell.

Rodo.   Adieu.   *Exit.*

Iago.   That *Caſſio* loues her, I do well beleeu't:
That ſhe loues him, 'tis apt, and of great Credite.   320
The Moore (howbeit that I endure him not)
Is of a conſtant, louing, Noble Nature,
And I dare thinke, he'le proue to *Deſdemona*
A moſt deere husband.   Now I do loue her too,
Not out of abſolute Luſt, (though peraduenture   325
I ſtand accomptant for as great a ſin)
But partely led to dyet my Reuenge,
For that I do ſuſpeſt the luſtie Moore
Hath leap'd into my Seate.   The thought whereof,   329

---

313. *if you can*] Ff, Rowe+, Steev.'85, Knt, Sing. Ktly, Del.   *if I can* Qq et cet.

316. *a Shore*] *aſhore* Q₁F₃F₄.

318. *Adieu*] *Adue* Qq.

Exit.] Om. Q₃.

[Scene VIII. Pope+, Jen.

319. *beleeu't*] Ff, Rowe, Cap.   *believe* Pope+.   *beleeue it* Qq et cet.

321. *howbeit*] *howbe't* Qq.

322. *conſtant, louing*] *constant-loving* Sta. Dyce iii.

louing, Noble] *noble, louing* Qq.

324. *do*] Om. Pope+.

325. *peraduenture*] *perapventure* Q₃.

326. *accomptant*] *accountant* Q₁Ff.

327. *led*] *lead* Qq.

328. *luſtie*] *luſtfull* Qq, Mal. Coll. i *luſty* Ff et cet.

329. *thought*] *thoughts* F₄, Rowe.

---

313. **if you can**] JENNENS: The sense requires *if I can;* Iago had brought the affair to opportunity by fixing on Roderigo for one of the watch; Roderigo's part remained to be done, viz.: provoking Cassio, which in this speech he promises to do, if opportunity offered to give him cause. KNIGHT: But Roderigo is not one of those who relies upon himself; and the reading of the Ff is far more characteristic. Iago replies to this expression of reliance on him, 'I warrant thee.' DYCE (ed. iii): Iago's reply, in fact, determines nothing; it suits equally well with either lection.

320. **him**] BOOTH: Pause, as though questioning the possibility of this.

322. **constant, louing**] WALKER (*Crit.* i, 29): I think Shakespeare wrote *constant-loving;* inasmuch as Othello's nature, with all its aptitude for true, manly affection, could hardly be described as, emphatically, a *loving* nature.

325, 327. **peraduenture . . . partely**] SWINBURNE (*A Study*, &c., p. 179, note). What would at least be partly lust in another man is all but purely hatred in Iago. For 'partly' read *wholly*, and for 'peradventure' read *assuredly*, and the incarnate father of lies, made manifest in the flesh, here speaks all but all the truth for once, to himself alone.

329. **seate**] COLERIDGE (*Notes*, &c., 255): This thought, originally by Iago's own

Doth (like a poyſonous Minerall) gnaw my Inwardes :   330
And nothing can, or ſhall content my Soule
Till I am eeuen'd with him, wife, for wiſt.
Or fayling ſo, yet that I put the Moore,
At leaſt into a Ielouzie ſo ſtrong
That iudgement cannot cure.   Which thing to do,   335
If this poore Traſh of Venice, whom I trace

331. *or*] *nor* Qq.

332. *eeuen'd*] *euen* Qq, Steev. Mal. Sing.

     wiſt] F₂.

334. *At leaſt*] *At last* Theob. ii, Warb. Johns.

336. *Traſh...trace*] *traſh...cruſh* Q₁, Mal. *brach...trace* Theob. *brach...cheriſh* Warb. *trash...trash* Steev.Var. Dyce, Sta. Wh. Glo. Cam. Del. Rlfe. *brach... trash* Coll. iii (MS), Sing. ii, Huds.

---

confession a mere suspicion, is now ripening, and gnaws his base nature as his own 'poisonous mineral' is about to gnaw the noble heart of his general.

330. **Minerall**] JOHNSON: This is philosophical. Mineral poisons kill by corrosion.

332. **eeuen'd**] According to SCHMIDT (*Lex.*), *even* is used as a verb in two other passages : *All's Well*, I, iii, 3 ; *Cymb.* III, iv, 184. SKOTTOWE (ii, 78) : Of this enterprise of Iago nothing afterwards is heard ; Shakespeare seems either to have forgotten his original intentions, or found that Iago had already enough business on his hands. BOOTH : This line should be very intense, 'not loud, but deep.'

336. **Trash . . . trace**] WARBURTON : 'A trifling insignificant fellow may perhaps be called *Trash*, but the metaphor of hunting is not preserved. I suppose therefore that the word is *brach*, which is a low species of hounds of the chase, and a term generally used in contempt. As to "trace," *crush* of Q₁ is plainly a corruption of *cherish*.' WARTON was the first to suggest that *trash* should be substituted for 'trace,' but he was not strictly accurate in his definition of its technical meaning ; he supposed that it meant simply to *rate*, to *check*, and cited Caratach's reply to Nennius (*Bonduca*, I, i) when Nennius taunted him with flying from the Romans : 'I fled too ; But not so fast,—your jewel had been lost then, Young Hengo there ; he *trash'd* me,' i. e., says Warton, he *stopped* me. At last STEEVENS (1793) discovered the meaning of *trash* which has since been generally accepted. 'To *trash* is still a hunter's phrase, and sig- nifies to fasten a weight on the neck of a dog, when his speed is superior to that of his companions. . . . . "Trash" in the first instance in this line may be used to signify a worthless hound, as the same term is afterwards employed to describe a worthless female : "I do suspect this trash" (V, i, 108). It is scarcely necessary to support the present jingle on the word, it is so much in our author's manner, although his worst.' KNIGHT upholds 'trace,' but was misled in his interpretation. 'Trash' and 'trace,' says Knight, 'are used with perfect propriety. The "trash" is the thing *traced, put in traces*—confined—as an untrained worthless dog is held, and hence the present meaning of *trash*.' DYCE (*Remarks*, p. 237) : Knight's explanation of 'trash' is boi rowed from Richardson's *Dict.*, where we find : 'A *trash*—anything (man, dog) *trashed* or *traced* or confined in *traces*, that it may not, because it would, run or pursue too fast, rashly ; like an untrained dog ; a worthless hound ; hence it is anything worth- less,' &c. But in this explanation Richardson is undoubtedly mistaken ; he gives to *trash* a meaning which it never did and never could bear. When used as a huntsman or dog-trainer's term, or metaphorically with an allusion to their practices, it invariably

For his quicke hunting, ſtand the putting on,   337
Ile haue our *Michael Caſſio* on the hip,

---

signifies *the thing* WHICH RESTRAINS: 'Above this lower roome shall be your hunts-
mans lodging, wherin hee shall also keep his cooples, liams, collars, *trashes*, boxes,'
&c.—Markham's *Countrey Contentments*, b. i. c., i, p. 15, 1615. The *trash*, whether a
strap, a rope dragging loose on the ground, or a weight, was fastened round the neck of
a too forward dog, to check his movements. COLLIER (ed. ii) in justification of his
(MS.) says that '*trash* and *trace* were used somewhat synonymously, as a mode of
keeping back *braches*, i. e. dogs, who hunted too quickly. Iago speaks of Roderigo as
a poor hound, who was so eager in the chase that it was necessary to restrain him.'
SINGER (ed. ii) thinks that Warburton's *brach* is correct, and that *crush* is a misprint
for *trash*. 'The converse has happened in the *Ind.* to the *Tam. of Shr.*, where *brach*
has been misprinted *trash*.' 'Roderigo is cheeked or *trashed* by Iago for his quick
hunting; i. e. he is in too great a hurry to come to an explanation with Desdemona.'
WHITE (ed. i): 'Whom I trash,' i. e. whom I restrain, whip in. 'Trace' seems to
have been only a varied form of *trash*. The misprint in the Qto is evidently due to the
likeness of *c* and *t*. STAUNTON cannot subscribe to Warburton's emendation *brach*,
'although persuaded that "*trash* of Venice" is a vitiation of what the poet wrote.
Trash signifying to *clog*, to *impede*, is surely the genuine word for "trace" of the
Folio.' BAILEY (ii, 108): It is plain to me that the genuine reading is *leash*, i. e.
whom I hold in leash for the quick hunting of the Moor. KEIGHTLEY (*Exp.* 302):
'The jingle,' Steevens says, 'being in Shakespeare's manner.' Now to this I object—
first, that this was not Shakespeare's manner, for the apparent instances of it are mostly
printers' blunders; and, secondly, that Roderigo did not require to be *trashed* or checked
'for his quick hunting,' for he was always hanging back and ready to give up the chase
till urged on by Iago. This last objection also applies to 'trace' in the sense of follow or accompany. It would apply also, though in a less degree, to *train*, which would
yield a tolerable sense. On the whole, I think that Iago's words may have been *praise*,
which would suit his sneering, ironical tone. As to *brach*, though we frequently find it
used of a woman, I believe it was never applied to a man. DYCE (ed. iii): I give the
reading of Steevens, but I now (1865) entertain great doubts if it be what Shakespeare wrote. [I have reserved HALLIWELL's note for the last, because it gives what
seems to me to be the true interpretation; the Folio needs no change; 'trace' bears
here one of its commonest meanings; '*For* his quick hunting' does not mean, *because
of* his quick hunting' but *in order to* make him, *for the purpose* of making him, hunt
quickly, a meaning of 'for' which White (ed. ii) especially notes, and, thus noting it, it
is strange that White should have missed the common meaning of the word 'trace.' It
was Steevens who gave a bias to the word from which it never recovered until Halliwell set it straight, whose note is as follows: 'The meaning seems to be—if this wretched
fellow, whose steps I carefully watch in order to quicken his pace, follows my directions,
I will have our Michael Cassio on the hip.'—ED.]

337. **the putting on]** ROLFE: This refers to h's picking a quarrel with Cassio.
not to his 'quick hunting' of Desdemona.

338. **hip]** JOHNSON: A phrase from the art of wrestling. DYCE (*Remarks*, p. 52):
But in his *Dictionary* Johnson derives the phrase, and with more probability, from hunting: 'the *hip* or *haunch* of a deer being the part commonly seized by the dogs.' [The
phrase occurs twice in *Mer. of Ven.* and here, the only three times in Shakespeare; as
nstances eisewhere are not common, Dyce gives four; in none of them, however, is it

Abuſe him to the Moore, in the right garbe
(For I feare *Caſſio* with my Night-Cape too)   340
Make the Moore thanke me, loue me, and reward me,
For making him egregiouſly an Aſſe,
And practiſing vpon his peace, and quiet,
Euen to madneſſe. 'Tis heere : but yet confus'd,
Knaueries plaine face, is neuer ſeene, till vs'd.   *Exit.*   345

---

339. *right*] Ff, Rowe, Pope, Theob.   *cap* Ff.
Johns. Knt.   *ranke* Qq et cet.   *too*] *to* Qq.
340. *Night-Cape*] *night cap* Qq. *Night-*   344. *madneſſe.*] *madneſſe :*— Q₁Q₃.

---

clear to me that the simile is derived from hunting. Halliwell gives three references;
two, like those of Dyce, are uncertain, one from Fuller's *Historie of the Holy Warre*,
1647, is decidedly from wrestling, 'fearing to wrestle with the king, who had him on
the hip, and could out him at pleasure for his bad manners.'—ED.]

339. **right garbe**] Since JOHNSON'S time, every modern editor, except KNIGHT,
has preferred *rank* of the Qto, which Steevens interprets as meaning '*grossly,* i. e
without mincing the matter,' and cites Marston's *Dutch Courtezan* [III, i], 'Whether,
in the ranke name of madnesse,—whether?' To this meaning MALONE adds, *lascivious,* as in *Mer. of Ven.* [I, iii, 81], 'The ewes, being rank.' For 'garbe' STEEVENS
cites, 'as perhaps employed in the sense here required,' Chapman's *Odyssey* [xviii,
482] where 'cheek-proud Melantho' rails at the disguised Ulysses: 'Or 'tis like To
prove your native garb, your tongue will strike On this side of your mouth.' [Despite
this array of authority, I cannot but think the Folio has the true reading. Iago's plans
are not settled, all is 'but yet confus'd,' details will depend on circumstances as they
arise; the main point is to get Cassio on the hip, and then abuse him to the Moor in
the right garb, in the best fashion, whatever that fashion may turn out to be. If *rank*
were the word here, I do not think that Iago would say '*the* rank garb,' as though
there were but one coarse way of dealing, but rather 'in *a* rank garb.' Whether 'garb'
is here used subjectively or objectively, as the style of address which Iago will himself
assume in approaching Othello or as the address which he will impute to Cassio, is
scarcely important; the question lies in the use of 'right' or *rank.* I prefer the former.
It is, probably, the fear which Iago expresses in the next line that has influenced the
preference for *rank* over 'right.' But this fear is only Iago's 'motive-hunting' for
dieting his revenge on Cassio; it does not specify the manner of his revenge, all that,
as he expressly says, is but yet confused, which would hardly be true if he had already
decided that the garb in which Cassio was to be abused should be *rank.* For references to 'garb' see *Lear*, II, ii, 92. SINGER (ed. ii) says that 'rank garb' is merely
in the *right down* or *straightforward* fashion, and in support refers to 'the right butterwoman's *rank* to market,' which is about as apt as would be the familiar phrase in
which Hamlet's uncle refers to his own offence. An appropriate support of the Folio
is to be found in *Mid. N. D.*, where Helena says, 'I am a right maid for cowardice,'
or in the 'right butterwoman' in Singer's own quotation from *As You Like It.*—ED.]

344. **madnesse**] HUDSON : Here we have perhaps the most appalling outcome of
Iago's proper character—namely, a pride of intellect, or lust of the brain, which exults
above all things in being able to make himself and others pass for just the reverse of

Scena Secunda.

Enter Othello's, Herald with a Proclamation.

Herald. It is *Othello's* pleaſure, our Noble and Valiant Generall.   That vpon certaine tydings now arriu'd,
importing the meere perdition of the Turkiſh Fleete: 5
euery man put himſelfe into Triumph.   Some to daunce,
ſome to make Bonfires, each man, to what Sport and
Reuels his addition leads him.   For beſides theſe bene-   8

---

1. Scena Secunda.] Om. Qq. Scæna
Secunda F₂. Scene IX. Pope+, Jen.
The Street. Pope.
2. Enter...] Enter a Gentleman reading a Proclamation. Q₁.
3. Herald.] Om. Qq.
   pleaſure,] *pleaſure;* Q₁.
4. *Generall.*] *Generall;* Ff, Rowe.
Generall, Qq et cet.
   arriu'd] *arriued* Qq.
6. *euery*] *that euery* Qq.

6. *Triumph.*] *triumph:* or *triumph;*
Qq et cet.
7. *to make*] *make* Qq.
   Bonfires] *bonefires* Q₁Q₃F₃, Pope,
Theob. Han. *bonefirs* Q₂. *Bone-fires* F₄,
Rowe.
8. *addition*] Ff. *minde* Q₁, Pope+,
Jen. *addiction* Q₂Q₃, Rowe et cet. *mind's
addiction* Anon. (ap. Cam.).
   theſe] *this* Rowe ii+.

---

what they are; that is, in being an overmatch for truth and Nature themselves.   And
this soliloquy is, I am apt to think, Shakespeare's supreme instance of psychologic sub-
tilty and insight; as it is also Iago's most pregnant disclosure of his real springs of
action, or what Coleridge aptly calls 'the motive-hunting of a motiveless malignity.'
For it is not that Iago really believes or suspects that either Cassio or Othello has
wronged him in the way he intimates; he is merely seeking to opiate or appease certain qualms of conscience by a sort of extemporized make-believe in that kind.

345. **seene**] JOHNSON: An honest man acts upon a plan, and forecasts his designs;
but a knave depends upon temporary and local opportunities, and never knows his own
purpose but at the time of execution.

5. **meere**] ABBOTT, § 15: That is, unmixed with anything else; hence, by inference, *intact, complete.*

6. **put himselfe into**] For instances of this reflexive use, see SCHMIDT (*Lex.*),
where, however, I find neither this passage nor that quoted by Steevens in *Per.* I, ii, 24.

8. **addition**] DYCE (ed. iii) calls this a 'stark misprint.' Is it?   Granting, for a
moment, that it is nonsense, would it be altogether out of place in the mouth of a
pompous Herald, who has just given us a taste of his quality in the stilted phrase,
'put himself into triumph'?   But is there not a glimmer of meaning to be discovered
in it?   That 'addition' may mean *title* we have seen in *Macb., Ham.,* and *Lear,*
and that it may so mean elsewhere, see examples in Schmidt, s. v.   Would it then
be a 'stark misprint' were the Herald to use it here in this military sense and
transfer the *title* to the holder of the rank himself?   Then the meaning is that the
soldiers are to enjoy themselves according to their rank—a somewhat superfluous
proclamation, it must be confessed; it is hardly to be supposed that Cassio and Iago
would fall to making bonfires; yet is it not in keeping with the rest of the Herald's

ficiall Newes, it is the Celebration of his Nuptiall. So
much was his pleafure fhould be proclaimed. All offi- 10
ces are open, & there is full libertie of Feafting from this
prefenr houre of fiue, till the Bell haue told eleuen. [319 *a*]
Bleffe the Ifle of Cyprus, and our Noble Generall *Othello.*   *Exit.*

Enter Othello, Defdemona, Caffio, and Attendants. 15
Othe. Good *Michael,* looke you to the guard to night.

---

9. *Celebration*] *Delebration* F₃.
  Nuptiall] Ff, Rowe, Pope, Han.
Knt, Dyce, Sta. Glo. Cam. Del. Huds.
Rlfe, Wh. ii. *Nuptialls* Qq et cet.
  11. *of Feafting*] Om. Qq.
  12. *prefenr*] F₁.
    fiue] *nine* Cap. conj. (p. 26 *b*).
    haue] *hath* Qq, Cap. Jen. Steev.
Mal. Var. Coll. Sing. Ktly.
    told] *toll' d* F₃F₄, Rowe, Pope, Han.
Wh. i.

13. *Bleffe*] Ff, Rowe+, Cap. Knt.
Heauen bleffe Qq et cet.
  Cyprus] *Cypres* Q₁.
  13, 14. *Bleffe*...Othello.] As a separate
line, Ff, Rowe, Pope, Han.
  14. *Exit.*] Om. Qq.
  Scene X. Han. Johns. Jen. Scene III.
Cap. et seq.
  The Castle. Theob.
  15. *Enter...*] Enter *Othello, Caffio,* and
Desdemona. Qq.

---

phrases? But there is an instance in *Tro. & Cress.* (I, ii, 24) where 'addition' seems
to stand for characteristic quality or natural bent; it is where Alexander says that Ajax
'hath robbed many beasts of their particular additions; he is as valiant as the lion,
churlish as the bear, slow as the elephant.' This is the meaning that I think it possible for 'addition' to bear here, certainly with enough plausibility to remove it from a
black list of 'stark misprints.' Each man is to betake himself to what sport or revel
his particular disposition leads him to indulge in; and if in 'addition' a military flavor
be found, it is all the more appropriate among soldiers. *Addiction* is a cacophonous
word, never used by Shakespeare, except in one other passage.—ED.

9. **Nuptiall**] RICHARDSON (*Dict.* s. v.): The noun is usually written with the plural termination *s.* Shakespeare writes it without. [This assertion of Richardson is an
illustration of the fact which we are all so liable to forget, viz.: that, omitting *V. &
A.* and *Lucrece,* we cannot know how Shakespeare wrote anything except through the
medium of the printers, whose work, it is believed, he never corrected. In this very
word we find the *s* of the plural in the Qq, which some editors think were fresher from
Shakespeare's hand than the Folio.—ED.]

10. **offices**] HALLIWELL: The rooms appropriated to the upper servants of great
families.

13. **Blesse**] WALKER (i, 215) supposes that the word *God,* softened in the Qq, was
omitted by the editor of the Folio in deference to the well-known act of Parliament; or
was, perhaps, expunged by the licenser of the press.

16. **Good Michael**] COWDEN-CLARKE (*The Shakespeare Key,* p. 91): These few
words, seemingly insignificant, are of important dramatic use. They give augmented
effect to Othello's subsequent anger at Cassio's being betrayed not only into neglect of
duty in preserving order, but into breach of order himself; while they set well before
the mind Othello's trust and confidence in Cassio as his chosen officer, and his liking
for him as a personal friend, calling him by his Christian name 'Michael,' which, after

Let's teach our felues that Honourable ftop,   17
Not to out-fport difcretion.
Caf.   *Iago*, hath direction what to do.
But notwithftanding with my perfonall eye   20
Will I looke to't.
Othe.   *Iago*, is moft honeft :
Michael, goodnight.   To morrow with your earlieft,
Let me haue fpeech with you.   Come my deere Loue,
The purchafe made, the fruites are to enfue,   25
That profit's yet to come 'tweene me, and you.
Goodnight.   *Exit.*

Enter Iago.

Caf.   Welcome *Iago* : we muft to the Watch.
Iago.   Not this houre Lieutenant : 'tis not yet ten   30
o'th'clocke.   Our Generall caft vs thus earely for the
loue of his *Defdemona* : Who, let vs not therefore blame;
he hath not yet made wanton the night with her : and
fhe is fport for *Ioue.*
Caf.   She's a moft exquifite Lady.   35

---

17. *that*] *the* Q₁.
19. *direction*] *directed* Q₁.
20. *notwithftanding*] *notwithftaning* F₄.
21. *to't*] *to it* Qq, Jen.
23. *your*] *our* Mal. Steev. Var.
24. *you.*] *you*, Qq.
   [To Desd. Johns.
26. *That*] *The* Q₁.
   profit's] *profits* Qq.
   'tweene] *'tween* F₃F₄, Rowe+, Knt,
Dyce, Sta. Glo. Cam. Wh. ii.   *tweene* F₂.
twixt Qq et cet.
27. *Goodnight*] Cas.   *Goodnight* Anon.

(ap. Cam.).
27.   Exit.] Exit *Othello* and *Defdemona.*
Qq.
30. *Lieutenant*] *Leiutenant* Q₁Q₂.
Lieutenant F₄.
31. *o'th'clocke*] *aclock* Qq.   *o'clock* Cap.
Steev. Mal. Coll. Sing. Ktly, Del.
32. Defdemona :] Defdemona. Q₁. Defdemona, Q₂Q₃.
   Who] Qq, Dyce, Sta. Glo. Cam.
Del. Huds. Rlfe, Wh. ii.   *Whom* Ff et cet.
33. *wanton the night*] *the wanton night*
Pope, Han.
35. *She's*] *She is* Qq, Jen.

---

the one final impressive appeal, 'How comes it, Michael, you are thus forgot?' he
never again uses.

22.   **honest**] D'HUGUES : Il semble, à partir de ce moment, que l'épithète 'honest'
soit devenue inséparable, dans la pensée d'Othello, du nom de ce scélérat.   La destinée a de ces ironies, et l'esprit humain de ces aberrations.

31.   **cast**] JOHNSON, perhaps forgetting that in I, i, 164, he had given to this word
the meaning which is now generally accepted, to *dismiss*, here interprets it as equivalent to 'appointed us to our stations.   To *cast the play*' he continues, 'is to assign to
every actor his proper part.'   See II, ii, 302, and V, ii, 400, where the meaning to *dismiss* is equally suitable.—ED.

Iago.   And Ile warrant her, full of Game.   36

Caſ.   Indeed ſh e s a moſt freſh and delicate creature.

Iago.   What an eye ſhe ha's ?

Methinkes it ſounds a parley to prouocation.

Caſ.   An inuiting eye :   40

And yet me thinkes right modeſt.

Iago.   And when ſhe ſpeakes,

Is it not an Alarum to Loue ?

Caſ.   She is indeed perfeƈtion.

Iago.   Well : happineſſe to their Sheetes. Come Lieu-   45

tenant, I haue a ſtope of Wine, and heere without are a

brace of Cyprus Gallants, that would faine haue a mea-

ſure to the health of blacke *Othello.*

Caſ.   Not to night, good *Iago,* I haue very poore,

and vnhappie Braines for drinking. I could well wiſh   50

Curteſie would inuent ſome other Cuſtome of enter-

tainment.   52

---

36. *her,*] *her* QqF$_4$, Rowe, Pope, Han.
Jen.

37. *ſhe s*] *ſhe is* Qq, Jen. Steev. Mal.
Var. Knt, Coll. Sing. Wh. i, Ktly, Del.
ſhe's Ff et cet.

38, 39. Prose, Pope et seq.

38. *ha's ?*] *has ?* QqF$_3$F$_4$. *has !* Han.

39. *to*] Ff, Rowe+, Knt, Dyce, Wh. i,
Cam. Del. *of* Qq et cet.

40–43. Two lines, Qq, Pope et seq.

43. *Is...Loue ?*] *tis an alarme to loue.*
Qq, Jen.

43. *Alarum*] *alarm* Mal. Steev.

44. *She is*] *It is* Q$_1$.

45. *Well :*] *Well,* Qq, Rowe et seq.
Sheetes.]*ſheetes—* Qq. *sheets !* Han.

46. *I haue*] *have* Jen. (misprint ?).
ſtope] *stoup* Glo. Cam. Rlfe, Wh. ii.
stoop Rowe et cet.

47. *Cyprus*] *Cypres* Q$_1$. *Cyprus'* Cap.

48. *of*] *of the* Qq, Theob.Warb. Johns.
Jen. Steev. Mal. Var. Coll. Sing. Wh. i,
Ktly.

---

39. BOOTH : Iago watches Cassio intently.

43. **Alarum**] JOHNSON : The *voice* may *sound* an *alarm* more properly than the *eye*
can *sound a parley.*   RITSON (p. 229) : The eye is often said to speak.   Thus we frequently hear of the *language* of the *eye.*   Surely that which can *talk* may, without any
violent stretch of the figure, be allowed to *sound a parley.*   STEEVENS : So in *Tro. &*
Cress. IV, v, 55 : ' There's language in her eye, her cheek, her lip, Nay, her foot speaks.'
BOOTH : So in *Mer. of Ven.* I, i, 164 : 'from her eyes I did receive fair speechless mes-
ſages.'

46. **stope**] It occurred to me that the uniformity of spelling in Qq and Ff might
nere betoken the pronunciation, especially as this form is given by SKEAT as Middle
English.   But a comparison of the five times where the word occurs in Shakespeare
ſhows that no such inference can be drawn.   It is 'stoope' in *Twelfth Night,* II, iii,
14 ; 'stope,' *Ib.* 129 ; 'stoupe,' *Ham.* V, i, 68 ; 'stopes,' *Ib.* 278.   The fact that the
spelling agrees in three cases out of the five might at best indicate that the pronunciation w ͵s in the transition state from the old to the new.—ED.

Iago.   Oh, they are our Friends : but one Cup, Ile   53
drinke for you.

Caſſio.   I haue drunke but one Cup to night, and that   55
was craftily qualified too *:* and behold what inouation
it makes heere.   I am infortunate in the infirmity, and
dare not taske my weakeneſſe with any more.

Iago.   What man ?   'Tis a night of Reuels, the Gallants deſire it.   60

Caſ.   Where are they ?

Iago.   Heere, at the doore *:* I pray you call them in.

Caſ.   Ile do't, but it diſlikes me.   *Exit.*

Iago.   If I can faſten but one Cup vpon him
With that which he hath drunke to night alreadie,   65
He'l be as full of Quarrell, and offence
As my yong Miſtris dogge.
Now my ſicke Foole *Rodorigo,*
Whom Loue hath turn'd almoſt the wrong ſide out,
To *Deſdemona* hath to night Carrows'd.   70

53. *Friends :*] *friends,—* Qq.
  Cup,] *Cup* F₄, Rowe.   *cup :* Qq,
Theob. ii et seq.
  55. *haue*] *ha* Qq.
  56. *too :*] *to,* Q₁Q₂.   Om. Johns.
  57. *infortunate*] *vnfortunate* Qq.
  59. *Reuels,*] *revels ;* Cap.
  63. Exit.] Om. Ff.
  67, 68. One line, Qq, Cap. et seq.
  67. *Miſtris*] *Miſtris's* F₃.   *Miſtriſs's*
F₄, Rowe, Pope.   *mistress'* Theob. et seq.
  67. *dogge.*] *dog :—* Qq.   *dog,* Ff.
  68. *Now my*] *Noy mw* Q₂.
  69. *Whom…out*] (*Whom…out*) Q₂Q₃.
  hath] *has* Qq.
  out] *outward* Qq, Jen. Steev. Mal.
Var. Coll. Wh. i.
  70. *Carrows'd.*] *carouſt* Qq.   *Carrows'd,*
F₂F₃.   *Carowz'd* F₄.

54. **Ile drink for you**] What does this mean?   Is it that Iago will use any and
every argument, even one as ridiculous as drinking by proxy, to induce Cassio to join
the revels ?—ED.

56. **craftily qualified**] JOHNSON : Slyly mixed with water.   [Cannot 'craftily'
here mean *strongly, powerfully ?*   'I have drunk but one cup, and that was "powerful weak," too.'   The necessity of his 'qualifying' his cup *furtively* is not clearly apparent to me, when he confesses the action thus freely to Iago.   To be sure, Cassio may
have accompanied the confession with a wink to indicate that he thought it a good
joke; but this jars a little with my conception of Cassio's character.   I prefer to think
that he openly and freely qualified that first cup, and the innovation it wrought made
him forget to qualify the second among the lads of Cyprus.—ED.]

57. **heere**] BOOTH : Merely a flushed face.

63. **it dislikes**] For similar instances of the use of impersonal verbs, see ABFOT₁,
§ 297.

64. **one Cup**] BOOTH : This should warn Cassio against overdoing the intoxication.

Potations, pottle-deepe; and he's to watch.   71
Three elſe of Cyprus, Noble ſwelling Spirites,
(That hold their Honours in a wary diſtance,
The very Elements of this Warrelike Iſle)
Haue I to night fluſter'd with flowing Cups,   75
And they Watch too.
Now 'mongſt this Flocke of drunkards   [319 *b*]
Am I put to our *Caſſio* in ſome Action
That may offend the Iſle.   But here they come.

Enter Caſſio, Montano, and Gentlemen.   80
If Conſequence do but approue my dreame,
My Boate ſailes freely, both with winde and Streame.
Caſ. 'Fore heauen, they haue giuen me a rowſe already.   83

71. *watch.*] *watch* Qq.
72. *elſe*] Ff, Rowe, Cap. Knt, Dyce i,
Wh. i.   *elves* Coll. (MS).   *lads* Qq et cet.
    Cyprus] *Cypres* Q₁.
73. *Honours*] *honour* Qq.
76, 77. One line, Qq, Rowe et seq.
76. *they*] *the* Qq.
77. *'mongſt*] *amongſt* Q₃.
78. *Am I*] *I am* Qq.   *And I* F₃F₄.
    in] *on* Cap. conj. (p. 26 *b*).
79. Two lines, Qq.

80. Enter...] Enter *Montanio, Caſſio,*
and others (after *Iſle,* line 79), Qq.   Re-
enter...(after line 79), Cap.
    Scene X. Pope, Warb.   Scene XI. Han.
Johns. Jen.
81. *dreame*] *Deem* Theob. Han. Warb.
Cap.
83. *'Fore heauen*] *Fore God* Qq, Cap.
Jen. Sta. Glo. Cam. Dyce iii, Huds. Rlfe,
Wh. ii.

---

71. **pottle-deepe**] DYCE (*Gloss.*): A pottle was a measure of two quarts ('A Pottle, *Quatuor libræ liquidorum, congii Anglicani dimidium,*' Coles's *Lat. and Eng.
Dict.*), but frequently meaning a drinking-vessel without reference to the measure.

72. **else**] DELIUS suggests, with great ingenuity, that this may have been meant for
Ls, the abbreviation of *Lords.*   DYCE (ed. iii): In my former edition I followed the
Folio (comparing *King John,* II, i, 276: 'Bastards and *else*'); but I now think it safer
to adhere to the lection of the Qq.

73. ROLFE: That is, are sensitive with regard to their honour, or quick to take
offence at a supposed insult.

74. **Elements**] JOHNSON: As quarrelsome as the *discordia semina rerum;* as
quick in opposition as fire and water.   SCHMIDT (*Lex.*): A pure extract, as it were,
the very quintessence of the isle.

80. **Montano**] BOOTH doubts if Shakespeare meant to have Montano take part in
this carouse, and therefore makes him enter later from a different direction just in time
to see Cassio stagger off.   STEEVENS felt the same impropriety; see his note line 85.

81. **Consequence**] An instance of the omission of the plural *s* in words whose
termination has a plural sound.   See WALKER'S *Vers.* Art. li, p. 243.   This line is not
there noted.   Or see ABBOTT, § 471.

81. **dreame**] THEOBALD suggested and adopted *deem,* i. e. opinion, judgement.
JOHNSON: I rather read *scheme.* But why should 'dream' be rejected?   Every scheme
subsisting only in the imagination may be termed a 'dream.'

Mon.   Good-faith a litle one : not paſt a pint, as I am a
Souldier.   85
   Iago.   Some Wine hoa.
And let me the Cannakin clinke, clinke:
And let me the Cannakin clinke.
A Souldiers a man : Oh, mans life's but a ſpan,
Why then let a Souldier drinke.   90
Some Wine Boyes.
   Caſ.   'Fore Heauen : an excellent Song.
   Iago.   I learn'd it in Fngland : where indeedthey are
moſt potent in Potting.   Your Dane, your Germaine,
and your ſwag-belly'd Hollander, (drinke hoa) are   95
nothing to your Engliſh.
   Caſſio.   Is your Engliſhmen ſo exquiſite in his drin-
king ?   98

84. *I am*] *I'm* Cap.
84, 104. Mon.] Gent. Booth.
84, 85. *as...Souldier*] Separate line, Qq,
Cap. Steev.'85, Mal.'90.
87. [Jago sings. Rowe.
87, 88. Cannakin] Cannikin Qq, Jen.
87. clinke, clinke :] clink, clink, clink.
Han. Johns. Cap.
88. clinke.] clinke, clinke : Qq.
89. One line, QqFf, Rowe+, Jen. Knt.
Two lines, Cap. et cet.
   Oh...life's] Ff, Rowe+, Jen. Knt,

Wh. i, Sta. Del. *Man's life's* Coll. iii. *a
life's* Qq et cet.
91. *Some Wine*] *Come, wine* Jen.
92. *'Fore Heauen*] *Fore God* Q₁, Cap.
Jen. Sta. Glo. Cam. Dyce iii, Huds. Rlfe,
Wh. ii.
96. *Engliſh*] *Englishman* Coll. ii (MS).
97. *Engliſhmen*] Engliſh *man* Qq.
Englishman Ff et cet.
   exquiſite] FfQ₂Q₃, Rowe+, Knt,
Coll. Sing. Wh. i, Ktly, Rlfe. *expert* Q₁
et cet.

84. **rowse**] GIFFORD (*The Duke of Milan*, Massinger, vol. i, p. 237, ed. 1805):
A 'rouse' was a large glass ('not past a pint' as Iago [sic] says) in which a health
was given, the drinking of which by the rest of the company formed a *carouse*.   Bar-
naby Rich is exceedingly angry with the inventor of the custom, which, however, with
a laudable zeal for the honour of his country, he attributes to an Englishman, who, it
seems, 'had his brains beat out with a pottlepot' for his ingenuity.   There could be no
rouse or *carouse* unless the glasses were emptied.   In process of time both these words
were used in a laxer sense. [See *Ham.* I, ii, 127; I, iv, 8.] BOOTH: Don't be *drunk*,
but silly,—absurdly polite.

85. **Souldier**] STEEVENS: If Montano was Othello's predecessor in the government
of Cyprus (as we are told in the Dramatis Personæ), he is not very characteristically
employed in the present scene, where he is tippling with people already *flustered*, and
encouraging a subaltern officer, who commands a midnight guard, to drink to excess.

87, &c. HALLIWELL: This song appears to be referred to in *The Knave in Grain
new Vampt*, 1640: '*Fub.* The drawers have drawne him out, sir.—*Lod.* Clinke,
boyes.—*Toma.* Drinke, boys.—*Stult.* And let the cannikin clinke, boyes.' The song
itself does not appear to have been discovered.   [This allusion I cannot find in Ingleby's *Centurie of Prayse.*—ED.]

Iago.   Why, he drinkes you with facillitie, your Dane
dead drunke.   He fweates not to ouerthrow your Al-   100
maine.   He giues your Hollander a vomit, ere the next
Pottle can be fill'd.

Caf.   To the health of our Generall.

Mon.   I am for it Lieutenant : and Ile do you Iuftice.

Iago.   Oh fweet England.   105
King Stephen was and-a worthy Peere,

100. *fweates*] *fweares* F₂F₃. *fwears*	dash after *England*, and with *king...peere*
F₄, Rowe.	in Roman) Q₁.
104. *Ile*] *I will* Qq, Jen.	106. and-a] Ff, Rowe, Pope, Han. and
105, 106. *Oh...Peere*] One line (with	a Q₂Q₃. *an a* Theob. Warb. Johns. a Q₁
	et cet.

97. **Englishmen**] STEEVENS : This accomplishment in the English is likewise mentioned in B. and F.'s *The Captain* [III, ii, p. 267, ed. Dyce] : ' *Lod.* Are the Englishmen Such stubborn drinkers ?   *Piso.* Not a leak at sea Can suck more liquor ; you shall
have their children Christen'd in mull'd sack, and, at five years old, Able to knock a
Dane down.'   SINGER (ed. ii) : Peacham, in his *Compleat Gentleman*, 1622, p. 193,
has a section entitled, ' Drinking the Plague of our English Gentry,' in which he says,
' Within these fiftie or threescore yeares it was a rare thing with us to see a drunken
man, our nation carrying the name of the most sober and temperate of any other in the
world.   But since we had to doe in the quarrell of the Netherlands . . . . the custom
of drinking and pledging healthes was brought over into England ; wherein let the
Dutch be their owne judges, if we equall them not ; yea I think rather excell them.

99. **you**] D'HUGUES : Comme on dit en français : 'il *vous* boit.'

103. BOOTH : Iago empties his own glass on the ground.

106, &c. STEEVENS : So in Greene's *Quippe for an Vpstart Courtier* [1592, vol. xi,
p. 234, ed. Grosart], ' I tell thee sawcy skipiack, it was a good and blessed time heer
in England when K. Stephen wore a pair of cloth breeches of a Noble a paire, and
thought them passing costlye.'   HALLIWELL : This ballad is alluded to in Dekker's
Guls Horn-book [1609, vol. ii, p. 210, ed. Grosart] : ' his breeches were not so much
worth as K. Stephen's, that cost but a poore noble.'   [These two allusions, together
with the version in Percy's *Reliques*, point to an English origin of this song.   The
earliest Scotch version (according to J. W. E., *N. & Qu.*, 1876, 5th, v, 249,) is in
Allan Ramsay's *Tea-Table Miscellany*, about 1728, certainly later than Percy's MS.
by three-quarters of a century, if not more.   CHAPPELL (*Pop. Mus.*, ii, 505) remarks
that the 'tune to "Take thy old Cloak about thee" is evidently formed out of *Green
Sleeves*,' an additional reason, perhaps, for assuming its English origin.   The version in
Percy's *Folio Manuscript*, ii, 324, is as follows :

> ' King Harry was a verry good K[*ing ;*]
>   I trow his hose cost but a Crowne ;
> he thought them 12ᵈ ouer to deere,
>   therfor he called the taylor Clowne.
> he was King & wore the Crowne,
>   & thouse but of a low degree ;
> itts pride *tha*t putts this cumtrye downe ;
>   man ! put thye old Cloake about thee ! '—ED.]

His Breeches cost him but a Crowne,   107
He held them Six pence all to deere,
With that he cal'd the Tailor Lowne:
He was a wight of high Renowne,   110
And thou art but of low degree:
'Tis Pride that pulls the Country downe,
And take thy awl'd Cloake about thee.
Some Wine hoa.

Cassio. Why this is a more exquisite Song then the o-   115
ther.

Iago. Will you heare't againe?

Cas. No : for I hold him to be vnworthy of his Place,
that do's those things.   Well : heau'ns aboue all : and
there be soules must be saued, and there be soules must   120
not be saued.

Iago. It's true, good Lieutenant.   122

---

108. them] 'em Qq.
  all to] all too Q₁F₃F₄ et seq.
110. wight] weight Han.
113. And] Ff, Rowe, Pope, Han. Knt.
Then Qq et cet.
  thy] Ff, Rowe, Pope, Han. Knt.
thine Qq et cet.
  awl'd] Ff, Rowe. *owd* Q₁. *old*
Pope, Han. auld Q₂Q₃ et cet.
115. Why] *Fore God* Q₁.
117. heare't] *hear it* Steev. Mal. Var.
Knt i, Coll.

117. againe] *agen* Qq.
118. to be] Om. Qq.
  of his] *in his* Jen.
119. things.   Well:] things : well, Q₁
things well, Q₂Q₃. things. Well— Rowe.
  heau'ns] Heauen's Q₂Q₃F₃F₄.
God's Q₁, Cap. Jen. Sta. Glo. Cam. Dyce
iii, Huds. Rlfe, Wh. ii.
120. must be] *that must bee* Qq, Rowe
ii+, Jen. Steev. Mal. Var.
120, 121. and...saued] Om. Qq.
122. It's] *It is* Qq, Jen. Coll. Del.

---

106. and-a] Compare 'He that has and—a little tiny wit,' *Lear*, III, ii, 74, and
'When that I was and—a little tiny boy,' *Twelfth N.* V, i, 398, where ABBOTT, § 96,
considers the use of 'and' as equivalent to *and that too.* [I doubt if ever in old Ballad
days it conveyed any more meaning than it does now.   It pieced out the line, giving
a swing to the rhythm and a charm of homeliness to the verse which are to me as inde-
scribable as they are indispensable.—ED.]

106. Peere] RITSON (p. 230): That is a worthy *lord,* a title frequently bestowed
upon *Kings* in our old romances.   So, in *Amadis de Gaule,* 1619: 'Sir, although you
be a *King* and a great *lord.*'   Spenser constantly uses the word 'peer' in this sense.

113. awl'd] This, the solitary indication of an unusual pronunciation, points, I
imagine, to a rustic rather than to a purely Scotch origin, although CAPELL seems to
assume that the whole ballad is Scottish.   Speaking of the line in which this word
occurs, Capell, in one of his characteristic notes, says that the usual version, 'something
unscotifies it to it's injury: (*a*) in "*take,*" and what is call'd the diphthong in "*auld,*"
should have the Scottish twang with them, namely—our (*ah*) sounded broader; and to
make out the line's Iambi, the first syllable of "*about*" must have a small thesis, and
"*thee*" a full one.'—ED.

Caſ.   For mine owne part, no offence to the Generall,   123
nor any man of qualitie : I hope to be ſaued.

Iago.   And ſo do I too Lieutenant.   125

Caſſio.   I : (but by your leaue) not before me.   The
Lieutenant is to be ſaued before the Ancient.   Let's haue
no more of this : let's to our Affaires.   Forgiue vs our
ſinnes : Gentlemen let's looke to our buſineſſe.   Do not
thinke Gentlemen, I am drunke : this is my Ancient, this   130
is my right hand, and this is my left.   I am not drunke
now : I can ſtand well enough, and I ſpeake well enough.

Gent.   Excellent well.

Caſ.   Why very well then : you muſt not thinke then,
that I am drunke.   *Exit.*   135

Monta.   To th'Platforme (Maſters) come, let's ſet the
Watch.   137

125. *too*] Om. Qq.
126. *I:*] *Ay*, Rowe et seq.   *Ay;* Coll.
(*but*] *but*, Theob.
127. *haue*] *ha* Qq.
128. *Forgiue*] *God forgiue* Q₁, Jen. Del.
vs our] *our* F₃F₄, Rowe+.
131. *this is*] *this* Q₃.
left] *left hand* Qq, Cap. Jen. Steev.
Mal. Var. Coll. Sing. Wh. i, Ktly, Del.
132. *I ſpeake*] Ff, Rowe+, Jen. Steev.

'85, Knt, Sta.   *ſpeake* Qq et cet.
133. Gent.] All. Qq, Cap. Steev. et seq.
134. *Why*] Om. Q₁.
thinke then] *thinke* Q₁.
Scene XI. Pope, Theob. Warb.   Scene
XII. Han. Johns. Jen.
136. *Platforme*] *plotforme* Q₁Q₂. *plet-
forme* Q₃. *plat-form* Cap.
Maſters] *maiſters* Q₁.
ſet] *ſee* Rowe, Pope, Han.

126. 'The habit which he [KEAN] had acquired in early life, and which led to such
important results, viz.: that of closely observing the expression of the human face
whenever he had the opportunity, continued with him to the last.   It was in a room at
the Castle one night that he was asked by a friend when he studied?   Indicating a
man on the other side of the room, who was very much intoxicated, but who was
labouring to keep up an appearance of sobriety, he replied, "I am studying now.   I
wish some of my Cassios were here.   They might see that, instead of rolling about in
the ridiculous manner they do, the great secret of delineating intoxication is the endeavour to stand straight when it is impossible to do so.   The only man who ever
played the drunken scene in *Othello* properly was Holland." —*Hawkins's Life of
Kean,* vol. ii, p. 360.

129. **sinnes**] BOOTH: The traditional 'business,' said to be Charles Kemble's, cannot be improved upon.   Cassio drops his handkerchief, and in his effort to recover it,
falls on his knees; to account for this position to his companions, he attempts to pray.
His clothes being awry, his sword has slipped to his right side, and this confuses him
for a moment as to which is his right or his left hand.   Whatever you do here, do 't
delicately and with great seriousness, and show a readiness to fight any one who *thinks*
you're drunk.   The more dignified your manner, the more absurd and yet correct your
performance will be.

131. **right . . . left**] PURNELL: A British soldier is not considered drunk if he
can go through his facings.

Iago.   You fee this Fellow, that is gone before,   138
He's a Souldier, fit to ftand by *Cæfar*,
And giue direction.   And do but fee his vice,   140
'Tis to his vertue, a iuft Equinox,
The one as long as th'other.   'Tis pittie of him :   [320 *a*]
I feare the truft *Othello* puts him in,
On fome odde time of his infirmitie
Will fhake this Ifland.   145
    Mont.   But is he often thus ?
    Iago.   'Tis euermore his prologue to his fleepe,
He'le watch the Horologe a double Set,
If Drinke rocke not his Cradle.
    Mont.   It were well   150
The Generall were put in mind of it :
Perhaps he fees it not, or his good nature   152

---

139. *He's*] *He is* Qq, Ff et cet.
141. *vertue*] *Virtues* F₃F₄, Rowe+.
143. *puts*] *put* Qq.
    him in] *in him* Cap. Coll. iii,
Huds.
147. *his prologue*] Ff, Rowe, Knt.   *the*

Prologue Qq et cet.
    148. *Horologe*] *Horolodge* Q₁Q₂.   *Horologue* Ff, Rowe+, Cap.
150, 151. One line, Qq.
150. *It were*] *Twere* Q₁.   *T'were* Q₂Q₃.
151. *were*] *wete* Q₁.

---

136. BOOTH : Montano enters here, in time to witness Cassio's conduct as he goes off.   D'HUGUES : On a jugé avec raison qu'une pareille exhibition de crapule n'etait pas absolument nécessaire à la marche ni à l'intelligence du drame, et que Shakespeare aurait aussi bien fait de supprimer toute cette scène.

140. **direction**] HUDSON : How differently the liar speaks of Cassio's soldiership to Montano and to Roderigo !   He is now talking where he is liable to be called to account for his words.

141. **Equinox**] ROLFE : Equal, counterpart ; the only instance of the word in Shakespeare.

143. **puts him in**] DYCE (ed. iii) quotes LETTSOM's approval of Capell's emendation : *puts in him.*   [I think that change is needless and the Folio is right.   The 'trust' that Othello put Cassio in was that of being Othello's 'own second,' referred to in line 159.—ED.]

148. **Horologe**] JOHNSON : If he have no drink, he'll keep awake while the clock strikes two rounds, or four and twenty hours.   HALLIWELL quotes a description by Admiral Smyth of an ancient clock, wherein the dial is described as 'divided into 24 hours, in two portions of 12 each, as was customary on the clockfaces of those days.' [This starts the question whether a 'double set' is twice twelve or twice twenty-four ; HALPIN (*Dram. Unities*, p. 18) affirms that as 'the Italian horologe numbers upon its dial-plate twenty-four hours, a "double set" or round, i. e. forty-eight hours, is the true time meant.'   It is, however, of small moment here ; Iago is not to be taken literally as to the very hours and minutes of Cassio's watchfulness.   To Halpin the term is important ; on it he bases his theory as to the limit of a dramatic action.—ED.]

Prizes the vertue that appeares in *Caſſio*,   153
And lookes not on his euills : is not this true ?
Enter Rodorigo.   155
Iago.   How now *Rodorigo* ?
I pray you after the Lieutenant, go.
Mon.   And 'tis great pitty, that the Noble Moore
Should hazard ſuch a Place, as his owne Second
With one of an ingraft Infirmitie,   160
It were an honeſt Action, to ſay ſo
To the Moore.
Iago.   Not I, for this faire Iſland,
I do loue *Caſſio* well : and would do much
To cure him of this euill, But he arke, what noiſe ?   165
Enter Caſſio purſuing Rodorigo.
Caſ.   You Rogue : you Raſcall.   167

---

153. *Prizes*] *Praiſes* Qq.
  vertue] *vertues* Q₁.
154. *lookes*] *looke* Q₁.
156, 157. [Aside. Cap. Mal. et seq.
157. [Aside. Wh. i.
  [Exit *Rod.* Qq, Rowe et seq. push-
ing him out. Cap.
160. *of an*] Om. Ff.
161, 162. One line, Qq. Two lines, the
first ending *ſay*, Mal. et seq. (except Knt,
Sta.).
162. *To*] *Unto* Pope+, Cap. Steev.'85.

162. *Moore*] *Moor, Iago* Anon. (ap.
Cam.)
163. *Not*] *Nor* Q₁.
164. [Helpe, helpe, within (*Italics, in
the margin*) Qq, Om. Ff, Rowe, Knt.
Within, *or*, A cry within, *or*, A cry without, *help ! help !* Theob. et cet.
165. *But*] Om. Pope+.
166. Enter...] Enter *Caſſio*, driuing in
Roderigo. Qq.   Re-enter... Pope.
167. *You Rogue*] *Zouns, you rogue* Q₁,
Jen. Cam.

---

160. **ingraft**] JOHNSON : An infirmity *rooted, settled* in his constitution.   HENLEY :
This explanation seems to fall short of the poet's meaning.   The qualities of a tree are
so changed by being engrafted, that its future fruits are not such as would have naturally sprung from the stock, but derive their qualities from the graft inserted in it.
Conformably to this idea is the assertion of Hamlet concerning the same vice of his
countrymen.   MALONE : Johnson's explanation is certainly just. So in *Lear*, I, i, 295;
' the imperfections of long-engrafted condition.'   See ABBOTT, § 342, for other instances
of the omission of the participial -*ed* after *t*.   BOOTH : This is not the language of one
who had taken part in the carouse.

161. **Action**] WALKER (*Vers.* 230) cites this as an instance in the middle of the
line of the old dissyllabic pronunciation of -*tion*, so very common at the end of a line.

161–236. My copy of Q₂ is imperfect and lacks the page containing these lines.   For
all references to that Qto within these limits I am indebted to the Cambridge Edition,
which we can all trust as implicitly as anything can be trusted which bears the common stamp of human imperfection.—ED.

164. DYCE justifies the stage direction here of the Qq, because Iago, line 252, says,
' There comes a fellow, crying out for helpe, And Cassio following him,' &c.

Mon.   What's the matter Lieutenant?   168

Caſ.   A Knaue teach me my dutie?   Ile beate the
Knaue in to a Twiggen-Bottle.   170

Rod.   Beate me?

Caſ.   Doſt thou prate, Rogue?

Mon.   Nay, good Lieutenant:
I pray you Sir, hold your hand.

Caſſio.   Let me go(Sir)   175
Or Ile knocke you o're the Mazard.

Mon.   Come, come : you're drunke.

Caſſio.   Drunke?

Iago.   Away I ſay : go out and cry a Mutinie.
Nay good Lieutenant.   Alas Gentlemen :   180
Helpe hoa.   Lieutenant.   Sir *Montano* :
Helpe Maſters.   Heere's a goodly Watch indeed.   182

169, 170. Prose, Qq, Pope +, Jen. Cam.
Dividing the lines at *duty!* Cap. et cet.

169. *Knaue...dutie?*] Ff, Rowe, Pope,
Han. *Knaue,...duty :* Qq. *Knave...duty!*
Theob. +, Jen. Sta. Glo. Cam. *Knave,...*
duty! Cap. *Knave to teach...duty!* Dyce
iii. *Knave. ...duty!* Steev. et cet.
Ile] but *I'le* Qq, Jen. Cam.

170. *Twiggen-Bottle*] *wicker bottle* Qq,
Cap. Jen. Coll. Cam.

171. *me?*] Qq, Jen. *me.* Ff. *me—*
Rowe +. *me!* Cap. et cet.

172. [Beats Rod. Cap. et seq.

173, 174. Prose, Qq, Jen. Cam.

173. *Nay*] Om. Qq.
[Staying him. Rowe et seq.

174. *I pray you*] *pray* Qq.

175, 176. Prose, Qq, Rowe +, Jen. Cam.

176. *knocke*] *know* Ff, Rowe.
o're] *on* Q₃.

177. *you're*] *you are* Qq, Jen.

178. [they fight. Qq.

179. [Aside. Cap. et seq.
[A bell rung. Q₁. Exit Rod. Q₂
Q₃.

180. *Alas*] *godſwill* Q₁. *God's-will*
Q₂Q₃, Cam. Del.

181. *Sir* Montano :] Ff, Rowe, Knt,
Sing. *Sir* Montanio, *ſir,* Q₁. *Sir,* Mon-
tanio, *ſir* Q₂Q₃. —*Sir, Montanio*— Pope,
Han. —*Sir*—*Montano*—Theob. +. *Sir,*
—*Montano*—*Sir*— Cap. et cet.

182. *Maſters*] *maſter* Q₃.
[A bell rings. Q₂Q₃, Rowe et seq.

---

168. BOOTH : Montano holds Cassio.

170. **Twiggen-bottle**] BOOTH : That is, slash him till he resembles a 'Chianti'
bottle covered with straw net-work; such a bottle as he has been drinking from, perhaps, is in his mind.   I have such a bottle used,—when I can get one.

178. BOOTH : Here they fight, and Cassio should utter incoherent sounds as though
'high in oath,' as Iago, line 261, states that he was.   I think Shakespeare intended
Cassio to 'cuss' a little.   Montano should not thrust, but merely defend, himself.   For
the same reason, to make his subsequent account of the fray correct, Iago should disappear with Roderigo at the word 'mutinie,' and before they return, almost immediately, let them both shout 'Mutiny! Mutiny!' behind the scenes.

181. **Sir Montano**] KNIGHT : Iago is pretending to separate the lieutenant and
Montano, but he is not familiar with Montano, the ex-governor, and he gives him a
title cf courtesy.

Who's that which rings the Bell. Diablo, hoa: 183
The Towne will rife.   Fie, fie Lieutenant,
You'le be afham'd for euer.   185

Enter Othello, and Attendants.

Othe. What is the matter heere?
Mon. I bleed ftill, I am hurt to th'death.   He dies.   188

---

183. *that which*] *that that* Qq, Cap. Jen. Steev. Mal. Var. Coll. Sing. Wh. i, Cam. Ktly. *that who* Pope+.

Bell: Diablo, hoa:] *bell? Diablo —ho,* Qq.

184. *Fie, fie Lieutenant*] Ff, Rowe, Pope, Han. Sing. *fie, fie Leiutenant, hold* Q₂Q₃, Theob. Warb. Johns. Jen. Knt. *godf-will Leiutenant, hold* Q₁, et cet.

185. *You'le*] Ff, Knt. *you will* Qq et cet.

afham'd] F₃F₄, Knt. *fham'd* Qq F₂ et cet.

186. *Enter…*] Enter *Othello*, and Gentlemen with weapons. Qq.

Scene XII. Pope, Warb. Scene XIII. Han. Johns. Jen.

187. *What is*] *what's* Q₂Q₃.

188. *I bleed*] Ff, Q₂Q₃, Rowe+, Cap. Jen. Steev. Knt. *Zouns, I bleed* Q₁, Mal. et cet.

hurt] *hurt*, Q₁. *hurt, but not* Ff, Rowe, Pope, Theob. Han. Warb.

He dies.] *—he dies.* Cap. Steev. Del. *He dies—* Knt. Om. Q₁, Ff, Rowe+, Jen. Mal. Var. Sing, Dyce i. [he faints. (*As Stage direction*) Q₂Q₃, Coll. Wh. Glo. Sta. Cam. Ktly, Dyce iii, Huds. Rlfe. [He is supported (*As Stage direction*) Coll. iii. [assailing Cassio again. Cap.

---

183. **Diablo**] COLLIER: An exclamation employed by other dramatists. M. Mason observes that 'it is a mere contraction of Diavolo, the Italian word for the devil.' Why should we go to a contraction of the Italian, when 'Diablo' is the ordinary Spanish word?

184. **Fie, fie**] In comparison with the vehement *God's will* of the Qq, this 'fie, fie' does sound weak; but is Iago in earnest? does he wish to be vehement? does he really want Cassio to hold? Between his desire to tarre Cassio on and yet to seem to hold him back, this half-hearted 'fie' seems to me a not unbefitting exclamation —ED.

185. DYCE pronounces this line, as compared with the Qq, 'most ridiculous.' It does not make *me* laugh. Indeed, to me, it is as much better than the Qq as an appeal to a man's own self-respect is higher than an appeal to the opinion the world may have of him. Unfortunately, we must not forget that it is Iago who utters it.—ED.

188. **He dies**] MALONE: The editor of the Folio, thinking it necessary to omit the first word of the line, absurdly supplied its place by adding these words at the end of the line. TOLLET: Montano thinks he is mortally wounded, yet by these words he seems determined to continue the duel and to kill his antagonist, Cassio. So, when Roderigo runs at Cassio in Act V, he says: 'Villain, thou diest.' STEEVENS: That is, *he shall die.* He may be supposed to say this as he is offering to renew the fight. Thus, Othello in his very next speech: '*he dies* upon his motion.' I do not therefore regard these words, when uttered by Montano, as an absurd addition in F₁. KNIGHT and DELIUS give the same explanation as Tollet's. COLLIER: These words are, in fact, nothing more than a printer's blunder, which F₂ corrects by making Montano say, 'I am hurt, but *not* to the death.' The true stage direction, for which 'He dies' was, no doubt, intended, is found in Q₂, 'He faints.' [It is not easy here to decide between the rival claims. As stage directions there are objections both to 'He dies' and 'He

Othe.   Hold for your liues.

Iag.   Hold hoa : Lieutenant, Sir *Montano*, Gentlemen :   190
Haue you forgot all place of fenfe and dutie?
Hold.   The Generall fpeaks to you : hold for fhame.
Oth.   Why how now hoa ? From whence arifeth this?
Are we turn'd Turkes ? and to our felues do that
Which Heauen hath forbid the *Ottamittes*.   195
For Chriftian fhame, put by this barbarous Brawle :
He that ftirs next, to carue for his owne rage,
Holds his foule light : He dies vpon his Motion.
Silence that dreadfull Bell, it frights the Ifle,   199

190. *Hold hoa :*] F₂F₃. *Hold, hold* Q₁Q₂, Jen. Steev. Mal. Var. Coll. *Holp, hold* Q₃. *Hold ho :* F₄, Rowe et cet.
Sir Montano,] F₂F₄, Jen. Knt, Sing. Wh. i. *fir* Montanio, Qq. *Sir* Montane, F₃. *Sir, Montano* Mal. Steev. Var. Coll. Ktly. *Sir—Montano—* Rowe et cet.
191. *place of fenfe*] QqFf, Rowe, Pope, Theob. Steev.'85. *sense of place* Han. et cet.
192. *Hold.*] Om. Pope +. *Hold, hold!*

Cap. Steev. Mal. Var. Coll. Wh. i, Ktly Closing line 191, Huds.
192. *hold for*] *hold, hold, for* Qq, Pope +, Jen. Glo. Cam. Huds. Rlfe, Wh. ii. *for* Wh. i.
193. *arifeth*] *arifes* Qq.
195. *hath*] *has* Qq.
Ottamittes] Ottamites QqF₄. Ottomites Q'95 et seq.
197. *for his*] *forth his* Q₁, Jen. Steev. '85, Mal. Var.

---

faints.' Assuredly Montano does not die ; and it is difficult to see with what propriety a man who had fainted could be adjured to stop fighting, both by Othello and Iago. If these words be not a stage direction, but a part of the text, there is to Tollet's interpretation this objection, viz. : that Montano was acting throughout in self-defence, as he himself tells Othello, line 227, which he would have scarcely presumed to assert had he renewed the attack with such bitterness before Othello's very eyes. This is one of the passages, I think, where it will not do to inquire too closely. The dramatic action demands a barbarous brawl, in which Montano shall be worsted, and latitude is given to the actors to portray the extent of his discomfiture. I am not sure that COWDEN-CLARKE'S course of omitting the words altogether be not the wisest.—ED.]

196. **barbarous Brawle**] WORDSWORTH (*Sh.'s Knowl. and Use of the Bible*, p. 225) : This line is one of those which make it difficult to believe that Shakespeare had altogether forgotten his schoolboy classics. Surely, when he wrote it he was thinking of Horace [Lib. I, Ode xxvii] : 'Natis in usum lætitiæ scyphis Pugnare Thracum est ; *tollite barbarum Morem*, verecundumque Bacchum *Sanguineis* prohibite *rixis*.' FECHTER : Othello speaks with passion.

197. **carue for**] STEEVENS : That is, supply food or gratification for his own anger. So in *Ham.* I, iii, 20 : 'he may not . . . . Carve for himself.' SCHMIDT : To indulge, to act at a person's pleasure.

198. BOOTH : Iago should go to assist Cassio, hoping that he is hurt. The Gentlemen enter in time to care for Montano, whom they place on the seat where Desdemona sat.

199. **dreadful bell**] WALKER (*Crit.* ii, 78) cites this as an instance of the use of dreadful' in an active sense, as in *Ham.* I, ii, 207 : 'This to me In dreadful secrecy

From her propriety.   What is the matter, Mafters?   200
Honeft *Iago*, that lookes dead with greeuing,
Speake *:* who began this?   On thy loue I charge thee?
   Iago.   I do not know : Friends all, but now, euen now.
In Quarter, and in termes like Bride, and Groome   204

200. *What is*] *what's* Qq, Jen.   et cet.
     Mafters] Om. Pope+.   202. *this?*] *this,* Qq.
201. *lookes*] QqF$_2$. *looks* F$_3$F$_4$, Rowe,   203. *not*] *not not* F$_2$.
Pope, Theob. Warb. Johns. *look'st* Han.   *all,*] *all* Qq, Cap. Steev. et seq.

impart they did.'   MALONE: When David Rizzio was murdered in Edinburgh, the
Provost ordered the *common bell* to be rung, and five hundred persons were immediately assembled.   So in Peacham's *Valley of Varietie,* where he is speaking of the use
of bells, 'they call for helpe when houses in cities and townes are on fire; or when
there is any mutinie or uproare.'   HALLIWELL: At the poet's native town, Stratford-
on-Avon, it has been the practice from time immemorial to ring the bell of the Guild
chapel on the alarm of fire being given.   ALGER (*Life of Forrest,* i, 308): From the
general group he [Forrest as Othello] turned to a single attendant who stood at his
elbow, and delivered the command in a subdued tone, as though it were not intended
for the ear of the multitude.   OTTLEY (*Fechter's Version,* &c., p. 19): This command
Fechter almost screams in passion, rushing up the stage the while.   Kean gave it calmly
and authoritatively, as a thing of course, and 'more in sorrow than in anger.'

   200. **propriety**] JOHNSON: From her regular and proper state.

   201. **lookes**] An instance (cited by WALKER, *Crit.* ii, 132) of *s* substituted for *st* in
the second person singular of the verb.   Compare IV, ii, 207; V, ii, 79; and two other
striking instances: *Ham.* I, iv, 53: 'That thou .... Revisits thus the glimpses,' &c.,
and *Lear,* IV, vi, 160: 'Thou hotly lusts to use her,' &c.   I think this usage should
be observed in even modern editions, when to give the full grammatical form would
result in harshness.—ED.

   204. **Quarter**] JOHNSON: In their quarters; at their lodging.   MALONE: That is,
on our station.   So in *Timon,* V, iv, 60: 'not a man Shall pass his quarter.'   Their
station or 'quarter' in the present instance was the guardroom in Othello's castle.   It
cannot mean lodgings, for Montano and the Gentlemen had continued, from the time
of their entrance, in the apartment of Othello's castle, in which the carousal had been;
and Cassio had only gone forth for a short time to set the watch.   On his return from
the platform to the apartment he meets Roderigo, and the scuffle ensues.   RITSON (p.
230): Rather, *at peace, quiet,* or, as Johnson elsewhere explains it, 'in friendship, amity,
concord.'   They had been on that very spot (the court or platform before the castle)
ever since Othello left them, which can scarcely be called be ng in their *quarters* or at
their *lodging.*   And, indeed, they could not have left it without being guilty of another
offence, as they were directed by Othello to keep the watch.   HENLEY denies that the
phrase ever meant *in quiet, at peace ;* it is evident, he says, that the 'quarter' referred to
was that apartment of the castle assigned to the officers on guard, where Othello, after
giving Cassio his orders, had, a little before, left him; and where Iago, with his companions, immediately found him.   PYE (p. 331): This word, in the military language
of the present day at least, seems to have no very precise meaning; but the meaning
on our station seems the leading signification, for the principal camp-guard of a regiment is called the quarter guard; but a regiment in quarters has no such guard.

Deuefting them for Bed : and then, but now :   205
(As if fome Planet had vnwitted men)
Swords out, and tilting one at others breaftes,   [320 *b*]
In oppofition bloody.   I cannot fpeake
Any begining to this peeuifh oddes.
And would, in Action glorious, I had loft   210
Thofe legges, that brought me to a part of it.
 Othe.   How comes it(*Michaell*)you are thus forgot?
 Caf.   I pray you pardon me, I cannot fpeake.
 Othe.   Worthy *Montano*, you were wont to be ciuill :
The grauitie, and ftillneffe of your youth   215
The world hath noted.   And your name is great
In mouthes of wifeft Cenfure.   What's the matter
That you vnlace your reputation thus,
And fpend your rich opinion, for the name
Of a night-brawler?   Giue me anfwer to it.   220
 Mon.   Worthy *Othello*, I am hurt to danger,

205. *Deuefting*] *Digefting* Q.'95. *Di-
vefting* Q.'81, Rowe ii+, Cap. Jen. Coll.
Wh. i.
 for Bed :] *to bed,* Qq, Cap.
 then,] Om. Q₃.
206. *men*] *them* Coll. (MS).
207. *Swords*] *Sword* F₃F₄, Rowe, Pope.
 breaftes] Ff, Rowe, Pope, Theob.
Han. Warb. *breft* Q₃. *breaft* Q₁Q₂ et cet.
208. *cannot*] *can't* Pope+.

211. *Thofe*] *Thefe* Q₁, Cap. Jen. Steev.
Mal. Sing. Ktly.
212. *comes*] *came* Qq, Jen. Coll. Wh. i,
Hal. Del.
 are] *were* Qq, Jen. Coll. Wh. i,
Hal.
214. *wont to be*] Ff, Rowe, Warb. Knt.
wont be Qq et cet.
217. *mouthes*] *men* Q₁.
220. *to it*] *to't* Qq, Cap. Jen. Sta.

209. **oddes**] STAUNTON : Headstrong or perverse quarrel.

212. **are thus forgot**] See ABBOTT, § 295, for other instances of the use of *to be*
with intransitive verbs.   Thus, 'I am declined,' III, iii, 309.   In BOOTH'S *Acting
Copy*, 'you' is italicized.   Cassio has staggered towards R. H. and rests against a column of the Castle.

213. FECHTER'S *Acting Copy :* 'I pray you pardon me (*Cassio speaks thickly, stops
short, and then, in deep humiliation*) I cannot speak !—'

214. **wont to be**] ABBOTT, § 349, following indirectly the text of the Qq, *wont be,*
cites it as an instance of the omission of *to* of the infinitive, which, of course, it may
be; but the presence of 'to' in the Ff shows that in the Qq it may be merely an instance of the absorption of the *to* in the *t* final of 'wont.'—ED.

215–217. BOOTH : Could it be possible, after this, to suppose that Montano was one
of the 'flock of drunkards'?

218. **vnlace**] JOHNSON : Slacken, or loosen.   Put in danger of dropping; or perhaps strip off its ornaments.

219. **spend**] JOHNSON : Throw away and squander a reputation so valuable as yours.

221. BOOTH : Montano is still seated, supported by gentlemen, one of whom staunches
the wound.

Your Officer *Iago*, can informe you,   222
While I fpare fpeech which fomething now offends me.
Of all that I do know, nor know I ought
By me, that's faid, o r done amiffe this night,   225
Vnleffe felfe-charitie be fometimes a vice,
And to defend our felues, it be a finne
When violence affailes vs.

   Othe.   Now by Heauen,
My blood begins my fafer Guides to rule,   230
And paffion(hauing my beft iudgement collied)
Affaies to leade the way. If I once ftir,   232

---

223. *me.*] *me,* Q₁Q₃. Om. Q₂.
224. *ought*] *aught* Theob. ii et seq.
225. *me,*] *me;* Ff. *me* Q.'95 et seq.
   faid] *fed* Q₁.
226. *fometimes*] *fometime* Qq, Cap.
Steev. Mal. Var. Coll. Wh. i.

231. *collied*] *coold* Qq.   *choler'd*
Rowe+. *quell'd* Cap. Coll. ii.   *cullied*
Bailey.
   232. *If I once*] *Zouns, if I* Q₁. *If once
I* Q₂Q₃.

---

223. **something**] See *Ham.* III, i, 173, and *Lear,* I, i, 20, for other instances of
this adverbial use like *somewhat.*

226. **selfe-charitie**] JOHNSON : Care of one's self.

227. **it**] ABBOTT, § 404: From this passage we may see how unnecessary and redundant our modern 'it' is. This is (if the order of the words be disregarded) as
good English as our modern 'Unless *it* be a sin to defend ourselves.' The fact is, this
use of the modern 'it' is an irregularity only justified by the clearness which it pro-
motes. 'It,' at the beginning of a sentence, calls attention to the real subject which is
to follow. '*It* is a sin, viz., to defend one's self.'

229. BOOTH : With restrained anger—not loud.

231. **collied**] STEEVENS : That is, passion having discoloured his judgement. To
colly anciently signified to *besmut,* to *blacken as with coal.* MALONE : Cole in his *Dict.,*
1679, renders '*collow'd* by *denigratus;* to *colly, denigro.*' COLLIER (ed. ii) : *Quelled,*
i. e. subdued or conquered, is precisely the word wanted, and we find it in the (MS).
It is to be remarked that if short-hand were employed in obtaining the copy of *Othello*
for the publisher, the very same letters which spell *quelled* would also spell 'collied,'
and even *cool'd.* SINGER (*Sh. Vind.,* p. 283) : To *quell* is never used by Shakespeare
in any other sense than that of killing or exterminating. I pity the man who could for
a moment think of displacing the effective, and now consecrated, word 'collied.' Its
obvious meaning is *darkened, obfuscated;* and a more appropriate and expressive word
could not have been used. DYCE (*Strictures,* &c., p. 199), after referring to the use of
'collied' in *Mid. N. D.* I, i, 145, and after citing with approval what Singer says of the
uniform meaning of *quell* in Shakespeare, and after quoting what Collier says about
short-hand spelling, goes on to say : Yet no one knows better than Mr Collier that the
Othello of F₁, which has the reading 'collied,' *was, beyond all doubt, printed from a
transcript belonging to the theatre, and that in stage-copies of plays (whether intended
for the use of the prompter or of the actors) short-hand was never employed.* [Italics,
Dyce's.] KEIGHTLEY (*Exp.* p. 302) : *Quelled* is not so absurd as Singer thinks it.
D'HUGUES : On s'étonne qu'Othello puisse trouver de si belles métaphores pour ex-
primer sa colère, au moment même où il commence à la ressentir. [See III, iii, 283.]

Or do but lift this Arme, the beft of you   233
Shall finke in my rebuke.   Giue me to know
How this foule Rout began : Who fet it on,   235
And he that is approu'd in this offence,
Though he had twinn'd with me, both at a birth,
Shall loofe me.   What in a Towne of warre,
Yet wilde, the peoples hearts brim-full of feare,
To Manage priuate, and domefticke Quarrell ?   240
In night, and on the Court and Guard of fafetie ?
'Tis monftrous : *Iago*, who began't ?   242

236. *this*] *his* Rowe ii, Pope, Han.
237. *twinn'd*] *twin'd* Q$_1$.
238. *Shall*] *should* Q$_3$.
  loofe] QqFf, Rowe i, Jen. Knt.
loosen Cap. *lose* Q.'95 et cet.
  me.] *me ever.* Lettsom.
  What in] Ff, Rowe i. *what, in*
Qq, Rowe ii, Pope. *What, and in* Han.
What ! in Cap. et seq. *What ! even in*
Huds. conj.
  of warre,] *with war* Daniel, Huds.

240. *Quarrell*] *quarrels* Qq, Jen.
241. *and guard of*] *of guard and*
Theob. Han. Johns. Cap. Mal. Var. Sing.
Ktly, Coll. iii (MS), Huds.
242. *monftrous*] *monsterous* Cap. Steev.
'85, Ktly.
  Iago] *Say, Iago* Pope +.
  began't] *began* Q$_1$Q$_2$. *degan* Q$_3$.
began it Mal. Steev. Var. Coll. Sing. Wh.
i, Ktly.

236. **approu'd**] JOHNSON : He that is convicted by proof of having been engaged in this offence.

238. **loose**] JENNENS : That is, be loose from me, or disjoined.   KNIGHT : The same word as *lose*, but differently applied. By the employment of *lose* we destroy the force of 'Thcugh he had *twinn'd* with me.'

238. **Towne of warre**] ABBOTT, § 163: In *Hen V*: II, iv, 7, 'towns of war' means *garrisoned towns*, and so probably here, like our 'man *of* war.'

241. **Court and Guard of safetie**] THEOBALD : *Guard of safety*, though couple, with a word of synonymous construction, was never soldiers' language. I have ver tured to make the conjunction and sign of the genitive case change places. So 'Court of Guard,' II, i, 251; 'look to the Guard,' II, ii, 16, and 'bear him to the Court of Guard,' *Ant. & Cleo.* IV, ix, 32.   MALONE : A similar mistake occurs in 'all place of sense and duty,' line 191. 'Court of guard' is established as a technical term by the uniform usage of the poets of Shakespeare's time. The *court of safety* may, in a metaphorical sense, be understood; but who ever talked of the *guard* (i. e. the *safety*) *of safety ?* STEEVENS : As a collocation of words, as seemingly perverse, occurs in *Mid. N. D.* III, i, 192, 'I shall desire *you of* more acquaintance,' I forbear to disturb the text. If *Safety*, like the Roman *Salus*, or *Recovery* in *Lear*, be personified, where is the impropriety of saying, under the guard *of* Safety ? Thus, Plautus, in his Captivi · 'Neque jam *servare Salus*, si vult, me potest.' DYCE (ed. iii) : Steevens defends the old reading not very satisfactorily. COWDEN-CLARKE : The text of the Ff means, in the very spot and guarding-place of safety.

242. **monstrous**] WALKER (*Vers.* 11) calls attention, as did MALONE before him, to the trisyllabic pronunciation here of this word; neither of them, however, noticed (nor did the CAMBRIDGE EDITORS, for that matter,) that CAPELL had long before so

   Mon.   If partially Affin'd, or league in office,   243
Thou doſt deliuer more, or leſſe then Truth,
Thou art no Souldier.   245
   Iago.   Touch me not ſo neere,
I had rather haue this tongue cut from my mouth,
Then it ſhould do offence to *Michaell Caſſio.*
Yet I perſwade my ſelfe, to ſpeake the truth
Shall nothing wrong him.   This it is Generall :   250
Montano and my ſelfe being in ſpeech,
There comes a Fellow, crying out for helpe,
And *Caſſio* following him with determin'd Sword
To execute vpon him.   Sir, this Gentleman,
Steppes in to *Caſſio*, and entreats his pauſe :   255
My ſelfe, the crying Fellow did purſue,
Leaſt by hiſc lamour (as it ſo fell out)
The Towne might fall in fright.   He,(ſwift of foote)
Out-ran my purpoſe : and I return'd then rather
For that I heard the clinke, and fall of Swords,   260
And *Caſſio* high in oath : Which till to night
I nere might ſay before   When I came backe
(For this was briefe) I found them cloſe together   263

---

243. *partially*] *partiality* Qq.
   Affin'd] *aſſign'd* Q.'81, Q.'95.
   league] QqFf, Rowe.   *leagu'd*
Pope et cet.
   244. *doſt*] *doeſt* Q₁Q₂.
   deliuer more,] *deliuer, more* Q₁.
   245. *no*] *mo* Q₃.
   247. *I had*] *I'd* Pope+.
   haue] *ha* Q₁.   *ha'* Q₂Q₃.
   cut from my] *out from my* Q₁.
out of my Q₂.   *out of his* Q₃.
   249. *ſpeake the*] *ſpeak ſo the* Ff, Rowe.

   250. *This*] Ff, Rowe, Knt, Sta.   *Thus*
Qq et cet.
      it is] *'tis* Pope+.
   252. *comes*] *coms* Q₃.
   253. *him*] Om. Pope+, Huds.
   255. *in to*] *into* Q₂F₂Q₃F₄, Rowe i.
   256. *My ſelfe,*] *my ſelfe* QqF₄ et seq.
   257. *Leaſt*] *Leſt* QqFf et cet.
   259. *and*] Om. Pope+.
      then] F₁, Knt.   *the* QqFf et cet.
   261. *oath*] *oaths* Q₁.
   262. *ſay*] *ſee* Q₁.

---

printed it in his text : *monsterous.* Walker goes on to show that Drayton, 'according
to his manner of marking a doubtful pronunciation by the spelling, writes *monsterous.*'
'There is also a third spelling, *monstruous*,' found in Surrey, and in the *Faerie Queene*,
I, ii, line 366 (ed. Grosart). See also 'mistress,' IV, ii, 104.—ED.

   243. **Affin'd**] STEEVENS : *Affin'd* is, bound by proximity of relationship ; but here
it means related by nearness of office.   In I, i, 42, it is used in the former sense.
STAUNTON : If, bound by partiality.   BOOTH : Montano should be in total ignorance
of the cause of the disturbance.

   253. **him**] CAPELL : This crept into the line from the line beneath.   DYCE and
WALKER also suspect that it is an interpolation.

At blow, and thruſt, euen as againe they were
When you your ſelfe did part them.   26ζ
More of this matter cannot I report,
But Men are Men : The beſt ſometimes forget,
Though *Caſſio* did ſome little wrong to him,
As men in rage ſtrike thoſe that wiſh them beſt,
Yet ſurely *Caſſio*, I beleeue receiu'd   270
From him that fled, ſome ſtrange Indignitie,
Which patience could not paſſe.

    Othe.   I know *Iago*.   [321 *a*|

Thy honeſtie, and loue doth mince this matter,
Making it light to *Caſſio* : *Caſſio*, I loue thee,   27ζ
But neuer more be Officer of mine.

    Enter Deſdemona attended.

Looke if my gentle Loue be not rais'd vp :
Ile make thee an example.   279

264. *againe*] agen Qq.
265. *When*] Whn Q₃.
266. *cannot I*] can I not Qq, Cap. Jen.
Steev. Mal. Var. Coll. Sing. Wh. i, Del.
Ktly.

268. *wrong*] woong Q₃.
269. *thoſe*] them Q₃.
277. Enter...] Enter *Deſdemona* with
others. Qq (after line 278) Q₂Q₃.
278. *rais'd*] raiſde Q₁.

274. COLERIDGE (*Notes*, &c., 255): Honesty and love! Ay, and who but the reader
of the play could think otherwise ?

275. **thee**] ABBOTT, § 231 : *Thou*, in Shakespeare's time, was very much like ' du '
now among the Germans, the pronoun of affection towards friends; good-humoured
superiority to servants; and contempt or anger to strangers.   It had, however, already
fallen somewhat into disuse, and, being regarded as archaic, was naturally adopted in
the higher poetic style and in the language of solemn prayer. . . . . In almost all cases
where *thou* and *you* appear at first sight indiscriminately used, further considerations
show some change of thought, or some influence of euphony sufficient to account for
the change of pronoun.   [In a foot-note, Abbott says that the Elizabethan distinction
between *thou* and *you* is remarkably illustrated in Early English, as detailed by Skeat
in *William of Palerne*.   The passage in SKEAT is as follows, and is the result of a
tabulation of the best examples in that Romance (about A. D. 1350) and also in the
Romance of *Alisaunder* (about A. D. 1340)] : ' *Thou* is the language of a lord to a
servant, of an equal to an equal, and expresses also companionship, love, permission,
defiance, scorn, threatening; whilst *ye* is the language of a servant to a lord, and of
compliment, and further expresses honour, submission, entreaty '—*Preface to William
of Palerne*, p. xlii.—ED.]

279. OTTLEY (p. 19) : Kean said these words, before preparing to go, solemnly and
sadly, as if justifying and explaining a painful act of duty.   And then his walk up the
stage ! so stately and grand, his cloak swaying gracefully with each well-measured step
—who that saw it shall forget it ?

Def.   What is the matter (Deere ?)   280
Othe.   All's well, Sweeting :
Come away to bed.   Sir for your hurts,
My felfe will be your Surgeon.   Lead him off :
Iago, looke with care about the Towne,
And filence thofe whom this vil'd brawle diftracted.   285
Come *Defdemona*, 'tis the Soldiers life,
To haue their Balmy flumbers wak'd with ftrife.   *Exit.*

Iago.   What are you hurt Lieutenant ?
Caf.   I, paft all Surgery.
Iago.   Marry Heauen forbid.   290
Caf.   Reputation, Reputation, Reputation : Oh I haue

---

280. *What is*] Q₁F₂, Cap. Steev.'85,
Mal. Knt.   *What's* Q₂Q₃F₃F₄ et cet.
   (*Deere ?*)] Ff.   *Dear ?* Rowe, Cap.
Jen. Steev. Mal. Var. Knt, Sing. Wh. i,
Ktly. Om. Qq et cet.
   281–283. *All's...off*] Lines end, *bed.* ...
Surgeon...off. Pope+, Jen. Steev.'85, Mal.
Coll. Dyce, Wh. Glo. Cam. Ktly, Del. Rlfe.
bed...hurts...off Steev.'93, Var. Sing.
   281. *All's*] *Aall's* Q₃.   *All is* Pope+.
   well,] Ff, Rowe+, Knt.   *well.*
Here Johns.   *well now* Qq et cet.
   282. *Come away*] *Com away* Q₃.   *Come,
away* F₄, Rowe, Pope, Theob. i, Han.
Come Theob. ii, Warb.   *Come, let's away*
Cap.
   283. *Surgeon.*] *surgeon.* [To Montano.

Johns.   To Mon. who is led off. Steev.
   283. *Lead him off*] Om. Huds.
   [Exeunt some with Mon. Cap.
   285. *vil'd*] *vile* QqFf.
   287. Exit] Exit Moore, *Defdemona*,
and attendants. (after line 288) Qq.
   Scene XIII. Pope, Warb.   Scene XIV.
Han. Johns. Jen.
   289. *I,*] *Ay*, Rowe.   Om. Pope+.
   290. *Marry Heauen*] *Mary God* Q₁.
Mary Heauen Q₂Q₃.
   291–294. Four lines, ending *my reputation...felfe...beaftiall, my reputation...
my reputation.* in Qq.
   291. *Reputation*] Only twice, Qq, Cap.
   Oh I] *I* Q₁, Cap.
   291, 292. *haue*] *ha* Qq.

---

281. Sweeting] STEEVENS : This surfeiting vulgar term of fondness originates from
the name of an apple distinguished only by its insipid sweetness.

283. Lead him off] MALONE : I am persuaded these words were originally a
stage direction.   In our old plays all the stage-directions were couched in imperative
terms :—Play music.—Ring the Bell.—Lead him off.   WHITE (ed. i) : Such is my
opinion, but for a different reason.   If Othello had ordered the removal of Montano,
he would have said, not 'Lead him off,' but 'Lead him *away*.'   We speak of a man's
being or having been led off, or on, in the sense of away, or onward ; but when we
direct a man to be taken from where we are, we say 'away,' unless we are upon a
staging, or some place of that kind, which, for Shakespeare's purposes, Othello was not.
The rhythm of this command, too, is not like that of Shakespeare's hemistichs.   But
as Qq and Ff agree, I do not venture to change it upon mere opinion.   ROLFE : Malone may be right.

285. BOOTH : Iago goes off.   Cassio braces himself for the sentence, but sinks to
the ground at Othello's exit.   At line 288, Iago hurriedly enters to Cassio.   In Cassio's
speech 'Reputation,' &c., don't preach ; be not violent ; avoid rant ; yet be impassioned,
—feel thoroughly disgusted with yourself, and you'll be natural.   Walk about, but don't
stamp or 'saw the air.'

loft my Reputation.   I haue loft the immortall part of   292
myfelfe, and what remaines is beftiall.   My Reputation,
Iago, my Reputation.

   Iago.   As I am an honeft man I had thought you had   295
receiued fome bodily wound; there is more fence in that
then in Reputation.   Reputation is an idle, and moft falfe
impofition; oft got without merit, and loft without de-
feruing.   You haue loft no Reputation at all, vnleffe you
repute your felfe fuch a loofer.   What man, there are   300
more wayes to recouer the Generall againe.   You are
but now caft in his moode, (a punifhment more in policie, then in malice) euen fo as one would beate his of-
fenceleffe dogge, ro affright an Imperious Lyon.   Sue to
him againe, and he's yours.   305

292. *part of*] *part fir of* Qq, Jen. Steev.
Mal. Var. Sing. Ktly.
   293. *my felfe*] *my falfe* Q₃.
   294. *remaines*] *remainrs* Q₃.
      Reputation.] *reputation*— Rowe
+, Jen.
   295. *I had*] Ff, Rowe+, Steev.'85,
Knt.   *I* Qq et cet.
   296. *receiued*] *receiu'd* Q₁Q₂.   *recei'd*

Q₃.
   296. *fence*] *offence* Qq, Jen. Steev. Mal.
Var. Coll. Sing. Ktly, Huds.
   300. *loofer*] *lofer* Qq.
   301. *more*] Ff, Rowe.   Om. Qq et cet.
      again] *agen* Qq.
   304. *ro*] *to.*
      Imperious] *impious* Han. ii (mis-
print).

296. **bodily wound**] GOULD (*The Tragedian*, p. 87): The simpler meaning is
conveyed by the usual emphasis on 'bodily.   But this emphasis would oppose bodily
to spiritual wounds, and Iago has no faith in the latter.   J. B. Booth, with fine penetration, emphasized both these words, as if there were no other wounds to suffer from.

   296. **sence**] KNIGHT: The *sense* of a wound is its *sensibility*.

   298, 299. **oft . . . deserving**] BOOTH: With significant glance at Cassio.   Do
not smile, or sneer, or glower,—try to impress even *the audience* with your sincerity.
'Tis better, however, always to ignore the audience; if you can forget that you are a
'shew' you will be natural.   The more sincere your manner, the more devilish your
deceit.   I think the 'light comedian' should play the villain's part, not the 'heavy
man;'   I mean the Shakespearian villains.   Iago should appear to be what all but the
audience believe he is.   Even when alone, there is little need to remove the mask
entirely.   Shakespeare spares you that trouble.

   299, 300. **You . . . looser**] DuBois (*Wreath*, p. 72) cites parallel passages from
Menander in Plutarch: Οὐδὲν πέπονθας δεινὸν, ἂν μὴ προσποιῇ—Thou hast suffered no
wrong, unless thou dost fancy so.   Also Epictetus, *Enchirid.*, c. 31 : Σὲ γὰρ ἄλλος οὐ
βλάψει, ἂν μὴ σὺ θέλῃς.   Τότε δὲ ἔσῃ βεβλαμμένος, ὅταν ὑπολάβῃς βλάπτεσθαι—No
one will hurt thee, unless thou art willing he should.   For then only wilt thou be hurt,
when thou dost think thyself hurt.   Also Marcus Antoninus, B. 7, § 14 : Ἐγὼ δὲ, ἐὰν
μὴ ὑπολάβω ὅτι κακὸν τὸ συμβεβηκὸς, οὔπω βέβλαμμαι—Unless I myself think that
which happens an evil, I am still unhurt.

   302. **cast**] JOHNSON: Ejected in his anger.   [See I, i, 164; II, ii, 31; V, ii, 400.]

Caf. I will rather fue to be defpis'd, then to deceiue   306
fo good a Commander, with fo flight, fo drunken, and fo
indifcreet an Officer. Drunke ? And fpeake Parrat? And
fquabble ? Swagger ? Sweare ? And difcourfe Fuftian
with ones owne fhadow ? Oh thou invifible fpirit of   310
Wine, if thou haft no name to be knowne by, let vs call
thee Diuell.

Iago. What was he that you follow'd with your
Sword ? What had he done to you ?

Caf. I know not.   315

Iago. Is't poffible ?

Caf. I remember a maffe of things, but nothing diftinctly : a Quarrell, but nothing wherefore. Oh, that
men fhould put an Enemie in their mouthes, to fteale a-
way their Braines ? that we fhould with ioy, pleafance,   320
reuell and applaufe, transforme our felues into Beafts.

307. *flight*] *light* Qq, Jen. Coll.
   and fo] *and* Qq.
308–310. *Drunke ?...fhadow ?*] Om.
Q₁.
   308. *fpeake Parrat ?*] *fpeak Parrat ?*
F₃, Cap. *fpeak, Parrot ?* F₄, Rowe, Pope.
fpeak ? Parrot, Theob. *fpeak ? parrot ?*
Han. *fpeak Parrot,* Johns. Jen. *fpeak
Parrot ?* Warb. et cet.
   310. *invifible*] *ivnifidle* Q₃. *invincible*
Theob. ii (mifprint ?), Warb.
   311. *Wine, if thou*] *wine ; thou* Q₃.
Wine ! if thou F₄, Rowe, Pope, Theob.
Han.Warb. Coll. Del. *wine ; if thou* Johns.
Jen.

311. *knowne...vs*] *konwen...ws* Q₃.
313, 314. *What...Sword ?*] One line as
verse, Qq.
   313. *follow'd*] *followed* Qq.
   316. *Is't*] *Is it* Steev. Mal. Var. Sing.
Ktly.
   318. *Oh,*] *O* Q₂Q₃. *O God,* Q₁, Jen.
Coll. Dyce, Sta.Wh. Glo. Cam. Del. Huds.
Rlfe.
   319, 320. *their...their*] *there...there* Q₁.
   320. *Braines ?*] *braines ;* Qq.
   320, 321. *pleafance, reuell*] *Reuell,
pleafure* Qq, Cap. Jen. Steev. Mal. Var.
Coll. Wh. i.

304. **affright**] As PURNELL says, this does not suit the comparison. STAUNTON
suggests *appease*, which certainly accords better with the sense.—ED.

308. **Parrat**] WARBURTON : That is, to act foolishly and childishly. [In proof,
Warburton cites a passage from Skelton, wherein it is true the two words 'speke' and
'Parrot' occur, but they occur as an address to the bird to speak, and not as in the
present phrase. The very title of the piece is *Speke, Parrot*, and Warburton's quotation runs thus : 'These maidens . . . . make swete my bowre, With, Speke, Parrot, I
pray you, full curtesly they say,' vol. ii, p. 2, ed. Dyce. Cassio's phrase bears its clear
meaning of senseless talk, but I have met no other instance of it. Parallel passages
are of use only where there is obscurity. Here there is none. For Shakespeare's references to parrots and their ways, see HARTING, p. 272.—ED.] MOREL : On pourrait
comparer l'expression familière du français, 'parler nègre.'

320. **pleasance**] MOREL : Marot chez nous disait encore au seizième siècle 'les
plaisances mondaines,' et le mot nous est resté dans les expressions telles que, *maison
de plaisance, bateau de plaisance.*

Iago.   Why ? But you are now well enough : how   322
came you thus recouered ?

Caf.   It hath pleas'd the diuell drunkenneſſe, to giue
place to the diuell wrath, one vnperfeƈtneſſe, ſhewes me   325
another to make me frankly deſpiſe my ſelfe.

Iago.   Come, you are too ſeuere a Moraller.   As the
Time, the Place, & the Condition of this Country ſtands
I could hartily wiſh this had not befalne : but ſince it is, as
it is, mend it for your owne good.   330

Caf.   I will aske him for my Place againe, he ſhall tell
me, I am a drunkard : had I as many mouthes as *Hydra*,
ſuch an anſwer would ſtop them all.   To be now a ſen-
ſible man, by and by a Foole, and preſently a Beaſt.   Oh
ſtrange! Euery inordinate cup is vnbleſs'd, and the Ingre-   335
dient is a diuell.

Iago.   Come, come : good wine, is a good famillar [321 *b*]
Creature, if it be well vs'd : exclaime no more againſt it.
And good Lieutenant, I thinke, you thinke I loue
you.   340

Caſſio.   I haue well approued it, Sir . I drunke ?

322. *Why ?*] Why, QqF₄ et seq.
324. *pleas'd*] *pleaſde* Q₁.
328. *& the*] *the* Qq, Han.
329. *not*] *not ſo* Q₁Q₂, Jen.
333. *them*] *em* Qq.
334. *Foole*] *foule* Q₃.
334, 335. *Oh ſtrange !*] Om. Qq, Pope +,
Jen.

335. *inordinate*] *vnordinate* Q₁.
335, 336. *Ingredient*] *ingredience* Qq,
Cap.
337. *famillar*] F₁.
341. *approued*] *approou'd* Q₁Q₂. *approv'd* Q₃.
Sir. I] *ſir,—I* Qq, Sing. ii.   *Sir,
I* Ff.

327. **Moraller**] For other instances of -*er* appended to nouns to signify the agent.
see ABBOTT, § 443.

328. **Time, the Place**] MOREL: Iago prend ainsi plaisir à rappeler à Cassio
les circonstances qui peuvent rendre sa faute plus criminelle et son remords plus
cuisant.

335. **Ingredient**] In that excellent contribution to Shakespearian literature, just
published, *Studies in Shakespeare* (alas! alas! that it should be posthumous!) GRANT
WHITE suggests that the form *ingredience* should be retained in *Macb.* I, vii, 11, in IV,
i, 34, and also in this present passage, on the ground that 'the idea is collective, not
separative.' This ground is valid in both instances in *Macb.*, but is less sure here, albeit
the Qq have *ingredience*. Not only are the Ff uniform in giving 'Ingredient,' but the
plural sound of *ingredience* would strike harshly before the singular verb.—ED.

337. **famillar**] MOREL: C'est le mot 'devil,' employé par Cassio, qui provoque cette
ironique repartie.

339. BOOTH: In tones whose subtlety cannot be described.

Iago. You, or any man liuing, may be drunke at a   342
time man. I tell you what you ſhall do : Our General's
Wife, is now the Generall. I may ſay ſo, in this reſpect,
for that he hath deuoted, and giuen vp himſelfe to the   345
Contemplation, marke : and deuotement of her parts
and Graces. Confeſſe your ſelfe freely to her : Importune her helpe to put you in your place againe. She is
of ſo free, ſo kinde, ſo apt, ſo bleſſed a diſpoſition,
ſhe holds it a vice in her goodneſſe, not to do more   350
then ſhe is requeſted. This broken ioynt betweene
you, and her husband, entreat her to ſplinter. And my
Fortunes againſt any lay worth naming, this cracke of
your Loue, ſhall grow ſtonger, then it was before.

Caſſio. You aduiſe me well.   355

Iago. I proteſt in the ſinceritie of Loue, and honeſt
kindneſſe.

Caſſio. I thinke it freely : and betimes in the mor-   358

342, 343. *a time*] Ff, Rowe, Knt, Dyce,
Wh. i, Glo. Rlfe. *ſome time* Qq et cet.

343. *man*] Om. Q₁.

    I tell] Ff, Rowe+. *Ile tell* Qq
et cet.

345. *hath*] *has* Qq.

346. *marke : and*] *marke and* Qq.
(*mark &* Q₃) Theob. ii, Warb. Cam.
mark : and F₄. —*mark,—and* Knt i, Sta.
—*mark !—and* Knt ii, Sing. Ktly. *mark,
and* Rowe et cet.

    deuotement] Q₁Q₂. *devotement*

FfQ₃, Rowe, Pope, Knt, Coll. i. *denote-·
ment* Theob. et cet.

348. *her helpe*] *her, ſhee'll helpe* Qq.
Jen. Steev. Mal. Var. Coll. Sing. Ktly. Del.

349. *of ſo*] *ſo* Qq.

350. *ſhe*] *that ſhe* Qq, Cap. Jen. Steev.
Mal. Var. Coll. Sing. Wh. i, Ktly, Del.

351. *broken ioynt*] *braule* Q₁.

354. *ſtonger*] *ſtronger* QqF₃F₄.

    it was] *twas* Q₁. *t'was* Q₂Q₃.

356. *honeſt*] Om. Q₃.

---

342. **at a time**] This is the Scotch 'ae,' meaning *one*. Compare 'Doth not rose-
mary and Romeo begin both with a letter' ? *Rom. & Jul.* II, iv, 187 ; 'these foils have
all a length,' *Ham.* V, ii, 232. See also ABBOTT, § 81.

346. **marke**] KNIGHT says that this is here used as an interjection ; 'to make the
matter still more ridiculous' ! exclaims DYCE (*Rem.*, p. 239), after condemning Knight's
preference for 'devotement' of F₁.

346. **deuotement**] THEOBALD : I cannot persuade myself that our Poet would ever
have said any one *devoted* himself to the *devotement* of anything. The mistake certainly arose from a single letter being turned upside-down at press. The three words,
Contemplation, mark, and denotement, are, indeed, in some degree tautological, but the
practice is allowed for the sake of energy. MALONE notes the frequent occurrence of
this accident in the Qq and Ff. Thus in *Merry Wives*, IV, vi, 39, 'deuote her to the
doctor ;' *Ham.* I, ii, 83, 'That can deuote me truly,' where in both cases it should be
denote. For other instances see his note on the passage in *Merry Wives*.

352. **splinter**] DYCE : To secure by splints.

353. **lay**] RITSON · Any bet, any wager.

ning, I will befeech the vertuous *Defdemona* to vndertake
for me : I am defperate of my Fortunes if they check me.   360
   Iago.   You are in the right : good night Lieutenant, I
muft to the Watch.
   Caffio.   Good night, honeft *Iago.*

                             Exit Caffio.

   Iago.   And what's he then,   365
That faies I play the Villaine?
When this aduife is free I giue, and honeft,
Proball to thinking, and indeed the courfe
To win the Moore againe.
For 'tis moft eafie   370
Th'inclyning *Defdemona* to fubdue
In any honeft Suite.   She's fram'd as fruitefull   372

359. *I will*] *will* *I* Qq, Jen. Mal. Steev.
befeech] *befech* Q₃.
360. *check me.*] Ff, Rowe, Pope, Knt.
checke me here. Qq et cet.
361. *You...right*] One line, Qq.
364. *Exit...*] Exit. Qq.
Scene XIV. Pope i, Warb.   Scene XV.
Han. Johns. Jen.   Scene II. Pope ii (misprint).
365, 366. One line, Qq, Rowe et seq.

368. *Proball*] *Probable* Rowe, Cap.
Steev.'85.   *Likely* Pope +.   *Provable*
Coleridge in quoting.
369, 370. One line, Qq, Rowe et seq.
369. *againe*] *agen* Qq.
371. *Th'*] Ff, Rowe+, Jen. Sing. Wh.
Ktly, Dyce iii, Huds.   *The* Qq et cet.
371, 372. *fubdue...Suite. She's*] *fub
due,...fuite, fhe's* Q₁.   *fubdue,...fuite fhe's*
Q₂Q₃.

363. **honest**] BOOTH : Not too pronounced.
365. BOOTH : Pause, and with a smile of satisfaction, look after him.
365. COLERIDGE (*Notes*, &c., 255): He is not, you see, an absolute fiend; or, at least, he wishes to think himself not so.
367. **free**] JOHNSON : This counsel has an appearance of honest openness, of frank goodwill.   HENLEY : Rather *gratis, not paid for*, as his advice to Roderigo was.   PYE (p. 333): His counsel has not the appearance only of honest openness and frank good-will, but was really such as honest openness and frank goodwill would give.   Henley's notion is completely absurd.
368. **Proball**] STEEVENS : There may be such a contraction of *probable*, but I have not met with it in any other book.   Abbreviations as violent occur in the works of Churchyard.   COLLIER : A colloquial contraction for *probable*.   Corresponding contractions are 'miseral' for *miserable* in Painter's *Palace of Pleasure*, i, 151; and in B. Rich's *Dialogue between Mercury and a Soldier*, 1574, we have 'varial' for *variable*.   SINGER : A contraction of *probable* or *proveable*.   HALLIWELL : A word of very rare occurrence.   I have met with it only once elsewhere, in Sampson's *Vow Breaker, or the Faire Maid of Clifton*, 1636: 'Didst thou not make me draw conveighances? Did not th'assurance of thy lands seeme *proball?*'   WHITE (ed. ii) : A word unknown elsewhere : but what cared Shakespeare for that !   [For other somewhat similar contractions, see ABBOTT, § 461.]
371. **inclyning**] MALONE : Compliant.

As the free Elements.   And then for her   373
To win the Moore, were to renownce his Baptifme,
All Seales, and Simbols of redeemed fin :   375
His Soule is fo enfetter'd to her Loue,
That fhe may make, vnmake, do what fhe lift,
Euen as her Appetite fhall play the God,
With his weake Function.   How am I then a Villaine,
To Counfell *Caffio* to this paralell courfe,   380
Directly to his good ?   Diuinitie of hell,
When diuels will the blackeft finnes put on,
They do fuggeft at firft with heauenly fhewes,
As I do now.   For whiles this honeft Foole
Plies *Defdemona*, to repaire his Fortune,   385
And fhe for him, pleades ftrongly to the Moore,
Ile powre this peftilence into his eare :
That fhe repeales him, for her bodies Luft'
And by how much fhe ftriues to do him good,
She fhall vndo her Credite with the Moore.   390
So will I turne her vertue into pitch,
And out of her owne goodneffe make the Net,
That fhall en-mafh them all.
How now *Rodorigo* ?   394

374. *were*] *wer't* Q₁Q₂. *were't* Q₃, Rowe
et seq.
375. *Simbols*] *fymboles* Q₃.
376. *enfetter'd*] *infetter'd* Qq.
379. *How am*] *Am* Pope+.
381. *Diuinitie of hell*] *' Tis hell's divin-
ity :* Pope, Han.
382. *diuels*] *Devils* F₃F₄.
    the] *their* QqF₄, Rowe+, Jen.
Steev. Mal. Var. Coll. Sing. Wh. i, Ktly,
Del.

384. *whiles*] *while* Q₁F₃F₄, Rowe+,
Cap. Jen. Steev. Mal. Var. Sing. Ktly.
whilft Q₂Q₃.
385. *Fortune*] Ff, Rowe+, Jen. Knt.
fortunes Qq et cet.
388. *for her*] *from her* Johns.
393, 394. One line, Pope et seq.
393. *en-mafh*] *enmefh* Q₁Q₂. *enemfh*
Q₃. *enmafh* F₃F₄, Rowe.
    them] *em* Q₁.
394. Rodorigo] *Rod'rigo* Pope, Han.

372. **fruitefull**] JOHNSON : Liberal, bountiful, as the elements, out of which all
things are produced.   [See III, iv, 46.]

379. **Function**] SCHMIDT (*Lex.*): The operation of the mental faculties.   [Very,
very doubtful.   See *Ham.* II, ii, 529; *Macb.* I, iii, 140.—ED.]

380. **paralell**] JOHNSON : That is, *level*, and *even with his design.*

380. **course**] WALKER (*Crit.*, i, 165): Perhaps *dele* comma after ' course.'

382. **put on**] That is, encourage, thrust forward.   A parallel inftance is in *Macb.*
IV, iii, 239 : ' the powers above put on their instruments.'

383. **suggest**] DYCE : To tempt, to incite, to seduce.

387. BOOTH : All this with a quiet chuckle and increasing intensity.

388. **repeals**] JOHNSON : That is, recalls him.   COLLIER : Its etymological sense.

Enter Rodorigo.   395

Rodorigo. I do follow heere in the Chace, not
like a Hound that hunts, but one that filles vp the
Crie. My Money is almoſt ſpent ; I haue bin to night
exceedingly well Cudgell'd : And I thinke the iſſue
will bee, I ſhall haue ſo much experience for my paines ; [322 *a*]
And ſo, with no money at all, and a little more Wit, re-   401
turne againe to Venice.

Iago.   How poore are they that haue not Patience ?
What wound did euer heale but by degrees ?
Thou know'ſt we worke by Wit, and not by Witchcraft   405
And Wit depends on dilatory time :
Dos't not go well ? *Caſſio* hath beaten thee,
And thou by that ſmall hurt hath caſheer'd *Caſſio:*
Though other things grow faire againſt the Sun,
Yet Fruites that bloſſome firſt, will firſt be ripe :   410

---

395. Enter...] After line 393, Qq.
Scene XV. Pope, Warb.   Scene XVI.
Han. Johns. Jen.
396. *do*] Om. Pope, Han.
398. *I haue*] *I ha* Qq.
399. *And*] Om. Qq.
400–402. *paines ... Venice*] *paines, as
that comes to, and no money at all, and
with that wit returne to Venice.* Q₁, Jen.
*paines, and ſo no mony at all, and with
a little more wit returne to Venice.* Q₂Q₃.
402. *againe*] Om. Qq, Jen. Steev. Mal.

Var. Knt.
403. *haue not*] *ha not* Q₁.
405. *know'ſt*] *knowſt* Qq.
407. *Dos't*] *Do'ſt* Q₁. *Doſt* F₃F₄,
Rowe i. *Does't* Rowe ii et seq.
   hath] *has* Qq.
408. *hath*] Sing. Dyce iii. *haſt* QqFf
et cet.
409. *grow*] *grew* Q₃.
410. *Yet*] *But* Q₁.
   will...ripe] *are not first ripe :* Han.
   firſt] *fire* Q₃.

---

398. **Crie**] DYCE : A pack, properly 'the giving mouth of hounds.' 'A crie of
Hounds have here a Deer in Chase.'—Sylvester's *Du Bartas, The Magnificence,*
p. 213, ed. 1632.

408. BOOTH : Roderigo shows delight at this, and is anxious to learn the particulars,
but Iago urges him to go ; then with triumphant haste speaks the concluding lines.

410. **ripe**] JOHNSON : Of many different things, all planned with the same art and
promoted with the same diligence, some must succeed sooner than others, by the order
of nature. Everything cannot be done at once ; we must proceed by the necessary
gradation. We are not to *despair* of slow events, any *more* than of tardy fruits, while
the causes are in regular progress and the fruits *grow fair against the sun.* MALONE :
The *blossoming,* or fair appearance of things, to which Iago alludes, is the removal of
Cassio. As their plan had already *blossomed,* so there was good ground for expecting
that it would *soon* be *ripe.* Iago does not mean to compare *their* scheme to *tardy*
fruits. DEIGHTON : Johnson says the meaning is that we are not to despair of slow
events, any more of tardy fruits, while the causes are in regular progress, and the
fruits *grow fair against the sun :* but Iago does *not* say that the fruits grew fair against

Content thy felfe, a-while.   Introth 'tis Morning;   411
Pleafure, and Action, make the houres feeme fhort.
Retire thee, go where thou art Billited :
Away, I fay, thou fhalt know more heereafter :
Nay get thee gone.   *Exit Rodorigo*.   415
Two things are to be done :
My Wife muft moue for *Caſſio* to her Miftris :
Ile fet her on my felfe, a while, to draw the Moor apart,
And bring him iumpe, when he may *Caſſio* finde   419

411. *a-while*] *awhile* Sing.
        Introth] F$_2$F$_3$. *In troth* F$_4$, Rowe +,
Knt, Wh.   *bi' the maſſe* Q$_1$.   *by' th maſſe*
Q$_2$Q$_3$.   *By th' mass* Cap. Jen. Huds.   *By
the mass* Steev. et cet.
    412. *houres*] *time* Jen.
    413. *Billited*] *bill ted* Q$_1$.
    415, 416. One line, Qq, Mal. et seq.
    415-418. Lines end *gone...move...on—
...apart*, Ktly.
    415. Exit...] Om. Qq.
    416. *Two*] *Some* Qq.

518. Two lines, the first ending *on*. Qq,
Theob. Warb. et seq.
        her on] Ff, Rowe, Pope.   *her on.*
Qq.   *her on*—Ktly.   *her on :* Theob. et cet.
        on...draw] *on to draw* Pope.   *on ;
so draw* Han.
        a while] FfQ$_2$Q$_3$, Rowe, Jen. Sing.
awhile Q$_1$.   *the while* Theob. Warb. et cet.
        to draw] *will draw* Johns. Steev.
'85.
    419. *when*] *where* Coll. MS.

---

the sun.   On the contrary, he says '*though other* things grow, &c., *yet*, &c.   I believe
the argument is this :—Iago compares Cassio to one tree, and himself and Roderigo to
another or others.   Cassio, he says, 'grew fair against the sun' while they were in the
shade, i. e., Cassio had an advantage over them in his position in life; but notwithstanding this, they had 'blossomed first,' i. e., had by their successful tumbling him out
of his lieutenancy, made better use of their time and opportunities; and arguing from
this, it was likely that they would 'first grow ripe,' i. e., would ultimately beat him in
the race by attaining their objects, while he would end in failure and disgrace.   Johnson's interpretation quite misses the point, while Malone does not touch the first of the
two lines, and fails to explain the blossoming *first* and getting ripe *first*, which are important words here.   HUDSON : The meaning seems to be, 'though in the sunshine of
good luck the other parts of our scheme are promising well, yet we must expect that
the part which first meets with opportunity, or time of blossom, will soonest come to
harvest, or catch success.'

    411. Introth] MALONE : One of the numerous arbitrary alterations made by the
Master of the Revels in the playhouse copies, from which a great part of the Folio was
printed.   WHITE (ed. i) : The change seems to be due rather to a care for the rhythm
than to the scruples of the Master of the Revels.

    418. THEOBALD : This unreasonable long Alexandrine was certainly a blunder of
the editors; a slight transposition and a change will regulate it.   [In Text. Notes,
see Theobald's division of the line, wherein he followed the Qq.]

    418. a while] JENNENS : Perhaps this means the same as *the while*, and may be a
contraction for *at the while*.

    418. to draw] STEEVENS : This is in keeping with the interrupted speech.   **Iago**
is still debating with himself the means to perplex Othello.

Soliciting his wife : I, that's the way :   420
Dull not Deuice, by coldneſſe, and delay.   *Exit.*

Actus Tertius. Scena Prima.

Enter Caſſio, Muſitians, and Clowne.

Caſſio. Maſters, play heere, I wil content your paines,
Something that's briefe: and bid, goodmorrow General.

Clo. Why Maſters, haue your Inſtruments bin in Na-   5
ples, that they ſpeake i'th'Noſe thus?

420. *wife :*] *wife—* Ktly.
421. *not Deuice*] *not deuiſe* Qq. *not, Device,* Theob. Warb.
Exit.] Exeunt. Qq.
1. Actus...] Om. Q₁. Actus 3. Scœna 1. Q₂Q₃. Actus...Scæna Prima. F₂.
Othello's Palace. Rowe.
2. Enter...] Enter *Caſſio,* with Muſitians and the Clowne, Q₁. Enter *Caſſio,* with Muſitians Q₂Q₃.
3. *Maſters*] *Maſter* Q₃.
4. *bid, goodmorrow*] F₂. *bid good morrow* QqF₃. *bid good morrow,* F₄, Rowe, Pope, Han. Coll. Dyce i, Wh. i, Sta. Rlfe.

bid, good morrow, Theob. Warb. Ktly. *bid, Good-morrow,* Johns. Jen. Knt. *bid—good morrow,* Cap. Steev. Mal. Var. Sing. *bid, good morrow to the* Coll. (MS). *bid 'Good morrow,* Glo. Cam. Del. Dyce iii, Wh. ii.
[They play, and enter the Clowne. Q₂Q₃. Music plays... Theob.
5. *haue*] *ha* Qq.
bin in] *bin at* Qq, Cap. Jen. Steev. Mal. Var. Sing. Ktly.
6. *ſpeake*] *play* Cap. (corrected in Errata). *squeak* Coll. ii (MS), Sing. ii.
i'th'] *i'the* Q₁. *i'th* Q₂Q₃. *ith'* F₃.

419. *iumpe*] Exactly; see Shakespeare *passim.*
419. *when*] COLLIER (ed. ii) *Where* of the (MS.) is probably wrong, since Iago is adverting more to time than to place.
2. THEOBALD (Nichols's *Illus.*, ii, 593): The direction for this entrance does not seem entirely right. The scene should be before Othello's palace. Cassio should speak with the musicians; after his speech they should play their serenade; and then the Clown should enter, as from the house. [This scene and the following scene are generally omitted, I believe, on the modern stage.—ED.]
3. **play heere**] BRAND (*Pop. Ant.*, ii, 176): The custom of awaking a couple the morning after the marriage with a concert of music, is of old standing. In the letter from Sir Dudley Carleton to Mr. Winwood, describing the nuptials of the Lady Susan with Sir Philip Herbert, it is stated that, 'they were lodged in the council chamber, where the King gave them a *reveille matin* before they were up.' CHAPPELL (*Pop. Music*, &c., p. 61): Any song intended to arouse in the morning was formerly called a *hunt's up.* See *Rom. & Jul.* III, v, 34. Cotgrave defines 'Resveil: A Hunts-vp, or morning song for a new-married wife, the day after the marriage.' RITSON: *Haut-boys* are the wind-instruments here meant.
5. **Naples**] JOHNSON: A loathsome disease first appeared at the siege of Naples. PARR (p. 36): There are few Clowns in Italy know this; but every clown there knows that Pulcinella is the Neapolitan mask, and that Pulcinella speaks through the nose. He generally knows, too, that the man who plays the puppet puts into his mouth a reed similar to that which is placed in the orifice of the haut-boy. COWDEN-CLARKE: The Neapolitans have a singularly drawling nasal twang in the utterance of their dialect.

Muf. How Sir? how?   7

Clo. Are thefe I pray you, winde Inftruments?

Muf. I marry are they fir.

Clo. Oh, thereby hangs a tale.   10

Muf. Whereby hangs a tale, fir?

Clow. Marry fir, by many a winde Inftrument that I
know.   But Mafters, heere's money for you : and the Generall fo likes your Muſick, that he defires you for loues
fake to make no more noife with it.   15

Muf. Well Sir, we will not.

Clo. If you haue any Muficke that may not be heard,
too't againe.   But (as they fay) to heare Muficke, the Generall do's not greatly care.

Muf. We haue none fuch, fir.   20

Clow. Then put vp your Pipes in your bagge, for Ile
away.   Go, vanifh into ayre, away.   *Exit Mu.*

Caffio. Doft thou heare me, mine honeft Friend?

Clo. No, I heare not your honeft Friend :
I heare you.   25

Caffio. Prythee keepe vp thy Quillets, ther's a poore
peece of Gold for thee : if the Gentlewoman that attends
the Generall be ftirring, tell her, there's one *Caffio* en-   28

7, 9, &c. Muf.] Boy. Qq.

8. *I pray you,*] *I pray, cald* $Q_1 Q_2$.   *I pray you, cald* Q_3, Jen. Steev. Mal. Var. Coll. Sing. Ktly, Del.

10, 11. *tale*] *tayle* Qq. *tail* Q.'81, Q.'95.

13. *heere's*] *heer's* Q_2. *hee's* F_2. *her's* Q_3.

14, 15. *for loues fake*] *of all loues* Q_1, Johns. Jen. Steev. Mal. Var. Sing. Ktly, Sta. Dyce iii, Coll. iii, Huds.

15. *no more*] *no* FfQ₃, Rowe, Pope, Han.

18. *too't*] *to't* Qq, Rowe et seq.

20. *haue*] *ha* Qq.

21. *put vp*] *put* Qq.
   for Ile] *and hye* Han. Warb. Jen.

22. *into ayre*] Om. Q_1, Jen.
   Exit Mu.] Om. Qq.

23. *heare me, mine*] *hear my* Qq. *hear, mine* Theob. +, Coll. Wh. *hear, my* Cap. et cet.

24, 25. One line, Qq, Rowe et seq.

26. *ther's*] *there's* $Q_1 F_3 F_4$.

28. *Generall*] *Cenerals wife* Q_1. *Generals wife* $Q_2 Q_3$, Rowe et seq.

---

14. **for loues sake**] KNIGHT: The Qto has the prettier phrase. [See ABBOTT, § 169, for other instances where *of* is used in appeals.]

18. **too't**] Is there a pun here? WHITE (ed. ii) says that 'in "the Generall" we have a punning allusion to the indifference of the general public to music,' and I think one pun is quite as likely, or as unlikely, as the other.—ED.

21. **for Ile away**] RITSON (p. 231): This must be wrong; possibly—*fly away*. [An unknown former owner of my copy of Jennens has here queried on the margin, *'fore all, away*, which is both ingenious and plausible.—ED.]

26. **Quillets**] MALONE: Nice and frivolous distinctions. [See *Ham.* V, i, 94].

treats her a little fauour of Speech.   Wilt thou do this?

Clo.   She is ſtirring ſir : if ſhe will ſtirre hither, I ſhall   30
ſeeme to notifie vnto her.   *Exit Clo.*

Enter Iago.

In happy time, *Iago*.

Iago.   You haue not bin a-bed then?

Caſſio.   Why no : the day had broke before we parted.   35
I haue made bold (*Iago*) to ſend in to your wife :
My ſuite to her is, that ſhe will to vertuous *Deſdemona*
Procure me ſome acceſſe.   [322 *b*]

Iago.   Ile ſend her to you preſently :
And Ile deuiſe a meane to draw the Moore   40
Out of the way, that your conuerſe and buſineſſe
May be more free.   *Exit*

Caſſio.   I humbly thanke you for't.   I neuer knew
A Florentine more kinde, and honeſt.   44

29. *her*] *of her* Rowe+.
Speech.] *ſpeech—* Qq.
30. *ſir :...hither,*] *ſir,...hither.* Jen.
31. *ſeeme to*] *soon so* Sing. ii (MS).
seem so to Coll. ii (MS).
Exit Clo.] Om. Q$_1$. (After *Iago*, line
33) Q$_2$Q$_3$.
33. *In happy*] Ff. Caſ. *Doe good my
friend : In happy* Qq, Steev. Mal. Var.
Knt, Coll. Sing. Wh. i, Ktly. Cas. *Do,
my good friend* [Enter Iago] *In happy*
Rowe+, Cap. (subs.). Cas. *Do, good my
friend* [To him Enter Iago] *In happy*
Jen. Dyce, Sta. Glo. Cam. Del. Huds. Rlfe,
Wh. ii.
34, 36. *haue*] *ha* Qq.
34. *bin*] *been* F$_4$.
a-bed] *a bed* QqF$_3$F$_4$.

35-37. *Why...Deſdemona*] Lines end,
parted...her.. Deſdemona Qq. Ending,
parted...wife;...her...Desdemona. Johns.
Ending, *broke...Iago...her...Desdemona*
Cap. et seq.
36. *Iago*] Om. Pope+.
wife :] *wife,—* Qq.
37. *to her*] Om. Pope, Theob. Han.
Warb.
vertuous] Om. Pope, Theob. Han.
Warb.
39. *to you*] Om. Pope+.
42. Exit.] After *for't*, line 43, Cap. Ktly,
Glo. Cam.
43. *for't*] *for it* Q$_1$.
43, 44. Lines end, *for't...honest.* Cap.
44. *A Florentine*] *a man* Cap.

30, 31. These lines are, of course, prose.   In the Globe Edition they chance to
divide at 'hither.'   WHITE overlooked this, and, in printing his second edition from
the Globe, has in his own text retained the division at 'hither' and printed as verse.
'To err is human,' and no divineness is needed to forgive so venial a slip as this.—ED.

31. to notifie vnto] DELIUS : A pedantic, affected phrase which the Clown purposely uses, and in such a way as to leave it uncertain that he himself understood it.

33. In happy time] *A la bonne heure.*   See *Rom. & Jul.* III, v, 110; *Ham.* V,
ii, 193, &c., &c.

38. acceſſe] For the accent, see ABBOTT, § 490.

43, 44. WALKER (*Crit.* i, 89) suggests in view of the very frequent interpolation of

Enter Æmilia. 45

Æmil. Goodmorrow(good Lieutenant) I am forrie
For your difpleafure : but all will fure be well.
The Generall and his wife are talking of it,
And fhe fpeakes for you ftoutly. The Moore replies,
That he you hurt is of great Fame in Cyprus, 50
And great Affinitie : and that in wholfome Wifedome
He might not but refufe you.But he protefts he loues you
And needs no other Suitor, but his likings
To bring you in againe.

Caffio. Yet I befeech you, 55
If you thinke fit, or that it may be done,
Giue me aduantage of fome breefe Difcourfe
With *Defdemon* alone. 58

47. *fure*] *foone* Qq, Cap. Jen. Steev.
Mal. Var. Coll. Sing. Wh. i, Ktly.
51. *wholfome*] Om. Pope, Theob. Han.
Warb.
52. *but*] *bat* Q₃.
refufe you] *refufe* Q₂Q₃, Cap.
he protefts] Om. Han.
53, 54. *likings To*] Ff, Rowe, Pope,

Theob. Han. Warb. *likings, To take the
fafeft occafion by the front* Qq et cet. (*firft
occafion* Johns. *faf'ft occafion* Cap. Steev.
'93, Var. Knt, Sing. Dyce, Wh. Ktly, Sta
Del.).
58. *Defdemon*] Ff, Rowe, Wh. i, Sta.
Del. Dyce iii. *Defdemona* Qq et cet.

---

a in the Folio, this division and reading: ' I humbly thank you for't | I ne'er knew
Florentine more kind and honest.' ' Perhaps,' he adds, ' we should arrange rather,—
" I humbly thank you for't; I ne'er knew Florentine | More kind and honest." ' [See
Capell's reading and division, in Textual Notes.]

43. humbly] DYCE (ed. iii): ' The word "humbly" is constantly used with
"thank," "pray," "beseech," and the like: hence, I suppose, a transcriber inserted
it here. Cassio was Iago's equal, or rather his superior, and would scarcely have used
the word even in his present dejected state.'—W. N. LETTSOM. Here, I apprehend,
' humbly ' is no more to be taken in its literal sense than is ' humble ' now-a-days when
some very courteous correspondent signs himself ' Your *humble* servant.'

44. Florentine] MALONE: In consequence of this line, a doubt has been entertained concerning the country of Iago. Cassio was undoubtedly a Florentine, as
appears by I, i, 22, where he is expressly called one. That Iago was a Venetian is
proved by what he says after having stabbed Roderigo, V, i, 112. All that Cassio
means to say here is, ' I never experienced more honesty and kindness even in any one
of my own countrymen than in this man.'

47. displeasure] STEEVENS: The displeasure you have incurred from Othello.

53. likings] WALKER (*Crit.* i, 250): Why the plural? In F₁ there is no stop after
the word; perhaps *s* has usurped the place of the comma, as it has elsewhere [in the
examples which Walker then proceeds to give].

58. Desdemon] This instance of the name thus spelled must have escaped
KNIGHT'S notice, or, I think, he would not have written, or at least would have modified, the following note, which he appends to III, iii, 64: ' In five passages in the

Æmil.   Pray you come in :
I will beftow you where you fhall haue time   60
To fpeake your bofome freely.
   Caffio.   I am much bound to you.

Scœna Secunda.

Enter Othello, Iago, and Gentlemen.

Othe.   Thefe Letters giue (*Iago*) to the Pylot,
And by him do my duties to the Senate :
That done, I will be walking on the Workes,   5
Repaire there to mee.
   Iago.   Well, my good Lord, Ile doo't.
   Oth.   This Fortification (Gentlemen) fhall we fee't ?
   Gent.   Well waite vpon your Lordfhip.   *Exeunt*   9

59. *Pray you*] *Pray* Ff, Rowe.
62. Om. Q₁.
   I am] *I'm* Pope, Theob. Han.
Warb.
   [Exeunt. QqF₃F₄.
1. Scœna...] Om. Qq, Rowe.
2. Enter ... Gentlemen] Enter ... other
Gentlemen. Qq.
3. *Pylot*] *Pilate* Q₁Q₂.   *Pilot* Q₃F₃F₄.

4. *by him*] *bid him* Cap. conj. (p. 28 *b*).
   Senate] *State* Qq, Cap. Steev. Mal.
Var. Coll. Wh. i.
5. *on the*] *to the* Q₂Q₃.
   Workes,] *works;* Coll. Dyce, Glo.
Cam. *works,*— Knt, Sta.
7. *Well*] Om. Pope+.
9. *Well*] *We* Qq, Jen. Coll.Wh. i.   *Weel*
F₂.   *We'll* F₃F₄ et cet.

Folio Desdemona is called *Desdemon.* The abbreviation was not a capricious one,
nor was it introduced merely for the sake of rhythm.   It is clearly used as an epithet
[sic] of familiar tenderness.   In the present instance [III, iii, 64] Othello playfully
evades his wife's solicitations with a rarely-used term of endearment.   In the next
case, IV, ii, 50, it comes out of the depth of conflicting love and jealousy—" Ah ! *Desdemon,* away, away, away ! "   In the next place where he employs it, V, ii, 29, it is
used upon the last solemn occasion when he speaks to her, " Have you prayed to-night,
Desdemon ? "   And, lastly, it is spoken by him when he has discovered the full extent
of his guilt and misery, " O *Desdemon !* dead *Desdemon,* dead."   The only other occasion on which it is employed is by her uncle Gratiano,—" Poor Desdemon ! "   Surely
we have no warrant for rejecting such a marked peculiarity.'   WALKER (*Crit.* i, 230)
suggests that Knight supposed the spelling in the present instance, the sixth, 'to be an
erratum ' ; but it is not ; the verse requires, as Walker says, that we should read *Desdemon,* and assuredly there can be no thought of 'familiar tenderness ' here, from Cassio.
This alone is a serious, perhaps fatal, objection to Knight's theory, which I regretfully
relinquish ; nor is the objection lessened when we find, as Walker points out, that a
double form of proper names is by no means uncommon.   There are half a dozen
instances of 'Helen' for *Helena* in *Mid. N. D.,* and again in *All's Well.*—ED.

Scœna Tertia.

Enter Defdemona, Caffio, and Æmilia.

Def. Be thou affur'd (good *Caffio*) I will do
All my abilities in thy behalfe.

Æmil. Good Madam do :   5
I warrant it greeues my Husband,
As if the caufe were his.

Def. Oh that's an honeft Fellow, Do not doubt *Caffio*
But I will haue my Lord, and you againe
As friendly as you were.   10

Caffio. Bounteous Madam,
What euer fhall become of *Michael Caffio*,
He's neuer any thing but your true Seruant.

Def. I know't : I thanke you : you do loue my Lord :
You haue knowne him long, and be you well affur'd   15
He fhall in ftrangeneffe ftand no farther off,
Then in a politique diftance.

Caffio. I, but Lady,   18

1. Scœna Tertia] Om. Qq. Scene II. Rowe.

An Apartment. Rowe. Before the Castle. Cap. The Garden of the Castle. Dyce.

3. *do*] *use* Quincy (MS).

5, 6. One line, Qq, Pope et seq.

6. *warrant*] *know* Qq, Pope+, Jen. Steev. Mal. Var. Coll. Sing. Ktly.

7. *caufe*] Ff, Rowe+, Knt, Sta. Del. *cafe* Qq et cet.

8. *Fellow,*] *fellow :—* Qq. *Fellow :* F₃ F₄, Rowe+. *fellow.* Johns. et seq.

Do not doubt] *doubt not* Pope+.

11. *Bounteous*] *Bountious* Q₁. *Moſt bounteous* Pope+, Cap.

14. *I know't :*] *O ſir*, Qq, Cap. Jen. Steev. Mal. Var. Coll. Sing. Ktly, Huds. *I know't*, Rowe, Pope, Theob. Han.Warb. Knt, Dyce, Sta. *I know't !* Wh. i.

15. *You haue*] *You've* Pope+, Dyce iii, Huds.

be you well] *be* Q₃.

16. *ftrangeneffe*] *ftrangeft* Qq. *ın ſ strangest* Anon (ap. Cam. ed.).

farther] *further* Steev.'93, Var Dyce, Glo. Del. Huds. Rlfe, Wh. ii.

FECHTER'S setting of the stage for this scene is noteworthy ; some of its details have been since adopted by eminent actors, and the public has not given due credit to the originator. It is thus : A Room in the Castle. At the back, an arched opening, looking over the sea. Right and left, in front,—and facing the public,—two large doorways closed with tapestry. At the left, a divan, and table covered with papers, maps, instruments of navigation, &c. On the right a low chair and stool ; around and about them, embroideries, music, musical instruments, &c. As the curtain rises, Desdemona, seated, winds off silk, which Emilia (sitting on the stool) holds to her ; Cassio stands respectfully before Desdemona, who continues her work as she speaks.

16. **strangenesse**] The. Anonymous conjecture recorded by the CAMBRIDGE EDITORS seems singularly happy.—ED.

That policie may either laſt ſo long,
Or feede vpon ſuch nice and wateriſh diet,   20
Or breede it ſelfe ſo out of Circumſtances,
That I being abſent, and my place ſupply'd,
My Generall will forget my Loue, and Seruice.

    Deſ.   Do not doubt that : before *Æmilia* here,
I giue thee warrant of thy place.   Aſſure thee,   [323 *a*]
If I do vow a friendſhip, Ile performe it   26
To the laſt Article.   My Lord ſhall neuer reſt,
Ile watch him tame, and talke him out of patience ;
His Bed ſhall ſeeme a Schoole, his Boord a Shrift,
Ile intermingle euery thing he do's   30
With *Caſſio*'s ſuite : Therefore be merry *Caſſio*,
For thy Solicitor ſhall rather dye,   32

19. *That*] *The* Q₁.
20. *wateriſh*] *watriſh* Q₁, Cap.
21. *Circumſtances*] Ff, Rowe+.   *circumſtance* Qq et cet.
22. *ſupply'd*] *ſupplied* Qq.

23. *will*] *would* Jen.
and] *an* Q₃.
24. *Æmilia*] *Emillia* Qq.
25. *place.*] *place?* Q₂.
27. *ſhall neuer*] *shan't* Han.

19. **That policie**] JOHNSON : He may either of himself think it politic to keep me out of office so long, or he may be satisfied with such slight reasons, or so many accidents may make him think my re-admission at that time improper, that I may be quite forgotten.

24. **doubt**] WHITE (ed. ii) : Do not imagine, fear, that.

25. **warrant**] COLERIDGE (p. 255) : The over-zeal of innocence in Desdemona.

28. **tame**] JOHNSON : It is said that the ferocity of beasts, insuperable and irreclaimable by any other means, is subdued by keeping them from sleep. STEEVENS : It is to the management of hawks and other birds that Shakespeare alludes. So, in Cartwright's *Lady Errant :* 'we'll keep you, As they do hawks, watching until you leave Your wildness.' Again, in *Monsieur D'Olive*, 1606: 'your only way to deal with women and parrots, is to keep them waking.' HARTING (p. 45) : A wild hawk was sometimes tamed by watching it night and day, to prevent its sleeping. So, in 'An approved treatyse of Hawks and Hawking,' by Edmund Berk, Gent, 1619 :—' I have heard of some who watched and kept their hawks awake seven nights and as many days, and then they would be wild, rammish, and disorderly.' PYE (p, 335) : This strumpet-like resolution of Desdemona takes off much from the interest we should take in her fate.   [In Pye's Preface, where he is pleased to speak favorably of Shakespeare (Pye was Poet Laureate, be it remembered), he observes that Shakespeare 'does not possess the power of Otway, and many inferior poets, in exciting pity.'   Should not a list of those poets who are superior to Shakespeare in exciting pity include Pye?   Is there anything in Shakespeare that excites more pity than this remark on Desdemona? Pye says that his Notes are the result of his 'perusal' of Shakespeare, which has been 'a favorite amusement in his hours of leisure.'   With what force is not the truth of the infant hymn driven home to us : ' For Satan finds some mischief still For idle hands to do'!—ED.]

Then giue thy caufe away.   3?

Enter Othello, and Iago.

Æmil. Madam, heere comes my Lord.   3¹

Caʃʃio. Madam, Ile take my leaue.

Deʃ. Why ftay, and heare me fpeake.

Caʃʃio. Madam, not now : I am very ill at eafe,
Vnfit for mine owne purpofes.

Deʃ. Well, do your difcretion.   *Exit Caʃʃ.ʳ.*   40

Iago. Hah? I like not that.

Othel. What doft thou fay ?

Iago. Nothing my Lord ; or if—I know not what.

Othel. Was not that *Caʃʃio* parted from my wife ?   44

---

33. *thy cauʃe*] *thee cauʃe :* Q₁.
Scene IV. Pope+, Jen.

33, 37. Lines end, *comes…stay…speak*
Steev.'93, Var. Knt, Sing.

34. Enter…] Enter *Othello, Iago,* and
Gentlemen Qq. …at distance. Theob.
After line 40, Dyce, Wh. Glo. Sta. Huds.
Rlfe.

37. *Why*] *Nay* Q₂Q₃, Jen.

38. *I am*] *I'm* Pope 'Iʀ↷ob. Han.
Warb. Dyce iii, Huds.

39. *purpoʃes*] *purpoʃe* Qq, Coll. i, Wh.
i, Ktly.

40. *Well*] Closing line 39, Sing. *Well,
well,* (closing line 39) Cap. Steev.'93, Var.

41. *Hah ?*] *Ha,* Qq.

43. *if—*] *if,* Q₁. *if;—*Q₂Q₃.

---

35 et seq. DELIUS : In short colloquies like this, Shakespeare is fond of using half
Alexandrines, which are usually cut up by the Editors into blank verse. CAPELL'S
emendation and division of line 40 occurred independently to WALKER (*Crit.* ii, 147).

40. FECHTER : Othello and Iago appear at the back, in the gallery. Emilia draws
the tapestry on the left, to give passage to Cassio. Iago (as by an involuntary movement) touches the arm of Othello, who raises his head at the moment when Cassio
bows to Desdemona and goes out. BOOTH : Enter Othello and Iago. Desdemona
and Emilia go with Cassio into the garden at back, and Cassio lingers just long
enough to be seen by Othello and Iago. The women remain for a moment after
his exit.

41. BOOTH : Don't growl this,—let it barely be heard by the audience.

44. FECHTER : Othello comes forward, opening dispatches and petitions, and followed by Iago. LEWES (*On Actors,* &c., p. 156) : It is one of Fechter's new arrangements that Othello, when the tempter begins his diabolical insinuation, shall be seated
at a table reading and signing papers. When I first heard of this bit of 'business' it
struck me as admirable ; and indeed I think so still ; although the manner in which
Fechter executes it is one of those lamentable examples in which the *dramatic* art is
subordinated to serve *theatrical* effect. (*Foot-note :* Having now seen Salvini in
Othello, I conclude that this 'business' was imitated from him,—but Fechter failed
to imitate the expression of emotion which renders such business significant.) That
Othello should be seated over his papers, and should reply to Iago's questions while
continuing his examination and affixing his signature, is *natural ;* but it is not natural,—that is, not true to the nature of Othello and the situation,—for him to be dead

Iago.   *Caſſio* my Lord *?* No ſure, I cannot thinke it   **45**
That he would ſteale away ſo guilty-like,
Seeing your comming.
  Oth.   I do beleeue 'twas he.
  Deſ.   How now my Lord?
I haue bin talking with a Suitor heere,   **50**
A man that languiſhes in your diſpleaſure.
  Oth.   Who is't you meane?
  Deſ.   Why your Lieutenant *Caſſio :* Good my Lord,
If I haue any grace, or power to moue you,
His preſent reconciliation take.   **55**
For if he be not one, that truly loues you,
That erres in Ignorance, and not in Cunning,
I haue no iudgement in an honeſt face.
I prythee call him backe.
  Oth.   Went he hence now?   **60**
  Deſ.   I footh ; ſo humbled,
That he hath left part of his greefe with mee
To ſuffer with him.   Good Loue, call him backe.   **63**

---

45. *Lord ?*] *Lord ?—* Qq.
46. *ſteale*] *ſneake* Q₁.
47. *your*] F₂, Knt. *you* QqF₃F₄, Rowe
et cet.
48. *do*] Om. Pope+.
48, 49. One line, Walker.
53. Caſſio :] Caſſio, Qq.   Caſſio. Ff.
60, 61. One line, Walker.
61. *I footh*] F₂. *Yes faith* Qq. *I, Sooth*

F₃F₄, Theob.Warb.   *In sooth* Rowe, Pope,
Han.   *I' sooth* Johns. Jen.   *Ay, sooth* Cap.
et cet.
        humbled] *humbl'd* Cap. (corrected
in Errata).
    62. *hath*] *has* Qq.
        greefe] *griefes* Qq.
    63. *To ſuffer*] *I ſuffer* Q₁, Mal. Steev.
Var. Sing. Ktly.

---

to the dreadful import of Iago's artful suggestions.   [I do not know when Salvini
first acted Othello, but Fechter, I believe, had acted Othello many times when his *Acting Copy* was printed in 1861.—ED.]

48. BOOTH: Exeunt Iago and Emilia.   Their presence would distract attention;
besides, it is proper for them to retire during an interview between their superiors.

49. FECHTER: Othello kisses Desdemona on the forehead.

55. **take**] WARBURTON: Cassio was to be reconciled to his General, not his General to him; therefore 'take' cannot be right.   We should read *make*.   JOHNSON: To
take his reconciliation, may be to accept the submission which he makes in order to be
reconciled.

57. **Cunning**] WARBURTON: *Design* or *purpose* simply.   MALONE: Perhaps,
rather, *knowledge*, the ancient sense of the word.   It is opposed to ignorance.

60. FECHTER: Othello seats himself in Desdemona's chair and returns to his papers,
as if to break the conversation.

61. **humbled**] WALKER (*Crit.* iii, 286): A trisyllable here.

Othel.   Not now (fweet *Defdemon*) fome other time.
Def.   But fhall't be fhortly?   65
Oth.   The fooner (Sweet) for you.
Def.   Shall't be to night, at Supper?
Oth.   No, not to night.
Def.   To morrow Dinner then?
Oth.   I fhall not dine at home: 70
I meete the Captaines at the Cittadell.
Def.   Why then to morrow night, on Tuefday morne,
On Tuefday noone, or night; on Wenfday Morne.
I prythee name the time, but let it not   74

64. Defdemon] F₂F₃Q₂, Knt, Sing.
Dyce, Wh. i, Sta. Hal. Del. Coll. iii, Huds.
Defdemona Q₁Q₃F₄, Rowe et cet.
  66. *The fooner*] *Sooner* Pope, Han.
  68. *No, not*] *Not* Pope+.
  72. *on*] Ff, Rowe, Knt.   *or* Qq et cet.
  73. *On Tuefday*] *Or Tuesday* Pope+,
Cap. Steev. Mal. Var. Sing. Ktly.
    noone] *morne* Qq.

73. *night; on*] night, *or* Qq, Pope+,
Jen. *night; or* Cap. Steev. Mal.Var. Sing.
Ktly.
    Wenfday] *wedenfday* Q₃. *wednef-
day* Q₂F₃F₄.
    7.†. *prythee*] *preethee* Q₁. *prethee* Q₂Q₃
F₃F₄. *praythee* F₂. *pray thee* Cap. Steev.
Mal. Var.

---

64. **Desdemon**] See III, i, 58. Booth: He leads her to the couch—they sit.
  67. **to night**] Heraud (p. 278): I know not whether the poet had any design in it, but it may be, and perhaps profitably, remarked that the action of the Third Act takes place on a Sunday. . . . . In the arrangements of the scene, the different persons engaged in it should appear as if coming from their devotions. In the next Act we find Othello derisively alluding to having seen the meretricious Emilia so engaged; and this event may have happened on this very Sunday, and probably had.
  70. Lewes (p. 158): These preceding short, evasive sentences are subtly expressive of Othello's mind; but Fechter misrepresents them by making Othello free from all misgiving. He 'toys with her curls,' and treats her as a father might treat a child who was asking some favour which could not be granted yet, which called for no explicit refusal. If the scene stood alone, I should read it differently; but standing as it does between the two attempts of Iago to fill Othello's mind with suspicion, the meaning is plain enough. He has been made uneasy by Iago's remarks; very naturally, his bearing towards his wife reveals that uneasiness. A *vague* feeling, which he dares not shape into a suspicion, disturbs him. She conquers him at last by her winning ways; and he vows that he will deny her nothing. If this be the state of mind in which the great scene begins, it is obviously a serious mistake in Fechter to sit down to his papers, perfectly calm, free from all idea whatever of what Iago has suggested; and answering Iago's insidious questions as if he did not divine their import. So clearly does Othello divine their import that it is *he*, and not Iago, who expresses in words their meaning. It is one of the artifices of Iago to make his victim draw every conclusion from prem- ises which are put before him, so that, in the event of detection, he can say, 'I said nothing, I made no accusation.' All he does is to lead the thoughts of Othello to the conclusion desired.
  72, 73. **On**] Knight: The repetition of 'on' is much more emphatic than *or*.

Exceed three dayes.   Infaith hee's penitent :   75
And yet his Trefpaffe, in our common reafon
(Saue that they fay the warres muft make example)
Out of her beft, is not almoft a fault
T'encurre a priuate checke.   When fhall he come?
Tell me *Othello.*   I wonder in my Soule   80
What you would aske me, that I fhould deny,
Or ftand fo mam'ring on?   What? *Michael Caffio,*
That came a woing wirh you? and fo many a time
(When I haue fpoke of you difpraifingly)   84

75. *Infaith*] *Ifaith* Qq. *In faith* Rowe et seq.

77. *warres*] *war* Cap.

77, 78. *example)...beft,*] Ff. *example... best,*) Rowe ii, Pope, Han. Knt, Sta. *examples...beft*) Qq et cet.

78. *her*] QqFf, Cap. Coll. i, Dyce i, Wh. i, Hal. Del. *the* Sing. ii, Huds. *our* Coll. iii (MS). *their* Rowe et cet.

almoft] *at most* Anon (ap. Cam.).

79. *T'encurre*] *T'incurre* F_2F_3. *T'in-*

cur F_4, Rowe+, Coll. Wh. i, Dyce iii, Huds.   *To incurre* Qq et cet.

81. *would*] *could* Qq, Cap. Jen. Steev Mal. Var. Coll. Sing. Wh. i, Ktly, Del.

I fhould] *I would* Ff, Rowe+.

82. *mam'ring*] *muttering* Q_1, Pope Theob. Warb. *mummering* Johns. *mammering* or *mamm'ring* Cap. et cet.

83. *fo*] Om. Pope+, Cap. Steev.'93.

84. *difpraifingly*] *disparagingly* Mrs Jameson.

78. **her best**] JOHNSON : The severity of military discipline must not spare the *best men* of their army when their punishment may afford a wholesome *example.* COLLIER (ed. i) : A personification of 'the wars,' which Shakespeare often treats as a substantive in the singular. COLLIER (ed. ii) : 'Her best' is a misprint for '*our* best,' as appears by the (MS.) DYCE (ed. i) : If we consider 'the wars' as used for *war generally,* the usual modern alteration, '*their* best,' is unnecessary. DYCE (ed. iii) : 'I must own I think "her" wrong. *The* is perhaps better than *their* or *our*.'—W. N. LETTSOM. [Would the difficulty be lessened by considering the *s* in 'Warres' that superfluous letter to which Walker, I, i, 31, calls attention, and of which, in this play, some eight instances are given?—ED.]

78. **not almost**] ABBOTT, § 29 : 'Almost' frequently follows the word which it qualifies. Hence, in negative sentences 'not-almost,' where we should use 'almost not,' or, in one word, 'scarcely,' 'hardly.' Thus, here, in this present instance, it is equivalent to, 'Is *not* (*I may almost say*) fault enough to,' &c., or, 'is *scarcely* fault enough to,' &c. It was natural for the Elizabethans to dislike putting the qualifying 'almost' before the word qualified by it. But there was an ambiguity in their idiom. 'Not almost-a-fault' would mean 'not approaching to a fault'; 'not-almost a fault, 'very nearly not a fault.' We have, therefore, done well in avoiding the ambiguity by disusing 'almost' in negative sentences.

82. **mam'ring**] HANMER (*Gloss.*) : To hesitate, to stand in suspense. HALLIWELL cites from Lyly's *Euphues* [p. 299, ed. Arber] : 'I ftoode in a great mamering, how I might behaue my felfe, least being too coye he might thinke mee proud, or vsing too much curtesie, he might iudge mee wanton.'

83. **with you**] See Note on I, ii, 64.

Hath tane your part, to haue fo much to do   85
To bring him in? Truft me, I could do much.

 Oth. Prythee no more : Let him come when he will :
I will deny thee nothing.

 Def. Why, this is not a Boone :
'Tis as I fhould entreate you weare your Gloues,   [323 *b*]
Or feede on nourifhing difhes, or keepe you warme,   91
Or fue to you, to do a peculiar profit
To your owne perfon. Nay, when I haue a fuite
Wherein I meane to touch your Loue indeed,
It fhall be full of poize, and difficult waight,   95
And fearefull to be granted.

 Oth. I will deny thee nothing.
Whereon, I do befeech thee, grant me this,
To leaue me but a little to my felfe.

 Def. Shall I deny you ? No : farewell my Lord.   10C

 Oth. Farewell my *Defdemona*, Ile come to thee ftrait.

86. *Truft me*] *Birlady* Q₁.
 much.] Q₁Ff. *much,*— or *much*—
Q₂Q₃ et cet.
 87. *Prythee*] *Preethee* Q₁. *Prethee* Q₂
Q₃F₃F₄. *Prithee* Q.'81.
 88. [Re-enter Iago and Em. Booth.
 90. *Gloues*] *cloths* Warb.
 91. *difhes*] *meats* Pope+.
 92. *you,*] *you* Cap.
  a] Om. Pope+, Cap. Steev.'93,Var.
Dyce iii, Huds.

 93. *a fuite*] *fuit* F₃F₄, Rowe+.
 95. *poize*] *poife* Qq.
  difficult waight] *difficulty* Q₁,
Pope+, Cap. Steev. Mal. Var. Sing. Ktly,
Sta.
  waight] *weight* Q₂Q₃F₃F₄.
 101. Defdemona] Defdomona Q₁. Def-
damona F₂. *Defdemon* Dyce iii.
  Ile] *I will* Cap. Steev. Mal. Var.
Sing. Ktly.
  to thee] Om. Pope+.

---

84. **difpraifingly**] BOOTH : Reprove her playfully. Throughout this colloquy gaze
lovingly in her face, and seem to encourage her to *coax* by your teasing silence.

86. BOOTH : Here she begins to 'pout' at her failure to obtain his consent, and he,
fearing that she has misconstrued his silence during her last appeal, stops her with a kiss.

91. **dishes**] WALKER (*Vers.* 267): The extra syllable in the body of the line
seems hardly allowable, where the pause is so slight; and yet '*dish*' for '*dishes*'
appears much too harsh.

92. **a**] WALKER (*Crit.* i, 88) suggests that this is one of the many instances where
ɪ is interpolated in the Folio, and, if it can be dispensed with, it should be omitted here
for the sake of rhythm. [See Text. Notes.]

95. **poize**] KNIGHT: In the sense before us 'poize' is *balance*, and Desdemona
means to say that, when she really prefers a suit that shall task the love of Othello, it
shall be one difficult to determine; and, when determined, hard to be undertaken.
DYCE (*Gloss.*): Weight, moment, importance. STAUNTON : Since 'poize' means
weight, the line in F₁ is apparently an error, arising probably from the poet's having,
in the first instance, written both *poize* and *weight*, uncertain which to adopt, and afterwards, forgotten to cancel the discarded word.

Def.   *Æmilia* come ; be as your Fancies teach you :   102
What ere you be, I am obedient.   *Exit.*

Oth.   Excellent wretch : Perdition catch my Soule
But I do loue thee : and when I loue thee not,   105
Chaos is come againe.

102. *come : be*] Ff, Rowe+, Knt. *come,*   Exeunt *Def.* and *Em.* Q₂Q₃.
be it Qq. *come ; be it* Cap. Jen. Steev. Mal.   Scene V. Pope+, Jen.
Var. Coll. Sing. Wh. i, Ktly. *Come. Be*   104. *wretch :*] *wretch,* Qq. *wretch :*
Johns. et cet.   Rowe. *wench !* Theob. Han. Wh. ii.
103. Exit] Exit *Defd.* and *Em.* Q₁.

---

104. FECHTER : Othello follows her with his eyes, and sends her a last kiss.

104–106. BOOTH : With joyousness,—yet there should be an undertone of sadness,
—as at their first embrace in Cyprus. Iago, at the back of the stage, watches him with
a sneering smile.

104. **wretch**] THEOBALD : This word can scarce be admitted to be used unless in
compassion or contempt. I make no question but that the Poet wrote *wench*, which
was not then used in that low and vulgar acceptation as at present. See ' ill-starr'd
wench,' V, ii, 335. UPTON (p. 289, n.) : Giraldi Cinthio calls Desdemona, in allusion
to her name, *la infelice Disdemona*. And I make no question but Othello, in his rapturous admiration, with some allusion to her name, exclaims, ' Excellent *wretch*.'
HEATH (p. 561) : The poison of jealousy has already begun to work in Othello, infused by the artful hints and half sentences of Iago, and by the frank and pressing
solicitations of Desdemona on behalf of Cassio. His assurance in her faith and virtue is already somewhat staggered, and he begins to consider it as a thing possible that
she may be unworthy of his love. To this state of mind this exclamation is admirably
well adapted, expressing the utmost fondness, and at the same time a distrust growing
upon him. If the etymology of the name had been known to Shakespeare, as Upton
suggests, he would not have spoiled it by changing it from Disdemona to Desdemona.
JOHNSON : The meaning of the word ' wretch ' is not generally understood. It is now,
in some parts of England, a term of the softest and fondest tenderness. It expresses
the utmost degree of amiableness, joined with an idea which, perhaps, all tenderness
includes, of feebleness, softness, and want of protection. Othello, considering Desdemona as excelling in beauty and virtue, soft and timorous by her sex, and by her situation absolutely in his power, calls her ' Excellent wretch ! ' It may be expressed :
' Dear, harmless, helpless excellence.' COLLIER : Such words of endearment are re-
sorted to when those implying love, admiration, and delight seem inadequate. [One
of Collier's best notes in this play.—ED.] HUDSON : As here used, ' wretch ' was the
strongest expression of endearment in the language. WHITE (ed. ii) : It is needless
to point out that ' wretch ' may be used as a term of fondest endearment ; but not in
connection with ' excellent.' The misprint [from *wench* to ' wretch '] was easy.

106. **Chaos**] JOHNSON : When my love is for a moment suspended by suspicion, ɪ
have nothing in my mind but discord, tumult, perturbation, and confusion. STEEVENS :
There is another meaning possible : ' When I cease to love thee, the world is at an
end,' i. e., there remains nothing valuable or important. The first explanation may be
more elegant ; the second is perhaps more easy. There is the same thought in *V. &
A.,* l. 1019 : ' For he being dead, with him is beauty slain, And, beauty dead, black
Chaos comes again.' [HUNTER (ii, 282) also cites this passage from *V. & A.* as one

Iago.   My Noble Lord.   107
Oth.   What doſt thou ſay, *Iago* ?
Iago.   Did *Michael Caſſio*
When he woo'd my Lady, know of your loue ?   110
Oth.   He did, from firſt to laſt :
Why doſt thou aske ?
Iago.   But for a ſatisfaction of my Thought,
No further harme.
Oth.   Why of thy thought, *Iago* ?   115
Iago.   I did not thinke he had bin acquainted with hir.
Oth.   O yes, and went betweene vs very oft.
Iago.   Indeed ?   118

107. *Lord.*] QqFf.   *lord,*— Theob. et
ſeq.
109, 110. *Did...Lady*] One line, Qq,
Pope et seq.
110. *he*] *you* QqFf et cet.
woo'd] *wooed* Qq.
111, 112. One line, Qq, Pope et seq.
113. *for a*] *for* Q₃.

113. *Thought,*] *thoughts.* Q_r.
114. *further*] *farther* Pope ii.
116. *he had*] *he'd* Pope, Theob. Han.
Warb.
hir] *it* Ff, Rowe +, Cap. Jen. Wh.
ii.   *her* Qq et cet.
117. *oft*] *often* Q_r.

---

of the many in this play, more than in any other, which remind us of that poem and of
R. of L.]   MALONE: Compare the same thought in *Wint. Tale,* IV, iv, 490 : ' It cannot fail but by The violation of my faith ; and then Let nature crush the sides o' the
earth together and mar the seeds within ! '   FRANZ HORN (i, 330) : Othello refers to
the chaos in his life before he knew Desdemona.

107. RYMER (p. 118) : One might think after what we have seen, that there needs
no great cunning, no great poetry and address to make the Moor jealous.   Such impatience, such a rout for a handsome young fellow, the very morning after her marriage,
must make him either to be jealous, or to take her for a *Changeling* below his jealousie.
After this scene, it might strain the Poet's skill to reconcile the couple, and allay the
jealousie.   Iago now can only *actum agere,* and vex the audience with a nauseous
repetition.   Whence comes it then that this is the top scene, the scene that raises
Othello above all other Tragedies on our Theatres ?   It is purely from the *Action ;*
from the Mops and the Mows, the Grimace, the Grins, and Gesticulation.   [It is to
be hoped that the reader comprehends the motive which prompts the occasional insertion of these criticisms by Rymer.   He has read his Shakespeare to little purpose
who does not appreciate the relief, amid tragic scenes, afforded by a dash of buf-
foonery.—ED.]

114. *harme*] BOOTH : With the merest shade of emphasis.   FECHTER : Othello,
at the table, throwing aside some of his papers and signing others.

116. *hir*] WHITE (ed. ii) : Cassio's acquaintance or non-acquaintance with Desdemona had no necessary connection with his knowledge of Othello's love.   [See Text.
Notes.]

118. BOOTH : Contract the brows, but do not frown,—rather look disappointed, and
merely mutter in surprise, ' Indeed ' !

Oth.   Indeed? I indeed. Difcern'ft thou ought in that?
Is he not honeft?   120
Iago.   Honeft, my Lord?
Oth.   Honeft? I, Honeft.
Iago.   My Lord, for ought I know.
Oth.   What do'ft thou thinke?
Iago.   Thinke, my Lord?   125
Oth.   Thinke, my Lord?   Alas, thou ecchos't me;

---

119. *I indeed*] *Indeed* Q₁. *Ay, indeed* Rowe et seq. Om. Steev. conj.
119, 123. *ought*] *aught* Theob. ii et seq.
119. *in that*] *of that* Rowe, Pope, Han.
122. *Honeft? I, Honeft*] *Ay, honest* (reading lines 120, 121, 122 as one line) Steev.'93.
124–126. *What...Lord?*] One line,
Steev.'93, Var. Coll. Sing. Dyce, Wh. Glo. Del. Rlfe.
126. *Alas...me;*] Separate line, Steev. '93, Var. Coll. Sing. Dyce, Wh. Glo. Del. Rlfe.
Alas, thou ecchos't] Ff, Rowe, Knt. *why doft thou ecchoe* Q₂Q₃, Johns. Jen. *why, by heav'n, thou eccho'st* Pope+. *By heauen he ecchoes* Q₁ et cet.

---

121. **Honest**] BOOTH: Hesitatingly.

122. **Honest?**] STEEVENS: It appears from many instances that where words were to be repeated at all, our old, blundering printers continued the repetition beyond propriety. [See Text. Notes.] KNIGHT: This re-echo of Iago's echo is rejected by Steevens, because it violates the measure. He could only see two syllables beyond the ten, without any regard to the force and consistency of the passage.

123. BOOTH: With indifference. FECHTER marks this as a broken speech, by a dash after 'know—'

125. BOOTH: With embarrassment.

126. COLERIDGE (*Note on Winter's Tale*, p. 243): The idea of this delightful drama [*The Winter's Tale*] is a genuine jealousy of disposition, and it should be immediately followed by the perusal of *Othello*, which is the direct contrast of it in every particular. For jealousy is a vice of the mind, a culpable tendency of the temper, having certain well-known and well-defined effects and concomitants, all of which are visible in Leontes, and, I boldly say, not one of which marks its presence in Othello;—such as, first, an excitability by the most inadequate causes, and an eagerness to snatch at proofs; secondly, a grossness of conception, and a disposition to degrade the object of the passion by sensual fancies and images; thirdly, a sense of shame of his own feelings exhibited in a solitary moodiness of humour, and yet from the violence of the passion forced to utter itself, and therefore catching occasions to ease the mind by ambiguities, equivoques, by talking to those who cannot, and who are known not to be able to, understand what is said to them,—in short, by soliloquy in the form of dialogue, and hence a confused, broken, and fragmentary manner; fourthly, a dread of vulgar ridicule, as distinct from a high sense of honour or a mistaken sense of duty; and lastly, and immediately consequent on this, a spirit of selfish vindictiveness.

126. **Alas**] MALONE: One of the numerous alterations made in the Folio by the licenser. KNIGHT: There is, in this reading, a quiet expression of dread,—a solemn

As if there were fome Monfter in thy thought   127
Too hideous to be fhewne.   Thou doft mean fomthing :
I heard thee fay euen now, thou lik'ft not that,
When *Caffio* left my wife.   What didd'ft not like ?   130
And when I told thee, he was of my Counfaile,
Of my whole courfe of wooing ; thou cried'ft,   Indeede ?
And didd'ft contract, and purfe thy brow together,
As if thou then hadd'ft fhut vp in thy Braine
Some horrible Conceite.   If thou do'ft loue me,   135
Shew me thy thought.
    Iago.   My Lord, you know I loue you.
    Oth.   I thinke thou do'ft :
And for I know thou'rt full of Loue, and Honeftie,
And weigh'ft thy words before thou giu'ft them breath,   140
Therefore thefe ftops of thine, fright me the more :
For fuch things in a falfe difloyall Knaue
Are trickes of Cuftome : but in a man that's iuft,
They're clofe dilations, working from the heart,   144

127. *thy*] Ff, Rowe+, Jen. Knt.   *his*
Q₁ et cet.
  128. *doft*] *didft* Q₁.
  129. *euen*] Ff, Rowe, Knt, Dyce, Glo.
Cam. Rlfe.   *but* Qq et cet.
    lik'ft] QqFf, Rowe.   *lik'dst* Pope
et cet.
  132. *Of my*] Ff, Rowe.   *In my* Qq et
cet.
  135. *Conceite*] *counfell* Q₁.   *conceits*
Rowe ii.
  138. *do'ft*] *doest* Theob. ii, Warb.
  139. *And for*] Qq, Rowe+, Cam.   *For*
Ff.   *And,—for* or *And, for* Cap. et cet.
    thou'rt] *thou't* F₃F₄.   *thou art*
Qq, Pope ii, Theob. Warb. Johns. Jen.

Steev. Mal. Var. Coll. Sing. Wh. i, Ktly.
  139. *Loue and*] Om. Han.
  140. *weigh'ft*] *weigheft* Qq.
    giu'ft them] *giue em* Q₁.   *giu'ft
'em* Q₂Q₃.
  141. *fright*] *affright* Q₁.
  142. *falfe difloyall*] *false-disloyal* Sta.
  144. *They're*] Ff, Rowe+, Knt, Dyce,
Wh. i, Sta. Cam. Del. Huds.   *They are*
Qq et cet.
    clofe] *cold* Ff, Rowe, Theob. Warb.
Om. Han.
    dilations] FfQ₂Q₃, Rowe, Theob.
Warb. Johns. Jen. Sta.   *denotements* Q₁,
Pope, Cap. Mal. Steev.'93, Var. Hal. *distillations* Han. *delations* Steev.'73 et cet.

foreboding of evil.   COLLIER : Tame and flat.   HUDSON : It is not easy to choose
between the three readings, but I am strongly inclined to prefer Q₂.   ROLFE : The
'alas' was, of course, put in to fill the gap made by the omission of the oath.

  128. BOOTH : Iago again pretends embarrassment.

  137. BOOTH : Reproachfully.   FECHTER : Taking his hand, across the table, and
grasping it with feigned emotion.

  144. dilations] UPTON (p. 291) : From the Latin *dilationes*, delayings, pauses, à
differendo.   [This is one of the very many instances cited by Upton to prove that
Shakespeare 'makes Latin words English, and uses them according to their original
idiom.']   WARBURTON : These stops and breaks are cold dilations, or cold keeping
back a secret, which men of phlegmatic constitutions, whose hearts are not swayed or

That Paſſion cannot rule.   145
   Iago.   For *Michael Caſsio,*
I dare be ſworne, I thinke that he is honeſt.   147

---

147. *be ſworne*] *preſume* Q₁.   147. *that he*] *he* Q₃.

---

governed by their passions, can do; while more sanguine tempers reveal themselves at
once, and without reserve.   JOHNSON: The reading of the earlier Quarto was changed
by the author not to 'dilations, but to *delations;* to *occult* and *secret accusations, working* involuntarily *from the heart,* which, though resolved to conceal the fault, cannot rule its *passion* of resentment.   STEEVENS: I should willingly have adopted Dr
Johnson's emendation, could I have discovered that the word *delation* was ever used
in its Roman sense of *accusation,* during the time of Shakespeare.   Bacon frequently
employs it, but always to signify *carriage* or *conveyance.*   MALONE: *Delation* is not
found in any Dictionary that I have seen, nor has any passage been quoted in support
of it.   On the contrary, we find in Minsheu the verb 'To delate,' not signifying to
accuse, but thus interpreted: '*to speak at large* of anything, vid. to *dilate*'; so that if
even *delations* were the word of the old copy, it would mean no more than '*dilations.*'
No reasonable objection can be made to *denotements,* i. e., indications, or recoveries,
not openly revealed, but involuntarily working from the heart, which cannot rule and
suppress its feelings.   Nothing is got by the change of the Folio to 'dilations,' which
was undoubtedly used in the sense of *dilatements,* or *large and full expositions.*   BOS-
WELL: In Todd's Johnson an authority is given for *delations* in the sense of *accusations,* from Wotten's *Remains,* p. 460, ed. 1651.   KNIGHT: We have adopted Johnson's
ingenious suggestion of *delations,* i. e., secret accusations.   STAUNTON: 'Dilations' may
be a contraction of *distillations* [see Text. N.], and the meaning of 'close dilations,'
secret droppings.   WHITE (ed. i): *Delations,* i. e., subtle, intimate confessions or in-
formations.   WHITE (ed. ii): *Delations,* i. e., revelations.   [To me the interpretations,
'secret accusation,' and the others, are here barely intelligible.   What has frighted
Othello is these 'stops,' these pauses, of Iago, which he would have disregarded in a
false knave, as a common trick, but in a man that's just, such 'stops,' such 'dilations'
indicate something deeper, some horrible conceit which he hesitates to disclose, and
which makes him weigh his words and protract the revelation.   For 'dilation' Shakespeare had the classical and common Latin word meaning to delay, as Upton pointed
out, and he had, besides, the very same word, exactly so spelled, in French.   Cotgrave
gives: 'Dilation: A deferring, delaying, prolonging, protraction.'   I do not think this
explanation pre-eminently happy.   I have seen better explanations of difficult passages
—and worse.—ED.]

   145. **Passion**] STAUNTON: Unless this word is here employed in the unusual
sense of *prudence, caution,* &c., we must understand Othello to mean,—working
from a heart that cannot govern its emotions.   [I prefer Warburton's interpretation in
the preceding note.—ED.]   HUDSON: It should be noted that in all this part of the
dialogue the doubts started in Othello by the villain's artful insinuations have reference only to Cassio.   There is not the least sign that the Moor's thoughts anywise
touch his wife; and Iago seems perplexed that his suspicions have lighted elsewhere
than he had intended.   The circumstance is very material in reference to Othello's
predispositions, or as regards the origin and nature of his jealousy.

   147. **sworne**] DYCE (ed. ii, 1866): 'Should not this be written with a break, as if
Iago were correcting himself?   "I dare be sworn—I think," &c.'—W. N. LETTSOM.

Oth.   I thinke fo too.   148

Iago.   Men fhould be what they feeme,

Or thofe that be not, would they might feeme none.   150

Oth.   Certaine, men fhould be what they feeme.

Iago.   Why then I thinke *Cafsio's* an honeft man.

Oth.   Nay, yet there's more in this ?

I prythee fpeake to me, as to thy thinkings,

As thou doft ruminate, and giue thy worft of thoughts   155

The worft of words.   [324 *a*]

Iago.   Good my Lord pardon me,

Though I am bound to euery Acte of dutie,

I am not bound to that : All Slaues are free :   159

---

148. *too*] *to* Qq.
149. *what*] *that* Q₁.
150. *feeme none.*] *feeme,* Q₃.
151. *Certaine, men*] *Certain men,* Q₃.
151, 152. *Certaine...Why then*] One line (reading *that Cassio is* in 152) Steev. '93.
153. *there's*] *ther's* Q₂Q₃.
this ?] *this,* Qq.
154. *prythee*] *pray thee* Ff, Rowe+, Cap. Steev. Mal. Var. Coll. Sing. Wh. i,

Ktly, Del.
154. *as to*] *to* Q₁.
thy] *my* Rowe ii.
155. *As...worft*] One line, Han.
thy...thoughts] *the...thought* Q₁.
thy thoughts Q₃.
156. *words*] *word* Q₁.
158. *Though I am*] *I am not* Rowe ii.
159. *that: All*] *that, all* Rowe+. *that all* Qq, Han. et seq.
free] Ff. *free to* Qq et cet.

[Five years earlier, FECHTER had so printed the line, and had also put a dash after 'Cassio.'—ED.]

149. **be**] BOOTH : With the least possible suggestiveness in tone and look.

150. **none**] WARBURTON : There is no sense in this reading. I suppose Shake speare wrote *knaves*. HEATH (p. 562) : I am rather inclined to think that it should be : 'they might *be known*.' That is, I wish there were any certain way of distinguishing and detecting them. JOHNSON : I believe the meaning is, ''would they might no longer seem, or bear the shape of men.' JENNENS : The old reading is plain enough. Those that seem honest should be honest, or those that be not what they seem, i. e., honest, would they might seem none, i. e., have no seeming or appearance of honesty.

151. FECHTER : Rising, without leaving the table; and smiling as if in raillery.

152. BOOTH : As though you would dismiss an unpleasant topic.

158. **Though I am**] The misprint in Rowe's ed. ii (see Text. Notes) POPE, in his edition, prints at the foot of the page, as though it were a genuine reading of the old text, and a proof of the fidelity of his collation. In his Preface Pope says that he had discharged the 'dull duty of editor with more labour than he expected thanks;' apparently at times the dulness was very great and the labour very small.—ED.

159. **free :**] MALONE [See Text. N.] : I am not bound to do that which even slaves are not bound to do. STEEVENS : So, in *Cymb.* V, i, 7 : 'Every good servant does not all commands : No bond but to do just ones.' ROLFE : We may say that 'free' is equivalent to *not bound*.

Vtter my Thoughts? Why fay, they are vild, and falce?   160
As where's that Palace, whereinto foule things
Sometimes intrude not? Who ha's that breaſt ſo pure,
Wherein vncleanly Apprehenſions
Keepe Leetes, and Law-dayes, and in Seſſions ſit
With meditations lawfull?   165
  Oth. Thou do'ſt conſpire againſt thy Friend (*Iago*)
If thou but think'ſt him wrong'd, and mak'ſt his eare
A ſtranger to thy Thoughts.
  Iago. I do beſeech you,
Though I perchance am vicious in my gueſſe   170

160. *Thoughts?*] thoughts: Q₂Q₃.
Why ſay,] Why, ſay Qq.   Why
ſay F₃F₄.   Why, say, Theob.
    they are] they're Pope+, Dyce iii,
Huds.
    vild] Ff, Rowe.   vile Qq et cet.
161. *As where's*] As, where's F₄, Rowe i.
162. *ha's*] has QqF₃F₄.
    that] Ff, Rowe, Knt, Coll. iii.   a
Qq et cet.
    ſo] of Q₃.
163. *Wherein*] Ff.   But ſome Qq et cet.

164. *Seſſions*] Ff, Rowe+, Jen. Knt,
Sing. Ktly, Del.   Seſſion Qq et cet.
167. *think'ſt...mak'ſt*] thinkeſt...mak-
eſt Qq.
169, 170. *you,...perchance*] QqFf,
Rowe, Pope, Cap.   you, Cauſe I perchance
Han.   you, Think I, perchance, Warb.
you, Though, I— perchance, Johns.   you,
Though I, perchance Theob. ii, Jen. Knt.
you,— Though I, perchance, Mal. Steev.
'93 et seq.
170. *gueſſe*] gheſſe Qq.

160. BOOTH: Don't speak this as though you held your thoughts to be really 'vile
and false,' nor *look* so; be frank in appearance.

161, 162. MALONE: So, in *R. of L.*, 854: 'But no perfection is so absolute, That
some impurity doth not pollute.'

163. **Wherein**] Qu. a misprint for *Where no?*—ED.

164. **Leetes**] WARBURTON: A metaphor wretchedly forced and quaint.   STEEV-
ENS: 'Leets' and 'law-days' are synonymous terms: 'Leet,' says Jacob, *Law Dict.*,
'is otherwise called a law-day.'   They are there explained to be courts, or meetings
of the *hundred*, 'to certify the King of the good manners, and government, of the
inhabitants,' and to enquire of all offences that are not capital.   MALONE: Who has
so virtuous a breast that some uncharitable surmises and impure conceptions will not
sometimes enter into it; hold a session there as in a regular court, and 'bench by the
side' of authorized and lawful thoughts?   We find the same imagery in the 30th *Sonnet;* 'When to the sessions of sweet silent thought.'

164. **Sessions**] DYCE (ed. iii): *Session* occurs in Shakespeare oftener than 'sessions.'   [See WALKER (*Crit.* i, 233), Art. xxxviii: The final *s* frequently interpolated,
and frequently omitted, in the first Folio.]

170. **Though**] THEOBALD, in a letter to Warburton (Nichols's *Illust.* ii, 593),
writes: 'I own I cannot understand the reasoning of this passage.—" *Though* I, per
haps, am vicious, &c., do not let your wisdom give you disturbance," &c.   *Hoc minime
videtur Shakespearianum.*   I have conjectured "*Think*, I perchance," &c.   [Theobald
did not repeat this in his ed., but WARBURTON did in his, without alluding to Theobald,
and complacently added that the sense thereby was made 'pertinent and perfect.'—ED.]

(As I confeſſe it is my Natures plague   171
To ſpy into Abuſes, and of my iealouſie
Shapes faults that are not) that your wiſedome
From one, that ſo imperfeƈtly conceits,
Would take no notice, nor build your ſelfe a trouble   175

172. *Abuſes*] *abuse* Pope+.
of my] Ff, Rowe i, Pope ii, Knt,
Dyce i, Wh. i. *oft my* Qq et cet.

173. *Shapes*] *Shape* Knt, Dyce i, Wh. i.
that your wiſedome] Ff, Rowe,
Knt, Sta. *I intreate you then* Q₂, Pope +,
Jen. Mal. Steev.'93, Var. *that your wiſedome yet* Q₂Q₃ et cet.

174. *imperfeƈtly*] *improbably* Johns.
conceits] *conieƈts* Q₁. *conjects*
Warb. Jen. Mal. Steev.'93, Var.

175. *Would*] *You'd* Q₁, Jen. Mal. Steev.
'93, Var. *Will* Q₃.
Would ... build] *Your wisdom
would not build* Pope+.

HEATH (p. 562): 'Vicious' doth not signify here, *wrong* or *mistaken*, but, apt to put
the worst construction upon everything. The sense then is, 'I beseech you, though I
for my own part am perhaps apt to see everything in the worst light, which is a fault in
my nature that carries its own punishment with it, yet let me intreat you that my imperfect conjectures, with the loose and uncertain observations on which they are founded,
may not be the means of raising disquiet in the breast of a person whose wisdom is so
much superior to mine.' The abrupt and broken character of the sentence was purposely intended, as it represents the artful perplexity of fraud and circumvention practising on the credulity of an open, honest heart. STEEVENS: Iago seems desirous by
his abruptness and ambiguity to inflame the jealousy of Othello, which he knew would
be more effectually done in this manner than by any expression that bore a determinate
meaning. The jealous Othello would fill up the pause in the speech, which Iago turns
off at last to another purpose, and find a more certain cause of discontent, and a greater
degree of torture in the doubtful consideration how it might have concluded, than he
could have experienced had the whole of what he inquired after been reported to him
with every circumstance of aggravation. We may suppose him imagining to himself
that Iago mentally continued the thought thus, 'Though I—know more than I choose
to speak of.' MALONE: The adversative 'though' does not appear very proper; but
in an abrupt and studiously clouded sentence like the present, where more is meant
than meets the ear, strict propriety may well be dispensed with. KNIGHT: The modern editors enter into a long discussion about abruptness, and obscurity, and regulation
of the pointing, without taking the slightest notice of the perfectly clear reading of the
Folio, which we give without the alteration of a point or letter. COWDEN-CLARKE:
'Though' is here used in the sense of 'inasmuch as' or 'since.' ROLFE: The reading of Q₁ for 'that your wisdom,' line 173, perhaps better suits the broken character
of the sentence. Possibly, in revising the play Shakespeare made the change to the
more logical form of the Folio, and overlooked the 'though,' which does not suit that
form so well. HUDSON: Iago here feigns self-distrust, and confesses that he has the
natural infirmity or plague of a suspicious and prying temper, that he may make Othello
trust him the more strongly. So men often prate about, and even magnify, their own
faults, in order to cheat others into a persuasion of their rectitude and candour.

174. imperfectly] CAMBRIDGE EDITORS: Johnson attributes the reading *improbably* to what he calls 'the old Quarto.' We have not found it in any copies.

174. conceits] MALONE: *Conject* of the Q₁ is to *conjecture*, a word used by other
writers HALLIWELL: 'Conceits' looks like a modernization by the compositor.

Out of his ſcattering, and vnſure obſeruance: 176
It were not for your quiet, nor your good,
Nor for my Manhood, Honeſty, and Wiſedome,
To let you know my thoughts.
 Oth. What doſt thou meane?   180
 Iago. Good name in Man, & woman(deere my Lord)
Is the immediate Iewell of their Soules;
Who ſteales my purſe, ſteales traſh:
'Tis ſomething, nothing;
'Twas mine, 'tis his, and has bin ſlaue to thouſands: 185
But he that filches from me my good Name,
Robs me of that, which not enriches him,   187

---

176. *his*] *my* Qq, Pope+, Jen.   *my Lord;* Q₁.
178. *and*] Ff, Rowe+, Knt, Sta. *or* 182. *their*] *our* Qq.
Qq et cet.   183, 184. One line, Qq, Rowe et seq.
180. *What...meane?*] *Zouns.* Q₁. 183. *ſteales my*] *ſtel es my* Q₃.
181. *woman...Lord)*] *woman's deere* 187. *enriches*] *inriches* Qq.

---

177. BOOTH: Not mysteriously as though you really have anything definite in your thoughts.

181–188. BOOTH: Don't fire this directly at Othello, but trust to the 'whiff and wind' of it, for your effect on him, and on the audience too, although it may not gain applause from them as do the scowls and growls of the stage-villain.

181. **and woman**] GOULD (p. 88): J. B. Booth, isolating the words 'and woman' by a pause before and after, and completing the isolation by uttering them in an altered, clear, low tone, aims directly at Othello's heart, and plants in it the first surmise of his wife's infidelity.

184. STAUNTON: This is invariably printed 'something, nothing'; but *something-nothing* [as in Staunton's text] appears to have been one of those compound epithets to which our old writers were so partial, and of which the plays before us afford very many more examples than have ever been noted. The precise meaning of the phrase is not easy to determine; the only instance of its use we have met with is the following: 'Before this newes was stale came a taile of freshe sammon to countermand it with certain newes of a *something nothing*, and a priest that was neither dead nor alive, but suspended between both.'—*A Watch Bayte to Spare Provender*, &c., 1604. It appears, however, to have been nearly equivalent to the expression, *neither here nor there.*

185. THEOBALD cites several passages from Greek and Latin authors concerning the uncertainty of wealth, 'which,' he says, 'might have given our author a hint for this sentiment.' [Is it not strange that it seems never to have occurred to the earlier editors of Shakespeare, who certainly had, especially Theobald, a great reverence for their 'poet,' as they termed him, that Shakespeare might be trusted to have conceived, now and then, here and there, and once in a while, an original idea, with quite as much likelihood as Lucian, or Apollodorus, or Publius Syrus?—ED.]

187. **not**] WHITE (ed. i): Were it not that this quite unexceptionable reading is found in both Qq and Ff, I should be inclined to regard 'not' as a phonetic misprint of *naught*.

And makes me poore indeed.   188

   Oth.   Ile know thy Thoughts.

   Iago.   You cannot, if my heart were in your hand,   190
Nor fhall not, whil'ft 'tis in my cuftodie.

   Oth.   Ha *?*

   Iago.   Oh, beware my Lord, of iealoufie,
It is the greene-ey'd Monfter, which doth mocke   194

---

189. *Ile*] FfQ₂Q₃, Rowe+, Cap. Knt.
By heauen I'le Q₁ et cet.
      Thoughts] *thought* Q₄, Cap. Steev.
Mal. Var. Sing. Ktly.
  192. Oth. *Ha ?*] Om. Q₁.

193. *Oh...iealoufie,*] *O beware iealoufie.*
Q₁.
  194. *It is the*] *It is a* Q₂Q₃, Pope+, Jen.
mocke] QqF₂. *mock* F₃F₄. *make*
Han. Johns. Cap. Mal. Var. Coll. Ktly,
Huds. Wh. ii.

---

188. **indeed**] HUNTER (ii, 283): There are several passages in Wilson's *Rhetorique* which remind one of Shakespeare, so many that it might be affirmed to be a book which Shakespeare had at some period of his life not only read but studied. The resemblance of this present passage to the following in the chapter on Amplification is remarkable: ' The places of Logique help oft for amplification.   As, where men have a wrong opinion, and think theft a greater fault than slander, one might prove the contrary as well by circumstances as by arguments.   And first, he might shew that slander is theft, and every slanderer is a thief.   For as well the slanderer as the thief do take away another man's possession against the owner's will.   After that he might shew that a slanderer is worse than any thief, because a good name is better than all the goods in the world, and that the loss of money may be recovered, but the loss of a man's good name can not be called back again; and a thief may restore that again which he hath taken away, but a slanderer cannot give a man his good name again which he hath taken from him.'

  189. BOOTH: Indignantly, not with rage.

  190, 191. BOOTH: Respectfully, not defiantly.

  192. BOOTH: With a tinge of anxiety.

  193, &c. BOOTH: In a tone of solicitude.

  194. **mocke**] In a letter to Warburton, dated ' March 31, 1730,' from his ' most affectionate and obliged friend and humble servant,' THEOBALD says: ' I am at a loss to form any idea to myself, how jealousy mocks its own food, or the cause on which it subsists.   No passion whatever is more in earnest than jealousy, or more intent on the object which exercises it.   But jealousy, we know, is generally mistaken in its object, and raises to itself uneasinesses from its own mistaken conceptions.   What if we should then read, " which doth *make,*" &c., i. e., jealous persons feed on the matter of their own suspicions.' Warburton's reply has not been preserved.   The future bishop required the punctilious return of all his letters to ' his dearest friend,' and perhaps destroyed them, but it is reasonable to suppose that he failed to commend the emendation, and probably criticised it with such severity that Theobald did not venture to allude to it ir his edition, nor did Warburton in his edition, where, instead, a note is found justifying ' mock ' and condemning *make,* which in the mean time had appeared in Hanmer's text. Whether or not the emendation is original with Hanmer it is impossible to say.   He rarely gives an authority for his changes.   It is possible that he may have received it from Warburton, who may have passed over to him Theobald's letters.   It was the use

[194. the greene-ey'd Monster, which doth mocke]

by Hanmer of Warburton's notes, without giving him credit, that drove Warburton to issue an edition of his own, in the Preface to which he thus meanly and haughtily refers to both Theobald and Hanmer: ' The one,' he says, 'was recommended to me as a poor man; the other as a poor critic; and to each of them, at different times, I communicated a great number of observations, which they managed, as they saw fit, to the relief of their several distresses.' The credit of this emendation (which Grant White asserts to be the 'surest ever made in Shakespeare,' and therefore well worth contending for) has been, I believe, generally accorded to Hanmer down to the appearance of the invaluable CAMBRIDGE EDITION, where for the first time it is rightly given as a conjecture of Theobald. Warburton's note in his edition is as follows: 'Mock,' i. e., loaths that which nourishes and sustains it. This being a miserable state, Iago bids him beware of it. The Oxford Editor [Hanmer] reads *make*, implying that its suspicions are unreal and groundless, which is the very contrary to what he would here make his General think, as appears from what follows, 'That cuckold lives in bliss,' &c. In a word, the villain is for fixing him jealous; and therefore bids him beware of jealousy, not that it was an *unreasonable*, but a *miserable*, state, and this plunges him into it, as we see by his reply, which is only 'Oh, misery!' GREY (ii, 318): That is, ''mock,' with an apostrophe for *mamock*, i. e., by continually ruminating or chewing, it makes *mammocks* of it, in a metaphorical sense. The verse will bear the whole word *mammock*, and will stand thus: 'which doth mamock The meat,' &c. [This note is so printed as to imply that it is due to ' Mr SMITH,' whom Grey, in his Preface, pronounced 'the most friendly and communicative man living;' surely, an enviable elevation above the vagueness of the patronymic.] HEATH: 'Mock' certainly never signifies to *loath*. Its common signification is, to disappoint, in which sense I think it is used here. The proper and immediate destination of food is to satisfy hunger; when this end is not attained by the use of it, the food may be metaphorically said to be mocked or disappointed. So the end proposed by that suspicious inquisitiveness, which is the natural food of jealousy, is certainty and satisfaction some way or other. But this end it very rarely attains, and those very doubts and suspicions are perpetually *mocked*, and disappointed of that satisfaction they are in such eager pursuit of. JOHNSON: I have received Hanmer's emendation; because to 'mock' does not signify to *loath;* and because, when Iago bids Othello 'beware of jealousy, the green-ey'd monster,' it is natural to tell why he should beware; and for caution he gives him two reasons, that jealousy *often* creates its own cause, and that, when the causes are real, jealousy is misery. FARMER: In this place, and some others, to *mock* seems the same with to *mammock* [vide GREY]. JENNENS: I am apt to think that Shakespeare had here the Crocodile in his eye, who, by its tears, is said to deceive and entice its prey. To 'mock' is used by our Author to signify to *delude* and *deceive*. But if this be the allusion, what is the meat that Jealousy feeds on? And the context seems to show that Shakespeare makes *Love* the food of Jealousy. 'That cuckold lives in bliss, who certain of his fate, loves not his wronger'; he feels not the pang of Jealousy, because he wants that which nourishes and supports it, viz.: Love. But how does Jealousy *mock* love? By pretending to be its friend, and by seeming to pity and condole with it, at the same time that it is its great enemy and destroyer. STEEVENS: If Shakespeare had written *a* green-ey'd monster, we might have supposed him to refer to some creature existing only in his particular imagination; but ' *the* green-ey'd monster' seems to have reference to an object as familiar to his readers as to himself. It is known that the *tiger* kind have *green eyes*, and always play with the victim to

[194. the greene-ey'd Monster, which doth mocke]
their hunger before they devour it.   So, in *R. of L.* 554, 'yet, foul night-waking *cat,*
he doth but *dally,* While in his hold-fast foot the weak mouse panteth.'   Thus, a jealous husband, who discovers no certain cause why he may be divorced, continues to
sport with the woman whom he suspects, and, on more certain evidence, determines to
punish.   There is no beast that can be literally said to *make* its own food, and therefore I am unwilling to receive Hanmer's emendation, especially as I flatter myself that
a glimpse of meaning may be produced from the old reading.   One of the ancient
senses of the verb to *mock* is to *amuse,* to play with.   Thus, in 'A Discourse of Gentlemen lying in London that were better keep House at Home in their Country,' 1593:
'A pretty toy to *mock* an ape withal,' i. e., a pretty toy to *divert* an ape, for an ape to
divert himself with.   The same phrase occurs in Marston, whose *Ninth Satire* is entitled 'Here's a Toy to mocke an Ape indeede,' i. e., afford an ape materials for *sport,*
furnish him with a plaything.   In *Ant. & Cleo.,* 'mock' occurs again: 'tell him He
mocks the pauses that he makes,' i. e., he plays wantonly with those intervals of time
which he should improve to his own preservation.   Should such an explanation be
admissible, the advice given by Iago will amount to this: Beware, my lord, of yielding
to a passion which, as yet, has no proofs to justify its excess.   Think how the interval
between suspicion and certainty must be filled.   Though you doubt her fidelity, you
cannot yet refuse her your bed, or drive her from your heart; but, like the capricious
savage, must continue to sport with one whom you wait for an opportunity to destroy.
A similar idea occurs in *All's Well:* 'so lust doth *play* With what it loaths.'   Such is
the only sense I am able to draw from the original text.   What I have said may be
liable to some objections, but I have nothing better to propose.   That jealousy is a
monster which often *creates* the suspicions on which it feeds may be well admitted,
according to Hanmer's proposition; but is it *the* monster? (i. e., the well-known and
conspicuous animal), or whence has it *green eyes? Yellow* is the colour which Shakespeare usually appropriates to jealousy.   It must be acknowledged that he afterwards
characterizes it as 'a monster, Begot upon itself, born on itself.'   But yet 'what damned
minutes tells he o'er,' &c. is the best illustration of my attempt to explain the passage.
To produce Hanmer's meaning a change in the text is necessary.   I am counsel for
the old reading.   M. MASON: It is so difficult, if not impossible, to extract any sense
from this passage as it stands, even by the most forced construction of it, and the slight
amendment proposed by Hanmer renders it so clear, elegant, and poetical, that I am
surprised the editors should hesitate in adopting it, and still more surprised that they
should reject it.   As for Steevens's objection that the definite article is used, not the
indefinite, he surely need not be told in the very last of these plays that Shakespeare
did not regard such minute inaccuracies, which may be found in every play he wrote.
When Steevens compares the jealous man, who continues to sport with the woman he
suspects, and is determined to destroy, to the tiger who plays with the victim of his
hunger, he forgets that the meat on which jealousy is supposed to feed is not the
woman who is the object of it, but the several circumstances of suspicion which jealousy itself creates, and which cause and nourish it.   So Emilia, III, iv, 183: 'They
are not jealous ever for the cause, But jealous, for they are jealous; 'tis a monster
Begot upon itself, born on itself.'   This passage is a strong confirmation of Hanmer's
reading.   The same idea occurs in Massinger's *Picture* [I, i], where Matthias, speaking of the groundless jealousy he entertained of Sophia's possible inconstancy, says:
'but why should I nourish A fury here, and with *imagin'd food,* Holding no real
ground on which to raise A building of suspicion.'   *Imagin'd food* is food created by

[194. the greene-ey'd Monster, which doth mocke]

imagination; the food that jealousy makes and feeds on. HENLEY: Mason's objections to 'mock' and to Steevens's most happy illustration of it, originate entirely in his own misconception, and a jumble of figurative with literal expressions. To have been consistent with himself, he should have charged Steevens with maintaining that it was the property of a jealous husband, first to *mock* his wife, and afterwards to *eat* her. In Act V the word *mocks* occurs in a sense somewhat similar to that in the passage before us : 'villainy hath made *mocks* with love.' MALONE: I have not the smallest doubt that Shakespeare wrote *make*. The words *make* and *mocke* are often confounded in these plays. Mr Steevens, in his paraphrase on this passage, interprets the word *mock* by *sport;* but in what poet or prose writer, from Chaucer and Mandeville to this day, does the verb *to mock* signify to *sport with ?* Besides, is it true, as a general position, that jealousy (*as* jealousy) *sports* or *plays with* the object of love (allowing this not very delicate interpretation of the words, *the meat it feeds on*, to be the true one)? The position certainly is not true. It is *Love*, not *Jealousy*, that sports with the object of its passion; nor can those circumstances which create suspicion, and which are *the meat it feeds on*, with any propriety be called the *food* of *Love*, when the poet has clearly pointed them out as the food or cause of *Jealousy;* giving it not only being, but nutriment. 'There is no beast,' it is urged, 'that can *literally* be said to make its own food.' It is, indeed, acknowledged that jealousy is *a* monster which often *creates* the suspicions on which it feeds, but is it, we are asked, '*the* monster? (i. e., *a well-known and conspicuous animal*), and whence has it *green eyes ?* *Yellow* is the color which Shakespeare appropriates to jealousy.' To this I answer that *yellow* is not the only colour which Shakespeare *appropriates* to jealousy, for we have in *Mer. of Ven.* III, ii, 110, 'shuddering fear, and *green-ey'd* jealousy'; and I suppose it will not be contended that he was *there* thinking of any of the tiger kind. If our poet had written only 'It is *the* green-ey'd monster; beware of it,' the other objection would hold good, and some particular monster must have been meant; but the words, 'It is *the* green-ey'd monster, *which* doth,' &c., in my apprehension have precisely the same meaning as if the poet had written, 'It is *that* green-ey'd monster, which,' or 'it is *a* green-ey'd monster.' When Othello says to Iago in a former passage, 'By heaven, he echoes me, as if there were some *monster* in his thought,' does any one imagine that any *animal* whatever was meant ? The passage in a subsequent scene, to which Steevens has alluded, strongly supports the emendation which has been made: '*jealousy* . . . . 'tis a *monster*, *Begot upon itself, born on itself.*' It is, *strictly* speaking, as false that any monster can be *begot*, or *born*, on itself, as it is that any monster can *make* its own food; but, poetically, both are equally true of that monster, jealousy. Steevens seems to have been aware of this, and therefore has added the word *literally :* 'No monster can be *literally* said to make its own food.' It should always be remembered that Shakespeare's allusions scarcely ever answer precisely on both sides; nor had he ever any care upon this subject. Though he has introduced the word *monster*,—when he talked of its *making its own food* and being *begot by itself*, he was still thinking of jealousy *only*, careless whether there was any animal in the world that would correspond with this description. That by the words, *the meat it feeds on*, is meant, not Desdemona herself, as has been maintained, but *pabulum zelotypiæ*, may be likewise inferred from a preceding passage in which a kindred imagery is found : 'That *policy* may either last so long, Or *feed* upon such nice and waterish *diet*,' &c. And this obvious interpretation is still more strongly confirmed by Daniel's *Rosamond*, 1592, a poem which Shakespeare had diligently read, and has more than once imitated in *Rom. & Jul. :* 'O jealousy . . . .

[194. the greene-ey'd Monster, which doth mocke]

Feeding vpon *suspect* that doth *renue* thee, Happy were louers if they neuer knew thee.' BECKET: I substitute *muck*, i. e., *bedaub* or *make foul;* and this is the true character of jealousy, it &c., &c.   For the 'green-eyed monster' I read the *agreinied*, i. e., sportive, with a mixture of pleasure or satisfaction in what it is engaged in ; in which sense the word is used by our earlier writers.   The lines thus altered will be highly descriptive of jealousy.   JACKSON : It may seem strange to my readers that a small domestic animal may have been the mighty *green-eyed monster* to which our ingenious Bard alludes—I mean the *mouse;* indeed, familiarly, it is often called *a little monster;* but its eyes are not to say *green;* however, a white mouse in Shakespeare's time would have been a very great curiosity, and if one had been produced with *green eyes*, it would have equally attracted the notice of the naturalist.   Now, the mouse has a peculiar propensity, 'which doth *muck* the meat it feeds on.'   The mouse, after it has glutted on a piece of nice meat, leaves as much defilement on the residue as it possibly can ; and thus treats that with indecency and contempt which it doted on until its hunger was perfectly appeased, &c., &c.   [Some years ago I announced the exhaustion of my patience with Andrew Becket and Zachary Jackson ; both of whom at times have been praised by my betters.   I know that only unfamiliarity with these two writers would impute to me this large omission as a fault ; and as an attempt to hush even this source of hostile criticism, I have inserted the two foregoing notes.   I feel that my vindication is complete.   There is a third Commentator, the sight of whose volume starts a shudder.   From him let me here add the last note that I will ever take from his pages, as follows : LORD CHEDWORTH : I think I have heard or read, though I cannot recollect where, of a sort of large dragon-fly, that voids a greenish foam from its mouth, and then gradually sucks it in again :—if there be such a creature, it would be sufficient to justify the expression, 'green-ey'd monster.' —ED.]   MARTINUS SCRIBLERUS (*Explanations*, &c., p. 19) : What if the poet meant to say that the meat mocked the monster, instead of the monster mocking the meat ? This is an inverted construction, to be sure, but it is admissible and gives a very good meaning.   Jealousy is certainly a monster which the meat it feeds on doth mock, that meat consisting of mere surmises and 'trifles light as air.'   'It is the green-eyed monster, which doth mock—The meat it feeds on!'   KNIGHT : One of the difficulties would be got over by adopting the indefinite article, '*a* green-eyed monster,' of Q_2 ; this leaves us the license of imagining that Shakespeare had some *chimera* in his mind, to which he applied the epithet 'green-eyed.'   We have no doubt that *mock* is the true word ; and that it may be explained, which doth play with,—half receive, half reject,— the meat it feeds on.   Farmer [sic] suggested that it was used for *mammock*, which is not unlikely.   COLLIER : Nothing could be much easier than for a compositor to misread *make* 'mocke.'   The sense seems indisputably to require *make*.   It was so altered by Southern in his copy of F_4, and such too is the emendation of the (MS.).   SINGER : Jealousy is personified, and like another *green-eyed* creature of the feline race, sports with its prey, mammocks and mocks the meat it feeds on.   COWDEN-CLARKE : 'Mock' bears the sense of 'disdain,' 'spurn,' 'tear wrathfully,' even while feeding on. . . . . Jealousy, even while greedily devouring scraps of evidence, and stray tokens of supposed guilt, bitterly scorns them, and stands self-contemned for feeding on them. KEIGHTLEY (*Exp.*, 303) : *Make* appears to me indubitable ; for this is the very thing which jealousy does—witness Ford and Leontes,—while I cannot see how jealousy, which is given to anything rather than mockery, should mock its food.   HUDSON [reading *make*] : That is, jealousy is a *self-generated* passion ; that its causes are subjective,

The meate it feeds on.   That Cuckold liues in bliſſe,   195
Who certaine of his Fate, loues not his wronger :
But oh, what damned minutes tels he ore,
Who dotes, yet doubts : Suſpeɔts, yet foundly loues ?   198

---

195. *The*] *That* Q₁.   198. *foundly*] Ff, Dyce i, Sta. Del.
     That] *What* Q₃.   *fondly* Knt, Sing. Wh. i, Coll. iii (MS)
196. *Fate, loues not his*] Om. Q₃.   *ſtrongly* Qq et cet.

---

or that it lives on what it imputes, not on what it finds. And so Emilia afterwards
describes it.   Iago is, in his way, a consummate metaphysician, and answers perfectly
to Burke's description : ' Nothing can be conceived more hard than the heart of a
thorough-bred metaphysician.   It comes nearer to the cold malignity of a wicked spirit
than to the frailty and passion of a man.'   WHITE (ed. ii) : Theobald's correction is
the surest ever made in Shakespeare.   Without it the passage is naught.   [I have
reserved Hunter and Staunton to the last, because both give what seems to me to be
emphatically the true explanation, and one which occurred to me before I had read
theirs.   How many times the sigh is breathed : ' Pereant qui ante nos,' &c.   The meat
that jealousy feeds on is the victim of jealousy, the jealous man, who is mocked with
trifles light as air.   Substitute *mind* for ' meat,' and is not the meaning clear ?   Is i
the mark of a monster to *make* his food ?   Then are cooks monsters,—and they some
times are.—ED.]   HUNTER (*New Illust.*, ii, 284) : Jealousy mocks the person whc
surrenders his mind to her influence, deluding him perpetually with some new show
of suspicion, sporting herself with his agonized feelings, just as the feline tribe sport
with the prey which they have got into their power.   The cat is ' green-eyed.'
STAUNTON : Strange that it should have occurred to no one that the meat the monster mocks (i. e., *scoffs, jibes*, or *ridicules*), while he feeds on it, may be his credulous
victim,—that thrice-wretched mortal,—' who dotes, yet doubts ; suspects, yet soundly
loves.'   [LUEDERS (p. 66) also gives the true explanation, and quotes as applicable to
Theobald's *make* that clever definition of jealousy by Saphir, as clever as it is untranslatable : ' Eifersucht ist eine Leidenschaft, die mit Eifer sucht, was Leiden schafft.'
My friend, Mr Edwin Booth, confesses his conversion to ' mock,' and suggests that
Iago can indicate by touching his own breast that the victim of jealousy is the meat
it feeds on.—ED.]
   196. *loues*] JENNENS calls attention to the reading *hates* in Steevens's Reprint,
which he ' finds in no other edition.'   CAMBRIDGE EDITION : In the Devonshire copy
of Q₁, which formerly belonged to Steevens, and which was the original of his reprint,
the word ' loues ' is partially obliterated by being changed with a pen to ' hates,' but
being still obscure, ' hates ' is written in the margin opposite in the same hand as the
stage direction mentioned [in a previous note].   Capell's ccpy has distinctly ' loues,'
and that this was originally the reading of the Devonshire copy is evident from the
traces of the letters which still remain.   [These marginal stage directions in the
Devonshire Qto, just alluded to, are, as the Cambridge Editors inform us, in a 17th
century hand. ' More than one hand seems to have been employed, and there are
other notes of a much later date in pencil.']
   198. *soundly*] COLLIER (ed. ii) : There is little or no doubt that this was a misprint for *fondly*.   The (MS.) and Singer's (MS.) both have the same alteration.   DYCE
(*Strictures*, p. 199) : The two MS. Correctors and Collier must have forgotten what
King Henry says to the Princess Katharine, ' O fair Katharine, if you will love me

Oth.   O miſerie.

Iago.   Poore, and Content, is rich, and rich enough,   200
But Riches fineleſſe, is as poore as Winter,
To him that euer feares he ſhall be poore :
Good Heauen, the Soules of all my Tribe defend
From Iealouſie.

Oth.   Why ? why is this ?   205
Think'ſt thou, I'ld make a Life of Iealouſie ;
To follow ſtill the changes of the Moone
With freſh fuſpitions ? No : to be once in doubt,
Is to be refolu'd : Exchange me for a Goat,
When I ſhall turne the buſineſſe of my Soule   210

---

201. *Riches...is as] rich...is* Q$_3$.
    fineleſſe] *endless* Pope, Theob.
Han. Warb.
        Winter] *want* Theob. conj. (with-
drawn).
203. *Heauen*] *God* Q$_1$.
205. *Why ? why*] *Why, why* Qq, Dyce,
Sta. Glo. Cam. Rlfe, Wh. ii.

205. *this ?*] *this, Iago ?* Cap.
206. *Think'ſt*] *Thinkeſt* Q$_3$.
    I'ld] *I'de* Qq.
208, 209. *With...Is*] One line, Han.
209. *Is*] *is At once* Han.   *Is— once*
Cap. Steev. Mal. Var. Sing.   *Is once* Qq
et cet.

---

soundly with your French heart,' *Hen. V :* V, ii.   WHITE (ed. i): I cannot hesitate,
on looking at the whole line, to believe that 'soundly' is a misprint for *fondly*.   True,
Henry V says to Katharine [as quoted by Dyce], but the sentiment and the occasion
of the two passages are entirely dissimilar.

199. **O miserie**] BOOTH : Spoken without reference to himself.   (I claim the credit
of curing Othello's 'Misery ! misery ! misery !' as formerly given by actors.   I directed
my father's attention to it when I was a boy, and he approved.)

201. **finelesse**] JOHNSON : Unbounded, endless, unnumbered treasures.

201. **Winter**] WARBURTON : Finely expressed; 'winter' producing no fruits.

204. BOOTH : A pause.   Spoken slowly and with significance ; watch him curiously
to observe the effect of your poison, suggest the 'evil eye.'   Othello now, for the first
time, begins to be conscious of a doubt—which, however, he immediately shakes off,
and turns, as though from a trance, to Iago with a clear front.

206. **Think'st thou**] HALLIWELL : There is nothing makes a man suspect much,
more than to know little; and, therefore, men should remedy suspicion by procuring
to know more, and not to keep their suspicions in smother.—*Bacon's Essays* [p. 528,
ed. Arber].

209. **resolu'd**] C. P. MASON (*Athenæum*, 22 Apr. 1876) : Schmidt explains this as,
'to be fixed in a determination.'   I would suggest that it here means 'to be freed from
uncertainty.'   The gist of Othello's speech is that, if once he doubts, he will make that
first occasion settle the whole question for ever, by having the doubt turned into a certainty, one way or the other.   This relation between *doubting* and *being resolved* is
repeated in lines 219, 220 : Ile see before I doubt, &c.

209. WHITE (ed. i) : A syllable is needed for the verse, and the omission of the
once of the Qq seems doubtless accidental.

To fuch exufflicate, and blow'd Surmifes,   211
Matching thy inference. 'Tis not to make me I ealious,
To fay my wife is faire, feeds well, loues company,
Is free of Speech, Sings, Playes, and Dances :
Where Vertue is, thefe are more vertuous.   215
Nor from mine owne weake merites, will I draw

211. *exufflicate*] QqF₂F₃, Rowe, Pope,
Theob. *exufflicated* F₄. *exsuffolate* Han.
Warb. Johns. Jen. Steev.'85. *exsufflicate*
Cap. et cet.

     blow'd] Knt, Sing. *blowed* Ff.
blowne Qq et cet.

212. *thy*] *the* Ff.

212. *Iealious*] *iealous* QqF₃F₄.
213. *feeds well*,] *feeds, well*, Q₃.
214. *Dances*] Ff, Knt, Sing. *dances well* Qq et cet.
215. *are more*] *are moſt* Ff, Rowe+. *make more* Warb.

---

211. **exufflicate**] HANMER defines his *exsuffolate* by 'whisper'd, buzz'd in the ears; from the Italian verb *suffolare*.' JOHNSON : The allusion is to a bubble. Do not think, says the Moor, that I shall change the noble designs that now employ my thoughts, to suspicions which, like bubbles *blown* into a wide extent, have only an empty show without solidity; or that, in consequence of such empty fears, I will close with thy inference against the virtue of my wife. MALONE : Whether our poet had any authority for the word *exsufflicate*, which I think is used in the sense of *swollen*, and appears to have been formed from *sufflatus*, I am unable to ascertain. BOSWELL : This may be traced to the low Latin *exsufflare*, to spit down upon, an ancient form of exorcising, and, figuratively, to spit out in abhorrence and contempt. It may thus signify *contemptible*. See Du Cange, s. v. *exsufflare*. RICHARDSON (*Dict*. s. v.) : Exsufflare, it is true, is explained by Du Cange (consequentially) to signify *contemnere, despuere, rejicere ;* arising from the custom in the Romish administration of baptism of renouncing the devil and all his works, *exsufflando et despuendo*, by blowing and spitting him away. Hence, also, the application of *exsufflare*, and *exsufflatio* (common words among early Latin ecclesiastical writers) to a species of exorcism. *Exsufflation* is used by Bacon in its ordinary sense. And 'exufflicate' in Shakespeare is not improbably a misprint for *exsufflāte*, i. e., *efflate* or *efflated*, puffed out, and consequently exaggerated, extravagant,—to which 'blow'd' is added, not so much for the sake of a second epithet, with a new meaning, as of giving emphasis to the first. COLLIER : The meaning of this word is more obvious than its etymology; and if we had any difficulty, it would be removed, perhaps, by the additional epithet 'blow'd.' It is one of the words, the origin of which must not be traced with too much lexicographical curiosity. DYCE (*Gloss*.) : *Exsufflicate*, swollen, puffed out. For my own part, I can see no reason to doubt that such was Shakespeare's word, and such the meaning he intended to convey. WHITE (ed. ii) : That is, puffed out, thin and bubble-like, or, spat upon, according to its derivation, as to which, and as to his own exact meaning, I think that Shakespeare himself was not clear.

212. **Iealious**] WALKER (*Vers.* 154) calls attention to this uniform spelling, in this play, in the Folio.

214. **Dances**] WHITE (ed. i) : The omission of *well* was doubtless accidental.

215. **vertuous**] JOHNSON : An action in itself indifferent grows *virtuous* by its end and application.

The fmalleft feare, or doubt of her reuolt,   217
For fhe had eyes, and chofe me.   No *Iago*,
Ile fee before I doubt ; when I doubt, proue ;
And on the proofe, there is no more but this,   220
Away at once with Loue, or Iealoufie.

   Ia.   I am glad of this : For now I fhall haue reafon   [324 *b*]
To fhew the Loue and Duty that I beare you
With franker fpirit.   Therefore (as I am bound)
Receiue it from me.   I fpeake not yet of proofe :   225
Looke to your wife, obferue her well with *Caffio*,
Weare your eyes, thus : not Iealious, nor Secure :
I would not haue your free, and Noble Nature,
Out of felfe-Bounty, be abus'd : Looke too't :   229

218. *chofe*] *chofen* Q₂Q₃.
221. *or*] *and* Q'81, Q'95, Han.
222. *I am*] *I'm* Pope, Theob. Han.
Warb. Dyce iii, Huds.
   this] *it* Qq, Coll. Dyce, Wh. Glo.
Cam. Del. Huds. Rlfe.
224. *I am*] *I'm* Pope, Theob. Han.

Warb. Huds.
225. *of*] *for* Q₃.
227. *Weare*] *Were* Q₃.
   eyes] Ff, Rowe, Knt, Sing. Ktly
eie Qq et cet.
   Iealious] *iealous* QqF₃F₄.
229. *too't*] *to't* Q₄F₃F₄, Rowe et seq.

---

   217. **doubt . . . reuolt**] See SCHMIDT (*Lex.*) for many other instances where the former means *apprehension, suspicion ;* and the latter, *faithlessness in love, inconstancy.* GOULD (p. 103) : This word, 'revolt,' was one of those strokes of genius in tone of which J. B. Booth furnished such numberless examples.   It came with an access of emphasis, as if he felt, for an instant, how dreadful a thing her revolt might be, then dismisses the thought at once.

   221. BOOTH : Touch your breast to signify that *love* is ' hearted ' and your head at *jealousy,* to denote that it is a brain disease which ' follows still the changes of the moon.'

   227. **thus**] BOOTH : With a side-glance to indicate a certain degree of watchful care.

   227. **nor Secure**] ALGER (*Life of Forrest,* i, 145) : Forrest represented Iago as a gay, dashing fellow on the outside, hiding his malice and treachery under the signs of a careless honesty and jovial good humour.   One point, strictly original, he made, which powerfully affected Kean.   Iago, while working insidiously on the suspicions of Othello, says to him [lines 226, 227].   All these words, except the last two, Forrest uttered in a frank, easy fashion ; but suddenly, as if the intensity of his under-knowledge of evil had automatically broken through the good-natured part he was playing on the surface, and betrayed his secret in spite of his will, he spoke the words *nor secure* in a husky tone, sliding down from a high pitch and ending in a whispered horror.   This fearful suggestiveness produced from Kean a reaction so truly artistic and tremendous that the whole house was electrified.   As they met in the dressing-room, Kean said excitedly, ' In the name of God, boy, where did you get that ? '   Forrest replied, ' It is something of my own.'   ' Well,' said he, while his auditor trembled with pleasure, ' everybody who speaks the part hereafter must do it just so.'

   229. **selfe-Bounty**] WARBURTON : That is, inherent generosity.   [Just as ' self charity ' in II, ii, 226, means charity to one's self, so here, it seems to me, ' self-bounty

I know our Country difpofition well :   230
In Venice, they do let Heauen fee the prankes
They dare not fhew their Husbands.
Their beft Confcience,
Is not to leaue't vndone, but kept vnknowne.
    Oth. Doft thou fay fo ?   235
    Iago. She did deceiue her Father, marrying you,
And when fhe feem'd to fhake, and feare your lookes,
She lou'd them moft.
    Oth. And fo fhe did.
    Iago. Why go too then :   240

230. *Country difpofition*] *country-dis-position* Johns. *country's disposition* Steev. '85.

231. *Heauen*] *God* Q_1.

232, 233. One line, Qq, Rowe et seq.

232. *not*] Om. Q_1.

234. *leaue't*] *leaue* Q_1, Cap. Jen. Steev.

Mal. Var. Knt, Sing. Dyce, Ktly.

234. *kept*] Ff, Rowe i. *keepe* Q_1, Cap. Jen. Steev. Mal. Var. Knt, Sing. Dyce, Ktly. *keepe't* Q_2. *keep't* Q_3 et cet.

235. *fo ?*] *fo.* Q_1.

240. *Why*] Om. Pope +, Cap. *too*] *to* F_3F_4, Rowe et seq.

means a little more than 'inherent generosity'; rather, is it not that 'bounty,' where 'self' is concerned, which approaches what we should call 'self-forgetfulness'?—ED.]

231. **Venice**] JOHNSON : Here Iago seems to be a Venetian.   HENLEY : There is nothing in any other part of the play, properly understood, to imply otherwise.

233, 234. BOOTH : Very confidentially.

235. FECHTER : With indignant menace.   BOOTH : Let your tone express unbounded faith in Iago's knowledge of 'human dealings.'

236. FECHTER : With a look of the basilisk, darting the sting which he had kept for the last.

237. **seem'd**] JOHNSON : This and the following argument of Iago ought to be deeply impressed on every reader.   Deceit and falsehood, whatever conveniences they may for a time promise or produce, are, in the sum of life, obstacles to happiness. Those who profit by the cheat distrust the deceiver, and the act by which kindness is sought puts an end to confidence.   The same objection may be made, with a lower degree of strength, against the imprudent generosity of disproportionate marriages. When the first heat of passion is over, it is easily succeeded by suspicion, that the same violence of inclination which caused one irregularity may stimulate to another; and those who have shown that their passions are too powerful for their prudence, will, with very slight appearances against them, be censured as not very likely to restrain them by their virtue.

238. **most**] HUDSON : This is one of Iago's artfullest strokes.   The instinctive shrinkings and tremblings of Desdemona's modest virgin love are ascribed to craft, and made to appear a most refined and elaborate course of deception.   His deep science of human nature enables him to *divine* how she appeared.

239. FECHTER : Othello stops at once, as struck by a thunderbolt ! His face changes by degrees, his eyes open as if a veil had been taken away ! BOOTH : Hoarsely and with despairing look.

240. FECHTER : Placing nimself behind him and speaking in his ear, as if better to

Shee that fo young could giue out fuch a Seeming   241
To feele her Fathers eyes vp, clofe as Oake,
He thought 'twas Witchcraft.
But I am much too blame:
I humbly do befeech you of your pardon   245
For too much louing you.
    Oth.   I am bound to thee for euer.
    Iago.   I fee this hath a little dafh'd your Spirits:
    Oth.   Not a iot, not a iot.   249

242. feele] feale QqF₃. *feal* F₄, Rowe+, Jen. Coll.

    Oake,] *oak—* Rowe et seq.
  243, 244. One line, Qq, Pope et seq.
  243. *Witchcraft.*] Ff, Coll.Wh. i. *witchcraft:* Qq, Cap. Steev. Mal.Var. Knt, Sing. Sta. *witchcraft—* Rowe et cet.

244, 247. I am] I'm Pope+, Dyce iii. Huds.

  244. *too blame]* to *blame* F₄, Rowe et seq.

  247. *to thee]* to to *thee* F₂. *to you* Rowe ii, Pope, Theob. Han. Warb.

---

instil his venom. [Although there is much, as I have said elsewhere, that is, to me, highly objectionable, not only in Fechter's style of acting, but even in his conception of character, yet in this instance he jumps with the very way in which it is barely possible that Burbadge spoke these lines while Shakespeare listened. See Appendix, where the ballad on *The Tragedie of Othello the Moore* is given, wherein it is said of Iago that ' He whisper'd at Othelloe's backe, His wife had chaungde her minde,' &c. —ED.]

  242. **seele**] See notes on I, iii, 297. COLLIER : The ordinary word *seal* seems here only intended.

  242. **Oake**] JOHNSON : There is little relation between *eyes* and *oak.* I would read *owls.* ' As blind as an owl ' is a proverb. [This note is repeated in Johnson and Steevens's Variorum editions of 1773 and 1778, but in that of 1785, after Dr Johnson's death, Steevens omitted it,—presumably out of respect to his friend's memory.—ED.] STEEVENS : The ' oak ' is, I believe, the most close-grained wood of general use in England. ' Close as oak ' means close as the grain of oak. D. (*N. & Qu.*, 1857, 2d, iv, 44) suggests that in connection with ' seel,' ' oak ' should be *hawk,* ' an alteration which,' so he says, ' gives significancy to a simile which has otherwise no meaning at all.' STAUNTON and HARTING make the same conjecture.

  243. FECHTER : Othello stands immovable as a statue. BOOTH : Othello should wince slightly at the recollection.

  244. **much too blame**] See also line 328 in this same scene. This phrase ' too blame ' is so common, not only in the Folio but in other Elizabethan authors, that ABBOTT, § 73, suggests that perhaps ' blame ' was considered an adjective, and that ' too ' may have been used as in Early English for ' excessively.' Even in modern editions, it seems to me, this ' too ' should be retained.—ED.

  245. **of**] See ABBOTT, § 174, for other instances where ' of ' means ' concerning,' ' about.'

  247. FECHTER : His eyes fixed—extending his hand to Iago, without looking at him. BOOTH : With great constraint.

  249. OTTLEY (p. 22) : Kean gave thefe words with a plaintive, choking cry, which

Iago.   Truſt me, I feare it has :   250
I hope you will conſider what is ſpoke
Comes from your Loue.
But I do ſee y'are moou'd :
I am to pray you, not to ſtraine my ſpeech
To groſſer iſſues , nor to larger reach,   255
Then to Suſpition.
   Oth.   I will not.
   Iago.   Should you do ſo (my Lord)
My ſpeech ſhould fall into ſuch vilde ſucceſſe,
Which my Thoughts aym'd not.   260
Caſſio's my worthy Friend :
My Lord, I ſee y'are mou'd :
   Oth.   No, not much mou'd :   263

250. *Truſt me*] *I faith* Q₁, Sta. Glo.
Cam. Dyce iii, Rlfe, Huds. Wh. ii.
   252, 253. One line, Qq, Rowe et seq.
   252. *your Loue*] *my loue* QqFf et cet.
   253. *y'are*] Ff, Wh. ii. *you are* Qq,
Cap. Jen. Steev. Mal. Var. Knt, Coll. Sing.
Wh. i, Ktly. *you're* Rowe et cet.
   259. *ſhould*] *would* Pope+, Jen.
   into ſuch] *into* Q₃.
   vilde] *vild* F₄, Rowe. *vile* Qq,
Pope et seq.
   ſucceſſe] *excess* Pope ii.

   260, 261. One line, Qq, Rowe et seq.
   260. *Which*] Ff, Rowe, Pope, Theob.
Han. Warb. Knt, Dyce i. *As* Qq et cet.
   aym'd not] F₂. *aim'd not* F₃F₄,
Knt, Dyce i. *aim'd not at* Rowe. *aime
not at* Qq et cet.
   261. *worthy*] *truſty* Q₁.
   Friend :] *friend.* Pope. *friend—*
Glo.
   262. *y'are*] Ff, Wh. i. *you are* Qq,
Cap. Jen. Steev. Mal.Var. Knt, Coll. Sing.
Ktly. *you're* Rowe et cet.

went to the heart. FECHTER : Crosses, and leans on the back of the low chair.
BOOTH : With forced indifference and trembling voice.

250. BOOTH : Soothingly.

253. BOOTH : A smothered moan.

253. **y'are**] Both here and in 262, this contraction, it seems to me, should be used
in modern editions in preference to the usual *you're*, or even to the *you are* of the Qq.
See also Walker, line 450, *post.*—ED.

255. **issues**] WARBURTON : Conclusions.

255. **reach**] WALKER (*Crit.* ii, 167) cites this as only an apparent rhyme with
'speech' in the preceding line; '*Ea* was pronounced nearly as *a* in *mate*.'

259. **succeſſe**] JOHNSON : If this be the right word, it seems to mean *consequence*
or *event*, as *succeſſo* is used in Italian. RICHARDSON (*Dict.* s. v.) : 'Success' is that
which is come to, arrived at, reached, or attained; whether good or bad. 'I haue bene
longer in describing, the nature, *the good or ill ſucceſſe*, of the quicke and hard witte,
than perchance you will thinke, this place and matter doth require.'—Ascham, *The
Scholemaster* [Book i, p. 35, ed. Arber].

261. FECHTER : Othello makes a step in advance, his hand on his poignard.
BOOTH : Give this as a stiletto-stab in the back—at which Othello groans aloud.

263. FECHTER : Supporting himself by the chair, and then sinking down on it.

I do not thinke but *Defdemona*'s honeft.

 Iago. Long liue fhe fo;   265

And long liue you to thinke fo.

 Oth. And yet how Nature erring from it felfe.

 Iago. I, there's the point:

As (to be bold with you)

Not to affeＣt many propofed Matches   270

Of her owne Clime, Complexion, and Degree,

Whereto we fee in all things, Nature tends:

Foh, one may fmel in fuch, a will moft ranke,

Foule difproportions, Thoughts vnnaturall.

But (pardon me) I do not in pofition   275

DiftinＣtly fpeake of her, though I may feare

Her will, recoyling to her better iudgement,

May fal to match you with her Country formes, 278

---

264. *I do*] *doe* Q₃.
265, 266. One line, Qq, Rowe et seq.
267. *it felfe.*] *it felfe*— F₂. *it felf*— F₃
F₄. *itfelf*— Warb. et seq.
268, 269. One line, Qq, Rowe et seq.
271. *her*] *our* Steev.'85.
272. *Whereto*] *Wherein* Q₃.
273. *Foh,*] *Fie* Qq. *Foh !* Rowe et seq.

273. *one*] *we* Qq.
moft] *muft* Q₃.
274. *difproportions*] Ff, Rowe +, Jen.
Knt, Sta. *difproportion* Qq et cet.
276. *Diftinctly*] *Deftinctly* Q₁.
278. *fal to match*] *fail to catch* Wh. ii
(misprint ?).

---

266. **think**] BOOTH : Perhaps a slight emphasis on this, though I doubt its value.

267. BOOTH : Referring to his color. (My Father indicated this by a glance at his hand as it passed down before his eyes from his forehead, where it had been pressed). Iago seizes this with eagerness and interrupts him.

269. **bold with you**] BOOTH : My Father interpreted this as a covert reference to Brabantio's assertion before the Senate (I, iii, 113) that Desdemona was 'a maiden never bold,' an assertion which Othello, with his knowledge of Desdemona's share in their wooing, might somewhat modify ; my Father, therefore, spoke the line not as an apologetic parenthesis addressed to Othello, as it is usually printed, but as though catching up and pursuing Othello's own train of thought, and thus insidiously summoning to Othello's memory secret occasions when Desdemona had shown a 'will most rank,' and had been 'bold' with him.   I wish I could describe the white-lipped, icy smile, the piercing glance at Othello's half-averted face, and eager utterance, with which my Father said, 'Ay, there's the point; as to be bold with *you*.'

273. **will**] JOHNSON : That is, wilfulness.   A 'rank will' is self-will overgrown and exuberant.   RITSON (p. 235) : To *smell* wilfulness and an overgrown self-will is a faculty peculiar to the learned critic.   But with all imaginable deference to him, the expression means, inclinations or desires most foul, gross, and strong-scented.

274. BOOTH : Othello repels this by a look of indignation.

274. **disproportions**] See I, i, 31.

275. **position**] COLLIER : The (MS.) reads *suspicion*, but if this were the word we should be inclined to think that 'not' had also been misprinted for *but*, the meaning of Iago then being, 'I *but* speak of her distinctly in *suspicion*.'

And happily repent.

   Oth.   Farewell, farewell :   280
If more thou dost perceiue, let me know more :
Set on thy wife to obserue.
Leaue me *Iago*.

   Iago.   My Lord, I take my leaue.

   Othel.   Why did I marry ?   285
This honest Creature (doubtlesse)
Sees, and knowes more, much more then he vnfolds.

   Iago.   My Lord, I would I might intreat your Honor [325 *a*]
To scan this thing no farther : Leaue it to time,
Although 'tis fit that *Cassio* haue his Place ;   290
For sure he filles it vp with great Ability ;
Yet if you please, to him off a-while :
You shall by that perceiue him, and his meanes :   293

---

279. *happily*] *haply so* Pope+.
   repent.] *repent*— Ktly.
280, 281. *Farewell, farewell : If more*]
Farewell, If more (as one line) Qq.
281, 283. *thou…*Iago.] Two lines, ending *on…Iago.* Qq.
281, 282. One line, Rowe et seq.
283. [*Going.* Rowe et seq.
284, 285. One line, Qq, Cap. et seq.
288. Continued to Oth. Q₁.
   Iago.] Om. Q₁.
   [*Returns.* Cap.
289. *To scan*] Iag. *To scan* Q₁.

289. *farther*] Ff, Rowe+, Knt, Coll.
Sta. *further* Qq et cet.
290. *Although 'tis fit*] *Tho it be fit* Q₁,
Jen. Var. Glo. Cam. Rlfe. *And though tis
fit* Q₂Q₃, Cap. Sing. *And though it be fit*
Steev. Mal.
292. *to him*] *to put him* Ff, Rowe, Pope,
Han. *to hold him* Qq et cet.
   off] *of* Q₁.
   a-while] F₂. *a while* Q₂Q₃F₃F₄,
Rowe+, Cap. Steev. Mal. Var. Ktly.
awhile Q₁ et cet.

---

279. *happily*] JENNENS : It is plain that *haply* or *perchance* is here meant. See,
to the same effect, ABBOTT, § 42.

280. GÉRARD : Othello n'est pas sans amour-propre. Il se rend justice sur ses traits
et son teint basané et il conviendra avec lui-même des désavantages de sa personne,
mais ce qu'il s'avoue tout bas il est fâché de l'entendre de la bouche d'un autre, et,
tranchant sur ce sujet, il congédie Iago. FECHTER : Dismissing Iago with a gesture,
but stopping him as he goes to the door. BOOTH : Impatiently ; unable to endure his
presence any longer ; line 282 he speaks as though overcome by shame at his own
baseness in the suggestion ; and at the close falls on a seat.

284. BOOTH : A quick, fiendish smile of triumph and a rapid clutch of the fingers,
as though squeezing his very heart (Othello's face is buried in his hands), is quite legitimate here, but do it unobtrusively, as you *vanish*. FECHTER : Iago pretends to go,
but stays on the threshold to watch Othello from the opening in the tapestry.

288. BOOTH : Othello assumes indifference for a while, but it leaves him at the mention of Cassio.

293. *meanes*] JOHNSON : You shall discover whether he thinks his best *means*, his
most powerful *interest* is by the solicitation of your lady.

Note if your Lady ſtraine his Entertainment
With any ſtrong, or vehement importunitie,   295
Much will be ſeene in that : In the meane time,
Let me be thought too buſie in my feares,
(As worthy cauſe I haue to feare I am)
And hold her free, I do beſeech your Honor.
    Oth.   Feare not my gouernment.   300
    Iago. I once more take my leaue.   *Exit.*
    Oth.   This Fellow's of exceeding honeſty,
And knowes all Quantities with a learn'd Spirit
Of humane dealings.   If I do proue her Haggard,   304

---

294. *his*] *her* Qq.

295. *importunitie*] *opportunity* Var.'03, '13, '21 (misprint).

299. *Honor.*] *Honor :* Ff.

301. Exit.] Om. Ff. Scene VI. Pope+, Jen.

303. *Quantities*] Q₂Q₃Ff, Rowe. *qualities* Q₁ et cet.

303. *learn'd*] Ff, Rowe, Pope, Wh. *learned* Qq et cet.

303, 304. *Spirit Of*] Q₁Q₂Ff, Coll. Sta. Wh. i. *ſpirit, Of* Q₃ et cet.

304. *humane*] *humaine* Q₁. *human* Rowe et cet.

dealings] *dealing* Q₁.

do] Om. Pope+.

---

294. **Entertainment**] JOHNSON : Press hard his re-admission to his pay and office. 'Entertainment' was the military term for admission of soldiers.

295. **importunitie**] WALKER (*Vers.* 201) : The *i* in *-ity* is almost uniformly dropped in pronunciation. [See 'satiety,' II, i, 261.]

299. BOOTH : Imploringly.

300. **gouernment**] JOHNSON : Do not distrust my ability to contain my passion GOULD (p. 104) : J. B. BOOTH indicated this meaning of self-control by a gesture strangely original and fine—the forefinger of the lifted hand pointed vertically to the top of the head.

301. FECHTER : He retires humbly—looking on from the back with a triumphant smile. At the door raises his shoulders in contempt; and exit. BOOTH : Iago should be rapid in all his actions except at this point—do nothing, but go slowly off with a tender respect : Othello should watch Iago keenly till he is gone.

303, 304. JOHNSON : The construction is, He knows with a learned spirit all quali ties of human dealings. WALKER (*Crit.* i, 160) : *Quære* whether the comma ought not to be expunged after 'spirit'? 'And knows all qualities with a spirit learned of (i. e., *in*) human dealings. (I believe I am wrong as to this passage.) [See Text. Notes, where Walker is anticipated.] LETTSOM [*Foot-note* to Walker] : Notwithstanding Walker's hesitation, I prefer the construction which he has suggested. *Quality* here, as frequently elsewhere, seems to mean *natural disposition.* In this passage the poet has unconsciously described himself.

304. **Haggard**] HARTING (p. 57) : A wild-caught and unreclaimed mature hawk, as distinguished from an 'eyess' or nestling. STEEVENS : From a passage in *The White Devil*, 1612, it appears that it was a term of reproach sometimes applied to a wanton : 'Is this your perch, you haggard? fly to th' stews'—[Webster's *Works*, vol. i, p. 120, ᵉd. Dyce]. It had, however, a popular sense, and was used for *wild* by those who

Though that her Ieffes were my deere heart-ftrings,   305
I'ld whiftle her off, and let her downe the winde
To prey at Fortune.   Haply, for I am blacke,
And haue not thofe foft parts of Conuerfation
That Chamberers haue : Or for I am declin'd   309

306. *I'ld*] *I'de* Qq.   307. *Haply*] *Happily* Qq.
    downe] *dewne* Q₂Q₃.   *I am*] *I'm* Pope+.
307. *prey*] *pray* Q₃.

---

thought not on the language of falconers.   FECHTER : Rousing himself, and trembling
with rage.   BOOTH : All this passage should be spoken more with anguish than with
anger.

305. **Iesses**] HARTING (p. 58) : These were two narrow strips of leather, fastened
one to each leg, the other ends being attached to a swivel, from which depended the
'leash.'   When the hawk was flown, the swivel and leash were taken off, the jesses and
bells remaining on the bird.   Turbervile, in his *Book of Falconrie*, 1575, speaking of
the trappings of a hawk, says : 'Shee must haue jesses of leather, the which must haue
knottes at the ende, and they should be halfe a foote long, or there about; at the least
a shaftmeete betweene the hoose of the jesse, and the knotte at the ende, whereby you
tye the hauke.'

306. **whistle**] JOHNSON : The falconers always let fly the hawk against the wind;
if she flies with the wind behind her, she seldom returns.   If, therefore, a hawk was
for any reason to be dismissed, she was 'let down the wind,' and from that time shifted
for herself and 'preyed at fortune.'   DYCE (*Few Notes*, p. 149) : '*Ajetter un oiseau.*
To cast, or whistle off, a hawke; to let her goe, let her flie.'—Cotgrave.   [It is needless to cite the numberless allusions throughout Shakespeare and Elizabethan authors
to every the minutest department of Hawking.   To WALKER (*Vers.* 68) I can simply
refer; in his enthusiasm for scansion he would be willing (if I understand him) to pronounce 'whistle her' as two syllables.—ED.]

307. **blacke**] FECHTER : Paces the stage, and starts on seeing his face in a glass.

308. **parts**] REED : This seems to be here synonymous with *arts*, as in '*Tis Pity
She's a Whore*, speaking of singing and music : 'They are *parts* I love' [II, i, ed.
Dyce].   MOREL : Le mot qui est resté courant dans la langue est commenté par Voltaire comme suit : ' *Great parts*,' de grandes parties.   D'où cette manière de parler qui
étonne aujourd'hui les Français peut-elle venir ?   D'eux-mêmes.   Autrefois nous nous
servions de ce mot de *parties* très communément dans ce sens-là.   Clélie, Cassandre,
nos autres anciens romans ne parlent que des parties de leurs héros et de leur héroïnes,
et ces parties sont leur esprit.   En effet, chacun de nous n'a que sa petite portion d'intelligence, de mémoire, de sagacité.   Les Français ont laissé échapper de leurs diction-
aires une expression dont les Anglais se sont saisis.   Les Anglais se sont enrichis plus
d'une fois à nos dépens.—*Dict. philosophique*, s. v. ' Esprit.'

309. **Chamberers**] STEEVENS : That is, men of intrigue.   So in the Countess of
Pembroke's *Antonius*, 1590 : 'Fall'n from a souldier to a chamberer.'   HENLEY : See
Romans, xiii, 13 : 'Let us walk honestly as in the day; not in rioting and drunkenness, not in chambering and wantonness.'   WRIGHT (*Bible Word-Book*) : Latimer, in
his remarks on Rom. xiii, 13, thus explains the word : 'St. Paul useth this word *chambering;* for when folks will be wanton, they get themselves in corners.'—*Rem.* p. 18

Into the vale of yeares (yet that's not much)   310
Shee's gone.   I am abus'd, and my releefe
Muft be to loath her.   Oh Curfe of Marriage!
That we can call thefe delicate Creatures ours,
And not their Appetites?   I had rather be a Toad,
And liue vpon the vapour of a Dungeon,   315
Then keepe a corner in the thing I loue
For others vfes.   Yet 'tis the plague to Great-ones,
Prerogatiu'd are they leffe then the Bafe,
'Tis deftiny vnfhunnable, like death:
Euen then, this forked plague is Fated to vs,   320
When we do quicken.   Looke where fhe comes:

310. *the vale*] *the valt* Q$_1$.   *a vale* Q$_3$.
311. *abus'd*] *aduis'd* Q$_3$.
    releefe] *releife* Q$_1$Q$_2$.
312. *Curfe*] *the curse* Pope+.
315. *of a*] *in a* Qq.
316. *corner*] *cornet* Q$_3$.
    the thing] *a thing* Qq.
317. *vfes*] *use* Pope+.

317. *plague to*] Ff, Rowe.   *plague of* Qq et cet.
    Great-ones] Ff, Rowe, Pope. *great ons* Q$_3$.   *great ones* Q$_1$Q$_2$, Theob. et seq.
318. *Prerogatiu'd*] *Prerogatiou'd* Q$_3$.
319. *'Tis*] *This* Q$_3$.
321. *Looke where fhe*] Ff, Rowe, Knt, Del.   *Defdemona* Q$_1$Q$_2$ et cet.

SCHMIDT defines it, but I am afraid on insufficient grounds: a man conversant with the arts of peace, opposed to a soldier; the same as 'carpet-monger.'

312. **Marriage**] WALKER (*Vers.* 176): Pronounce *dissolutè*.

314. **Appetites**] BOOTH: This word may bother the many, so touch your *heart* to signify, *likings*, or *longings*.

318. **Prerogatiu'd**] MALONE: Compare *As You Like It*, III, iii, 58, where Touchstone holds forth a contrary opinion.   'Shakespeare would have been more consistent if he had written: Prerogativ'd are they *more* than the base?'   Othello would then have answered his own question: '(No:) 'Tis destiny unshunnable,' &c.   STEEVENS soothingly remarks: 'Allowance must be made to the present state of Othello's mind: passion is seldom correct in its effusions.'

319. **vnshunnable**] MALONE: To be consistent, Othello must mean that it is destiny unshunnable by 'great ones,' not by all mankind.

320. **forked plague**] PERCY: That is, the horns of the cuckold.   MALONE: See, in proof, *Tro. & Cress.* I, ii, 178; and *Wint. Tale*, I, ii, 186.   One of Harrington's *Epigrams* contains the very expression: 'Actæon .... Was plagu'd with hornes; .... Wherefore take heed, ye that are curious, prying, With some such forked plague you be not smitten,' &c.

321. **comes**] 'The burst of mixed passions with which Forrest uttered the first part of this speech was terrific.   His voice then sank into tones the most touching, expressive of complaining regret.   The conclusion seemed to have excited him to the utmost pitch of loathing and disgust, and, as he sees Desdemona advancing, he, for a few moments, gazed upon her with horror.   The feeling gave way, and all his former tenderness seemed to return as he exclaimed, "If she be false," &c.'—Alger's *Life of Forrest*, i, 308.

Enter Defdemona and Æmilia.   322

If fhe be falfe, Heauen mock'd it felfe:
Ile not beleeue't.

Def.   How now, my deere *Othello*?   325

Your dinner, and the generous Iflanders
By you inuited, do attend your prefence.

Oth.   I am too blame.

Def.   Why do you fpeake fo faintly?

Are you not well?   330

Oth.   I haue a paine vpon my Forehead, heere.

---

322. Enter...] After line 323, Qq, Dyce,
Sta. Del.

323. *falfe*] *fals* Q₃.

    Heauen mock'd] Ff.   *O then
heauen mocks* Qq et cet.

324. *beleeue't*] *beleeue it* Qq, Jen. Steev.
Mal. Var. Coll. Sing. Ktly, Del.

326. *Iflanders*] *Ilander* Qq.

328. *too*] *to* Qq, F₃F₄ et seq.

329, 330. One line, Qq, Cap. Steev.
Mal. Var. Coll. Sing. Ktly.

329. *Why...faintly*] *Why is your fpeech
fo faint* Qq, Cap. Steev. Mal. Var. Coll.
Sing. Ktly.

331. *heere*] *heare* Q₂Q₃.

323, 324. COLERIDGE (p. 255): Divine! the effect of innocence and the better
genius!

323. **mock'd**] MALONE: That is [see Text. Notes], renders its own labours fruit-
less, by forming so beautiful a creature as Desdemona, and suffering the elegance of
her person to be disgraced and sullied by the impurity of her mind,—such, I think, is
the meaning,—the construction, however, may be different.   If she be false, Oh, then,
even *heaven itself* cheats us with 'unreal mockery,' with false and specious appearances, intended only to deceive.   STEEVENS: The first of the foregoing explanations
is, I believe, the true one.   If she be false, heaven disgraces itself by creating woman
after its own image.   To have made the resemblance perfect, she should have been
good as well as beautiful.   KNIGHT: By the reading of the Folio we may understand
that, if Desdemona be false,—be not what she appears to be,—heaven, at her creation,
instead of giving an image of itself, mocked itself,—gave a false image.   The reading
of the Qq is more forcible and natural.

324. BOOTH: I strike my forehead as if to kill the devilish thought.   After Desdemona and Emilia have entered it is better for the latter to retire, for the reason given at
line 48 of this scene.   Moreover, it is better for her on her re-entrance to find the handkerchief than to steal it.

326. **generous**] STEEVENS: The islanders of rank, distinction.   So, in *Meas. for
Meas.* IV, vi, 13, 'The generous and gravest citizens.'   See also *Ham.* I, iii, 74, 'select
and generous.'

328. **too blame**] See *supra*, III, iii, 244.

331. **Forehead**] RYMER (p. 121): Michael Cassio came not from Venice in the
ship with Desdemona, nor till this morning could be suspected of an opportunity with
her.   And 'tis now but dinner time; yet the Moor complains of his forehead.   He
might have set a guard on Cassio, or have lockt up Desdemona, or have obferv'd their
carriage a day or two longer.   He is on other occasions phlegmatic enough: this is

Def. Why that's with watching, 'twill away againe.   332
Let me but binde it hard. within this houre
It will be well.

Oth. Your Napkin is too little :   335

332. *Why*] *Faith* Q$_1$, Mal. Steev.'93, Var. Coll. Dyce,Wh. Glo. Cam. Del. Huds. Rlfe.

 'twill] *t'will* Q$_1$Q$_2$.   *t'wll* Q$_3$.

333. *it hard*] *your head* Q$_1$.

334. *well.*] *well againe.* Q$_1$, Jen.

335. [She drops her Handkerchief Rowe.

---

very hasty. [Rymer's innuendo that in the pain upon his forehead Othello here covert ly alludes to the forked plague is, I am afraid, only too correct. Delius, also, thus inter prets it. Note the use of 'upon.' If this reference was understood by Shakespeare's auditors,—and it seems as though it were scarcely possible in those days to refer to the forehead other than as a groundwork for this plague,—then, in Desdemona's tender response they perceived a proof of her unconscious innocence which is otherwise lost on us.—ED.]

333. BOOTH : She kneels to do so,—he is sitting.

335. **Napkin**] WARNER (*Letter to Garrick*, p. 35) : This word is still used to sig nify a Handkerchief in Scotland and in the North of England, especially about Shef field in Yorkshire. We meet with it in that sense in the Proceedings in Scotland in the Douglass cause : ' Lady Jane never admitted any person to see her till she was fully dress'd . . . . with a large Napkin on her breast.' [' Oft did she heave her nap kin to her eyne '—*Lover's Complaint*, 21.—ED.]

335. COLLIER (ed. i) : We take this necessary stage direction [*'Let's fall her Nap kin'*] from a MS. note, in a hand-writing of the time, in the Duke of Devonshire's Q$_1$. DYCE (*Remarks*, p. 239) : The stage direction inserted by other modern editors is far better, viz. [*' He puts the handkerchief from him, and it drops'*]. There can be no doubt that, while Othello pushes away the handkerchief, Desdemona lets it fall : Emilia (who is now on the stage) says presently : '*she* let it drop by negligence; And I,' &c. COLLIER (ed. ii) : This stage direction [' *The napkin falls to the ground'*] and others [*'Offering to bind his head,* after line 333] are from the (MS.) [Where stage directions occur in the Qq or Ff they are to be reverently accepted, and they are also respectable in Rowe, as indications of stage tradition, but in other cases, where they are devised by editors, they are apt to be intrusive and are mostly superfluous. They belong more to the province of the actor than to that of the editor. We editors readily lose sight of the fact that we are, for the most part, mere drudges, humble diggers and delvers in forgotten fields, and from close poring over the words of a dramatic character we are apt to forget ourselves, and bound in imagination for one wild moment on the stage to dictate action to the player-folk themselves. Picture Dr Johnson in the rôle of Mercutio ! Yet when Dr Johnson modified or inserted stage directions, be they ever so slight, as he has in Mercutio's speeches, did not his imagination, for an instant, play him that same fantastic trick ? To editorial stage directions far more than to æsthetic illustrations the phrase 'sign-post criticisms' may be properly applied, as it seems to me. The stage directions of actors stand on a different footing. Here lies the actor's true province, and to his interpretations must be applied the supreme test of public judgement, wherein we, as a part of that public, have a right to give our voice. Here FECHTER decides that it is Othello who throws down the handkerchief, and does it in a rage; but BOOTH, with finer insight, lets Othello gently push the hand kerchief aside and Desdemona drop it.—ED.]

Let it alone : Come, Ile go in with you.   *Exit.*   336
  Def.   I am very forry that you are not well.
  Æmil.   I am glad I haue found this Napkin :
This was her firſt remembrance from the Moore,
My wayward Husband hath a hundred times   340
Woo'd me to ſteale it.   But ſhe ſo loues the Token,
(For he coniur'd her, ſhe ſhould euer keepe it)
That ſhe reſerues it euermore about her,
To kiffe, and talke too.   Ile haue the worke tane out,
And giu't *Iago :* what he will do with it   345
Heauen knowes, not I :

336. Exit.] Ex. Oth. and Defd. (after *napkin,* line 338) Qq. Exeunt Ff. After line 337, Rowe et seq.
337. Om. Cap. (corrected *Notes,* ii, 148 *b*).
  Scene VII. Pope+, Jen.
338. *Napkin :*] *napkin here.* Han.
341. *Woo'd*] *Wooed* Qq.
342. *ſhould*] *would* Var.'03, '13, '21, Sing. i.
344. *talke too*] *talke to* QqFf.
  haue] *ha* Qq.

344, 345. *Ile...he will*] *I will have the work | Ta'en out, and give it to Iago, but | What he'll* (reading *What he'll...not I* in lines 345, 346 as one line) Han.
345, 346. Lines end, *Iago...I :* Johns. Cap. Jen. Steev. Mal.Var. Sing. Dyce, Del. Huds.
345. *giu't*] *give it* Steev. Mal.
  he will] *hee'll* Q₁, Pope+, Jen. Steev. Mal. Var. Sing.   *he'l* Q₂Q₃.
346, 347. One line, Ktly.

336. **Exit**] Booth : Take time, gently push the handkerchief from her hand as she is in the act of binding it on your forehead.   Pass her, while on her knees, with forced indifference, but turn lovingly, and holding your arms for her to enter them, say ' Come, I'll go in with thee.'   Then with a long soulful look into her eyes, fold her tenderly to your heart and go slowly off.   *Keep time.*   Don't *drawl* in either speech or movement, yet be not abrupt nor rapid.   Every movement, gesture, look, and tone should be in harmony.

338. Fechter : Comes forward with caution, and seizes the handkerchief, which she has watched narrowly since Othello threw it down.   Booth : Emilia, by chance, sees the handkerchief and picks it up.

339. **remembrance**] Staunton : That is, *memorial,* or *forget-me-not.*

344. **tane out**] Johnson : The meaning is not, to have the work picked out and leave the ground plain, but to have this work copied in another handkerchief.   Steevens : So in Middleton's *Women Beware Women,* I, i, ' she intends To *take out* other works in a new sampler.'   Again, in the Preface to Holland's Pliny : ' Thus Nicophanes (a famous painter in his time) gave his mind wholly to antique pictures, partly to exemplifie and take out their patternes.'   Blackstone : Her first thoughts are to have a copy made of it for her husband, and to restore the original to Desdemona.   But the sudden coming in of Iago, in a surly humour, makes her alter her resolution, to please him.   Malone : This scheme of having the work copied was to render Emilia less unamiable.   It is remarkable that when she perceives Othello's fury on the loss of this token, though she is represented as affectionate to her mistress, she never attempts to relieve her of her distress, which she might easily have done.   Shakespeare fell into this incongruity by departing from Cinthio's novel.

I nothing, but to pleafe his Fantafie.   347

Enter Iago.

Iago.   How now ? What do you heere alone ?

Æmil.   Do not you chide : I haue a thing for you.   350

Iago.   You haue a thing for me ?   [325 *b*]

It is a common thing————

Æmil.   Hah ?

Iago.   To haue a foolifh wife.

Æmil.   Oh, is that all ? What will you giue me now   355

For that fame Handkerchiefe.

Iago.   What Handkerchiefe ?

Æmil.   What Handkerchiefe ?

Why that the Moore firft gaue to *Defdemona*,

That which fo often you did bid me fteale.   360

Iago.   Haft ftolne it from her ?

Æmil.   No : but fhe let it drop by negligence,

And to th'aduantage, I being heere, took't vp :

Looke, heere 'tis.

Iago.   A good wench, giue it me.   365

---

347. *nothing...his*] *nothing know, but for his* Q₁, Johns.

348. Enter...] After line 345, Qq.

351, 352. One line, Qq, Cap. Steev. et seq.

351. *You haue*] Ff, Rowe+, Jen. Steev. '85. Om. Qq et cet.

352. *thing*—] *thing.* Q₁. *thing:* Cap.

354. *wife*] *thing* Q₁.

356, 357, 358. *Handkerchiefe*] *handkercher* Q₁.

361. *ftolne*] *ftole* Qq, Cap. Jen. *ftoln* F₃. *ftollen* F₄, Rowe, Pope.

362. *No: but fhe*] Ff, Rowe+, Cap. Jen. Steev.'85, Knt. *No faith, fhe* Qq et cet.

363. *th'*] Ff, Rowe+, Jen. Coll. Dyce iii, Huds. *the* Qq et cet.

took't] *tooke it* Q₂Q₃, Steev.'85, Mal.

364. *'tis*] Ff, Rowe+. *it is* Qq, Han. et cet.

349–352. WALKER (*Crit.* iii, 287) : Arrange, perhaps,—How now ! | What do you here alone ? *Emil.* Do not you chide ; | I have a thing for you. *Iago.* A thing for me ? | It is a common thing.

350. **chide**] BOOTH : Note this. Iago's manner is brusque,—disappointed at not finding Othello here ; he had come to drive the dagger deeper in his heart.

357. FECHTER : Earnestly. BOOTH : Indifferently. Up stage.

361. BOOTH : Turn quickly, with delighted expectancy.

362. **No**] COLLIER (ed. i) : The Master of the Revels seems to have been capriciously scrupulous in this play ; here, according to the Folio, '' faith ' was erased as an oath, and this not for the first time. In line 332 the same thing occurs.

363. **to th' advantage**] JOHNSON : I, being *opportunely* here, took it up.

365. BOOTH : Snatch at it eagerly.

Æmil.   What will you do with't, that you haue bene   366
ſo earneſt to haue me filch it?

Iago.   Why, what is that to you?

Æmil.   If it be not for ſome purpoſe of import,
Giu't me againe.   Poore Lady, ſhee'l run mad   370
When ſhe ſhall lacke it.

Iago.   Be not acknowne on't:
I haue vſe for it.   Go, leaue me.   *Exit Æmil.*
I will in *Caſſio's* Lodging looſe this Napkin,
And let him finde it.   Trifles light as ayre,   375
Are to the iealious, confirmations ſtrong,
As proofes of holy Writ.   This may do ſomething.   377

366, 367. *What...ſo*] *What...So* (As
verse) Q₁. (As verse, the first line ending *with it*) Q₂Q₃. Prose Ff, Rowe, Pope.
What...earneſt] One line, Theob.
et seq.

366. *with't*] *with it* Qq, Jen. Steev.
Mal. Var. Sing. Ktly.

that] Om. F₃F₄, Rowe+.

you haue] *you've* Huds.

367. *filch*] *fetch* Q₃. *filtch* F₄, Rowe.

368. *what is*] Ff, Rowe+, Jen. Steev.
'85. *what's* Qq et cet.

[*Snatching it.* Rowe.

369. *If it*] *If't* Q₂Q₃, Pope+, Cap. Jen.
Cam. Dyce iii, Huds.

for] Om. Coll. (MS).

370. *Giu't me*] *Giue mee't* Q₁Q₂. *Give
me't* Q₃, Jen. *Give it me* Steev. Mal. Var.

372, 373. One line, Qq, Jen. *Be...for
it* One line, Cap. et seq. (except Ktly and
Dyce iii).

372. *not acknowne on't*] F₂. *not you
knowne on't* Q₁Q₃, Pope+, Cap. Jen. *not
you acknowne on't* Q₂, Dyce iii, Coll. iii.
not you known of't Mal. Steev.'93, Var.
not acknown on't F₃F₄ et cet. *not you
known in't* Johns. conj.

373. *for it.*] *for it:—* Qq. *for't* Walker
Go, leaue me] Separate line, Cap
et seq. (except Ktly and Dyce iii).

Exit Æmil.] Exit Em. (after *napkin*, line 374) Qq.

374. *looſe*] *loſe* Qq.

376. *iealious*] *iealous* QqFf.

377. *Writ.*] *Wright*, Q₃.

---

368. **Why**] BOOTH: Pause mysteriously, 'Why ——,' as if about to give her some
wonderful reason.   Then snatch it, with 'What's that to you?'

372. **acknowne**] STEEVENS: That is, do not acknowledge anything of the matter.
The word occurs in Golding's *Ovid*: 'Howbeit I durſt not be ſo bolde of hope ac
knowne to bee' [p. 91, Lib. vii, 632, 'nec me ſperare fatebar']. Again in Puttenham's *Arte of Poesie* [p. 260, ed. Arber]: 'ſo would I not haue a tranſlatour to be
aſhamed to be acknowen of his tranſlation.' PORSON: Again in *The Life of Ariosto*, in
Harrington's translation of Orlando, ed. 1607: 'Some ſay, he was married to her privi-
lie, but durſt not be acknowne of it.'

373. BOOTH: Many 'Iagos' kiss her, and coax her to leave him,— he is given rather
to chiding than to caressing.

374. **Napkin**] BOOTH: Why may not Cassio bind this about his wounded leg at
close of the next Act?   'Tis traditional, and reasonable,—do it.

375, 376. HUNTER (ii, 281): Compare *V. & A.* 1023: 'Trifles unwitnessed with
eye or ear   Thy coward heart with false bethinking grieves.'

The Moore already changes with my poyſon :   378
Dangerous conceites, are in their Natures poyſons,
Which at the firſt are ſcarſe found to diſtaſte :   380
But with a little acte vpon the blood,
Burne like the Mines of Sulphure.   I did ſay ſo.

Enter Othello.

Looke where he comes : Not Poppy, nor Mandragora,   384

378. Om. Q$_1$.
    poyſon] *poyſons* Ff, Rowe+.
379. Om. Rowe ii.
    Natures] *nature* Pope+.
380. *diſtaſte*] *diſtaſt* Qq.
381. *acte vpon*] *art, vpon* Q$_1$.
382. *Mines*] *mindes* Q$_1$.

383. Enter...] (After *blood,* line 381)
Q$_1$Q$_2$. Om. Q$_3$.   After *yesterday,* line
387, Knt, Sing. Dyce, Wh. Ktly, Sta.
Huds.
    Scene VIII. Pope+, Jen.
384. *nor*] Om. F$_4$.

---

378. **my poyson**] STAUNTON : The repetition of 'poison' here is so inelegant that
we may well suspect the word in one line was caught by the compositor's eye from the
other, but it is hard to say in which the corruption lies.   WALKER (*Crit.* i, 287) : I
once thought that we should read 'with my *practise ;*' but it would seem that the word
required should be similar in termination, or general appearance, to 'poison' ; for this
line has dropt out, most probably from that cause, in Q$_1$.   Therefore I conjecture *potion.*

382. **I did say so**] To BLACKSTONE this exclamation was most unmeaning in the
mouth of such a speaker, at such a time ; he therefore suggested that as Iago has the
handkerchief in his hand there may be a reference to it, and that the phrase is 'Hide
it !—so—so' ; but he 'readily retracted' his emendation (though still thinking the
phrase obscure) after reading the following note by STEEVENS : Iago first ruminates on
the qualities of the passion which he is labouring to excite ; and then proceeds to comment on its effects.   'Jealousy (says he), with the smallest operation on the blood, flames
out with all the violence of sulphur,' &c.   'I did say so ; Look where he comes—!'
i. e., I knew that the least touch of such a passion would not permit the Moor to enjoy
a moment of repose :—I have just said that jealousy is a restless commotion of the mind ;
and look where Othello approaches, to confirm the propriety and justice of my observation.   HUDSON : The moment Iago's eye lights on Othello, he sees that his devilish insight of things was punctually prophetic of Othello's case ; that his words are exactly
verified in the inflamed looks of his victim.   BOOTH's dramatic instinct clears any difficulty by a stage direction—'Othello groans.'

383. In a note on *Tro. & Cress.,* DYCE, in his *Remarks,* p. 147, shows that these
stage directions were not meant to be taken as the actual entrance of the actor, but that
they were merely, as in the present case, to show that towards the end of a soliloquy
the actor who spoke next was to prepare himself (or be summoned) to enter,—not that
he was to come on the stage before the conclusion of the soliloquy.   It is the same in
IV. i, 116, where 'Enter Cassio' occurs four lines before Iago addresses him.   [I suppose it was on this fact that Dyce founded his positive assertion (see note on II, ii, 231)
that F$_1$ was printed from a stage transcript, and not from one where shorthand had been
used.   KNIGHT was the first to indicate Othello s entrance at the proper word, although
Capell had 'Enter Othello, *at a distance.*'—ED.]

384. **Mandragora**] STAUNTON quotes from Holland's *Pliny,* Bk. xxv, ch. 13 :
'This herbe Mandragoras, some writers cal Circeium ; and two kinds there be of it :

Nor all the drowfie Syrrups of the world   385
Shall euer medicine thee to that fweete fleepe
Which thou owd'ft yefterday.

    Oth. Ha, ha, falfe to mee?

    Iago. Why how now Generall? No more of that.

    Oth. Auant, be gone : Thou haft fet me on the Racke: 390
I fweare 'tis better to be much abus'd,
Then but to know't a little.

    Iago. How now, my Lord?

    Oth. What fenfe had I, in her ftolne houres of Luft?   394

---

387. *owd'ft*] *owedft* Qq, Han. Warb.
Johns. Jen. Glo. Cam. Huds. *had'st* Pope,
Theob.

    yesterday] *yester-night* Edwards
(in jest).

388. *Ha, ha,*] *Ha!* Pope+, Cap.

    falfe to mee?] *falfe to me, to me?*
Q₁Q₂, Jen. *falfe to me to me?* Q₃. *False?
To me! to me!* Johns. *false to me? to me?*
Steev. Mal. Var. Coll. Sing. Wh. i, Ktly.

390. *Thou haft*] *thou'st* Pope+.

391. *fweare*] *fware* Q₃.

392. *know't*] *know* Q₁, Rowe, Pope,
Theob. Han. Warb.

393. *now*] Om. Pope+.

394. *fenfe*] *fence* Q₂Q₃. *fent* F₂F₃.
fcent F₄, Rowe.

    in her] Ff, Rowe, Pope, Han. Knt.
of her Qq et cet.

    of Luft] *or luft* Theob. ii, Warb.
Johns. [See Commentary.]

---

the white which is supposed the male; and the black which you must take for the
female. . . . . It may be used safely enough for to procure sleep, if there be good regard
nad in the dose. . . . . Also it is an ordinarie thing to drink it . . . . before the cutting
or cauterizing, pricking or launcing of any member to take away the sence and feeling
of such extreme cures. And sufficient it is in some bodies to cast them into a sleep
with the smel of Mandrage, against the time of such Chirurgery.'   HUNTER (ii, 286):
It may be suspected that when Shakespeare used the word, mandragora had but a traditional and historical claim to be reckoned among the 'drowsy syrups of the world.'
BUCKNILL (p. 217): Shakespeare refers to this plant altogether six times, and it is
noteworthy that on the two occasions where its real medicinal properties are mentioned,
the Latin term *mandragora* is used; the vulgar appellation, *mandrake*, is employed when
the vulgar superstition is alluded to. [See notes on 'mandrake' in *Rom. & Jul* IV,
iii, 47.]

    387–389. STEEVENS reads and divides: Which thou ow'dst yesterday. *Oth.* Ha!
ha! false to me? | To me? *Iago.* Why, how now, general? no more of that. |

    388. BOOTH: Mournfully. Iago addresses him as though not expecting him.

    394. **in**] KNIGHT: *Sense of* is the modern use of the term *knowledge of;* 'sense
in' is the more proper and peculiarly Shakespearian use, which implies the impression
upon the senses, and not upon the understanding. The difference is the same as be
tween *a sensible man* and *a man sensible to pain.*

    394. **of**] At first sight, in Theobald's ed. ii, this looks like *or*, but closer scrutiny
shows the *r* to be simply a battered, mutilated *f;* in one of my copies of this edition,
the *l* of the following word is totally lost, and half of the *u*, presumably from the same
accident that destroyed the upper half of this *f.* But Warburton, who had denounced
Hanmer for not comparing Pope's edition with Theobald's, falls here under his own

I faw't not, thought it not : it harm'd not me : 395
I flept the next night well, fed well, was free, and merrie.
I found not *Caffio's* kiffes on her Lippes :
He that is robb'd, not wanting what is ftolne,
Let him not know't, and he's not robb'd at all.

    Iago. I am forry to heare this ? 400

    Oth. I had beene happy, if the generall Campe,
Pyoners and all, had tafted her fweet Body, 402

---

395. *faw't*] *faw it* F₄, Rowe, Steev.
Mal. Var. Coll. Del.
396. *fed well*] Ff, Rowe, Knt, Sing.
Wh. i, Ktly, Del. Om. Qq et cet.
399. *know't*] *know it* Steev.

400. *I am*] *I'm* Huds.
402. *Pyoners*] QqF₂. *Pioners* Cap.
Dyce, Sta. Wh. Glo. Cam. Del. Rlfe.
Pioneers F₃F₄ et cet.

---

condemnation; he accepted the *or*, without comparing it with any edition, and incorporated it in his own text bare of comment. So likewise did Dr Johnson, who, while using Theobald's text to print from, sneered at him in his Preface, and raised a laugh against him by saying : ' I have sometimes adopted his restoration of a comma, without inserting the panegyric in which he celebrated himself for his achievement.' Sir, he who accepts a text to print from on the one hand, and vilifies his benefactor on the other, is, on this occasion, removed alike either from the claims of consideration or the requirements of respect.—ED.

394 et seq. STEEVENS calls attention to certain passages in Middleton's *Witch* resembling this and other passages in this scene, to which, apparently, he attached importance as indications that Shakespeare nad followed Middleton, but MALONE afterwards showed that *The Witch* must have been produced after 1613. [See *Macbeth, Appendix*, p. 388.]

396. **fed well**] KNIGHT : The rejection of these words by the modern editors can be accounted for only by the fact that they would make any sacrifice of sense or poetry, and prefer the feeblest to the strongest expression, if they could prevent the intrusion of a line exceeding ten syllables. This sacrifice, for the sake of a tame and uniform rhythm, is even more ludicrous when they strive to make an heroic line out of the broken sentences of two or more speakers, as in line 122, where ' Honest ' is omitted. COLLIER (ed. i) : A strange corruption, for which it is difficult to account. COLLIER (ed. ii) : An absurd insertion, as if Othello meant to say that he had *fed well* in the night, while he was ' free and merry,' a corruption of the verse for which, however, it is not difficult to account.

396. FECHTER : In a feverish agony of rage.

398. **wanting**] BOOTH : I prefer *knowing*, for surely Othello did ' want ' Desdemona's love at all times and forever. [But ' wanting ' is here used not in the sense of *needing*, but of *missing*,—and yet even in this sense it has a lack of tenderness.—ED.]

398, 399. HALLIWELL quotes Milton, ix, 756 : ' For good unknown sure is not had ; or had And yet unknown, is as not had at all.'

401. GOULD (p. 105) : We may imagine the guileless hospitality of the gentle lady to her guests, maddening her husband, so that he leaves them abruptly, and re-enters on the scene to Iago.

402. **Pyoners**] GROSE : ' A soldier ought ever to retaine and keepe his arms in safetie and forth comming, for he is more to be detested than a coward, that will lose

So I had nothing knowne.　Oh now, for euer　　　403
Farewell the Tranquill minde ; farewell Content ;
Farewell the plumed Troopes, and the bigge Warres,　　405
That makes Ambition, Vertue ! Oh farewell;
Farewell the neighing Steed, and the ſhrill Trumpe,
The Spirit-ſtirring Drum, th'Eare-piercing Fife,　　　408

---

403. *knowne*] *knowen* Q$_3$.

405. *Troopes*] F$_2$. *Troops* F$_3$F$_4$, Rowe+, Cap. Knt, Sta. Wh. i, Del. *troope* Qq et cet.

Warres] *war* Rowe ii+, Cap.

406. *makes*] Qq, Johns. Cap. Ktly. *make* Ff et cet.

farewell ;] *farewell,* QqFf, Rowe, Cam. *farewell !* Pope et cet.

408. *th'*] Ff, Rowe+, Cap. Jen. Dyce iii, Huds. *the* Qq et cet.

---

or play away any part thereof, or refuse it for his ease, or to avoid paines; wherefore such a one is to be dismissed with punishment, or to be made some abject pioner.'—Davies's *Art of War and England Traynings*, 1619. So, in *The Laws and Ordinances of War*, established by the Earl of Essex, printed in 1640: 'If a trooper shall loose his horse or hackney, or a footman any part of his arms, by negligence or lewdnesse, by dice or cardes; he or they shall remain in qualitie of pioners, or scavengers, till they be furnished with as good as were lost, at their own charge.' WALKER (*Vers.* p. 217) shows that the spelling *pioner*, from the flow of the verse, were there no other indication, should be retained. [See *Ham.* I, v, 163.]

404 et seq. MALONE quotes two passages, one from a 'very ancient drama entitled *Common Conditions*,' and another from a *Farewell* by Peele, which he intimates may have suggested these lines to Shakespeare. STEEVENS: I know not why we should suppose that Shakespeare borrowed so common a repetition as those diversified *farewells* from any preceding drama. A string of *adieus* is perhaps the most tempting of all repetitions, because it serves to introduce a train of imagery as well as to solemnify a speech or composition. Wolsey, like Othello, indulges himself in many *farewells ;* and the Valete, aprica montium cacumina ! Valete, opaca vallium cubilia ! &c., are common to poets of different ages and countries. I have now before me an ancient MS. English poem, in which sixteen succeeding verses begin with the word *farewell,* applied to a variety of objects and circumstances. BOOTH : Utter this, looking off,—towards Desdemona. My Father once said to me, 'No human voice could surpass, if equal, Edmund Kean's in his delivery of this passage.' Begin slowly, with suppressed emotion; gradually increase the volume and intensity of voice,—never loud, nor let your tones be too tearful or tremulous,—it becomes monotonous.

405. **plumed**] DANIEL (*Athenæum*, 14 Jan. 1871) calls attention to the change of this word to *plumped*, in a quotation of these two lines in Suckling's *Goblins*, 1696, and queries whether it be a misprint, or a misquotation, or the reading of some copy of *Othello* now lost. Its meaning, he adds, would be *in serried ranks ;* in proof, several illustrations are given from Hall's *Chronicle*, a book with which Shakespeare must have been familiar. TIFFIN (*Athenæum*, 28 Jan. 1871) asserts that *plumped* is merely a misprint of the 1696 edition of *The Goblins ;* in the edition of 1658 it is correctly quoted 'plumed.'

408. **Eare-piercing**] WARBURTON : I would read *fear-'spersing,* i. e. *fear-dispersing ;* whereupon EDWARDS (p. 34) suspects a misprint, and that Warburton intended to say, 'I would *write ;* for no man living can *read* such a cluster of consonants.

The Royall Banner, and all Qualitie,
Pride, Pompe, and Circumſtance of glorious Warre: 410
And O you mortall Engines, whoſe rude throates
Th'immortall Ioues dread Clamours, counterfet,
Farewell : *Othello's* Occupation's gone.   413

410. *Pride, Pompe*] *Prid. Pompe* Q₃.
411. *you*] *ye* Qq, Jen.
    rude] *wide* Qq.
412. *Th'*] Ff, Rowe+, Jen. Dyce iii.

The Qq et cet.
412. *dread*] *great* Qq.
    Clamours] *clamor* Qₓ.
    counterfet] *counterfeit* QqFf.

408. **Fife**] WARTON: In mentioning the *fife* joined with the *drum*, Shakespeare, as usual, paints from the life; those instruments accompanying each other being used in his age by the English soldiery. The *fife*, however, as a martial instrument, was afterwards entirely discontinued among our troops for many years. It was first used within the memory of man, among our troops, by the British guards, by order of the Duke of Cumberland, when they were encamped at Maestricht, in the year 1747. They took it from the Allies, with whom they served. This instrument, accompanying the drum, is of considerable antiquity in the European armies, particularly the German. In a curious picture in the Ashmolean Museum at Oxford, painted 1525, representing the siege of Pavia by the French King, where the Emperor was taken prisoner, we see *fifes* and *drums*. In Rymer's *Fœdera*, in a diary of King Henry's siege of Bulloigne, 1544, mention is made of the *drommes* and *viffleurs* marching at the head of the King's army. The *drum* and *fife* were also much used at ancient festivals, shows, and processions. Gerard Leigh, in his *Accidence of Armorie*, printed in 1576, describing a Christmas magnificently celebrated at the Inner Temple, says, 'we entered the prince his hall, where anon we heard the noyse of *drum* and *fife*.' At a stately masque on Shrove-Sunday, 1510, in which King Henry VIII was an actor, Holinshed mentions the entry 'of a *drum* and *fife* appareled in white damaske and grene bonnettes'— *Chron.* III, 805, col. 2. KNIGHT: Among the French regiments the fife is not found, and is so completely unknown to the French in the present day, that M. Alfred de Vigny, in his translation of this passage of *Othello*, gives us only the drum. [It is to be feared that Knight drew a conclusion from insufficient premises. The instrument was known in France in the days of Shakespeare. Cotgrave gives 'Fifre: m. A Fife; a Flute, or little pipe accorded with a Drumme, or Taber,' and that it was never 'completely unknown' may be inferred, I think, from the fact that from LE TOURNEUR in 1776, down through LAROCHE, GUIZOT, HUGO, and CAYROU, to AICARD in 1882, the word 'fife' is translated 'fifre,' and DE VIGNY is the solitary exception where it is not found, the omission being presumably due to the exigencies of his rhythm.—ED.]

410. **Circumstance**] HUNTER (ii, 286): So singular a use of this word requires something to show that it was not without precedent. Take the following from Langley's Translation of Polydore Virgil, where we find that the Romans celebrated their dead 'with great pomp and circumstance'—Fol. 122, *b*. [Steevens, in his Preface, refers to the 'ambition in each little Hercules to set up pillars, ascertaining how far he had traveled through the dreary wilds of black letter.' There have been, however, very, very few contributions to Shakespearian literature more valuable, or more attractive, than Hunter's *New Illustrations.*—ED.] ROLFE: Shakespeare uses the singular and plural indifferently. See *R. of L.*, 1262 and 1703.

413. GILES (p. 227) Othello does not here allude once to his real grief, or to his

Iago.   Is't poſſible my Lord?

Oth.   Villaine, be ſure thou proue my Loue a Whore;   415

---

414. *Is't*] *Is it* Steev. Mal. Var. Coll.   Sing. Sta. Ktly, Del. *poſſible, my Lord!*
    poſſible my Lord?] *poſſible?*—   QqFf, Booth's Reprint et cet.
My Lord,— Cap. Steev. Mal. Var. Coll.

---

recent happiness; but, with a terrible spring of the mind, he leaps the chasm of affliction into which he cannot dare to look, and alights on the other side, amidst the tur-
moils of his youth, amidst the noise and glories of his soldiership. This is the instinct
of the mind to save itself from madness. The mind thus blots out the present from its
view, and takes refuge in the past. Othello will not front his deadliest loss; he shrinks
from it, to grasp with associations which restore him for an instant to the vigorous grandeur of his manhood; when *that* instant is over, his energies collapse; then comes the
depressing sense that for him no more is either hope or action; and so he murmurs
' Othello's occupation's gone.' Othello, in this passage, reveals the casuistry with which
the mind blinds itself to ruin; the sophistry in which it quibbles with despair; the
maniac strength with which it wrestles against fate and fact. It is as when we fall
asleep with a heavy trouble on the soul; the soul takes advantage of this silent hour to
escape from its bondage; again it is on the sunny hills; the strength of youth comes
back, with the gladness of love and the hopes of life; not once does the spectre of ill
throw its shadow on the dream; the vision is bright while the eyes are shut; but no
sooner do they open than the dismal reality is present, and it cannot be dismissed.

413. GOULD (p. 106): In the mere word 'farewell' his [J. B. Booth's] great heart
seemed to burst as in one vast continuing sigh. The phrase, 'the tranquil mind,' immediately succeeding, came in clear brain-tones, with a certain involved suggestiveness
of meaning almost impossible to define, but as if the tranquil mind *had* flown. The
whole passage, with its successive images of glorious war filing and disappearing before
the mind's eye, employed some of the grandest elements of voice, subdued to retro-
spective and mournful cadences. 'Othello's occupation's gone.' And he stood with a
look in his large blue eyes,—the bronzed face lending them a strange sadness,—as if
all happiness had gone after. Kean's manner in this scene was very different. At the
close of the 'farewell' he raised both hands, clasped them, and so brought them down
upon his head, with a most effective gesture of despair. But the action seems to us like
transferring Othello into Edmund Kean. FECHTER: Othello falls back on his seat,
quite humbled.

415. LEWES (p. 4): Kean's range of expression was very limited. His physical apti-
tudes were such as confined him to the strictly tragic passions; and for these he was
magnificently endowed. Small and insignificant in figure, he could at times become
impressively commanding by the lion-like power and grace of his bearing. I remember the last time I saw him play Othello, how puny he appeared beside Macready,
until in the Third Act, when, roused by Iago's taunts and insinuations, he moved
towards him with a gouty hobble, seized him by the throat, and, in a well-known explosion, 'Villain! be sure,' &c., he seemed to swell into a stature which made Macready
appear small. On that very evening, when gout made it difficult for him to display
his accustomed grace, when a drunken hoarseness had ruined that once matchless
voice, such was the irresistible pathos,—manly, not tearful,—which vibrated in his tones
and expressed itself in looks and gestures, that old men leaned their heads upon their
arms and fairly sobbed. It was, one must confess, a patchy performance considered as
a whole; some parts were miserably tricky, others misconceived, others gabbled over

Be fure of it : Giue me the Occular proofe,   416
Or by the worth of mine eternall Soule,   [326 *a*]
Thou had'ft bin be?ter haue bin borne a Dog
Then anfwer my wak'd wrath.

   Iago.   Is't come to this?   420

   Oth.   Make me to fee't : or (at the leaft) fo proue it,
That the probation beare no Hindge, nor Loope,
To hang a doubt on : Or woe vpon thy life.

   Iago.   My Noble Lord.

   Oth.   If thou doft flander her, and torture me,   425
Neuer pray more : Abandon all remorfe
On Horrors head, Horrors accumulate :
Do deeds to make Heauen weepe, all Earth amaz'd ;   428

---

416. *Occular*] *ocular* Q$_1$. *ocular* Q$_2$Q$_3$ Ff.

[Catching hold on him. Rowe.

417. *mine*] *mans* Q$_1$, Warb. Sta. Glo. Cam. Dyce iii, Huds. Rlfe, Wh. ii.   *my* Q$_2$Q$_3$, Cap.

418. *had'ft bin*] *hadft* Q'81.   *hadst much* Quincy (MS).

419. *Then*] *That* Q$_3$.

420. *Is't*] *Is it* Steev. Mal. Var. Coll. W?. i, Del.

421. *fee't*] *see it* Steev. Mal. Var.

424. *Lord.*] QqFf, Rowe.   *lord—*Pope et seq.

426. *remorfe*] *remorce.* Q$_1$.   *remorce :* Q$_2$.   *remorfe :* Q$_3$.

427. *Horrors head*] *horror's head* Han. Johns. et seq.

accumulate] *accumilate* Q$_1$.

---

in haste to reach the 'points'; but it was irradiated with such flashes that I would again risk broken ribs for the chance of a good place in the pit to see anything like it. BOOTH : As before, with smothered intensity, not loud, gradually increasing, till 'If thou dost slander her'—when the full force of Othello's wrath breaks forth in violent tones and he seizes Iago, who cowers.

415. *Loue*] MAGINN (p. 273) : We may observe that he still, though his suspicions are so fiercely aroused, calls her his 'love.' It is for the last time before her death. After her guilt is, as he thinks, proved, he has no word of affection for her. She is a convicted culprit, to be sacrificed to his sense of justice.

417. *mine*] STEEVENS : An opposition may have been designed between *man* and 'dog.' [See Text. Notes. BOSWELL, in the *Var.* of '21, gives *man's* as the reading of a Quarto for 'my' in line 419. I think it is merely a misprint in the reference, and that the *varia lectio* refers to 'mine' in this present line, and not to the 'my.' It apparently puzzled Collier, or I should not have referred to it.—ED.]

418. **have been**] See *Ham.* V, i, 232, or ABBOTT, § 360.

426. **remorse**] MALONE : All tenderness of nature, all pity. [See *post*, line 532.] HUDSON : That is, apparently here, *conscience ;* 'Cast off the restraints and regards of conscience altogether.' The sense of *pity*, however, is included and interfused with it. What an appalling disclosure this speech is, of Othello's excruciating agony of mind !

427. **Horrors accumulate**] WALKER (*Crit.* i, 253) : Read *horror.* The corruption originated in the preceding 'horrors.' [See I, i, 31.]

428. **weepe**] STEEVENS : Compare *Meas. for Meas.* II, ii, 121 : 'Plays such fantastic tricks before high Heaven As make the angels weep.'

For nothing canſt thou to damnation adde,
Greater then that.   430
   Iago.   O Grace! O Heauen forgiue me!
Are you a Man? Haue you a Soule? or Senſe?
God buy you : take mine Office.   Oh wretched Foole,
That lou'ſt to make thine Honeſty, a Vice!
Oh monſtrous world! Take note, take note (O World)   435
To be direƐt and honeſt, is not ſafe.
I thanke you for this profit, and from hence
Ile loue no Friend, ſith Loue breeds ſuch offence.
   Oth.   Nay ſtay : thou ſhould'ſt be honeſt.
   Iago.   I ſhould be wiſe ; for Honeſtie's a Foole,   440
And looſes that it workes for.
   Oth.   By the World,
I thinke my Wife be honeſt, and thinke ſhe is not: 443

429, 430. One line, Qq.

431. *forgiue*] *defend* Qq, Pope+, Cap.
Jen. Steev. Mal.Var. Coll. Sing. Cam. Ktly.

433. *buy*] QqF₂F₃. *b'w'* F₄, Jen. *be
w'* Theob.Warb. Johns. *b'wi'* Sing. Dyce,
Wh. Huds. *be wi'* Rowe et cet.
  mine] *my* Q₂Q₃.
  Office.] *office,—* Qq.
  Oh] Om. Pope, Han.

434. *lou'ſt*] Ff, Rowe, Cap. Knt, Wh.
ii. *lieuſt* Qq et cet.
  thine] *thy* Q'95.

435. *world!*] *world,* Qq.

438. *ſith*] *ſince* Qq, Jen. Mal. Steev.'93,
Var. Coll. Sing. Wh. i, Ktly, Huds.

439. *ſtay :*] *ſtay,* Qq. *stay—* Rowe+.
stay. Johns. Jen. Coll. Wh. Ktly, Del.
  honeſt.] *honest—* Rowe+, Jen.

441. *looſes*] *loſes* Ff.
  that] *what* Pope+.

442-449. Om. Q₁.

443. *be*] *is* F₃F₄, Rowe+, Cap.
  and] Om. Cap.

---

430. BOOTH : I carry no weapon in this scene, but seeing Iago's dagger I clutch it in frenzy and am about to stab him, when the Christian overcomes the Moor, and throwing the dagger from me, I fall again upon the seat with a flood of tears.   To this weeping Iago may allude in his next speech, where he says contemptuously, 'Are you a man?'

433. buy] See I, iii, 215. This spelling must not mislead us as to the pronunciation; 'buy' should not be pronounced like our present *bye;* the *y* is merely phonetic, and represents not *ye* but *wi'*, and should be pronounced like it, as, indeed, it is indicated by Singer.   See Text. Notes.—Ed.

434. lou'st] KNIGHT : Surely the man that *loves* to carry his honesty so far that it becomes a vice is what Iago means when he calls himself a *fool.*

438. sith] See *Ham.* II, ii, 6, where Marsh points out the distinction between *sith* and *since,* viz.: that *sith* belongs to logic and *since* to time, a distinction which the printers of Shakespeare's plays were not always careful to preserve.

439. BOOTH : Peremptorily, as to your subaltern, and Iago halts at the word of command.

443. be . . . is] ABBOTT, § 299: *Be* expresses more doubt than *is* after a verb of thinking.   Very significant is this difference in this line of the doubtful Othello where *is* is the emphatic word and the line contains the extra dramatic syllable.

I thinke that thou art iuſt, and thinke thou art not:
Ile haue ſome proofe.   My name that was as freſh   445
As *Dians* Viſage, is now begrim'd and blacke
As mine owne face.   If there be Cords, or Kniues,
Poyſon, or Fire, or ſuffocating ſtreames,
Ile not indure it.   Would I were ſatisfied.

Iago.   I ſee you are eaten vp with Paſſion: 450
I do repent me, that I put it to you.
You would be ſatisfied?

Oth.   Would? Nay, and I will.

Iago.   And may : but how *?* How ſatisfied, my Lord?
Would you the ſuper-viſion groſſely gape on?   455
Behold her top'd?

445. *My*] Ff, Rowe, Mal. Knt.   *her*
Q₂Q₃ et cet.
446. *begrim'd*] begrimd Q₂. *begrimed*
Q₃.
448. *ſtreames*] steams Pope, Han.
450. *I ſee*] Ff, Rowe. *I ſee ſir*, Qq et
cet.
452. *ſatisfied ?*] *ſatisfied.* Qq.
453. *Would ?*] *Would,* Qq, Rowe i.
and I] Ff, Rowe, Knt, Ktly. *and*
Pope+. *I* Qq et cet.

454. *how ?*] *now ?* Rowe i.
455. *you the ſuper-viſion*] Ff, Rowe,
Knt, Coll. Ktly. *you, the ſuperuiſor* Q₁
you, the ſuperuiſion Q₂Q₃. *you be super-*
visor, Pope+. *you, the supervisor,* Cap.
et cet.
on ?] *on,* Qq. *on—* Dyce, Wh.
Glo. Sta.
456. *top'd*] Warb. *topt* Qq. *topp'd*
Ff, Rowe, Pope i, Knt, Sing. Glo. Ktly,
Cam. Wh. ii. *tupp'd* Pope ii et cet.

445. **My name**] KNIGHT: There is probably not a more fatal corruption of the mean
ing of the poet [than *her* of Q₂] amongst the thousand corruptions for which his editors
are answerable.   It destroys the master-key to Othello's character.   It is his intense
feeling of *honour* that makes his wife's supposed fault so terrific to him.   It is not that
Desdemona's name is begrimed and black, but that *his own name* is degraded.   This
one thought, here for the first time exhibited, pervades all the rest of the play; and
when we understand how the poison operates upon Othello's mind, we are quite prepared fully to believe him when he says, in conclusion,—'For naught I did in hate,
but all in honour.'   The thought that his own name is now tarnished drives him at
once into a phrenzy.   He has said, '*I'll have some proof*'; but the moment that the
idea of dishonour comes across his sensitive nature he bursts into uncontrolled fury:
' If there be cords, ... *I'll not endure it.*'   DYCE (*Remarks*, p. 240): The word
' own ' in the phrase ' mine own face,' is alone sufficient to refute Knight's long and
laborious defence of ' My.'   Othello would not have said, ' MY name is now as black
as mine OWN face.'   Mr Knight's text of the present tragedy is, on the whole, as bad
as his text of *Hamlet ;* and a worse text of either play could hardly be produced.   [These
harsh expressions of opinion are apt to make one antagonistic and far from willing to
accept them as decisive.   In justice to Dyce it should be noted that when, a dozen years
later, he became himself an editor of Shakespeare, his tone to his fellow-editors became
much less supercilious and dogmatic.—ED.]

450. **I see you are**] WALKER (*Crit*. iii, 287) prefers this to the *I see, sir* of the
Qq, and contracts 'you are' to *y'are*.   See line 253 above.

Oth.   Death, and damnation.   Oh!   457
  Iago.   It were a tedious difficulty, I thinke,
To bring them to that Profpect : Damne them then,
If euer mortall eyes do fee them boulfter   460
More then their owne.   What then ? How then ?
What fhall I fay? Where's Satisfaction ?
It is impoffible you fhould fee this,
Were they as prime as Goates, as hot as Monkeyes,
As falt as Wolues in pride, and Fooles as groffe   465
As Ignorance, made drunke.   But yet , I fay,
If imputation, and ftrong circumftances,
Which leade directly to the doore of Truth,
Will giue you fatisfaction, you might haue't.   469

457. *damnation.   Oh !*] *damnation—*
oh Qq.
  459. *bring them*] *bring em* Qq, Rowe+,
Cap. Jen. Steev.'85, Mal. *bring* Ff. *bring*
it Coll. (MS).
  Damne them] *dam em* Qq, Cap.
Jen.
  460. *mortall*] *morall* Q$_3$.
  do fee] *did fee* Qq.

  461. *How then ?*] *how then, say you ?*
Cap.
  462. *What...fatisfaction ?*] *Where's fat-*
isfaction ? What shall I say ? Cap.
  469. *you might*] Ff, Rowe+, Jen.
Steev.'85, Knt, Del. *you may* Qq et cet.
haue't] *ha't* Qq. *have it* Steev.
Mal. Var. Coll. Del.

---

457. HAZLITT (Hawkins's *Life of Kean,* ii, 209) : Kean was great, as we expected,—
surpassingly great.   In the Third Act he let himself loose on the ocean of his passion, and drove on in darkness and in tempest, like an abandoned barque.   The agony
of his heart was the fiery Moorish agony, not cramped in within an actor's or a school-
man's confines, but fierce, ungovernable, dangerous.   You knew not what he would do
next in the madness of his spirit,—he knew not himself what he should do.   One of
the finest instantaneous actions of Kean was his clutching his black hand slowly round
his head as though his brain were turning, and then writhing round and standing in
dull agony with his back to the audience,—what other performer would so have forgotten himself ?

  461, 462. CAPELL indicates a quotation by Italics in his text, and thus prints these
two lines : 'More than their own! *What then ? how then,* say you? | *Where's satis-*
faction ? What shall I say ?'   Thereupon he has the following wellnigh unwedge-
able note : What is spoke in another's person ought ever to be distinguish'd from what
a speaker says in his own; and this fitness is greatest in such a case as the present,
where interrogations follow interrogations; for want of such distinction, the two members of [line 462] (by what accident transpos'd, we know not; but, probably, of the
press) keep through all prior copies the perverse order that accident put them in, the
latter member preceding : Was all other proof wanting that what is now the first member stands in it's due place, we might receive it from what the speaker concludes with,
in which is mention of 'satisfaction' as a thing of Othello's *asking:* to which asking
the insertion [of *say you* in line 461] is as favorable on the score of perfpicuoufness,
as it is to the verse's numbers which are now first compleated.

Oth.   Giue me a liuing reafon fhe's difloyall.   470
  Iago.   I do not like the Office.
But fith I am entred in this caufe fo farre
(Prick'd too't by foolifh Honefty, and Loue)
I will go on.   I lay with *Caffio* lately,
And being troubled with a raging tooth,   475
I could not fleepe.   There are a kinde of men,
So loofe of Soule, that in their fleepes will mutter
Their Affayres : one of this kinde is *Caffio :*
In fleepe I heard him fay, fweet *Defdemona,*
Let vs be wary, let vs hide our Loues,   480
And then (Sir) would he gripe, and wring my hand :
Cry, oh fweet Creature : then kiffe me hard,
As if he pluckt vp kiffes by the rootes,   [326 *b*]
That grew vpon my lippes, laid his Leg ore my Thigh,
And figh, and kiffe, and then cry curfed Fate,   485

470. *reafon*] *reafon, that* Qq, Jen. Mal. Var.

471. Iago.] Iogo. F$_2$.

472. *fith*] *since* Theob. ii, Warb. Johns. *I am*] *I'm* Pope+, Sta. Dyce iii, Huds.

   in] *into* Qq, Jen.

473. *too't*] *to't* QqF$_3$F$_4$. *to it* Steev. Mal. Var.

474. *on*] *one* Q$_3$.

475–478. Ff, followed by Rowe, Han. Cap. Ktly. Lines end, *fleep...foule...affaires...Cafsio.* Qq. Ending, *tooth,...sleep ...soul...affairs...Cassio* Pope et cet.

476. *could*] *colud* Q$_3$.

477. *fleepes*] *fleep* Q'81, Q'95.

478. *Their*] *All their* Han. *Of their* Cap.

480. *wary*] *merry* Q$_1$.

482. *Cry, oh*] *Cry out,* Qq. *then*] Ff, Rowe, Knt. *and then* Qq et cet.

484–486. Ff, Rowe, Knt. Ending lines, *leg...then...Moore.* Qq et cet.

484. *That*] *And* Rowe ii, Pope, Han. *laid*] Ff. *then layed* or *laied* Qq. *lay* Rowe, Knt. *then lay* Pope+. *and lay* Steev.'85. *then lay'd* Cap. et cet. *ore*] Ff, Rowe. *ouer* Qq et cet.

485. *figh ... kiffe ... cry*] Ff, Rowe+, Steev.'85 Knt. *figh'd...kiffed...cried* Qq et cet.

---

470. **liuing**] MALONE: A reason founded on fact and experience, not on surmise and conjecture.

477. **sleepes**] See *Ham.* IV, vii, 30.   The use of this plural form is so common that the *s* can scarcely be regarded as an interpolation under Walker's Art. xxxviii (*Crit.* i, 233; see I, i, 31); it is rather a genuine plural, like 'loves,' *Ham.* I, i, 173, 'consents,' 'wills,' 'sights,' &c.

481. BOOTH: Holds Othello's hand, which Othello draws with disgust from his grasp.

482. WALKER (*Crit.* ii, 20), in a list of many instances where *creature* is pronounced as a trisyllable, cites this line, but doubts whether the common reading, which adopts *and then* of the Qq, is not preferable; in this case *creature* would be a dissyllable. LETTSOM (in a foot-note to Walker) thinks the Qq far superior, in which, however, the

That gaue thee to the Moore.   486

   Oth.   O monftrous ! monftrous !

   Iago.   Nay, this was but his Dreame.

   Oth.   But this denoted a fore-gone conclufion,

'Tis a fhrew'd doubt, though it be but a Dreame.   490

   Iago.   And this may helpe to thicken other proofes,

That do demonftrate thinly.

   Oth.   Ile teare her all to peeces.

   Iago.   Nay yet be wife ; yet we fee nothing done,

She may be honeft yet : Tell me but this,   495

Haue you not fometimes feene a Handkerchiefe

Spotted with Strawberries, in your wiues hand ?

   Oth.   I gaue her fuch a one : 'twas my firft gift.   498

487. *O monftrous*] *O monfterous* Q₃.

488. *Nay*] Om. Pope, Han.

489 *denoted*] *deuoted* Q₁.

   fore-gone] *fore-gon* Q₂Q₃.

490-492. *'Tis...thinly*] Given to Iago by Q₁, Warb.

490. *fhrew'd*] *fhrewd* Qq. *fhrewde* F₄.

494. *Nay yet*] Ff, Rowe. *Nay, but* Qq et cet.

496, 499. *Handkerchiefe*] *handkercher* Q₁.

497, 500. *wiues*] *wife's* Rowe et seq.

then would be better away, for *cry* and *kiss* are most closely connected, and this *then* may have crept in from the *then* two lines below.

489. **conclusion**] MALONE : An experiment, or trial. See *Ant. & Cleo.* V, ii, 358. 'She hath pursued conclusions infinite Of easy ways to die.' [See *Ham.* III, iv, 195.] DELIUS finds here an allusion to the 'conclusion' in II, i, 295.

490. JOHNSON : I think this line is more naturally spoken by Othello, who, by dwell ing so long upon the proof, encouraged Iago to enforce it.

490. **doubt**] Suspicion. See line 217 of this scene.

493. FECHTER : Othello crosses with the fierceness of a tiger, and with action as if destroying Desdemona's work. BOOTH : Here you may let the *savage* have vent,—but for a moment only ; when Othello next speaks he is tame again and speaks sadly. Iago has caught and held him as he was about to rush off to 'tear her all to pieces.' Do not stoop to the old stage-trick of displaying Desdemona's handkerchief, as if by accident, while Othello's back is turned.

494. **we see**] WARBURTON : An oblique and secret mock at Othello's saying, 'Give me ocular proof.' HUDSON : Iago is exulting in his intellectual mastery, as shown in the success of his lies. Truth prevails by her own might ; lies by the skill of the liar ; hence, gaining his ends by falsehood is to Iago just the sweetest thing in the world.

497. **spotted**] HALLIWELL : Mr Fairholt sends me the following curious note : 'The ladies of the Shakespearian era were great adepts in the use of the needle ; the designs they made use of were consequently conventional like those worked by our grandmothers in the school sampler. Flowers and fruits were depicted in a sort of heraldic fashion, and repeated mechanically over the surface to be ornamented.' 'The habit of wearing curiously wrought handkerchiefs, which prevailed in our author's day, was derived from the East, where it was customary for both sexes to carry them.'— *Nott.*

Iago.   I know not that : but such a Handkerchiefe
(I am sure it was your wiues) did I to day   500
See *Caſſio* wipe his Beard with.
Oth.   If it be that.
Iago.   If it be that, or any, it was hers.
It ſpeakes againſt her with the other proofes.
Othel.   O that the Slaue had forty thouſand liues :   505
One is too poore, too weake for my reuenge.
Now do I ſee 'tis true.   Looke heere *Iago*,
All my fond loue thus do I blow to Heauen.   'Tis gone.
Ariſe blacke vengeance, from the hollow hell,   509

---

500. *Iam*] *I'm* Pope +, Dyce iii, Huds.
502. *If it*] *If't* Qq, Cap. Jen.
　　that.] *that—* Rowe et seq.
503. *any, it was hers.*] *any, it was hers,*
Qq.   *any, if 'twas hers,* Ff, Rowe +, Cap.
Jen. Steev.'85, Knt.   *any that was hers,*
Mal. et cet.
507. *do I*] *I doe* Q₂Q₃.
　　true] *time* Q₁, Warb.

508. *Heauen.   'Tis*] *heauen,—tis* Qq.
heaven : 'Tis Pope et seq.
　　'Tis gone] Separate line, Pope et
seq. (except Coll. Wh. i, Ktly).
508, 509. *'Tis...hell*] One line, Ktly.
509. *the hollow hell*] *thy hollow cell* Qq,
Johns. Jen. Steev. Mal. Var. Coll. Sing.
Glo. Ktly, Cam. Wh. ii.   *th' unhallow'd
cell* Warb.

---

503. **it was hers**] MALONE : For the emendation *that* in place of ʻit,' I am answerable.   The mistake probably arose from *yt* only being written in the manuscript.   STEEV-
ENS : I prefer Mr Malone's correction to that of F₂, though the latter gives sense where
it was certainly wanting.   KNIGHT prefers F₂ [as does also the present ED.].

505. **forty thousand**] ELZE (Note on *Ham.* V, i, 257) calls attention to Shakespeare's fondness for this number as an expression of indefiniteness.   BOOTH : Whether
this refers to Cassio or Desdemona I'm uncertain.   He would prepare swift means of
death for her and tear her all to pieces, yet ʻslave' seems very inappropriate to apply
to a woman.   I think he has Cassio in mind, and his reference to him in the Fifth
Act, ʻHad all his hairs been lives,' seems to give an additional warrant.   [Assuredly,
it was Cassio.   I doubt if Othello even heard what Iago had just said.—ED.]

507. **true**] WARBURTON upholds Q₁ as an ʻallusion to what Othello had said before,
line 221 : " Away at once with love or jealousy."   This *time* has now come.'

508. **fond love**] BOOTH : Although the savage blood is up, let a wave of humanity
ʻweep over his heart at these words.   Breathe out ʻ'Tis gone ' with a sigh of agony
which seems to exhale love to heaven.

509. **the hollow hell**] WARBURTON : ʻ Hollow ' as applied to ʻ hell ' is a poor
unmeaning epithet.   It is corrupt, and should be read *unhallow'd cell*, i. e. the infernal
regions.   STEEVENS : The same phrase occurs in Jasper Heywood's translation of Seneca's *Thyestes*, 1560 : ʻ Where most prodigious vgly thinges the hollowe hell doth
hyde.'   HOLT WHITE : Again in *Paradise Lost*, i, 314 : ʻ He call'd so loud, that all
the hollow deep Of hell resounded.'   MALONE : Also, line 542 of the same book :
ʻ the universal host up sent A shout that tore hell's concave.'   KNIGHT : It seems perfectly incredible that Johnson, Steevens, and Malone should have rejected the magnificent reading ʻ hollow hell '; if it had failed to impress them by its power, the imitations
of it by Milton should have rendered it sacred.   But let us only mark the opposition

Yeeld vp (O Loue) thy Crowne, and hearted Throne   510
To tyrannous Hate.   Swell boſome with thy fraught,
For 'tis of Aſpickes tongues.
  Iago.   Yet be content.
  Oth.   Oh blood, blood, blood.
  Iago.   Patience I ſay : your minde may change.   515
  Oth.   Neuer *Iago.*   Like to the Ponticke Sea,

---

510. *hearted*] *harted* Q₁. *parted* Warb.
511. *boſome*] *booſome* Q₃.
512. *Aſpickes*] *Aſpecks* Q₁.
   [he kneeles. Q₂Q₃.
513. *Yet*] *Pray* Qq, Cap. Steev. Mal.
Var. Coll. Sing. Ktly.
   [he kneeles. Q₁.
514. *blood, blood, blood.*] *blood, Iago,*

blood Qq, Cap. Jen. Steev. Mal. Var. Coll.
Sing. Ktly.
514. *blood.*] *blood*— Rowe +.
515. *minde may*] Ff, Rowe, Pope, Han.
Knt. *mind perhaps may* Qq et cet.
516–523. Iago...*Heauen*] Om. Q₁
516. Two lines, Q₂Q₃.
Like to] *Like* Pope, Han. Warb.

---

of the two lines : 'All my fond love thus do *I blow to heaven.*   Arise, black vengeance, from the hollow *hell.*'

510. **hearted**] JOHNSON : The heart on which thou wast enthroned.   MALONE :
So, *Twelfth Night*, II, iv, 21 : 'It gives an echo to the very seat Where Love is
throned.'

511. **Swell**] WARBURTON : Because the fraught is of poison.

513. BOOTH : Iago affects remorse for having 'put this to him,' &c.

514. FECHTER : He rushes about as if seeking his prey.

515. FECHTER : Exciting him.   BOOTH : Eagerly, as if to clinch the nail he has
driven home.

516. **Ponticke Sea**] POPE : This simile is omitted in the first edition; I think it
should be so, as an unnatural excursion in this place.   STEEVENS : Every reader will,
I durst say, abide by Mr Pope's censure on this passage.   When Shakespeare grew
acquainted with such particulars of knowledge, he made a display of them as soon as
opportunity offered.   He found this in Holland's *Pliny*, Bk. ii, chap. 97, 1601 : 'And
the sea Pontus euermore floweth and runneth out into Propontis, but the sea neuer
retireth backe again within Pontus.'   Edwards, in his MS. notes, conceives this simile
to allude to Sir Philip Sidney's device, which was the Caspian Sea, with this motto, *Sine
reflexu.*   KNIGHT : It is delightful to see how Shakespeare's knowledge impresses
itself, even in technicalities, upon practical men whose minds are not clouded by the
low pedantry of such critics as Steevens.   A gentleman, who writes to us as 'a sailor,'
begs us to notice this passage as exhibiting a proof of the poet's knowledge 'of the
continual flow of the tide through the Gut of Gibraltar.'   HUNTER (ii, 279) : Few persons will doubt that Steevens's quotation from Holland's *Pliny* was substantial and
good, a valuable contribution to the illustration of the play; Knight's correspondent's
in the highest degree vain and ridiculous.   SWINBURNE (p. 183) : In their version of
Othello, remarkably enough, the 'player-editors,' contrary to their wont, have added to
the treasure-house of their text one of the most precious jewels that ever the prodigal
afterthought of a great poet bestowed upon the rapture of his readers.   Some of these,
by way of thanksgiving, have complained with a touch of petulance that it was out of
place and superfluous in the setting; nay, that it was incongruous with all the circumstances,—out of tone and out of harmony and out of keeping with character and tune

Whofe Icie Current, and compulfiue courfe,   517
Neu'r keepes retyring ebbe, but keepes due on
To the Proponticke, and the Hellefpont:
Euen fo my bloody thoughts, with violent pace   520
Shall neu'r looke backe, neu'r ebbe to humble Loue,
Till that a capeable, and wide Reuenge
Swallow them vp.   Now by yond Marble Heauen,   523

518. *Neu'r*] *Ne'r* Q₂Q₃. *Nev'r* F₂.   521. *neu'r*] *ne're* Q₂Q₃F₃F₄.
Ne're F₃F₄.   *Ne'er* Rowe et seq.   522. *capeable*] *capable* Ff.
  keepes] Ff, Knt. *knows* Coll. Wh.   523. *by yond*] *be yond* Q₃. *by yond'*
i. *feels* Q₂Q₃ et cet.   Cap.

and time.   In other lips, indeed, than Othello's, at the crowning minute of culminant agony, the rush of imaginative reminiscence which brings back upon his eyes and ears the lightning foam and tideless thunder of the Pontic sea might seem a thing less natural than sublime.   But Othello has the passion of a poet closed in, as it were, and shut up behind the passion of a hero.   For all his practical readiness of martial eye and ruling hand in action, he is also in his season ' of imagination all compact.'   Therefore it is that in the face and teeth of all devils akin to Iago that hell could send forth to hiss at her election, we feel and recognize the spotless exaltation, the sublime and sunbright purity, of Desdemona's inevitable and invulnerable love.   When once we likewise have seen Othello's visage in his mind, we see, too, how much more of greatness is in this mind than in another hero's.   For such an one, even a boy may well think how thankfully and joyfully he would lay down his life.   Other friends we have of Shakespeare's giving whom we love deeply and well, if hardly with such love as could weep for them all the tears of the body and all the blood of the heart; but there is none we love like Othello.

517. **Icie**] SINGER (ed. ii): This is a palpable misprint for *yesty*.

518. **keepes . . . keepes**] MALONE: Many similar repetitions in the same line, due to the compositor's mistakes, may be found in F₁. See *Ham.* II, ii, 52; *Ib.* III, iii, 14. KNIGHT: The repetition would not be objectionable if in the first instance it gave us a clear meaning,—the same meaning as in the second instance,—but it is not so.   And yet *feels* does not seem to be the right word.   COLLIER (ed. ii): Southern altered it to *knows* in his F₄, and it is *knows* in the (MS).   WHITE (ed. i) ' cannot but regard *feels* as a mere sophistication,' but in his ed. ii he silently adopts it.   WALKER (*Crit.* i, 314): *Feels* is wrong; *brooks* would be better, though not, I think, the true word.   KEIGHTLEY (*Exp.* 303): I doubt much if the original word was not *makes*, which I have given, corresponding with ' keeps ' in not personifying.

523. **marble**] In that delightful book, *The Plain Speaker* (p. 483, Bohn's ed.), HAZLITT discerns, with an insight keen and poetic, a meaning here which at first sight is so taking that I cannot but regret that a closer scrutiny will hardly justify it, or at most accept it only as one of those interpretations which it is the prerogative of a fine critic to find where he will.   Hazlitt says: ' when Othello swears " By yon *marble* heaven," the epithet is suggested by the hardness of his heart from the sense of injury; the texture of the outward object is borrowed from that of the thoughts; and that noble simile, " Like the Propontic," &c., seems only an echo of the sounding tide of passion, and to roll from the same source, the heart.'   If this passage in Othello were the only

In the due reuerence of a Sacred vow,
I heere engage my words.   525
  Iago.   Do not rife yet :
Witneffe you euer-burning Lights aboue,
You Elements, that clip vs round about,
Witneffe that heere *Iago* doth giue vp
The execution of his wit, hands, heart,   530

524. *of*] *to* Q₃.
  [He kneels. Rowe et seq.
525. *engage*] *ingage* Qq.
  words.] *words*— Ff, Rowe+, Jen.
526. [Iago kneels. Q₂, Rowe et seq.
527. *Witneffe you*] *Witneffe the* Q₂Q₃.

Witnefs your F₄, Rowe. *Witness, ye* Johns
528. *You*] *Ye* Johns.
  [Iago kneeles. Qₓ.
530. *execution*] *excellency* Qₓ.
  hands] *hand* Qq, Cap.

instance in Shakespeare where 'marble' is applied to the 'heavens,' this fine interpretation might stand without question. But it is used elsewhere in passages where it cannot have a subjective meaning, and it is these passages and others, which, I think, should determine its meaning here. In Timon's wild address to the earth (IV, iii, 191) he bids it 'Teem with new monsters, whom thy upward face Hath to the marbled mansion all above Never presented;' again, twice in *Cymb.* (V, iv) where Sicilius first invokes Jupiter to 'Peep through thy marble mansion,' and then when Jupiter retires, he exclaims, 'The marble pavement closes.' In these three instances 'marbled' is, it seems to me, purely objective, and is not a quality projected by the emotions of the speaker; it is suggestive of all the imposing pomp of masonry with cloud-capt towers and glistening domes. Furthermore, Marston uses the same phrase, as Steevens and Malone pointed out, in *Solyman and Perseda,* 1599: 'Now by the marble face of the welkin,' &c., and in *Antonio and Mellida,* 1602: 'And pleas'd the marble heavens,' &c. Lastly, Milton (*Par. Lost,* iii, 564) describes how Satan 'into the world's first region throws His flight precipitant, and winds with ease Through the pure marble air his oblique way.' We are safe in ascribing a classic origin to many a Miltonic phrase, and it was Upton (p. 25) who, in vindicating *Paradise Lost* from the strictures of Bishop Burnet, shows that 'marble' is used by Milton 'in its thoroughly classic sense from μαρμαίρω, to sparkle, to glow, or, as in the "æquor marmoreum" of Vergil, the sea shining or resplendent like marble.' This, then, is the meaning in which, I think, it was always used by Shakespeare, of course without a thought, or perhaps even knowledge, of its classic origin. 'Marble' refers, I think, to color, aglow with lacing streaks, and not to texture or to substance.—ED. SCHMIDT (*Lex.* s. v.) queries whether 'marble' is applied to the heavens on account of their eternity.

523. BOOTH: Kneels. Both hands above the head, with upturned palms and fingers towards the back. I used this gesture impulsively, in England first, and it was spoken of as suggestive of the Orient. Iago watches Othello keenly—sidewise—during his next speech; while Othello seems absorbed and with upturned eyes.

528. **clip**] DYCE: That is, embrace. PURNELL: Originally, 'to hold tight'; and then, as the shears press down on the cloth in the act of cutting, the later meaning superseded the earlier.

530. **execution**] MALONE: That is, employment, exercise. STEEVENS: So in *Tro. & Cres* V, vii, 6, 'In fellest manner execute your arms.'

To wrong'd *Othello*'s Seruice.   Let him command,   531
And to obey fhall be in me remorfe,
What bloody bufineffe euer.
   Oth.   I greet thy loue,
Not with vaine thanks, but with acceptance bounteous,   535
And will vpon the inftant put thee too't.
Within thefe three dayes let me heare thee fay,   537

---

532. *And to obey*] *And to obey*, Qq,
Warb. Johns.   *Not to obey* Pope.   *Nor to
obey* Theob. Han.   *And not to obey* Jen.
    be in me remorfe] *be remorce* Q₁.
be in me. Remord Warb.   *be in me no remorse* Upton, Cap.
   533. *bufineffe euer*] *worke fo euer* Qq,

Jen. Steev. Mal. Var. Sing. Ktly.   *work
soe'er* Coll. Huds.
   533. *euer.*] *ever—* Knt.
    [Rising. Cap.
   536. *thee*] *the* Q₃.
    too't] *to't* QqF₃F₄.

---

532. **And to obey**] THEOBALD changed POPE'S *Not* to *Nor,* 'that is, let your com
mands be ever so bloody, remorse and compassion shall not restrain me from obeying
them.'   UPTON (p. 200): A negative particle has slipped out here, we must read 'And
to obey shall be in me *no* remorse.'   JOHNSON: Iago devotes himself to wronged
Othello, and says, 'Let him command whatever bloody business, and in me it shall be
an act, not of cruelty, but of tenderness, to obey him; not of malice to others, but of
tenderness to him.'   STEEVENS: 'Remorse' is used for *pity* in Surrey's translation of
the Fourth Æneid: 'Sister, I crave thou have remorse of me.'   Again, in *King Edward III.* 1599: 'But for yourselves, look you for no remorse,' and in many more
instances, but I shall content myself to observe that the sentiment of Iago bears no
small resemblance to that of Arviragus in *Cymb.* IV, ii, 168: 'I'ld let a parish of such
Cloten's blood, And praise myself for charity.'   REED quotes MASON as saying that
Shakespeare seldom, if ever, uses the word in any other sense.   [It is the only sense
given by DYCE (*Gloss.*)].   TOLLET: That is, let him command any bloody business,
and to obey him shall be in me an act of pity and compassion for wrong'd Othello.
FARMER: I read, 'let him command *An*' to obey shall be in me remorse What bloody
business ever ——' 'And' for *if* is sufficiently common; and Othello's impatience
breaks off the sentence, I think, with additional beauty.   KNIGHT: It is quite clear
that Othello interrupts the conclusion of Iago's speech.   At the moment when he has
said that 'obedience to Othello shall stand in the place of remorse (mercy)—What
bloody business ever' (Othello may command), Othello, jumping at his meaning, at
once sets him upon the murder of Cassio.   SINGER (ed. ii): 'To remord—to prey
upon continually and repeatedly; and hence Iago's prefigured remorse; a feeling that
will continually prey upon his mind—Mordax—Edax-cara.'   [This Latin I do not
understand.—ED.]   I owe this admirable solution of a difficult passage to the kindness of Dr Richardson.   HUDSON: 'Remorse' for *conscience,* simply.   Iago has said
before, 'I hold it very stuff o' the conscience to do no contrived murder.'   So the meaning here is, 'Let him command whatever bloody work he may, to perform it shall be
with me a matter of conscience.'   This explanation is Joseph Crosby's.   WHITE (ed.
ii): 'Remorse,' a doubtful reading, or else a very forced use of the word in the
sense of pity, for Othello.   BULLOCH (p. 250): I would read, '—— shall be in *mere*
remorse What bloody business *severs.*'   That is the ordinary pity experienced at the
separation of soul and body in others.   [See III. iii, 426.]

That *Caſſio*'s not aliue.   538
   Iago.   My Friend is dead:
'Tis done at your Requeſt.   540
But let her liue.
   Oth.   Damne her lewde Minx:
O damne her, damne her.
Come go with me a-part, I will withdraw
To furniſh me with ſome ſwift meanes of death   545
For the faire Diuell.
Now art thou my Lieutenant.
   Iago.   I am your owne for euer.   *Exeunt.*   548

539, 540. One line, Cap. Steev. et seq.	542, 543. *Damne*] *Dam* Qq.
540, 541. One line, Qq, Rowe+, Jen.	542. *Minx*] *minks* Qq.
540. *at your*] *as you* Qq, Cap. Jen.	543. *O...her.*] Ff, Rowe+, Jen. Knt,
541, 543. As one line, Steev.'93 et	Ktly. *O dam her.* Qq et cet.
seq.	546, 547. One line, Qq, Rowe et seq.
542, 543. One line, Qq, Rowe et seq.	546. *Diuell*] *deuill* Q₂Q₃. *Devil* F₃F₄.

538. BOOTH: Iago is shocked, of course, and slightly shudders as he rises to his feet. Line 541 he speaks beseechingly.

539. THEOBALD: In like manner Jonson in his *Cataline* [III, iii] expresses the impetuosity of Cethegus for the death of Cicero, 'He shall die. *Shall* was too slowly said; he's dying, that Is yet too slow; he's dead.' But this is a copy from Seneca's *Hercules Furens* [v. 644]: 'Si novi Herculem Lycus Creonti debitas poenas dabit. Lentum est, dabit; dat; hoc quoque lentum est; dedit.'

542. **Minx**] PURNELL: Possibly short for *minikin*.

543. BOOTH: Take a liberty here and 'damn her' *four* times; the first savagely, the second time less so, melt with the third, and choke with tears at the fourth; the merest pause—then recover and 'Come, go with me,' &c. Iago shows deep grief till 'Now art thou my lieutenant,' then, quickly kneeling, he kisses Othello's hand, and his face reveals his triumph. FECHTER's Othello returns as he is going out, and, striking Iago on the shoulder, with a savage smile of triumph says, 'Now art thou my lieutenant.'

545. **death**] RYMER (p. 92): Othello is made a Venetian General. We see nothing done by him, nor related concerning him, that comports with the condition of a General, or, indeed, of a Man, unless the killing himself, to avoid a death the Law was about to inflict on him. When his jealousy had wrought him up to a resolution of 's taking revenge for the suppos'd injury, He sets Jago to the fighting part, to kill Cassio; And he chuses himself to murder the silly Woman his Wife, that was like to make no resistance.

548. BOOTH: To portray Iago properly you must seem to be what all the characters think, and say, you are, not what the spectators know you to be; try to win even *them* by your sincerity. Don't *act* the villain, don't *look* it or *speak* it (by scowling and growling, I mean), but *think* it all the time. Be genial, sometimes jovial, always gentlemanly. Quick in motion as in thought; lithe and sinuous as a snake. A certain bluffness (which my temperament does not afford) should be added to preserve the military flavour of the character; in this particular I fail utterly, my Iago lacks the soldierly quality. My consolation is that we know him more as a courtier than as a soldier.

Scæna Quarta.

Enter Defdemona, Æmilia, and Clown.

Def. Do you know Sirrah, where Lieutenant *Caſſio*
lyes?

Clow. I dare not ſay he lies any where.   5

Def. Why man?

Clo. He's a Soldier, and for me to ſay a Souldier lyes,
'tis ſtabbing.

Def. Go too : where lodges he?

Clo. To tell you where he lodges, is to tel you where   10
I lye.

Def. Can any thing be made of this?

Clo. I know not where he lodges, and for mee to deuiſe a lodging, and ſay he lies heere, or he lies there, were
to lye in mine owne throat.   15

Def. Can you enquire him out? and be edified by re
port?

Clo. I will Catechize the world for him, that is, make
Queſtions, and by them anſwer.   19

1. Scæna Quarta.] Om. Qq, Rowe.
Scene IX. Pope+, Jen.
  Another Apartment in the Palace.
Theob. Before the Castle. Dyce.
  2. Enter...] Enter *Defdemonia, Emill-
la* and the Clowne. Qq (*Defdemona* Q₂Q₃).
  3. *Lieutenant*] *the Leiutenant* Qq, Jen.
Coll. Wh. i.
  7. Clo.] Om. Qᵣ.
    He's] Ff, Rowe+, Dyce, Glo. Cam.
Huds. Rlfe, Wh. ii. *He is* Qq et cet.
    me] Ff, Rowe+, Steev. Mal. Var.
Knt, Sing. Ktly. *one* Qq et cet.
  8. *'tis*] Ff, Rowe+, Knt. *is* Qq et cet.

9. *too:*] *to,* Q₁Q₂. *to* Q₃. *to:* Ff. *to't*
Knt.
  10, 11, 12. Om. Qᵣ.
  14. *lies...there*] *lies there* Qq.
  15. *mine own*] *my* Qᵣ. *my own* Cap.
Mal. Steev.'93, Var. Sing. Ktly.
  16. *enquire*] *inquire* Qᵣ.
    and be] *and* Q₃.
    by] *to* Coll. (MS).
  18. *Catechize*] *cathechize* Qq.
  19. *and...anſwer*] Separate line, Qq.
    by them] *make them* Q₃, Jen. Steev.
  '85. *bid them* Theob.+, Cap.

3–24. These lines are, I believe, invariably omitted on the stage. FECHTER continues the scene, that is, it is still III, i. BOOTH at line 25 begins IV, i.

2. **Clown**] DOUCE (ii, 272): He appears but twice in the play, and was certainly
intended to be an allowed, or domestic, *fool* in the service of Othello and Desdemona.

4. **lyes**] Shakespeare was not above sharing the weakness of his contemporaries in
making puns on this word. See also *Ham.* V, i, 116.

15. **throat**] JOHN HUNTER : This meant, to utter a wilful lie. ' To lie in the teeth '
was less intentional, and gave less offence.

19. **by them**] WARBURTON : The Clown was to go seek for one; he says he will
ask for him, and by his own questions make answer. Without dcubt we should read—

Def. Seeke him, bidde him come hither : tell him, I   20
haue moou'd my Lord on his behalfe, and hope all will
be well.

Clo. To do this is within the compaffe of mans Wit,
and therefore I will attempt the doing it.   *Exit Clo.*

Def. Where fhould I loofe the Handkerchiefe, Æ-   25
milia?

Æmil. I know not Madam.

Def. Beleeue me, I had rather haue loft my purfe
Full of Cruzadoes. And but my Noble Moore
Is true of minde, and made of no fuch bafeneffe,   30

---

21. *moou'd*] *moued* Qq.
    on] *in* Qq, Cap. Steev. Mal. Var.
Coll. Sing. Wh. i, Ktly, Del.
23. *of mans Wit*] *of a man* Q₁.
24. *I will*] *I'le* or *Ile* Qq.
    doing it] *doing of it* Qq, Rowe+,
Jen. Steev.'85, Mal. *doing* Rlfe.

24. Exit Clo.] Exit. Qq.
25. *loofe*] *lofe* Q'81 et seq.
    the] Ff, Rowe, Pope, Han. Knt,
Wh. i. *that* Qq et cet.
25, 62, 68, 105, &c. *Handkerchiefe*]
handkercher Q₁. *Handkerchiffe* F₃.
28. *haue loft*] *loofe* Qq. *lofe* Q'81.

---

and *bid* them answer; i. e., the world; those whom he questions. HENLEY: His
design was to propose such questions as might elicit the information sought for from
him, and, therefore, *by* his *questions* he might be enabled to answer. MALONE: That
is, and by them, *when answered*, form my own answer to you. ROLFE states it clearly :
By them be enabled to answer, or get the information to use in my answer.

24. **the doing it**] For a full exposition of verbals, followed by an object, see
ABBOTT, § 93, or *Macb.* I, iv, 8.

25. **should I loose**] ABBOTT, § 325: 'Should,' in a direct question about the past,
seems to increase the emphasis of the interrogation, since a doubt about the past (time
having been given for investigation) implies more perplexity than a doubt about the
future.

25. **the**] WHITE (ed. i): *That* of the Qq has a loss of significance. To Desdemona this handkerchief was at any time *the* handkerchief, and now more so than ever.

27. HUDSON: Objection has been made to the conduct of Emilia in this scene as
inconsistent with the spirit she afterwards shows. I can discover no such inconsistency. Want of principle and strength of attachment are often thus seen united.
Emilia loves her mistress deeply, but she has no *moral* repugnance to theft and false
hood, apprehends no *fatal* consequences from the Moor's passion, and has no soul to
conceive the agony her mistress must suffer by the charge of infidelity; and it is but
natural that when the result comes she should be the more spirited for the very remembrance of her own guilty part in the process. BOOTH: Emilia speaks with slight embarrassment.

28. **rather**] Cited by WALKER (*Vers.* 108) as an instance of its contraction into a
monosyllable. See also, to the same purpose, ABBOTT, § 466.

29. **Cruzadoes**] GREY: A Portuguese coin, in value three shillings. JOHNSON:
So called from the crofs stamped on it. FECHTER: Desdemona turns over her work
and materials to find the handkerchief.

As iealious Creatures are, it were enough   31
To put him to ill-thinking.

Æmil.   Is he not iealious ?

Def.   Who, he? I thinke the Sun where he was borne,
Drew all ſuch humors from him.   35

Æmil.   Looke where he comes.

Enter Othello.

Def.   I will not leaue him now, till *Caſſio* be
Call'd to him. How is't with you, my Lord ?

Oth.   Well my good Lady . Oh hardnes to diſſemble !   40
How do you, *Deſdemona* ?

Def.   Well, my good Lord.

Oth.   Giue me your hand.
This hand is moiſt, my Lady.   \

Def.   It hath felt no age, nor knowne no ſorrow.   45

Oth.   This argues fruitfulneſſe, and liberall heart :
Hot, hot, and moyſt.   This hand of yours requires   47

31, 33. *iealious*] * iealous* Q₁Q₂. *jealious*
F₂. *jealous* Q₃F₃F₄.
37. *Enter...*] After *him* line 35, Qq.
After *ſorrow* line 45, F₃. After *Lord ?*
line 39, F₄, Rowe+, Steev. Mal. Var. Knt,
Sing. Ktly. After *him* line 39, Jen. Dyce,
Sta. Glo. Cam. Del. Rlfe, Huds. Wh. ii.
38, 39. Lines end, *now...Lord ?* Qq,
Cap. Ending, *Caſſio...Lord ?* Steev.'93,
Var. et seq. Prose, Mal.
38. *till*] *Let* Q₁.
39. *is't*] *is it* Qq, Pope, Theob. Han.
Warb. Jen. Steev.'85.

Scene X. Pope+, Jen.
40. *Oh...diſſemble*] As Aside, Han.
Johns. et seq.
42. Def.] Lef. F₂.
    good] Om. Pope+.
43, 44. One line, Qq, Rowe et seq.
45. *It hath*] Ff, Rowe ii.   *It yet hath*
Rowe i+, Jen. Steev.'85, Dyce, Glo. Rlfe,
Huds. Wh. ii.   *It yet has* Qq et cet.
47. *Hot, hot*] *Not hot* Q₁.
    moyſt.] Ff, Johns. Jen. Ktly.   *moiſt*
Qq.   *moist—* Rowe+.   *moist :* Cap. et cet.

---

35. RYMER (p. 126) : By this manner of speech one wou'd gather the couple had
been yoak'd together a competent while, what might she say more, had they been man
and wife seven years ?

39. **to him**] FECHTER : Exit Emilia R. at the moment when Othello appears at the
terrace. He observes them an instant ; then comes down, straight to where Desdemona
has been deranging her work and materials, looking at them with mistrust ; when he
speaks he represses his anger. BOOTH : Othello addresses Desdemona as he passes
her, then he suddenly changes his tone and manner from indifference to sadness.

42. FECHTER : Coaxing by placing her hands, clasped, on the shoulders of Othello,
who releases himself from her caress and takes her hand.

45. BOOTH : At the word 'sorrow' he looks anxiously into her eyes, and with a sigh
proceeds.

46. **fruitfulnesse**] DELIUS : That is, liberal, bountiful, as 'fruitful' is used in II, ii,
372.

47. **moyst**] BUCKNILL (*Med Knowledge of Sh.* p. 273) : This appears to express

A fequefter from Liberty : Fafting, and Prayer,   48
Much Caftigation, Exercife deuout,
For heere's a yong, and fweating Diuell heere   50
That commonly rebels : 'Tis a good hand,
A franke one.   52

48. *Prayer*] *praying* Qq, Jen. Coll. i,   50. *yong*] *ftrong* Warb.
Wh. i.   *fweating*] *fweatie* Q₃.
49. *deuout*] *devoted* Q₃.   52. *franke one*] *very frank one* Han.
50. *heere's*] *there's* Daniel.   *frank one too* Cap. Ktly.

an old opinion that 'a moist palm indicates a hot liver,' one, however, which Primrose
considered a vulgar error, and to the refutation of which he devoted a chapter. BOOTH :
Examining its lines as in palmistry.

   49. **Exercise**] MALONE: This was the term for religious duties. 'Henry VII,'
says Bacon, 'had the fortune of a true Christian as well as of a great king, in living
exercised, and dying repentant.'

   49, etc. GOULD: As he uttered these words, J. B. Booth held up the innocent hand
between his two in momentary, but fervent, attitude of prayer.   Then, still holding her
hand in one of his and pointing with the other, and looking keenly, but without
unkindness, into her palm, he adds, with heightening and ringing accent : ' For here's,'
&c.   The three words, ' That commonly rebels,' in changed tone, and with the voice
sustained at the close, and given in such a manner that the attentive listener supple-
mented the meaning—' and I fear must do so in your case.' So, at the first performance. On the second, a fine variation—' For here's a young and sweating—*devil* here,'
with the same searching intensity ; then a kindly doubt seems to rise in his mind, and
he gives her the benefit of it in saying—' That *commonly* (slight pause) *rebels*.'

   51, etc. WALKER (iii, 288): Arrange, perhaps,—' 'Tis a good hand, a frank one. |
Desd. You may indeed say so ; for 'twas that hand | That gave away my heart.' [I
record this note, like many another of Walker, simply because I lack the moral courage to omit it.   When Walker spends his time and ours in cutting up verses, and frag-
ments of verses spoken by different characters, into lines, what else is it but scanning
by the eye and for the eye ? If the words do not flow musically, cutting them into lines
will not make them musical. If they do flow musically, the lines will take care of
themselves. Is it to be imagined that Shakespeare ever followed any guide but his
ear ? What does the ear know of lines ? recurrent or uncurrent rhythm is all that ever
it can note.—ED.]

   51, 52. **hand, . . . one.**] As questions in FECHTER'S copy.

   52. KEIGHTLEY (*Exp.* 304): I have given in my edition 'A frank one *too*,' but no
addition was necessary.   I made an error for the sake of metre, and, I think, weakened the passage. [And was anticipated by Capell, after all.—ED.]

   52. BOADEN (*Life of Kemble*, i, 259): During this speech of Othello, Mrs Siddons's
face had a beauty of expression that offered one of the most striking and varying pictures ever contemplated. The surprise, arising to astonishment, a sort of *doubt* if she
heard aright, and that being admitted, what it could *mean ;* a hope that it would end
in nothing so unusual from him as an *offensive* meaning ; and the slight relief upon
Othello's adding—' 'Tis a good hand, a frank one ' ; all this commentary was quite as
legible as the text.

Def. You may (indeed) fay fo :   53
For 'twas that hand that gaue away my heart.
    Oth. A liberall hand. The hearts of old, gaue hands :   55
But our new Heraldry is hands, not hearts.

---

55. *hand.*] Ff, Rowe+, Jen. Ktly.   55. *hearts ... hands*] *hands ... hearts*
hand, Qq.   *hand :* Cap. et cet.   Han. Warb. Cap.

---

53. **You**] ABBOTT, § 483 : Emphasized pronouns sometimes dispense with the un-
accented syllable. Here *you* is emphatic. ' A fránk | one.   *Yó* | *u* máy | indéed |
say só.

55, 56. In these lines WARBURTON discerned a satirical allusion to the creation of
baronets by James the First, and founded on it the date of the composition of the play.
For his arguments in this regard and Malone's reply to them, see Appendix, *Date of
the Composition.*   Warburton also asserted that ' it is evident that line 55 should be
read : " The *hands* of old gave *hearts* "; otherwise it would be no reply to " For 'twas
that *hand* that gave away my heart."   Not so, says her husband, " The hands of old
indeed gave hearts ; but the custom now is to give hands without hearts." '   JOHNSON :
Of emendation there is no need. She says that her hand gave away *her heart.*   He
goes on with his suspicion, and the hand which he had before called *frank*, he now
terms *liberal ;* then proceeds to remark that *the hand was formerly given by the heart ;*
but now it neither gives it, nor is given by it.   STEEVENS : The phrase ' our new heraldry ' is only figurative, without the least reference to James's creation of baronets.
The absurdity of making Othello so familiar with British heraldry, the utter want of
consistency as well as policy in any sneer of Shakespeare at the badge of honours
instituted by a Prince whom, on all other occasions, he was solicitous to flatter, and at
whose court this very piece was acted in 1613, most strongly incline me to question the
propriety of Warburton's historical explanation.   MALONE : The hearts of old, says
Othello, dictated the union of *hands*, which formerly were joined with *the hearts* of the
parties *in them ;* but in our modern marriages, *hands* alone are united, without *hearts.*
Such is the plain meaning of the words.   I do not, however, undertake to maintain
that the poet, when he used the word ' heraldry,' had not the new order of baronets in
his thoughts, without intending any satirical allusion.   KNIGHT : We do not think that
Shakespeare would have gone out of his way to introduce a covert sarcasm at a passing
event, offensive as it must have been if understood, and perfectly useless if not understood.   The obvious meaning of the words, without any allusion, is plain enough ; and
' our new heraldry,' if it be any more than a figurative expression, may be easily referred
to the practice of quartering or joining the arms of husband and wife.   DYCE (*Remarks*,
p. 241) : The reader will probably recollect with dismay the immense mass of annota-
tion which this passage has called forth in consequence of Warburton's ridiculous idea
that the poet alluded here to the new order of baronets created by King James. I have
only to observe : first,—that the word ' heraldry ' (which the commentators are surprised
at finding here) was evidently suggested to Shakespeare by the words in the preceding
line, ' gave hands ' (to ' give arms ' being a heraldic term) ; secondly, that Warner, in
his *Albion's England*, p. 282, ed. 1596, has, ' My hand shall neuer giue my heart, my
heart shall giue my hand.'   WHITE (ed. i and ed. ii) adopts Warburton's idea.   In his
ed. ii he says : ' This seems to be the new heraldry Othello speaks of ; but in that case,
the passage was probably added after the first production of the play.'

 Def. I cannot fpeake of this :   57
Come, now your promife.
 Oth. What promife, Chucke ?
 Def. I haue fent to bid *Caffio* come fpeake with you. 60
 Oth. I haue a falt and forry Rhewme offends me :
Lend me thy Handkerchiefe.
 Def. Heere my Lord.   [327 *b*]
 Oth. That which I gaue you.
 Def. I haue it not about me.   65
 Oth. Not ?
 Def. No indeed, my Lord.
 Oth. That's a fault : That Handkerchiefe
Did an Ægyptian to my Mother giue :   69

57, 58. One line, Qq, Rowe et seq.

58. *Come, now*] Ff, Rowe +, Jen. *Come, come,* Q₁. *Come now* Q₂Q₃, Han. Mal. Steev.'93, Var. *Come now,* Cap. et cet.

60. *I haue*] *I've* Pope, Theob. Warb. Johns. Dyce iii, Huds.

61. *forry*] *fullen* Qq, Steev. Mal. Var. Coll. Sing. Ktly.

 Rhewme] *rhume* Qq. *rheum* Rowe.

66. *Not ?*] *Not.* Qq.

66–68. *Not ?...fault :*] As one line, Steev.'93, Var. Knt, Coll. Sing. Dyce, Wh. Sta. Glo. Rlfe.

67. *No indeed,*] *No faith* Q₁.

68. *That's*] Ff, Rowe +, Jen. Sing. Cam. *Thats* Qq. *That is* Cap. et cet.

 That Handkerchiefe] Separate line, Steev.'93, Var. Knt, Coll. Sing. Dyce, Wh. Sta. Glo. Del. Rlfe.

69. *Ægyptian*] *Ægypttan* F₂.

---

 61. sorry] JOHNSON's interpretation of *sullen* of the Qq is 'a rheum obstinately troublesome.' COLLIER (ed. ii): Perhaps the word is *sudden,* to which it is altered in the (MS.). FECHTER : Stretching out his hand, without looking at her.

 64. BOOTH : Quickly—hoping to see the one he gave her.

 68. Handkerchiefe] THEOBALD : Cinthio Giraldi only says it was the Moor's gift upon his wedding to Desdemona ; that it was most curiously wrought after the Moorish Fashion, and very dear both to him and his wife, 'il qual pannicello era lavorato alla moresca sottilissimamente, & era carissimo alla Donna & parimente al Moro.' BOOTH : All this description of the Handkerchief should be told with an air of intense and earnest mystery. Desdemona should listen in wonder and speak like a frightened child. [This description, with its witchcraft, is among those passages which KNIGHT (*Biography*, p. 438) cites to prove that Shakespeare probably visited Scotland in the autumn of 1601. I cannot see that the inference can be drawn from anything stronger than that in the information against Isobell Straquhan for witchcraft it is averred that she made a charm out of a bent penny, a clout, and a piece of red wax, wherewith the face being stroked, love and marriage would follow.—ED.]

 68, etc. RYMER (p. 135) : So much ado, so much stress, so much passion and repetition about an Handkerchief ! Why was not this call'd the *Tragedy of the Handkerchief ?* .... The Wardrobe of obsolete Romances, one might think, were a fitter place for this Handkerchief than that it, at this time of day, be worn on the stage, to raise everywhere all this clutter and turmoil.

 69 Ægyptian] HUNTER (ii, 284) : By this, Shakespeare may mean either an

She was a Charmer, and could almoſt read   70
The thoughts of people.   She told her, while ſhe kept it,
'Twould make her Amiable, and ſubdue my Father
Intirely to her loue : But if ſhe loſt it,
Or made a Guiſt of it, my Fathers eye
Should hold her loathed, and his Spirits ſhould hunt   75
After new Fancies.   She dying, gaue it me,
And bid me (when my Fate would haue me Wiu'd)
To giue it her.   I did ſo ; and take heede on't,
Make it a Darling, like your precious eye :
To looſe't, or giue't away, were ſuch perdition,   80
As nothing elſe could match.

  Deſ.   Is't poſſible ?

  Oth.   'Tis true : There's Magicke in the web of it :
A *Sybill* that had numbred in the world
The Sun to courſe, two hundred compaſſes,   85

---

72. *and ſubdue*] *ſubdue* Ff, Rowe+.

73. Repeated at the top of the next page in Q₁.

 Intirely] Q₁Q₂Ff, Rowe+, Jen. Steev.'85.   *Intierly* Q₃.   *Entirely* Cap.

74. *Guiſt*] *gift* QqF₃F₄.

75. *loathed*] *lothely* Q₁.   *loathly* Cap. Steev. Mal. Var. Knt, Sing. Sta. Ktly.
 his] *her* Jen. (misprint ?).
 Spirits] *ſpirit* Q'81, Wh. i.
 ſhould] Om. Pope+.

77. *Wiu'd*] Ff, Rowe+,Wh. Del. *wiue* Qq, Cap. et cet.

78. *on't*] *of't* Mal. Steev.'93, Var.

80. *looſe't*] F₂, Rowe ii, Pope. *looſe* Q₁Q₂. *loſe* Q₃, Jen. Steev.'93, Var. Coll. Wh. i, Sing.   *loos't* F₃F₄, Rowe i.   *loſe't* Theob. et cet.
 perdition] *prediction* Q₃.

82. *Is't*] *Is it* Steev. Mal. Var.

84. *had*] *hath* Han. ii.
 numbred] *numbered* Q₃.

85. *The…courſe*] *The Sun to make* Q₁, Mal. Steev.'93, Var.   *Of the sun's course* Han.

Ægyptian properly so called, or a Gypsy or Bohemian, as the same people are called in many parts of the continent.   Presents of this kind from Gypsies proper occur in Italian Poetry; thus Ariosto: 'About her neck a jewel rich she ware, A cross all set with stones in gold well tried; This relick late a Boem pilgrim bare, And gave her father other things beside,' &c.   But the mention of 'mummy,' and other points in the passage, seem to guide us to the true Egyptians, neighbours of the Moors.   ELZE (*Sh. Jahrbuch*, xi, 299) calls attention to Maudlin's description of her 'browder'd belt,' which 'A Gypsan lady, and a right beldame Wrought by moonlight,' in Jonson's *Sad Shepherd*, II, i.   Elze finds a noteworthy similarity therein with this passage in *Othello*.

77. **Wiu'd**] It is not necessary to adopt the Qq here.   'Wiu'd' is in the same construction as 'loathed,' line 75.—ED.

85. **to course**] JOHNSON : The expression is not very infrequent; we say, I counted the clock to strike four; so she number'd the sun to course, to run, two hundred compasses, two hundred annual circuits.

In her Prophetticke furie fow'd the Worke :   86
The Wormes were hallowed, that did breede the Silke,
And it was dyde in Mummey, which the Skilfull
Conferu'd of Maidens hearts.
   Def. Indeed ? Is't true?   90
   Oth. Moſt veritable, therefore looke too't well.
   Def. Then would to Heauen, that I had neuer ſeene't?   92

86. *ſow'd*] Ff, Rowe+, Cap. *ſowed*
Qq. *sew'd* Johns.
   87. *hallowed*] *hollowed* Q₃. *hallow'd*
Cap. et seq.
   88. *dyde*] *died* Qq. *dyede* F₂. *di'd* F₃F₄.
Mummey] *Mommy* Q₃.
which] *with* Q₁Q₃, Jen.
   89. *Conferu'd*] *Conferues* Q₁, Jen. *Con-*
cerue Q₂. *Conferue* Q₃.
   90. *Indeed ?*] *Ifaith* Q₁. *Indeed,* Q₂Q₃.

90. *Is't*] *is it* Steev.'85, Mal.
   91. *too't*] *to't* QqF₃F₄. *to it* Steev.'85,
Mal.
   92. *to Heauen*] *to God* Qq, Jen. Dyce,
Sta. Glo. Cam. Rlfe, Huds. Wh. ii. *the
Heaven* Ff.
   ſeene't ?] *ſeene it.* Qq, Jen. Steev.
Mal. Var. Knt, Coll. Sing. Wh. i, Ktly.
ſeene't. Ff. *seen't !* Rowe et cet.

86. **Prophetticke furie**] HUNTER (ii, 285): There is something more classical in
this expression than is, perhaps, anywhere else to be found in these plays; but the
phrase may have presented itself to Shakespeare in the writings of Sylvester, where it
often occurs.

88. **Mummey**] STEEVENS: The balsamic liquor running from mummies was formerly celebrated for its anti-epileptic virtues. This fanciful medicine still holds a place
in the principal shops where drugs are sold. DYCE: A preparation for magical purposes, made from dead bodies. Steevens's note seems irrelevant. [I doubt if the word
conveyed, of necessity, any reference to Egyptian mummies; that reference was perhaps
restricted to *mummia*. Falstaff refers to himself as being turned by drowning into a
'mountain of mummy,' and we have 'Witches' mummy' in *Macb.* IV, i, 23, which
see with the notes. In Johnson's *Dict.* s. v. there is a full account of the medicinal
preparation, from Dr Hill's *Materia Medica*, and in Latham's *Johnson* a passage is
given from Sir T. Herbert's *Travels*, &c. 1677, which shows that that traveler not only
did not associate 'mummy' with Egypt, but not even with dead bodies:—'In or near this
place is a precious liquor or *mummy* growing; . . . . a moist, redolent gum it is, sovereign against poisons.' Steevens cites from *The Microcosmos* of John Davies of Here-
ford (1603, p. 77, ed. Grosart): 'That's *Mummey* made of the meere Hart of *Love*.'
That Davies was well read in Shakespeare's *Sonnets* is felt throughout the *Microcosm*,
but the date of the latter is rather too early to permit the supposition that it had been
influenced by *Othello*.—ED.]

92. MRS. JAMESON (ii, 38): Desdemona, whose soft credulity, whose turn for the
marvellous, whose susceptible imagination had first directed her thoughts and affections
to Othello, is precisely the woman to be frightened out of her senses by such a tale as
this, and betrayed by her fears into a momentary tergiversation. It is most natural in
such a being, and shows us that even in the sweetest natures there can be no completeness and consistency without moral energy. There is an incident in the original tale
which could not well be transferred to the drama, but which is very effective, and adds, I
think, to the circumstantial horrors of the story. Desdemona does not accidentally drop
the handkerchief; it is stolen from her by Iago's little child, an infant of three years

Oth. Ha? wherefore?   93
Def. Why do you fpeake fo ftartingly and rafh?
Oth. Is't loft? Is't gon? Speak, is't out o'th'way?   95
Def. Bleffe vs.
Oth. Say you?
Def. It is not loft : but what and if it were?
Oth. How?
Def. I fay it is not loft.   100
Oth. Fetcht, let me fee't.
Def. Why fo I can : but I will not now :
This is a tricke to put me from my fuite,
Pray you let *Caffio* be receiu'd againe.
Oth.   Fetch me the Handkerchiefe,   105
My minde mif-giues.

94. *ftartingly*] *ftaringly* F₃F₄.
rafh] *rafhly* Q₁.
95. *Is't...Is't*] *Is it...Is it* Steev.'85.
is't out] Ff, Rowe, Knt, Sta. *is it
out* Qq et cet.
o'th'] *o'the* Qq. *oth'* F₃. *of the* Steev.
96. *Bleffe*] Q₂Q₃Ff, Rowe+, Cap. Knt.
Heauen bleffe Q₁ et cet.
98. *and if*] QqFf, Rowe, Pope, Theob.
i, Jen. Knt. *an if* Theob. ii et cet.
99. *How?*] *Ha.* Qq. *Ha!* Pope+,
Cap. Jen. Steev. Mal. Var. Sing. Ktly.
101. *Fetcht*] F₂. *Fetcht'* F₃. *Fetch it*

Steev.'85, Mal. *Fetch't* QqF₄ et cet
101. *fee't*] *fee it* Qq, Jen. Steev. Mal.
Var. Knt, Cam.
102. *can :*] Ff. *can fir*, Qq et cet.
104. *Pray you*] *I pray* Qq, Cap. Jen.
Steev. Mal. Var. Coll. Wh. i, Sing. Ktly,
Del.
105, 106. One line, Qq et seq.
105. *the*] *that* Qq, Cap. Jen. Steev. Mal.
Var. Coll. Sing. Ktly, Del.
106. *mif-giues.*] *misgives—* Rowe,
Pope, Theob. Han. Warb. *misgives me—*
Ktly.

---

old, whom he trains or bribes to the theft. The love of Desdemona for this child,
her little playfellow,—the pretty description of her taking it in her arms and caressing
it, while it profits by its situation to steal the handkerchief from her bosom, are well
imagined, and beautifully told; and the circumstance of Iago employing his own innocent child as the instrument of his infernal villainy adds a deeper, and, in truth, an
unnecessary touch of the fiend, to his fiendish character. [It is so common among the
critics to accuse Desdemona of telling a falsehood here, that gratitude is due to Mrs
Jameson for the milder term 'tergiversation.' Although Desdemona herself says,
'where should I *lose* the handkerchief?' she did not believe it to be actually lost, irre-
coverably gone; it was merely mislaid, and a further search would reward her with
discovery. If she had not been terrified she might have told all this to Othello (and
we should not have had the tragedy, which would be a relief), but, as it is, I think in
her soul she believed she was telling the truth.—ED.]

94. **startingly and rash**] WALKER (*Crit.* i, 220) cites this, among others, as an
instance of the termination *-ly* attached to one adjective and affecting others. See also
ABBOTT, § 397, or SCHMIDT, p. 1419.

105-115. BOOTH: This little 'bit' is difficult to act without being tame, or too violent. I have never *hit* it. [At line 114, FECHTER actually directs Othello to seize
Desdemona violently, and raise his hand as if to strike her!—ED.]

Def.   Come, come : you'l neuer meete a more fuffici-   107
ent man.

Oth.   The Handkerchiefe.

Def.   A man that all his time   110
Hath founded his good Fortunes on your loue ;
Shar'd dangers with you.

Oth.   The Handkerchiefe.

Def.   Infooth, you are too blame.

Oth.   Away.   *Exit Othello.*   115

107. *Come, come :*] Separate line, Cap.
Steev. et seq.
    Come...neuer] Come, *you'll ne'er*
Pope+.
    109, 113. *Handkerchiefe.*] *handker-
chief!* Dyce, Sta. Glo. Ktly, Cam. Coll.
iii, Rlfe, Huds. Wh. ii. *Handkerchief—*
Rowe et cet.
    109, 110. *Handkerchiefe.* Def. *A man*]
handkercher. Def. *I pray talke me of Cafsio.* Oth. *The handkercher.* Def. *A man*
Q₁, Johns. Jen. et seq.

111. *founded his*] *founded* Q₃.
    112–115. *Shar'd...Away.*] Two lines,
first ending *sooth,* Ktly.
    112. *you.*] *you :* Cap. Steev. Mal. Var.
Knt, Coll. Sing. Wh. i, Del. *you—* Steev.
'73, Dyce, Sta. Glo. Ktly, Cam. Rlfe,
Huds. Wh. ii.
    114. *Infooth*] *Ifaith* Q₁. Separate line,
Steev.'93.
    too] *to* Q₃F₄.
    115. *Away.*] *Zouns.* Q₁.

109, 110. It is easy to see how the printer came to omit the sentences given in the
Q₁.—ED.

109. When De Vigny makes his dashing attack on the French Classic School, ridi-
culing its horror at the word *mouchoir,* which, under the hands of the fastidious Ducis,
becomes a 'bandeau de diamants, que l'héroïne (as De Vigny says) voulut garder même
au lit de peur d'être vue en négligé,' our hearts and admiration go entirely with him,
and an almost instinctive contempt arises for any one who can find in such a word, as
'handkerchief,' at such a time, anything unworthy of this tragic scene.   But will not
the curl of our lips at Ducis straighten, and even some fellow-feeling for him spring
up, if we imagine the word as it is in the Qto, uttered by Othello with passionate vehemence ?   As this word sounds to us, so must *mouchoir,* on the stage, have sounded to
Ducis.—ED.

110. **A man**] BODENSTEDT (*Sh. Jahrbuch,* ii, 263): With the same recklessness
and self-will with which Desdemona, out of love to Othello, had exposed herself to
the anger of her Father, she now defies the anger of her husband out of friendship
to Cassio.

115. **Away**] FIELDING: Nothing can be more provoking to the human temper, nor
more dangerous to that cardinal virtue, Patience, than solicitations of extraordinary
offices of kindness in behalf of those very persons with whom we are highly incensed.
For this reason Shakespeare hath artfully introduced his Desdemona soliciting favours
for Cassio of her husband, as the means of inflaming not only his jealousy, but his rage,
to the highest pitch of madness ; and we find the unfortunate Moor less able to command his passion on this occasion than even when he beheld his valued present to his
wife in the hands of his supposed rival.   In fact, we regard these efforts as insults to
our understanding ; and to such the pride of man is with great difficulty brought to
submit.—*Tom Jones,* ix, 3, quoted by HALLIWELL.

Æmil.   Is not this man iealious?   116
   Def.   I neu'r faw this before.
Sure, there's fome wonder in this Handkerchikfe,
I am moft vnhappy in the loffe of it.

   Æmil.   'Tis not a yeare or two fhewes vs a man :   120
They are all but Stomackes, and we all but Food,
They eate vs hungerly, and when they are full
They belch vs.
                Enter Iago, and Caffio.

Looke you, *Caffio* and my Husband.   125

Scene XI. Pope+, Jen.	119. *the loffe of it.*] *the loffe.* Q,.
116. *iealious*] *iealous* or *jealous* Qq	121. *They are*] *They're* Dyce iii, Huds.
F₃F₄.	*are all*] *are* Rowe ii, Pope, Han.
117. *neu'r*] *ne're* Q,. *nere* Q₂Q₃. *never*	122. *they are*] *they're* Pope+, Dyce iii,
F₃F₄, Rowe. *ne'er* Pope et cet.	Huds.
118. *Sure*] *Sir* Q₃.	123, 125. One line, Qq et seq.
there's] *ther's* Q₂Q₃.	124. Enter...] Ff, Rowe, Coll. Wh. i.
Handkerchikfe] F₁.	After line 119 Qq. After line 125 Pope
119. *I am*] *I'm* Pope+, Dyce iii, Huds.	et cet. Enter Cassio and Iago. Dyce.

120. RYMER (p. 126): As if for the first year or two Othello had not been jealous ?
This Third Act begins in the morning, at noon she drops the Handkerchief, after dinner
she misses it, and then follows all this outrage and horrible clutter about it. If we
believe a small Damosel, in the last scene of this Act, this day is effectually seven days.
Our Poet is at this plunge, that whether this Act contains the compass of one day, of
seven days, or of seven years, or of all together, the repugnance and the absurdity
would be the same. For Othello, all the while, has nothing to say or to do, but what
loudly proclaim him jealous; her friend and confident Emilia again and again rounds
her in the ear that *the Man* is jealous; yet this Venetian dame is neither to see, nor to
hear; nor to have any sense or understanding, nor to strike any other note but *Cassio,
Cassio.* STEEVENS: This line has no reference to the duration of the action, or to the
length of time that Desdemona had been married. What Emilia says is a sort of proverbial remark, of general application, where a definite time is put for an indefinite.
Besides, this 'year or two' may refer to the beginning of the acquaintance and intimacy between the couple. PYE (p. 342): Emilia's saying, 'it is not a year or two
shews us a man,' may be well supposed to insinuate, how then should a month or two,
or even a day or two ?

121. WHITE (ed. ii): Emilia means, They are nought but stomachs, and we nought
but food. The obscurity results from an inversion of, They are but all stomach, and
we but all food. [There may be an inversion here, but I do not think that it is the
inversion which White points out. 'All' does not qualify 'stomachs,' or 'food,' but
'They' and 'we.' The meaning is that they, every one of them, are merely stomachs
for which we, every one of us, are merely food. When White represents Shakespeare
as making man revert to the Gasteropods or to the Amœbas, his admiration and exaltation of our demi-god go one step farther than mine. 'We know what we are, but
we know not what we may be,' as Ophelia says, so that I may even yet be brought to
believe that Shakespeare anticipated Darwin,—but not from this passage.—ED.]

125. BOOTH: As if glad to change the subject.

Iago.   There is no other way : 'tis fhe muſt doo't: 126
And loe the happineſſe : go, and importune her.

Def.   How now (good *Caſſio*) what's the newes with [328 *a*]
you?

Caſſio.   Madam, my former fuite.   I do befeech you,   130
That by your vertuous meanes, I may againe
Exiſt, and be a member of his loue,
Whom I, with all the Office of my heart
Intirely honour, I would not be delayd.
If my offence, be of fuch mortall kinde,   135
That nor my Seruice paſt, nor preſent Sorrowes,
Nor purpos'd merit in futurity,
Can ranſome me into his loue againe,
But to know ſo, muſt be my benefit:
So ſhall I cloath me in a forc'd content,   140
And ſhut my felfe vp in ſome other courſe

126. *doo't*] *doe it* Qq.   *do't* F₃F₄, Rowe
et seq.

131. *I may againe*] *I doe befeech you :*
Q₃.

133. *Office*] *duty* Q₁, Johns. Jen. Steev.
Mal. Var. Sing. Ktly.

134. *delayd*] *delayed* Q₁Q₂. *delayde* Q₃.

136. *nor my*] *neither* Q₁, Johns. Steev.
Mal. Var. Sing. Ktly.   *not my* Q₂Q₃Ff,

Rowe+, Jen.

136. *Sorrowes*] *sorrow* Walker.

140. *cloath*] *cloth* Q₁, Cap.   *cloathe* F₃.
clothe Johns.

141. *ſhut...in*] *ſhoote...in* Q₁, Johns.
Jen.   *shoot myself upon* Cap. Rann.   *ſhape
myself upon* Rann conj.   *suit...in* and
shoot myself forth in Anon. conj. ap.
Cam.

127. **happineſſe**] HUDSON: That is, good hap, or lucky chance; referring to the
timely and opportune meeting with Desdemona.   MOREL: C'est bien l'équivalent du
français : ' Quel bonheur' !

127. **importune**] ROLFE: For the accent, see also *Rom. & Jul.* I, i, 138; and
Ham. I, iii, 110.

131. **vertuous**] MOREL: 'Vertuous,' *puiſſant,* nous rappelle le sens primitif du français *vertu*   'Vertu me done [donne-moi force] vers cele gent haïe (*Roland à Ronce-
vaux,* cité par Littré).

133. **Office**] SINGER: 'Office' and *duty* of the Qq are synonymous.   Thus Baret
—' *Dutie, office,* dutie of behaviour in honestie and reason : *officium.*

136. **Sorrowes**] Another instance, according to WALKER (*Crit.* i, 246), of the interpolated *s ;* see I, i, 31.

141. **shut**] STEEVENS: That is, I will put on a constrained appearance of being
contented and shut myself up in a different course of life, no longer to depend on my
own efforts, but to wait for relief from the accidental hand of charity.   See the same
expression, ' shut up In measureless content,' *Macb.* II, i, 16.   MASON prefers *shoot,*
that is, to *push suddenly,* or *forward.*   ' Cassio means that he will push forward into
some other line of life and seek his fortune.'   COLLIER (ed. ii) : We formerly suggested
that ' And *set* myself *upon* some,' &c., may have been the true lection; but the (MS.)
tells us to put it, ' And *shift* myself *upon* some other course.'

To Fortunes Almes.   142
   Def.   Alas (thrice-gentle *Caffio*)
My Aduocation is not now in Tune;
My Lord, is not my Lord ; nor fhould I know him,   145
Were he in Fauour, as in Humour alter'd.
So helpe me euery fpirit fanctified,
As I haue fpoken for you all my beft,
And ftood within the blanke of his difpleafure
For my free fpeech.   You muft awhile be patient :   150
What I can do, I will : and more I will
Then for my felfe, I dare.   Let that fuffice you.
   Iago.   Is my Lord angry ?
   Æmil.   He went hence but now :
And certainly in ftrange vnquietneffe.   155
   Iago.   Can he be angry ? I haue feene the Cannon
When it hath blowne his Rankes into the Ayre,
And like the Diuell from his very Arme
Puff't his owne Brother : And is he angry ?
Something of moment then : I will go meet him,   160
There's matter in't indeed, if he be angry.   *Exit*
   Def.   I prythee do fo. Something fure of State,
Either from Venice, or fome vnhatch'd practife
Made demonftrable heere in Cyprus, to him,
Hath pudled his cleare Spirit : and in fuch cafes,   165

---

142. *Almes*] *arms* Pope.
143. *thrice-gentle*] *thrice gentile* Q₃.
146. *alter'd*] *altred* Q₁Q₂. *altr'd* Q₃.
149. *ftood*] *ftoop* Q₃.
159. *is he*] Ff, Rowe, Sing. Wh. i. *can he be* Qq et cet.
161. Exit.] Om. Qq. After *fo* line 162,

Cap.
Scene XII. Pope+, Jen.
163. *or fome*] *of some* Johns.
164. *demonftrable heere*] *here demonftrable* Pope+, Jen.
heere] *her* Han. ii (misprint ?).
165. *pudled*] *pulld* Q₃.

---

142. **Almes**] MALONE : That is, waiting patiently for whatever bounty or chance may bestow upon me.   See 'at fortune's alms,' *Lear*, I, i, 277.

146. **Fauour**] JOHNSON : That is, in look, in countenance.   See I, iii, 371.

149. **blanke**] JOHNSON : Within the *shot* of his anger.   STEEVENS : The *white* mark at which the shot or arrows were aimed.—[Note on *Ham.* IV, i, 42.]

153. BOOTH : With surprise.

159. **Brother**] MALONE : Something is suppressed here.   Iago means to say 'and his own brother puffed from his side,—*and meanwhile have seen him cool and unruffled.*'   BOOTH : What is apparently omitted here, my Father, following, I presume, old ftage traditions, always supplied by adding ' yet he stood unmoved.'

163. **vnhatch'd practise**] JOHNSON : Some treason that has not taken effect.

165. **pudled**] ROLFE : Muddied, disturbed, or the Yankee ' riled.'

Mens Natures wrangle with inferiour things,   166
Though great ones are their obiect. 'Tis euen fo.
For let our finger ake, and it endues
Our other healthfull members, euen to a fenfe
Of paine. Nay, we muft thinke men are not Gods,   170
Nor of them looke for fuch obferuancie
As fits the Bridall. Befhrew me much *Æmilia*,
I was (vnhandfome Warrior, as I am)
Arraigning his vnkindneffe with my foule:
But now I finde, I had fuborn'd the Witneffe,   175

167–170. *Though…Gods*] Lines end, *object,…ake,… members,… thinke,… gods,* Qq, Cap.
167. *Though*] *Tho* Q₁Q₂. *The* Q₃.
  their] *the* Qq.
168. *endues*] *endures* Q₃. *induces* Ktly conj.
169. *euen to a*] Ff, Rowe, Steev.'85, Knt, Sta. *with a* Pope+. *Euen to that* Qq et cet.
171. *Nor*] *Not* Q₃.

171. *obferuancie*] *obferuances* Qq, Mal. Steev.'93, Var. Coll. Sing. Glo. Ktly, Wh. ii. *obferuance* Ff. *observance always* Rowe+, Jen.
172. *fits*] *fit* Mal. Steev.'93, Var. Coll. Sing. Wh. Glo. Ktly.
173. *Warrior*] *wrangler* Han. Warb.
174, 175. *Arraigning…vnkindneffe… fuborn'd*] *Arraingning…unkinkneffe.. fubborne* Q₃.

167–170. WALKER (*Crit.* iii, 288) proposed, for the sake of ocular scansion, a division of these lines that happens to be the same as that of the Qq (which was pointed out by LETTSOM), and also of Capell (which was not pointed out by Lettsom).

168. endues] JOHNSON: I believe it should be, rather, *subdues* our other healthful members to a sense of pain. MALONE: The meaning is, this sensation so gets possession of, and is so infused into, the other members, as to make them all participate of the same pain. DYCE (*Gloss.*), after quoting this paraphrase of Malone, adds,— 'rightly perhaps.'

171. obseruancie] HUDSON: That is, watchful, tender, and devout attention. So in *As You Like It*, V, ii, 102, where Silvius describes 'what 'tis to love': 'It is to be . . . . All adoration, duty, and observance, All humbleness, all patience,' &c. ROLFE: Not used by Shakespeare elsewhere.

172. As fits] ROLFE: Another suggestion of 'long time.'

172. the Bridall] DELIUS: Used as a noun by Shakespeare only here.

173. Warrior] JOHNSON: Evidently, *unfair assailant*. COWDEN-CLARKE: A lovely reminiscence of her husband's having called her 'my fair warrior' in the joy of his first meeting, on arrival.

174, 176. Arraigning . . . falsely] HEARD (*Sh. as a Lawyer*, p. 76, ed. ii): This is clearly a reference to the crime of subornation of perjury, which is an offence at common law, and consists in the procuring another to take such a false oath as constitutes perjury in the principal, or person taking it.

175. Witnesse] WALKER (*Vers.* 244 and 246) gives this, among many others, as an instance of a plural, but which, because it already ends in *s*, lacks that additional plural sound. In many of these examples Walker would end the word with an apostrophe to indicate that although it is the singular both in spelling and in pronunciation,

And he's Indited falfely.   176

Æmil.   Pray heauen it bee
State matters, as you thinke, and no Conception,
Nor no Iealious Toy, concerning you.

Def.   Alas the day, I neuer gaue him caufe.   180

Æmil.   But Iealious foules will not be anfwer'd fo;
They are not euer iealious for the caufe,
But iealious, for they're iealious.   It is a Monfter
Begot vpon it felfe, borne on it felfe.

Def.   Heauen keepe the Monfter from *Othello's* mind.   185

Æmil.   Lady, Amen.

Def.   I will go feeke him.   *Caffio*, walke heere about :
If I doe finde him fit, Ile moue your fuite,
And feeke to effect it to my vttermoft.   *Exit*

Caf.   I humbly thanke your Ladyfhip.   190

Enter Bianca.

Bian.   'Saue you (Friend *Caffio*.)   192

176. *Indited*] *indicted* Coll. et seq.
(except Del.).

177–179. Lines end, *thinke...toy...you.*
Qq, Cap. et seq.

178. *State matters*] *State-matters* F$_4$.
State-matter Pope.

no] *on* Steev.'93 (misprint).

179. *Nor no*] *Nor* Rowe+.

179, 181, 183, 212. *Iealious*] F$_1$F$_2$.

182. *iealious*] F$_1$.

the caufe] *a cause* Pope+.

183. *they're*] Ff, Rowe+, Knt, Sta.
Dyce iii, Huds.   *they are* Qq et cet.

It is] Ff, Rowe, Knt, Sta.   *It's*
Pope+.   *tis* Qq et cet.

184. *vpon*] *unto* Q$_3$.

185. *the*] Ff, Rowe, Cap. Knt.   *that*
Qq et cet.

Othello's] *Othell's* F$_2$.

187. *heere about*] F$_2$.   *here about* Qq,
Jen. Ktly.   *hereabout* F$_3$F$_4$ et cet.

187–IV, ii.] Om. Booth.

189. *to effect*] *t'effect* Pope+, Dyce iii,
Huds.

vttermoft] *utmoft* Q$_3$.

Exit.] Exeunt *Defd.* and *Emillia*
(opposite to lines 189, 190) Qq.   Ex. Des-
dem. and Æmil. at one door ; Cassio, at
the other. Theob.

Scene XIII. Pope+, Jen.   Changes to
the street before the Palace. Theob.

191. Enter...] After line 192, Q$_1$.   Re-
enter Cassio meeting Bianca. Theob.

---

yet it is, in reality, a plural.   In this present passage, however, if I understand Walker
aright, he would have the full plural form, *witnesses*, because it seems 'more natural.'
But I do not think it would be correct.   The word here is singular, not plural.   There
was but one 'Witness,' viz. : this solitary instance of discord in her advocation, and
this it was that had been 'suborned,' by falsely interpreting, as a lack of observance,
that which was in truth due to 'something of state.'—ED.

179, etc. **Iealious**] WHITE (ed. ii) : It is worth while to remark that this word **was**
pronounced *jelyus* in Shakespeare's time   It is almost invariably spelled *jealious*, **as**
here five times within five lines.   [See WALKER'S note on III, iii, 212, where he is more
cautious than White, and restricts the peculiarity of this spelling to the First Folio.   It

Caſſio.   What make you from home ?   [328 *b*]
How is't with you, my moſt faire *Bianca* ?
Indeed (ſweet Loue) I was comming to your houſe.   195
   Bian.   And I was going to your Lodging, *Caſſio.*
What? keepe a weeke away ? Seuen dayes, and Nights ?
Eight ſcore eight houres ? And Louers abſent howres
More tedious then the Diall, eight ſcore times ?
Oh weary reck'ning.   200
   Caſſio.   Pardon me, *Bianca* :
I haue this while with leaden thoughts beene preſt,
But I ſhall in a more continuate time
Strike off this ſcore of abſence. Sweet *Bianca*
Take me this worke out.   205
   Bianca.   Oh *Caſſio*, whence came this ?
This is ſome Token from a newer Friend,
To the felt-Abſence : now I feele a Cauſe :   208

---

193. *make*] *makes* F₄, Rowe+, Var.
Huds.
   194. *is't*] *is it* Qq, Rowe et seq.
   195. *Indeed*] Q₂Q₃Ff, Rowe+, Knt.
Ifaith Q₁ et cet.
     comming] *going* Q₃.
     houſe] *lodging* Cap. (misprint ?)
   198. *Louers*] Qq. *Loves* Ff, Rowe.
lover's Pope, Han. *lovers'* Theob. et cet.
   200. *Oh*] *No* Q₁.
     reck'ning] *reckoning* Q₁Q₂, Jen. et
seq. *reckning* Q₃.
   202. *leaden*] *laden* Q₁.

203. *continuate time*] *conuenient time*
Q₁, Pope+, Cap. Jen. Coll. iii. *continuate :
of time,* Q₃.
   204. Giving her Desdemona's handkerchief. Rowe et seq.
   206. *Oh*] Om. Han.
   207. *a*] Om. Johns. (misprint.)
   207, 208. *Friend,...now*] Ff. *friend,
To the felt abſence, now* Q₁. *friend To
the felt abſence, now* Q₂Q₃. *friend ; To
the felt-absence, now* Rowe, Jen. *friend.
Of thy felt absence, now* Pope+. *friend.
To the felt absence now* Cap. et cet. (subs.).

---

is almost uniformly *Iealous* in the Qq. See Textual Notes in this scene, lines 31, 33,
and 116.—ED.]

   193. **make**] COLLIER (eds. i and ii) : A Saxon idiom, which Malone destroyed by
printing *makes*. [See Text. Notes.]

   195. **I was**] WALKER (*Crit.* ii, 202) cites this instance, with others, as a proof that
I was, from its position in the line, must have been pronounced as one syllable, in
whatever manner the contraction was effected. See also *Ham.* IV, v, 14.

   197. **weeke**] HUDSON : It would seem by this that seven days at least have elapsed
since Cassio was cashiered ; perhaps much more, as the 'leaden thoughts' may have
been kept off for some time by the thoughts of Desdemona's promise of intercession,
and brought on again by the unexpected delay.

   203. **continuate**] JOHNSON : That is, less interrupted, time which I can call more
my own.

   204. **score**] DELIUS finds here a punning allusion to Bianca's 'eight *score.*'

   205. **Take . . . out**] See 'coppied' line 219, and III, iii, 344.

Is't come to this? Well, well.

    Caſſio.   Go too, woman: 210
Throw your vilde geſſes in the Diuels teeth,
From whence you haue them.   You are iealious now,
That this is from ſome Miſtris, ſome remembrance;
No, in good troth *Bianca.*

    Bian.   Why, who's is it?   215

    Caſſio.   I know not neither:
I found it in my Chamber,
I like the worke well ; Ere it be demanded
(As like enough it will) I would haue it coppied :
Take it, and doo't, and leaue me for this time.   220

    Bian.   Leaue you ? Wherefore?

    Caſſio.   I do attend heere on the Generall,
And thinke it no addition nor my wiſh
To haue him ſee me woman'd.

    Bian.   Why, I ptay you?   225

    Caſſio.   Not that I loue you not.

    Bian.   But that you do not loue me.
I pray you bring me on the way a little,
And ſay, if I ſhall ſee you ſoone at night?   229

---

209. *Is't*] *Is it* Steev. Mal. Var. Coll.
Wh. i.

    Well, well.] Om. Q₁. *Well, well,
well—* Ktly.

210. *Go too, woman:*] *Go to woman,*
Qq. *Well, go to, woman;* Han. *Woman,
go to!* Cap. Steev.'93.

211. *vilde geſſes*] *vile gheſſes* Q₁Q₂. *vile
gueſſes* Q₃.

212. *them*] *'em* Cap.

214. *in good troth*] *by my faith* Q₁, Cam.
in good truth Johns.

215. *who's*] *whoſe* Q₂Q₃F₃F₄.

216, 217. One line, Qq, Rowe et seq.

216. *neither:*] Ff, Rowe+, Cap. Knt,
Dyce, Sta. Del. *ſweete,* Qq et cet.

219. *I would*] Ff, Rowe. *I'de* Qq et
cet.

223. *nor my*] *nor do I*] Quincy (MS).

224. *him*] *h m* F₂.

225, 226. One line. Q₁.

225. *ptay*] F₁.

227. *But…me*] *Nor that you love me.*
Han.

229. *night ?*] *night.* Qq.

---

221. **Wherefore**] WALKER (*Vers.* 112): With the stronger accent on the latter
syllable.

223. **addition**] ROLFE: That is, credit.

224. **woman'd**] ABBOTT, § 294: That is, accompanied by a woman.

229. **soone at**] WHITE (ed. i, note on *Merry Wives,* I, iv, 8): This phrase was
used with a meaning which it is not very easy to express. It may, perhaps, be taken
to signify *surely,* or *without let or hindrance,* which is, probably, the radical meaning
of 'soon.' See Richardon's *Dict.* Marston has two instances of it,—'O wee will
mount in triumph: soone at night Ile set his head up.'—*Antonio and Mellida,* Part I,

Caßio.   'Tis but a little way that I can bring you,   230
For I attend heere : But Ile ſee you ſoone.
Bian.   'Tis very good : I muſt be circumſtanc'd.

                                            Exeunt omnes.   233

Actus Quartus. Scena Prima.

Enter Othello, and Iago.

Iago.   Will you thinke ſo?
Oth.   Thinke ſo, *Iago*?
Iago.   What, to kiſſe in priuate ?   5
Oth.   An vnauthoriz'd kiſſe ?

233. Exeunt...] Exeunt. Qq.
1. Actus...] Actus. Q₁. Actus 4. Q₁. Actus 4.
Scœna 1. Q₂Q₃ (Scæna Q₃).
A Room of State. Rowe. A Court before
the Palace. Theob. An open place, before the Castle. Steev.
2. Enter...] Enter *Iago* and *Othello*.

Qq.
3–52. Om. Fechter.
3–5. *Will... What*] One line, Cap. et
seq.
4. *Iago ?*] Iago. Qq.
6. *kiſſe ?*] Ff, Rowe+, Knt. *kiſſe.* Qq,
Johns. et cet.

Act III. 'Gentlemen, as yet I can but thanke you; but I must bee trusted for my
ordinarie soone at night.'—*What You Will*, V, i. Dyce (*Gloss.*) : About. Schmidt :
This very night, so early as to-day in the evening.

231. **soone**] Cassio here uses this word in the sense of *nightfall*, an acceptation to
which Arrowsmith (p. 7) first, as far as I know, called attention by the following
quotation from Gil's *Logonomia Anglica*, ed. 1619 :—'Quickly cito, sooner citior aut
citius, soonest citissimus aut citissime, nam 'soon' hodie apud plurimos significat ad
primam vesperam, olim cito.' Whether or not this acceptation of 'soon' lies perdu in
the preceding phrase, 'soon at night,' I do not feel competent to say, but I suspect
that it does.—Ed.

232. **'Tis very good**] Deighton : Said with bitterness.

232. **circumstanc'd**] Mason : I must give way to circumstances.

3–6. Walker (*Crit.* iii, 288) : Arrange, perhaps,—Will you think so ? | Think so,
Iago ? What, to kiss in private ? | An unauthóriz'd kiss. Lettsom [in a foot-note] :
Walker, intentionally or otherwise, has placed a full stop after *kiss*. So the Qq, I
believe, and Dyce; the F₁ has a note of interrogation. [See Text. Notes.] Are these
short speeches properly distributed ? Iago seems to have been pretending that, if
Othello had caught Cassio kissing Desdemona, that would have been no proof of guilt
in the lady and her friend; from this Othello seems to have dissented. *Qu.,*—'Thinks
so, Iago ! what, to kiss in private ! | An unauthoriz'd kiss !' Deighton is inclined to
think that lines 3 and 5 should be also given to Othello, and that Iago first speaks at
line 7.

6. **vnauthoriz'd**] For the accent, 'unauthóriz'd,' see Walker (*Vers.* Art. xxxvii,
p 194) or Abbott, §491.

Iago.   Or to be naked with her Friend in bed,   7
An houre, or more, not meaning any harme *?*
   Oth.   Naked in bed (*Iago*) and not meane harme ?
It is hypocrifie againft the Diuell: 10
They that meane vertuoufly, and yet do fo,
The Diuell their vertue tempts, and they tempt Heauen.
   Iago.   If they do nothing, 'tis a Veniall flip:
But if I giue my wife a Handkerchiefe.
   Oth.   What then ?   15
   Iago.   Why then 'tis hers (my Lord) and being hers,
She may (I thinke) beftow't on any man.
   Oth.   She is Protectreffe of her honor too:
May fhe giue that ?   19

7. *Friend*] *Friends* Ff.

7, 9. *in bed*] Ff, Rowe+, Cap. Knt, Dyce, Sta. Glo. Cam. Coll. iii, Wh. ii. *abed* Qq et cet.

8. *harme ?*] *harme.* Q$_1$.

12. *tempts, and*] *tempts not ;* Warb. Han.

13. *If they*] Ff, Rowe+, Knt, Coll.

Sing. Sta. Wh. i, Ktly, Del.   *So they* Qq et cet.

14. *But if I*] *But I* F$_3$F$_4$.

14, 22. *Handkerchiefe.*] *handkercher.* Q$_1$. *Handkerchiffe.* F$_3$. *handkerchief*— Rowe et seq.

18. *Protectreffe*] *proprietor* Warb. conj. Han. *propertied* Warb. *proprietress* Cap. *too :*] *to,* Q$_1$.

7 and 9. **naked**] DYCE, in both his Second and his Third Edition, prints these words with an accent, thus: 'nakèd.' I wish I knew why; especially since a similar forethought for heedless readers of this word is not extended by Dyce elsewhere; after having learned to lean on our accented *è*'s, we are liable to read, in his edition, that Emilia wishes rascals to be lashed 'nak'd through the world,' and that Othello threatens Gratiano that he will assault him 'nak'd as he was.'—ED.

10. **Diuell**] JOHNSON: This means, hypocrisy to cheat the devil. As common hypocrites cheat men by seeming good, and yet living wickedly, these men would cheat the devil, by giving him flattering hopes, and at last avoiding the crime which he thinks them ready to commit. RYMER (p. 128): At this gross rate of trifling, our General and his Auncient March on most heroically; till the jealous Booby has his Brains turn'd; and falls in a Trance. Would any imagine this to be the Language of Venetians, of Souldiers, and mighty Captains? no Bartholomew Droll cou'd subsist upon such trash. [According to ALLIBONE (*Dict.*), Pope considered Rymer, 'on the whole, one of the best critics we ever had'; Dryden and Sir Walter Scott quote him with respect; Dr Johnson was disgusted at his 'ferocity'; Sergeant Talfourd praises his acuteness at the expense of his judgement, and Lord Macaulay deems him 'the worst critic that ever lived.'—ED.]

12. **Heauen**] HENLEY; The true key to the explanation of this passage may be found in St. Matthew, iv, 7. The poet's idea is, that the devil tempts their virtues by stirring up their passions, and they tempt heaven by placing themselves in such a situation as makes it scarcely possible to avoid falling, by the gratification of them.

Iago.   Her honor is an Eſſence that's not ſeene,   [329 *a*]
They haue it very oft, that haue it not.   21
But for the Handkerchiefe.
Othe.   By heauen, I would moſt gladly haue forgot it :
Thou ſaidſt (oh, it comes ore my memorie,
As doth the Rauen o're the infeƈtious houſe :   25
Boading to all) he had my Handkerchiefe.
Iago.   I : what of that ?
Othe.   That's not ſo good now.
Iag.   What if I had ſaid, I had ſeene him do you wrong?
Or heard him ſay (as Knaues be ſuch abroad,   30
Who hauing by their owne importunate ſuit,
Or voluntary dotage of ſome Miſtris,   32

25. *infectious*] Ff, Rowe, Cap. Knt, Sta. Del.   *infected* Qq et cet.
26. *all*) *he*] Ff.   *all.*) *He* Qq.   *all, he* Rowe.   *ill,—he* Pope ii, Theob. Warb.   *all, —he* Han. et cet.
　Handkerchiefe] *hankercher* Q₁.   *hankerchief* Warb.

27–29. *I...What*] As one line, Dyce, Glo. Cam. Huds. Rlfe, Wh. ii.
29. *had ſaid, I had*] *said, I'ad* Pope, Theob. Warb. Johns.   *said, I had* Han.
30. *heard*] *heare* F₂.   *hear* F₃F₄.   *ſay* (*as*] *say ? as* Han.
32. *Or*] *Or by the* Q₁.

23. **forgot**] DE VIGNY: Il est bien beau, à mon avis, qu'Othello ait oublié cette circonstance, légère en apparence, et qu'il faut lui rappeler souvent.   Cela diminuera beaucoup le reproche que l'on fait à Shakespeare d'avoir construit toute l'intrigue sur un fondement aussi peu solide que le mouchoir perdu.

25. **Rauen**] HARTING (p. 99): Go where we will over the face of the wide world, the hoarse croak of the raven is still to be heard.   He was seen perched on the bare rocks, looking over the dreary snows of the highest points visited in Arctic expeditions Under the burning sun of the equator he enjoys his feast of carrion.   He was discovered in the islands of the Pacific by Captain Cook; and in the lowest Antarctic regions travellers have found him pursuing his cautious predatory life, just as in England.   From the earliest times, with his deep and solemn voice he has always commanded attention, and in his croakings the superstitious have found something unearthly and ominous.   By the Romans he was consecrated to Apollo and regarded as a prophet of good or of evil. Through a long course of centuries this character has clung to him; and even at this day there are many who believe that the raven's croak predicts a death.   No wonder then that Shakespeare has used this widespread belief, and has introduced the raven into many of the solemn passages of his Plays.   MALONE quotes these fine lines of Marlowe, *Jew of Malta*, II, i, 1: 'Thus, like the sad presaging raven, that tolls The sick man's passport in her hollow beak, And in the shadow of the silent night Doth shake contagion from her sable wings.'

27. **PURNELL:** Iago would attach no importance to that.   Othello says that that is unlike his usual wisdom.

28, 29. **That's . . . wrong**] WALKER (*Crit.* iii, 288): Arrange, perhaps,—That's not so good now.   What if I had said | I had seen him do you wrong ? |

Conuinced or fupply'd them, cannot chufe   33
But they muft blab.)

   Oth.   Hath he faid any thing?   35

   Iago.   He hath (my Lord) but be you well affur'd,
No more then he'le vn-fweare.

   Oth.   What hath he faid?

   Iago.   Why, that he did : I know not what he did.

   Othe.   What? What?   40

   Iago.   Lye.

   Oth.   With her?

   Iago.   With her? On her : what you will.

   Othe.   Lye with her? lye on her? We fay lye on her,
when they be-lye-her.   Lye with her : that's fullfome :   45
Handkerchiefe : Confeffions : Handkerchiefe.   To con-

---

33. *Conuinced or] Coniured or* Q$_2$. *Con-jured or* Q$_3$. *convinc'd or* Theob. Han. Warb. Johns. Cap. *convinc'd her and* Ktly.

   fupply'd] Ff, Wh. *suppled* Theob. Han. Warb. Johns. *suppl'd* Cap. *fupplied* Qq et cet.

   cannot] *they cannot* Theob. Warb. Johns. *then cannot* Han. *straight cannot* Cap.

34. *blab.*)] *blab.* Q$_1$, Rowe, Pope, Han. Steev.'85, Del. *blab :* Cap. *blab*— Jen. Mal. et seq.

39. *Why*] Q$_2$Q$_3$Ff, Rowe+, Cap. Steev. 85, Knt. *Faith* Q$_1$ et cet.

   he...did.] *he did I know not what; he did.* Rann.

   he did : I] Ff. *he did—I* Qq et cet.

40. *What? What?*] *But what?* Q$_1$, Jen. *What?* Q$_2$Q$_3$.

41. *Lye.*] *Lye*— Rowe et seq.

43. *her? On her :*] *her, on her,* Qq. *her? on her*— Rowe, Pope. *her; on her*— Theob. Warb. Johns. *her! on her*— Han. *her, on her*— Jen. *her;—on her;*— Knt, Sta. *her, on her;* Cap. et cet.

   will.] *will*— Rowe+, Jen.

44, 45. *We...be-lye-her*] Om. Pope, Theob. Han. Warb.

45. *be-lye-her.*] *bely her;* Qq, Cap. *be-lye her* F$_3$F$_4$.

   her : that's] *her, Zouns, that's* Q$_1$. *her! Zouns, that's* Jen. Cam.

46. *Handkerchiefe : Confessions : Handkerchiefe.*] *handkerchers, Confeffion, han-kerchers.* Q$_1$. *handkerchiefs, confeffion, handkerchiefs* Q$_2$Q$_3$. *handkerchief—con-feffions—handkerchief—handkerchief—* Theob. Warb. Johns.

46–52. *To confeffe...diuell*] Om. Q$_1$.

46–48. *To confeffe...confeffe*] Om. Pope, Han.

---

33. **Conuinced or supply'd**] THEOBALD : I read 'convinced or *suppled*,' and the meaning is, there are some such long-tongued knaves in the world, who, if they through the *force of importunity extort* a favour from their mistress, or if through *her own fond-ness* they make her *pliant* to their desires, cannot help boasting of their success.   To *convince*, here, is not, as in the common acceptation, to make sensible of the truth of anything by reasons and arguments ; but to '*overcome, get the better of*,' &c.   JENNENS : I see no reason for this alteration ; Iago is here describing two sorts of gallants ; one who by their importunities have *convinced*, or overcome, their mistresses ; the other, who, when their mistresses voluntarily doated on them, have *supplied* them with the effects of love.   STEEVENS : 'Supplied' is certainly the true reading.   See *Meas. for Meas.* V, i, 212.

   44–52. Here, as in *Lear*, IV, vi, 127, the highest passion of all, as ABBOTT (§ 511) says, is expressed in prose   Compare lines 198 et seq. of this Scene.

feſſe, and be hang'd for his labour.   Firſt, to be hang'd,   47
and then to confeſſe : I tremble at it.   Nature would not
inueſt her ſelfe in ſuch ſhadowing paſſion, without ſome
Iuſtruction.   It is not words tha*t* ſhakes me thus, (piſh)   50

47. *and be hang'd*] *and be hanged* Q₃,
Var. Knt, Coll. Dyce, Sta.
48. *then to confeſſe :*] *then—to confeſs !*
Theob. Warb. Johns.
49. *ſhadowing*] *shuddering* Coll. (MS).
paſſion] Om. Pope, Theob. Han.

Warb.

50. *Iuſtruction*] F₁.   *induction* Warb.
Han. Cap.
   not] *no* Rowe ii.
   ſhakes] QqFf, Cap. Cam. Del. *shake*
Rowe et cet.

46–52. **To . . . diuell**] POPE: No hint of this trash in the first edition.   MALONE :
See Marlowe's *Jew of Malta*, IV, i : 'Blame not us, but the proverb,—Confess and be
hanged.'   HALLIWELL : Again in Shirley's *Love Tricks* [IV, vi] : *Ruf.* Did you hear
him confess it ?   *Bub.* Here's right *confess and be hanged* now.'   WALKER (*Crit.* iii,
289) : In the confusion of Othello's mind, 'handkerchief,' from the sound and its coming in connection with 'confessions,' suggests the idea of hanging.

50. **Instruction**] WARBURTON : The starts and broken reflections in this speech
have something very terrible, and show the mind of the speaker to be in inexpressible
agonies.   But the words we are upon have a sublime in them that can never be enough
admired.   The ridiculous blunder of writing 'instruction' for *induction* (for so it should
be read) has, indeed, sunk it into arrant nonsense.   Othello is just going to fall into a
swoon; and, as is common for people in that circumstance, feels an unusual mist and
darkness, accompanied with horror, coming upon him.   This, with vast sublimity of
thought, is compared to the season of the sun's eclipse, at which time the earth becomes
shadowed by the *induction* or bringing over of the moon between it and the sun.   This
being the allusion, the reasoning stands thus, My nature could never be thus overshad-
owed, and falling, as it were, into dissolution for no cause.   There must be an *induction* of something; there must be a real cause.   My jealousy cannot be merely imaginary.   Ideas, *words* only, could not shake me thus, and raise all this disorder.   My
jealousy must be grounded, therefore, on matter of fact.   This word is used in this
sense in *Rich. III :* IV, iv, 5.   JOHNSON : This is a noble conjecture, and, whether
right or wrong, does honour to its author.   Yet I am in doubt whether there is any
necessity of emendation.   There has always prevailed in the world an opinion that,
when any great calamity happens at a distance, notice is given of it to the sufferer by
some dejection or perturbation of mind, of which he discovers no external cause.   This
is ascribed to that general communication of one part of the universe with another,
which is called sympathy and antipathy ; or to the secret monition, *instruction*, and
influence of a Superior Being, which superintends the order of nature and of life.
Othello says, Nature could not invest herself in such shadowing passion without
instruction.   It is not words that shake me thus.   This passion which spreads its
clouds over me is the effect of some agency, more than the operation of words; it is
one of those notices which men have of unseen calamities.   HEATH (p. 569) : Othello
feels all his faculties failing him on the sudden, and a cloudy or misty darkness creeping
very fast upon him.   This circumstance suggests to him the thought that his very nature,
which sympathizes with him in his present agony, must have received some secret mysterious instruction, intimation, or instinctive knowledge of the reality of that calamity
which so deeply oppresses him, otherwise she would never have spontaneously invested

Noſes, Eares, and Lippes : is't poſſible.   Confeſſe? Hand-   51
kerchiefe ? O diuell.   *Falls in a Traunce.*

    Iago.   Worke on,
My Medicine workes.   Thus credulous Fooles are caught,
And many worthy, and chaſt Dames euen thus,   55
(All guiltleſſe) meete reproach : what hoa ? My Lord ?
My Lord, I ſay : *Othello.*

Enter Caſſio.

How now *Cvſſio ?*
    Caſ.   What's the matter ?   60

---

   51. *poſſible.*] *poſſible ?* Q₂Q₃. *poſſible !*
Rowe.

   51, 52. *Confeſſe ? Handkerchiefe ?*] *Con-*
feſs !—Handkerchief !— Rowe.

   52. *Falls...*] He fals downe. Q₁. Falles
...trance. Q₂Q₃F₄.

   53–59. Prose, Qq.

   53, 54. One line, Cap.

      on, My Medicine workes.] Ff,

Rowe, Pope, Han. *on my medicine, worke:*
Qq. *on, My medicine, work !* Theob. et cet.

   55, 56. *Dames...guiltleſſe*)] *dames, euen*
thus all guiltleſſe, Q₁.

   57. *Othello.*] Othello,— Qq, Theob.
Johns.

   58. *Enter...*] After line 59, Qq.
Scene II. Pope+, Jen.

   60. *What's*] *What is* Steev.'93, Vaɪ.

---

herself in that horrid darkness which he now felt overwhelming him. Sɪʀ J. Rᴇʏ-
ɴᴏʟᴅs : Othello alludes only to Cassio's dream, which had been invented and told him
by Iago.   When many confused and very interesting ideas pour in upon the mind all
at once, and with such rapidity that it has not time to shape or digest them, if it does
not relieve itself by tears (which we know it often does, whether for joy or grief) it
produces stupefaction and fainting.   Othello, in broken sentences and single words, all
of which have a reference to the cause of his jealousy, shows that all the proofs are
present at once to his mind, which so overpowers it that he falls into a trance, the natural consequence.   Mᴀʟᴏɴᴇ : *Induction*, in Shakespeare's time, meant *introduction* or
prelude, and at no time signified *bringing over*, as Warburton interprets it.

   50. **that shakes**] See I, iii, 312.

   51. **Lippes**] Sᴛᴇᴇᴠᴇɴs : Othello is imagining to himself the familiarities which he
supposes to have passed between Cassio and his wife.   If this be not the meaning, we
must suppose he is meditating a cruel punishment for the guilty lovers.

   53. Fᴇᴄʜᴛᴇʀ here begins his Act IV.   Othello and Iago discovered.   Othello is
stretched, unconscious, on the divan.   Iago behind, contemplating him with a diabolical sneer.

   54. **workes**] An interpolated *s*, according to Wᴀʟᴋᴇʀ.   See I, i, 31.

   57–200. Sᴀʟᴠɪɴɪ justifies his omission of this portion of the scene on the ground
that it is not in accord with Othello's character.   'Is it to be imagined,' he asks, 'that
a man of the Moor's haughty and violent temper could command himself during the
recital of his dishonour from the lips of his wronger ?   Would you not suppose that he
would spring like a tiger on Cassio and tear him to pieces ?   To be sure, Cassio would
gain enough time to clear up the misunderstanding, and the Tragedy would fall through.
Hence, either this scene must be retained to the injury of Othello's character, or it must
be omitted.'   The gap in the story Salvini considers as filled by Othello's assertion in
the last scene, that he had seen the Handkerchief in Cassio's hand.

Iago.   My Lord is falne into an Epilepfie,   61
This is his fecond Fit : he had one yefterday.
   Caf.   Rub him about the Temples.
   Iago.   The Lethargie muft haue his quyet courfe :
If not, he foames at mouth : and by and by   65
Breakes out to fauage madneffe.   Looke, he ftirres :
Do you withdraw your felfe a little while,
He will recouer ftraight : when he is gone,
I would on great occafion, fpeake with you.
How is it Generall ? Haue you not hurt your head ?   70
   Othe.   Doft thou mocke me ?
   Iago.   I mocke you not, by Heauen:
Would you would beare your Fortune like a Man.
   Othe.   A Horned man's a Monfter, and a Beaft.
   Iago.   Ther's many a Beaft then in a populous Citty,   75
And many a ciuill Monfter.
   Othe.   Did he confeffe it ?
   Iago.   Good Sir, be a man :
Thinke euery bearded fellow that's but yoak'd   79

61. *falne*] QqFf, Rowe, Pope. *fell*
Theob. Warb. *fallen* Steev. Mal. Var.
Knt, Coll. Sing. Wh. i, Ktly. *fall'n* Han.
et cet.
   62. *is his*] *is the* F$_4$, Rowe+.
   64. Iago. *The*] Iag. *No, forbeare, The*
Qq (*forbare*, Q$_3$) Pope et seq.
      haue his] *have* Q$_3$.
   65. *at*] *at'* Ed. conj.
   66. *he ftirres*] *he ftarres* Q$_3$.
   68, 69. *gone...fpeake*] *gon...fpake* Q$_3$.
   69. [Exit Cassio. Rowe et seq.
   70. *head ?*] *hand ?* Ff (*hand ;* F$_4$)

   71. *Doft thou*] *Doft* Q$_3$, Cap.
      me ?] *me ?* Exit *Caf.* Q$_2$Q$_3$.
   72. *you not, by*] Ff, Rowe+.   *you no
by* Q$_3$.   *you ? no by* Q$_1$Q$_2$ et cet.
      Heauen :] *heaven ; I mock you not.*
Cap.
   73. *Fortune*] Ff, Rowe, Pope, Han.
Cap. Knt, Dyce, Sta. Glo. Cam. Del. Coll.
iii, Wh. ii.   *fortunes* Qq et cet.
      like] *life* F$_2$.
   77. *confeffe it ?*] *confeffe ?* Qq.
   79. *euery*] *ever* Q$_3$.

61. **Epilepsie**] BUCKNILL (*Med. Knowledge of Sh.* p. 274): This designation
appears a mere falsehood.   It is to be observed, however, that Shakespeare's knowledge of epilepsy here goes farther than in *Jul. Cæs.* I, ii, 256, since he describes the
maniacal excitement which so often follows the fit.   When Cassio has been persuaded
to withdraw, Iago applies to the patient himself the truthful and correct designation
of his morbid state.

   62. **yesterday**] COWDEN-CLARKE: Iago is so solid a liar that this cannot be taken
literally; but it aids to give the effect of long dramatic time.

   64. WHITE (ed. i): The words [supplied by the Qq, see Text. Notes,   were omitted
from the Folio, accidentally we may be sure.

   71. **mocke**] JOHN HUNTER: As if Iago had meant the hurt done to the head **when**
one is made a horned monster.

May draw with you.   There's Millions now aliue,   80
That nightly lye in thofe vnproper beds,
Which they dare fweare peculiar.   Your cafe is better.
Oh, 'tis the fpight of hell, the Fiends Arch-mock,
To lip a wanton in a fecure Cowch;
And to fuppofe her chaft.   No, let me know,   [329 *b*]
And knowing what I am, I know what fhe fhallbe.   86

   Oth.   Oh, thou art wife : 'tis certaine.

   Iago.   Stand you a while apart,
Confine your felfe but in a patient Lift,
Whil'ft you were heere, o're-whelmed with your griefe   90
(A paffion moft refulting fuch a man)

80. *you.   There's*] *you, there's* Qq.
There's Millions] *Millions are*
Pope+.
   now] *uow* F₂.
81. *lye*] *lyes* Qₓ.
82. *peculiar*] *prculiar* F₂. *peculior* Q₃.
cafe] *caufe* Ff, Rowe.
83. *Oh, 'tis*] *O this* Q₃. *Oh, it is* Han.
82–88. Lines end, *cafe...hell,...in,...
chaft....am...wife:...apart,* Han. (reading *you now* line 88).

85. *let me*] *let not me* Q₃.
87. *'tis*] *that's* Cap. (Corrected in Errata).
88. *Stand you*] *Stand you now* Han.
89. *Lift,*] *lift :* Qq.   *list.* Rowe.
90. *heere, o're-whelmed*] *here ere while,
mad* Qₓ, Steev. Mal. Rann. Var.
91. *refulting*] Ff, Rowe. *vnfuting* Qₓ.
vnfitting Q₂Q₃, Pope, Han. Cap. Coll.
Dyce iii.   *unsuiting* Theob. et cet.

81. **vnproper**] DYCE: Not peculiar to an individual, common.   ROLFE: Shake-speare uses it only here; *improper*, that is, not becoming, only in *Lear*, V, iii, 222.

82. **peculiar**] WHITE (ed. ii): Equivalent to belonging to one; that is, to each one of them (the millions) respectively.

83. **spight**] SCHMIDT (*Lex.* s. v.): Vexation, mortification.   ROLFE: It rather seems to be malice.   The 'spite of hell' is explained by 'the fiend's arch-mock.'   The man is not *mortified*, for he does not know his disgrace.

84. **secure**] MALONE: In a couch on which he is lulled into a false security.   So, 'though Page be a secure fool,' &c., *Merry Wives*, II, i, 241.   [For other instances of the accent on the first syllable, see WALKER (*Vers.* 292) or ABBOTT, § 492.]

85–87. WALKER (*Crit.* iii, 289) proposes an arrangement, 'if the reading be right,' of these lines, wherein he was anticipated by Hanmer.   See Text. Notes.

86. **she**] STEEVENS: Redundancy of metre, without improvement of sense, inclines one to consider this word as an intruder.   Iago is merely stating an imaginary case as his own.   'When I know what I am, I know what the result of that conviction shall be.'   To whom, indeed, could the pronoun 'she' grammatically refer?

89. **List**] COLLINS: That is, barrier, bound.   Keep your temper, says Iago, within the bounds of patience.

90. **o're-whelmed**] KNIGHT: These words, in the Qq, afford one evidence, amongst many, that both his texts were printed from a manuscript.

91. **resulting**] COLLIER (ed. ii): That *unfitting* was the word usually recited on the stage we may infer, perhaps, from its having been thus altered in the (MS.).

Caffio came hither.   I fhifted him away,   92
And layd good fcufes vpon your Extafie,
Bad him anon returne : and heere fpeake with me,
The which he promis'd.   Do but encaue your felfe,   95
And marke the Fleeres, the Gybes, and notable Scornes
That dwell in euery Region of his face.
For I will make him tell the Tale anew;
Where, how, how oft, how long ago, and when
He hath, and is againe to cope your wife.   100
I fay, but marke his gefture : marry Patience,
Or I fhall fay y'are all in all in Spleene,
And nothing of a man.
　　Othe.   Do'ft thou heare, *Iago*,
I will be found moft cunning in my Patience :   105
But (do'ft thou heare) moft bloody.
　　Iago.   That's not amiffe,
But yet keepe time in all : will you withdraw ?
Now will I queftion *Caffio* of *Bianca*,
A Hufwife, that by felling her defires   110
Buyes her felfe Bread, and Cloath.   It is a Creature

92. *hither.*] *hither,* Qq.
93. *layd*] *layed* Qq. *laid* Ff.
　fcufes vpon] *fcufe, vpon* Q₁. *fcufes
on* Ff, Rowe+ *fcufe vpon* Q₂Q₃ et cet.
94. *Bad*] *Bid* Q₁. *Bade* Johns, Steev.
et seq.
　　returne:] *retire,* Qq.
　　heere fpeake] *her fpeake* Q₃.
95. *Do but*] *but* Qq, Coll. Wh. i.
　encaue] *incaue* Qq.
96. *Fleeres*] *Ieeres* Q₁. *geeres* Q₂Q₃.
　Gybes] *Iibes* Q₁.
98. *Tale*] *rale* Q₃.
100. *hath*] *has* Qq.
101. *gefture: marry*] *ieafture, mary*
Qq.

102. *y'are*] Ff, Rowe, Wh. Dyce iii,
Huds. *you're* Pope, Han. *you are* Qq
et cet.
　all in all] *all-in-all* Sta. Huds.
　in Spleene] *a spleen* Johns. conj.
Cap. *one spleen* Lettsom conj. Huds.
104. *thou*] Om. Cap.
107. *Iago.*] *aago.* F₂.
108. *But yet*] *But* Q₃.
　　[Othello withdraws. Rowe. Othello conceals himself. Cap.
109. *Bianca,*] *Bianca ?* Q₃.
111. *Cloath*] *cloathes* Qq. *cloth* F₃F₄,
Rowe+. *clothes* Steev.'93 et seq.
　It is a Creature] Om. Q₃.

93. **scuses**] WALKER (*Crit.* i, 239) cites this in the same article referred to at I, i,
31, adding 'it is possible that Shakespeare may have written 'scuses *on*.' Neither
Walker nor his Editor noticed that this is the reading of all the Ff but the First. For
the dropped prefix, see ABBOTT, § 460.

102. **in Spleene**] STEEVENS : We still say, such a one is *in* wrath, *in* the dumps,
&c. The sense, therefore, is plain. DYCE (ed. iii) : Lettsom suggests '*one* spleen.'

110. **Huswife**] WHITE (ed. ii) : Pronunciation, *husif;* sense, *hussy.*

111. **It is**] ROLFE : Used contemptuously, as in *Rom. & Jul.* IV, ii, 14.

That dotes on *Caſſio*, (as 'tis the Strumpets plague 112
To be-guile many, and be be-guil'd by one)
He, when he heares of her, cannot reſtraine
From the exceſſe of Laughter.   Heere he comes. 115

Enter Caſſio.

As he ſhall ſmile, *Othello* ſhall go mad :
And his vnbookiſh Ielouſie muſt conſerue 118

---

113. *be-guile ... be-guil'd*] *beguile ...*
beguil'd QqF₃F₄.
114. *reſtraine*] Ff, Rowe, Sta. *refraine*
Qq et cet.

116. Enter...] After line 113, Qq. After
wrong line 120, Dyce, Sta. Wh.
Scene III. Pope+, Jen.
118. *conſerue*] *conſter* Qq. *construe*
Rowe et seq.

---

116. See note, III, iii, 383.

118. **vnbookiſh**] WHITER (p. 112), after citing many instances where Shakespeare has used the imagery of a *book* in connection with *love*, ends with the celebrated description of Cressida (*Tro. & Cress.* IV, v, 54) wherein Ulysses speaks of 'unclasping the tables of their thoughts To every ticklish reader;' and the same metaphor, Whiter is persuaded, Iago uses here. 'The "unbookish" jealousy of Othello,' says Whiter, 'is that which confounds his knowledge in the *Books of* LOVE, and blinds his discernment respecting the *language of* LOVERS. It will cause him to mistake the artless smiles and gestures of Cassio for the significant expressions of *amorous parley*. Whether our Poet intended to comprehend the whole of this meaning, I am not able to decide: I am convinced, however, that this remote epithet " unbookish," as applied to jealousy, was suggested to his mind by the above very singular imagery of the *Lover* and the *Book*.' WALKER (*Crit.* iii, 289) noticed what had escaped Whiter, that 'unbookish' is connected with 'construe,' but when he adds that 'it is explained by it,' he does not take me wholly with him. 'Unbookish' is certainly used here in an unusual sense; it is as though there were Books of *Jealousy*, like Saviolo's *Practise of Honorable Quarrels*, which should guide Othello, but did not. WARBURTON'S explanation, followed by Dyce and others, that it is equivalent to *ignorant*, is scarcely sufficient. The use of 'bookish' in the first scene of this play, in its manifest meaning (where Iago talks of the 'bookish Theoric'), shows that more is meant by 'unbookish' than mere lack of knowledge or of skill. Until a better can be given, Whiter's explanation seems the nearest, viz.: that Shakespeare having so frequently compared *love* and *lovers* to *books*, here, by the association of ideas, makes Othello's misconstruction of Cassio's smiles due to Othello's lack of learning in the books of love.—ED.

118. **conſerue**] This is a mere misprint, of one letter, for *construe*, which is spelled in the Qq as it was probably pronounced. It is spelled *conster* in the Ff *Twelfth Night*, III, i, 54; thus also in F₁F₂F₃ *Tam. of Shr.* III, i, 30 and 40; *construred* in Qq *Merry Wives*, I, iii, 42; *consture* in *Love's Lab.* V, ii, 341; *consters* in *R. of L.* 324, and *conster* in *Pass. Pil.* 14, 8; *construe* in all other instances, viz.: *Two Gent.* I, ii, 56; Ff *Merry Wives*, I, iii, 42; Ff *Love's Lab.* V, ii, 341; *Jul. Cæs.* I, ii, 44; I, iii, 34; II, i, 307; *2 Hen. IV:* IV, i, 103. Collier, in all honesty doubtless, says that F₁ has *conserve*, which shows how necessary it is to have the *ipsissimæ literæ* of the original text in sight, where the *u*'s are not converted to *v*'s. DYCE (*Remarks*, p. 54, note on the

Poore *Caſſio's* ſmiles, geſtures, and light behauiours
Quite in the wrong.　How do you Lieutenant?　　**120**
　　Caſ.　The worſer, that you giue me the addition,
Whoſe want euen killes me.
　　Iago.　Ply *Deſdemona* well, and you are ſure on't:
Now, if this Suit lay in *Bianca's* dowre,
How quickely ſhould you ſpeed?　　**125**
　　Caſ.　Alas poore Caitiffe.
　　Oth.　Looke how he laughes already.
　　Iago.　I neuer knew woman loue man ſo.
　　Caſ.　Alas poore Rogue, I thinke indeed ſhe loues me.
　　Oth.　Now he denies it faintly : and laughes it out.　　**130**
　　Iago.　Do you heare *Caſſio*?
　　Oth.　Now he importunes him
To tell it o're : go too, well ſaid, well ſaid.
　　Iago.　She giues it out, that you ſhall marry her.
Do you intend it?　　**135**
　　Caſ.　Ha, ha, ha.
　　Oth.　Do ye triumph, Romaine? do you triumph?　　**137**

---

119. *Poore*] *Our* Theob. conj. (with-drawn).

　　behauiours] Ff, Rowe. *behauiour* Qq et cet.

120. *you*] Ff, Rowe.　*you now* Qq et cet.

　　Lieutenant] *Leiutenant* Qq.

121. *worſer*] *worſe* Q₃.

　　giue] *gave* Ff, Rowe, Pope, Han.

123. *on't*] *of't* Mal. Steev.'93, Var.

124. [Speaking lower. Rowe.

　　dowre] Ff, Rowe, Knt, Sta. Del. *power* Qq et cet.

126. *Caitiffe*] *catiue* Qq.

127, 130, 132, 137, 141, 145, 149, 154, 158, 176. As Aside, Theob. Warb. et seq.

128. *woman*] Ff, Knt, Coll. Dyce i, Sta. Wh. Glo. Del. Rlfe.　*a woman* Qq et cet.

129. *indeed*] Ff, Rowe+, Cap. Steev. '85, Knt.　*ifaith* Q₁ et cet.

130. *it out*] *out* Pope+.

132, 133. *Now...o're*] One line, Qq.

132. *importunes*] *in portunes* Q₃.

133. *it o're*] *it on* Q₁Q₂.　*it out* Q₃. *go too*] *go to* QqFf.

　　well ſaid, well ſaid] *well ſaid* Qq.

137. *Do ye*] Ff, Rowe, Pope.　*Doe you* Qq et cet.

Mer. of Ven. II, ii) says that the form *misconster* is common in our early writers, and gives several instances.—ED.

119. **behauiours**] See I, i, 31, or WALKER (*Crit.* i, 241).

124. **dowre**] KNIGHT : *Dower* in the sense of gift.　COLLIER : The letter *d* having been turned in the Folio, 'power' there became *dower*.　DELIUS thinks that 'dower' accords better with what Iago afterwards insinuates, viz.: 'she gives it out that you ſhall marry her.'

133. **well said**] See II, i, 192.

137. **Romaine**] WARBURTON : Never was a more ridiculous blunder than the word 'Roman.'　Shakespeare wrote *rogue*, which, being obscurely written, the editors mistook for *Rome*, and so made *Roman* of it.　JOHNSON : Othello calls him 'Roman'

Caſ. I marry. What ? A cuſtomer ;prythee beare   138
Some Charitie to my wit, do not thinke it
So vnwholeſome.   Ha, ha, ha.   140
Oth.   So, ſo, ſo, ſo : they laugh , that winnes.
Iago.   Why the cry goes, that you marry her.
Caſ.   Prythee ſay true.
Iago.   I am a very Villaine elſe.
Oth.   Haue you ſcoar'd me ? Well.   145

138–140. *I...ha.*] Two lines, ending
wit...ha. Q₁. Three lines, ending *Cuſtomer...wit,...ha.* Q₂Q₃, Walker. Prose, Pope
et seq.
   138. *I marry.*] Ff, Rowe, Pope, Han.
Knt. *I marry her?* Qq et cet.
   What ? A Cuſtomer] Om. Q₁.
   prythee] *I prethee* Qq, Jen. Steev.
Mal. Var. Coll. Sing. Wh. i, Ktly, Cam.
Del.
   141. *So, ſo, ſo, ſo*] *So,ſo* F₃F₄, Rowe+.
   they laugh] *laugh* Q₁, Cap.
   winnes] Ff. *wins* Q₁Q₂, Cap.

wines Q₃. *win* F₄, Rowe et cet.
   142. *Why*] FfQ₂Q₃, Rowe+, Cap.
Steev.'85, Knt. *Faith* Q₁ et cet.
   that you] F₂, Knt. *you ſhall*
Q₁. *that you ſhall* Q₂Q₃F₃F₄, Rowe et
cet.
   marry] *merry* Q₃.
   144. *very*] Om. Han.
   145. *Haue...me ?*] Om. Coll. (MS).
   Haue] *Ha* Qq.
   ſcoar'd me ? Well.] *ſtor'd me well.*
Q₁. *ſcoar'd me ; well.* Ff. *scor'd me ? Well.*
Theob. ii et seq.

---

ironically. 'Triumph,' which was a Roman ceremony, brought Roman into his
thoughts. 'What !' says he, 'you are now triumphing as great as a Roman ?' COLLIER
(ed. ii) : The (MS.) informs us that for 'Roman' we ought to substitute *o'er me.* This
may be so, and the reason for 'Roman,' in reference to 'triumph,' is not obvious ; but
as the change is somewhat violent, and in no respect compulsory, we do not make it.
PURNELL : Shakespeare had been studying for the Roman plays about this time.

   138. **customer**] JOHNSON : A common woman, one that invites custom. WHITE
(ed. ii) : Both Iago and Cassio are led by the occasion to make out Bianca worse, or at
least lower in condition, than she was. WISE, in his *Glossary* appended to his *Shakespeare and his Birthplace,* gives this word as in use in this sense among the peasantry
of Warwickshire at this day.

   139. **Charitie**] WALKER (*Vers.* 201) : The *i* in *-ity* is almost uniformly dropped in
pronunciation. See also III, iii, 295.

   141. **winnes**] See I, iii, 312.

   145. **scoar'd**] JOHNSON : Have you made my reckoning ? have you settled the term
of my life ? STEEVENS : To score originally meant no more than to cut a notch upon
a tally, or to mark out a form by indenting it on any substance. But it was soon figuratively used for setting a *brand* or *mark* of disgrace on any one, and it is employed
in this sense here. COLLIER (ed. ii) : In view of the reading of the Qq, we cannot be
by any means sure that 'scored' is the true lection ; possibly some other word ought to
be substituted. The sense usually attached to the phrase has been : Have you marked
me like a beast, which you have made me, by giving me horns. STAUNTON : That is,
branded, unless the word is a misprint. DELIUS : Othello applies to Desdemona Iago's
words, 'you shall marry her,' and asks, 'Have you made out my reckoning ? Are
you finished with me ?' it is not until Othello is out of the way that a marriage with
her is possible. HUDSON : I am not clear as to the meaning of this. To *score* was to

Caſ.   This is the Monkeys owne giuing out: 146
She is perſwaded I will marry her
Out of her owne loue & flattery, not out of my promiſe.

Oth.   *Iago* becomes me : now he begins the ſtory.   [330 *a*]

Caſſio.   She was heere euen now : ſhe haunts me in e-   150
uery place.   I was the other day talking on the Sea-
banke with certaine Venetians, and thither comes the
Bauble, and falls me thus about my neck.

Oth.   Crying oh deere *Caſſio*, as it were: his ieſture imports it.   155

Caſſio.   So hangs, and lolls, and weepes vpon me :
So ſhakes, and pulls me.   Ha, ha, ha.

Oth.   Now he tells how ſhe pluckt him to my Chamber : oh, I ſee that noſe of yours, but not that dogge, I
ſhall throw it to.   160

Caſſio.   Well, I muſt leaue her companie.

Iago.   Before me : looke where ſhe comes.   162

146–148. Prose, Qq, Pope et seq.
146. *Monkeys*] *monkies* QqF₃F₄.
149. *becomes*] *becons* F₂.   *beckon's* F₃.
beckons QqF₄ et cet.
151. *the other*] *tother* Qq, Jen.
152. *thither*] *theither* Q₃.
   comes the] *comes this* Qq, Jen. Var.
Coll. i, Wh. i.
153. *and...thus*] *by this hand ſhe fals
thus* Q₁, Jen. Steev. Mal. Var.   *fals me
thus* Q₂Q₃.   *and, by this hand, she falls
me thus* Coll. Wh. Del. Glo. Cam. Rlfe.
   neck.] FfQq, Jen.   *neck—* Rowe.
neck : Cap.

154. *ieſture*] *geſture* Q₂Q₃Ff.
156, 157. Prose, Qq, Pope et seq.
156. *lolls*] *iolls* Q₂.   *jolls* Q₃.
157. *ſhakes*] Ff, Rowe +, Knt. *hals* Q₃.
hales Q₄Q₂ et cet.
   pulls] *pu* Q₂.   *puls* Q₃.
158–160. Two lines, ending *chamber..
to.* Qq.   Three, ending *chamber...dog...
to.* Ktly.
159. *oh, I*] *I* Qq.
   but not] *but now* Ff.
160. *throw it*] *throw't* Qq, Jen.
162, 164. Iago., Caſ.] Om. Q₂Q₃.

----

cut notches in a stick, and accounts were formerly kept by scoring the items thus ir
what were called tally-sticks.   In *All's Well*, IV, iii, we have the line, ' After he *scores,*
he never *pays the score*'; and the context there shows the meaning to be, that when he
has sworn a woman into granting his wish, he never keeps his oaths ; or what the Poet
elsewhere calls ' beguiling virgins with the brokens seals of perjury.'   So, in the text,
the meaning may be, ' Have you run up an account against me, which I must pay ?
very well, I'll see you paid.'   Or it may be, ' Have you squared the account with me
for cashiering you ? '

159. **nose . . . dogge**] DEIGHTON (p. 62) : I see your nose, which I shall soon
tear from your face and fling to the first dog that comes in my way.

162. **Before me**] SCHMIDT interprets this as equivalent to ' by my soul,' and refers
to *Twelfth Night*, II, iii, 194.   PURNELL considers it as a euphemism for ' before God,'
and refers to *Cor.* I, i, 124.

Enter Bianca. 163

Caf. 'Tis fuch another Fitchew:marry a perfum'd one?
What do you meane by this haunting of me? 165

Bian. Let the diuell, and his dam haunt you : what
did you meane by that fame Handkerchiefe, you gaue
me euen now ? I was a fine Foole to take it : I muft take
out the worke? A likely piece of worke, that you fhould
finde it in your Chamber, and know not who left it there. 170
This is fome Minxes token, & I muft take out the worke?
There, giue it your Hobbey-horfe, wherefoeuer you had
it, Ile take out no worke on't.

Caffio. How now, my fweete *Bianca*?
How now ? How now? 175

Othe. By Heauen, that fhould be my Handkerchiefe.

Bian. If you'le come to fupper to night you may, if
you will not, come when you are next prepar'd for. *Exit*

Iago. After her : after her.

Caf. I muft, fhee'l rayle in the ftreets elfe. 180

Iago. Will you fup there?

Caffio. Yes, I intend fo.

Iago. Well, I may chance to fee you : for I would very faine fpeake with you.

Caf. Prythee come : will you? 185

163. Enter...] After line 161, Qq. After
line 164, Dyce.

Scene IV. Pope +, Jen.

164. Caf.] Om. Q₁.

Fitchew] *ficho* Q₁.

164, 165. *one? What*] *one, what* Q₁.
one: What Q₂Q₃F₃F₄.

167, 176, 190. *Handkerchiefe*] *handkercher* Q₁. *Handkerchiffe* or *Hanker-
chiffe* F₃.

169. *the worke*] *the whole worke* Q₁,
Jen. Steev. Mal. Var. Sing. Ktly.

170. *know not*] Ff, Rowe +, Cap. Knt,
Coll. Sta. Wh. i, Del. *not know* Qq et cet.

171. *worke?*] *worke;* Qq, Han. *work!*
Knt, Sing. Sta.

172. *it your*] *it the* Qq, Jen.

174, 175. One line, Qq, Pope et seq.

177. *If...if*] Ff, Rowe +, Knt, Sing.
Ktly. *An...an* Qq et cet.

180. *I muft*] Ff, Rowe +, Cap. Steev.
'85, Knt. *Faith I muft* Q₁ et cet.
in the] *i'the* Qq, Cap. Jen.
ftreets] Ff, Rowe +, Knt, Sta.
Wh. i. *ftreete* Q₁. *ftreet* Q₂Q₃ et cet.

181. *Will...there?*] *You fup there.*
Q₂Q₃. *You fup there?* Johns.

182. *Yes,*] FfQ₂Q₃, Rowe +, Cap. Jen.
Steev.'85, Knt, Dyce iii, Huds. *Faith* Q₁
et cet.

185. *Prythee*] *Preethee* Q₁. *Prethe* Q₂
Q₃. *Prethee* F₃. *Prithee* F₄.

164. **such another**] See Schmidt (s. v. *another*), for other instances of this kindly
contemptuous phrase, to which Schmidt gives as equivalent the German 'auch so eine.

164. **Fitchew**] Dyce (*Gloss.*): A polecat, and the cant term for a strumpet. [The
Qq give what was probably the pronunciation. Cotgrave has *Fissau.*—Ed.]

172. **Hobbey-horse**] Dyce (*Gloss.*): An abandoned woman.

Iago. Go too : fay no more.   186
Oth. How fhall I murther him, *Iago.*
Iago. Did you perceiue how he laugh'd at his vice ?
Oth. Oh, *Iago.*
Iago. And did you fee the Handkerchiefe ?   190
Oth. Was that mine ?
Iago. Yours by this hand : and to fee how he prizes
the foolifh woman your wife : fhe gaue it him, and he
hath giu'n it his whore.
Oth. I would haue him nine yeeres a killing :   195
A fine woman, a faire woman, a fweete woman ?
Iago. Nay , you muft forget that.
Othello. I, let her rot and perifh, and be damn'd to
night , for fhe fhall not liue. No, my heart is turn'd to
ftone : I ftrike it, and it hurts my hand. Oh, the world   200
hath not a fweeter Creature : fhe might lye by an Em-
perours fide, and command him Taskes.   202

186. *too : fay*] *to, fay* Q₁. *to fay* Q₂Q₃. *to ; fay* Ff.
    more.] *more.* Exit *Caffio.* Qq. *more.* Exit. Ff.
    Scene V. Pope+, Jen.
    [Coming hastily from his conceal-ment. Cap. Advancing. Coll.
187. *murther*] Ff, Rowe+, Cap. Knt, Wh. i, Rlfe. *murder* Qq, Johns. et cet.
    Iago.] Iago? QqF₃F₄, Rowe et seq.
188. *laugh'd*] *laughed* Qq.

189. Iago.] Iaga. Q₂.
192–194. Om. Qq.
195, 196. Prose, Qq, Cap. Jen. Coll. et seq.
196. *woman ?*] *woman.* Qq. *woman !*— Rowe et seq.
197. *forget that.*] *forget.* Q₁. *forget that* Q₂Q₃.
198. *I,*] *And* Qq. *Ay,* Rowe et seq.
    damn'd] *damb'd* Qq.
200. *ftone*] *a ftone* Q₂Q₃.
201. *hath*] *has* Qq.

192–194. JENNENS: The omission of this speech in Q₁ evidently appears to be a blunder of the compositors; for Othello's speech, 'Was that mine ?' concludes the page; and the catchword to the next page is *Iag.*, which shows that this speech of Iago was in the MS.; otherwise the catchwords would have been 'I would.'

195. *a killing*] See ABBOTT, § 24, for instances of *a-* before verbal nouns where it represents *on ;* as here, 'nine years on, or in the act of killing.'

198–202. This speech is assuredly *metric prose.* In moments of wild passion the least restraints of verse, even to Shakespeare it seems, are choking, yet the phrases will fall rhythmically. I cannot find that any one has ever attempted to cut it up into lines, and yet WALKER (*Crit.* ii, 23) says that 'creature,' in line 201, is 'probably a dissyllable' where the innuendo is that it occurs in verse. To my ear 'crĕature' is better.—ED.

200. **stone . . . hand**] STEEVENS: This thought, as often as it occurs to Shake-speare, is sure to be received, and as often counteracts his *pathos.* See *Ant. & Clea.* IV, ix, 16.

Iago.   Nay, that's not your way.   203

Othe.   Hang her, I do but fay what fhe is : fo delicate
with her Needle : an admirable Mufitian. Oh fhe will   205
fing the Sauageneffe out of a Beare : of fo high and plenteous wit, and inuention ?

Iago.   She's the worfe for all this.

Othe.   Oh, a thoufand, a thoufand times :
And then of fo gentle a condition ?   210

Iago.   I too gentle.

Othe.   Nay that's certaine :
But yet the pitty of it, *Iago* : oh *Iago*, the pitty of it
Iago.   [330 *b*]

Iago.   If you are fo fond ouer her iniquitie : giue her   215
pattent to offend, for if it touch not you, it comes neere
no body.

Oth.   I will chop her into Meffes : Cuckold me ?

Iago.   Oh, 'tis foule in her.   219

---

204. *do but*] *do not* Q_2Q_3.
206. *high and*] *high a* Ff, Rowe.
206, 207. *plenteous*] *plentious* Q_1F_3.
plentions Q_3.
207. *inuention ?*] *inuention*. Qq. *invention !*— Rowe.
209, 210. Prose, Qq, Cap. et seq.
209. *Oh, a*] *A* Qq.
 thoufand, a thoufand] Ff,
Rowe+, Cap. Steev. Mal. Var. Knt, Del.
thousand-thousand Sta. Dyce iii, Huds.
thoufand thoufand Qq et cet.
210. *a condition ?*] *a condition.* Q_1Q_2,

Jen. *a condition,* Q_3. *condition !* Pope+.
a condition ! Cap. et seq.
212–214. One line, Qq. Prose, Cap. et
seq.
212. *Nay*] *I* Q_1.
213, 214. *oh* Iago,...Iago.] *the pitty.* Q_1.
oh the pitty. Q_2Q_3, Jen.
215. *you are*] *you be* Qq, Cap. Jen.
216. *touch*] *touches* Qq, Cap.
218. *Meffes :*] *meffes*— Q_1. *meffes,*—
Q_2Q_3. *messes.* Johns.
me ?] *me !* Qq.

---

203. **your way**] DEIGHTON (p. 63): That is, it won't do for you to let your thoughts
dwell upon her many excellences, or you will be unmanned.
206. MALONE: So in *V. & A.* 1096: 'when he hath sung The tiger would be tame.'
210. **condition**] See II, i, 282.
212. MRS JAMESON (ii, 35): Desdemona displays at times a transient energy, arising
from the power of affection, but gentleness gives the prevailing tone to her character,—
gentleness in its excess,—gentleness verging on passiveness,—gentleness which not only
cannot resent, but cannot resist. Here in this passage the exceeding softness of Desdemona's temper is turned against her by Iago, so that it suddenly strikes Othello in a new
point of view, as the inability to resist temptation ; but to us, who perceive the character
as a whole, this extreme gentleness of nature is yet delineated with such exceeding
refinement that the effect never approaches to feebleness. It is true that *once* her
extreme timidity leads her, in a moment of confusion and terror, to prevaricate about
the fatal handkerchief.
216. **pattent**] See CHALMERS, on Date of Composition, in Appendix.

Oth. With mine Officer?   **220**

Iago. That's fouler.

Othe. Get me ſome poyſon, *Iago*, this night. Ile not
expoſtulate with her : leaſt her body and beautie vnprouide my mind againe : this night *Iago*.

Iago. Do it not with poyſon, ſtrangle her in her bed,   **225**
Euen the bed ſhe hath contaminated.

Oth. Good, good :
The Iuſtice of it pleaſes : very good.

Iago. And for *Caſſio*, let me be his vndertaker :
You ſhall heare more by midnight.   **230**

Enter Lodouico, Deſdemona, and Attendants.

Othe. Excellent good : What Trumpet is that ſame?

Iago. I warrant ſomething from Venice,
'Tis *Lodouico*, this, comes from the Duke.
See, your wife's with him.   **235**

---

220. *Officer?*] *Officer.* Qq. *officer!*
Rowe.

222. *night. Ile*] *night Ile* Qq.

223. *beautie*] *her beauty* F₃F₄, Rowe+.

224. *againe :*] *agen*, Qq.

225, 226. Prose, Qq, Cap. Steev. et seq.

225. *her in*] *here in* Q₃.

226. *Euen*] *Even* in Pope+.

227, 228. One line, Qq; or prose, Cap.
et seq.

228. *pleaſes : very*] *pleaſes very* Q₁.
pleaſes, very Q₂Q₃.

229, 230. Prose, Qq, Cap. Steev. Mal.
Var. Dyce, Sta. Glo. Cam.

230. *midnight.*] *midnight.* A Trumpet.
Qq.

230. [A trumpet within. Theob. After
good. line 232, Dyce.

Scene VI. Pope. After line 233, Han.
After line 235, Warb. Johns. Jen.

231. Enter...] After *Lodovico* line 234,
Cap. After line 235, Steev.

232. Two lines, Qq.

233–235. *I...him.*] Ff, Rowe, Pope,
Knt. *Something from* Venice *ſure*, (*ſure ;*
Q₂. *ſure* Q₃) *tis* Ludouico, *Come from the
Duke, and ſee your wife is with him.* Qq
et cet. (subs.). *I warrant you 'tis something come from Venice. Oh ! it is Lodovico
from the Duke. And ſee your wife is with
him.* Han.

234. *this, comes*] F₂, Knt. *this comes*
F₃F₄, Rowe, Pope.

222–229. WALKER (*Crit.* i, 11) thus divides these lines : ' I'll not expostulate with
her, lest her body | And beauty unprovide my mind again : | This night, Iago. | Do't
not with poison, strangle her in her bed, | Even the bed she hath contaminated. | Good,
good : | The justice of it pleases ; very good. | And, | For Cassio, let me be his under-
taker.' | But the latter part is very doubtful. DYCE (*Rem.* 241) anticipated Walker
as regards 225, 226. ' This speech,' says Dyce, ' (printed by all the modern editors as
prose) is, I suspect, two lines of blank verse.'

223. **vnprouide**] ROLFE : Used by Shakespeare only here.

233–235. According to WALKER (*Vers.* 65), ' warrant ' is a monosyllable, and (*Crit.*
i, 223) *something* is pronounced *something*. [The lines in the Qq are smoother.—
ED.]

Lodo. Saue you worthy Generall. 236

Othe. With all my heart Sir.

Lod. The Duke, and the Senators of Venice greet you.

Othe. I kiſſe the Inſtrument of their pleaſures.

Deſ. And what's the newes, good cozen *Lodouico*? 240

Iago. I am very glad to ſee you Signior:
Welcome to Cyprus.

Lod. I thanke you : how do's Lieutenant *Caſſio*?

Iago. Liues Sir,

Deſ. Cozen, there's falne betweene him, & my Lord, 245
An vnkind breach : but you ſhall make all well.

Othe. Are you ſure of that?

Deſ. My Lord?

Othe. This faile you not to do, as you will——

Lod. He did not call : he's buſie in the paper, 250
Is there deuiſion 'twixt my Lord, and *Caſſio*?

Deſ. A moſt vnhappy one : I would do much
T'attone|them for the loue I beare to *Caſſio*. 253

---

236. *Saue you*] *God ſave the* Q₁, Jen.
God save you Mal.
238. *the Senators*] Ff, Rowe, Pope,
Theob. Warb. Johns. *Senators* Qq, Han.
Cap. et seq.
[*Gives him a letter.* Rowe.
239. *pleaſures*] *good pleaſures* Han.
Cap.
[*Opens and peruses it.* Cap.
241, 242. One line, Q₁, Cap. *I...Wel-
come* One line, Ktly.
241. *very*] Om. Cap.

241. *Signior:*] *Seignior:*— Q₁Q₂.
243. *you*] *you, sir* Cap.
244. *Sir,*] *ſir.* Q₁, Ff.
247. [Aside. Theob. Warb.
248. *Lord?*] *Lord.* Qq.
249. [Reads. Theob. et seq.
will—] *will.*— Q₁Q₂.
251. *'twixt my*] *betweene thy* Q₁. *'twixt
thy* Cap. Steev. Mal. Var.
253. *T'attone*] Ff, Rowe+, Wh. i, Dyce
iii, Huds. *To attone* Qq et cet.

---

237. MALONE : This does not relate to what Lodovico has just said, but is spoken by
Othello while he salutes him. STEEVENS : I know not how the meaning of this speeh
can be ascertained, unless by reference to the salutation of Lodovico. The distracted
Othello, considering his own happiness at an end in this world, readily catches at the
idea of future felicity suggested by the words : ''Save you, general!' In his reply,
therefore, he must be supposed to welcome the pious wish expressed in his behalf. In
Meas. for Meas. II, ii, 157, two replies of Angelo, equally equivocal, are derived from
similar premises : '*Isab.* Heaven keep your honour safe! *Ang.* Amen!' Again, at
the conclusion of the same scene : '*Isab.* 'Save your honour! *Ang.* From thee : even
from thy virtue!' If it be urged that ''save you' only means *preserve you in this* world,
my sense of the passage will not be much weakened : as our protection, even '*here*,
upon this bank and shoal of time,' depends on the Almighty.

253. **attone**] JOHNSON : Make them *one;* reconcile them HENLEY : The verb is
fo med by the coalesceⁱce of the words *at one.*

Oth.   Fire, and brimeſtone.

Deſ.   My Lord.   255

Oth.   Are you wiſe?

Deſ.   What is he angrie?

Lod.   May be thLetter mou'd him.

For as I thinke, they do command him home,

Deputing *Caſsio* in his Gouernment.   260

Deſ.   Truſt me, I am glad on't.

Othe.   Indeed?

Deſ.   My Lord?

Othe.   I am glad to ſee you mad.

Deſ.   Why, ſweete *Othello*?   265

Othe.   Diuell.

254. *brimeſtone*] *Brimſtone* QqF$_3$F$_4$.

255. *Lord.*] *Lord!* Pope.

258. *May be*] '*May be*, Theob.

261. *Truſt me*] *By my troth* Q$_1$, Jen. Steev. Mal. Var. Coll. Sing. Ktly, Cam. *I am*] *I'm* Steev.'93.

262. *Indeed?*] *Indeed.* Qq.   *Indeed!* Rowe.

263. *Lord?*] *Lord.* Qq.   *Lord!* Rowe.

265. *Why*] *How* Qq, Jen. Mal. Steev Var. Coll. Sing. Wh. i, Ktly. *Othello?*] *Othello*— Glo.

266. [Striking her. Theob.

256. **Oth.**] FECHTER gives this speech to Iago, directing him to seize the arm of Othello across the table and stop him violently. Othello, 'rising furiously,' had just uttered line 254. [Much as I dislike the Porte St. Martin, or Bowery, style of Fechter's Othello, I must confess that here his suggestion strikes me as worthy of consideration. There is no small degree of propriety in representing the cool Iago as recalling Othello to his senses; and even if Iago's attempt be obtrusive or unmilitary, it is, perhaps, a less dramatic fault than what might seem the anticlimax of a sedate expostulation, addressed to Desdemona after the furious explosion, 'Fire and brimstone.'—ED.]

259. THEOBALD: Othello is but just arrived at Cyprus; the Senate could hardly yet have heard of the Ottoman fleet being scattered by the tempest; and Othello is at once remanded home, without any imputation suggested on his conduct, or any hint of his being employed in a more urgent Commission. Tis true, the deputation of Cassio in his room seems designed to heighten the Moor's resentment; but some probable reason should have been assigned for his recall. As to what Iago says afterwards, that Othello is to go to Mauritania, this is only a lie of his own invention to carry his point with Roderigo. LLOYD: The news that Othello is superseded recalls the impressions of the judicial deliberations of the Venetian Senate in the First Act, and seems to complete the proof of the infallible instincts of the statesmen.

264. COWDEN-CLARKE: We cannot help thinking that the author probably wrote, 'I am *mad* to see you *glad.*' But we have not ventured to alter the text; because Othello's reply, as it stands, allows the meaning to be understood of 'I am glad to see you unwise,' in reference to his having asked, 'Are you wise?'

265. **Othello?**] DANIEL (p. 79): This speech should be marked as exclamatory. It is one of the innumerable instances where the printers use the '?' for the '!'

266. That THEOBALD added the proper stage direction here there can be, unfortu-

 Def. I haue not deferu'd this.   267

 Lod. My Lord, this would not be beleeu'd in Venice,
Though I fhould fweare I faw't. 'Tis very much,
Make her amends : fhe weepes.   270

 Othe. Oh diuell, diuell :
If that the Earth could teeme with womans teares,
Each drop fhe falls, would proue a Crocodile :
Out of my fight.

 Def. I will not ftay to offend you.   275

 Lod. Truely obedient Lady :
I do befeech your Lordfhip call her backe.

 Othe. Miftris.   [331 *a*]

 Def. My Lord.

 Othe. What would you with her, Sir ?   280

 Lod. Who I, my Lord?

 Othe. I, you did wifh, that I would make her turne :
Sir, fhe can turne, and turne : and yet go on
And turne againe. And fhe can weepe, Sir, weepe.
And fhe's obedient : as you fay obedient.   285
Very obedient : proceed you in your teares.

---

269. *faw't*] *saw it* Steev. Mal. Var. Coll. Sing. Wh. i, Ktly, Del.

  much,] *much;* Theob. *much.* Johns.

272. *womans*] *womens* Qq.

273. *Crocodile*] *crocadile* Qq.

275. *to offend*] *t'offend* Pope+, Dyce iii, Huds.

 [Going. Rowe.

276. *Truely*] Ff, Rowe. *Truely an* Qq et cet.

282. *I,*] *I!* Rowe, Pope. *Ay,* Theob.

285. *fhe's*] *fhe is* Q₃.

---

nately, no doubt. This blow is the ineffaceable blot in Othello's history which leaves, upon me at least, a more painful impression than even the smothering. This, is simply the rage of a coward ; that, is an act of supposed justice. FECHTER strikes with the letter which he holds ; this is a shade better than the backhanded blow which SALVINI delivers full on those sweet lips, and which makes your own lips grow white as death, at the sight.—ED.

272. **teeme**] JOHNSON : If women's tears could impregnate the earth. By the doctrine of equivocal generation, new animals were supposed producible by new combinations of matter. See Bacon, vol. iii, p. 70, ed. 1740. MALONE : 'It is written,' says Bullokar, 'that the crocodile will weepe ouer a man's head when he hath deuoured the body, and then will eate vp the head two. Wherefore in Latine there is a proverbe, *Crocodili Lachrymæ*, crocodiles teares, to signifie such teares as are fained, and spent onely with intent to deceiue or doe harme.'—*Expositor*, 1621.

273. **falls**] For other instances of intransitive verbs used transitively, see ABBOTT, § 291.

286. **teares.**] WARNER suggests an interrogation-mark : 'What ! will you still continue to be a hypocrite by a display of this *well-painted passion ?*'

Concerning this Sir, (oh well-painted paſſion)   287
I am commanded home : get you away :
Ile ſend for you anon.   Sir I obey the Mandate,
And will returne to Venice.   Hence, auaunt :   290
Caſſio ſhall haue my Place.   And Sir, to night
I do entreat, that we may ſup together.
You are welcome Sir to Cyprus.
Goates, and Monkeys.   *Exit.*

     Lod.   Is this the Noble Moore, whom our full Senate   295
Call all in all ſufficient ? Is this the Nature
Whom Paſſion could not ſhake ? Whoſe ſolid vertue
The ſhot of Accident, nor dart of Chance   298

288. *home :*] *here :—* Q₁. *home :—* Q₂
Q₃. *home—* Rowe.
  289. *anon.*] *anon :—* Q₁Q₂. *anone :—*
Q₃. *anon—* Rowe.
    Mandate] *mandat* Qq.
  290. *Venice.*] *Venice :—* Qq.
    auaunt :] *auant*, Qq. *avant !—*
Rowe.
    [Exit Desd. Rowe.
  293, 294. One line, Qq, Cap. et seq.
  293. *You are*] *You're* Cap.
    Cyprus.] *Cypres,—* Qq.

Scene VII. Pope+, Jen.
  296. *all in all*] QqFf, Rowe, Jen. Glo.
Cam. Rlfe, Wh. ii. *all-in-all* Pope et cet.
    Is this the] *This the noble* Qq, Jen.
Steev. Mal. Var. Coll. Sing. Ktly. *this the*
Pope+, Cap. Coll. ii, Cam.
  297. *Whom*] *Which* Pope+.
  298. *Accident*] *accidents* Jen.
    nor] *or* Han.
    Chance] *Change* Warb. conj
Theob.

290. FECHTER : Othello, finding in the dispatch the name of 'Cassio,' which he
mutters, tears it violently, and turns in his rage to Desdemona, who shrinks affrighted.
  291. **Place**] STEEVENS : Perhaps this is addressed to Desdemona, who had just
expressed her joy on hearing Cassio was deputed in the room of her husband.
  294. MALONE : Iago, in III, iii, 464, alludes to 'goates' and 'monkeyes' where he
says that ocular proof of Cassio's and Desdemona's guilt was impossible. These words,
we may suppose, still ring in Othello's ears. STEEVENS : A reference to a distant scene
but ill agrees with the infuriation of Othello's mind. His fancy, haunted by still growing images of lewdness, would scarce have expressed his feelings in recollected phraseology. BOSWELL : They were words which he was not likely to have forgotten. FECH-
TER : Aside,—and as if comprising the whole world in a bitter sarcasm. As he goes out
he casts a last infuriated glance at Desdemona's door.
  296. **Is this the**] DYCE (*Rem.* 242) : The word *noble* in the Qq was undoubtedly
inserted by a mistake of the compositor, his eye having caught it from the preceding
line.
  298. THEOBALD : I cannot see, for my heart, the difference betwixt the shot of *accident* and dart of *chance*. The words, and things they imply, are purely synonymous ;
but that the Poet intended two different things seems plain from the *discretive* adverb.
Chance may afflict a man in some circumstances ; but other distresses are to be
accounted for from a different cause. I am persuaded our Author wrote : 'nor dart
of *change*.' In several other places he industriously puts these two words in opposition to each other. HEATH (p. 569) : There is no occasion for Theobald's alteration.

Could neither graze, nor pierce?

   Iago.   He is much chang'd.   300

   Lod.   Are his wits fafe? Is he not light of Braine?

   Iago.   He's that he is : I may not breath my cenfure.

What he might be : if what he might, he is not,

I would to heauen he were.

   Lod.   What? Strike his wife?   305

   Iago.   'Faith that was not fo well : yet would I knew

That ftroke would proue the worft.

   Lod.   Is it his vfe?

Or did the Letters, worke vpon his blood,

And new create his fault?   310

   Iago.   Alas, alas :

It is not honeftie in me to fpeake   312

299. *graze*] *raze* Warb. Theob. Han.
300. *chang'd*] *changed* Qq.
301. *light of*] *of light* Ff, Rowe, Pope.
302. *He's*] *He is* Steev. Mal. Var. Knt. *He's—* Sta.
   that] *what* Pope+.
   breath] F₂Q₂Q₃, Rowe, Cap. *breathe* Q₁F₃F₄, Pope et cet.
   cenfure.] *cenfure,* Qq. *censure* Jen. Cam. Wh. ii. *censure:* Coll. iii.
303. *be:*] Ff, Jen. Cam. Wh. ii. *be,* Qq.

be,— or *be,* Rowe et cet.
   303. *if what*] FfQ₂Q₃, Rowe+, Jen. Sing. Wh. Ktly, Glo. Cam. Huds. Rlfe. *if as* Q₁. *if, what* Cap. et cet.
   305. *What? ...wife?*] *What,...wife.* Qq. *What,...wife?* Ff. *What,...wife!* Rowe ii et seq.
   308. *Is it*] *It is* Q₃.
   310. *new create*] *new-create* Pope et seq.
   his] Ff, Rowe, Knt. *this* Qq et cet.

'Accident' is commonly used to denote personal calamities; 'chance,' to distinguish those in which we are involved in consequence of more general revolutions of fortune.

   299. graze] WARBURTON : 'Tis no commendation to the most solid virtue to be free from the attacks of fortune, but that it is so impenetrable as to suffer no impression. Now, to 'graze' signifies only *to touch the superficies* of anything. That is the attack of fortune; and by that virtue is try'd, but not discredited. We ought certainly, therefore, to read *raze*, i. e., neither lightly touch upon nor pierce into. The ignorant transcribers being acquainted with the phrase of a *bullet grazing*, and 'shot' being mention'd in the line before, they corrupted the true word. JOHNSON : To 'graze' is not merely to touch superficially, but to strike not directly, not so as to bury the body of the thing striking in the matter struck. Theobald trifles, as is usual. 'Accident and 'chance' may admit a subtle distinction ; 'accident' may be considered as the *act*, and 'chance' as the *power* or *agency* of Fortune; as, It was by *chance* that this *accident* befel me. At least, if we suppose all corrupt that is inaccurate, there will be no end of emendation. MALONE : I do not see the least ground for supposing any corruption. As 'pierce' relates to 'the dart of chance,' so 'graze' is referred to 'the shot of accident.'

   302, 303. That the punctuation of these lines is puzzling may be inferred from the fact that the Cambridge Editors, in 1866, did not follow their own punctuation of 1864 I do not think that the F₁ can be much improved.—ED.

   306, 307. yet . . . worst] PURNELL : Probably this is an aside.

What I haue feene, and knowne. You fhall obferue him,   313
And his owne courfes will deonte him fo,
That I may faue my fpeech : do but go after   315
And marke how he continues.
Lod. I am forry that I am deceiu'd in him.   *Exeunt.*

Scena Secunda.

Enter Othello, and Æmilia.

Othe. You haue feene nothing then *?*   3

313. *him*] Om. Q₂Q₃.
314. *deonte*] *denote* QqFf.
315. *after*] *after him* Q₂Q₃, Jen.
317. *I am*] *I'm* Pope+, Dyce iii, Huds.
    that I am] *that I was* Han.

1. Scena...] Scene VIII. Pope+, Jen.
An Apartment. Rowe.   A room in the
Castle. Mal.
3. *then ?*] *then.* Qq.

317. FECHTER : They go out as following Othello ; who, as soon as they are out of
sight, appears from the tapestry on the left, bringing forward Emilia, and speaks as continuing to interrogate. [Of course the Scene continues. Here begins BOOTH'S Second
Scene, Act Fourth.]   LLOYD : When this Scene, in which the fainting Othello appears
as the suffering and passive instrument of Iago, is left out in representation, the best
acting in the world, or to be in the world, will not preserve the Scene in the bed-chamber from having, to well-ordered sympathies, all the shockingness of a contrived, cold-
blooded murder.

Scena Secunda] MALONE : There are great difficulties in ascertaining the place
of this Scene.   Near the close of it, Iago says to Desdemona, ' Go *in*, and weep not,'
which would lead us to place it in the court before Othello's castle.   These words
may, indeed, be explained to mean, ' Go *into* the supper-room ' (though I do not think
that the meaning) ; but immediately afterwards Roderigo enters and converses with
Iago, which decisively ascertains the scene not to be in Othello's house ; for Roderigo,
who had given the first intelligence to Brabantio of his daughter's flight, and had
shortly afterwards drawn his sword on Othello and his partisans, certainly would not
take the liberty of walking into his house at pleasure.   On the other hand, what
Othello says early in the scene to Emilia, line 35, '*shut the door*,' and his subsequent
address to her as he goes out, as decisively point out a room in Othello's castle as the
place of the Scene, and compel us to place the several interlocutors there, however
inconsistent with Roderigo's entry and Iago's address to Desdemona.   The truth is,
that our poet and his audience, in this instance as in many others, were content, from
want of scenery, to consider the very same spot, at one and the same time, as the
outside and inside of a house.   COWDEN-CLARKE : But if it be remembered that a
portion of the mansion is used as a guard-room, it would be natural enough that Roderigo should seek Iago there, and, not finding him, should pursue his search in some of
the apartments adjacent ; moreover, it should be remembered that Roderigo is partially
disguised, and therefore not likely to be recognized as the man who gave Brabantio
intelligence of Othello's having married Desdemona.

3–5. WALKER (*Crit.* iii, 289) : Arrange, perhaps,—' You have seen nothing then ? Nor
ever heard, | Nor ever did suspect. Yes, you have seen | Cassio and she together.' BOOTH :
Othello should look her steadily in the eyes while questioning her with incredulous tones

Æmil.   Nor euer heard : nor euer did fufpeᵉt.

Othe.   Yes, you haue feene *Caffio,* and fhe together.   5

Æmi.   But then I faw no harme : and then I heard,
Each fyllable that breath made vp betweene them.

Othe.   What ? Did they neuer whifper ?

Æmil.   Neuer my Lord.

Othe.   Nor fend you out o'th'way ?   10

Æmil.   Neuer.

Othe.   To fetch her Fan, her Gloues, her Mask, nor no-

Æmil.   Neuer my Lord.   (thing ?

Othe.   That's ftrange.

Æmil.   I durft (my Lord) to wager, fhe is honeft :   15
Lay downe my Soule at ftake : If you thinke other,
Remoue your thought.   It doth abufe your bofome:
If any wretch haue put this in your head ,
Let Heauen requit it with the Serpents curfe,   19

5 *Yes,*] *Yes, and* Qq.
   fhe] *her* Pope+, Coll. Wh. i, Ktly.
7 *them*] *'em* Qq, Jen.
8. *What ?*] Ff, Rowe+. *What !* Coll.
Wh. i, Ktly. *What,* Qq et cet.
10. *Nor*] *Never* Q₃.
11. *Neuer*] *Never, my lord.* Ktly.
12. *her Gloues, her Mask*] *her mask,*

her gloues Qq.
12,13. *nothing ?*] *nothing.* Q₄. *nothing,*
Q₃.
18. *wretch*] *wreatch* Q₃.
   haue] *ha* Qq. *hath* F₃F₄, Rowe+,
Cap. Jen. Steev. Mal. Var. Sing. Ktly.
19. *Heauen*] *heauens* Qₓ.
   requit] *requite* QₓFf. *require* Q₂Q₃.

5. she] See ABBOTT, § 211, and to the instances there given of this use of 'she'
for *her,* add : 'the earth hath swallow'd all my hopes but *she,*' *Rom. & Jul.* I, ii, 14.
SCHMIDT also gives, '*she* that was thy Lucrece,' *R. of L.* 1682; 'I will detest myself
also as well as *she,*' *Meas. for Meas.* II, i, 76; '*She* should this Angelo have married,'
Ib. III, i, 221; 'but *she* I can hook to me,' *Wint. Tale,* II, iii, 6; 'for *she* that scorned
at me, now scorned of me,' *Rich. III:* IV, iv, 102. WHITE (ed. ii): Mere carelessness; not the 'grammar' of Shakespeare's time.

12. Fan] HALLIWELL quotes from Fairholt that the most ordinary fan used by
Venetian ladies was the flag or vane-shaped fan, moving round an upright handle.

12. nor] ELZE (*Notes,* &c. p. 189): Although this line, as far as my knowledge
goes, has never been queried, yet I cannot but think it faulty; I feel certain that
Shakespeare wrote, 'her mask, *her* nothing.' Compare *Cor.* II, ii, 81 : 'To hear my
nothings monster'd,' although it seems doubtful whether *nothing* is to be understood in
the same sense in these two passages. *Wint. Tale,* I, ii, 295 : 'nor nothing have these
nothings, If this be nothing.'

15. durst . . . to] For other instances of the insertion and omission of *to* before
the infinitive, see ABBOTT, § 349.

15-22. BOOTH : During this Othello is a little moved. He takes a chair from
behind the arras and sits.

16. other] For this adverbial use, equivalent to *otherwise,* see ABBOTT, § 12, p. 24.

For if ſhe be not honeſt, chaſte, and true,   [331 *b*]
There's no man happy.   The pureſt of their Wiues   21
Is foule as Slander.
   Othe.   Bid her come hither : go.   *Exit Æmilia.*
She ſaies enough : yet ſhe's a ſimple Baud
That cannot ſay as much.   This is a ſubtile Whore: 25
A Cloſſet Lockeand Key of Villanous Secrets,
And yet ſhe'le kneele, and pray ; I haue ſeene her do't.

                Enter Deſdemona, and Æmilia.

   Deſ.   My Lord,what is your will ?
   Othe.   Pray you Chucke come hither.   30
   Deſ.   What is your pleaſure ?
   Oth.   Let me ſee your eyes : looke in my face.
   Deſ.   What horrible Fancie's this ?
   Othe.   Some of your Function Miſtris :
Leaue Procreants alone, and ſhut the doore: 35
Cough, or cry hem ; if any bodycome :
Your Myſtery, your Myſtery : May diſpatch. *Exit   Æmi.*   37

---

21. *their Wiues*] *her Sex* Q₁, Jen.
23. Exit...] After *Slander* line 22, Qq.
25. *Whore*] *one* Han.
26. *Cloſſet Lockeand Key*] *cloſet, locke and key*, Qq. *cloſſet-lock and key* Rowe, Pope. *closet-lock-and-key* Mal. Steev.'93, Var. Knt, Coll. Sing. Dyce, Sta. Wh. i, Ktly, Del. Huds.
27. *I haue*] *I ha* Qq. *I've* Pope+, Dyce iii, Huds.
28. Enter...and] Reenter...with Cap.

Scene IX. Pope+, Jen.
30. *Pray you*] Ff, Rowe+, Knt, Sta. *Pray* Qq et cet.
32. *eyes : looke*] *eyes—looke* Qq, Jen. *eyes. Look* Johns.
32, 33. *looke...this ?*] As one line, Cap. Steev. et seq.
34. [To Æmilia. Han. Johns. et seq.
36. *Cough*] *Coffe* Qq.
37. *May*] *nay* QqFf. Exit...] Om. Q₂Q₃.

---

27. **pray**] HERAUD (p. 279): Emilia's supposed hypocrisy embitters Othello both against her and her calumniated mistress.   Perhaps, too, the poet intended his free-thoughted and noble Moor to entertain a customary protest against superstitious cere-monies ; and here we have a glimpse vouchsafed of his religious tendency.   It is in this furtive manner that Shakespeare always alludes to the theological aspects of his theme.   Never will he altogether neglect them ; but nowhere will he thoroughly unveil them.   Both political and religious prudence are evidently observed by Shakespeare in the treatment of all his subjects.   The spirit of the time compelled him to this reticence. [See HERAUD, III, iii, 67.]

   32. BOOTH : She looks up, but, frightened by his piercing glare, drops her eyes again.

   37. COWDEN-CLARKE : Othello taunts Emilia with having made a traffic in conni-vance at stolen meetings between Cassio and Desdemona, and now bids her give a specimen of her proficiency in her avocation.   HUDSON : As in mere wantonness of self-torture, Othello here fondles the most agonizing conceptions, and seeks a morbid

Def. Vpon my knee, what doth your fpeech import?　38
I vnderftand a Fury in your words.

Othe. Why ? What art thou ?　40

Def. Your wife my Lord : your true and loyall wife.

Othello. Come fweare it : damne thy felfe, leaft
being like one of Heauen, the diuells themfelues fhould
feare to ceaze thee. Therefore be double damn'd : fweare
thou art honeft.　45

Def. Heauen doth truely know it.

Othe. Heauen truely knowes, that thou art falfe as hell.

Def. To whom my Lord ?
With whom ? How am I falfe ?

Othe. Ah *Defdemon*, away, away, away.　50

Def. Alas the heauy day : why do you weepe ?
Am I the motiue of thefe teares my Lord ?
If happely you my Father do fufpect,
An Inftrument of this your calling backe,　54

38. *knee*] Ff, Rowe+, Knt. *knees* Qq
et cet.

　doth] *does* Qq.

39. *words.*] Ff, Rowe. *words, But not
the words.* (As a separate line) Qq et cet.
(*your words* Pope+).

40. *Why ?*] Ff, Rowe+, Jen. *Why*, Qq
et cet.

41, 42. *your true...felfe*] As one line,
Cap. Steev. Mal. *and...felfe* as one line,
Steev.'93, Var. Coll. Sing. Dyce, Wh. Glo.
Ktly, Rlfe.

42–45. *Come...honeft*] Verse, lines ending *felfe ... themfelues...damn'd ... honeft*
Qq, Cap. et seq. Three lines, ending *one...
thee...honeft* Rowe+, Jen.

42. *leaft*] *Left* Q₂Q₃. Om. Ff, Rowe.

44. *ceaze*] *ceafe* Qq. *ceife* F₃. *feize* F₄.
47. Dividing the line at *knowes* Rowe+.
48, 49. One line, Qq, or prose, Cap. et
seq.

50. *Ah* Defdemon,] Ff, Rowe, Pope,
Knt, Dyce, Sta. Del. Huds. *Ah, Defdemona !* Theob. Han. Warb. Johns. Jen.
O Desdemon Wh. i, Coll. iii. *O Defde*
mona, Qq et cet.

　[Sits. Booth.

51. *heauy*] *heavenly* Q₃.
52. *motiue*] *occafion* Qq, Jen. Steev.
Mal. Var. Coll. Sing. Ktly.

　thefe] *thofe* Qq, Jen.

　[Kneels beside him. Booth.

53. *happely*] F₂F₃. *happily* F₄, Rowe.
haply Qq et cet.

relief in thinking of Emilia as doing the office or mystery of a procuress. A master-
stroke of delineation.

38. RYMER (p. 130) : Here follows another storm of horrour and outrage against the
poor Chicken, his Wife. Some Drayman or drunken Tinker might possibly treat his
drab at this sort of rate, and mean no harm by it ; but for his excellency, a My Lord
General, to Serenade a Senator's Daughter with such a volly of scoundrel filthy Language, is sure the most absurd Maggot that ever bred from any Poets addle brain.

43. **Heauen**] COWDEN-CLARKE : These few words serve to paint Desdemona's look
of angelic purity, as well as the impression it creates, even on her husband's jaundiced
sight.

50. **Desdemon**] See III, i, 58.

Lay not your blame on me : if you haue loft him,   55
I haue loft him too.

    Othe. Had it pleas'd Heauen,
To try me with Affliction, had they rain'd
All kind of Sores, and Shames on my bare-head:
Steep'd me in pouertie to the very lippes,   60
Giuen to Captiuitie, me, and my vtmoft hopes,
I fhould haue found in fome place of my Soule
A drop of patience.   But alas, to make me
The fixed Figure for the time of Scorne,
To point his flow, and mouing finger at.   65

---

55. *you haue*] *you've* Pope.

55, 56. *loft...loft*] *left...left* Q₁.

56. *I*] *Why I* Qq, Rowe et seq.

57. *Heauen*] *heavens* Johns. Ktly.

58. *they*] Ff, Johns. Dyce, Glo. Cam. Ktly, Del. Rlfe, Wh. ii.   *it* Han.   *hè* Qq et cet.

    rain'd] *ram'd* Q₁.

59. *kin l*] Ff, Rowe+, Cap. Steev.'85. *kindes* Q₁Q₂.   *kinds* Q₃ et cet.

    on] *no* Q₃.

    bare-head] *bare head* QqF₄.

61. *Giuen*] *Give* Q₃.

    vtmoft] Om. Qq, Pope, Theob. Han. Warb.

62. *place*] *part* Qq, Cap. Mal. Steev.'93, Var. Coll. Sing. Ktly.

63. *drop*] *prop* Theob. conj. withdrawn.

64. *The fixed Figure*] Ff, Knt, Dyce i, Sta. Del.   *A fixed figure*, Qq et cet.

    for...of] *of...for* Hunter, Sta.

    time] *hand* Rowe+, Cap. Jen. Coll. ii.

65. *flow, and mouing*] Ff, Rowe, Pope, Theob. Han. Knt, Dyce i, Sta. Del.   *cold unmoving* Cartwright.   *flow vnmouing* Qq et cet.

    finger] *fingers* Q₁.

    at.] *at—* Rowe+, Knt, Sing. Dyce i, Sta. Del. Ktly.   *at;* Coll. Wh. i.   *at!* Glo. Cam. Dyce iii, Huds. Rlfe, Wh. ii.   *at— oh, oh,* Qq, Cap. Jen. Steev. Mal. Var. (*O! O!* in separate line, Cap. Steev. Mal. Var.).

---

57 et seq. BOOTH: With all the pathos you are capable of.

58. **they**] WALKER (*Crit.* ii, 110) shows that 'Heaven' is used as plural, by instances not alone from Shakespeare, but from Massinger, Beaumont and Fletcher, Shirley, Ford, and others. See *Ham.* III, iv, 173, 175.

64, 65. STEEVENS: We call the hour in which we are to die, 'the hour of death,'—the time when we are to be judged, 'the day of judgement,'—the instant when we suffer calamity, 'the moment of evil'; and why may we not distinguish the time which brings contempt along with it by the title of 'the time of scorn'? Othello takes his idea from a clock. 'To make me (says he) a fixed figure (on the dial of the world) for the hour of scorn to point and make a full stop at!' By '*slow unmoving* finger' our poet could have meant only 'so slow that its motion was imperceptible.' Thus, in *Ant. & Cleo.* III, iii, 22, the messenger, describing the gait of the demure Octavia, says, she creeps; Her motion and her station are as one,' i. e., she moved so slowly that she appeared as if she stood still. MALONE: Might not Shakespeare have written 'for *the scorn of time*,' &c., 1. e., the marked object for the contempt of all ages and all time? So in *Ham.* III, i, 70, 'the whips and scorns of time.' However, in support of the old copies it may be observed that 'scorn' is personified in the 88th *Sonnet:* 'And place my merit in the eye of scorn.' The epithet *unmoving* may likewise derive some

[64, 65. **time of Scorne . . . slow, and mouing finger.**]

support from the 104th *Sonnet*, in which this very thought is expressed : ' Ah! yet doth
beauty, like a dial-hand, Steal from his figure, and no pace perceiv'd ; So your sweet
hue, which methinks still doth stand, Hath motion, and mine eye may be deceiv'd.'
In the clocks of the last age there was, I think, in the middle of the dial-plate, a
figure of Time, which, I believe, was in our poet's thoughts when he wrote the passage
in the text.   The *finger* of the dial was the technical phrase.   So in *Albovine*, by
D'Avenant, 1629 : ' Even as the slow finger of the dial Doth in its motion circular
remove To distant figures.'   The reading of F₁, ' and moving,' certainly agrees with
the image presented, and its counterpart, better than *unmoving*, which can be applied
to a clock only by license of poetry (*not appearing to move*), and as applied to ' scorn '
has but little force, to say nothing of the superfluous epithet ' slow ' ; there needs no
ghost to tell us that that which is *unmoving* is ' slow.'   ' Slow ' implies some sort of
motion, however little it may be, and therefore appears to me to favour the reading
of F₁.   M. MASON : Perhaps we should read, ' *slowly moving* finger at.'   HUNTER (ii,
287) : I have little doubt that the particles ' of ' and ' for ' have changed places ; and
that, on the whole, the true reading is, ' The fixed figure of the time, for Scorn To
point his slow and moving finger at.'   It is of the nature of that feeling which leads a
person to suppose himself an object of scorn and derision, to think of himself also as
an object of universal attention.   Thus, Othello represents to himself that he shall be
' the fixed figure of the time,' the one object of public attention, every passer-by pointing at him the finger of scorn.   KNIGHT : There is certainly the most extraordinary
confusion in Malone's interpretation ; if the figure of Time be in the middle, the dial-
hand points from it, and not at it, and there is nothing more remarkable in one numeral
of a clock than in another.   But why are we to have the notion of a clock at all ?   There
is nothing whatever in the passage to warrant us in believing that the poet meant such
a metaphor.   By the ' fixed figure ' we understand, literally, a living man exposed to
public shame ; or an effigy exhibited to a multitude, as Butler has it, ' To punish in
effigie criminals.'   By ' the time ' we receive the same idea as in *Ham.* III, i, 70, where
' time ' is used distinctly to express the *times*, the *age ;* and it is used in the same way
by Ben Jonson : ' Oh, how I hate the monstrousness of time ! '   In the expression before
us, then, the ' time of scorn ' is *the age of scorn*.   The ' slow finger ' is the *pausing*
finger, pointing at the fixed figure ; but while it points it *moves in mockery*.   Shakespeare was probably thinking of the *Digito Monstrari* of the ancients, and it may be,
also, of the finger gesticulations of the Italians.   COLLIER (ed. ii) reads, with his
(MS.), ' *hand* of scorn ' and ' *slowly moving* finger ' ; but returns to the Qq in ed. iii.
WHITE (ed. i) ; ' Unmoving ' may mean either that the finger of scorn does not move
from its object, or that it moves so slowly that its motion is not perceived.   So in Lyly's
Euphues : ' You were ignorant of the practices, thinking the Diall stands still, because
you cannot perceive it to move.'—Sig. E e, ed. 1597.   ' The tongue of a Louer should
be like a poynt in a Dial, which though it goe none can see it going.'—*Ib.* Sig. Y, 3, b.
I was once in favour of Hunter's transposition.   But ' the time of scorn ' is a phrase
like ' the day of sorrow,' ' the hour of joy,' ' the age of progress.'   BAILEY (ii, 112)
makes ' the passage run ' thus : ' A fixèd figure for the time, *in* scorn, To point his *sly
and mocking* finger at, ——' and then adds : ' These epithets greatly enhance the
expression of Othello's horror of the ridicule of the world.'   KEIGHTLEY (*Exp.* 305) :
I see no need of changing the text of the Qto.   ' The Time of scorn ' is the scornful
age or world, a frequent sense of ' time ' ; and we should print, ' To point his slow—
unmoving finger at,' the latter term being a correction of the former.   DELIUS : ' Slow

Yet could I beare that too, well, very well :   66
But there where I haue garnerd vp my heart,
Where either I muſt liue, or beare no life,
The Fountaine from the which my currant runnes,
Or elſe dries vp : to be diſcarded thence,   70
Or keepe it as a Ceſterne, for foule Toades
To knot and gender in.   Turne thy complexion there :   72

---

67. *there where*] *there : where* Q₁. *there,*   71. *Toades*] *Taodes* Q₃.
where Q₂Q₃.   72. *in.*] *in :* Qq.
  69. *Fountaine*] *foundation* Q₃.   *there :*] *there,* Qq. *thence* Warb.
  71. *Ceſterne*] *ceſtern* F₃. *Ciſtern* F₄.   *there !* Steev. Mal. Var. Sing.

---

and moving,' according to Shakespeare's use of the copula, forms one idea [like ' by night and negligence,' I, i, 83]. MASSEY (*The Secret Drama*, &c. p. 257) : Othello cannot mean that he is made into a clock or a dial, but the *laughing-stock* of the time. R. H. LEGIS (*N. & Qu.* 5th, vi, 25), having appropriated Hunter's emendation, and changed 'slow' to *low*, asserts ' the image ' to be ' absolutely correct in both sense and artistic rectitude.' BULLOCH (p. 252) assumes that Othello ' had in view the scurrilous writers of pithy lampoons, those vile scoffing wits who ridiculed misfortune and enjoyed the degradation of others,' and therefore thus emended : ' A fixed figure for the *rhymer's* scorn, To point his *foul* unmoving finger at.' COWDEN-CLARKE : We take the ' time of scorn ' to be an impersonation of the scornful spirit of the epoch, and alluding to the image of Time which many ancient clocks bore. To our minds the combination ' slow, unmoving,' serves exactly to describe the hand of a dial, with its onward-stealing yet apparently still finger; so that, in every way, the idea of the clock is presented to the imagination by this passage. JOHN HUNTER : ' For the time of scorn ' is *for scorn's opportunity*. HUDSON : ' The time of scorn ' means, I think, the *age* of scorn, that is, the whole period during which scorn may be said to live. The ' fixed figure ' is simply the speaker himself. As to *slow unmoving*, the sense of it can be better felt than expressed; we can see the sneer darting from the inexorable finger, ever slowly moving *with* the object, never moving *from* it. ROLFE : That Shakespeare should be supposed to have written ' slow and moving,' shows what a poet may suffer at the hands of a pro-saic critic. The mistake in the Folio was doubtless one of the ear in transcribing the MS. [I am afraid that this may be classed among those readings to which Steevens elsewhere refers as having hitherto disunited the opinions of the learned, and which ' will continue to disunite them as long as England and Shakespeare have a name.'— ED.]

67. **garner'd**] JOHNSON : The ' garner' and the ' fountain' are improperly conjoined. ROLFE : But a *succession* of metaphors is not a fault, like the *mixing* of them. DELIUS : The word is finely chosen; to ' garner' is to store that on which life depends.

67–70. This passage Salvini adduces as proof that Othello was not jealous, but that his love was of a purely poetic nature, untainted with passion.

72–74. JOHNSON : At such an object do thou, *Patience*, thyself *change colour ;* at this do thou, even thou, *rosy cherub* as thou art, *look grim as hell*. The old editions and the new have it : ' *I* here look grim as hell.' *I* was written for *ay*, and not since corrected. [It was hard, very hard, for Dr Johnson to be just to Theobald, ' poor pid-dling Tibbald.' The foregoing note is substantially the same as Theobald's, and for

Patience, thou young and Rofe-lip'd Cherubin,   73
I heere looke grim as hell.

   Def.   I hope my Noble Lord efteemes me honeft.   75

   Othe.   Oh I, as Sommer Flyes are in the Shambles,
That quicken euen with blowing. Oh thou weed:
Who art fo louely faire, and fmell'ft fo fweete,
That the Senfe akes at thee,
Would thou had'ft neuer bin borne.   80

   Def.   Alas, what ignorant fin haue I committed?

---

73. *thou*] *thy* Qq.

74. *I heere*] *I here* QqF₃F₄, Rowe, Pope, Warb. *Ay, there* Theob. *There, there* Han. *Ay, here* Johns. Jen. *Ay, there,* Cap. et seq.

75. *my Noble*] *my* Ff.

76. *Sommer Flyes*] *fummers flies* Qq. *Summer-flies* Rowe, Pope, Han. *Shambles*] *fhamples* Q₃.

77–79. *Oh...thee*] Two lines, ending *faire...thee* Qq, Warb. Jen.

77. *thou weed:*] *thou blacke weede,* Qq, Jen. *thou bale weed* Warb. *thou base weed*

Heath.

78. *Who...faire,*] *Why...faire?* Qq, Warb. Jen.

  and fmell'ft] *Thou fmell'ft* Qq, Warb. Jen.

79, 80. *That...borne.*] One line, Cap. Steev. et seq.

79. *akes*] *askes* F₂. *asks* F₃F₄, Rowe i.

80. *thou had'ft*] *thad'ft* F₃. *thou'dft* F₄, Rowe.

  neuer] Ff, Rowe. *ne're* Qq. *ne'er* Pope et cet.

  bin] *been* F₃F₄.

---

over thirty years, when Dr Johnson wrote, Theobald's text had read *Ay* for *I.* To S. T. P. (*N. & Qu.* 5th, vi, 405), Dr Johnson's interpretation seems very forced and inapplicable. The suggestion is then ventured that 'possibly the words were meant as addressed to Desdemona, who first blushes at Othello's gross accusations. He then bursts out in admiration of her beauty; and then when she looks gravely indignant, challenges her to "look grim as hell."'   S. T. P. demands no verbal change, but apparently finds the passage cured by an heroic exhibition of exclamation-marks.—ED.]

73. **Cherubin**] It is not to be supposed that either Shakespeare, or his contemporaries, knew or cared that this is a Chaldee Plural. Cotgrave translates '*Cherubin*, a cherubin,' and it is probably through the French that the word was introduced into English.—ED.

76. **Sommer Flyes**] These words might serve, in F₄ as an approximate test, among the various copies, of priority in printing. The CAMBRIDGE EDITION notes between them a hyphen. In one of my copies of F₄, this hyphen is distinct and unmistakable; in the second, it is quite faint; in the third, it has vanished, leaving behind a warning to all not to lean too confidingly on the punctuation of the old texts.—ED.

79, 80. WALKER (*Crit.* iii, 289) reduces these two lines to the rhythmical standard by omitting 'That' and contracting 'thou hadst': 'The sense aches at thee,—Would th' hadst ne'er been born!'   [See Text. N.]

79. **akes**] Thus the verb is uniformly spelled throughout the Folio; one of the instances, we have had before in this play, III, iv, 168; the noun is spelled *ache*, and its plural is dissyllabic, from which it is reasonable to infer that the singular was pronounced *aatsh.* There 's an oversight in Ellis's *Early Eng. Pronunciation*, p. 930, where this present line is cited as an instance of a 'Monosyllabic Plural.'—ED.

Othe. Was this faire Paper ? This moſt goodly Booke   82
Made to write Whore vpon ? What commited,
Committed ? Oh, thou publicke Commoner,   [332 *a*]
I ſhould make very Forges of my cheekes,   85
That would to Cynders burne vp Modeſtie,
Did I but ſpeake thy deedes.   What commited ?
Heauen ſtoppes the Noſe at it, and the Moone winks :
The baudy winde that kiſſes all it meetes,
Is huſh'd within the hollow Myne of Earth   90

82. *Paper ?*] *paper*, Qq.
83. *vpon ?*] *on ?—* Q₁, Jen.
 What] *What*, Q₁. *what, what*
Theob. Warb. Han. Johns. Cap. *What*
sin Ktly.
84–87. Om. Q₁.
87. *Did*] *ſhould* Cap. (Corrected in
Errata).

87. *I but*] *but I* F₃F₄, Rowe, Pope,
Theob. Warb. Johns.
 deedes.] *deed.* Jen. Steev.'85.
 What] *What, what* Theob. Han.
Warb. Johns. Cap. *What sin* Ktly.
 commited] F₁. *committad* Q₃.
90. *hollow*] *hallow* Q₁.

82, 83. STEEVENS : Massinger has imitated this in *The Emperor of the East*, IV, v.
GIFFORD, in a note (p. 321) to this passage in Massinger, observes that there are several other short passages in that same scene copied from *Othello*.   ROLFE : For the
metaphor, compare *King John*, II, i, 485; *Rom. & Jul.* I, iii, 87; III, ii, 83; *R. of
L.* 615, 1253, &c.

83. **commited**] MALONE : This word, in Shakespeare's time, besides its general
signification, seems to have been applied particularly to unlawful acts of love.   [Might
not this have been due to its use in the Seventh Commandment ?—ED.]   KNIGHT :
Othello, indignant at Desdemona's question, with a mocking fury repeats it four
times,—' what committed ? '   The commentators have changed it into an interjectional
phrase, telling us that ' committed ' had a peculiar signification.   The plain and natural
interpretation seems the true one.   DEIGHTON agrees with Knight; ' Othello repeats
interrogatively, over and over again, the last word of Desdemona's speech, which is
here used in its ordinary sense.'

84. BOOTH : Not too violently,—more of indignation than anger.

85. **my**] WHITE (ed. i) : I suspect that Shakespeare wrote *thy*.   The misprint is
common.   Othello has already, when with Iago, spoken Desdemona's imputed deeds
very plainly ; and would Shakespeare have forgotten that Othello's cheeks were too
dark to show a blush ? or, still more, would he have referred the blush in such a case
to the countenance of the man when the woman was present ?   In *Tit. And.* IV, ii,
Aaron the Moor speaks of Chiron's ' beauty ' as a ' treacherous hue, that will *betray
with blushing*,' whereas his own blackamoor child is a ' lad fram'd of *another leer*.'
DYCE (ed. iii) : But, as LETTSOM observes, ' Othello is speaking not of blushes, but of
heat.'   WHITE (ed. ii) : A doubtful reading.   Shakespeare surely may have written
' *thy* cheeks.'   Not only was it Desdemona's part to flush, but Othello's cheek was
black.

89. **baudy**] MALONE : So in *Mer. of Ven.* II, vi, 16.   HALLIWELL : The wind is
more elegantly alluded to in *Hen. V*, as the ' chartered libertine.'   ROLFE : So, *Mid.
N. D.* II, i, 129.

And will not hear't.　What commited *?*　　　91
　Def.　By Heauen you do me wrong.
　Othe.　Are not you a Strumpet?
　Def.　No, as I am a Chriftian.
If to preferue this veffell for my Lord,　　　95
From any other foule vnlawfull touch
Be not to be a Strumpet, I am none.
　Othe.　What, not a Whore?
　Def.　No, as I fhall be fau'd.
　Othe.　Is't poffible?　　　　100
　Def.　Oh Heauen forgiue vs.
　Othe.　I cry you mercy then.
I tooke you for that cunning Whore of Venice,
That married with *Othello.*　You Miftris,
　　　　　Enter Æmilia.　　　105
That haue the office oppofite to Saint *Peter,*
And keepes the gate of hell.　You, you : I you.　107

---

91. *hear't.*] *hear't :—* Qq.　*hear of it*
Ktly.　*hear it* Steev. et seq.
　What commited ?] Ff, Rowe, Pope,
Knt.　*what committed,—impudent ſtrum-
pet.* Qq.　*Committed ?—impudent strumpet !* Han.　*Committed ! what committed !
Impudent strumpet !* Cap.　*What sin committed ! Impudent strumpet !* Ktly.　*What
committed ?—Impudent strumpet !* Theob.
et cet.
　Reading *Impudent strumpet* as if of
ᴌne 92, Cap. Coll. et seq.
　96. *other*] *hated* Q₁, Jen. Wh. i.
　99. *fau'd.*] *faued.* Enter *Emillia* Q₁.
faued. Q₂Q₃.
　100. *Is't*] *Is it* Steev. Mal. Var. Coll.
Wh. i, Del.
　101. *forgiue vs*] *forgiueneffe* Q₁.
　102. *mercy then.*] *mercy,* Q₁.

103. *Venice,*] *Venice,* Enter *Emillia.*
Q₂Q₃.
　104. *Othello.　You*] *Othello.* [Raising
his voice] *You* Glo. Cam. Wh. ii.
　Scene X. Pope +, Jen.
　　You Miſtris,] *Come you, mistress,*
Han.　*You, mistress, there !* Cap.　*You,
misteress,* Ktly.
　105. Enter...] After *you.* line 107, Knt,
Coll. iii.　After *hell* line 107, Dyce, Sta.
Wh. Glo. Cam. Del.
　106. *Saint* Peter] *S. Peter* Qq.　*Saint
Peter's* Ktly.
　107. *keepes*] QqF₂.　*keeps* F₃F₄.　*keeþ*
Rowe et cet.
　gate of] *gates in* Qq.
　hell.] *hell,* Q₁.　*hell ;* Q₂Q₃.
　You, you : I you.] *I, you, you, you,*
Q₁.　*you, you, I, you* Q₂Q₃.　*you, you ! Ay
you !* Rowe et seq.

---

95. **vessell**] UPTON (p. 219): Thus, in *1 Thess.* iv, 4 : ' To possess his vessel in
sanctification.'

104. **Mistris**] WALKER (*Vers.* 48): That is, ' mist(e)ress.'　[See Keightley, Text.
N., and II, ii, 242.]

106. **opposite**] HUDSON: The opposition is between Emilia, as keeper of the gate
of Hell, and Saint Peter, as keeper of the gate of Heaven.　The sense, therefore,
requires that the special emphasis, if there be any, should be laid on ' opposite.'

107. BOOTH : Desdemona sinks to the floor, whence Emilia, at line 111, raises her.

We haue done our courſe : there's money for your paines :　108
I pray you turne the key, and keepe our counſaile.　*Exit.*

Æmil.　Alas, what do's this Gentleman conceiue?　110
How do you Madam ? how do you my good Lady?

Def.　Faith, halfe a ſleepe.

Æmi.　Good Madam,
What's the matter with my Lord?

Def.　With who?　115

Æmil.　Why, with my Lord, Madam ?

Def.　Who is thy Lord?

Æmil.　He that is yours, ſweet Lady.

Def.　I haue none : do not talke to me, *Æmilia,*
I cannot weepe : nor anſweres haue I none,　120
But what ſhould go by water.　Prythee to night,
Lay on my bed my wedding ſheetes, remember,
And call thy husband hither.

Æmil.　Heere's a change indeed.　*Exit.*

Def.　'Tis meete I ſhould be vs'd ſo : very meete.　125
How haue I bin behau'd, that he might ſticke
The ſmall'ſt opinion on my leaſt miſvſe ?　127

108. *We haue*] *We ha* Qq. *We've* Dyce iii.

113, 114. One line, Qq, Rowe et seq.

115. *who*] *whom* Ff, Rowe +, Jen. Coll. Ktly. *whom, Æmilia ?* Han.

116. *Why,*] Om. Cap. Steev.'85.

117, 118. Om. Q₁.

119. *I haue*] *I ha* Qq.

120. *anſweres*] F₂. *anſwers* F₃F₄, Rowe. *anſwer* Qq et cet.

121. *Prythee*] *Pray* Pope +.

122. *my wedding*] *our wedding* Q₁, Jen.

124. *Heere's*] *Here is* Qq, Cap. Jen. Steev. Mal. Var. Coll. Sing. Ktly.

125. *vs'd*] *vſde* Q₁Q₂. *uſed* Q₃. *very meete.*] *very well ;* Q₁.

127. *ſmall'ſt*] *ſmalleſt* Q₁, Rowe i, Jen. *on*] *of* Pope, Theob. Han. Warb. *leaſt miſvſe ?*] *greateſt abuſe* Q₁, Jen. *great'ſt abuse* Steev. Mal. Rann. Var. Sta. Dyce iii, Huds. *least misdeed* Coll. (MS).

---

108. **paines**] HUDSON quotes WHITE : Othello, who in his relations towards women is one of the most delicate and sensitive of men, in the bitterness of his soul *pays* his wife's own maid as he leaves the former's bed-chamber; not either to reward or to offend Emilia, but that he may torment his own soul by carrying out his supposition to its most revolting consequences.　FECHTER : He throws a purse on the table and exit. BOOTH : Don't use a purse, it is absurd, and 'tis not likely that Iago would pass it by ; he confesses himself a thief in his dealings with Roderigo, and he would never leave a purse of money unheeded on the floor.　This purse once tempted me so annoyingly that I picked it up, and very properly was reproved for it,—but I could not help it.

121. **water**] HUDSON : That is, *be expressed by tears.*　Surely a conceit quite out of place.　Laertes, in *Ham.* IV, iv, vents a similar one on learning that his sister is drowned.

127. **misvse**] SINGER : 'On' must be understood to signify *of.*　The ſense appears

Enter Iago, and Æmilia.   128

Iago.   What is your pleaſure Madam?
How is't with you?   130
   Deſ.   I cannot tell : thoſe that do teach yong **Babes**
Do it with gentle meanes, and eaſie taskes.
He might haue chid me ſo : for in good faith
I am a Child to chiding.
   Iago.   What is the matter Lady?   135
   Æmil.   Alas (*Iago*) my Lord hath ſo bewhor'd her,
Throwne ſuch diſpight, and heauy termes vpon her
That true hearts cannot beare it.
   Deſ.   Am I that name, *Iago?*
   Iago.   What name, (faire Lady?)   140
   Deſ.   Such as ſhe ſaid my Lord did ſay I was.
   Æmil.   He call'd her whore : a Begger in his drinke :
Could not haue laid ſuch termes vpon his Callet.   143

Scene XI. Pope+, Jen.
129, 130. One line, Pope et seq.
130. *is't*] *is it* Steev. Mal. Var. Coll. Wh. i.
131. *yong*] *young* Qq. *your* Ff, Rowe, Pope, Theob. Han. Warb.
133. *haue*] *ha* Qq.
134. *to*] *at* Q₁, Jen.
135. *What is*] *What's* F₄, Rowe, Pope, Theob. Warb. Johns. Steev.'93, Var. Coll. Sing. Dyce, Sta. Wh. Glo. Cam. Ktly, Del.

138. *That*] Ff, Rowe+, Knt. *As* Qq et cet.
   beare it] Ff, Rowe+, Knt. *beare* Qq et cet.
141. *ſaid*] Ff, Rowe+, Jen. Knt, Sta *ſayes* Qq et cet.
143. *laid*] *layed* Q₁Q₂. *laied* Q₃.
   ſuch] *worse* Cap. conj.
   Callet] *callat* Coll. Dyce, Sta. Wh. Glo. Cam. Del. Rlfe.

to be : ' How have I behaved that he can attach the smallest notion *of* the least mis-conduct?' HUDSON [adopting Q₁]: A very harsh and awkward expression, but mean-ing, ' What have I been doing, that upon my worst act he should fasten the slightest imputation of crime?' We cannot take 'on' here as equivalent to *of*, for the connec-tion is 'stick on' and not 'opinion on'; so that 'least' of F₁ does not give the right sense. ['How have I been behaved that he could find the smallest possible fault with my smallest possible misdeed?' a paraphrase which is substantially the same as Cowden-Clarke's.—ED.]

136–138. COWDEN-CLARKE: This shows that Emilia, among her other objection-able characteristics, is a listener,—a mean listener at doors.

139. **that name**] MRS JAMESON (ii, 42): A stroke of consummate delicacy, sur-prising, when we remember the latitude of expression prevailing in Shakespeare's time, and which he allowed his other women generally. So completely did Shakespeare enter into the angelic refinement of the character.

143. **Callet**] GIFFORD (Note in Jonson's *Volpone*, IV, i, p. 277): *Callet, callat,* or *calot* is used by all our old writers for a strumpet of the basest kind. It is derived, as Urry observes, from *calote*, Fr., a ſort of cap once worn by country-girls; and, like a

Iago.   Why did he fo?

Def.   I do not know : I am fure I am none fuch.   145

Iago.   Do not weepe, do not weepe : alas the day.

Æmil.   Hath fhe forfooke fo many Noble Matches?
Her Father? And her Country? And her Friends?
To be call'd Whore? Would it not make one weepe?   [332 *b*]

Def.   It is my wretched Fortune.   150

Iago.   Befhrew him for't :
How comes this Tricke vpon him?

Def.   Nay, Heauen doth know.

Æmi.   I will be hang'd, if fome eternall Villaine,
Some bufie and infinuating Rogue,   155
Some cogging, cozening Slaue, to get fome Office,

---

145. *I am fure*] *I'm sure* Pope+, Dyce iii.

147. *Hath*] *Has* Qq, Cap. Mal. Steev. '93, Var. Knt, Coll. Sing. Ktly.

148. *And her Friends*] *all her friends* Q₁.

151, 152. One line, Qq, Rowe+, Jen.

151. *for't*] *for it* Qq, Jen. Steev. Mal. Var. Coll. Wh. i.

---

hundred other terms of this nature, from designating poverty or meanness, finally came, by no unnatural progress, to denote depravity and vice.   DYCE (*Gloss.*) cites Cotgrave : ' *Goguenelle*, A fained title, or tearme, for a wench; like our Gixie, Callet, Minx, &c.' WEDGWOOD (s. v. ed. ii) : Probably an unmeasured use of the tongue is the leading idea.   NE. *to callet*, to rail, or scold; *calleting*, pert, saucy, gossiping.   [I do not find it in SKEAT.—ED.]

150. Othello echoes this with ' Who can control his fate ?' V, ii, 328.—ED.

154. FECHTER : Suspiciously eyeing Iago.   COWDEN-CLARKE: Emilia, by no means, here refers to her husband, but to some one who, as she thinks, has misled both Iago and Othello.   She has before told the Moor, ' If any wretch have put this in your head, let Heaven requite it with the serpent's curse.'   Her suspicion never for an instant falls on her own husband.   [Witness her incredulity, in the last Scene, when Othello tells her it was ' her husband ' who first told him Desdemona was false to wedlock.—ED.] BOOTH : This is spoken without intended reference to Iago.

154. **eternall**] WALKER (*Crit.* i, 62) cites this passage and *Ham.* I, v, 21 ; V, ii, 352, and *Jul. Cæs.* IV, ii, 160, as instances of the inaccurate use by Shakespeare of ' eternal ' for *infernal*.   See also, to the same effect, ABBOTT, *Introduction*, p. 16. [Walker's instances from *Hamlet* may be well chosen ; in ' this eternal blazon,' and in ' what feast is toward in thine eternal cell,' Shakespeare may have used the word inaccurately ; it is also possible that the error is the printer's.   But here in *Othello* and in *Jul. Cæs.* (' There was a Brutus once, that would have brook'd Th' eternal devil,' &c.) the supposition of inaccuracy is, I think, far from probable.   Walker himself says that the phrase ' eternal villain ' seems to be still in use among the common people, and antici- pates the thought which rises in every American mind, when he adds : ' I need scarcely notice the Yankee '*tarnal*.'   When needs must, nowadays, we speak of our friends as ' everlasting fools ' ; I think, therefore, that here Emilia means what she says.—ED.]

156. **Slaue**] WALKER (*Crit.* ii, 307) : Does ' slave ' here mean anything more than

Haue not deuis'd this Slander : I will be hang'd elſe.   157

   Iago.   Fie, there is no ſuch man : it is impoſſible.

   Deſ.   If any ſuch there be, Heauen pardon him.

   Æmil.   A halter pardon him :   160

And hell gnaw his bones.

Why ſhould he call her Whore ?

Who keepes her companie ?

What Place ? What Time ?

What Forme ? What liklyhood ?   165

The Moore's abus'd by ſome moſt villanous Knaue,

Some baſe notorious Knaue, ſome ſcuruy Fellow.

Oh Heauens, that ſuch companions thou'd'ſt vnfold,

And put in euery honeſt hand a whip

To laſh the Raſcalls naked through the world,   170

Euen from the Eaſt to th'Weſt.

   Iago.   Speake within doore.

   Æmil.   Oh fie vpon them : ſome ſuch Squire he was

That turn'd your wit, the ſeamy-ſide without,   174

---

157. *Haue*] *Has* Ff, Rowe+, Cap.
Steev.'85.

    deuis'd] *deuiſde* Q₁Q₂. *deviſed*
Q₃.

    I will] Ff, Rowe, Knt. *I'le* Q₁.
Ile Q₂Q₃. *I'll* Pope et cet.

158. *Fie*] Separate line, Dyce iii.

159. *there be*] *there are* Q₂Q₃.

160–165. Three lines, Qq, Rowe et seq.

166. *moſt villanous*] *outragious* Q₁.

168. *Oh Heauens*] Ff, Rowe i. *O heauen*
Qq et cet.

    companions] *companion* Han.
Cap.

168. *thou'd'ſt*] *thoudſt* Q₁Q₂. *ſhouldſt*
Q₃.

170. *Raſcalls*] *raſcall* QqFf, Rowe+,
Cap. Mal. Steev.'93, Var. Sing. Coll. iii.

171. *Euen*] *Ev'n* Pope+.

    to th'] Ff, Rowe+, Wh. i.   *to'th*
Q₂Q₃.   *to the* Q₁ et cet.

172. *doore*] *dores* Qq, Jen.

173. *them*] *him* Qq, Han. Cap. Steev.
Mal. Var. Sing.

    Squire] *'Squire* F₄, Rowe+, Jen

173–175. *ſome...Moore*] Aside to Iago
Sta.

174. *ſeamy-ſide*] *ſeamy ſide* QqF₃F₄.

---

villain, abandoned wretch ?   This use of ' slave' (compare the Italian *cattivo*, whence
our *caitiff*) is frequent in old plays.

   158. WALKER (*Vers.* 272): Arrange and write, perhaps,—' Fie | There's no such
man, it is impossible.'   [DYCE (ed. iii) adopted this.]   BOOTH : Wait until the effect
of her speech is past.   FECHTER : Iago has not even frowned, but looks at her with
cold self-possession.

   167. **notorious**] JOHNSON : For *gross*, not in its proper meaning for *known*.

   168. **companions**] MALONE : Used as a word of contempt, in the same sense as
fellow is at this day.

   172. JOHNSON : Do not clamour so as to be heard beyond the house.   BOOTH : Goes
to her and speaks low.

   174. **seamy-side**] JOHNSON : That is, inside out.   STEEVENS : Compare II, ii, 69 :
' Whom Love hath turn'd almost the wrong side out.'

And made you to fufpeჭt me with the Moore.   175

   Iago.   You are a Foole : go too.

   Def.   Alas *Iago,*

What fhall I do to win my Lord againe ?

Good Friend, go to him : for by this light of Heauen,

I know not how I loft him. Heere I kneele :   180

If ere my will did trefpaffe 'gainft his Loue,

Either in difcourfe of thought, or aჭtuall deed,

Or that mine Eyes, mine Eares, or any Sence   183

---

176. [Aside to Emilia. Sta.
    too] *to* QqFf.
177. *Alas*] Ff, Rowe+, Cap. Knt,
Dyce, Sta. Wh. i, Coll. iii. *O good* Qq et
cet.
179. *for*] Om. Pope+.

180. Two lines, Q₂Q₃.
180–193. *Heere…me*] Om. Q₁.
180. [kneeling. Rowe+, Cap. Jen.
182. *Either*] *Or* Pope+.
    of thought] *or thought* Q₂Q₃,
Pope+, Jen. Steev.'85, Huds.

---

176. BOOTH : Angrily, but *sotto voce.*

181. BOOTH : Iago replaces chair behind the arras.

182. **discourse of thought**] This phrase is no easier of comprehension than the similar phrase in *Ham.* I, ii, 150, to which MALONE refers : ' discourse of reason.' The precise meaning which our ancestors attached to ' discourse ' it is now very difficult to determine, as Gifford says in a note, cited in this edition, on the passage in *Hamlet.* Johnson, in his *Dict.*, defines it as ' the act of the understanding, by which it passes from premises to consequences,' which is little else than a paraphrase of his own illustration from Glanville, which reads : ' The third act of the mind is that which connects propo-sitions, and deduceth conclusions from them ; and this the schools call *discourse ;* and we shall not miscall it, if we name it reason.' But that it was not mere ' reason,' as Shakespeare used it, is clear from the phrase ' discourse of reason,' nor that it was merely ' the reasoning faculty,' as some have defined it, as is shown by this phrase in *Othello,* ' the discourse of thought.' May it not be that in the few instances where Shakespeare uses it in reference to the operations of the mind (I speak with great hesitation) that its Latin origin was uppermost in his thought, vaguely, perhaps, but still operative, espe-cially if, as is not unlikely, he pronounced the word ' discoorse,' *Hibernicè* ? This would lead to SINGER's paraphrase, *discursive range,* which, although somewhat tauto-logical, is, perhaps, as satisfactory as any that has been yet proposed. Why may we not omit the *discursive,* and say that ' discourse when applied to the mind means the *range ?* ' Thus, ' a beast that wants *the range* of reason ' ; ' he that made us with so large *a range,* looking before and after.' This, too, will explain what Guildenstern says to Hamlet (III, ii, 320), ' put your discourse into some frame,' i. e., ' restrict the range of your fancies.' And here, too, in *Othello,* Desdemona says, ' either in range of thought, or actual deed.'—ED. STEEVENS gives a note, signed ' C,' to the effect that the Qq are right, and that Desdemona refers to the three ways of committing sin, men-tioned in the Catholic Catechisms [and in our Liturgy, adds Steevens], viz. : in *thought, word,* and *deed.* VERPLANCK and HUDSON prefer the Qq. The former says : ' The *on* of the Qq appears to me more probable in itself, because more impressive, and more in unison with the particularity of Desdemona's asseveration of innocence in every possi-ble manner.'

Delighted them : or any other Forme.

Or that I do not yet, and euer did, 185

And euer will, (though he do ſhake me off

To beggerly diuorcement) Loue him deerely,

Comfort forſweare me.   Vnkindneſſe may do much,

And his vnkindneſſe may defeat my life,

But neuer taynt my Loue.   I cannot ſay Whore, 190

It do's abhorre me now I ſpeake the word,

To do the Act, that might the addition earne,

Not the worlds Maſſe of vanitie could make me.

   Iago.   I pray you be content : 'tis but his humour :

The buſineſſe of the State do's him offence. 195

   Deſ.   If 'twere no other.

   Iago.   It is but ſo, I warrant,

Hearke how theſe Inſtruments ſummon to ſupper :

The Meſſengers of Venice ſtaies the meate, 199

---

184. *them : or*] Ff. *them on* Rowe+.
them in Q₂Q₃ et cet.
    Forme.] *forme;* Q₂Q₃. *form :*
F₃F₄.
   188. *forſweare me.*] *for ſware me* Q₃.
   190. *cannot*] *can't* Pope+, Cap.
   191. *do's*] *doth* Q₂Q₃.
   192. *the addition*] *th' addition* Q₂Q₃,
Pope+, Jen. Dyce iii.
   195. *offence.*] Ff, Rowe. *offence, And
he does chide with you* Qq et cet.
   196. *'twere*] *t'ware* Q₃.
    other.] QqFf, Rowe. *other!* Knt,
Sta. Wh. i. *other—* Pope et cet.

197. *It is*] Ff, Rowe+, Cap. Steev. Mal.
Var. Knt, Sing. Sta. Ktly. *Tis* Qq et cet.
   warrant,] *warrant you*, Qq, Jen.
Steev. Mal. Var. Sing. Ktly.
    [Trumpets. Rowe.
   198. *ſummon*] *ſummon you* Qq, Jen.
   199. *The...meate*] *And the great Meſ-
ſengers* of Venice *ſtay*, Q₁, Johns. Jen.
Steev. Mal. Var. Sing. *The meate, great
Meſſengers* of Venice *ſtay;* Q₂Q₃.
    Meſſengers] *Meſſenger* Ff, Rowe,
Pope, Theob. Han. Warb. Cap.
    ſtaies the meate] *ſtayes the meat*
F₃F₄, Ktly. *stay the meat* Knt et seq.

---

191. **abhorre**] ROLFE: It is abhorrent to me, it fills me with horror; the only
instance of this sense in Shakespeare.   ['Here hung those lippes . . . . now they
abhorre me,' *Ham.* Q₁, line 1946.—ED.]

193. **vanitie**] WHITE (ed. ii): Splendor, finery, as in 'Vanity Fair.'

194. BOOTH : Iago assists Desdemona to rise.

195, 196. In the line here regained from the Qq, many editors, following STEEVENS
and MALONE, note that 'chide with' is the phraseology of the time, and adduce examples.

199. KNIGHT : Steevens calls the reading of the Folio 'poor,' but its precision and
familiarity make it more dramatic and characteristic. WHITE (ed. ii) : 'Stay the meat,'
that is, for the meat.   In some parts of England a visitor is still invited to 'stay dinner.'
Vice-regal persons and grandees had, and in some courts still have, all their movements
announced by trumpets.   [Either 'Messengers' is wrongly in the Plural or 'staies'
is wrongly in the Singular, and at first sight the 'extravagant and erring' *s* might be
thought to come under WALKER'S *Article* (cited at I, i, 31), but I am inclined to think
that 'staies' is in the Singular by attraction with 'Venice.'—ED.]

Go in, and weepe not : all things ſhall be well.   200
                          Exeunt Deſdemona and Æmilia.

                          Enter Rodorigo.

How now *Rodorigo ?*

Rod.   I do not finde
That thou deal'ſt iuſtly with me.

Iago.   What in the contrarie ?   205

Rodori.   Euery day thou dafts me with ſome deuiſe
Iago, and rather, as it ſeemes to me now, keep'ſt from
me all conueniencie, then ſupplieſt me with the leaſt aduantage of hope : I will indeed no longer endure it.   Nor   210
am I yet perſwaded to put vp in peace, what already I
haue fooliſhly ſuffred.

Iago.   Will you heare me *Rodorigo ?*
                                                        213
Rodori.   I haue heard too much ∶ and your words and [333 *a*]

---

200. *well*] *will* Q₃.
201. Exeunt...] Exit women. Qq.
Scene XII. Pope+, Jen.   Scene III.
Booth.   Scene II. Fechter.
204, 205. One line, Qq, Pope et seq.
205. *deal'ſt*] *dealſt* Qq.   *dealest* Dyce,
Glo. Cam. Rlfe.
207–212. *Euery...ſuffred*] Six lines,
verse, ending *Iago...from me,...leaſt...it
...already...ſuffred.* Q₁.
207. *dafts*] Knt.   *dofftſt* Qq. *dofts* Ff.
doffeſt Q'81.   *doft'ſt* Rowe+, Jen. Cap.
daff'ſt Coll. Sta. Wh. Del. Huds.   *daffest*
Dyce, Glo. Cam. Rlfe.   *doff'ſt* Han. et
cet.

207. *deuiſe*] *device* Ff.
208. *me now,*] *me, thou* Q₁.
       keep'ſt] *keepeſt* Q₁.   *kee'pſt* Q₂Q₃.
209. *then*] *thou* F₄.   *that* Warb. *than*
Rowe.
212. *ſuffred*] *ſufferd* Q₁.   *ſuffered* Q₂
Q₃.   *ſuffer'd* F₃F₄.
214, 215. Two lines, the first ending
words, Q₁.   Three, ending *much...per-
formance...together* Q₂Q₃.
214. *I*] Ff, Rowe, Pope, Han. Johns.
Knt.   *Sir, I* Q₂Q₃, Cap.   *Faith I* Q₁ et cet.
       and your] Ff, Rowe+, Cap. Knt.
for your Qq et cet.

---

200. BOOTH : Sometimes the scene ends here, in which case, exit Iago with an
angry glance at Emilia.

203. BOOTH : They run against each other,—Iago somewhat embarrassed. Roderigo refuses his proffered hand, and while the former is speaking 207 et seq. Iago is
somewhat nervous.

207. **Every day**] COWDEN-CLARKE : Effect of 'long time' given; though they
have been in Cyprus, according to 'short time,' but one day.

207. **dafts**] An instance, under WALKER'S *Article* (*Crit.* ii, 128), on the substitution of *s* for *st* in the second person singular of the verb.   See II, ii, 201.

209. **aduantage of hope**] COLLIER (ed. ii) : Ought we not to read, 'the least
hope of advantage'?   [If Collier can thus ask, should he not have been contented
with merely converting 'the time of scorn,' line 64 of this scene, into 'the scorn of
time,' and not have changed it to the '*hand* of scorn'?   The two phrases are parallel,
if we choose to make them so; but it is not necessary.   'Advantage of hope' is the

Performances are no kin together.   215

    Iago.   You charge me moſt vniuſtly.

    Rodo.   With naught but truth : I haue waſted my
ſelfe out of my meanes.   The Iewels you haue had from
me to deliuer *Deſdemona*, would halfe haue corrupted a
Votariſt.   You haue told me ſhe hath receiu'd them,   220
and return'd me expectations and comforts of ſodaine
reſpect, and acquaintance, but I finde none.

,   *Iago.*   Well, go too : very well.

    Rod.   Very well, go too : I cannot go too, (man) nor
tis not very well.   Nay I think it is ſcuruy : and begin to   225
finde my ſelfe ſopt in it.

    Iago.   Very well.

    Rodor.   I tell you, 'tis not very well : I will make my
ſelfe knowne to *Deſdemona*.   If ſhe will returne me my
Iewels, I will giue ouer my Suit, and repent my vnlaw-   230
full ſolicitation.   If not, aſſure your ſelfe, I will ſeeke
ſatisfaction of you.

    Iago.   You haue ſaid now.   233

---

215. *Performances*] *performance* Qq.

217. *With...truth*] Om. Q₁.

218. *out of my*] *out of* Qq, Cap.

219. *deliuer*] Ff, Rowe. *deliuer to* Qq
et cet.

220. *hath*] *has* Qq, Mal. Steev. Var.
Coll. Sing. Wh. i, Ktly.

    them] *em* Qq.

221. *expectations*] *expectation* Qq.
comforts] *comforst* Q₃.

222. *acquaintance*] *acquittance* Q₁,
Theob. Han. Warb. Cap. Jen. Mal. Steev.
'93, Var. Sing. *acquaintance* Q₃.

223. *very well*] *very good* Q₁.

224, 225. *nor tis*] *it is* Q₁.

225. *Nay I think it is*] *by this hand,
I ſay tis very* Q₁, Jen. Steev. Mal. Var.
Coll. Sing. Wh. i, Cam. Ktly. Del. (all
read *it is* except Jen. Cam.). *I ſay t'is
very* Q₂Q₃.

226. *fopt*] QqFf. *fob'd* Rowe+, Cap.
Jen. *fobb'd* Steev. Mal. Wh. *fopped* Dyce,
Cam. Del. *fobbed* Var. et cet.

228. *I tell you,'tis*] *I ſay it is* Qq, Jen.

231. *I will*] *I'le* Q₁. *Ile* Q₂Q₃.

233. *now.*] *now—* Theob. Warb. Johns.

---

advantage tc be derived from hope; it was because Iago doffed him with devices that
he had no hope, and had lost even that advantage.—ED.

   214, 215. COLLIER : Here we meet with an extraordinary variation in copies of F₁;
that belonging to the Duke of Devonshire has the following at the top of the page :
'I have heard too much : And hell graw his bones Performances.' CAMBRIDGE EDIT-
ORS : The mistake was discovered and corrected in other copies. This accounts for the
'and' which the corrected copies still retain instead of 'for.'

   223. BOOTH : With nonchalance, walking up and down, both here and at 227, but
Roderigo's threat to make himself known to Desdemona arrests Iago, and he instantly
plans the removal of Roderigo as well as Cassio.

   229. **knowne**] Can this refer to anything else but his disguise ? his favour, defeated
with an usurp'd beard ?—ED.

Rodo. I : and faid nothing but what I proteſt intend-
ment of doing.   235

Iago. Why, now I fee there's mettle in thee : and
euen from this inſtant do build on thee a better o-
pinion then euer before : giue me thy hand *Rodorigo.*
Thou haſt taken againſt me a moſt iuſt excepti-
on : but yet I proteſt I haue dealt moſt directly in thy   240
Affaire.

Rod. It hath not appeer'd.

Iago. I grant indeed it hath not appeer'd : and
your fuſpition is not without wit and iudgement.
But *Rodorigo,* if thou haſt that in thee indeed, which   245
I haue greater reaſon to beleeue now then euer (I
meane purpoſe, Courage, and Valour) this night
ſhew it. If thou rhe next night following enioy not
Deſdemona, take me from this world with Treache-
rie, and deuiſe Engines for my life.   250

Rod. Well : what is it ? Is it within, reaſon and compaſſe ?

Iago. Sir, there is eſpeciall Commiſſion come from
Venice to depute *Caſſio* in *Othello's* place.

Rod. Is that true ? Why then *Othello* and *Deſdemona*   255
returne againe to Venice.

---

234. *and faid*] *and I haue faid* Q₁,
Jen. Steev. Mal. Var. Coll. Sing. Wh. i,
Ktly, Del.

234, 235. *intendment*] *entendment* Qq.

237. *inſtant*] *time* Q₁.

  do] *do I* Rowe+.

239, 240. *exception*] *conception* Qq.

240. *but yet*] *but* Rowe ii+.

241. *Affaire*] *affaires* Q₁.

242. *appeer'd*] *appeared* Qq.

245. *in thee*] *within thee* Qq, Cap. Jen.
Steev. Mal. Var. Coll. Sing. Wh. i, Ktly,
Del.

248. *enioy*] *enioyeſt* Qq, Jen. Steev.
Mal. Var. Coll. Wh. i, Del.

250. *for*] *from* Q₃.

251. *what is it ?*] Om. Qq.
  within,] *within* QqFf.

253-264. *Sir...braines*] Eleven lines,
ending : Venice...*place*...Deſdemona...
Venice...*him*...*linger'd*...*fo* (Q₁. *deter
minate* Q₂Q₃)...Caſsio...*him ?*...*place*...
braines Qq.

253. *eſpeciall*] *a special* Mal. conj
  Commiſſion] *command* Q₁.

---

238. giue . . . hand] BOOTH : Roderigo does not, but Iago wheedles, and gets his
hand laughingly.

243-250. BOOTH : This, very earnestly.

250. Engines] RITSON : This seems to mean, to contrive *racks, tortures,* &c. DYCE
(*Gloss.*) : Does it not rather signify ' contrive artful means to destroy my life ? ' (' An
Engine [device], *Artificium, Ingenium.*'—Coles's *Lat. and Eng. Dict.*) [See *Lear,*
I, iv, 262].

256. BOOTH : Roderigo is elated at the thought of Desdemona's return to Venice,

Iago. Oh no : he goes into Mauritania and taketh   257
away with him the faire *Defdemona*, vnleffe his a-
bode be lingred heere by fome accident. Wherein none can be fo determinate, as the remouing of   260
Caffio.

Rod. How do you meane remouing him ?

Iago. Why, by making him vncapable of *Othello's*
place : knocking out his braines.

Rod. And that you would haue me to do.   265

Iago. I : if you dare do your felfe a profit, and a
right. He fups to night with a Harlotry : and thither
will I go to him. He knowes not yet of his Honourable
Fortune, if you will watch his going thence (which
I will fafhion to fall out betweene twelue and one)   270
you may take him at your pleafure. I will be neere
to fecond your Attempt, and he fhall fall betweene
vs. Come, ftand not amaz'd at it, but go along with
me : I will fhew you fuch a neceffitie in his death, that
you fhall thinke your felfe bound to put it on him. It   275
is now high fupper time : and the night growes to waft.
About it.

Rod. I will heare further reafon for this.

Iago. And you fhalbe fatisfi'd.   *Exeunt.*   279

257. *taketh*] Ff, Rowe+, Cap. Jen.
Steev.85, Knt. *takes* Qq et cet.

259, 260. *Wherein*] *whereof* Cap. conj.
(p. 35 *b*).

262. *him*] Ff, Rowe+, Cap. Knt, Sta.
of him Qq et cet.

263. *by making*] *making* Cap. conj.
(p. 35 *b*).
vncapable] *incapable* Warb. Johns.

265. *do.*] FfQq, Rowe, Cap. *do ?* Pope
et seq.

266. *if*] *and if* Qq.

266. *and a*] *and* Qq.

267. *Harlotry*] *harlot* Q$_1$, Pope+, Jen.
Steev. Mal. Var.

268. *him. He*] *him ;—he* Q$_1$Q$_2$. *him—
he* Q$_3$.

276. *high*] *nigh* Mason.
waft] *wafte* F$_3$. *waift* Mal. conj.

277. [*Enter* Othello, Defdemona, Lodouico, Emillia, *and Attendants* Q$_1$.

279. *fhalbe*] *shall ; be* Sta.
fatisfi'd] *fatisfied* Qq.
Exeunt.] Ex. *Iag.* and *Rod.* Q$_1$.

his home as well as hers ; and is correspondingly disappointed when Iago says it is to
Mauritania. The 'removing of Cassio' Iago speaks slowly, and mysteriously.

259. **Mauritania**] THEOBALD : This is only a Lie, of Iago's own invention, to carry
a point with Roderigo. [See *Othello's Color*, in Appendix.]

266. BOOTH : Utter all this rapidly,—don't give Roderigo a chance to think.

267. **Harlotry**] See *Rom. & Jul.* IV, ii, 14.

276. **high**] STEEVENS : That is, *full complete* time.

276. **wast**] MALONE : The night is wasting apace. [See *Ham.* I, ii, 198 : 'the
dead vast,' where Malone makes the same conjecture as here. See Text. Notes.—ED.]

Scena Tertia.   [333 b]

Enter Othello, Lodouico, Defdemona, Æmilia,
and Atendants.

Lod. I do befeech you Sir, trouble your felfe no further.

Oth.   Oh pardon me : 'twill do me good to walke.   5

Lodoui.   Madam, good night : I humbly thanke your
Ladyfhip.

Def. Your Honour is moft welcome.

Oth. Will you walke Sir ? Oh *Defdemona.*

Def. My Lord.   10

Othello.   Get you to bed on th'inftant,   I will be return'd forthwith : difmiffe your Attendant there : look't
be done.   *Exit.*

Def.   I will my Lord

Æm. How goes it now? He lookes gentler then he did.   15

Def. He faies he will returne incontinent,
And hath commanded me to go to bed,
And bid me to difmiffe you.   18

---

1. Scena...] Scene XIII. Pope+, Jen.
A Room in the Castle. Cap.

4. *I do befeech*] '*Beseech* Cap.

5. *pardon me*] *pardon* F_3F_4, Rowe,
Pope, Han.

'*twill*] *it fhall* Qq.

6. *Madam*] *Madame* Q_x.

9. Dividing the line at *Sir ?* Cap. Steev.
'93 et seq. (except Huds.).

Sir ? Oh] Ff, Pope+, Knt, Ktly.
fir :—O Qq, Rowe.   *sir ?—O*, Jen.
Huds.   *sir ?—O,*— Cap. et cet.

Defdemona.] *Desdemona !*— Rowe
+. *Desdemona,*— Cap. et seq.

[*Ex.* Lod, &c. Han. Stepping back.

Cap.

11. *bed...inftant,*] *bed, o'the inftant* Qq.
on th'] Ff, Rowe+, Wh.   *o'the* Qq,
Cap. Jen.   *on the* Steev. et cet.

11, 12. *return'd forthwith :*] *return'd,
forthwith,* Q_r.   *return'd, forthwith* Q_2Q_3.

12. *difmiffe*] *difpatch* Qq.
there :] *there,*— Qq.
look't] Ff, Rowe, Pope, Han. Dyce,
Wh. i, Huds.   *looke it* or *look, it* Qq et cet.

13. Exit.] Exeunt. Qq.

17. *And*] Ff, Rowe+, Knt, Sta.   *He*
Qq et cet.

18. *bid*] Ff, Rowe+.   *bad* Q_r, Cap.
Jen.   *bade* Q_2Q_3 et cet.

---

279. **shalbe**] Note STAUNTON's ingenious punctuation, which is likely to give an
editor pause.—ED.

5. **walke**] COWDEN-CLARKE: This shows the restlessness of the body, with fever
of the mind.

9. **walke**] SCHMIDT: That is, withdraw; as in *Lear,* IV, vii, 83.

15. HAZLITT (p. 51): In this short speech of Emilia's there occurs one of those
side-intimations of the fluctuations of passion which we seldom meet with but in Shakespeare.   After Othello has resolved upon the death of his wife and bids her dismiss her
attendant for the night, Emilia says 'he looks gentler than he did.'   Shakespeare has
here put into half a line what some authors would have spun out into ten set speeches.

Æmi. Difmiffe me ?

Def. It was his bidding : therefore good *Æmilia,*   20
Giue me my nightly wearing, and adieu.
We muft not now difpleafe him.

Æmil. I, would you had neuer feene him.

Def. So would not I : my loue doth fo approue him,
That euen his ftubborneffe, his checks, his frownes,   25
(Prythee vn-pin me) haue grace and fauour.

Æmi. I haue laid thofe Sheetes you bad me on the bed.

Def. All's one : good Father, how foolifh are our minds?
If I do die before, prythee fhrow'd me
In one of thefe fame Sheetes.   30

Æmil. Come, come : you talke.

Def. My Mother had a Maid call'd *Barbarie,*   32

19. *Difmiffe*] *To dismiss* Ktly.

23. *I, would*] *Would* Q₂Q₃. *Ay, would*
Knt. *I would* Q₁Ff et cet.

25. *checks*] *cheeks* Jen. (misprint ?).
his frownes] *and frownes* Qq, Pope
ii, Theob. Warb. Johns. Cap. Jen. Steev.
Mal. Var. Coll. Sing. Wh. i, Ktly, Del.

26. *and*] *ond* F₂.
fauour.] *fauour in them.* Qq, Rowe
et seq.
[beginning to undress. Cap.

27. *I haue*] *I've* Dyce iii, Huds.
laid] *laied* Q₁Q₂.
thofe] *thefe* Q₁.
bad] *bade* Q₁.

28. *one : good Father,*] Ff. *one, good
father ;* Q₂Q₃. *one : good Father !* Rowe +,
Cap. Jen. Steev. Mal. Var. Knt, Coll. i,
Sing. Wh. i, Del. *one good faith :* Q₁.
one. Good faith, Dyce, Coll. ii, Sta. Glo.
Ktly, Cam. Coll. iii, Huds. Rlfe, Wh. ii.
minds ?] Ff, Rowe +. *minds ;* Q₂
Q₃. *minds !* Han. et cet.

29. *before,*] *before thee,* QqFf et cet.
fhrow'd] *fhrowd* QqFf.

30. *thefe*] Ff, Rowe +. *thofe* Qq et cet.

31. *talke.*] *talk—* Ktly.

32, 39. Barbarie] Barbary Qq. Barbara
Ff et cet. (line 39, Brabarie F₁).

---

26. WALKER (*Crit.* i, 92) : Whence *in them ?* it is not in the Folio.   *Qu.,* 'have *a*
grace and favour.'   LETTSOM (Foot-note to Walker) : The words 'in them' appear in
Q₁. The Folio reading, as emended by Walker, is such as Shakespeare might well
have written ; on the other hand, the additional words do not look either like a sophistication or a printer's blunder.

29. CORNHILL MAGAZINE (Oct. 1866) : This presentiment of Desdemona does not
bear the same tests as that of Romeo [see note *ad loc.* V, i, 1], nor Hamlet [V, ii, 207].
She had no reason to apprehend a violent death, but she had enough to apprehend from
Othello's anger.   He had struck her and called her the vilest names.   Naturally, these
unkindnesses would throw her into a deep state of depression.   ' A sort of gain-giving '
would naturally trouble her and exclude every chance of a real presentiment, the essence
of which is, that it shall be spontaneous, at a time when you have no reason to look for
it, when you are not under the influence of any fear or anxiety from known causes, and
when, perhaps, you have some difficulty in its interpretation.

31. **talke**] For other instances where this means to *talk idly,* to *prattle,* see SCHMIDT.

32. **Maid**] See LE TOURNEUR, in Appendix, ' Othello's Colour.'

32. **Barbarie**] KNIGHT : Barbarie is a pretty word, and we would not willingly

She was in loue : and he fhe lou'd prou'd mad,   33
And did forfake her.   She had a Song of Willough,
An old thing 'twas : but it exprefs'd her Fortune,   35
And fhe dy'd finging it.   That Song to night,
Will not go from my mind : I haue much to do,
But to go hang my head all at one fide
And fing it like poore *Brabarie* : prythee difpatch.

    Æmi.   Shall I go fetch your Night-gowne?   40
    Def.   No, vn-pin me here,
This *Lodouico* is a proper man.
    Æmi.   A very handfome man.
    Def.   He fpeakes well.   44

33, 34. *and...her.*] *and he, she lov'd, forsook her, And she prov'd mad :* Warb.
34. *had*] *has* Q₁.
34. &c. *Willough*] *willow* QqF₄.
35. *old*] *odd* Quincy (MS).
36. *dy'd*] *died* Qq.
37. Two lines, Q₂Q₃.
    go] *grow* Rowe i.
    mind :] *mind*— Q₁.
37-58. *I haue...next.*] Om. Q₁.

37. *I haue*] *I've* Pope+, Dyce iii, Huds.
    to do] *ado* Pope+.   *to-do* Huds.
38, 39. Prose, Q₂Q₃.
38. *But*] *Not* Theob. conj. (withdrawn), Han. Cap.
    at one] *on one* Han.   *o' one* Cap Steev.'85.
40. *go*] Om. Cap.
44. *He*] *And he* Cap. Steev.'93, Var.

---

change it; but it would appear like an affectation of singularity to retain it.   WALKER (*Crit.* iii, 290): The form is not yet obsolete among the common people.   [It is still frequently so pronounced in New England.   I doubt if any New England old lady who *can* sing 'Barbara Allen,' would pronounce it otherwise than 'Barbarie Allen.'—ED.]

    **33. mad*] JOHNSON: I believe that 'mad' only signifies *wild, frantic, uncertain* RITSON: Here it ought to mean *inconstant*.   KEIGHTLEY: For 'mad,' which is certainly wrong. Theobald read *bad*, and I think he was right.   'Proved bad' answers to our present *turned out bad*.   Regarding *bad* as rather low and trivial, I read in my Edition *false*, as that is the term in the ballad.   I thought 'mad' might have been suggested by 'maid' in the preceding line.   [Theobald proposed *bad* in a letter to Warburton (Nichols, *Illust.* ii, 599), but did not allude to it in his edition, where the text is 'mad.' Capell reads *bad ;* no one else.—ED.]   COWDEN-CLARKE: We see no reason to suppose it used in any other sense than *insane*.

    37, 38. JOHNSON: This is, perhaps, the only insertion made in the latter editions which has improved the play.   The rest seem to have been added for the sake of amplification, or of ornament.   When the imagination had subsided, and the mind was no longer agitated by the horror of the action, it became at leisure to look round for specious additions.   This addition is natural.   Desdemona can at first hardly forbear to sing the song; she endeavors to change her train of thoughts, but her imagination at last prevails, and she sings it.

    **37. to do*] For instances where this is equivalent to *ado*, see SCHMIDT, s. v. *b*, or *Ham.* II, ii, 338.   But, as ROLFE well observes, in this present passage it 'may have no more than its ordinary meaning: *I have to do much*, that is, make a great effort.'

    **38. But*] For instances of 'but' signifying *prevention*, see ABBOTT, § 122.

Æmil. I know a Lady in Venice would haue walk'd   45
barefoot to Paleftine for a touch of his nether lip.

Def. *The poore Soule fat finging, by a Sicamour tree.*   47

45. *I...walk'd*] One line, as verse, Cap. Ktly.

    would] *who would* Steev.'93, Var.

46. *barefoot*] *barefooted* Q₂, Q'81, Dyce iii.

    for] *fore* Q₃.

46. *nether*] *neither* Q₂F₂F₃, Theob. i.

47. Def.] *Defdemona* fings Q₂Q₃. Singing. Rowe.

    finging] Ff, Rowe+, Steev.'85, Knt. finghing Q₃. fighing Q₂, Cap. et cet.

47. COLLIER (ed. i) referred to a ballad, 'of which some of the stanzas ended with "For all the grene wyllow is my garland," by old John Heywood, preserved in MS. in B. H. Bright's library.' [This ballad is printed in *The Shakespeare Society's Papers*, vol. i, p. 44; it has nothing in common with Desdemona's song except the refrain. WARTON (*Hist. Eng. Poetry*, iii, 287, note) mentions a song, called The Willow-Garland, attributed to Edwards, and which he thinks is the same, that is licensed to T. Colwell in 1564 (22 July,—Arber's *Transcript*, i, 270), beginning, ' I am not the fyrst that hath taken in hande, The wearynge of the willowe garlande.' PERCY (*Reliques*, 1765, vol. i, p. 175) gives a black-letter ballad from the Pepys Collection thus entitled, ' A Lovers complaint, being forsaken of his love. To a pleasant tune.' The stanzas which correspond to those of Shakespeare are as follows :]

> A poore foule fat fighing under a ficamore tree,
>   O willow, willow, willow !
> With his hand on his bofom, his head on his knee ;
>   O willow, willow, willow !
>   O willow, willow, willow !
> Sing, O the greene willow fhall be my garland.
>   *   *   *   *   *   *
> The cold ftreams ran by him, his eyes wept apace,
>   O willow, &c.
> The falt tears fell from him, which drowned his face ;
>   O willow, &c.
> Sing, O the greene willow, &c.
>
> The mute birds fate by him, made tame by his mones ;
>   O willow, &c.
> The falt tears fell from him, which foftned the ftones.
>   O willow, &c.
> Sing, O the greene willow, &c.
>
> Let nobody blame me, her fcornes I do prove ;
>   O willow, &c.
> She was borne to be fair ; I, to die for her love ;
>   O willow, &c.
> Sing, O the greene willow, &c.

This ballad, Collier says, is obviously a comparatively modern re-impression (about the year 1640 or 1650) of a much older production. CHAPPELL (i, 206): The song, which Desdemona sings, is contained in a MS. volume, with accompaniment for the

[Sing Willough, Willough, Willough.]

lute, in the British Museum (Addit. MSS. 15,117). Mr Halliwell considers the transcript to have been made about the year 1633; Mr Oliphant (who catalogued the Musical MSS.) dates it about 1600; but the manuscript undoubtedly contains songs of an earlier time, such as,—'O death! rock me asleep, Bring me to quiet rest,' &c., attributed to Anne Boleyn, and which Sir John Hawkins found in a MS. of the reign of Henry VIII. ['The music is older than 1600. It is found in Thomas Dallis's MS. "Lute Book," with the title, "All a greane willow." Dallis taught music at Cambridge; and his book, dated 1583, is now in the Library of Trinity College, Dublin.'—*Shakspere's Songs*, p. 50, New Sh. Soc. 1884. In this same excellent publication of *The New Shakspere Society* ten compositions of this song are enumerated. ZELTER'S composition is given in Voss's *Othello*, Jena, 1806; in Le Tourneur the composition by MARTINI is given; and for Ducis's *Romance du Saule* the music was composed by GRÉTRY. Of course the song is also to be found in the Opera of *Otello* by ROSSINI. The music here given is from Chappell's *Popular Music of the Olden Time*, i, 207; however lovely the melody, its charm is heightened by the knowledge that its plaintive notes once 'sighed along' the traverses of the Globe Theatre.—ED.]

Sing all a greene Willough :   48
Her hand on her bofome her head on her knee,
Sing Willough, Willough, Wtllough.   50
The frefh Streames ran by her, and murmur'd her moanes
Sing Willough, &c.
Her falt teares fell from her, and foftned the ftones,
Sing Willough, &c.   (Lay by thefe)
Willough, Willough. (Prythee high thee : he'le come anon)   55
Sing all a greene Willough muft be my Garland.
Let no body blame him, his fcorne I approue.
(Nay that's not next.   Harke, who is't that knocks ?
  Æmil.   It's the wind.
    Def. I call'd my Loue falfe Loue : but what faid he then?   60
Sing Willough, &c.
If I court mo women, you'le couch with mo men.   62

52, 61. Willough, &c.] willow, willow,
willow; Q₂Q₃, Cap. Jen. Coll. Dyce, Sta.
Wh. Glo. Cam. Del. Huds. Rlfe.

53. Her falt] *The falt* Cap. (corrected
in Errata).

and] which Q₂Q₃, Jen.

54. Sing Willough, &c.] Ff. fing willow, &c. Q₂, Rowe +, Jen. Steev.'85. fling-
willow &c. Q₃. Om. Cap. et cet.

(*Lay by thefe*)] Rowe i, Johns. Jen.
(*Lady by thefe*) Ff, Rowe ii. Om. Pope,
Theob. Han. Warb.   Separate line, no
parenthesis, Cap. et cet.

[giving her her Jewels. Cap. Jen.

55. Willough, Willough.] willow, willow. QqFf, Rowe, Pope, Han. Jen. *Willow, willow, &c.* Theob. Warb. Johns.
Sing willow, willow, willow. Cap. et cet.

(*Prythee...anon*)] Ff, Rowe, Pope,
Theob. i, Han. Jen.   Separate line, Q₂Q₃,
Theob. ii, Warb. Johns.   Separate line, no
parenthesis, Cap. et cet.

high] *hie* Q₂Q₃.

57. Marked as Second Stanza, Cap.
Steev. Mal. Var. Knt, Sing. Ktly, Coll. iii.

approue.] approue : Q₂Q₃. *approve,*
— Cap. et seq.

58. *Nay...next.*] In parenthesis, Jen.
Harke.] *Hark ! hark !* Cap.

who is't that] *who's that* Qq. *who
is it that* Theob. ii, Warb. Johns. Jen.
Steev. Mal. Var. Coll. Sing. Wh. i, Ktly,
Del.

59. *It's*] *It is* Q₁, Jen. Steev. Mal. Var.
Coll. Sta. Wh. i, Del.   *T'is* Q₂Q₃.

60-62. Def. I...men.] Om. Q₁.

60. falfe Loue] falfe, Q₂Q₃.

62. mo women] no women F₃F₄. *more
women* Rowe +, Jen. Steev.'85, Dyce iii.
moe women Glo. Ktly, Cam. Del. Rlfe,
Wh. ii.

couch] *touch* Upton.

mo men] *more men* Rowe +, Jen.
Steev.'85, Dyce iii.   *moe men* Glo. Ktly,
Cam. Del. Rlfe, Wh. ii.

---

54. **Lay by these**] After this Aside, nearly every modern editor, even Keightley
(for whose punctuation I have much respect), puts a colon or a semicolon, as though
the sentence were incomplete.   Almost the same can be said of the punctuation after
' anon ' in the next line ; a few editors do put a full stop there.   Let the record of the
punctuation of these lines at least, be red-lettered for Isaac Jaggard.—ED.

58. **knocks**] W. N. (*Memorials of Sh.* p. 364) : What gives a finishing stroke to
the terror of this midnight scene is the rustling of the wind, which the affrighted imagination of Desdemona supposes to be one knocking at the door.   This circumstance,

So get thee gone, good night : mine eyes do itch :   **[334 *a*]**
Doth that boade weeping ?

   Æmil, 'Tis neyther heere, nor there·   65

   Def.   I haue heard it faid fo. O thefe Men, thefe men !
Do'ft thou in confcience thinke (tell me *Æmilia*)
That there be women do abufe their husbands
In fuch groffe kinde ?

   Æmil.   There be fome fuch, no queftion.   70

   Def.   Would'ft thou do fuch a deed for all the world ?

   Æmil.   Why, would not you ?

   Def.   No, by this Heauenly light.

   Æmil.   Nor I neither, by this Heauenly light:
I might doo't as well i'th'darke.   75

   Def.   Would'ft thou do fuch a deed for al the world ?

   Æmil.   The world's a huge thing :
It is a great price, for a fmall vice.

   Def.   Introth, I thinke thou would'ft not.

   Æmil.   Introth I thinke I fhould, and vndoo't when   80
I had done.   Marry, I would not doe fuch a thing for a
ioynt Ring, nor for meafures of Lawne, nor for Gownes,   82

63. *So*] *Now* Q₁.
63, 64. *mine…weeping*] One line, Q₁.
64. *Doth*] *does* Qq, Cap.
66–70. Om. Q₁.
69. *kinde*] *kindes* Q₂Q₃.
71. *deed*] *thing* Q₂Q₃, Cap.
74,75. Prose, Han. Cam. Del. Dyce iii.
Nor…might, as one line, Ktly.
74. *Nor*] *No, nor* Cap.
75. *doo't as well*] *doe it as well* Q₁. *as well doe it* Q₂Q₃.
  i'th'] Ff, Rowe+, Jen. Wh. *in the* Qq. *i' the* Cap. et cet.
76. *Would'ft*] *Would* Q₁.
  deed] *thing* Q₁, Jen.
77, 78. Prose, Han. Jen. Knt. *The…* Qq.

price, as one line, Qq, Cap. Steev. Mal. Var. Coll. et seq.
77. *world's*] *world is* Qq, Johns. Cap. Jen. Steev. Mal. Var. Coll. Sing. Wh. ₁, Ktly, Del.
78. *It is*] Ff, Rowe+, Jen. Dyce, Glo. Cam. Rlfe, Wh. ii. '*Tis* Cap. et cet.
79. *Introth*] *Good troth* Q₁, Mal. Steev. '93, Var. Sing. Ktly.
80. *Introth*] *By my troth* Q₁, Mal. Steev.'93, Var. Sing. Ktly.
  vndoo't] *unswear't* Han.
81. *done.*] *done it*, Qq.
82. *ioynt Ring*] *join'd-ring* Wh. i.
  nor for meafures] *or for meafur:* Qq.

---

which would have been overlooked as trifling by an inferior writer, has a most sublime effect in the hands of Shakespeare.

62. **mo**] WALKER (*Crit.* iii, 290): Why write 'mo' [in modern editions] ? This, indeed, is the spelling of F₂, but F₁ has 'mo' or 'moe' in numberless places where no one has thought it necessary so to read, unless the rhyme demanded it.

71–94. COLLIER (ed. ii) : These lines are struck out with a pen in the (MS.), as if not acted in the time of the old annotator.

78 DYCE (ed. iii) : A quotation evidently. [Printed by Dyce as a distich.]

82 **ioynt Ring**] STEEVENS : These rings will be best described by a passage in

Petticoats, nor Caps, nor any petty exhibition. But for   83
all the whole world : why, who would not make her hus-
banda Cuckold, to make him a Monarch? I fhould ven-   85
ture Purgatory for't.

Def.   Befhrew me, if I would do fuch a wrong
For the whole world.

Æmil.   Why, the wrong is but a wrong i'th'world;
and hauing the world for your labour, 'tis a wrong in   90
your owne world, and you might quickly make it right.

Def.   I do not thinke there is any fuch woman.

Æmil.   Yes, a dozen : and as many to'th'vantage, as
would ftore the world they plaid for.

But I do thinke it is their Husbands faults   95
If Wiues do fall : (Say, that they flacke their duties,
And powre our Treafures into forraigne laps;
Or elfe breake out in peeuifh Iealoufies,
Throwing reftraint vpon vs : Or fay they ftrike vs,
Or fcant our former hauing in defpight)   100
Why we haue galles : and though we haue fome Grace,

<hr>

83. *Petticoats*] *or Petticotes* Q₁.
 nor Caps] *or Caps* Q₂Q₃.
 petty] *fuch* Q₁.
84. *all the*] *the* Qq, Cap.
 world :] *world?* Q₁. *world!* Han.
world,— Cap. et seq.
 why,] *vds pitty,* Q₁.
85. *Cuckold*] *cuckole* Q₁.
86. *for't*] *for it* Qq, Jen.
87, 88. Prose, Jen. Steev.'93, Var. Knt,
Coll. Sing. Ktly, Huds.
87. *a wrong*] *wrong* Q₂Q₃.
89. *i'th'*] Ff, Rowe+, Cap. Jen. Wh.

i' th Q₂Q₃. *i' the* Q₁ et cet.
91. *right*] *wright* Q₃.
93. *to'th'*] Ff, Rowe+, Jen. Wh. *to the*
Qq et cet.
93, 94. As verse, Theob. Warb. Cap.
Mal. *Yes...many* one line, Steev.'93, Var.
Coll. Sing.
94. *plaid*] *played* Qq.
95–112. Om. Q₁.
97. *powre*] *poure* Q₂. *pouer* Q₃. *pour*
F₃F₄.
 our] *out* Rlfe.
99. *vpon*] *on* Rowe ii+.

<hr>

Dryden's *Don Sebastian :* '—— a curious artist wrought them, With *joints* so close as
not to be perceiv'd; Yet are they both each other's counterpart : Her part had Juan
inscrib'd, and his had Zayda, (You know those names are theirs) and, in the midst, A
heart divided in two halves was plac'd. Now if the rivets of these rings inclos'd, Fit
not each other, I have forg'd this lye : But if they *join*, you must forever part.'

83. **exhibition**] DYCE (*Gloss.*) : An allowance, a pension. See *Lear*, I, ii, 25.

89. **wrong i' th' world**] WHITE (ed. ii) : That is, a wrong in the world's eye, a
conventional wrong. Emilia is quibbling. PURNELL : It is only wrong if it becomes
known to the world; now, if one is to gain the worlc for it, the world is at your command, and therefore it is no matter.

93. **vantage**] STEEVENS : That is, to boot, over and above.

100. **hauing**] JOHNSON : Our former allowance of expense.

101. **Grace**] In a theological sense.—ED.

Yet haue we fome Reuenge.   Let Husbands know,   102
Their wiues haue fenfe like them : They fee, and fmell,
And haue their Palats both for fweet, and fowre,
As Husbands haue.   What is it that they do,   105
When they change vs for others *?* Is it Sport?
I thinke it is : and doth Affe&ion breed it *?*
I thinke it doth.   Is't Frailty that thus erres *?*
It is fo too.   And haue not we Affe&ions *?*
Defires for Sport? and Frailty, as men haue *?*   110
Then let them vfe vs well : elfe let them know,
The illes we do, their illes inftru& vs fo.

   Def.   Good night, good night :
Heauen me fuch vfes fend,
Not to picke bad, from bad ; but by bad, mend.   *Exeunt*   115

---

108. *Is't*] *It's* Var. (misprint).
110. *Sport*] *sports* Warb. Johns.
111. *them...them*] *em...em* Q$_2$Q$_3$.
112. *The illes*] *The ill* Q$_3$.
    fo.] *to.* Ff, Rowe ii+, Cap. Jen.

Steev. Coll. ii.   *too* Rowe i.
113, 114. One line, Qq, Rowe et seq.
114. *Heauen*] *God* Q$_1$.
    vfes] *vfage* Q$_2$, Johns. Cap. Steev.
Mal. Var.

---

103. **sense**] MALONE and DYCE: That is, sensual appetite.   [As Hamlet uses it in his interview with his mother.]

114, 115. HUNTER (ii, 288): Shakespeare having remarked in *King John*, 'How oft the sight of means to do ill deeds Makes ill deeds done,' we may probably take these words of Desdemona as, beside their purpose in the drama itself, intended as a hint and warning to the audience not to be infected by the fearful instance, about to be presented, of the higher paroxysms of passion.   We have noticed similar cautions on other occasions.

114. **vses**] JOHNSON: *Usage* is an old word for *custom*, and, I think, better than 'uses.'   COLLIER (ed. ii): We may almost suspect that neither 'uses' nor *usage* is correct; perhaps 'uses' ought to be *issues*, i. e., *results;* in *Tim.* I, i, 23, we have seen 'issues' misprinted *uses.*   STAUNTON: It may be doubted whether either 'uses' or *usage* is the poet's word.   [' Uses,' it seems to me, is emphatically right.   It is merely a repetition of Emilia's own word.   Emilia has threatened that if 'husbands do not "*use* us well," it will be their fault if we follow their example.'   Desdemona prays that she may receive such 'uses' that, instead of imitating the bad by bad, she may be able even to mend and become better thereby.   The noble, self-forgetting music in which Æmilia dies, goes far to drive away the shadow that envelops her theft of the handkerchief, for which, in the retrospect, we are ready to make every excuse.   But no excuses can be suggested for her here.   Her insidious references to Lodovico, and her allusion to Othello's blow, while Desdemona's lips are still bruised from it, stone our hearts, and we can see in her here only the dark foil to Desdemona's snow-white purity.—ED.]

Actus Quintus. Scena Prima.

Enter Iago, and Rodorigo.

Iago.   Heere, ftand behind this Barke,
Straight will he come :
Weare thy good Rapier bare, and put it home :   5
Quicke, quicke, feare nothing ; Ile be at thy Elbow,
It makes vs, or it marres vs, thinke on that,
And fixe moft firme thy Refolution.

  Rod.   Be neere at hand, I may mifcarry in't.   [334 *b*]

  Iago.   Heere, at thy hand : Be bold, & take thy ftand.   10

  Rod.   I haue no great deuotion to the deed,
And yet he hath giuen me fatisfying Reafons :
'Tis but a man gone.   Forth my Sword : he dies.

  Iago. I haue rub'd this yong Quat almoft to the fenfe,   14

1. Actus...] Actus. 5. Q₁.   Actus 5.
Scœna 1. Q₂Q₃.
   The Street. Rowe. A Street before the
Palace. Theob.
   3, 4. One line, Qq, Rowe et seq.
   3. *Barke*] F₂. *Bulke* Qq. *Bark* F₃F₄.
balk Sing. Wh. i. *bulk* Rowe et cet.
   7. *on*] *of* Qq.
   8. *moft*] *more* Q₂Q₃.
   10. *Be bold*] *Behold* Ff, Rowe.

10. *ftand*] *fword* Q₁, Pope, Theob.
Han. Warb. Jen. Steev. Mal. Var.
   [Retires to a little distance. Cap.
   11. *deed*] *dead* Q₁.
   12. *And*] Om. Pope+.
      hath] *has* Qq, Cap. Mal. Steev.'93,
Var. Coll. Sing. Wh. i, Del.
   13. [Stands apart. Theob.
   14. *I haue*] *I've* Pope+, Dyce iii.
      Quat] *gnat* Q₁, Pope, Warb.   *knot*
Theob.   *quab* Han.

3. **Barke**] KNIGHT : We prefer the more intelligible reading *bulk*, although we
have little doubt that 'bark' was correctly used by Shakespeare in this instance as a
projecting part of the fortification,—a buttress.   SINGER : I feel assured that *balke* was
intended, and not *bulk*.   Palsgrave renders that word by *pouste*, and Huloet defines it,
'the chief beame or *piller* of a house.'

8. **Resolution**] WHITE (ed. ii) : Five syllables.

14. **Quat**] JOHNSON : Hanmer reads *quab*, a *gudgeon ;* not that a *gudgeon* can be
rubbed to much *sense*, but that a man grossly deceived is often called a *gudgeon*.
Upton reads *quail*, which he proves, by much learning, to be a very cholerick bird.
Theobald would introduce *knot*, a small bird of that name.   A 'quat' in the midland
counties is a *pimple*, which by rubbing is made to smart, or is *rubbed to sense*.   Roderigo is called a 'quat' by the same mode of speech as a low fellow is now termed in
low language a *scab*.   [Dr Johnson forgot that Shakespeare uses this word too.—
ED.]   To rub to the sense is to rub to the quick.   STEEVENS cites several instances of
the use of 'quat' in Dekker and others, but more to the purpose is it that WISE (p. 156)
gives it in his *Glossary of Warwickshire Words*, as in use at this day, in the same sense
as here.

And he growes angry.   Now, whether he kill *Caſſio*,   **15**
Or *Caſſio* him, or each do kill the other,
Euery way makes my gaine.   Liue *Rodorigo*,
He calles me to a reſtitution large
Of Gold, and Iewels, that I bob'd from him,
As Guifts to *Deſdemona*.   **20**
It muſt not be : If *Caſſio* do remaine,
He hath a dayly beauty in his life,
That makes me vgly : and beſides, the Moore
May vnfold me to him : there ſtand I in much perill :
No, he muſt dye.   But ſo, I heard him comming.   **25**

              Enter Caſſio.

Rod.   I know his gate, 'tis he : Villaine thou dyeſt.

Caſ.   That thruſt had beene mine enemy indeed,
But that my Coate is better then thou know'ſt :
I will make proofe of thine.   **30**

---

15. *angry. Now,*] *angry now :* Q₁.
angry, now, Q₂.   *angry, now* Q₃.
   17. *gaine*] *game* Qq, Jen. Coll. Wh. i,
Ktly, Rlfe.
   19. *Of*] *For* Qq.
   22. *hath*] *has* Qq.
      dayly] *daynty* Jabez (N. & Qu. 5,
vii, 83).
   24. *him : there*] *him there ;* Q₃.
      much perill] *perill* Q₁, Pope+, Jen.
   25. *But ſo,*] *be't ſo,* Qq, Jen. Sing. Ktly.
Be it so, Pope+.   *be't so ;* Coll. Wh. i, Dyce

iii, Huds.   *Be't so.* Cam.
   25. *heard*] *heare* or *hear* QqFf et cet.
      [Exit Iago. Rowe.
   27. *gate*] *gait* Johns.
      [He runs at Cassio and wounds him.
Rowe.
   28. *mine*] *my* Qq.
   29. *know'ſt*] *think'ſt* Q₁, Jen. Steev.
Mal. Var. Sing. Ktly.
   30. [Fight. Iago cuts Cassio behind in
the Leg, and Exit.   Then Rod. and Cassio fall. Theob.

---

17. **Liue**] For instances where the subjunctive may be indicated by placing the
verb before the subject, see ABBOTT, § 361.

19. **bob'd**] MALONE: That I fool'd him out of.   [Both Malone and Dyce cite
Coles's *Latin Dict.*, 1679, as an authority for this word; but Rider's *Latin Dict.* of
1626, half a century earlier, gives 'A bob or mocke, *sanna*.'   It is still current slang
here in America.—ED.]

25. **But so**] DYCE (ed. iii): Qy. if intended for 'But, soft'?   HUDSON: And so I
suspect it should be.

29. **Coate**] MALONE supposes that Iago overhearing this, and inferring from it that
Cassio wears secret armour, afterwards wounds Cassio in the leg.   KNIGHT says that
the characteristics, according to Vecellio, of the costume of a 'soldato disarmato,' which
would be that of Cassio and Iago when off guard, were the 'buff jerkin and the scarf
of company,' and that it is to this 'buff jerkin' that Cassio refers, and not to any secret
armour.   THEOBALD asserts, however, that Shakespeare 'copied his Italian Novelist in
this incident,' wherein it is stated that the Ancient 'dirrizzò un colpo alle gambe, per
farlo cadere.'

Rod.   Oh, I am flaine.   31

Caffio.   I am maym'd for euer :

Helpe hoa : Murther, murther.

Enter Othello.

Oth.   The voyce of *Caffio, Iago* keepes his word.   35

Rod.   O Villaine that I am.

Oth.   It is euen fo.

Caf.   Oh helpe hoa : Light, a Surgeon.

Oth.   'Tis he : O braue *Iago*, honeft, and iuft,

That haft fuch Noble fenfe of thy Friends wrong,   40

Thou teacheft me.   Minion, your deere lyes dead,

And your vnbleft Fate highes : Strumpet I come :

For of my heart, thofe Charmes thine Eyes, are blotted.

Thy Bed luft-ftain'd, fhall with Lufts blood bee fpotted.

Exit Othello.   45

Enter Lodouico and Gratiano.

Caf.   What hoa? no Watch? No paffage ?

Murther, Murther.

Gra.   'Tis fome mifchance, the voyce is very direfull.   49

---

31. [Fight, and both fall. Rowe.

32, 33. One line, Qq, Pope et seq.

32. *I am*] *I'm* Pope+, Dyce iii, Huds.
maym'd] maind Q₁.

33. *Helpe*] *light* Qq, Cap. Coll.
Murther, murther.] murder, Q₂Q₃.

34. Enter...] Enter Othello, above at a
Window. Rowe.

Scene II. Pope+, Jen.

37. *It is*] *Harke tis* Q₁Q₃. *Harke, tis*
Q₂, Jen. Steev. Mal. Var. Sing. Ktly. '*Tis*
Knt, Sta.

euen] *e'en* Coll. Wh. i.

41. *me. Minion*] Ff, Rowe, Coll. Sing.
Wh. Glo. Ktly, Cam. Rlfe. *me ;—minion*
Qq, Knt, Dyce iii. *me—minion* Pope et
cet.

42. *vnbleft Fate highes :*] *fate hies apace*
Q₁, Pope+, Cap. Jen. Steev. Mal. Var.
Sing. *vnbleft fate hies ;* Q₂Q₃. *unbleft fate
hies apace ;* Ktly.

43. *For of*] *For off* Ff, Rowe. *From
off* Pope, Theob. Han. Warb. *Forth of*
Qq, Johns. et seq.

are] *have* Han. ii.

44. *Bed luft-ftain'd*] *Bed-left-ftain'a*
F₃F₄.

45. Exit...] Ex. Q₁. Exit. Q₂Q₃.

46. Enter...] Enter ... at a distance.
Theob.

Scene III. Pope+, Jen.

47, 48. One line, Qq, Rowe et seq.

49. *voyce*] Ff, Rowe+, Cap. Knt, Dyce
i, Sta. *cry* Qq et cet.

39–44. INGLEBY (*Shakespeare, the Man,* &c. ii, 192), believing that Shakespeare did
not intend Othello to speak at all in this Scene, denies that Shakespeare wrote these
lines, which he calls 'atrocious stuff.'

43. **For of**] Unquestionably a misprint for *Forth of,* of which form see other
instances in ABBOTT, § 156.

47. **passage**] JOHNSON : No passengers ? nobody going by ?   SINGER : A *passen-
ger* anciently fignified a *passage-boat* or *vessel,* and could not, therefore, be ufed in its
modern fenfe without an equivoque.

Caſ. Oh helpe. 50
Lodo. Hearke.
Rod. Oh wretched Villaine.
Lod. Two or three groane. 'Tis heauy night ;
Theſe may be counterfeits : Let's think't vnſafe
To come into the cry, without more helpe. 55
Rod. Nobody come : then ſhall I bleed to death.
Enter Iago.
Lod. Hearke.
Gra. Here's one comes in his ſhirt, with Light, and
Weapons. 60
Iago. Who's there *?*
Who's noyſe is this that cries on murther ?
Lodo. We do not know.
Iago, Do not you heare a cry ?
Caſ. Heere, heere : for heauen ſake helpe me. 65
Iago. What's the matter ?
Gra. This is *Othello*'s Ancient, as I take it.
Lodo. The ſame indeede, a very valiant Fellow.
Iago. What are you heere, that cry ſo greeuouſly ? 69

51. *Hearke.*] *Hark, hark!* Ktly.
53. *groane*]*grones* Qq. *groans* Pope+,
Cap. Jen. Steev. Mal. Var.
'Tis] Ff, Rowe, Knt. *it is a* Qq et
cet.
55. *into*] QqFf, Rowe+, Jen. Sing.
Ktly. *in to* Cap. et cet.
56. *come :*] Ff, Rowe, Pope. *come,* Qq.
come ? Theob. et cet.
57. Enter Iago] Enter *Iago* with a light.
Qq. Enter Jago in his shirt. Rowe.
59. *Light*] *lights* Qq.

60. [Re-enter Iago with a light. Dyce.
61, 62. One line, Qq, Pope et seq.
62. *on*] *out* Ff, Rowe+, Cap. Jen. Steev.
'85.
murther ?] *murther thus ?* Coll.
(MS).
63. *We*] *I* Qq, Jen.
64. *Do*] Ff, Rowe+, Cap. Knt. *Did*
Qq et cet.
65. *heauen*]*heauens* Qq. *heaven's* Han.
et seq.

---

52. JOHN HUNTER : Roderigo here reproaches himself.
53. **groane**] KNIGHT : Lodovico does not merely say that there are two or three
groans from one man, but that two or three men groan ; and he adds, 'these may be
counterfeits.' LETTSOM (Walker, *Crit.* iii, 290, foot-note) : How could people at a distance distinguish whether groans proceeded from one person or from more, when the
groaners were lying close together ? [Probably they did not both groan in the same
key.—ED.]
53. **heauy**] JOHNSON : A *thick, cloudy* night, in which an ambush may be com-
modiously laid. PURNELL : 'Gloomy.' Used elsewhere only of the eye in this sense.
62. **cries on**] MALONE : So in *Eastward Hoe*, 1605 : 'Who cries on murder ?
Lady, was it you ?' That line is a parody on a line in *The Spanish Tragedy.* See
also *Ham.* V, ii, 351. WHITE (ed. i) : That is, cries continually murder.

Caſ. *Iago* ? Oh I am ſpoyl'd, vndone by Villaines :   7C
Giue me ſome helpe.

Iago.   O mee, Lieutenant !
What Villaines haue done this ?

Caſ.   I thinke that one of them is heereabout,   74
And cannot make away.   [335 *a*]

Iago.   Oh treacherous Villaines :
What are you there ? Come in, and giue ſome helpe.

Rod.   O helpe me there.

Caſſio.   That's one of them.

Iago.   Oh murd'rous Slaue ! O Villaine !   80

Rod.   O damn'd *Iago* ! O inhumane Dogge !

Iago.   Kill men i'th'darke ?
Where be theſe bloody Theeue s ?
How ſilent is this Towne ? Hoa, murther, murther.   84

70. Iago?] Iago, Qq.
   I am] *I'm* Pope+, Dyce iii, Huds.
72, 73. One line, Qq, Pope et seq.
72. *mee,*] *my* Q₁. *me* Q₃. *me*, Q₂Ff
et cet.
74. *that one*] *the one* Qq.
77. [To Lod. and Gra. Theob.
78. *me there.*] *me ! here.* Coll. Wh. 1.
   there] Ff, Rowe+, Jen. Sta. *here*
Qq et cet.
79. *them*] *em* Qq.

80. *murd'rous*] Ff, Rowe+, Cap. Wh.
ii. *murderous* Qq, Johns. et cet.
   [Thruſts him in. Q₂Q₃. Jago stabs
him. Rowe.
81. *inhumane*] *inhumaine* Q₁Q₄. *in
humaine* Q₃.
   Dogge !] *dog,—o, o, o.* Qq, Cap. Jen.
Steev. Mal. Var.
   [Dies. Han.
82, 83. One line, Qq, Rowe et seq.
82. *men*] *him* Q₁.
83. *theſe*] *thoſe* Qq.

79. BOOTH : Cassio takes Desdemona's handkerchief,—the gift of Othello,—from
his pocket and binds his leg.

80. HAWKINS (*Life of Kean*, i, 253) : Previous actors of Iago did not appear to have
remembered that the whole fortune of the Ancient hinged upon this event ; they stabbed
Roderigo, and then walked away with perfect ease and satisfaction. Not so Kean. He
gave and repeated the murderous thrust till no life could be supposed to remain ; but
feeling this to be too important a matter to be left in doubt, he, though conversing
coolly with those about him, threw his eye continually towards the prostrate body, with
an intensity as if he would pierce its vital recesses to ascertain the important fact.
Sometimes he walked by it carelessly and surveyed it with a glance too rapid to be
observed ; sometimes he deliberately approached it and looked at it with his candle, as
if to satisfy the spectators that it was the villain who had attacked his friend Cassio,
and thus he continued to watch and hover over it until he left the stage, his manner
perfectly cool, while his eye expressed the most restless anxiety.

83. **be**] ABBOTT, § 299 : *Be* is used in questions implying doubt : ' where can they
be ? '

84. BOOTH : As Iago is about to stab Cassio, he sees Lodovico and Gratiano approaching with servants and torches.

What may you be? Are you of good, or euill?   85
   Lod.   As you fhall proue vs, praife vs.
   Iago.   Signior *Lodouico*?
   Lod.   He Sir.
   Iago.   I cry you mercy : here's *Caſſio* hurt by Villaines.
   Gra.   *Caſſio?*   90
   Iago.   How is't Brother?
   Caſ.   My Legge is cut in two.
   Iago.   Marry heauen forbid :
Light Gentlemen, Ile binde it with my ſhirt.

Enter Bianca.   95

   Bian.   What is the matter hoa? Who is't that cry'd?
   Iago.   Who is't that cry'd?
   Bian.   Oh my deere *Caſſio*,
My ſweet *Caſſio :* Oh *Caſſio, Caſſio, Caſſio.*
   Iago.   O notable Strumpet. *Caſſio*, may you ſuſpect   100
Who they ſhould be, that haue thus mangled you?
   Caſ.   No.
   Gra.   I am ſorry to finde you thus ;
I haue beene to ſeeke you.
   Iago.   Lend me a Garter. So :———Oh for a Chaire   105
To beare him eaſily hence.
   Bian.   Alas he faints. Oh *Caſſio, Caſſio, Caſſio.*
   Iago.   Gentlemen all, I do ſuſpect this Traſh
To be a party in this Iniurie.
Patience awhile, good *Caſſio.*   Come, come ;   110

87. Lodouico?] Lodouico. QqFf, Rowe, Pope.

88, 89. *He...hurt*] As one line, Steev. '93, Var. Sing. Ktly.

90. Caſſio?] Caſſio. QqF₃F₄. *Cassio!* Cap.

91. *is't*] *is it* Qq, Cap. Jen. Steev. Mal. Var. Coll. Sing. Wh. i, Ktly. Scene IV. Pope+, Jen.

96. *cry'd?*] *cried?* Qq.

97. As a quotation. Sta. *cry'd?*] *cried.* Q₁Q₂. *cry'd!* Han. Coll. Dyce, Glo. Cam. Rlfe, Wh. ii.

98, 99. Thus divided, Ff, Rowe+, Jen. One line, Qq. Prose, Cam. Rlfe, Huds.

Oh...ſweet Caſſio : as one line, Cap. et cet.

99. *My...*Caſſio.] *O my ſweete* Cafsio, Cafsio, Cafsio. Qq.

101. *haue thus*] *thus haue* Qq, Jen

103, 104. One line, Qq, Cap. et seq. *I am*] *I'm* Theob. Warb. Johns. Dyce iii, Huds.

104. *I haue*] *I've* Dyce iii, Huds.

105, 106. Om. Q₁. Prose, Q₂Q₃.

109–111. Two lines, ending, *Cafsio.. no?* Q₁. Three, ending, *Cafsio...light :... no?* Q₂Q₃.

109. *be a party*] *beare a part* Qq. *this Iniurie*] *this* Q₁.

110. *Come, come ;*] Om. Q₁.

101. **should**] See III, iv, 25.

Lend me a Light : know we this face, or no ?   111
Alas my Friend, and my deere Countryman
Rodorigo? No : Yes fure : Yes, 'tis *Rodorigo*.

   Gra.   What, of Venice ?

   Iago.   Euen he Sir : Did you know him ?   115

   Gra.   Know him? I.

   Iago.   Signior *Gratiano* ? I cry your gentle **pardon**:
Thefe bloody accidents muft excufe my Manners,
That fo neglećted you.

   Gra.   I am glad to fee you.   120

   Iago.   How do you *Caffio* ? Oh, a Chaire, a **Chaire**.

   Gra.   *Rodorigo* ?

   Iago.   He, he, 'tis he :
Oh that's well faid, the Chaire.
Some good man beare him carefully from hence,   125
Ile fetch the Generall's Surgeon.   For you Miftris,
Saue you your labour.   He that lies flaine heere (*Caffio*)
Was my deere friend.   What malice was between **you**?

   Caf.   None in the world : nor do I know the man ?

   Iago.   What? looke you pale? Oh beare him o'th'Ayre.   130
Stay you good Gentlemen.   Looke you pale, Miftris ?

---

112. *Countryman*] *countrey man :* Qq.
113. *Yes, 'tis*] Q₂Q₃, Cap. Knt. *Yea, 'tis* Ff, Rowe+. *O heauen* Q₁, Jen. et cet.
    Rodorigo] Rederigo Q₂Q₃.
114. *What*] *Roderigo ? what* Cap. conj. (p. 36 *b*).
116. *I*] QqFf. *Ah !* Rowe+. *Ay.* Han. et cet.
117. *your*] Ff, Rowe+, Cap. Knt, Sta. *you* Qq et cet.
120. *I am*] *I'm* Dyce iii.
123, 124. One line, Qq, Rowe et seq.
123. *He, he,*] *He,* Qq.
    [Enter Some with a Chair. Cap.

124. *the*] *a* Qq.
126. *Generall's*] *General* F₄. [To Bianca. Johns.
127. *labour. He*] *labour, he* Qq. (Caffio)] Om. Han.
128. *between*] *betwixt* Q₁Q₃. *betwix* Q₂.
129. *man ?*] *man :* F₄. *man.* Qq, Rowe et seq.
130. [To Bianca. Johns.
    o'th'] *out o'th* Q₁. *out oth'* Ff. *out o' th'* Rowe+, Jen. Dyce iii, Wh. ii. *o' the* Knt. *out o' the* Q₂Q₃ et cet.
131. *Gentlemen.*] *Gentlewoman,* Qq, Mal. Vər.

---

112. **Countryman**] STEEVENS : This passage inconteſtably proves that Iago was meant for a Venetian.   BOOTH : Iago is very much overcome.

124. **well said**] See II, i, 192.

131. **Gentlemen**] MALONE upholds the Qq : ' No reason can be assigned why Lodovico and Gratiano should leave before they had heard from Iago further particulars of the attack on Cassio, merely because Cassio was borne off ; whereas, Bianca would naturally endeavour to accompany Cassio, to render him assistance.'   BOSWELL agrees with Malone, and thinks that Iago stops Bianca under a pretended suspicion

Do you perceiue the gaftneffe of her eye?   132
Nay, if you ftare, we fhall heare more anon.
Behold her well : I pray you looke vpon her:
Do you fee Gentlemen? Nay, guiltineffe will fpeake   135
Though tongues were out of vfe.
 Æmil.   Alas, what is the matter?
What is the matter, Husband?
 Iago.   *Caffio* hath heere bin fet on in the darke
By *Rodorigo*, and Fellowes that are fcap'd :   140
He's almoft flaine, and *Rodorigo* quite dead.   [335 *b*]
 Æmil.   Alas good Gentleman : alas good *Caffio.*
 Iago.   This is the fruits of whoring.   Prythe *Æmilia*,
Go know of *Caffio* where he fupt to night.   144

132. *gaftneffe*] *ieaftures* Q_1Q_2. *jeftures*
Q_3. *geftures* Q'81. *ghastness* Knt, Sing.
Ktly, Del.
 [To Bianca. Rowe.
133. *if you ftare*] *an you ftirre* Qq.
(*ftirr* Q_3). *an you stir :—* Coll. Hal.
heare] *haue* Qq.
134. *well :...you*] *well...you,* Qq. *well,
...you* Rowe.
135. *Do...guiltineffe*] One line, Qq,
Pope+, Jen.
136. *vfe.*] *vfe.* Enter Em, Qq. (Emi.
Q_2Q_3).
 Scene V. Pope+, Jen.
137, 138. One line, Qq, Cap. et seq.
(except Knt).

137, 138. *Alas, what is... What is*] Ff,
Rowe+, Knt.   *Alas! what's...what's*
Coll. Wh. i, Ktly, Hal. Rlfe.   *'Las, what's
...what is* Sta.   *'Las what's...what's* Qq
et cet.
139. *hath heere bin*] *has here bin* Qq,
Cap.   *has heen* Q'81.   *has been* Q'95.
hath there been Theob. Warb. Johns.
141. *quite*] Ff, Rowe, Knt.   Om. Qq,
Pope et cet.
143. *fruits*] Ff, Rowe, Knt, Sta. Wh.
i, Del.   *fruite* Qq et cet.
 Prythe] *pray* Q_1, Pope+, Jen.
prithee $Q_2F_3F_4$, Rowe, Knt, Dyce, Glo.
Cam. Rlfe, Wh. ii.   *Prethee* F_2Q_3. *'Pr'ythee*
Sing. Ktly.   *Pr'ythee* Cap. et cet.

---

that she would try to escape.   REED defends the Ff on the ground that it was more
proper for the two gentlemen to leave with Cassio in order to assist him, than to stay
and gratify their curiosity.   Respect for Othello's successor, if not personal regard,
would have dictated such a proceeding had they not been stopped by Iago's desiring
them not to go.

135. **will**] MOREL: Ce n'est pas un futur, mais une forme emphatique on fréquenta-
tive.   Le latin donne parfois une valeur analogue aux désinences du futur : Cantabit
vacuus coram latrone viator.'—*Juvenal.*

136. **use**] STEEVENS: So in *Ham.* II, ii, 569: 'For murder, though it have no
tongue, will speak With most miraculous organ.'

144. **to night**] MALONE: In the last Scene of the preceding Act, Iago informs
Roderigo that Cassio was to sup with Bianca; that he would accompany Cassio to her
house, and would take care to bring nim away from thence between twelve and one.
Cassio, too, had himself informed Iago (IV, i) that he would sup with Bianca, and Iago
had promised to meet him at her house.   Perhaps, however, Iago chose to appear ignorant of Cassio's movements during the evening.   STEEVENS: Yet how happens it that

What, do you fhake at that? 145

 Bian. He fupt at my houfe, but I therefore fhake not.

 Iago. O did he fo? I charge you go with me.

 Æmil. Oh fie vpon thee Strumpet.

 Bian. I am no Strumpet, but of life as honeft,

As you that thus abufe me. 150

 Æmil. As I? Fie vpon thee.

 Iago. Kinde Gentlemen:

Let's go fee poore *Caffio* dreft.

Come Miftris, you muft tel's another Tale.

Æmilia, run you to the Cittadell, 155

And tell my Lord and Lady, what hath happ'd:

Will you go on afore? This is the night

That either makes me, or foredoes me quight. *Exeunt* 158

Scœna Secunda.

Enter Othello, and Defdemona in her bed.

 Oth. It is the Caufe, it is the Caufe (my Soule) 3

148. *Oh fie*] Ff, Rowe+, Cap. Knt, Coll. Wh. i. *Fie* Q₂Q₃. *Fie, fie* Q₁ et cet.
151. *Fie*] Ff, Rowe+, Knt, Coll. Wh. i. *fough, fie* Q₁, Jen. *now fie* Q₂Q₃. *foh! fie* Cap. et cet.
152, 153. One line, Qq, Rowe et seq.
153. *go*] Om. Pope+.
154. *tel's*] *tell us* Steev. Mal. Var. Rann. Knt.
155. *you*] Om. Pope, Theob. i, Han.
156. *hath*] *has* Qq, Mal. Steev.'93, Var. Sing. Ktly.
157. *on afore?*] *on, I pray*, Q₁. *on, I pray?* Jen. Steev. Mal. Var. Coll. Sing.

Rlfe. *on? I pray:* Q₂Q₃. *on? I pray.* Glo. Cam. Wh. ii.
157. [Aside. Steev. et seq.
158. *makes*] *markes* Q₁.
1. Scœna...] Om. Qq. Scene VI. Pope+, Jen.
2. Enter...] Enter *Othello* with a light. Q₁. Enter *Othello* with a light, and *Defdemona* in her bed. Q₂Q₃. A Bed-chamber: Desdemona is discover'd asleep in her bed. Enter Othello. Rowe. Enter Othello with a light and a sword. Pope. ...A light burning. Steev.

Bianca, instead of replying,—'He supp'd,' &c., did not answer, addressing herself to Iago: 'Why, you well know | He supp'd,' &c. The former line being imperfect, some such words might have been omitted. Or, perhaps, our author was unwilling that Bianca should say, in the presence of Iago's wife, that he too had been of Cassio's supper-party; and hence this seeming inconsistency. SINGER: We must suppose that Iago thought it more secure to waylay Cassio, as we find he does, without actually joining him at supper-time.

 157. BOOTH: Watch them well off, then take a look at Roderigo and speak hoarsely.

 158. **foredoes**] See *Ham.* II, i, 103.

 2. KNIGHT is at some pains to explain the setting of the stage for this Scene in Shakespeare's time, and, with the aid of Tieck and Ulrici, devises a satisfactory arrangement, whereby we have a stage within the stage. But I do not think that

[2. *Enter Othello, and Desdemona in her bed.*]

much real information has been added to that which Malone has left us; certainly Dyce and Collier found nothing to add, and all that Malone was able to discover was, substantially, that there was a balcony, or upper stage, at the back of the principal stage, and that, in addition to the principal curtain in the front, there were others, as substitutes for scenes, which were called *traverses*, and could be drawn aside, disclosing inner compartments. It is really not difficult to imagine that even these simple resources were adequate to all the needs of this last scene.—ED.   FECHTER : Desdemona's Chamber.   At the back a large window with balcony, overlooking the sea.   On the left of the window an arch discovering an oratory; by the half-raised curtain is seen a prie Dieu, surmounted by a Madonna, and lighted by a red lamp.   On the same side, in front, a bed raised by two steps.   A door at the right.   A high and elegant Venetian lamp burns at the head of the bed, where Desdemona lies asleep; a small toilette glass, fallen from her hand, lies near her.   Her clothes scattered about.   On the balcony, Othello, motionless, enveloped in a long white burnous, is looking at the stars.   Far off,—at sea,—is heard the Song of *Willow*.   As the voices die away, Othello, who, during the last couplet, comes slowly forward to the bed to look at Desdemona, accidentally touches the glass in which he sees his bronzed face,—(*With bitter despair*) : ' It is the cause, it is the cause, my soul ! (*returning to the window, his eyes fixed on the heavens.*)   Let me not name it to you, you chaste stars !—(*looking at his face once again*).   It is the cause ! (*He violently throws the glass into the sea, goes to the door, locks it, advances to the bed, half drawing his sword ; then suddenly stops, and returns it to the scabbard*)   Yet I'll,' &c.   BOOTH : A Bed-chamber in the Castle.   Raised Bed L., opposite to large Window R.   Moonlight streams through window and falls upon Bed.   Door C.   Divan C.   A Light burning on Table.   Desdemona in Bed, asleep, discovered.   Othello also discovered.   BOOTH (MS.) : I prefer the bed at the side of the stage, with the head towards the audience; it is of more importance that Othello's face should be seen than Desdemona's dead body, and the killing is partly hidden at the same time.   MRS F. A. KEMBLE (*Temple Bar*, July, 1884) : This last Scene presents technical difficulties in its adequate representation which have never yet been even partially overcome.   The audience, of course, cannot be expected to sit by and see Desdemona smothered; the curtains of the alcove in which the bed is, are therefore lowered during that operation, but it is very desirable, if not absolutely necessary that she should be both heard and seen when she gasps out her dying exculpation of her husband, and while she is perpetually apostrophized by Emilia, Othello, and Lodovico.   The lines addressed to the lamp, ' If I quench thee, thou flaming minister,' should certainly be spoken with the light in near juxtaposition to the bed, and the intense pathos of the following ones, ' When I have plucked the rose,' &c., can only be given with due effect,—and what effect Salvini's voice would give to them !—by Othello leaning over his sleeping wife. . . . . The position of the bed (which for all the purposes of the Scene would be altered with advantage to the side of the stage), by which Othello is constrained to turn his back to the audience while addressing Desdemona, if she remains in it, has, we suppose, induced Signor Salvini to make her come from the alcove and speak the greater part of the dialogue standing in front of it ; an alteration of the stage tradition which hurts the effect of the Scene, and is untrue to the intention of Shakespeare, who makes Othello tell his wife that she is on her deathbed, and in reply to his furious command, ' Peace, be still,' receives the answer, ' I will; what is the matter ? ' with which the terrified woman cowers down upon her pillow like a poor, frightened child.   Indeed, the whole Scene loses its most pitiful

Let me not name it to you, you chaſte Starres,
It is the Cauſe.   Yet Ile not ſhed her blood,   5
Nor ſcarre that whiter skin of hers, then Snow,

---

element, by allowing Desdemona to confront Othello standing, instead of uttering the piteous pleadings for mercy in the helpless prostration of her half-recumbent position; although we have no doubt that a most powerful effect might be produced by any actress equal to the situation, who should herself rush from the bed to Othello's feet, as she utters the piercing denial, 'No, no, no; send for the man and ask him.'

3, 4. JOHNSON: The abruptness of this soliloquy makes it obscure.   The meaning, I think, is this :—I am here (says Othello in his mind) overwhelmed with horror.   What is the reason of this perturbation?   Is it want of resolution to do justice?   Is it the dread of shedding blood?   No; it is not the action that shocks me, but 'it is the cause, it is the cause, my soul.'   STEEVENS: Othello, full of horror at the cruel action which he is about to perpetrate, seems at this instant to be seeking his justification, by representing to himself *the cause*, i. e., the greatness of the provocation he had received. He may, however, mean,—It is the *cause* of chastity and virtue that I maintain.   HUDSON: Othello means that Desdemona's crime is the sole motive or reason that impels him to the present act; that in this alone he has a justifying cause, a 'compelling occasion,' for what he is about to do; so that he cannot justly lie under the reproach of having acted from any subjective or self-generated *animus* of revengeful jealousy. WHITE (ed. ii): This is, to me, one of the most doubtful and perplexing passages in all these plays.   Which is the emphatic word, 'it' or 'is' or 'cause,' and what is 'the cause,' and of what it is the cause, I confess that I am not ready to decide.   That 'it' in the second line refers to Desdemona's supposed unchastity is plain enough; but that her unchastity is 'the cause' is not so certain.   For Othello to say to himself, and at this moment, that Desdemona's conduct is the cause of his intended murder, seems very tame; and the [eighth] line, with its conclusion, 'else she'll betray more men,' seems to imply that Othello has deluded himself into looking upon his act as providential rather than retributive, and that 'cause' is his emphatic word.   [If 'cause' is the emphatic word, and assuredly it is when it first occurs, it should not receive an equal emphasis twice in the same line; then White's perplexity falls on all of us.   Is the second 'it' or the second 'is' to be emphatic?   I should prefer to let the emphasis fall on 'is.'   But is it necessary to emphasize any one word?   Is not the mere repetition of each word in itself an emphasis of each word?—ED.]

4. chaste Starres] HUDSON: In classical poetry the Moon is Diana, the goddess of *chastity*, and the stars are the train of *virgins* attending on her.   The epithet 'chaste' thus applied suggests the nature of the cause which the *purity* of the stars forbids to be named in their presence.   *The Athenæum* (10 April, 1875): After delivering the speech, 'It is the cause,' slowly, the first lines being spoken close to the door by which he enters, Othello [Salvini] kisses his sleeping wife, then goes to the window, and stands with the lightning playing upon his face.

6. whiter] For many instances of this transposition of the adjective, see ABBOTT, § 419 *a*, and WALKER (*Crit.* i, 160).

6. of hers] ABBOTT, § 239 : 'This of yours' is now, as in E. E., generally applied to one out of a class, whether the class exist or be imaginary.   We could say 'this coat of yours,' but not (except colloquially) 'this head of yours.'   It is, however, commonly used by Shakeſpeare, as in the present instance, where even the conception of a class is impoſsible.

And fmooth as Monumentall Alablafter: 7
Yet fhe muft dye, elfe fhee'l betray more men:
Put out the Light, and then put out the Light: 9

7. *as*] *and* Pope ii.
    Alablafter] QqF₂F₃, Rowe ii, Pope. *Alabafter* F₄, Rowe i.
    [Lays down the sword. Theob.

9. *Light,...Light:*] QqFf, Mal. Steev. '93, Var.'03, Var.'13, Var.'21, Dyce i, Glo. Cam. Del. Wh. ii. *Light, and then put out the Light,* Rowe i. *Light, and then put out the Light,* Rowe ii. *light, and then put out the light;* Pope. *light, and, then, put out the light;* Theob. *light: and*

then—put out thy *light.* Han. *light, and then—Put out the light?* Warb. Jen. Knt, Coll. i, Coll. ii. *light, and, then—Put out the light?* Johns. *light, and then—Put out the light!* Cap. Steev.'78, Steev.'85, Rann, Sing. Sta. Ktly, Rlfe. *light, and, then—Put out the light!* Steev.'73. *light, and then put out the light.* Wh. i. *light,— and then put out thy light:* Dyce ii, Dyce iii, Coll. iii, Huds. *light, and then put out the light?* Hal.

7. **Alablaster**] HUNTER (ii, 281): Compare with this, *R. of L.*, 'Where, like a virtuous monument she lies.'—391. And again, 'Without the bed her other fair hand was, On the green coverlet; whose perfect white Shew'd like an April daisy on the grass.'—*Ib.* 393. And again, 'With more than admiration he admired Her azure veins, her alabaster skin, Her coral lips, her snow-white dimpled chin.'—*Ib.* 418. MURRAY (*New Eng. Dict.*): The spelling in the 16–17th centuries is almost always *alablaster;* apparently due to a confusion with *arblaster,* a cross-bowman, also written *alablaster.*

8. **more men**] HUNTER (ii, 288): I confess the sense is not clear to me. It seems as if it should be that Othello is the 'betrayed,' not Cassio, or any other person whom the Moor, in his disordered mind, may suppose to be a second Cassio. I would therefore suggest as worthy of consideration, that the words may have been originally, 'else she'll betray *me more.*' This conjecture is, to a certain extent, supported by the use of the word 'betray' in the following passage of Beard's *Theatre of God's Judgment,* 1531: 'Out of the same fountain sprang the words of Queen Hecuba in Euripides, speaking to Menelaus touching Helen, when she admonished him to enact this law, that any woman which should betray her husband's credit and her own chastity to another man, should die the death.'—p. 387.

9. UPTON (p. 177): Othello enters with a taper (not with a sword, for he intended all along to strangle his wife in her bed), and in the utmost agony of mind says, he has cause for his cruelty, a cause not to be named to the chaste stars; 'tis fit, therefore, Desdemona should die. 'I'll put out the light, and then,'—strangle her, he was going to say; but this recalls a thousand tender ideas in his troubled soul; he stops short—If I quench the taper, how easy 'tis to restore,' &c. WARBURTON: The meaning is, I will put out the light, and *then* proceed to the execution of my purpose. But the expression of *putting out the light,* bringing to mind the effects of the extinction of the light of life, he breaks short, and questions himself about the effects of this metaphorical extinction, introduced by a repetition of his first words, as much as to say, But hold, let me first weigh the reflections which this expression so naturally excites. FARMER: Warburton's punctuation gives a spirit which, I fear, was not intended. It seems to have been only a play upon words. 'To put out the light' was a phrase for 'to kill.' FIELDING (*A Journey from this World to the Next,* Miscellanies, 1743, vol. ii, p. 65): I then observed Shakespeare standing between Betterton and Booth, and deciding a Difference between those two great Actors, concerning the placing an Accent in one of hi

[9. **Put out the Light, and then put out the Light :**]

lines; this was disputed on both sides with a Warmth, which surprised me in Elysium, till I discovered by Intuition that every Soul retained its principal Characteristic, being, indeed, its very Essence. The Line was that celebrated one in *Othello :* ‘Put out the Light, and then put out the Light,’ according to Betterton. Mr Booth contended to have it thus : ‘Put out the Light, and then put out *the* Light.’ I could not help offering my Conjecture on this Occasion, and suggested it might perhaps be : ‘Put out the Light, and then put out *thy* Light.’ Another hinted a Reading very *sophisticated* in my Opinion, ‘Put out the Light, and then put out *thee*, Light,’ making ‘Light’ to be in the vocative Case. Another would have altered this last Word, and read, ‘Put out thy Light, and then put out thy Sight.’ But Betterton said, if the Text was to be *disturbed*, he saw no reason why a Word might not be changed as well as a Letter, and instead of ‘put out thy Light,’ you might read, ‘put out thy *eyes*.’ At last it was agreed on all sides to refer the matter to the decision of Shakespeare himself, who delivered his Sentiments as follows : ‘Faith, Gentlemen, it is so long since I wrote the Line I have forgot my Meaning. This I know, could I have dreamt so much Nonsense would have been talked and writ about it, I would have blotted it out of my Works ; for I am sure, if any of these be my Meaning, it doth me very little Honour.’ He was then interrogated concerning some other ambiguous Passages in his Works, but he declined any satisfactory Answer, saying, if Mr Theobald had not *writ about it* sufficiently, there were three or four more new Editions of his Plays coming out, which he hoped would satisfy every one ; Concluding, ‘I marvel nothing so much, as that Men will gird themselves at discovering obscure Beauties in an author. Certes, the greatest and most pregnant Beauties are ever the plainest and most striking ; and, when two Meanings of a Passage can in the least balance our Judgements which to prefer, I hold it matter of unquestionable Certainty that neither of them are [*sic*] worth a farthing.’ MALONE : The poet, I think, meant merely to say : ‘I will now put out the lighted taper which I hold, and then put out the light *of life ;*’ and this introduces his subsequent reflection and comparison, just as aptly, as supposing the latter words of the line to be used in the same sense as in the beginning of it, which cannot be done without destroying that equivoque and play of words of which Shakespeare was so fond. I believe, however, that Shakespeare wrote, ‘and then put out *thy* light’ ; and the reading of Q₁ in line 12, ‘but once put out *thine*,’ seems to me to countenance this emendation. [This very line in the Folio KNIGHT adduces as strengthening Warburton’s interpretation.] BOSWELL : If Warburton’s explanation be an error, it is *demptus per vim*, and I, for one, am very sorry to part with it. Broken sentences are very much in Shakespeare’s manner, and are surely natural in the perturbed state of Othello’s mind. I am unwilling to persuade myself that a regulation of the text which contains so much beauty could be merely the refinement of a critic, and that our great author, in one of his most highly-wrought scenes, instead of it, intended nothing but a cold conceit. [Both Steevens and Malone cite many instances from Shakespeare, his predecessors, and contemporaries, to prove that ‘to put out the light’ means ‘to kill’ or to die. As if the inverted torch were not as old as mortuary symbolism !—ED.] WHITE (ed. i) : Warburton’s ingenious reading makes the second clause the lively expression of stimulated intelligence ; to me it is the despairing utterance of the profoundest woe. WALKER (*Crit.* iii, 291) : Read, I believe, ‘then put out *thy* light !’ or, possibly, ‘*her* light.’ CAMBRIDGE EDITORS : Mr Goldwin Smith, regarding the line in question as a stage direction which has crept into the text, suggests to us that the passage ought to be printed as follows : ‘Yet she must die, else she’ll betray more men.’ [*Takes off his sword, and then puts out the light.*] If I

If I quench thee, thou flaming Minifter,   10
I can againe thy former light reftore,
Should I repent me.   But once put out thy Light,
Thou cunning'ft Patterne of excelling Nature,
I know not where is that *Promethæan* heate
That can thy Light re-Lume.   15
When I haue pluck'd thy Rofe,
I cannot giue it vitall growth againe,
It needs muft wither.   Ile fmell thee on the Tree.
Oh Balmy breath, that doft almoft perfwade   19

---

12. *me*] Om. Pope+.

thy Light] *thine* Qq, Jen. Rann,
Steev.'93, Var. Sing. Ktly.

13. *cunning'ft*] *cunning* Q₁, Jen.

14. Promethæan] *promethian* Qq. Pro-
methean Ff.

heate] *fire* Cap. conj. (p. 37 *a*).

15, 16. One line, Qq, Cap. et seq.

15. *re-Lume*] F₂F₃. *returne* Q₁. *relum-
ine* Q₂Q₃, Cap. Jen. Steev.'85. *re-lumine*
Rowe+. *re-lume* F₄. *relume* Mal. et cet.

[Sets down the Taper. Theob. ...

not putting it out. Han.

16. *thy*] *the* Qq, Han. Jen. Rann, Glo.
Cam. Dyce iii, Coll. iii, Huds. Rlfe, Wh. ii.

18. *needs muft*] *muft needes* Qq, Glo.
Cam. Rlfe, Wh. ii.

thee] Ff, Rowe+, Cap. Knt.   *the*
F₃.   *it* Qq, Johns. et cet.

[Kiffes her. Q₂Q₃.]   He kiffes her
(after lines 22, 23) Q₁.

19. *Oh*] *A* Qq.   *O* Rowe.   *Ah* Glo.

doft almoft] *doth almost* Qq, Knt.
almost dost Jen.

---

quench thee,' &c., or thus : '——— alabaster.   [*Takes off his sword.*]   Yet she must die,
else she'll betray more men.   [*Puts out the light.*]   If I quench thee,' &c.   DYCE
(ed. iii) : I agree with Malone and Walker that [*thy* light] is the true reading, though
Boswell objects to it as introducing 'a cold conceit' (he, we may suppose, having suddenly forgotten what a crop of 'conceits' there is in Shakespeare).   Compare the context : 'but once *put out thy light*, ... that can *thy light* relume.'   [Surely Malone
knew that his change to '*thy* light' was not original.   Farmer's reference to Fielding
is quoted in Malone's own edition; it was this casual reference to Fielding that led me
to look up the passage.   Ought not Dyce to have known that it was at least as old as
Hanmer?   Dyce is unsparing in his criticisms of mistakes or oversights in others, yet
he is no more infallible than the rest of us.   In the interpretation of the present line
every one will decide, and for the nonce rightly, according to his own temperament.
Warburton's suggestion suits mine.—ED.]   THEOBALD gives us a glimpse of the stage
business of his day where he says : 'The players in all the companies wherever I have
seen this tragedy performed, commit the absurdity of making Othello put out the candle.'   He goes on to say, 'Desdemona is discovered in her bed in the dark; Othello
enters the chamber with a taper.   If there were any other lights in the room, where
would be the drift of putting out *his ?*   If there were no others, and that he put out
his, how absurd is it for Desdemona in the dark to talk of his "eyes rolling," and his
"gnawing his nether lip."'   The difficulty is solved, Theobald thinks, by making
Othello set down the light while he goes to kiss Desdemona; this wakens her, and so
'they continue in discourse together till he stifles her.'   [How vapid is the Italian
translation : Ch' io spenga questa face, E poi la vita sua.']

16. *thy Rose*] To me, this is far preferable to *the rose* of the Qq.   This is 'beauty's
Rose' of the *S nnets.*—ED.

Iuftice to breake her Sword.   One more, one more :   20
Be thus when thou art dead, and I will kill thee,
And loue thee after.   One more, and that's the laft.
So fweet, was ne're fo fatall.   I muft weepe,
But they are cruell Teares : This forrow's heauenly,
It ftrikes, where it doth loue.   She wakes.   25

 Def.   Who's there ? *Othello* ?
 Othel.   I *Defdemona.*
 Def.   Will you come to bed, my Lord?
 Oth.   Haue you pray'd to night, *Defdemon* ?
 Def.   I my Lord.   30
 Oth.   If you bethinke your felfe of any Crime
Vnreconcil'd as yet to Heauen, and Grace,
Solicite for it ftraight.   33

---

20. *Iuftice*] *Iuftice her felfe* Qq, Jen.
Steev.'85, Mal. Rann.

 Sword.   One more, one more :]
fword once more, Q₁. *fword: one more ;*
Q₂Q₃. *Sword.—Once more—* Jen. Steev.
'85, Mal. Rann.

 22. *One more*] *Once more* Q₄, Jen. Steev.
'85, Mal. Rann.

 and that's] Ff, Rowe, Knt, Dyce,
Sta. *that's* Pope+. *and this* Qq et cet.

25. *where*] *when* Q₁, Jen.
doth] *does* Qq.

 She wakes.]—*She wakes*— Pope.
She wakes— Steev.   A Stage direction,
reading *It*...*Othello* ? as one line, Anon.
ap. Cam.

27. *I*] *I*, QqF₃F₄.   *Ay*, Rowe.

29. *pray'd*] *prayed* Qq.

Defdemon] F₂, Knt, Dyce, Sta.
Del.   Defdemona QqF₃F₄ et cet.

---

23. **weepe**] BOOTH : Remember how often he is moved to tears,—therefore I do not attempt to restrain them in the excess of passion here, in Act III, and elsewhere. [Yet Othello himself says that his eyes are 'unused to the melting mood.'—ED.]

24. **heauenly**] JOHNSON : 'This tenderness, with which I lament the punishment which justice compels me to inflict, is a holy passion.' I wish these two lines could be honestly ejected. It is the fate of Shakespeare to counteract his own pathos. STEEVENS : The 'cruel tears' seem adopted from the fabulous history of the crocodile [ROLFE quotes this, and befittingly adds an exclamation mark]; the 'heavenly sorrow' from a passage in the Scriptures. DEIGHTON : Othello surely means, 'I cannot help weeping at your fate, but my tears do not soften my heart, so as to change my determination to kill you.' HUDSON : The tears are cruel, because, while heart-wringing pity is streaming from the eyes, an overmastering strain of duty is forcing him to what is, objectively, an act of cruelty. And the very loveliness of the victim only works to intensify his purpose, lest love should usurp the crown that belongs to a higher passion,—a passion, too, that *must* wear the crown, else love itself will fall from its propriety. Pathos carried to the most soul-searching height ! And the 'sorrow is heavenly,' because it is baptized and washed into holiness by the sacred and divine regards of justice.

33. **Solicite**] WALKER (*Crit.* iii, 291) : That is, *plead*, as in the old sense of *solicitor ;* yet I do not know that *plead* exactly expresses the meaning.

Def. Alacke, my Lord,
What may you meane by that ?   35
   Oth. Well, do it, and be breefe, I will walke by :
I would not kill thy vnprepared Spirit,
No , Heauens fore-fend) I would not kill thy Soule.
   Def. Talke you of killing ?
   Oth. I, I do.   40
   Def. Then Heauen haue mercy on mee.
   Oth. Amen, with all my heart.   [336 *a*]
   Def. If you fay, I hope you will not kill me.
   Oth. Humh.
   Def. And yet I feare you : for you're fatall then   45
When your eyes rowle fo.
Why I fhould feare, I know not,
Since guiltineffe I know not : But yet I feele I feare.
   Oth. Thinke on thy finnes.
   Def. They are Loues I beare to you.   50
   Oth. I, and for that thou dy'ft.
   Def. That death's vnnaturall, that kils for louing.
Alas, why gnaw you fo your nether-lip ?
Some bloody paffion fhakes your very Frame :
Thefe are portents : but yet I hope, I hope,   55

34, 35. One line, Qq, Cap. et seq.
34. *Alacke*] Ff, Rowe +, Knt, Dyce, Sta. Huds. *Alas* Qq et cet.
35. *may*] *doe* Q₂Q₃, Glo. Rlfe, Wh. ii.
38. *Heauens*] Ff, Rowe +, Knt. *heauen* Qq et cet.
41, 42. *haue...heart*] As one line, Cap. Steev. et seq. (except Cam.).
43. *fay*] *fay fo* QqFf et cet.
44. *Humh*] *Hum* Qq. *Humph !* Mal.
45. *you're*] Ff, Rowe +, Dyce iii, Huds. *y'are* Q₂Q₃. *you are* Q₁ et cet.
46, 47. One line, Qq, Theob. et seq.

48. *guiltineffe*] *guilt* Pope +.
   But] Om. Pope +.
50. *They are*] *They're* Pope +, Dyce iii, Huds.
   Loues] *love* Ff.
   I beare] *to beare* Q₃.
51. *I, and*] *And* Qq.
   dy'ft] *dieft* Qq.
52. *vnnaturall...louing*] *unnatural ; what ! kill for loving !* Han.
53. *gnaw*] *knaw* Q₂Q₃.
   nether-lip] *neather lip* Qq.
55. *I hope, I hope*] *I hope* Qq.

---

36. **walke by**] BOOTH : Paces the room.

38. **Soule**] STEEVENS : Othello appears to have been a favourite of his author ; he has bestowed on him that piety which he had refused to Hamlet. See *Ham.* III, iii, 94.

42. BOOTH : Say it with all your heart and soul.

52. **vnnaturall**] MALONE : Compare *Rich. III :* I, ii, 134, 'It is a quarrel most unnatural, To be revenged on him that loveth you.'

54. FECHTER : She throws back the coverlet, rises, and sits on the bed.

55. **portents**] For other instances of 'portent' thus accented on the last syllable, see ABBOTT, § 190.

They do not point on me.   56
 Oth. Peace, and be ftill.
 Def. I will fo : What's the matter?
 Oth. That Handkerchiefe
Which I fo lou'd, and gaue thee, thou gau'ft to *Caſſio.*   6c
 Def. No by my Life, and Soule : fend for the man,
And aske him.
 Oth. Sweet Soule, take heed, take heed of Periury,
Thou art on thy death-bed.
 Def. I, but not yet to dye.   65
 Oth. Prefently.
Therefore confeffe thee freely of thy finne :
For to deny each Article with Oath,
Cannot remoue, nor choake the ftrong Conception
That I do grone withall. Thou art to dye.   7c
 Def. O Heauen haue mercy on me.
 Oth. I fay, Amen.
 Def. And haue you mercy too. I neuer did
Offend you in my life : neuer lou'd *Caſſio,*
But with fuch generall warrantie of Heauen,   75
As I might loue. I neuer gaue him Token.
 Oth. By Heauen I faw my Handkerchiefe in's hand.
O periur'd woman, thou do'ft ftone my heart,   78

---

58. *will ſo :*] Ff, Rowe+, Cap. Jen. Steev. Mal. Var. Knt, Sing. Ktly. *will, ſo,* Q₁Q₂. *will ſo,* Q₃. *will so.* Johns. et cet.

59, 60. *That...thee*] One line, Qq, Cap. Steev. et seq.

59, &c. *Handkerchiefe*] *handkercher* Q₁.

60. *gau'ſt*] *gaueſt* Qq.
 to] Om. F₃F₄, Rowe+.

61, 62. Lines end, *Soule :...him.* Qq, Cap. Steev. et seq.

63, 64. Lines divided, *heed,...death-bed.* Cap. Steev. et seq.

64. *Thou art*] *thou'rt* Steev.'93, Var. Knt, Coll. Sing. Wh. i, Ktly, Dyce iii, Huds.

66. *Prefently*] Ff, Rowe, Pope, Theob. Warb. Johns. *Yes, prefently* Qq et cet

69. *Conception*] *conceit* Q₁, Jen.

71. *O Heauen*] Ff, Rowe+, Cap. Jen. Steev.'85, Knt. *Then Lord* Qq et cet.

73, 74. *I...*Caffio] One line, Qq.

74. *life : neuer*] *life,—neuer* Qq.

77. *in's*] *in his* Qq, Jen. Steev. Mal. Var. Sing. Ktly.

78. *periur'd...do'ſt*] *periured...doeſt* Q₁. *my*] *thy* Q₁.

---

58. **will so :**] Note the punctuation of Q₁Q₂; indicating what seems to me to be the true reading : 'I will.—So.—What's,' &c.—ED.

65. BOOTH : Desdemona comes from her bed, and rests tremblingly against it.

66. **Presently**] ABBOTT, § 59 : That is, 'at the present time,' 'at once,' instead of, as now, 'soon, but *not* at once.'

71. BOOTH : Sinking on her knees. During the rest of this, down to line 98, she is half reclining on the steps and dais of the bed.

And makes me call, what I intend to do,
A Murther, which I thought a Sacrifice.   80
I faw the Handkerchiefe.
    Def.   He found it then :
I neuer gaue it him : Send, for him hither.
Let him confeffe a truth.
    Oth.   He hath confeſt.   85
    Def.   What, my Lord ?
    Oth.   That he hath vs'd thee.   87

---

79. *makes*] *makeſt* Q₄Ff. *makſt* Q₂Q₃.

80. *Murther*] Ff, Rowe+, Cap. Knt, Wh. Rlfe.   *murder* Qq, Johns. et cet.

84. *Let*] *And let* Q₁, Jen. Steev. Mal. Var. Sing. Ktly.

85. *hath*] *has* Qq.

87. *hath vs'd thee.*] Ff, Rowe, Knt, Dyce, Wh. Glo. Cam. Del. Rlfe. *hath— vds death.* Q₁.   *hath—vſde thee.* Q₂Q₃ et cet.

---

80. **Sacrifice**] JOHNSON : This line is difficult. 'Thou hast hardened my heart, and makest me kill thee with the rage of a murderer, when I thought to have sacrificed thee to justice with the calmness of a priest striking a victim.'   I suspect '*thy* heart' of Q₁ to be genuine.   The meaning then will be,—'Thou forcest me to dismiss thee from the world in the state of the murdered without preparation for death, when I intended that thy punishment should have been a sacrifice atoning for thy crime.'   I am glad that I have ended my revisal of this dreadful scene.   It is not to be endured. HALLIWELL : Many readers will probably sympathize with Dr Johnson's concluding observation.   Without disputing the masterly power displayed in the composition of the present tragedy, there is something to my mind so revolting, both in the present Scene and in the detestable character of Iago, which renders a study of the drama of *Othello* rather a painful duty than one of pleasure.   [I do not shrink from saying that I wish this Tragedy had never been written.   The pleasure, however keen or elevated, which the inexhaustible poetry of the preceding Acts can bestow, cannot possibly, to my temperament, countervail, it does but increase, the unutterable agony of this closing Scene. --ED.]

85-98. HALES (p. 112) : For the most part Shakespeare delights in tracing the action of the great moral laws of the world, and showing how fearful is the penalty of trans-gression.   But sometimes he exhibits a yet more dreadful spectacle,—a spectacle mysterious, inscrutable, soul-prostrating.   It is Fate blind, inexorable, rapacious.   Desdemona is one of Fate's choicest victims.   Her 'graces serve' her 'but as enemies.'   Her very virtues bring on her ruin.   What is most innocent is construed into evidence against her.   In obeying the best instincts of her clear spirit she excites the evilest suspicions and secures the bitterest condemnation.   The truth from her lips is turned into a lie.   In the present passage, her answers, by an almost incredible infelicity, are, through the very purity of her nature, just such as to confirm Othello's detestable impeachment.   Could replies be more unfortunate ?   She lies in the toils of Fate, and there is no escape for her.   We may go further than her name in Greek, δυσδαίμων, 'ill-starred,' and say it is merely a variation of δυσδαιμονία, 'ill-starredness.'   She is not only unhappy, she is unhappiness itself.

87. **vs'd thee**] COLLIER (ed. iii) : The First Qto gives an important reading, as if Othello were choked and unable to utter the words.   [To be sure 'uds death' is not

Def. How? vnlawfully ? 88

Oth. I.

Def. He will not fay fo. 90

Oth. No : his mouth is ftopp'd :

Honeft *Iago* hath 'tane order for't.

Def. Oh, my feare interprets. What is he dead?

Oth. Had all his haires bin liues, my great Reuenge

Had ftomacke for them all. 95

Def. Alas, he is betray'd, and I vndone.

*Oth.*Out Strumpet : weep'ft thou for him to my face?

Def. O banifh me, my Lord, but kill me not.

Oth. Downe Strumpet.

Def. Kill me to morrow, let me liue to night. 100

Oth. Nay, if you ftriue.

Def. But halfe an houre.

Oth. Being done, there is no pawfe.

Def. But while I fay one prayer. 104

---

93. *Oh,...interprets.*] *My feare inter-
prets then,*— Qq, Theob. Warb. Johns.
Cap. Jen. Mal. Steev. Var. Coll. Sing.
Ktly. *My fear interprets. Oh!* Han.

94, 95. *my...all.*] One line, Qq.

95. *them*] *'em* Q₁, Jen. *em* Q₂Q₃.

96. *betray'd*] *betrayed* Q₃.

I] *I'm* Han.

97. *Out Strumpet :*] *O ftrumpet,*— Qq.

97. *weep'ft*] *weepeft* Qq.

101. *if*] *an* Qq.

ftriue.] QqFf, Rowe, Pope, Knt.
strive— Theob. et cet.

102. *houre.*] *hour*— Rowe, Pope, Har.

103 is omitted, joining in one lines 102,
104, by Q₁, Pope, Han. Dividing it at *done*
Cap. Steev. Mal. Var. Knt, Coll. Sing. Sta.
Wh. i, Ktly.

---

an uncommon exclamation in the old dramas ('vds pitty' occurs in Q₁ at IV, iii, 84),
but Desdemona's next question shows clearly, I think, that it is out of place here.—
ED.]

92. **'tane order**] STEEVENS: That is, has taken measures. [See SCHMIDT, s. v. 2.]

94. **liues**] STEEVENS: This thought appears to have been very common; it occurs
frequently in dramas prior to *Othello.*

97. BOOTH: Enraged. After his next speech there is a struggle, during which
Othello hides her from the audience while she gets back upon the bed.

103. **Being done**] KNIGHT: A correspondent suggests that the reading should be,
'being *down*, there is no pause.' We cannot agree to receive Othello's meaning so
literally. He certainly has already said, 'Down, strumpet,' and has probably at that
moment commenced the death-struggle; for he adds, 'nay, if you *strive.*' But the
words 'being done' appear to us to have a much greater depth of meaning. They are
not addressed to Desdemona, but exhibit what is passing in Othello's mind. The conflict between his love and his wounded honour is over; he looks upon the act of retribution as *done* when he has lifted his murderous hand against his wife. It is done.
For the mere completior of the violence, which will then be mercy, 'there is no
pause.'

Oth.   It is too late.   *Smothers her.*   105
      Æmilia at the doore.
Æmil.   My Lord, my Lord? What hoa?
My Lord, my Lord.   [336 *b*]
   Oth. What noife is this? Not dead? not yet quite dead?
I that am cruell, am yet mercifull,   110
I would not haue thee linger in thy paine?
So, fo.   112

105. *It is too*] *Tis too* Q₁, Jen. *Tis to*
Q₂Q₃.
   Smothers her.] he ftifles her. Q₁.
he ftifles her. (after line 104) Q₂Q₃. At-
tempts to smother her. Rowe ii.
   105, 107. *late.* Æmil. *My Lord*] *late.*
Def. *O Lord, Lord, Lord.* Em. *My Lord*
Q₁, Jen. Coll. Ktly.

Scene VII. Pope+, Jen.
   106. Æmilia...] *Emillia* calls within.
Qq.
   107, 108. One line, Qq, Pope et seq.
   109. *noife*] *voyce* Qq, Jen.
   111, 112. One line, Qq.
   112. [Stabbing her. Rann.

---

105. STEEVENS: After this speech, Q₁ adds an invocation from Desdemona, consisting only of the sacred name thrice repeated. As this must be supposed to have been
uttered while she is yet struggling with death, I think an editor may be excused from
inserting such a circumstance of supererogatory horror. SINGER was misled by this
note of Steevens, as was pointed out by the Cambridge Editors, and 'invented a reading of Q₁'; he says that Desdemona's invocation was 'God! God! God!' COLLIER
(ed. i) having adopted these exclamations, which, as he said, are found only in Q₁, DYCE
(*Rem.* 242), adds: 'And there Collier ought (with the other modern editors) to have
left them; for they were most probably foisted into the text by the players. So far is
"O Lord, Lord, Lord!" from adding to the terror or pathos of the scene, that [*sic*] it is
disgustingly vulgar; and being immediately followed by Emilia's " My *lord*, my *lord!*
what ho! my *lord*, my *lord!*" the effect of the whole is not a little comic.' COLLIER,
nothing intimidated, calmly printed the Quarto's words in his next edition. Whereupon DYCE, in *his* next edition, observed that though he had protested against the
insertion of 'Oh Lord, Lord, Lord,' as disgustingly vulgar, &c., his 'protest appears to
have had no other effect than to make Mr Collier the more determined to retain it in
his second edition.' In his third and last edition COLLIER again imperturbably prints
the invocation from the Qto, and says that the words are 'exclamations by Desdemona,
to show that she is not killed, and she speaks afterwards.'

105. BOOTH: Long pause. Emilia's rap must not be loud.

112. In the Appendix will be found the Ballad which was discovered among the Egerton Papers by Collier. From this ballad we learn that the earliest actor of Othello, Bur
badge, Shakespeare's friend and fellow-actor, stabbed Desdemona, and 'dyed to gory
red, his hands of blackest shade.' Collier, however, shows that the writer 'spoke at
random' in it, with regard to Burbadge's early career, and its antiquity has been recently
questioned, so that its authority as to the 'stabbing' must pass for what it is worth.
From the tone of FRANCIS GENTLEMAN's remarks in the *Dramatic Censor* (i, 148) in
1770, where he is presumably criticising Garrick, we may infer that the stabbing of
Desdemona was an innovation which needed justification. Gentleman says: 'The
revival of Desdemona from a state of suffocation, and her expiring without any fresh
violence, we apprehend to be rather absurd, therefore, highly approve Othello's stabbing

[112. **I would not haue thee linger in thy paine? So, so.**]

her with a dagger,—drawing blood accounts naturally for gaining power of speech, and yet may be mortal.' The editors and commentators, in the Variorum Editions, are singularly silent. STEEVENS alone alludes to the question, and he approves of 'stabbing' on the ground, suggested by Gentleman, of its relief to congestion, and believes that a stage direction to that effect had been accidentally omitted. This omission was supplied by RANN, the solitary editor who has inserted it. KNIGHT thinks it is 'most probable' that Othello stabs Desdemona, 'according to the practice of the modern stage. His previous resolution, "I'll not shed her blood," is forgotten in the agony and terror of the moment, when he says "not dead, not yet quite dead."' DELIUS believes that if Shakespeare had 'intended Othello to stab Desdemona, he would have given us in the context some hint, no matter how slight, from which it might be inferred. The lack of this hint, coupled with the express stage directions, compels us to suppose that with the "So, so" Othello again stifles Desdemona.' COLLIER says, in reference to the stabbing, that 'it may be so.' HUDSON thinks the stage custom of stabbing 'may be right.' COWDEN-CLARKE believes that '"So, so" may merely be intended to represent that Othello heaps more clothes around her, pressing the pillow more closely upon the mouth.' DYCE, STAUNTON, WHITE, ROLFE, and PURNELL are silent. FECHTER: Passing his poignard under the pillow and turning away his eyes. BOOTH: Hide your face in trembling hand while you stab and groan 'So, so'; the steel is piercing your own heart. SALVINI: I think that this 'So, so' means that Othello kneels on her breast to hasten her death.

Thus far Editors and Actors, with a ground-tone from the public at large to the effect that there does seem to be something not altogether true to physiology in the subsequent revival of Desdemona; yet, such is the Anglosaxon faith in Shakespeare, that, in any variance between him and Nature, Shakespeare is considered quite able to hold his own.

It was the phrase 'Pale as thy smock' which first caught my attention; it seemed to reveal either an oversight on Shakespeare's part, or that he had intended, contrary to the directions in the QqFf, that Desdemona should be stabbed. As far as I know, no one has ever noticed the bearing, on the manner of Desdemona's death, of this exclamation. To my layman's small knowledge there seemed here a violation of physiological laws so downright, in representing a smothered person as pale, that I knew Shakespeare, who could note the 'crimson drops i' the bottom of a cowslip,' never could have committed it. The reality before our very eyes cannot be as vivid as the coinage of his brain was to Shakespeare. What he saw, he spoke; so that he must either have known of a case where congestion of blood in the face did not follow stifling, or he must have intended Othello to stab Desdemona; which, after all, would only half solve the difficulty; the stabbing would leave the face pale, but the smock red, as I thought. For Shakespeare's credit I felt no concern, but I did feel mortified for Nature, on whose behalf it seemed that if ever our best medical wisdom were to be unmuzzled, this was the hour. To this trial, in which Nature is the defendant (not Shakespeare, perish the thought!) I hoped to summon such an array of experts that their verdict would be accepted as final wherever the masters in medicine are known and honored, or any faith exists in diagnosis. To each one of the following eminent men, whose friendship I am glad to own, I sent a copy of this last Scene, with the following passages underscored: '*Yet I'll not shed her blood*'; '*So, so*'; '*She's Dead*'; '*Ha, No More Moving? Still as the Grave*'; '*I think she stirs again,—No*'; all Desdemona's words after the smothering: '*Your niece, Whose breath, indeed, these hands have newly stopped*'; and lastly, '*Pale as thy smock,*' accompanying which were these questions: 1. Do you think it likely that

[112. **I would not haue thee linger in thy paine? So, so.**]

Othello stabbed Desdemona at ‘So, so’?   2. If he stabbed her, could her smock be pale?   3. If she were smothered, could she be pale?   4. In either case, could she speak after apparent death?   5. If she could speak, why did she not quite revive? 6. From what cause, then, did she really die?

To these questions there came the following answers:—

DR D. HAYES AGNEW: In answer to your inquiry, I would say that Shakespeare has been most unfortunate in killing Desdemona.   Death by strangulation, inferred from the language used by Othello: ‘*Whose breath indeed, these hands have newly stopp'd,*’ cannot readily be reconciled with a temporary revival and ability to speak at three different times on the part of the victim, after all signs of life had apparently disappeared nor with the post-mortem appearances, in which the color of the face and of the smock are compared (both presumably white).

Against the theory of death by stabbing, we have the declaration of Othello himself, ‘*Yet I'lt not shed her blood,*’ and the supposed absence of blood-stains on the clothing of Desdemona, indicated by the expression, ‘*pale as thy smock*’; and yet all the phenomena before and after death are comprehensible on the theory of internal hemorrhage, namely, the possibility of a stab in a vital region of the body, without more than a few drops of blood being seen externally; syncope, resembling actual death, causing a temporary arrest of bleeding and a return to consciousness and to speech, followed by the recurrence of a rapidly-fatal hemorrhage, leaving the face bloodless and pale.

There is, however, a theory which (though somewhat strained) would meet all the conditions of the text; namely, that death ensued from the secondary effects of injury to the larynx.   It is true that in fatal cases following laceration or fracture of that organ, the patient dies from a slow asphyxia, and may be rendered voiceless by the lesion; but surgical writers refer to instances in which, after violence applied to the neck and the person apparently suffocated, partial recovery has followed with ability to speak, and yet death suddenly followed from shock, with probably some spasm of the glottis.   In shock the blood retreats from the superficial vessels, giving to the surface the pallor of death.   Probably such were the conditions in the case of Desdemona.

DR D. G. BRINTON: There is not a word in the text about stabbing, and several passages make directly against it.   In describing Desdemona's death, Othello distinctly states that he ‘stopped her breath,’—smothered her.   Death by stabbing, therefore, could not have been in the mind of the author at all.

This leads to the further result that her death is not represented as the immediate act of her husband; he is not the murderer that he thinks himself; his hands refused the deed and failed at the second attempt, as they did at the first.   Again she moves and speaks.   But her frail body has been put to too severe a strain.   Anxiety and fear have been too much for her debilitated heart, and her last and superhuman effort to exculpate her loved husband completely exhausts her vital powers; the central organ fails, and she falls back dead from ‘cardiac exhaustion.’   We may call it ‘paralysis of the heart,’ like that brought about by certain potent poisons, or that which supervenes in feeble subjects on sudden and violent emotions, either of fear or joy.   We know little of the intimate pathology of this fatal process.   Writers say that such physical or mental shocks ‘extinguish life by their action on the cardiac plexus.’   The phrase sounds well, but leaves us where we were before.

Such instances are by no means rare, and must have come to the knowledge of the author of *Othello*.   A number of them were quoted for the defence in a trial in New

[112. I would not haue thee linger in thy paine? So, so.]

York City a few years ago. The victim, wife of a physician, was smothered by the assassin. The defence was, that the attempt at suffocation was abortive, that she revived, but died of heart-shock from fright and struggling. The theory of her death thus advanced by the defence is my theory of the death of Desdemona. It consistently explains the appearance of her face, her smock, her recovery of speech, &c., and relieves us from the painful and repugnant contemplation of her husband as her actual murderer. I shall be delighted if these crude remarks aid you in any degree in throwing light on the train of thought in this wonderful literary creation.

Dr J. M. DA COSTA : The features of Desdemona's death cannot, I believe, be reconciled to strict scientific facts; it is best to accept them as not transgressing poetic license. That she should have spoken after being smothered is not possible; if she had regained consciousness sufficiently to speak intelligently, as she did, recovery would have ensued, though death might have happened, after a time, from injuries induced by the violence.

Concerning the pallor of the countenance, it is contrary to the customary conception of death by strangulation; the face is held to be suffused and swollen, of dusky or violet hue; but the great poet, in assuming it otherwise, has not been guilty of error. The countenance in strangulation may be pale and sunken; indeed, so eminent an authority as Casper declares his observation to have taught him that the greater number of persons strangled have neither a turgid nor a livid countenance, but one simply like that of any other corpse.

These statements deal with the supposition that Desdemona's death was caused by strangling. If the stage tradition of her being also stabbed be admitted as correct, a view suggests itself which removes all difficulties. The effect of the bleeding would be to relieve the cerebral and pulmonary congestion occurring in strangulation. She revives sufficiently to speak; the internal hemorrhage continues; she dies exhausted, and, as always in death from loss of blood, with extreme pallor marked. 'Pale as thy smock' Othello might well say; nor need a poet's words be so literally construed as to exclude the thought of some blood-stains on the white garment; though in point of fact a stab severing large vessels in the chest may prove fatal without giving rise to external bleeding.

The stabbing subsequent to the smothering makes, then, the death of Desdemona one which is described with the closest attention to truth. Whether the stage tradition represent Shakespeare's thought is, of course, an open question. There is that in the text, however, which supports the supposition of the stabbing, notwithstanding Othello's first-declared intention of not shedding blood. He sees her linger, and he determines on quick, decisive measures. The words 'So, so,' when he is supposed to stab her, are short, abrupt expressions, very suitable to rapid, sudden movements as in stabbing.

Dr WILLIAM A. HAMMOND : The matter that engrosses your attention has many features of interest to me, and your questions lead up to several important points.

Without going into details, I may say, first, I do not think Othello stabbed Desdemona; he expressly says, ' I will not shed her blood.' I am of the opinion that, at the words ' So, so,' he pressed the pillow more forcibly against her face.

If he stabbed her, I think it possible, though not probable, that her smock might be pale.

If she were smothered she might be pale. Persons who are smothered do not ordinarily show any signs of having suffered a violent death. For my views in full on this point, permit me to refer you to my novel, *Mr Oldmixon*, chap. xiii, in which Hogarth Oldmixon smothers his wife.

[112. **I would not haue thee linger in thy paine? So, so.**]

If she were smothered sufficiently, she certainly could not speak after the act. A person smothered, and speaking afterwards, would not die from the smothering. The mere fact of her speaking shows that she was not smothered to the extent necessary to cause death.

As to what really killed her, I think it is clearly apparent that Shakespeare was ignorant of the *modus operandi* of smothering. She ought not to have died at all so far as any act of Othello's is directly concerned, except, perhaps, from what is called a 'broken heart,' or from extreme shock to her nervous system.

Dr WILLIAM HUNT: You have asked me some interesting questions about Desdemona's death. I am happy to be able to answer you positively and at once; her sad end is no pathological puzzle to me. She died of fracture of the cricoid cartilage of the larynx. Shakespeare is entirely consistent, and must have had, as in everything else, an intuitive, if not practical, knowledge of the subject. Years ago I wrote an Article upon that fracture, founded upon a case of it. The Article is quoted as authority to this day. I collected all the reported cases I could find, and several of them were like Desdemona's. It was a piece of unpardonable oversight in me that I did not put her in the list. The poet's story is exactly in accordance with the ordinary sequence of symptoms. There is nothing for a school-boy or anybody else to laugh at in it.

Othello, true to his stated purpose, did not 'shed her blood, nor scar that whiter skin of hers than snow.' He first tried a very ineffectual method of smothering with pillows. His poor victim was simply dazed, 'not dead.' Seeing this, he grasps her neck with his powerful hands, his thumbs being over the larynx, and with two strong squeezes and a 'So, so,' garrotes her.

The cricoid cartilage breaks, and under the shock there is 'no more moving.' She is 'still as the grave.' But I have no doubt she did 'stir again'; had any good auscultator placed his ear to her chest he would have heard her heart beating feebly and rapidly. Paleness, not lividity, would accompany this condition. I have seen it so in others. A short time passes. Desdemona slowly and temporarily reacts. An exciting conversation is held in her presence. She hears, and in a smothered, hoarse whisper, perfectly audible, she speaks; there is a slight spitting of blood, for which, in her nicety, she uses a handkerchief she had about her, and which must have reminded her of that other fatal one 'spotted with strawberries,' and so her smock is left pale and undefiled. In my case the patient was pale as a ghost, and his speech as hoarse as a raven's. Gradually Desdemona succumbs to the pressure of swelling and emphysema, and to the nervous shock. Tracheotomy was the only thing that might have saved her, but there was nobody there to perform it, and the chance was slim. I have thus, I think, answered all your questions. Does not Othello himself acknowledge my method when he says, 'There lies your niece, whose breath indeed *these hands* have newly stopped'? There was never a clearer case. Is not Shakespeare's universality wonderful?

Rest assured, Desdemona died of fracture of the larynx. The history and the sequences are without flaws.

In future, let no Othello stab; and let Desdemona learn a hoarse, grating, audible whisper that will rasp the audience into sympathetic agony.

Dr AD. LIPPE: To the first question, I answer No; Othello stifles, but does not stab Desdemona; he had said 'I will not shed her blood'; at 'So, so,' he stifles her the more.

Had she been stabbed, her smock would have been saturated with blood.

If she were smothered, she could be nothing else but pale.

Æmil. within.   What hoa? my Lord, my Lord?   113
Oth.   Who's there?

113. within.] Om. Qq.

Had she been stabbed and the dirk or knife not withdrawn, she might have spoken. If the dagger had been withdrawn, she could not have spoken. If smothered, and, since Othello says ' I think she stirs again,' not fully dead, a few drops remaining in the left heart would permit of a contraction, and the lungs not being completely clogged would allow the utterance of a few words. These last few contractions of the left heart must have been caused by the violent mental emotions produced by Emilia's relation and her questions. These few remaining drops having been expelled, her ability to speak ceased, and she was fully dead. The real cause of her death was suffocation and stifling. In Wharton and Stillé's *Medical Jurisprudence*, ii, 802, we find a complete vindication of Shakespeare : ' *Homicidal Suffocation.* Those who are usually the victims of this form of murder are infants and the aged, or those who are otherwise helpless. So slight a degree of resistance is necessary to defeat the purpose of the assassin, that a great disproportion of strength must exist for the attempt to be successful. Nevertheless, those miserable wretches, Burke and his accomplices, reduced murder by suffocation to a system, choosing it as a mode of death most likely to leave no mark of crime behind it. The murderer bore with his whole weight upon the breast of his victim, and with his hands forcibly covered the mouth and nostrils till death came on. The body of one of the victims presented, according to Dr Christison, so few traces of injury, that without the assistance of proof from other sources, it would have been impossible to have declared that the death was not a natural one.' How well Shakespeare knew the difference between suffocation and strangulation is evident from his masterly description of the latter in the case of Gloucester in *2 Hen. VI*: III, ii. Suffocation alone caused the death of Desdemona, and the suffocation was slow. Violent mental emotion caused the heart to expel the last few drops of blood, and when the right side of the heart became filled with dark venous blood, she died. How violent mental emotions can affect the heart belongs to the deep mysteries of Nature. Materialists cannot solve the question.

Dr S. Weir Mitchell : I suppose Shakespeare would have put in a stage direction at ' So, so,' if he had meant that Othello used a dagger. Were I an actor I should simply throttle her fiercely again and again as I said ' So, so.' With this view her smock need not trouble us. Death by strangling leaves the face horribly congested, not pale. Believing that Othello simply choked Desdemona, how could she have been pale of visage and spoken several distinct sentences with so clear a brain as the relevancy of her words displays, and yet have been *fatally* strangled ?

It could not have been; but I fancy Shakespeare cared little for realism when he desired an explanatory dramatic effect.

If there is evidence that Shakespeare meant that Othello choked her insufficiently, and finished with a dirk, it becomes clearer, because then speech, partial recovery, death from bleeding, help us to understand the passage. At the same time the face would have been paling from blood-loss, and as to the smock, all wounds do not bleed externally ; then a little blood on the smock would not have made less for him its general whiteness.

Again, where Othello says he has ' newly stopp'd her breath,' he does not speak of what would have been the more striking object to the spectator, the dagger-wound. For him, too, that would have been *the* murder, not the ineffectual throttle.

Æmil.   Oh good my Lord, I would ſpeake a word   115
with you.

Oth.   Yes : 'Tis *Æmilia* : by and by.   Shee's dead.
'Tis like ſhe comes to ſpeake of *Caſſio*'s death :
The noiſe was high.   Hah, no more moouing ?
Still as the Graue.   Shall ſhe come in ? Wer't good ?   120
I thinke ſhe ſtirres againe   No, what's beſt to do ?
If ſhe come in, ſhee'l ſure ſpeake to my wife :
My wife, my wife : what wife ? I haue no wife.
Oh inſupportable ! Oh heauy houre !
Me thinkes, it ſhould be now a huge Eclipſe   125
Of Sunne, and Moone ; and that th'affrighted Globe
Did yawne at Alteration.

Æmil.   I do beſeech you
That I may ſpeake with you.   Oh good my Lord.   129

115, 128. Æmil.] Emil. within. Mal.
115. *good my*] *my good* F₃F₄, Rowe+.
I would] *I'de* Qq, Cap. Jen.
117. Æmilia: *by and by :*] Emilia, *by
and by :* Qq. Æmilia—*by and by*—
Rowe+, Cap. Jen.
119. *high*] *here* Q₁, Jen. Glo. Cam.
Rlfe, Wh. ii.
119, 120. *moouing ? Still*] *moving ;
Still* Jen.
121. *beſt to do*] *the beſt* Qq, Pope+,
Cap. Jen. Steev. Mal. Var. Coll.
122. *ſhe come*] *ſhe'll come* Coll. iii.
123. *wife : what wife ?*] *wife, my wife ;*
Q₁.
I haue] *I ha* Qq.

126. *th'*] Ff, Rowe ii+, Jen. Coll. Wh.
i, Dyce iii.   *the* Qq et cet.
127. *Did*] Ff, Rowe i, Knt.   *Should*
Qq et cet.
Alteration.] *Alteration—* Rowe,
Pope, Theob. Han. Warb.
128, 129. *I do…Lord*] One line, Qq.
*Good my lord, | I do beſeech you I may
ſpeak with you.* Cap.   *I do…with you.*
One line, Johns. Jen. Steev. Mal. Var.
Coll. Sta. Wh. i, Del.
128. *do*] Om. Pope, Theob. Han. Warb.
129. *That I*] *I* Qq, Johns. Jen. Steev.
Mal. Var. Coll. Wh. i, Del.
Oh good] *good* Q₁.

---

119. **noise . . . high**] BOOTH : That is, of the ſtruggling with Desdemona, whose
cries were mingled with Othello's angry voice.   (Irving supposes this to refer to Emilia's
knock.)   [Does not this refer to Roderigo's attack on Cassio ?—ED.]

119. WALKER, in his Article 'On the omission of repeated words' (*Crit.* ii, 144),
queries if *still* be not omitted at the end of this line ?   HUDSON answered in the affirm
ative by adding it, 'because,' as he says, 'the metre certainly wants it, and the sense
even more, perhaps, than the metre.'

122. **wife**] BOOTH : At this word he pauses as if stunned, or, rather, puzzled by so
strange a word, and mutters it twice inquiringly, then, under the full force of the horror,
he almost screams, 'I have no wife !' and falls prostrate on the divan in centre of the
stage, where he writhes while speaking the lines that follow.

125–127. THEOBALD : Let the Poet account for the profanation, if he has committed
any ; but it is very obvious to me his allusion is grounded on a certain *solemn* circumstance, when *darkness* is said to have *covered the whole face of the land ;* when *rocks*
were *rent ;* and *graves opened.*

Oth.   I had forgot thee : oh come in *Æmilia.*   130
Soft, by and by, let me the Curtaines draw.
Where art thou? What's the matter with thee now?
Enter Æmilia.

Æmil.   Oh my good Lord, yonders foule Murthers
done.   135
Oth.   What? now?
Æmil.   But now, my Lord.
Oth.   It is the very error of the Moone,
She comes more neerer Earth then ſhe was wont,
And makes men mad.   140
    Æmil. Caſſio, my Lord, hath kill'd
A young Venetian, call'd *Rodorigo.*
Oth.   *Rodorigo* kill'd? and *Caſſio* kill'd?
Æmil.   No, *Caſſio* is not kill'd.
Oth.   Not *Caſſio* kill'd? Then Murther's out of tune,   145
And ſweet Reuenge growes harſh.
Deſ.   O falſely, falſely murder'd.   147

---

130. *forgot*] *forgotten* Q₂Q₃, Cap.
oh come] *come* Q₂Q₃, Cap.
132. [Unlocks the door. Theob.
133. Enter...] After *draw* line 131, Qq.
After *thou ?* line 132, Dyce.
134. *my good*] *good my* Steev.'93, Var.
Coll. i, ii.
    yonders] *yonder's* Qq.
    Murthers] Ff, Rowe, Pope, Han.
Cap. Knt, Wh. ii. *murders* Qq, Sing.
Dyce i, Glo. Ktly, Cam. *murther* Theob.
Warb. Wh. i, Rlfe. *murder* Johns. et cet.
136. *What?*] FfQ₂Q₃, Rowe+, Steev.

Knt, Coll. Sing. Wh. i, Ktly, Del. *What,*
Q₁ et cet.
    139. *neerer*] *neere the* Qq, Pope+, Cap.
Jen. Steev. Mal. Var. Coll. Sing. Wh. i,
Ktly, Dyce iii.
    141, 142. *Caſſio... Venetian*] One line,
Qq, Cap. et seq.
    141. *hath*] *has* Qq, Cap. Mal. Steev.
Var. Coll. Sing. Wh. i, Del.
    143. Two lines, Cap. Steev. et seq.
    147. *murder'd*] *murdered* Qq. *mur-
ther'd* Theob. Han. Warb. Knt, Wh.
Rlfe.

---

130. FECHTER : Othello goes to the door, which, in his agitation, he tries to open at the hinges ; and, perceiving his mistake, leans against the wall distracted, wiping the cold damps from his forehead.

134. **my good**] DYCE: Perhaps Steevens and the others may be right ; Emilia has just before twice used that form of expression.

134. **murther**] BOOTH : Othello starts at this word.

139. **more neerer**] Compare *Ham.* II, i, 11, or ABBOTT, § 11, for instances of double comparatives and superlatives.

147. KEIGHTLEY : It would not be possible, in the whole compass of poetry, to find a more glaring absurdity than this of making Desdemona speak after she had been smothered. [The following extract, involving, as it does, a name around which still cluster holy memories in living hearts, is of a date so recent that I should hesitate to use it here did I imagine that any service in the illustration of Shakespeare could bring aught·but honour, or that I should hereby lightly treat him whose voice appeared to

Æmil.   Alas! what cry is that?   148
Oth.   That? What?
Æmil.   Out, and alas, that was my Ladies voice.   150
Helpe, helpe hoa, helpe.   Oh Ladie fpeake againe,
Sweet *Defdemona*, oh fweet Miftris, fpeake.
Def.   A guiltleffe death, I dye.
Æmil.   Oh who hath done this deed?
Def.   No body : I my felfe, farewell :   155
Commend me to my kinde Lord : oh farewell.
Oth.   Why, how fhould fhe be murdred?   157

148. *Alas*] *O Lord* Q₁, Cap. Jen. *Ahlas*
Q₂.
    cry is] *cry's* Steev.'93.
150. *that was*] *it is* Q₁, Jen. *it was*
Q₂Q₃.
154. *hath*] *has* Qq.

154. *this deed*] As beginning 155, Cap.
Steev. Mal. Var. Knt, Coll. Sing. Wh. i,
Ktly, Dyce iii.
156. [She dies. Qq.
157. *murdred*] *murdered* Qq.

me the solitary one worth listening to, on a London Sunday, thirty years ago.—ED.]
'When I returned at 5 A. M. next day, copious effusion had taken place in one of the
pleura, and death was close at hand . . . . almost immediately afterwards, without any
struggle, all was over,—as it seemed.   We remained kneeling around the bed.   No
sound came from the motionless chest, the beating of the artery under my finger was
no longer perceptible; the hand, which a moment before was grasping mine, had relaxed
its hold; the countenance was no longer scored by lines denoting difficulty in breathing;
the spark in the eye had gone out, and nowhere, so far as I could see, was there any
reason for thinking that the fire of life was still smouldering.   I could find no such
reason then, I can find no such reason now.   And yet shortly afterwards, he, who
seemed to have died, and to have been dead for several minutes, or moments, minutes
rather than moments, as I remember them, slowly raised himself upon one of his
elbows into a half-sitting posture, and said distinctly, "The peace of God, which pass-
eth all understanding, keep your—*our*—hearts and minds in the knowledge and love
of God, and of his Son Jesus Christ our Lord; and the blessing of God Almighty, the
Father, the Son, and the Holy Ghost, be amongst *us* and remain with *us* always;" and
having so said, without another word, he lay down and died—again.   The voice in
which these words were uttered was the old familiar voice, clear and solemn. . . . .
Between them and the preceding words, which were hurried and scarcely coherent,
and almost lost in distracting sounds connected with lack of breath, a broad line of
separation must be drawn.   In uttering these last words no difficulty in breathing or
speaking was noticeable. . . . . I cannot confound these words with any ordinary
death-bed utterances.'—DR C. B. RADCLIFFE (*Life of Frederick Denison Maurice*, 2d
ed., vol. ii, p. 645, London, 1884).

150. BOOTH : Emilia rushes to the bed and throws back the curtains.

155, 156. BOOTH : This should affect Othello; he believes her dying with a lie on
her lips, and he shows how it pains him.   His next speech is in half-choked utterances.   FECHTER says that this line 157 is spoken 'looking at Emilia with steady
effrontery.'   ELZE (*Notes*, &c., 2d Ser. p. 157) would divide these lines at 'me,' read-
ing the second, 'To my | kind lord. | O, fáre | well.'

Æmil. Alas : who knowes?   158

Oth. You heare her fay her felfe, it was not I.

Æmil. She faid fo : I muft needs report the truth.   160

Oth. She's like a Liar gone to burning hell,

'Twas I that kill'd her.

Æmil. Oh the more Angell fhe, and you the black-

er Diuell.

Oth. She turn'd to folly : and fhe was a whore.   165

Æmil. Thou do'ft bely her, and thou art a diuell.

Oth. She was falfe as water.

Æmil.   Thou art rafh as fire, to fay

That fhe was falfe. Oh fhe was heauenly true.   169

---

159. *heare*] Ff, Rowe. *heard* Qq et cet.
160. *the truth*] *a truth* Qq, Coll. Wh. i.
161. *burning*] *burne in* Q₃, Cap.
163, 164. Two lines, Cap. Steev. et seq.

168. *Thou art*] *Thou as* Q₁. *Thou'rt*
Cap.
168, 169. *to fay...true*] One line, Qq.

161, 162. FECHTER: With a burst of triumph. BOOTH: With deep emotion, not harshly.

163. **Angell**] HUDSON: Emilia evidently means that Desdemona is the more angel for having spoken the falsehood in question.   And surely all well-ordered minds must agree with her; at all events, I, for one, cannot choose but love and honour Desdemona the more for that lie.   For, indeed, the sweet, dear sufferer knows that Othello is driven onward by some monstrous delusion; that some hideous inspiration has put him clean out of his native self; that he is sure to have the worst of it, and so is even more an object of compassion than herself; and the unspeakable agony legible in his features wrings her pure soul with a pity so intense as to take from her all sense of the pangs of death; and so her last breath is hallowed with a tender yearning to shield him, as far as she possibly can, from the dreadful retributions which await him, both from without and from within, when the truth shall be known.   So deep and sacred is the head and spring of Desdemona's dying falsehood!   It is a lie born of the very holiness of truth itself!

165. **folly**] MALONE: This signifies here, as in the sacred writings, *wantonness* or unchastity.   So in *R. of L.*, 556: 'Her sad behaviour feeds his vulture folly.'   STEEVENS: So in *Deut.* xxii, 21 : 'She hath wrought *folly* in Israel.'   MOREL: C'est une vieille acception du français 'folie' qui a persisté jusqu' au dix-septième siècle.   La Fontaine dit encore 'faire la folie' pour 'se livrer à la débauche.'   PROF. GEORGE ALLEN (MS note): So also in Greek.   Cf. Euripides, *Hippolytus*, 644: ἡ δ'ἀμήχανος γυνὴ | γνώμη βραχεία μωρίαν ἀφηρέθη.   Monk says: μωρία, *impudicitia*, vel *libido*, quâ significatione adhibitur etiam in *Ion*, 557.

167. **as water**] JOHNSON: As water that will support no weight, nor keep any impression.   PURNELL: The comparison is as old as Jacob's farewell to his sons: 'Reuben, unstable as water.'—*Gen.* xlix, 4.

168. **Thou art**] WALKER (*Crit.* ii, 203): To be pronounced as one syllable. See I, ii, 34; III, iv, 195.

Oth. *Caſſio* did top her : Ask thy husband elſe.   170
O, I were damn'd beneath all depth in hell:
But that I did proceed vpon iuſt grounds
To this extremity.   Thy Husband knew it all.

Æmil.   My Husband?   [337 *a*]
Oth.   Thy Husband.   175
Æmil.   That ſhe was falſe to Wedlocke?
Oth.   I, with *Caſſio* : had ſhe bin true,
If Heauen would make me ſuch another world,
Of one entyre and perfeƈt Chryſolite,
I'ld not haue ſold her for it.   180

Æmil.   My Husband?
Oth.   I, 'twas he that told me on her firſt,
An honeſt man he is, and hates the ſlime
That ſtickes on filthy deeds.

Æmil.   My Husband?   185
Oth.   What needs this itterance, Woman?

170. *top*] QqFf, Rowe, Pope i, Knt,
Coll. i, Sing. Glo. Ktly, Cam. Wh. ii. *tup*
Pope ii et cet.

173. *extremity*] *extreme* Steev. conj.

174. *Husband?*] *husband :* Q₂Q₃.

177. Two lines, Cap. Steev. Var. Knt,
Sing.

  I, with] *Ay, and with* Ktly.
  had] Ff, Rowe +, Cap. Knt. *nay,
had* Qq et cet.
  true] *but true* Coll. (MS.)

180. *for it*] *for't* Cap.

182. *me on her firſt*] Ff, Knt. *me firſt*
Qq et cet.

184. *on*] *one* Q₃.

186, 187. One line, or prose, Qq, Cap.
Steev. et seq.

186. *itterance, Woman?*] *iteration?
woman,* Qq, Ktly. *iteration, woman?*
Pope (subs.) +, Jen. Steev. '85, Mal. Coll
Sing. Glo. Cam. Wh. ii.

171, 172. BOOTH: With vigour; in justification of what he has done.

179. **Chrysolite**] Holland's Translation of *Pliny's Naturall Historie*, The seuen and
thirtieth Booke, *Chap.* viii: 'The Topaze or Chrysolith, hath a singular green colour
by it selfe, for which it is esteemed very rich, and when it was first found, it surpassed
all others in price. . . . . It is said, that the first that tooke a liking vnto the stone, was
queene *Berenice* the mother of *Ptolome* the second, and that by the meanes of *Philemon* (lieutenant generall to her son in those countries) who presented one of them to
the said queen. Of which Chrysolit, *Ptolomæus Philadelphus* K. of Egypt, caused the
statue of his wife *Arsinoë* to be made, 4 cubits long; and in honour of the said queene
his wife, dedicated it in a chappell named the Golden temple.' [This passage in Holland's *Pliny* is referred to by Plumptre. Can it be doubted that it was the story of this
precious statue which suggested 'chrysolite' to Shakespeare?—ED.] WHITE (ed. ii): A
greenish, yellow stone of no rarity and small value. It is little worn: probably Shakespeare never saw one; but the word promises largely, and it sounded well in his verse.

185. ROLFE: Emilia's astonishment here is ſufficient proof that she did not before
ſuspect Iago of being the 'eternal villain' that had devised this slander. See IV, ii, 154.

186 itterance] See note on 'Reprobance,' line 261, *post.*

I ſay, thy Husband. 187

Æ*mil.* Oh Miſtris,

Villany hath made mockes with loue

My Husband ſay ſhe was falſe? 190

Oth. He, Woman;

I ſay thy Husband : Do'ſt vnderſtand the word?

My Friend, thy Husband; honeſt, honeſt *Iago.*

Æ*mil.* If he ſay ſo, may his pernicious Soule

Rot halfe a graine a day : he lyes to'th'heart, 195

She was too fond of her moſt filthy Bargaine.

Oth. Hah?

Æ*mil.* Do thy wotſt:

This deede of thine is no more worthy Heauen,

Then thou was't worthy her. 200

Oth. Peace, you were beſt.

Æ*mil.* Thou haſt not halfe that powre to do me harm,

As I haue to be hurt. Oh Gull, oh dolt,

As ignorant as durt : thou haſt done a deed

(I care not for thy Sword) Ile make thee known, 205

188–193. Om. Q₁.

188, 189. One line, Q₂Q₃, Rowe et seq.

189. *hath*] *had* F₄. *has* Rowe+.

190. *ſay ſhe*] Ff, Rowe+. *ſay that ſhe* Q₂Q₃ et cet.

191, 192. One line, Q₂Q₃.

193. *honeſt, honeſt*] *honest-honest* Sta.

194. *ſay*] *says* Theob.

195. *to'th'*] QqFf, Rowe+, Jen. Wh. i, Huds. *to the* Cap. et cet.

196. *too fond*] *to fond* Q₃.

198. *wotſt*] F₁.

202. *that powre*] *the power* Qq, Jen. Mal. Steev. Var. Coll. Sing. Ktly, Huds.

203. *be hurt*] *bear hurt* Han.

204. *thou haſt*] *thou'st* Pope+.

204. *deed*] Ff, Rowe i. *deed—* Qq et cet.

205. *Sword*] *word* F₄.

205. *known*] *know* Qq.

---

189. **mockes**] JOHNSON: 'Villainy' has taken advantage to *play upon* the weakness of a violent passion. HUDSON: That is, villainy has made a sport and mockery of love, by playing upon it, and beguiling it into a conflagration of its own home. Emilia probably refers to Desdemona's friendly efforts in Cassio's behalf.

195. **to'th'heart**] The Cambridge Editors note that Johnson reads 'o' th' heart.' In my copy of Johnson the *t* of 'to' is very faint, but I think it is unmistakably present. There is, however, no indication whatever of an apostrophe after the *o*. Let the vanity be pardoned which prompts me to show how exact is my collation, by comparing it with that of the Cambridge Editors.—ED.

202, 203. JOHNSON: She means to say, 'I have in this cause power to endure more than thou hast power to inflict.' MALONE: Compare *Hen. VIII:* III, ii, 387, 'I am able. . . . . Out of a fortitude of soul, I feel, To endure more miseries. . . . . Than my weak 'earted enémies dare offer'; and *2 Hen. VI:* IV, i, 130: 'More can I bear than you dare execute.'

203. **As**] See ABBOTT, § 109, for an instance of 'as' for *that* without the antecedent *so.*

Though I loſt twenty liues.   Helpe, helpe, hoa, helpe :   206
The Moore hath kill'd my Miſtris.   Murther, murther.

Enter Montano, Gratiano, and Iago.

Mon.   What is the matter ? How now Generall ?

Æmil.   Oh, are you come, *Iago* : you haue done well,   210
That men muſt lay their Murthers on your necke.

Gra.   What is the matter ?

Æmil.   Diſproue this Villaine, if thou bee'ſt a man :
He ſayes, thou told'ſt him that his wife was falſe :
I know thou did'ſt not : thou'rt not ſuch a Villain.   215
Speake, for my heart is full.

Iago.   I told him what I thought,
And told no more
Then what he found himſelfe was apt, and true.

Æmil.   But did you euer tell him,   220
She was falſe ?

Iago.   I did.

Æmil.   You told a Lye an odious damned Lye :
Vpon my Soule, a Lye ; a wicked Lye.   224

206. *hoa, helpe*] *O helpe* Qq.

207. *hath*] *has* Qq, Steev. Mal. Var. Coll. Sing. Wh. i, Ktly, Del.

208. *Enter...and Iago*] *Enter...Iago, and others.* Qq. (Gragantio Q₂Q₃).
Scene VIII. Pope+, Jen.

209. [*Staying him.* Cap.

210. *you haue*] *you've* Dyce iii, Huds.

211. *Murthers*] *murder* Qq.

212. Gra.] All. Qq.

213. *Diſproue this Villaine*] *Disprove it, villain* Cap. *Disprove this villany* Cap. conj. Rann.

215. *did'ſt*] *diſt* Q₂Q₃.
thou'rt] *thou art* Qq.

217, 218. One line, Qq, Rowe et seq.

219. *Then*] *But* Cap.

220, 221. One line, Qq, Rowe et seq

206. BOOTH : Othello goes to the bed, and lies moaning there, not loudly.

211. BOOTH : Iago, of course, is much astonished.

213. **this Villaine**] CAPELL (having misprinted *it* inſtead of 'this,' has the follow-ing note, which is unusually lucid) : One of the present Editor's oversights is corrected in the 'Errata.'   At discovery, and in ruminating upon it, it appears to him that there is a further mistake by the old printers made in the same line : '*villaine,*' as they point it, is predicated of Othello ; suppose their pointing erroneous, and make *villaine* a voca-tive, it then belongs to Iago ; but this direct application, and to their face, of such a term as is *villaine* to parties standing in such relation as both do to the speaker, is a trespass on character ; and may easily be remov'd by supposing the word intended was—*villainy,* which takes off the directness.

214. BOOTH : Iago hardens himself, as it were, looking straight before him ; immov-able,—and answers after a pause, and doggedly.

222. BOOTH : Short and sharp.   He darts a quick, steely glance at her in defiance, but quails as she proceeds, and speaks line 227 with desperation.

Shee falfe with *Caffio*?   225
Did you fay with *Caffio*?
  Iago. With *Caffio*, Miftris?
Go too, charme your tongue.
  Emil. I will not charme my Tongue;
I am bound to fpeake,   230
My Miftris heere lyes murthered in her bed.
  All. Oh Heauens, forefend.
  Emil. And your reports haue fet the Murder on.
  Othello. Nay ftare not Mafters,
It is true indeede.   235
  Gra. 'Tis a ftrange Truth.
  Mont. O monftrous Acte.
  Emil. Villany, villany, villany: [337 *b*]
I thinke vpon't, I thinke : I fmel't : O Villany:
I thought fo then : Ile kill my felfe for greefe.   240

225–230. Three lines, Qq, Rowe et seq.
225. *Shee falfe*] She was falfe Q₃.
230. *I am*] *I'm* Pope+, Dyce iii.
231–241. Om. Q₁.
231. *heere lyes*] lies here Pope+.
  murthered] murdered Q₂Q₃.
murther'd Pope et seq.
  bed.] bed, Q₃, Cap. Dyce, Sta.
Huds.

232. *All.*] Mon. Gra. Cap. Dyce iii,
Huds.
232–241. Put in margin. Pope, Han.
233. *Murder*] murderer Q₂, Johns.
Murther F₃F₄.
234, 235. One line, Q₂Q₃, Rowe, Theob.
Warb. et seq.
239. *I fmel't : O Villany*] *I fmell a
villany* Q₂Q₃.

---

228. **charme**] JOHNSON: I know not whether I have read, or whether my own
thoughts have suggested, an alteration here. It seems to me not improbable that
Shakespeare wrote *clam* your tongue; to *clam* a bell is to cover the clapper with felt,
which drowns the blow and hinders the sound [qu., *hinders* the blow and *drowns* the
sound? The Cambridge Editors record '*chain*, Anon. conj.'—ED.] MALONE: That
is, compel to be silent, as if by the power of enchantment. STEEVENS: Thus Jonson,
Cynthia's Revels [I, i]: 'Charm your skipping tongue.' Also *Faerie Queene*, V, ix
[line 350]: 'That well could charme his tongue, and time his speach.' [For additional examples in Shakespeare, see SCHMIDT.]

236. **strange**] STAUNTON: This is one of the many words which have lost weight
and emphasis since Shakespeare's time. With us it imports no more than *unusual, not
customary*, &c.; but when Desdemona spoke of the Moor's adventures as 'strange,'
she meant that they were *wonderful, incredible;* and it is in this deeper sense of the
word that Gratiano employs it here.

239. In the punctuation of this line the Ff are followed by the Globe, Hudson, Rolfe,
White ii. All other editions substantially follow Rowe in separating the first clause:
'I think upon't—I think—I smell't—O villainy!' except STAUNTON, whose punctua-
tion seems, to me, the best: 'I think upon't,—I think I smell't;—O, villainy!—'—ED.

240. **then**] STEEVENS: That is, at the instant when she gave Desdemona's handkerchief to Iago; for even *then* Emilia appears to have suspected it was sought after

O villany! villany!　　　　　　　　　　241
　Iago.　What, are you mad?
I charge you get you home.
　Emil.　Good Gentlemen, let me haue leaue to fpeake:
'Tis proper I obey him; but not now:　　245
Perchance *Iago*, I will ne're go home.
　Oth.　Oh, oh, oh.
　Emil.　Nay, lay thee downe, and roare:
For thou haft kill'd the fweeteft innocent,
That ere did lift vp eye.　　　　　250
　Oth.　Oh fhe was fowle!
I fcarfe did know you Vnkle, there lies your Neece,
Whofe breath (indeed) thefe hands haue newly ftopp'd:
I know this acte fhewes horrible and grim.
　Gra.　Poore *Desdemon:*　　　255

242, 243. One line, Qq, Rowe et seq.
246. *Perchance*] *Perhaps* Q₂Q₃.
247. *Oh, oh, oh.*] *Oh! oh! oh! oh!* Cap.
Steev.'93, Ktly.
　[Oth. fals on the bed. Qq. (falls Q₂Q₃).

251. [Rising. Theob.
254. *horrible*] *terrible* Qq, Coll. Wh. i.
255, 256. One line, Qq, Rowe et seq.
255. Defdemon] F₂, Knt, Dyce, Sta. Del. Huds. *Desdemone* Cap. *Defdemona* QqF₃F₄ et cet.

for no honest purpose, and there asks her husband: 'What will you do with it?' &c., III, iii, 366. COWDEN-CLARKE: In allusion to her suspicions at IV, ii, 154; she seems to be about to say, 'I thought then that there was villainy going on, but little thought my husband was the author.' The very thought that Iago could be capable of such villainy, causes her to interrupt her half-uttered sentence with 'I'll kill myself for grief.' ROLFE agrees with Cowden-Clarke.

246. I will] ABBOTT, §319: Some passages which are quoted to prove that Shakespeare used *will* with the first person without implying *wish, desire*, &c., do not warrant such an inference [see *Ham.* V, ii, 167]. . . . . There is a difficulty in the expression 'perchance I *will*'; but, from its constant recurrence, it would seem to be a regular idiom. Compare this passage in *Othello* with *Com. of Err.* IV, i, 39: 'Perchance I will be there as soon as you,' and *Mer. of Ven.* II, v, 52: 'Perhaps I will return immediately.' In all these passages 'perchance' precedes, and the meaning seems to be in the last example, for instance: 'My purpose may, perhaps, be fulfilled,' and 'my purpose is to return immediately,' or, in other words, 'If possible, I intend to return immediately.' In all these cases the 'perhaps' stands by itself. It does not qualify *will*, but the whole of the following sentence.

247. BOOTH: Iago gloats over this quietly. Emilia sits on divan, C.

252. Vnkle] BOOTH: Gratiano falls into a seat near the bed, soon after his entrance, when he discovers his niece dead.

255. Desdemon] See III, i, 58. DELIUS: Gratiano appears to have come to Cyprus to bring to Desdemona the news of her Father's death. [In that 'the gentle lady' never knew of her Father's death, is the one tiny glimmering ray of comfort in this blackness. —ED.]

I am glad thy Father's dead,   256
Thy Match was mortall to him : and pure greefe
Shore his old thred in twaine. Did he liue now,
This fight would make him do a defperate turne :
Yea, curfe his better Angell from his fide,   260
And fall to Reprobance.

    Oth. 'Tis pittifull : but yet *Iago* knowes
That fhe with *Caffio*, hath the Act of fhame,
A thoufand times committed. *Caffio* confeft it,
And fhe did gratifie his amorous workes   265
With that Recognizance and pledge of Loue
Which I firft gaue her : I faw it in his hand :
It was a Handkerchiefe, an Antique Token
My Father gaue my Mother.   269

---

256. *I am*] *I'm* Pope +, Dyce iii, Huds.
258. *in twaine*] *atwaine* Q₁.
261. *Reprobance*] Ff, Cap. Knt, Dyce, Wh. i, Del. Huds. Rlfe. *reprobation* Qq et cet.
263. *hath*] *had* Q₂Q₃, Theob. Warb. Johns.

266. *that*] ;*he* Q₁.
267. *gaue her*] *gave* Pope, Har..
268. *a*] *an* Pope +, Steev.'85.
268, 280. *Handkerchiefe*] *handkercher* Q₁.
268. *Antique*] *Antick* F₃F₄, Rowe.

---

260. **side**] MALONE : So in *Sonn.* 144 : 'My female evil Tempteth my better angel from my side.'

261. **Reprobance**] In his Article on 'the instance of error in the beginning or earlier parts of words, WALKER (*Crit.* ii, 241) says : 'By the way, terminations in *ance* for *ation* are not infrequent.' He then gives five or six instances in addition to the present. His Editor, LETTSOM, in a foot-note, says : 'So we have a little above "iterance," which is necessary for the metre. Collier reads *iteration* and *reprobation* with the Qq, because there is no authority for the other forms. That is the very reason why they were corrupted in the Qq.'

262. BOOTH : Iago, who has turned aside, now faces them as all look towards him.

264. **thousand**] PYE (p. 342) : This is merely hyperbolical, and is used every day by impatient men in common speech for *five* or *six*. COWDEN-CLARKE : Merely an indefinite number ; used here to convey the effect of long time. See 'a hundred times,' III, iii, 339.

265. **gratifie**] WALKER (*Crit.* iii, 291) : That is, express her gratitude for, recompense.

269. **Mother**] STEEVENS : In III, iv, 69, Othello says that 'an Egyptian' gave this handkerchief to his Mother ; and here he says it was his Father. This has been censured as an oversight in Shakespeare, but perhaps it is only a fresh proof of his art. The first account of the handkerchief, as given by Othello, was purposely ostentatious, in order to alarm his wife the more. When he mentions it a second time, the truth was sufficient for his purpose. COWDEN-CLARKE : Even this slight deviation from truth works its own retribution. Had not Othello over-excited Desdemona's fears by his description of the handkerchief, she might not have been led to prevaricate and into falsehood.

Emil.   Oh Heauen ! oh heauenly Powres !   270
Iago.   Come, hold your peace.
Emil.   'Twill out, 'twill out.   I peace ?
No, I will fpeake as liberall as the North ;
Let Heauen, and Men, and Diuels, let them all,
All, all, crie fhame againft me, yet Ile fpeake.   275
Iago.   Be wife, and get you home.
Emil.   I will not.
Gra.   Fye, your Sword vpon a Woman.
Emil.   Oh thou dull Moore,
That Handkerchiefe thou fpeak'ft of   280
I found by Fortune, and did giue my Husband :
For often, with a folemne earneftneffe,
(More then indeed belong'd to fuch a Trifle)
He begg'd of me, to fteale't.
Iago.   Villanous Whore.   285
Emil.   She giue it *Caffio*? No, alas I found it,
And I did giu't my Husband.
Iago.   Filth, thou lyeft.   288

270. *Oh...Powres*] O God, O heauenly
God Q₁, Sta.
271. *Come*] Zouns Q₁, Sta.
272. *'Twill out, 'twill out.*] FfQ₂Q₃,
Cam. *'Twill out, 'twill :* Q₁. *'Twill out,
'twill out*— Rowe+, Jen. *'Twill out,
'twill out !* Sta. Huds. *'Twill out, 'twill
out ;*— Cap. et cet.
  I peace ?] Ff, Cap. *I peace !* Rowe,
Pope, Theob. Han. Dyce, Wh. Glo. Cam.
Huds. Rlfe. *I, peace !* Warb. *I hold my
peace fir, no,* Qq, Johns. et cet.
273. *No*] Om. Qq, Jen. Sing. Ktly.
  I will fpeake as] *Ile be in fpeaking,*
Qq, Jen. Sing. Ktly.

273. *North ;*] *ayre* Q₁, Pope, Theob.
Han. Warb. Cap. Jen. Mal. Steev. Var.
Sing. Ktly.   *wind* Coll. (MS).
274. *them*] em Qq, Jen.
277. [Jago offers to stab his wife. Rowe.
278. *Fye*] As closing line 277, Cap.
Steev. et seq.
279, 280. One line, Qq, Pope et seq.
280. *of*] on, Qq, Jen.
284. *fteale't*] F₂F₃, Sing. Ktly, Sta.
fteale it QqF₄ et cet.
286. *giue*] gaue Qq, Johns.
  No, alas] Alas F₃F₄, Rowe+.
  found] find Q₃.
287. *giu't*] give it Steev.'85, Mal.

271. BOOTH : Iago had not thought of her betraying him, and now starts and trem-
bles violently.

273. **North**] Compare *Cymb.* I, iii, 36 : 'the tyrannous breathing of the north Shakes
all our buds from growing.'   Also *R. of L.* 1335 : '—— hie as fast As lagging fowls
before the northern blast.'   It was the wind which, it seems to me, symbolized masterful
rudeness.   Steevens cites from Webster's *White Devil* [p. 92, ed. Dyce] : 'And let th'
irregular north wind sweep her up,' which does not help us much.—ED.

281. **by Fortune**] MOREL : Cf. la locution française : 'Comme elle difait ces mots
| Le loup, *de fortune,* passe.'—La Fontaine.

288. **Filth**] DYCE (*Few Notes*, p. 149) : Here Iago uses a term synonymous with
the word he has juft applied to her.   Compare Greene's *Notable Discouery of Coosnage,*

Emil. By Heauen I do not, I do not Gentlemen:
Oh murd'rous Coxcombe, what fhould fuch a Foole   290
Do with fo good a wife?
   Oth. Are there no ftones in Heauen,
But what ferues for the Thunder?
Precious Villaine.
   Gra. The woman falles: 295
Sure he hath kill'd his Wife.
   Emil. I, I: oh lay me by my Miftris fide.
   Gra. Hee's gone, but his wife's kill'd.
   Mon. 'Tis a notorious Villain: take you this weapon   299

290. [To Oth. Cap.
291. *wife*] *woman* Qq, Coll. i, ii, Glo.
Wh. ii.
   [The Moore runnes at *Iago. Iago*
kils his wife. Qq.   Jago breaks through,
and wounds his Wife, then runs out. Rowe.
Oth. offers to stab Iago but is disarmed by
Mont. Dyce.
293, 294. One line, Qq, Rowe et seq.

293. *But...for*] *For what then serves*
Warb.
   ferues] QqF$_2$F$_3$, Cap. *ferve* F$_4$ et
cet.
294. *Precious*] *pretious* Q$_1$. *pernitious*
Q$_2$Q$_3$.
295, 296. One line, Qq, Rowe et seq.
297. [Exit Iago. Qq.
299. *you this*] *your* Qq.   *this* Pope +
Cap.

&c., 1592 [p. 44, ed. Grosart]: 'To him will some common filth (that neuer knew
loue) faine an ardent and honest affection.'   HALLIWELL: 'Filth,' applied to man or
woman, was a term implying the greatest possible degree of contempt.
   291. wife] DYCE (*Remarks*, p. 243): It is absolutely necessary to adopt here the
reading of the Folio.
   292, 293. WARBURTON: Without question Shakespeare wrote and pointed thus:
'Are there no stones in heaven?   For what then serves the thunder?' i. e. are there
no bolts in heaven for this villain? for what purpose then serves the thunder, that
instrument of vengeance?   [Kean adopted this emendation; see Wood's *Personal Recollections*, &c., p. 264.—ED.]   STEEVENS: Othello does not demand a thunder-bolt for
Iago.   He only asks, if there are no lesser degrees of chastisement more proportioned
to the guilt of mortals, ready to drop down on such villains as Iago, though Omnipotence withholds its thunder as too noble an instrument for the punishment of crimes
like his?   Shakespeare might, however, mean, Does heaven reserve its thunder only to
make a noise? has it no implements of mischief to punish as well as terrify?   MALONE:
Has not heaven one supernumerary bolt, to hurl directly at the head of this atrocious
villain?   Must all the stores of its arsenal be reserved for common and ordinary thunder?
   294. Precious] COLLIER: *Pernitious* of the Qq does not suit the measure.   DYCE
(ed. iii): '"*Precious* villain" is more in the style of Cloten than of Othello: qu. *Pernicious* with Q$_2$.   This could scarcely have crept in from "pernicious caitiff" 80 lines
below.   Collier's metrical objection is "naught."   See Walker, *Vers.*, &c., Art. ix.'—
LETTSOM.   [I have failed to find this passage in Walker; it certainly is not in Art. ix.
I therefore give it on Lettsom's authority.—ED.]
   299. notorious] See IV, ii, 167.   ROLFE: Iago was not a *notorious* villain in its
modern sense; his villainy had but just then become known.

Which I haue recouer'd from the Moore :   300
Come guard the doore without, let him not paſſe,
But kill him rather.   Ile after that ſame villaine,
For 'tis a damned Slaue.   *Exit.*

Oth.   I am not valiant neither :   [338 *a*]
But euery Punie whipſter gets my Sword.   305
But why ſhould Honor out-liue Honeſty ?
Let it go all.

Æmil.   What did thy Song boad Lady ?
Hearke, canſt thou heare me ? I will play the Swan,
And dye in Muſicke : *Willough, Willough, Willough.*   310
Moore, ſhe was chaſte : She lou'd thee, cruell Moore,
So come my Soule to bliſſe, as I ſpeake true :
So ſpeaking as I thinke, alas, I dye.

Oth.   I haue another weapon in this Chamber,   314

---

300. *haue recouer'd*] *haue here re-couered* Qq. *recouer'd have here* Pope i. *have here recouer'd* Pope ii et seq.

301. *Come guard*] *Some guard* Theob. conj. (withdrawn).

303. Exit.] Exit *Mont.* and *Gratiano.* Qq.   Exit Montano. Knt.

Scene IX. Pope +, Jen.
308–310. *What...Willough*] Om. Q₁.
310. [Singing. Dyce.
313. *alas, I dye.*] Ff, Rowe +, Knt, Wh. i.   *I die, I die.* Qq et cet.
[She dies. Qq.

---

303. **Slaue**] See IV, ii, 156.

305. **Punie**] BOOTH : Can we infer from this that Othello was a large man ? Yet, further on he speaks of his 'little arm.' The Moors, I believe, are usually slight of build and wiry.   [I think it is more an expression of contempt in both cases, without any reference to physical size.   Is the contemptuous inferiority implied in 'whipster' due to a survival of the feeling of feminine weakness involved in the feminine termina-tion ?—ED.]

306. **Honor . . . Honesty**] WALKER (*Crit.* i, 22) suggests that 'Honor' belongs to birth, dignity, grace of mind or person, while 'Honesty' is equivalent to virtue, and cites *Wint. Tale*, II, i, 66 : 'She is a goodly lady . . . . 'Tis pity she's not honest-honourable' (the hyphen is Walker's), i. e., honourable with honesty.   Also *Hen. VIII :* I, i, 39 : 'As I belong to worship, and affect In honour honesty.'   'Each of these words, by the way,' adds Walker, '"honour" and "honesty," was, at times, used in both meanings.'

309. **Swan**] STEEVENS : Compare, for the same thought : *Mer. of Ven.* III, ii, 44, and *King John*, V, vii, 21.   ROLFE adds 'And now this pale swan in her watery nest Begins the sad dirge of her certain ending,'—*R. of L.* 1611 ; and 'death-divining swan.'—*Phœn. & Turt.* 15.   DOUCE (i, 262), in a note on the passage from *Mer. of Ven.*, cited by Steevens, proves the antiquity, from Plato to Luther, of the belief in the swan's dving song.

It was a Sword of Spaine, the Ice brookes temper: 315
Oh heere it is : Vnkle I muſt come forth.
    Gra.   If thou attempt it, it will coſt thee deere;
Thou haſt no weapon, and perforce muſt ſuffer.
    Oth.   Looke in vpon me then, and ſpeake with me,
Or naked as I am I will aſſault thee.   320
    Gra.   What is the matter?
    Othel.   Behold, I haue a weapon:
A better neuer did it ſelfe ſuſtaine
Vpon a Soldiers Thigh.   I haue ſeene the day,
That with this little Arme, and this good Sword,   325
I haue made my way through more impediments
Then twenty times your ſtop.   But (oh vaine boaſt)
Who can controll his Fate? 'Tis not ſo now.
Be not affraid, though you do ſee me weapon'd:
Heere is my iournies end, heere is my butt   330
And verie Sea-marke of my vtmoſt Saile.
Do you go backe diſmaid? 'Tis a loſt feare: 332

---

315. *It was*] Ff, Rowe+, Cap.   *It is*
Qq et cet.
    the Ice brookes] *the Iſebrookes* Qq.
the Ice brooks F_3F_4.   *the Ebro's* Pope,
Theob. Han. Warb. Cap.
    temper:] *temper;*— Cap. *temper.*
— Coll.
    316, 317. *forth.* Gra.] *forth. Gra.* with-
n. Gra. Qq.   *forth.* Gra. [within] Pope.
forth. Gra. [without] Sta.
    319. *with me*] *to me* Qq, Coll.

320. [Re-enter Gra. Theob.
322. *Behold*] *Lo!* Pope+.
324. *I haue*] *I've* Pope+, Dyce iii,
Huds.
326. *I haue made*] *I made* Pope, Han.
I've made Theob. Warb. Johns. Dyce iii,
Huds.
327. *your ſtop*] *you ſtop* $Q_1F_3F_4$.
329–335. Om. Q_1.
331. *And verie*] *The very* Q_2Q_3,
Theob. Warb. Johns. Jen. Steev.'85.

---

315. **Ice brookes**] JOHNSON : Steel is hardened by being put red-hot into very cold
water.   STEEVENS identifies the 'ice brook' with the river called Salo (now Xalon),
near Bilbilis, by citations from Martial [*Epig.* IV, lv, 15, and I, xlix, 12] and Justin, l,
44.   POPE'S needless change was thus justified by BLACKSTONE: I incline to read '*'tis
ebroes* temper.'   If we suppose that the words, '*tis ebroes*, were huddled together, either
in transcribing or composing, thus, '*tisebroes*, the compositor, in running it over with his
eye, might (to make it sense, as he thought) add a couple of letters, and divide the
words thus : th'*iſebrokes*, which is nearly as it stands in the old Qto.   I doubt whether
'ice-brooks' are usual in the climate of Spain.   MALONE: How this fact may be, I
know not; and I am confident Shakespeare did not inquire.
    320. **naked**] WHITE (ed. ii) : That is, weaponless, as Gratiano supposes him.
    327. **stop**] STEEVENS: So in *Cor.* I, i, 72 : 'cracking ten thousand curbs Of more
strong link asunder, than can ever Appear in your impediment.'
    328. **Fate**] The echo of Desdemona's 'It is my wretched Fortune.'—ED.

Man but a Rufh againſt *Othello's* breſt,   333
And he retires.   Where ſhould *Othello* go ?
Now : how doſt thou looke now? Oh ill-Starr'd wench,   335
Pale as thy Smocke : when we ſhall meete at compt,
This looke of thine will hurle my Soule from Heauen,
And Fiends will ſnatch at it.   Cold, cold, my Girle ?
Euen like thy Chaſtity.   O curſed, curſed Slaue !
Whip me ye Diuels,   340
From the poſſeſſion of this Heauenly ſight :
Blow me about in windes, roaſt me in Sulphure,
Waſh me in ſteepe-downe gulfes of Liquid fire.
Oh *Deſdemon* ! dead *Deſdemon* : dead. Oh, oh !   344

335. *Now : how*] Ff. *How* Q_2Q_3. *Now*
—*how* Rowe+, Jen.   *Now, how* Cap. et
cet.

  ill-Starr'd] *ill ſtor'd* Q_3.
  336. *compt*] *count* Q_1.   *'count* Jen.
  339, 340. Three lines, Rlfe.   *O...Diuels*
one line, Cap. Steev. Mal. Var. Knt.
  339. *curſed, curſed*] *curſed* Qq,
Pope+, Jen. Coll. Glo. Cam. Wh. ii.
  340. *ye*] *you* Qq.
  342. *roaſt*] *and roaſt* F_3F_4, Rowe.
  343. *ſteepe-downe*] *ſteepe downe* Qq.
     gulfes] *Gulf* Rowe ii.
  344. *Oh...oh* !] Knt.   *O Desdemon !
dead, Desdemon ! dead ! O, O !* Sta. Huds.
O Deſdemona, Deſdemoua, *dead, O, o, o.*
Q_1.   *O* Deſdemona, Deſdemona; *dead, O,
o, o.* Q_2Q_3.   *Oh Desdemona, Desdemona !
dead ! oh, oh, oh !* Jen.   *O Desdemona !*

Desdemona ! dead ? O, O, O ! Coll.   *O
Desdemona ! Desdemona ! dead !* | *Oh !
Oh ! Oh !* Glo. Cam. Rlfe, Wh. ii.   *Oh
Deſdemon ! dead* Deſdemon : *dead. dead.
Oh, oh !* F_2.   *Oh* Deſdemona ! *dead* Deſ-
demona : *dead, dead. Oh, oh !* F_3. *Oh* Deſ-
demona ! *Dead,* Deſdemona : *Dead, dead.
Oh, oh !* F_4, Rowe.   *Oh Desdemona ! Des-
demona ! dead, dead ! oh, oh !* Pope+.   *O
Desdemona ! dead, Desdemone ? dead ?
dead ?* | *O, o, o !* Cap.   *O Desdemona !
Desdemona ! dead ?* | *Dead ? O ! O ! O !*
Steev.'73, '78, '85, Mal. Rann, Steev.'93,
Var.'03, '13, '21, Sing. Ktly.   *O Desde-
mon ! dead, Desdemon ! dead ! O !* Dyce,
Wh. i, Del.   *O Desdemona ! Desdemona !
dead ? O !* Hal.   *O Desdemona ! Desdemona ! dead ! Oh, oh, oh !* Clarke.

---

333. An allusion, says STAUNTON, to the mock tournaments, in which the combat-
ants were armed with *rushes* in place of spears.   This leads DELIUS to conjecture that
the reading should be ' *Run* but a rush,' &c.

  334. BOOTH : Goes towards the bed, near which his sword falls from his hand.

  335. wench] STEEVENS : This originally signified only a *young* woman.   Cassandra, in Whetstone's *Promos and Cassandra*, 1578, says of herself : ' O wretched wench,
where may I first complayne ? '   Again : ' Therefore, sweet wenche, helpe me to rue
my woe.'   It is used without any dishonourable meaning in the Bible : ' Now Jona-
than and Ahimaaz stayed by En-rogel ; . . . . and a wench went and told them,' &c.—
2 Sam. xvii, 17.   And by Gawin Douglas, in his version of the *Æneid :* ' audetque
viris concurrere virgo.   This wensche stoutlye rencounter durst with men.'   HALLI-
WELL : Here we find it applied to a princess : ' For Ariodant so lov'd the princely
wench, That Neptune's floods unneth his flames cold quench.'—Har. *Ariost.* v, 20.
[There was, nevertheless, I think, a faint subaudition of inferiority of some kind.—ED.]

  336. compt] DYCE : That is, the reckoning at the Judgement-day.

Enter Lodouico, Caſſio, Montano, and Iago,   345
with Officers.

Lod.   Where is this raſh, and moſt vnfortunate man?

Oth.   That's he that was *Othello :* heere I am.

Lod.   Where is that Viper?

Bring the Villaine forth.   350

Oth.   I look down towards his feet ; but that's a Fable,
If that thou bee'ſt a Diuell, I cannot kill thee.

Lod.   Wrench his Sword from him.

Iago.   I bleed Sir, but not kill'd.

Othel.   I am not ſorry neither, Il'd haue thee liue :   355
For in my ſenſe, 'tis happineſſe to die.

Lod.   Oh thou *Othello,* that was once ſo good,   357

---

345. Enter...] Enter *Lodouico, Montano, Iago,* and Officers, *Caſſio* in a Chaire. Qq. (*Iago* Om. Q₂Q₃). Enter Lodovico, Cassio led in wounded, Montano, and Iago Prisoner, with Officers. Rowe.
Scene X. Pope +, Jen.

347. *vnfortunate*] *infortunate* Qq.

348. Othello: *heere*] *Othello ;* [pointing to his wife] *here* Cap.

349, 350. One line, Qq, Rowe et seq.

349. *that*] *this* Q₁.

352. *If that*] *If* Q₁.
[Oth. wounds Jago. Rowe.

353. *Wrench*] *Wring* Q₁.

354. *bleed...not*] *bleed, but am not* Han. ii.

357. *that was*] Ff, Steev.'85, Var. Knt, Sing. Ktly. *wast* Rowe +, Cap. Mal. Steev. *that wert* Qq et cet.

---

339. **Slaue**] BOOTH : By gesture show that you mean Iago. [Until now, I had always thought that this referred to Othello himself.—ED.]

342. **Blow . . . windes**] DOUCE calls attention to that immortal passage in *Meas. for Meas.* III, i, 124: ' To be imprison'd in the viewless winds, And blown with rest less violence round about The pendent world.'

344. See III, i, 58. COLLIER (ed. ii) says that the 'line ends strictly at "dead," ' but then Collier reads ' Desdemona.'

345. **Cassio**] COLLIER : From the omission in the Folio of the stage direction here found in the Qq, we may infer that the practice of our old stage in this respect was not uniform. In modern times Cassio walks in lame, and supported, with the handker chief as a bandage about his wounded leg.

350. BOOTH : Othello draws the bed-curtains close at Iago's entrance, that Desde mona's corpse may not be polluted by Iago's gaze. All eyes are fastened on Iago, thus giving Othello the chance to assault him unobserved.

351. **feet**] JOHNSON : To see if, according to the common opinion, his feet be cloven.

354. **I bleed**] MAGINN (p. 260, note) : This is strange language. Should it not be, ' I [i. e., Ay, as usual in Shakespeare], *bled,* sir, but not killed ' ?

356. BOOTH : ' If 't were now to die, 'twere now to be most happy.' The same sad refrain first heard in the very heaven of his happiness, now in his hell of misery. Let it be faintly heard wherever possible through your performance of this cnaracter.

357. **so good**] BOOTH : Not a savage brute. Remember this.

Falne in the practife of a curfed Slaue,   358
What fhall be faide to thee.

Oth.   Why any thing :   360
An honourable Murderer, if you will :
For nought I did in hate, but all in Honour.

Lod.   This wretch hath part confeft his Villany :
Did you and he confent in *Caffio*'s death.

Oth.   I.   365

Caf.   Deere Generall, I neuer gaue you caufe.

Oth.   I do beleeue it, and I aske your pardon :
Will you, I pray, demand that demy-Diuell,
Why he hath thus enfnar'd my Soule and Body.   [338 *b*]

Iag. Demand me nothing : what you know, you know :   370
From this time forth, I neuer will fpeake word.

Lod.   What? not to pray ?

Gra.   Torments will ope your lips.   373

---

358. *curfed*] Ff, Rowe+, Cap. Steev. Mal. Var. Knt, Sing. Wh. i, Ktly. *damned* Qq et cet.

  359. *fhall*] *fhould* Qq.
    thee.] *thee ?* QqF₄ et seq.

362. *I did in*] *did I in* Qq, Jen. Sta. Cam. Del. *I did* F₄.

366. *neuer gaue*] *did neuer giue* Qq, Jen.

367. *your*] *you* Qq, Coll. i, Glo. Del. Rlfe.

368. *I pray*] *pray* Q₁.

369. *enfnar'd*] *infnar'd* Qq.

373. *ope*] *op'e* Q₁.

---

358. **in**] WALKER (*Crit.* iii, 291) : 'In' for *into, ut sæpe ;* for Shakespeare can scarcely have written, 'Fall'n into th' practise.'

358. **practise**] JOHNSON : In the snare, by the stratagem.

358. **cursed**] DYCE (ed. iii) : I prefer the Qq, because Othello has a little before exclaimed 'O cursèd, cursèd slave !'

371. SWINBURNE (p. 179) : Iago has within him a sense or conscience of power incomparable : and this power shall not be left, in Hamlet's phrase, 'to fust in him unused.' A genuine and thorough capacity for human lust or hate would diminish and degrade the supremacy of his evil. He is almost as far above or beyond vice as he is beneath or beyond virtue. And this it is which makes him impregnable and invulnerable. When once he has said it, we know as well as he that henceforth he never will speak word. We could smile almost as we can see him to have smiled at Gratiano's most ignorant and empty threat, being well assured that torments will in no wise ope his lips ; that as surely and as truthfully as ever did the tortured philosopher before him, he might have told his tormentors that they did but bruise the coating, batter the crust, or break the shell of Iago. Could we imagine a far other lost spirit than Farinata degli Uberti's endowed with Farinata's might of will, and transferred from the sepulchres of fire to the dykes of Malebolge, we might conceive something of Iago's attitude in hell,—of his unalterable and indomitable posture for all eternity. BOOTH : I grind my teeth at this, not because it 'takes,' but because I feel that it expresses determination never to speak again.

Oth. Well, thou doſt beſt.

Lod. Sir,   375
You ſhall vnderſtand what hath befalne,
(Which, as I thinke, you know not) heere is a **Letter**
Found in the pocket of the ſlaine *Rodorigo*,
And heere another, the one of them imports
The death of *Caſſio*, to be vndertooke   380
By *Rodorigo*.

Oth. O Villaine!

Caſſio. Moſt Heatheniſh, and moſt groſſe.

Lod. Now, heere's another diſcontented paper
Found in his pocket too : and this it ſeemes   385
Rodorigo meant t'haue ſent this damned villaine :
But that (belike) *Iago* in the interim
Came in, and ſatisfi'd him.

Oth. Oh thou pernitious Caitiffe ;
How came you (*Caſſio*) by that Handkerchiefe   390
That was my wiues ?

Caſſio. I found it in my Chamber :
And he himſelfe confeſt it but euen now,
That there he dropt it for a ſpeciall purpoſe,
Which wrought to his deſire.   395

374. *doſt*] *doeſt* Qq.
375, 376. One line, Qq, Rowe et seq.
377. *not*] Om. Johns.
    heere is] *here's* Pope, Theob. Han.
Warb. Dyce iii.
379. *the one*] *one* Pope+.
380, 381. One line, Qq.
    vndertooke By] *vndertooke — by*
Q₁.
386. *t'haue*] Ff, Rowe+, Dyce iii,
Huds. *to haue* Qq et cet.

387. *interim*] *nicke* Q₁, Jen.
388. *ſatisfi'd*] *ſatisfied* Qq.
389. *Oh thou*] Ff, Rowe+, Knt, Sta
Del. *O the* Qq et cet.
    Caitiffe] *catieffe* Qq.
390. *that*] *a* Qq, Jen.
    Handkerchiefe] *handkercher* Q₁.
391. *wiues*] *wifes* Qq. *wife's* Rowe.
393. *it but*] Ff, Rowe+, Jen. *it* Q₁.
but Cap. et cet.
394. *ſpeciall*] *ſpeaciall* Q₃.

377. **Letter**] KOESTER (*Sh. Jahrbuch*, i, p. 142) finds here, in the needlessness of
these letters, and in the fact that they rehearse only what is already known to the
audience, a proof that the scenes, in which the events related in these letters occur,
were omitted in the representation.

382. **Villaine**] RITSON: Read, for the sake of both sense and metre: *villainy*
'Of course,' says WALKER (*Crit.* ii, 45).

388. **satisfi'd**] WHITE (ed. ii): Gave him enough; killed him. [See IV, ii, 279.]

390. BOOTH: After a pause,—looking wonderingly at the handkerchief.

393. **it**] MALONE: This was manifestly caught by the compositor's eye glancing on
the next line.

Othel.   O Foole, foole, foole!   396
Caſſio.   There is beſides, in *Rodorigo*'s Letter,
How he vpbraides *Iago*, that he made him
Braue me vpon the Watch : whereon it came
That I was caſt : and euen but now he ſpake   400
(After long ſeeming dead) *Iago* hurt him,
Iago ſet him on.
Lod.   You muſt forſake this roome, and go with **vs** :
Your Power, and your Command is taken off,
And *Caſſio* rules in Cyprus.   For this Slaue,   405
If there be any cunning Crueltie,
That can torment him much, and hold him long,
It ſhall be his.   You ſhall cloſe Priſoner reſt,
Till that the Nature of your fault be knowne
To the Venetian State.   Come, bring away.   410
Oth.   Soft you ; a word or two before you goe :
I haue done the State ſome ſeruice, and they know't :   412

398. *vpbraides*] *obraides* Q₂Q₃. *up-braipes* F₃.
Iago] *Iagos* Q₃.
400. *but*] Om. Rowe ii +.
ſpake] *ſpeake* Q₃. *said* Rann conj.
405. *For*] *Fore* Q₃.
410. *bring*] Ff, Rowe, Pope, Han. Johns. Cap. Steev.'93, Knt, Dyce, Sta.
Cam. Coll. iii, Huds.   *them* Coll. (MS). *bring him* Qq et cet.
411. *before you goe*] Om. Qₓ.
412. *I haue*] *I've* Pope+, Dyce iii, Huds.
know't] *know it* Steev. Mal. Var. Rann, Coll. Wh. i.

---

396. HAWKINS (*Life of Kean*, i, 229): Booth, Garrick, Barry, and Kemble raved, tore their hair, and became convulsed with passion when expressing these words, but Kean knew better; he felt no agony at the moment, because neither Shakespeare nor Nature taught him to feel any, 'and he repeated the word quickly and almost inarticulately, and with a half smile of wonder at his incredible stupidity in having been such a "fool." ' OTTLEY (p. 32): It is needless to remind those who saw Kean in this passage, of the marvellous use he made of the occasion,—his eye wandering in vacancy, as stupefied by amazement, remorse, and despair,—and the clasped hands, palms upwards, gathered across the head, as if to crush a fevered brain, which threatened to burst out into a volcano,—exclaiming the while with trembling, gasping utterance, and in agonized tones: 'Fool! fool! fool!' BOOTH: From this onward, I imagine Othello to be on the very verge of pure insanity.

400. **cast**] See I, i, 164; II, ii, 31; II, ii, 302.

411. **Soft you**] GOULD (p. 116): As J. B. Booth begins this speech he takes a silken robe and carelessly throws it over his shoulder; then reaches for his turban, possessing himself of a dagger he had concealed therein. BOOTH: Othello opens the curtains,—pauses,—kisses Desdemona,—slowly and with deepest feeling of remorse,—turns towards the others, who, in respectful sympathy, droop their heads, and, therefore, do not see his purposed suicide until it is too late.

No more of that.   I pray you in your Letters,   413
When you ſhall theſe vnluckie deeds relate,
Speake of me, as I am.   Nothing extenuate,   415
Nor ſet downe ought in malice.
Then muſt you ſpeake,
Of one that lou'd not wiſely, but too well :
Of one, not eaſily Iealious, but being wrought,
Perplexed in the extreame : Of one, whoſe hand   420
(Like the baſe Iudean) threw a Pearle away

---

415. *of me, as I am*] *of them as they
are* Q₂, Jen.
416, 417. One line, Qq, Pope et seq.
417. *muſt you*] *you muſt* Q₂Q₃.
418. *too well*] *to well* Q₃.
419. *Iealious*] F₂. *iealous* or *jealous*
QqF₃F₄.

420. *Perplexed*] *Perplext* Qq. *per-
plex'd* Rowe.
421. *baſe*] *bare* Cartwright.
Iudean] Indian QqF₃F₄. *Judian*
Theob. Warb. *Judean* Han. Johns. Steev.
Mal. Var. *Indian* F₂ et cet.

---

420. **Perplexed**] WALKER (*Crit.* iii, 291) : This word, as Shakespeare understood
it, meant much more than with us.   [In proof, many instances are cited, *Cymb.* V, v,
108; *Two Gent.* II, iii, 9, &c., and a striking one from Sidney's *Arcadia*, Bk. ii, p. 189,
l. 4: 'But the truth indeed is, that partly with the shame and sorrow she took of her
father's faultiness, partly with the fear, that the hate I conceived against him, would
utterly disgrace her in my opinion, whensoever I should know her, so vehemently perplexed her, that her fair colour decayed, and daily and hastily grew into the extreme
working of sorrowfulness,' &c.]

421. **Iudean**] POPE : In the first edition it is *Judian*, occasion'd, probably, by the
word *Tribe* just after, but the common reading is better; as the word *Tribe* is applicable to any race of people, and the thought of an ignorant *Indian's* casting away a pearl
very natural in itself, whereas to make sense of the other, one must presuppose some
particular story of a *Jew* alluded to, which is much less obvious.   THEOBALD adopted
Judian on the grounds that no Indian was so ignorant as not to know the value of
pearls; that an Indian would have been called *rude* and not 'base'; that 'pearl' is
metaphorical, and by it 'our author very properly means *a fine woman*.'   To Pope's
objection to *Judian*, that it must contain a reference to some particular Jew, Theobald
opposes the story of 'Herod, who in a fit of blind jealousy threw away such a jewel
of a wife as Mariamne,' whose story was dramatized in 1613 by Lady Elizabeth Carew.
Lastly, that the accent was no obstacle to a poet who shortens the second syllable in
Euphrates.   WARBURTON agrees with Theobald, and adds that from the phrase 'out-
herod Herod' applied to a poor player in Hamlet, the existence of a tragedy on Herod
is to be inferred.   [Malone afterwards showed that the Herod here alluded to was a
character in one of the ancient Mysteries.]   UPTON (p. 255) : In the First book of the
Ethiopian romance of Heliodorus there is the story of Thyamis, an Aegyptian robber,
who fell in love with Chariclea; stung with jealousy, and despairing of possessing her
himself, he resolves to murder her; and thinking he had killed her (but it happened to
be another), he cries out, 'Alas, poor maid, these are the nuptial gifts I present thee.'
This story is alluded to in *Twelfth Night*, V, i, 121; and it is this same story, it seems
to me, that Othello refers to here, and the phrase should therefore be, 'Like the base

[421. (Like the base Iudean) threw a Pearle away].

Egyptian, threw,' &c.   This exactly agrees with the Romance.   'Twas Thyamis's own
hand, and he, too, in a strong fit of love and jealousy, that committed this murder.
Brabantio had called Othello 'a foul thief.'   These circumstances crowd into Othello's
mind, and with great propriety he calls himself 'the base *Egyptian.*'   As for Theobald's reference to Herod and Mariamne, very little will be found in it applicable to
Desdemona's case.   Othello was a private murderer, Herod brought his wife to public
justice; Desdemona was fond of the Moor, the Jewess hated her husband, and always
treated him with scorn and contempt.   On the other hand, the story of the Egyptian
thief is very minutely applicable, and the passage in *Twelfth Night* shows that our
author was pleased with the allusion.   It seems the corruption was owing to some sort
of ill-written abbreviation, that might be in the original, as *Egpⁱᵃⁿ,* and which could
not be easily understood by printer or player.   HEATH (p. 571) defends *Indian*
against Theobald's objections by asserting, first: That Indians do not know the value
of pearls.   'Nay, even at this day the various tribes of Indians who inhabit the continent of North America, would joyfully exchange the most valuable pearl that might
accidentally fall into their hands for a bottle of rum, or a flask of gunpowder.'   Secondly: 'Base' is used to signify not only villainous and treacherous, but mean, vulgar,
uninstructed in the arts of polished life.   Thirdly: That the 'pearl' doth not mean a
fine woman in virtue of a metaphor, but is only likened to one, to wit, to Desdemona,
in virtue of a comparison or similitude.   On the other hand, there are three unanswerable objections to *Judian.*   First: There is no such word, and the verse will not permit
Judæan.   Secondly: It contradicts the probable truth of the manners, as it is in the
highest degree improbable that Othello, born a Negro or Moor, and bred in the tented
field, and rude in speech, should have ever heard of Herod and Mariamne.   Thirdly:
There is not the least resemblance between the two stories, except that both Othello
and Herod put their wives to death, the one privately, the other publicly.   STEEVENS:
I cannot join with the learned critics in conceiving this passage to refer either to the ignorance of the natives of India, in respect of *pearls,* or to the well-known story of Herod
and Mariamne.   The poet might just as fairly be supposed to have alluded to that of
Jephthah and his Daughter.   Othello, in detestation of what he had done, seems to compare himself to another person who had thrown away a *thing of value,* with some circumstances of the *meanest villainy,* which the epithet *base* seems to imply in its general
sense, though it is sometimes used only for *low* or *mean.*   The Indian could not properly be termed *base* in the former and most common sense, whose fault was *ignorance,*
which brings its own excuse with it; and the crime of Herod surely deserves a more
aggravated distinction.   I do not believe the poet intended to make the present simile
coincide with all the circumstances of Othello's situation, but merely with the single act
of having *basely* (as he himself terms it) destroyed that on which he ought to have set
a greater value.   As the *pearl* may bear a *literal* as well as a *metaphorical* sense, I
would rather choose to take it in the *literal* one, and receive Pope's rejected explanation, *presupposing some story of a Jew alluded to,* which might be well understood at
that time, though now, perhaps, forgotten, or, at least, imperfectly remembered.   I have
read in some book, as ancient as the time of Shakespeare, the following tale, though at
present I am unable either to recollect the title of the piece or the author's name [That
obliging, and yet treacherous, memory!—ED.]: 'A Jew, who had been prisoner for
many years in distant parts, brought with him at his return to Venice a great number
of pearls, which he offered on the 'change among the merchants, and (one alone
excepted) disposed of them to his satisfaction.   On this pearl, which was the largest

[421. (Like the base Iudean) threw a Pearle away].

ever shown at market, he had fixed an immoderate price, nor could be persuaded to make the least abatement. Many of the magnificoes, as well as traders, offered him considerable sums for it, but he was resolute in his first demand. At last, after repeated and unsuccessful applications to individuals, he assembled the merchants of the city, by proclamation, to meet him on the Rialto, where he once more exposed it to sale on the former terms, but to no purpose. After having expatiated, for the last time, on the singular beauty and value of it, he threw it suddenly into the sea before them all.' Though this anecdote may appear inconsistent with the avarice of a Jew, yet it sufficiently agrees with the spirit so remarkable at all times in the scattered remains of that vindictive nation. 'Richer than all his tribe' seems to point out the Jew again in a mercantile light, and may mean that 'the pearl was richer than all the gems to be found among a set of men generally trading in them.' Neither do I recollect that Othello mentions many things but what he might fairly have been allowed to have had knowledge of in the course of his peregrinations. Of this kind are the similes of the Euxine Sea flowing into the Propontick, and the Arabian trees dropping their gums. The rest of his speeches are more free from mythological and historical allusions than almost any to be found in Shakespeare, for he is never quite clear from them; though in the design of this character he seems to have meant it for one who had spent a greater part of his life in the field, than in the cultivation of any other knowledge than what would be of use to him in his military capacity. It should be observed, that most of the flourishes merely ornamental were added after the first edition; and this is not the only proof to be met with, that the poet, in his alterations, sometimes forgot his original plan. FAR-MER: I abide by the old text *Judian,* and to the allusion to Herod in the play of Mariamne: 'I had but one inestimable *jewel*—Yet I in suddaine choler cast it downe, And dasht it all to pieces.' MALONE: I once thought that the accent here given to *Júdean* was a strong objection to this reading: and that the word must have been *Judèan* or *Judæan* (as a derivative from *Judæ*), which would not suit the metre. But the objection was founded on a mistake; for derivative words of this kind were thus accented in Shakespeare's time. Thus, in *Merry Wives,* we have in the old copies, 'an *Epicurian* rascal,' which ascertains the pronunciation of that word to have been different formerly from what it is now. The word is also thus spelt in North's *Plutarch.* Again, in *Ant. & Cleo.* II, i, 24: 'Keep his brains fuming, Epicurean cooks.' Those who would adopt the original reading, *Indian,* may urge in its support that the pearl naturally brings a people of the East to Shakespeare's mind; the connection in his time being considered so strong, that a contemporary author has distinguished the inhabitants of *India* by an epithet founded on the circumstance of their abounding in pearls: 'where the bright sun with neighbour beams Doth early light the pearled Indians.'—*Cornelia,* by T. Kyd, 1594. On the other hand, the word 'tribe' is strongly in favour of 'Júdean,' and I have now no doubt that it is the true one. Webster, in his *Appius and Virginia,* 1654, has 'the jewels that she wore, More worth than all her tribe' [p. 217, ed. Dyce]. BOSWELL: Read *Indian.* 'Tribe' is not peculiarly applicable to Jews; it meant, as we learn from Cockeram, *a kindred,* and is constantly used at this day in speaking of Indians. The Jews are not in general described as willing to throw away what is valuable; and it is not likely that Shakespeare would allude to an anecdote of a single individual, of which, perhaps, none of his auditors had ever heard; but in our author's time, when voyages of discovery to America were common, each 'putter-out of five for one' was probably stimulated by a description of the riches he might find there, and of the facility with which the Indians, *base,* on account of their ignorance, would part

[421. (Like the base Iudean) threw a Pearle away].

with them.   [Boswell here cites two allusions to the casting away of pearls and gems by Indians, one from Howard's *The Woman's Conquest*, 1671, and another from Habington's *Castara*, 1634, p. 67, ed. Arber].   COLERIDGE (*Notes*, &c., p. 256, referring to Warburton's note): Thus it is for no-poets to comment on the greatest of poets! To make Othello say that he, who had killed his wife, was like Herod, who killed Mariamne!—Oh, how many beauties, in this one line, were impenetrable to the ever thought-swarming, but idealess, Warburton! Othello wishes to excuse himself on the score of ignorance, and yet not to excuse himself,—to excuse himself by accusing. This struggle of feeling is finely conveyed in the word 'base,' which is applied to the rude Indian, not in his own character, but as the momentary representative of Othello's. *Indian*,—for I retain the old reading,—means American, a savage *in genere*.   KNIGHT: We might have thought that there was in F₁ only a substitution of *u* for *n*, had we not turned to all the passages in that edition where 'Indian' occurs, and found it invariably spelt *I-n-d-i-a-n*. . . . . To show how far conjecture may be carried, we may mention that a correspondent wishes to impress upon us that the allusion was to Judas Iscariot. COLLIER: The meaning is very clear, the allusion obscure; and the probability is, that Shakespeare referred to some known fable of the time, now lost.   DYCE (*Remarks*, p. 243): It was rather unnecessary in Boswell to refer to Cockeram, since, *in the present play*, Iago says, 'the souls of all my *tribe* defend From jealousy!'—III, iii.   The latter part of Boswell's note [i. e., the citations from Habington and Howard] (the most valuable of Boswell's contributions to the illustration of Shakespeare) proves, I think, that Othello alludes to no particular story, but to 'the Indian' as generally described; and to the passages just cited the following may be added: 'The wretched Indian spurnes the golden ore.'—Drayton, *Legend of Matilda*, sig. F, f 7,—*Poems*, n. d. WHITE (*Shakespeare Scholar*, p. 443): There appears to me not a doubt that F₁ is right, and that the allusion is to Herod and Mariamne.   [White here gives a long extract from George Lunt, of which the following is an abstract]: The expression is one of generalization, demanding the ready understanding of the reader.   Whether he understand the particular allusion or not, at least it should be of that character that he might, or ought to have known it; and not drawn from a source so remote as to be out of his reach.   On this ground we are willing to set up any possible *Judean* against any *Indian* that can be imagined.   In the first place, 'tribe' is a word peculiarly appropriate to the Jewish people.   Next, 'base' would be held peculiarly descriptive of the Jewish people; in common understanding, it would fit any Jew and all Jews.   There would have been a manifest impropriety in the epithet as denoting the characteristics of East Indians in general.   Lastly, the word 'Judean,' in reality, means something more than *Jew*.   A 'Judean' is, in fact, an *inhabitant of Judea ;* and thus, in correspondence with Shakespeare's common mode of expression, the word might naturally, and with more force would, refer to Herod, King of Judea, as the *Judean, par excellence,*—as representing the State.   [Thus far Lunt.   White then resumes, and emphasizes the absolute necessity of a reference to a particular story.   In Boswell's citations and in Dyce's, not only] is the Indian generally described, but the act.   No specific deed is referred to ; there is a mere allusion to a characteristic of the Indian.   Not so in Othello's speech. In that, a particular person and a particular act must be alluded to, because Othello likens himself, not to the Indian who *throws* a pearl away, but to 'the base Júdean' who '*threw* a pearl away.'   The reference is to some story, specific and unmistakable ; can there be a shadow of a doubt that Herod's was the story referred to, and that we should not disturb the F₁?   [Six years later, in his edition, WHITE says]: To my

Richer then all his Tribe : Of one, whofe fubdu'd Eyes,   422
Albeit vn-vfed to the melting moode,
Drops teares as faft as the Arabian Trees   424

---

422. *fubdu'd*] *fubdued* Qq. Om. Pope,   424. *Drops*] Q₁, Ktly. *Dropt* Jen.
Theob. Han. Warb.   *Drop* Q₂Q₃Ff et cet.

---

maturer judgement and more careful consideration, the allusion appears to be to the
ignorance of the *Indians* in regard to the value of their gold and jewels, which was a
matter of more common remark two hundred and fifty years ago than it is at present.
[In White's Second Edition there is no note whatsoever on the passage.] WALKER
(*Crit.* iii, 292): *Indian*, certainly. STAUNTON: We follow the Qq, but must admit
that a good case has been made out for the reading of the Folio. JOHN HUNTER: As
there are several allusions in old poetry to the wretchedness or ignorance of the Indians
in spurning the golden ore and casting away pearls and gems, we have no doubt that
Indian was our author's word. COLLIER (ed. iii): We may add, what has never been
referred to, that in G. Fenton's translation of *Guevara*, 1582, p. 277, 'Judea' is misprinted *India*,—'Titus having subdued the countrey of India, and taken the great city
of Hierusalem,' &c. This would rather show that the true reading is *Judean ;* but
either way the sense is precisely the same. THOS. M'GRATH (*N. & Qu.* 4th, iii, 120)
elaborates Steevens's allusion to the story of Jephthah and his Daughter, and maintains
that no parallel could be much closer than that between the Judean and Othello : 'We
have a story of *a Jew*, a member of the *tribe* of Ephraim or Manasseh, *base* in birth,
who, with *his own hand*, threw away *a treasure*, the pearl of his tribe. A story also
well known to Shakespeare, for we find it commented on in his other plays.' [That
Othello killed his wife, and Jephthah his daughter, does not disconcert M'Grath, for he
philosophically adds, 'we cannot expect every minute detail' to be exact in counterpart.] HUDSON: Whether Shakespeare meant an allusion to any particular story of an
Indian, or to the Indians as generally described, is not quite clear; probably the latter.
COWDEN-CLARKE: Even though we follow the Qq, we confess to entertaining considerable doubts whether the Folio may not, after all, give what Shakespeare wrote.
PURNELL: Read Judæan, and refer to Herod and Mariamne. [In *N. & Qu.* 6th,
iii, 264, H. K. gives two citations to show the common repute of an Indian's indifference to the value of gems; one is from Carew, '*To A. D.*,' and is given by Walker (*Crit.*
iii, 292), and the other is from *Pierce Pennilesse*, p. 80. In the next volume, p. 245,
of the same periodical, A. E. QUEKETT adds a passage, to the same effect, from Chapman's *Revenge for Honour*, IV, ii. Again, in *The Academy*, 14 April, 1883, H. A
EVANS calls attention to the words 'Indian' and 'pearle' in Bullen's Reprint of Glap-
thorne's *The Lady Mother*, p. 121. And I dare say many and many another allusion
can yet be found,—but to me all are idle that are subsequent to the date of *Othello*, and
are general in expression, without referring to any particular Indian, who, on some especial occasion, threw away a pearl. I have reserved HALLIWELL'S opinion to the last,
because, to me, it gives the true explanation. It is as follows : 'The epithet 'base'
appears to support 'Iudean,' which, if correct, I cannot but think, notwithstanding that
the idea has been ridiculed, refers to Judas Iscariot.' Is there not, may I be permitted
to add, suggestion even in the identity of the two first syllables, *Jud*as and *Jud*ean ?
Once before in this Scene, Othello's agonized thoughts had turned for a fit comparison
to that dread time when the affrighted globe yawned and darkness covered the face of
the earth.— ·ED.]

Their Medicinable gumme.   Set you downe this :   425
And fay befides, that in *Aleppo* once,
Where a malignant, and a Turbond-Turke
Beate a Venetian, and traduc'd the State,
I tooke by th'throat the circumcifed Dogge,
And fmoate him, thus.   430

---

425. *Medicinable*] Ff, Knt, Del. Rlfe.
med'cinable Cap. Steev.'85, Mal. Dyce,
Sta. Wh. i.   *medicinall* Qq et cet.
gumme] *gums* Johns.
427. *Where*] *When* Coll. (MS).
malignant] Malignant Q$_r$.
Turbond-Turke] Turb and Turke

Q$_r$.   *Turband* Turke Q$_2$Q$_3$.   *Turband
Turk* Rowe i.   *Turban'd Turk* Pope.
429. *by th'*] Ff, Rowe, Pope i, Han.
Johns. Jen. Wh. i.   *bi' th* Qq.   *by* Cap.
by the Theob. et cet.
430. [He ftabs himfelfe. Qq.

---

425. **Medicinable**] ROLFE : Shakespeare has the word in four other passages
(*Much Ado*, II, ii, 5 ; *Tro. & Cress.* I, iii, 91 ; *Ib.* III, iii, 44, and *Cymb.* III, ii, 33) ;
in all it is equivalent to medicinal, and in all pronounced as here *med'cinable*. *Medicinal*, in the only instance in which Shakespeare uses it (*Wint. Tale*, II, iii, 37 : 'Do
come with words as medicinal as true'), is pronounced *med'cinal*, which would nct
suit the measure here.

425. **gumme.**] HUNTER (ii, 289) thinks from the description in *The Great Herbal*,
that this is the gum called 'Bernix,' which was used in medicine. BUCKNILL (p. 274) :
Probably not gum arabic, but myrrh.

426. **Aleppo**] STEEVENS : I am told that it is immediate death for a Christian to
strike a Turk in Aleppo.   Othello is boasting of his own audacity.

427. **Turbond**] DELIUS : Shakespeare seems to have connected the idea of arro-
gance with turbans.   See in *Cymb.* III, iii, 6 : 'that giants may jet through And keep
their impious turbans on.'   FECHTER : Othello here seizes and forces Iago, still bound,
to kneel before Desdemona, but promptly intercepted by Lodovico and Montano, he
draws his poignard, and suiting the action to the word utters the last two lines 429,
430 ; stabs himself, and throws the dagger at the feet of Iago ; then, tottering, walks
to the bed ; but, unable to reach Desdemona, falls in despair and dies.

430. HAWKINS, *Life of Kean* (i, 75) : Kean's falling on his back in the last Scene of
Othello was suggested by an incident in nature.   He was giving a young officer some
instruction in fencing, when he accidentally received an alarming wound in the breast,
from the effect of which, becoming insensible, he fell to the ground on his back.   When
he recovered his senses he asked, 'How did I fall ?'   BOOTH : At the word 'thus'
Othello stabs himself, cries 'O, Desdemona !' makes an effort to reach the bed, clutching (not much) for the curtains as he falls back dead.

430. DYCE (ed. iii) : When Othello offers to stab Iago he is disarmed by Montano,
but he has 'another weapon,—a sword of Spain.'   Of that weapon, after wounding
Iago, he is also deprived ; this is shown not only by the exclamation of Lodovico,
'Wrench his sword from him,' but by the remark of Cassio, 'This I did fear, but
thought he had no weapon.'   The instrument he now uses must, therefore, have been
a dagger, which was concealed about his person.   [See GOULD, line 411.]

430. SALVINI upholds his disregard of the usage of Shakespeare's own stage, as
shown by the directions in the Qq, and prefers cutting the throat to stabbing, on the
following grounds : 'First, it is the use and wont of African tribes thus to execute

431

Lod. Oh bloody period.

Gra. All that is fpoke, is marr'd.

Oth. I kift thee, ere I kill'd thee : No way but this,
Killing my felfe, to dye vpon a kiffe.   *Dyes*

Caf. This did I feare, but thought he had no weapon : [339 *a*]
For he was great of heart.

437

Lod. Oh Sparton Dogge :

---

432. *that is*] Ff, Rowe+, Steev.'85,
Mal. Knt, Sta. *that's* Qq et cet.
434. *kiffe*] *kiffo* Q₃.

434. Dyes.] He dies. Qq.
437. *Sparton*] *Spartane* Qq. *Spartan*
Ff.

---

criminals or armed prisoners of war ; secondly, the shape of their weapons is more adapted to a blow than a thrust ; thirdly, Shakespeare does not forbid my mode of death ; Othello simply says : " I took by the throat the circumcised dog, and smote him thus;" allusion having been made to the throat, it seems to me more natural that the action should lie there where attention was directed and 'the dog' was seized. A fourth and last reason is, that the critics of this mode of death adduce only two trifling arguments against it ; namely, that a man after his throat is cut cannot speak ; as though a single artery were not enough, but that the carotid must be severed ! The second argument is even more trifling, almost absurd, namely : *tradition*, to which, with all respect be it said, I will not subject myself.' [—Translation of a *Lecture* delivered in Florence by the eminent Tragedian, and contributed by him to Lewinsky's *Vor den Coulissen*, Berlin (ii, 219). A translation by Mr Botta from the original Italian appeared in *The Century* for November, 1881.—ED.]

430. To divert all suspicion, Kean simulated a pride in his punishment of the turbaned Turk, and as his eyes wandered with searching brilliance from face to face in order to see whether any suspicion as to his object lurked in their minds, he went through the concluding words with inimitable strength and beauty : 'And smote him,—*thus!*' and as he spoke the glistening steel entered his breast ; a frozen shudder swept over his frame,—every physiological indication of his suffering was faithfully and distinctly marked ; and in the attempt to imprint a last kiss on the cold, rigid face of his wife, he fell backwards,—dead.—HAWKINS, *Life of Kean*, i, 231. We only object to the virulence with which he stabs himself,—a virulence which Othello would feel neither against himself at the moment, nor against the 'turbaned Turk' (whom he had slain) at such a distance of time.—HAZLITT, quoted in *Ib.*, p. 234.

431, 432. BOOTH : Let Cassio speak these lines sorrowfully, while all show grief by pose and action as the slow curtain falls.

433. **No way but this**] Must not this phrase have floated through Macaulay's memory? See *Lays of Ancient Rome, Virginia:* 'Then clasp me round the neck once more, and give me one more kiss ; And now, mine own dear little girl, there is no way but this.'—ED.

434. **Dyes**] The winds have blown, till they have waken'd death, and after this tempest, comes the calm.—II, i, 213.—ED.

437. **Sparton**] HANMER : The dogs of Sparta were reckoned among those of the most fierce and savage kind. SINGER : The reference seems to be to the determined silence of Iago, and to the proverbial silence of the Spartans under suffering, as well as to the savageness of the dogs.

More fell then Anguifh, Hunger, or the Sea :
Looke on the Tragicke Loading of this bed :   438
This is thy worke :
The Obiect poyfons Sight,   440
Let it be hid.   *Gratiano,* keepe the houfe,   [339 *b*]
And feize vpon the Fortunes of the Moore,
For they fucceede on you.   To you, Lord Gouernor,
Remaines th eCenfure of this hellifh villaine :
The Time, the Place, the Torture, oh inforce it :   445
My felfe will ftraight aboord, and to the State,
This heauie Act, with heauie heart relate.   *Exeunt.*

FINIS.

439. *Tragicke*] *targicke* Q₃.
Loading] *lodging* Qq.
440, 441. One line, Qq, Rowe et seq.
443. *feize*] *ceaze* Qq.

444. *on you*] *to you* Qq, Rowe+, Jen.
Mal. Steev. Var. Sing. Ktly.
445. *Cenfure*] *fenfure* Q'81.
446. *Torture, oh*] *torture :* O Qq.
448. Exeunt.] Exeunt omnes. Qq.

443. seize vpon] WALKER (*Crit.* iii, 293): That is, take possession of; the law
term, as in *Rich. II:* II, i, 160: 'we do seize to us The plate, &c. Whereof our uncle
Gaunt did die possess'd.'   So also *Ib.* IV, i, 181: 'Here, cousin, seize the crown,' and
Much Ado, V, iv, 53: 'Which is the lady I must seize upon.'

444. COLLIER (ed. ii): Gratiano was uncle to Desdemona, and it is hardly to be
supposed that Othello left any known heirs behind him.   Gratiano, therefore, took
possession of the 'fortunes of the Moor' in right of his niece.

448. COLERIDGE (*Notes*, &c., p. 256): Let me repeat that Othello does not kill Desdemona in jealousy, but in a conviction forced upon him by the almost superhuman
art of Iago, such a conviction as any man would and must have entertained who had
believed Iago's honesty as Othello did.   We, the audience, know that Iago is a villain
from the beginning; but in considering the essence of the Shakespearian Othello we
must perseveringly place ourselves in his situation and under his circumstances.   Then
we shall immediately feel the fundamental difference between the solemn agony of the
noble Moor, and the wretched fishing jealousies of Leontes, and the morbid suspicious-
ness of Leonatus, who is, in other respects, a fine character.   Othello had no life but in
Desdemona; the belief that she, his angel, had fallen from the heaven of her native
innocence, wrought a civil war in his heart.   She is his counterpart; and, like him, is
almost sanctified in our eyes by her absolute unsuspiciousness, and holy entireness of
love.   As the curtain drops, which do we pity the most?

The Names of the Actors.

(:*₊*:)

Thello, *the Moore.*
Brabantio, *Father to Desdemona.*
Cassio, *an Honourable Lieutenant.*

Iago, *a Villaine.*   5

1-16. Om. Qq.

1. *The Names*...] *The Actors Names.*
Ff. (At the beginning of the Play in F₄)
Dramatis Personæ. Q'81 et seq.

2. *Othello*...] Othello...General of the
Army in Cyprus. Q'81. *Othello*...General
for the *Venetians* in *Cyprus.* Rowe.

3. *Brabantio*...] *Brabantio,* a Magnifico,... Q'81. *Brabantio,* a noble *Venetian.* Rowe.

4. *Cassio*...] *Cassio,* his Lieutenant General. Q'81.

5. *Iago*...] *Jago,* standard-bearer to the
Moor; a Villain. Q'81. his Ancient. Cap.

2. **Othello**] STEEVENS: It is highly probable that Shakespeare met with this name
in some tale that has escaped our researches: as I likewise find it in Reynolds's *God's
Revenge against Adultery,* standing in one of his Arguments as follows: 'She marries
Othello, an old German soldier.' This History (the eighth) is professed to be an *Italian* one. Here also occurs the name of *Iago.* It is likewise found, as Dr Farmer
observes, in *The first and second part of the History of the famous Euordanus, Prince
of Denmark. With the strange Adventures of Iago, Prince of Saxonie: And of both
theyr severall fortunes in Love. At London, printed by I. R. for R. B.* 1605. It may,
indeed, be urged that these names were adopted from this tragedy, but I trust that every
reader who is conversant with the peculiar style and method in which the work of honest John Reynolds is composed, will acquit him of the slightest familiarity with the scenes
of Shakespeare. B. H. C. (*N. & Qu.,* 2d, x, 269): In 1606, *M. A. Othelio,* a learned
jurisconsult, wrote a reply to the Bull of Excommunication which Pope Paul V. issued
against the Doge, Senate, and Republic of Venice. RUSKIN (*Munera Pulveris,* p. 126):
This means, I believe, 'the careful'; all the calamity of the tragedy arising from the
single flaw and error in his magnificently-collected strength. MRS F. A. KEMBLE
(*Records of Later Life,* 1884, p. 88): I have two drawings which Mrs Somerville
made for me; one, a delicate outline sketch of what is called Othello's House in Venice, and the other, a beautifully-executed coloured copy of his shield, surmounted by
the Doge's cap, and having three mulberries for a device,—proving the truth of the
assertion that the *Otelli del Moro* were a noble Venetian folk, who came originally
from the Morea, whose device was the mulberry, and showing how curious a jumble
Shakespeare has made, both of name and device, in calling him a *Moor,* and embroider-
ing his arms on his handkerchief as *strawberries.* In Cinthio's novel the husband is a
Moor, and, I think, called by no other name.

5. **Iago**] RUSKIN (*Munera Pulveris,* p. 127): 'Iago' and 'Iachimo' have, evi
dently, the same root,—probably the Spanish Iago, Jacob, 'the supplanter.' W. C.
HAZLITT (*Shakespeare's Library,* Pt. I, vol. ii, 284): So far as I can judge, there is a
certain inconsistency in the form which this name (a form of *James*) is allowed to take
in the modern editions. When the *I* or *i* of the old printed copies is otherwise altered

Rodorigo, *a gull'd Gentleman.* 6
Duke of Venice.
Senators.
Montano, *Gouernour of Cyprus.*
Gentlemen of Cyprus. 10
Lodouico, *and* Gratiano, *two Noble Venetians.*
Saylors.
Clowne.

Deſdemona, *Wife to Othello.*
Æmilia, *Wife to Iago.* 15
Bianca, *a Curtezan.*

---

6. *Rodorigo...*] *Roderigo,* a fooliſh Gentleman, that follows the Moor in hopes to
Cuckold him. Q'81. *Rodorigo,* a fooliſh Gentleman in love with Desdemona.
Rowe.

8. Senators.] Om. Rowe.

9. *Montano...*] *Mtaoanio,* the Moors
Predeceſſor in the Government of Cyprus.
Q'81. (*Montanio...*Predeſſor...Q'95).

11. *Lodouico*] *Lodovico* their kinſman.
Q'81. [i. e. to Brabantio and Gratiano].
Gratiano] *Gratiano,* his Brother.
Q'81. [i. e. to Brabantio].

13. Clowne.] Clown, Servant to the
Moor. Q'81.

15. *Æmilia...*Iago.] *Emillia...Jago.*
Q'81. *Æmilia...Jago.* Rowe.

16. *Bianca...*] *Bianca,Caſſio's* Wench.
Q'81.

Officers, Gentlemen, Meſſengers, Mu-
ſicians, Herald, Attendants. Q'81.

Scene Cyprus. Q'81. Scene for the
First Act in Venice; during the rest of
the Play in Cyprus. Rowe.

Throughout the play the names are
spelled *Roderigo* and *Emillia* in the Qq.
And *Jago* in Q'81, Q'95. Rowe, Pope.

---

to *J* or *j,* Iago alone remains unchanged,—perhaps to meet rhythmical exigencies. It
is, in fact, the same name as Jago, which is still a common appellation in Cornwall.

9. **Montano**] STEEVENS: Though Montano's rank in Cyprus cannot be exactly
ascertained, yet, from many circumstances, we are sure he had not the powers with
which Othello was subsequently invested.

14. **Desdemona**] SHAFTESBURY was the earliest to call attention to a meaning in this
name (see I, iii, 168), but he translated it 'superstitious.' UPTON (p. 288) corrected it,
saying that 'the name is not derived from Δεισιδαίμων, but Δυσδαίμων, that is, the "unfortunate"; and Cinthio, making the word feminine, calls her *Disdemona.*' [See HALES,
V, ii, 85.]

APPENDIX

THE TEXT

IN the *Registers of the Stationers' Company* (Arber's *Transcript*, vol. iv, p. 59) occurs the following Entry:

6° October 1621

Thomas Walkley   Entred for his copie vnder the handes of Sir GEORGE BUCK, and Master **Swinhowe** warden, *The Tragedie of OTHELLO the Moore of Venice* . . . . vj^d

During the next year this 'copie' was published with the following title page:

THE | Tragœdy of Othello, | The Moore of Venice. | *As it hath beene diuerse times acted at the* | Globe, and at the Black-Friers, by | *his Maiesties Seruants.* | Writ-*ten by* VVilliam Shakefpeare. | [Vignette] | *LONDON,* | Printed by *N. O.* for *Thomas Walkley,* and are to be fold at his | fhop, at the Eagle and Child, in Brittans Burffe. | 1622.

N. O. stands, probably, for Nicholas Oakes, and as the Vignette is the same as that on the title page of the Pide Bull edition of *King Lear,* it may be that he was the printer of the latter also (see *Lear,* p. 357).

To this edition, which, following the Cambridge Editors, I have called the FIRST QUARTO, or Q₁, is prefixed the following:

The Stationer to the Reader.

To set forth a booke without an Epistle, were like to the old English prouerbe, A blew coat without a badge, *& the Author being dead, I thought good to take that piece of worke vpon mee : To commend it, I will not, for that which is good, I hope euery man will commend, without intreaty : and I am the bolder, becaufe the Authors name is fufficient to vent his worke.   Thus leauing euery one to the liberty of iudgement : I haue ventered to print this Play, and leaue it to the generall cenfure.*

Yours,
Thomas VValkley.

On p. 20 it has *Actus 2 Scœna* 1, a division which corresponds to all other editions; and so also does *Actus* 4, on p. 61, and *Actus* 5, on p. 77.   There is no reference to Actus 3.   Up to p. 74 the pagination is correct; from there to the last page it is quite irregular.   The last page is 99, in reality it is 91.

In the next year we find the following Entry in the *Register of the Stationers' Company* (Arber's *Transcript*, iv, 107):

8° Nobembris 1623

Master Blounte **Isaak Jaggard**	Entred for their Copie vnder the hands of Master Doctor WORRALL and Master **Cole** warden Master WILLIAM SHAKSPEERS *Comedyes Histories, and Tragedyes* soe manie of the said Copies as are not formerly entered to other men. . . . *vizt* . . . . **vij^s**

COMEDYES	*The Tempest* *The two gentlemen of Verona* *Measure for Measure* *The Comedy of Errors* *As you like it* *All's well that ends well* *Twelfe night* *The winters tale*
HISTORIES	*The thirde parte of* HENRY *ye* SIXT HENRY *the* EIGHT
TRAGEDIES	CORIOLANUS TIMON *of Athens* JULIUS CÆSAR MACKBETH ANTHONIE *and* CLEOPATRA CYMBELINE

It will be noted that in accordance with the terms of the Entry, no play is included in this list of which an authentic Quarto had been already printed; yet when the volume was published, it contained these Quarto plays. From which it is to be presumed that the interests in these Quartos had become vested in various ways, by purchase, inheritance, or marriage, in the proprietors of the Folio: Jaggard, Blount, Smithwicke, and Apsley. But there is a mystery about *Othello*. It certainly appeared in Quarto, and it certainly appeared in the Folio, and yet Thomas Walkley had not resigned all his interest in it in 1623. For in the *Stationers' Registers* (Arber, iv, 194) we find the following:

i^{mo} Martii 1627 [i. e., 1628]

Master Richard **Hawkins**	Assigned ouer vnto him by **Thomas Walkley**, and Consent of a Court holden this Day all the estate right title and Interest which he hath in these Copies following . . . . **xviij^d**

> *vizt*
> *A kinge and no kinge.*
> PHILASTER *or love lies ableeding.*
> ORTHELLO *the more of Venice.*

It is not easy to reconcile this proof of property still vested in Walkley with the appearance of *Othello* in the First Folio. Collier suggests that, 'most likely, the publishers of the Folio purchased Walkley's interest at a date posterior to the entry of their undertaking at Stationers' Hall, and thus became entitled to include it in their noble volume,' which does not help us. Although the Folio was issued in 1623, the printing must have been in hand long before that. Indeed, there are not wanting copies which are supposed to bear the genuine date 1622, the very year in which Walkley issued his Quarto, so that the two books must have been in the hands of the printers at the same time. Can we here infer some private understanding between the publishers? Was it to emphasize his possession of the Quarto, while acquiescing in its appearance in the Folio, that Walkley put forth his unusual address 'to the Reader'? But speculations are idle; even if they led to assurance, what should we gain? Merely a better knowledge of the private affairs of Thomas Walkley. 'When all's done, you look but on a stool.' Of more importance is it that two years later, in 1630, Richard Hawkins put his assignment to use by issuing a Quarto *Othello* with exactly the same title-page, except that there is a different Vignette, and that it is stated to be: 'Printed by *A. M.* for *Richard Hawkins*, and are to be fold at | his fhoppe in Chancery-Lane, neere Sergeants-Inne. | 1630.'

This is the *Second Quarto*, or Q$_2$.

We next meet 'Orthello' in the *Stationers' Register* (Arber, iv, p. 420), when on the 29° Maij, 1638, **vrsula Hawkins** widdow (late wife of **Richard Hawkins** deceased) assigned to 'Master **Mead** and Master **Meredith**' certain 'Copies' 'which did belong vnto her said husband;' in the list of twenty-five titles, which follows, appears 'ORTHELLO *the More of Venice* a play.' Master Mead and Master Meredith did not long retain possession of *Orthello;* on the 25th of January of the following year, 1639, they assigned over to Master **William Leake** 'these Copies,' 'following which were Entred vnto them from Mistris **Hawkins**.' Again in this list also we have 'Orthello the More of Venice a Play.' For sixteen long years did Master Leak permit the dust to settle on *Orthello* before he published what he called, on the Title-page, 'The fourth Edition.' The rest of the title-page is exactly the same, barring a Crown for a Vignette, as in the preceding Quartos, except that it is: 'Printed for *William Leak* at the *Crown* in *Fleet-* | *ftreet*, between the two Temple Gates, 1655.'

This is the *Third Quarto*, or Q$_3$.

A Player's Quarto appeared in 1681, as 'now [acted] at the Theater Royal, by His Majesties Servants.' It is 'Printed for *W. Weak*, and are to be fold by *Richard Bent* | *ley* and *M. Magnes* in *Ruffel Street* near *Covent-* | *Garden*, 1681.' Halliwell suggests that 'Weak' is a misprint for *Leak*. If it be the same W. Leak that published the Third Qto, who was presumably the same W. Leake that was 'called as an Assistant' to the Stationers' Company, seventy-seven years before, in 1604, it may be a misprint, it cannot possibly, after such a protracted existence, be a misnomer. Reprints of this Quarto followed in 1687 and 1695.

Meanwhile the *First, Second, Third,* and *Fourth Folios* had appeared in 1623, 1632, 1663, and 1685.

Here bibliographic interest in all of them ceases. Their value to us as texts is all that is of importance now. Although this value is somewhat difficult of adjustment, there is greater harmony among Editors with regard to it in this play than usually falls to the lot of a play which has attendant satellites in the shape of Quartos.

We have Four Folios and Three Quartos. How many independent texts are there and what are their respective values?

The Four Folios are practically one. For any changes introduced after the First was issued, there is no more authority to be yielded than is due to the intelligence, more or less keen, of a compositor. For the text of the First Folio there must have been used either the original MS of Shakespeare (Heminge and Condell asserted that they had so used it, but then we know that in the case of certain other plays this was 'a grace snatched beyond the bounds of truth') or else a stage copy, which, perhaps, contained no single word written by Shakespeare's own hand.

Considering the twenty years since Shakespeare's ink was dry on the original, and considering the burning, between whiles, of 'The Globe' and its contents (it *was* a conflagration of the world to us), this latter supposition, that the Folio was printed from a stage copy, seems the more probable. In either case Shakespeare's personal friends vouched for its accuracy, and no similar authority vouches for any other. This, then, the text of the Folio of 1623, becomes the text of the play; and in any claim for preference put forth by other texts the burden of proof lies on the claimants, the presumption of authenticity is all in favour of F_1. As we have seen at II, ii, 231, Dyce, whose opinion on such matters is of very great weight, asserts that this play in F_1 was 'beyond all doubt printed from a transcript belonging to the theatre.'

On the other side stand the three Quartos.

The FIRST, as we have seen, was issued by a Stationer named Walkley. What manuscript he used, or how he obtained it, we cannot know. He says in his address 'to the reader,' that the author is dead; it is, therefore, not likely that he received the MS from Shakespeare during Shakespeare's lifetime and kept it lying idle for five or six years. Nor is it likely that Walkley's text was taken down surreptitiously by short-hand from a performance on the stage: the stage directions are not sufficient in number, nor descriptive enough in character, to indicate an eye-witness; and although four of the Acts are noted, there are no divisions into Scenes. Yet there can be no doubt that Walkley's text is an original text, and that it is not the same as that of the Folio. In a comparison of the two, mere omissions go for nothing. Counting every line of the Folio, not as verses but as lines, as is done in the preceding pages of this volume, and counting the lines in the Quarto in the same way, there are, roughly speaking, more than three hundred and fifty lines in the Folio that are omitted in the Quarto. Knight, who with closer accuracy, computed the verses, reckons the number at 'a hundred and sixty-three.' But additions are important; they are presumably from the hand of the author; and in the way of additions there are ten or fifteen lines in the Quarto, Knight says less than ten, which are not to be found in the Folio. This alone goes far to stamp the Qto as an independent text. But the most noticeable difference, one that strikes every reader at once, from the beginning to the end, in the first speech of Iago and among the last speeches of Emilia, and in Cassio's drunken scene, lies in the use of oaths and adjurations. 'Zounds,' 'God,' ''Sblood,' etc., scattered through the First Quarto, are either omitted altogether or are toned down, in the Folio. Hence there can be no reasonable doubt that in the First Quarto we have a genuine text, and since it cannot be supposed to have come from Shakespeare, and was not taken down by short-hand, we are forced to conclude that it too was a play-house copy, and, I think, an old one, possibly 'stolne.' It is not worth while here to enter upon a minute comparison of the two texts. The very purpose of the Textual Notes in the foregoing pages is to enable the student to do that for himself. It is not hard to grow interested in minute collation, but then one must do it for himself, at first hand. Simply to repeat another's work is most tolerable and not to be endured. It is no better than proof-reading, proof-reading, too, uncheered by the hope of blunders.

The older Editors, from JOHNSON to the time of KNIGHT, were influenced in favour of this Qto, which they considered older and more authentic. Knight followed the Folio, upholding its text always through thick, and sometimes through thin. COLLIER leaned to the Second Qto, but since his time the balance of favour has been on the side of the Folio, which is, to me, far and away the better.

Perhaps it is well to mention that Pope, in his 'Table of the Several Editions' which he had used, closed his list with the title of an *Othello*, undated, but 'Published by Tho. Walkely, Quarto, (soon after his Death, as appears by the Preface.)' Overlooking Pope's somewhat startling announcement of 'Walkely's' posthumous performance, Malone conjectured that this Quarto was simply Q_r, whose date had been 'cut off, which frequently happens in old plays.' Capell, both in his 'Table of Plays' and in his Appendix, refers to this undated Qto, but it is on the authority of Pope. The Cambridge Editors think that the reference to the publisher's preface is conclusive that Pope's Qto was the Qto of 1622. No undated Qto having been discovered from Pope's day to the present, we may safely acquiesce in Malone's opinion.

The SECOND QUARTO appeared in 1630. Have we here an independent text, or merely a reprint? MALONE dismissed it as 'an edition of no authority,' but COLLIER espoused its cause with zeal, on the ground that it 'was unquestionably printed from a manuscript different from that used for the Qto of 1622 or for the Folio of 1623; and presents a number of various readings, some of which singularly illustrate the original text of *Othello*.' Collier cites III, iii, 518, where Q_2 gives the word *feels* adopted by the majority of Editors, instead of 'keepes,' of the Ff. GRANT WHITE, however, does not estimate this Qto as highly as Collier does (DYCE and STAUNTON do not even mention it in their Prefaces); he says, in reference to it, in his Introduction: 'After a careful consideration of its readings, I have come to the conclusion that it is 'only a reprint of the Qto of 1622, corrected by the text of the Folio, having some 'typographical errors peculiar to itself, and a very few unimportant corrections and 'sophistications, such as crept into almost every dramatic reprint of the period. I 'therefore regard it as of no authority, and make no mention of its readings.' The CAMBRIDGE EDITORS agree in the main with Grant White. 'After a minute compari- 'son,' they say, 'of the two [Quartos] it appears to us clear that the Quarto of 1630 'must have been printed from a copy of the Quarto of 1622, which had received addi- 'tions and corrections in manuscript. The resemblances between the two are too close 'to allow of any other supposition. These additions and corrections, though agreeing 'for the most part with the First Folio, which had appeared in the interval, were derived 'from an independent source.'

It by no means follows that 'this independent source' was Shakespeare or his MS.; a compositor or an actor would be competent to have suggested the changes. With this understanding, I quite agree with this conclusion, to which, I think, any one would the more readily come if the two copies and the Folio were placed open side by side. Where F_r supplies the omissions of Q_r, Q_2 follows F_r, and even where it differs from F_r there seems to be more an attempt to correct than to rewrite. For instance, II, i, 45, 'Euen till we make the Maine, and th' Eriall blew,' is not in Q_r; in Q_2 the line is found, but it is evidently an attempt to convert nonsense into sense, and not an original reading: 'Euen till we make the Maine and th' Ayre all blue.' Again, oaths and adjurations are sometimes omitted and sometimes retained, even on the same page, as though the excision had been attempted but done carelessly. Once more, let the Textual Notes suffice for any further investigation, if the subject be worth it.

The THIRD QUARTO is a reprint of Q_2; if it were a good reprint, it would be to that extent respectable; as it is, it is worthless. I have recorded its separate readings only here and there as mere curiosities. I can say nothing worse of it than that, having been issued in the same year with the Third Quarto of *King Lear*, I think Jane Bell must have printed them both, and tried her 'prentice hand on *Othello*.

THE DATE OF COMPOSITION.

THE earliest attempt to fix the Date of the Composition of this Play was made by WARBURTON, who asserted that there was an allusion to the creation of baronets by James the First, in the words of Othello to Desdemona in III, iv, 55 : 'The hearts of old, gaue hands : But our new Heraldry is hands, not hearts.' 'The expression ' of " new heraldry," ' says Warburton, ' was a satirical allusion to the times. Soon after ' King James the First came to the crown, he created the new dignity of baronets for ' money. Amongst their other prerogatives of honour, they had an addition to their ' paternal *arms*, of a HAND *gules* in an Escutcheon *argent*. And we are not to doubt ' but that this was the *new heraldry* alluded to by our author : by which he insinuates ' that some then created had *hands* indeed, but not *hearts ;* that is, *money* to pay for ' the *creation*, but no *virtue* to purchase the *honour*. But the finest part of the poet's ' address in this allusion is the compliment he pays to his old mistress, Elizabeth. For ' James's pretence for raising money by this creation, was the reduction of Ulster, and ' other parts of Ireland ; the memory of which he would perpetuate by that addition ' to their arms, it being the arms of Ulster. Now the method used by Elizabeth in the ' reduction of that Kingdom was so different from this, the dignities she conferred being ' on those who employed their *steel*, and not their *gold*, in this service, that nothing could ' add more to her glory, than the being compared to her successor in this point of view : ' nor was it uncommon for the dramatic poets of that time to satirize the ignominy of ' James's reign. So, Fletcher, in *The Fair Maid of the Inn.* One says, ' I will send ' ' thee to Amboyna in the East Indies for pepper.' The other replies, ' To Amboyna ? ' ' so I might be pepper'd.' Again, in the same play, a Sailor says, ' Despise not this ' ' pitch'd canvas, the time was, we have known them lined with Spanish ducats.' '

This 'satirical allusion' of Warburton would fix the date at 1611, the year in which James instituted the order of Baronets, and in this date there arose general acquiescence. MALONE, in his first edition, 1790, accepted it, but under protest. After quoting Warburton's note, ' our Hibernian coadjutor,' as Steevens calls him, proceeded thus to criticise it :

' By what chemistry can the sense which Warburton has affixed to this passage be ' extracted from it ? Or is it probable that Shakespeare, who has more than once ' condescended to be the encomiast of the unworthy founder of the order of Baronets, ' who had been personally honoured by a letter from his majesty, and substantially ' benefited by the royal license granted to him and his fellow-comedians, should have ' been so impolitic, as to satirize the king, or to depreciate his new-created dignity ? ' . . . . On every marriage the arms of the wife are *united* to those of the husband. ' This circumstance it was, that suggested *heraldry* in this place. . . . . It was the office ' of the herald to *join*, or, to speak technically, to *quarter* the arms of the new-married ' pair. Hence with his usual license, Shakespeare uses ' heraldry' for *junction*, or ' *union* in generall. Thus in *R. of L.* 64, the same term is employed to denote that ' *union* of colours which constitutes a beautiful complexion. This passage not afford- ' ing us any assistance, we are next to consider one in *The Alchemist*, by Ben Jonson, ' which, if it alluded to an incident in *Othello*, as Steevens seems to think it does, ' would ascertain this play to have appeared before 1610, in which year *The Alchemist* ' was first acted : ' *Lovewit*. Didst thou hear a cry, says't thou ? *Neighbour*. Yes, sir, ' ' like unto a man that had been strangled an hour, and could not speak.' But I doubt ' whether *Othello* was here in Jonson's contemplation. Old Ben generally spoke out ; ' and if he had intended to sneer at the manner of Desdemona's death, I think he

'would have taken care that his meaning should not be missed, and would have writ-
'ten—'like unto a *woman*,' &c.' Although *Othello* was not printed until 1622, Malone
said 'it was acted at court early in the year 1613'; and, as an authority for this statement, cited 'MS. Vertue,' for an account whereof see Chalmers, *post*. Malone continues: 'I have persuaded myself that *Othello* was one of Shakespeare's latest per-
'formances; a supposition to which the acknowledged excellence of the piece gives
'some degree of probability. It is here [i. e., in Malone's edition of 1790] attributed
'to the year 1611, because Warburton's comment on the passage may convince others,
'though, I confess it does not satisfy me. *Emilia* and *Lodovico*, two of the characters
'in this play, are likewise two of the persons in *May-day*, by Chapman, first printed in
'1611.'

The value of Warburton's citation from Fletcher's *Fair Maid of the Inn*, Malone
destroyed in his note on III, iv, 55, where he says 'that play indeed never was per-
'formed before King James, being the last play but one that Fletcher wrote, and not
'produced till the 22nd of Jan. 1625–6, after the death both of its author and King
'James; but when it was written, he must, from the circumstances already mentioned,
'have had the court before his eyes.'

Malone died in 1812, and when the Variorum of 1821 appeared, it was found that
he had abandoned the date of 1611 and adopted 1604, but before this change became
known, two other dates had been proposed.

First: CHALMERS (*Supplemental Apology*, 1799, p. 457) urged a date later even than
Warburton, 'who,' said Chalmers, 'is partly right, and partly wrong. By what chem-
'istry could this critic extract such a sense from this passage? asks Mr Malone. The
'answer must be, the same sort of chemistry, which so frequently enabled the observant
'dramatist to captivate his audience, by his striking allusions to the passing scene; to
'satyrise without lampoon; and to throw out sarcasms without scoffing. In IV, i, Iago,
'working on the jealousy of Othello, artfully remarks: 'If you are so fond over her
'"iniquity, give her [a] *patent* to offend.' The audience, who knew from their feel-
'ings, how much vexation had arisen from the *patents of monopoly*, which Queen Eliz-
'abeth and King James had so frequently granted, and so often retracted, must have
'been electrified by this fine stroke of well-timed satire. . . . . Warburton was right in
'supposing that the stroke at the *new* heraldry was, incidentally, aimed at the creation
'of baronets, which was attended with uncommon circumstances. The epoch of this
'order was undoubtedly May, 1611. But, unluckily, for the speculation of Warburton,
'the additional armorial bearing, of the bloody hand, was not given by the patent of
'creation. The order had scarcely been created when a dispute arose, during those
'punctilious times, about precedence, between the baronets and the younger sons of
'viscounts, and barons. On this difficult point King James sat *personally*, during three
'several days, to hear the learned counsel; to take the information of Heralds; and to
'consider the proofs: And, in the end, he decided against the baronets, declaring he
'had not had any purpose to wrong *third parties tacitly*, whatever he might intend to
'confer, by his creation, on others: But the King, wishing to ampliate his favour towards
'the baronets, granted them by a *second* patent, dated 28 May, 1612, among other *pre-
heminences*, 'the arms of Ulster, that is, in a field argent, a hand *geules*, or a *bloudie
'hand*.' Spenser will inform us, in his *State of Ireland*, 'that the *bloody hand* is
'*O' Neel's badge*.' Such, then, was the *new* heraldry, which Shakespeare played with,
in order to please his audience! Yet we see clearly, from the second patent, in 1612,
that the epoch, which was assigned to *Othello* in 1611, cannot be supported. And we
must, therefore, look for the true date in some subsequent year. The fact is, that the

'baronets had to encounter a severer shock. A great noise was made in the House of
'Commons on the 23 May, 1614, about the creation of Baronets. This clamour against
'the King's right to create such an order was silenced in committee. . . . . There was,
'a few days before, a still louder outcry raised, in the House of Commons, with much
'greater cause, against patents of monopoly. Owing to those remarkable coincidences,
'and powerful reasons, I am of opinion, that *Othello* was written in 1614; and, being
'written at this epoch, was the last, as it was one of the greatest, of his labours.'

Malone had stated, as we have seen, that *Othello* 'was acted at Court early in the
year 1613,' and gave as his authority 'Vertue's MS.' This date, if authentic, would
overthrow Chalmers's chronology; wherefore Chalmers set to work 'making some
'inquiries by a friend what manuscript of Vertue's it were, which I saw so often quoted
'about scenic matters, and Mr Steevens was so obliging as to say: 'The books, from
''which those extracts were made, with several others lost, belonged to Secretary Pepys,
''and afterwards to Dr Rawlinson, who lent them to Mr Vertue. There is a MS note
''subjoined to the MSS of Vertue, which, about thirty years ago, were lent to Mr Steev-
''ens by Mr Garrick.' Much is it to be lamented that any MS or book which furnished
'an illustration of Shakespeare, and having once been seen, should ever disappear. I
'would bow to any register of the time; but I will not allow Vertue, though a very dili-
'gent collector, to draw deductions for me which are to militate against the strongest
'probabilities.'

Second: though Chalmers discarded Vertue's MS, DRAKE (*Shakespeare and his
Times*, ii, 528) accepted it; and taking its date, viz: the '1st of January, 1613,' as a
final limit in one direction, and the date of the '*Second* Patent' to the Baronets, viz:
the '28th of May, 1612, as a starting-point on the other, Drake felt 'no hesitation in
expressing 'the belief that *Othello* was written in the interval between the two.'

We now come to MALONE'S final decision in the Variorum of 1821; a decision,
which, although formed on evidence now lost, has been generally concurred in down
to the present day. To his note in 1790 (quoted above), Malone now adds: 'A passage
'in the Essays of Sir Wm Cornwallis, the younger, 1601, may have suggested to Shake-
'speare the mention of the new heraldry upon which Warburton has put, what I think,
'a most erroneous interpretation: 'We of these later times full of a nice curiositie mis-
''like all the performances of our *forefathers;* we say they were honest plaine men,
''but they want the capering wits of this ripe age. . . . . *They had wont to give their
''hands and their hearts together, but we think it a finer grace to looke asquint, our
''hand looking one way and our heart another.*' If the simile of the 'Pontick Sea,'
'in III, iii, is an allusion to Pliny, translated by Philemon Holland in 1601, this will
'assist us further in ascertaining the date of this play. We know it was acted in 1604,
'and I have, therefore, placed it in that year.'

On this last very noteworthy sentence, BOSWELL has the following: 'Mr Malone
'never expresses himself at random. I therefore lament deeply that I have not been
'able to discover upon what evidence he *knew* this important and decisive fact.'

Here, for the moment, we must leave the discussion of this final date of Malone, and
proceed chronologically.

In 1836, COLLIER (*New Particulars*, p. 58) announced his discovery of the proof
that *Othello* was written not in 1604, according to Malone's chronology, but as early as
1602. This fact was obtained from the Accounts preserved at Bridgewater House in
the handwriting of Sir Arthur Mainwaring, of the expenses incurred by Sir Thomas
Egerton, afterwards Lord Ellesmere, in entertaining Queen Elizabeth and her Court
for three days at Harefield. 'It is headed, '31° July et 1° et 2° Augusti, 1602, the

''Queenes Matie beeing at Harefield iij nights,' and among the particulars is the fol-
'lowing: '6 Aug. 1602. Rewardes to the Vaulters Players and Dauncers. Of this £10
''to Burbidge's players for Othello . . . . 64 18 10.'' 'It is indisputable,' says Collier,
'from this evidence, that *Othello* was acted at Harefield in 1602.'

KNIGHT accepted this date in his edition which followed shortly after Collier's an
nouncement.

A few years after this, PETER CUNNINGHAM, a man of literary and antiquarian tastes,
was appointed to a situation in the Audit Office, Somerset House, and forthwith started
on a search for 'old papers,' rummaging 'in dry repositories, damp cellars, and still
damper vaults, for books of accounts, for warrants, and for receipts.' He found many
documents of value, but still nothing of commanding interest, until at last his perseverance was rewarded. 'My last discovery,' he says, 'was my most interesting; and
'alighting as I now did upon two official books of the Revels,—one of Tylney's and
'one of Buc's,—which had escaped both Musgrave and Malone, I at last found some-
'thing about Shakespeare,—something that was new, and something that was definitive.
'This was my little Guanahana' [*sic*]. And this was all. Cunningham was destined
to find no more. Still it was a great 'find'; any 'find' connected with Shakespeare is
great. Malone's Transcripts from ten of the Books of the Revels are printed in vol. iii
of the Variorum of 1821, pp. 364–409, and at the close of the last, ending in 1587–88,
Malone adds: 'There is no subsequent Revels Account in the reign of Queen Eliza-
'beth now extant,' wherein he was probably correct. Cunningham's discovery, which
he calls 'Book XII,' opens with November, 1605.

These 'Revels Books' are the Accounts of the expenses incurred for the entertainment of Royalty by the Master of the Revels, a title which sufficiently defines itself.
From 1579 to 1610 this office was filled by one man, Edmund Tylney, who deserves
a fame which has not been vouchsafed to him. His term extended over nearly the
whole of Shakespeare's dramatic life; through his hands and under his eyes must
have passed the original manuscripts ('O happy reader, by no critic vex't!') of upwards
of thirty of those immortal plays. Since Edmund Tylney adorns no tale, let him at
least point a moral. The first, fresh inhalation of Shakespeare's poetry in Shakespeare's own handwriting ought to have proved a liberal education, but, alack the
day! in Tylney's case it did not; witness the following uncouth description of his
office; its lack of polish can be accounted for, I fear, only by the fact that he read the
text without the help of the commentators: 'The Office of ye Revells consistethe of
'a Wardropp, and other several Roomes, for Artificers to worke in, viz. Taylors, Im-
'brotherers, Propertimakers, Paynters, Wyerdrawers, and Carpenters, togeather with a
'convenient place for ye Rehearsalls and settinge forthe of Playes and other Showes
'for those Services.' It is the infinite variety of expenses, big and little, necessarily
connected with these duties that composes these Revels Books, whereof the whole
Series was printed by *The Shakespeare Society* in 1842 under Cunningham's editorial
supervision. For the most part it is weary, dreary reading, wherein it is inconceivable
that human intelligence can find present interest, an endless repetition of the most insignificant items, which would require Dickens's immortal 'pair of million-magnifying gas
microscopes, of hextra power' to enlarge into even a languid interest. We find page
after page embalming the facts that the Master of the Revels spent so many pence for
'A peece of small corde,' 'A pound of glewe,' 'A peece of greate corde,' 'For pynnes,'
'For allom,' 'For broomes,' &c., &c., &c. But on pp. 203, 204, we are startled broad
awake by the sight of the 'greatest name in all literature;' it is true that in 'Shaxberd'
its favour, like Roderigo's, is defeated, literally, with an vsurp'd beard,—but it is there'

We read :

The Plaiers	1605	The Poets wch
By the Kings	Hallamas Day being the first of Nouembar	mayd the plaies
Maties plaiers	A play in the Banketinge house att Whithall	Shaxberd
	called The Moor of Venis.	

(In the original, 'Shaxberd' is not placed here, but opposite the play of *Mesur for Mesur.*) Then follows a list of twelve or thirteen plays, such as 'the Merry Wiues of Winsor,' 'Mesur for Mesur,' 'The Plaie of Errors,' 'How to larne of a woman to wooe,' &c., with the names of 'Shaxberd,' 'Hewood,' &c., in the margin, a practice observed nowhere else in the volume. Although this is headed 1605, internal evidence in the rest of the entries shows that the true date is 1604.

This date of the performance of *Othello* in 1604, of course, corroborated Collier's of 1602, and it is safe to say that it influenced every editor down to, and including, Dyce in 1866. The original MS volume, from which Cunningham printed, disappeared.

VERPLANCK, who wrote shortly after Cunningham's publication, unwillingly, on æs-thetic grounds, relinquished the later dates of Malone and Chalmers. The emotions and passions depicted in *Othello* are not, so he thought, such as could be reasoned out from a young Poet's mind, or portrayed by any effort of an inexperienced imagination. 'Richard and Romeo, and *The Tempest* (whatever may have been their actual dates) 'might have been the creations of youthful genius, but *Othello* required actual experi-'ence, or close observation, of the workings of bitter passions, in however humble a 'form, yet in actual life.' So impressed was Verplanck with this belief that, in order to reconcile the *Othello* of 1602 with the *Othello* of 1622, he suggested that the former 'may have been, like the original *Hamlet*, barely an outline, sufficient for dramatic 'effect, containing all the incidents and characters, but wanting some of the heightened 'poetry and intense passion of the drama we now read.'

The controversy that arose in 1859 over the genuineness of the MS Corrections in Collier's Second Folio, extended to the other Shakespearian documents put forth by Collier in his *New Facts* and *New Particulars*, and among them to the papers in Bridge-water House, with the item of £64 paid to 'Burbidge's players for *Othello*' in 1602, the only one which concerns us here. I do not find that this paper is anywhere, early in the controversy, specifically mentioned as spurious. Halliwell, to whose opinion as to the genuineness of the five Bridgewater documents great weight is deservedly attached, did not see this *Othello* item (Hamilton's *Inquiry*, p. 81), and although Hamilton, in his *Inquiry* (p. 84), says that 'these [five] documents are given in Appendix I,' yet when we turn to Appendix I, this *Othello* item is not there, and it is stated (p. 109) that there are *six* documents, and when we come to count them we find that there are, in all, *seven* documents; and had the *Othello* item been given, there would have been *eight*. I dare say this confusion, or discrepancy, is all my own, and shall accept with equanimity any imputation on my editorial fidelity or capacity. I might as well con-fess, at once, not merely to an indifference, but to an aversion, to all this discussion over the authorship of these documents. It is one thing to prove a document a forgery, but it is another, and a very different thing, to say who is the forger. The imputation of dishonesty, and a motiveless dishonesty at that, cast upon one to whom every student of dramatic history is under lasting obligations, is so painful that I have always avoided the whole matter; and while ready to accept results, as to genuineness, arrived at by my betters, must beg to be suffered to retain my private judgement as to the hand by which the dishonesty was committed. While thus confessing that my reading has not been thorough, I wish it understood that, from what I have read, I have received the deep impression that if these documents, and the MS corrections in F_2, are forged, it was not Collier who was guilty; he must have been the dupe, not the forger. In the department of 'the Collier controversy' my library is incomplete, and will remain so. I have felt that this obtrusive personal reference is necessary to explain the omission of all discussion as to the character, genuine or otherwise, of this reference by Collier to the performance of *Othello* in 1602. DYCE, in his first edition (vol. i, p. lxix), quotes Collier, but with a *caveat*. STAUNTON is more outspoken. In his Preface to *Othello*, alluding to this Bridgewater item, he says, 'the suspicion long entertained that the Shakespearian documents in that collection are modern fabrications having now deepened almost into certainty, the extract in question is of no historical value.' HALLIWELL, in his Folio Edition (1865, vol. i, p. 188), while stating the questionable character of all the Bridgewater documents, passes no judgement on the *Othello* item, because that one, as he says, he had not seen. In his Preface to *Othello* in that same edition, he passes it over in silence. DYCE, in his Second Edition (1866, vol. i, p. 77), quotes Staunton's verdict, and adds, from Hardy's *Review of the Present State of the Shakespearian Controversy*, p. 60: 'The writing, the ink, and the signature [of the paper containing the *Othello* item] equally condemn it at once.' I can find no notice of it in HALLIWELL-PHILLIPPS's *Outlines of the Life of Shakespeare*, 1885, 5th edition.

Here we must leave its further consideration, and turn to the Editors in chronological order. The next in point of time is GRANT WHITE, who, in his First Edition, was strongly influenced by Warburton's theory, and inclined to place the date in 1611. ' It seems impossible to avoid the conclusion that this passage [i. e., ' our new heraldry '' is hands, not hearts '] was written after the creation of the first baronets '; ' although ' it is possible that the play was written before the creation, and that the allusion was ' introduced immediately afterwards, it is not probable.' Collier's Bridgewater document has been ' pronounced a forgery,' but even should it ' prove genuine, the perform- ' ance of a play called *Othello* by ' Burbidge's players,' in 1602, cannot, for reasons to be presently given, be accepted as conclusive evidence that Shakespeare's tragedy was ' then written. As to the genuineness ' of Cunningham's item from the Revels Account, there can be no doubt; and ' the probability seems strong that the play in question was ' Shakespeare's *Othello*. But is it certain? Not quite, in my opinion. It may have ' been a play founded on Giraldi Cinthio's story, and called *The Moor of Venice*, which ' was written by another playwright, and which, being the property of his company, ' Shakespeare afterwards entirely re-wrote, taking the names of Othello and Iago from ' the *History of the Prince of Denmark*, before mentioned. This supposition is so ' much in accordance with Shakespeare's practice, and the heraldic allusion before ' mentioned is entitled to such weight in the decision of the question, that, although ' there seems no sufficient ground for a fixed opinion upon the subject, I am inclined to ' place the date of the composition of this tragedy rather after 1611 than before that ' year. There is yet another fact which leads towards this conclusion. . . . . *Troilus ' and Cressida* and *Pericles* were published in 1609; and after a lapse of thirteen ' years without the appearance of one of Shakespeare's dramas from the press, this trag- ' edy was published in 1622, although there were then nineteen of no inferior rank ' among his works which were known to the public only upon the stage. Why this ' long interval passed thus unimproved by the dealers in dramatic literature, and why ' this play was chosen from among so many, to be published only a year before the ' appearance of the collected edition, (the intentions in regard to which could hardly ' have been unknown to the trade, or even to the public,) can only be a matter of very

' vague conjecture. We know that it was high in general favour; but I am inclined
' to the opinion that in addition to this claim upon a publisher's notice, it had also that
' of being one of its author's very latest productions. It certainly seems strange that
' after thirteen years had passed without the publication of one of Shakespeare's plays,
' during the first half of which period he produced works which were as well adapted for
' the press as any that had previously been issued, a publisher should go back at least
' eighteen years for one, which was the case if *The Moor of Venise* performed before King
' James, in 1604 was Shakespeare's *Othello*, in the only form in which it is known to us.'

If there were in those days only one play called *The Moor of Venis*, and if the
heraldic allusion were not a later insertion, it was reserved for SIR FREDERIC MADDEN
to overthrow completely Warburton's date of 1611. Among the MSS in the British
Museum there is an account of the journey in England of Lewis Frederick, Prince of
Wirtemberg, in 1610, 'which has been briefly penned in the French language by me,
Hans Jacob Wurmsser von Vendenheym.' In this journal Madden found the following entry in the month of April: 'Lundi, 30. S. E. alla au Globe lieu ordinaire ou l'on
joue les Commedies, y fut representé l'histoire du More de Venise.'

HALLIWELL in his Folio edition, relying on the Revels Book, puts the date of composition 'some time previously to November 1st, 1604,' and adds a reference to the performance of the play seen by the Prince of Wirtemberg; and, 'again, in an account of
' plays acted before Prince Charles, the Lady Elizabeth, and the Prince Palatine Elector,
' early in the year 1613, in both instances under its title of the 'Moor of Venice.' . . . .
' The twelfth Public Act, which was passed in the first Parliament of James, some time
·between March 19th and July 7th, 1604, was levelled 'against conjuration, witch-
'' crafte, and dealinge with evill and wicked spirits.' [Cited by GREY, see I, iii, 76.]
' In the course of this Act it is enacted, that 'if any person or persons shall, from and
'' after the feaste of Saint Michaell, the Archangell next comminge, take upon him or
'' them *by witchcrafte, inchantment, charme or sorcerie*, to tell or declare in what place
'' any treasure of golde or silver should or might be founde or had in the earth or other
'' secret places, or where goodes or thinges loste or stollen should be founde or become,
'' *or to the intent to provoke any person to unlawfull love*,' then such person or persons,
' if convicted, 'shall for the said offence suffer imprisonment by the space of one whole
'' yere without baile or maineprise, and once in everie quarter of saide yere shall, in some
'' markett towne upon the markett day, or at such tyme as any faire shal be kepte there,
'' stande openlie upon the pillorie by the space of sixe houres, and there shall openlie
'' confesse his or her error and offence.' It seems probable that part of the First Act
' of *Othello* would not have assumed the form it does, had not the author been familiar
' with the statute, in common with the public of the day, the Duke referring to such
' a Law when he tells Brabantio, that his accusation of the employment of witchcraft
' shall be impartially investigated. If this be the case, the date of the composition of
' this tragedy may be positively assigned to the year 1604.' To this note Halliwell-
Phillipps adds in his *Outlines*, &c., 5th ed., p. 541: 'Although the offence named in
' the statute refers not to the use of charms to make people love one another, but to the
' employment of them for the provocation of unlawful love, yet still this may be said to
' have an oblique application to the story of the tragedy in the surreptitious marriage of
' Othello. By the Act of James, a previous one, 5 Eliz. c. 16, of a similar character
· was 'utterlie' repealed, and the object of the second Act appears to have been to
' punish the same offence more severely.' [The existence of an Act of a 'similar
character' already in force, somewhat weakens this argument, as it seems to me.]

In a note on III, iii, 183: 'Who steals my purse steals trash,' Halliwell observes

'This is imitated by one J. M. in an unpublished manuscript, ' *The Newe Metamorphosis, or a Feaste of Fancie, or Poeticall Legendes*, written by J. M., gent., 1600.' This imitation would give the date of the play to an earlier period than is stated [above], but the year 1600, attached to the manuscript, appears to indicate the era in which the poem was commenced:

> " The highwayman that robs one of his purse
> " Is not so bad; nay, these are ten tymes worse !
> " For these doe rob men of their pretious name,
> " And in exchange give obloquie and shame." '

STAUNTON in his note on the same passage cites this reference of Halliwell, and adds: ' But the reflection is sufficiently trite, and in both instances, as in many others ' where it occurs, was probably founded ' on passages in *Homily* XI, pt. 2, *Homily* XII, pt. 1. HALLIWELL-PHILLIPPS (*Outlines*, p. 163, first ed.) now pronounces the passage from J. M. to be ' of no critical value to the enquiry. Although the date of 1600 appears ' on the title-page of that poem, the manuscript itself contains a distinct allusion by name ' to Speed's *Theatre of Great Britaine*, a work first published in 1611.' (For a fuller account of *The New Metamorphosis*, see p. 98, and Appendix C of the 2nd edition of that fine revelation of Shakespeare's early and wide influence, INGLEBY'S *Centurie of Prayse*, which, in this 2nd Edition, revised and added to by MISS LUCY TOULMIN SMITH, adds another instance of enduring, scholarly work, in the Shakespearian field, done by a woman.)

In 1868, *The Athenæum* (20th of June) announced a painful discovery in connection with the Revels Books, edited for *The Shakespeare Society* by Cunningham. In *The Galaxy* of November following, the story of the discovery was re-told by GRANT WHITE with fuller details, which he had ' learned from authentic sources.' It is substantially as follows : ' The story about the finding of the Revels Book had passed out of mind, ' though not out of memory, when about three months ago an oldish man, broken down ' by hard drinking, appeared at the British Museum and presented for sale an old manu- ' script volume, which contained, he said, records of much value about the early English drama, and which ' his friend, Mr Collier, said was worth sixty guineas.' It was Peter Cunningham, and the volume was that one of the ' Revels Accounts,' which contained the record of the performance of nine plays by Mr Shaxberd. The volume was retained for examination before purchase, was found to be public property, and was, of course, held as such. So interesting a volume attracted at once the attention of the experts of the Audit Office, and they at once discovered that, although the book was genuine, that part of it which was of greater interest than all the rest, the leaves containing the ' record of the performance of Shakespeare's plays, was a forgery, a gross forgery from ' beginning to end. Mr Duffus Hardy, of the Rolls Court, than whom there is no better ' authority in England, not excepting Sir Frederic Madden himself, so pronounces it, ' and so do the distinguished Shakespearian scholars, the Rev Alexander Dyce and Mr ' J. O. Halliwell, although they have founded part of their editorial labours upon it. . . , . ' It is to be remarked, that the important entries are made upon two leaves lying loose ' in the volume, and that these leaves, and these only of all the volume, have in the ' margin the names of the writers of the plays. There is other writing upon the mar- ' gins, usually mere index words for convenience of reference; but here only in the ' course of thirteen books, which when put into print make two hundred and twenty- ' six octavo pages, is the name of the author of a play, mask, or interlude given. This ' circumstance in itself, of which no notice seems to have been taken, casts great sus

'picion upon the pages on which these records appear, and when it is found that they
'are loose and were never bound into the volume, suspicion approaches certainty. But
'the evidence of the writing itself is said to settle the question at once for any person
'familiar with old manuscript. . . . . And now who is the forger? The conclusion that
'Peter Cunningham is the man seems unavoidable.'

From an Article in *The British Quarterly Review* of January, 1869, we learn, in
reference to this MS volume which Cunningham offered to the British Museum, that
'it only required a glance of the experts to discover that the list of Shakespeare's plays
'performed before the Court in the years alluded to, had been appended to the old doc-
'uments by a modern hand. The trifling and uninteresting items of expenditure are
'genuine, but the book containing these appears to have also contained some blank
'pages, into which the forger has crammed the whole of the writings referring to
'Shakespeare.'

But the mystery connected with these entries in the Revels Book by no means ends
here. Recent revelations have shown that Malone was right when he said that he
knew *Othello* was acted in 1604; and the proof of this knowledge, which Boswell
failed to find, has been discovered, and it turns out to be this very list, which, or a copy
of it, Cunningham is accused of forging in 1842. These revelations are made in that
inestimable volume, for which too much gratitude to the author cannot be shown, especially by us Americans, debarred as we are from all access to original records, the *Outlines of the Life of Shakespeare*, by Halliwell-Phillipps. From the Fifth Edition, 1885,
p. 607, I quote the following :

'There are substantial reasons for believing, that although the manuscript [of the
'pages of Cunningham's Revels Book] itself is spurious, the information which it yields
'is genuine.

'In the year 1791 Sir William Musgrave, the First Commissioner of the Board of
'Audit, made arrangements for Malone's inspection of the ancient manuscripts then in
'his office, these including what he termed 'records of the Master of the Revels for
''1604 and 1605.' These facts are derived from explicit notes that will be found in
'the Variorum Shakespeare, ed. 1821, iii, 361, 363. That Malone availed himself of
'the opportunity, and visited Somerset House for the express purpose of examining
'the whole collection of the documents that pertained to the Office of the Revels, is
'evident from his own statement in the work just quoted, iii, 361; and amongst the
'papers that came with that portion of his library which was added to the treasures of
'the Bodleian in 1821 is a leaf which contains the following memoranda no clue, how-
'ever, being given to the source whence they were derived :—'1604 & 1605—Ed^d.
''Tylney—Sunday after Hallowmas—Merry Wyves of Windsor perf^d by the K's play-
''ers—Hallamas—in the Banquetting ho^s. at Whitehall the Moor of Venis—perf^d. by
''the K's players—on S^t. Stephens Night—Mesure for Mesur by Shaxberd'' [as in the
case of the Revels Book, only so much is cited here as applies to *Othello* and Shax-
berd].

'Although the contents of this leaf are not in Malone's handwriting, there is no
'doubt whatever that it belonged to his collection of materials, it being one with others
'of an analogous character that were in a loose bundle of scraps which formed part of
'the original gift to the Bodleian, and had remained uncatalogued and inaccessible to
'students until they were bound in recent years under the direction of Mr H. S. Har-
'per, one of the officials of that library. The leaf containing the abridged transcript
'just given is now preserved in MS. Mal. 29; and Mr Harper, who well recollects
arranging the papers for the formation of that volume, assures me that there is no

'possibility of any of its contents having been acquired subsequently to the reception
'of the Malone Collection in 1821. There is nothing either in the character of the
'handwriting or in the form of the transcript, to justify the faintest suspicion that it is
'in itself a forgery. It has, on the contrary, every indication of being a faithful abridge-
'ment, sent most probably to Malone from the Audit Office, of the list which was
'printed in 1842. There now arises the crucial enquiry for the period at which
'Malone became acquainted with the information yielded by that list, for, unless he
'met with the latter for the first time nearly at the end of his career, it is incredible
'that he should have accepted the genuineness of any of its important details without
'a personal examination of the original. Such an assumption is incompatible with the
'numerous traces of the unwonted assiduity that pervaded his Shakespearian researches.
'Now, although there is at present no direct evidence of the fact, the little that is known
'favours the belief that he was in possession of the contents of the existing forgery
'within a few years after his invitation to the Audit Office in 1791, while nothing has
'been produced which is in the slightest degree inconsistent with that opinion. Let
'the following intimations be carefully weighed: The material novelties that are intro-
'duced into that forgery are restricted to the dates therein given of the performances
'of *Othello* and *Measure for Measure*, and the entries respecting these are the only
'items which Malone would have been absolutely compelled to notice in his disserta-
'tion on the order of Shakespeare's plays. With respect to the first, he took the new
'chronological fact for granted when he made the following decisive statement,—' we
'' *know* it (*Othello*) was acted in 1604, and I have therefore placed it in that year,'—
'important words that were penned before his death in 1812 (*Variorum Shakespeare,*
'ed. 1821, ii, 404); and there can hardly be a reasonable doubt that he was relying on
'the same testimony when he observed in another work: 'I formerly thought that
'' *Othello* was one of our great dramatic poet's latest compositions, but I now know,
'' from indisputable evidence, that was not the case'—note to a passage in Dryden's
'*Grounds of Criticism,* ed. 1800, pp. 258, 259. If the former work, the Variorum of
'1821, had not been impaired by the disadvantages attending its posthumous com-
'pilation, it being the product of Malone's imperfectly revised text and essays, the con-
'firmation of his assertion respecting the date of the tragedy would no doubt have been
'given; and to the same unfortunate accident must be imputed the circumstance of his
'observations on the date of *Measure for Measure* in that edition being a mere reprint
'of those which had appeared in 1790. It is altogether impossible that so experienced
'a record-student as Malone could have been even transiently deceived by the forgery
'now in existence, while the character of its ink encourages the suspicion that it could
'not have been perpetrated until long after his death in 1812. The latter opinion is to
'some extent supported by its entries not belonging to the more graphic species of lite-
'rary frauds that were current before that period. Then there is the extreme improb-
'ability that Malone should have lighted upon two documents, each of them yielding
'the unexpected information of the early date of *Othello*, while his acknowledged rigid
'integrity excludes the very thought that he would have been accessory to a deception
'in the matter. It may, therefore, on the whole, be fairly presumed that he had access
'in or before 1800 to a genuine manuscript that included in some form the entries that
'are given in the abridged transcript; for we may feel sure that he would never have
'used the words 'indisputable evidence' in respect to one of them until he had made
'a personal scrutiny of the original, even if his residence had not been, as it was, within
'less than an hour's walk from the Audit Office. There appears to be only one solution
'that reconciles all the known facts of the case. It is that the forger had met with,

'and reproduced in a simulated form, trustworthy extracts from a genuine record that
'had disappeared from that Office. This view of the case is essentially supported by
'what is, in respect to the present inquiry, the important discovery at Hatfield of the
'note of Sir Walter Cope, which mentions the revival of *Love's Labour's Lost* by the
'King's Company in or shortly before January, 1605, an evidence that could not have
'been known to the imposter, and one of a fact that would have been beyond even the
'remote probability of a successful conjecture. On the other hand, with the single excep-
'tion of the day assigned for the performance of that comedy, there are no questionable
'indications of any kind in the contents of the fabricated list, nothing that cannot be either
'explained or corroborated. The only other feature that could really justify a suspicion
'is the quaint orthography of the poet's name, but this no doubt is to be ascribed to the
'illiteracy of the original scribe; and it may be added that similar forms were in pro-
'vincial use, e. g., *Shaxber*, Chapel-lane deed, 1572, and Stratford MS., 1704; *Shax-*
'*bere*, Henley-street conveyance, 1573; *Shaxbeer*, Stratford MS., 1737.' [Halliwell-
Phillipps here gives six confirmatory facts of the performance of the plays from the
accounts of the *Treasurer of the Chambers*, and two for the performance of the maskes
from Winwood's *Memorials ;* four of these confirmatory facts from the accounts of the
Treasurer of the Chambers, Cunningham also reprinted in the Preface to his Revels
Books, pp. xxxvi, xxxvii. Halliwell-Phillipps then continues] : 'It would appear from
'these notices either that the fabricator had not before him a complete list of the plays
'that had been acted, or that he intentionally omitted a number of entries. Whatever
'may have been the exact nature of his proceedings, it is certain that the particulars
'of the forgery were not based upon the defective information given in the official
'accounts of the *Treasurer of the Chambers*. If that had been the case, it would be
'necessary to assume that he went recklessly out of his way to insert a fictitious notice
'of a performance on a day that was not sanctioned by those accounts, the high proba-
'bility of the accuracy of that solitary discrepancy having, moreover, been lately revealed
'by the discovery of an evidence to which he could not have had access. This singular
'coincidence may fairly be held to outweigh the suspicion attending the omission in the
'Treasurer's ledger, an oversight of a very unusual character, and yet an error infinitely
'more likely to occur than the preternatural ratification of what would have been by
'itself an extravagant conjecture. Upon a balance of probabilities there can thus
'hardly be a doubt that *Love's Labour's Lost* was revived at Court very early in Janu-
'ary of 1605 in a representation that was not honoured by the presence of the Queen.
'When, therefore, a play was to be selected almost immediately afterwards for the
'entertainment of Her Majesty at Lord Southampton's, it was natural that Burbadge,
'who had only one day's notice of the intended performance, should have recom-
'mended a drama which his company had just then in hand, and which at the same
'time would have been a novelty to the only spectator whose approval was regarded.'

WARD, whose valuable *History of English Dramatic Literature* preceded Halliwell-Phillipps's discovery of Malone's transcript, says: According to internal evidence
of character and manner there can be no difficulty in assigning to this play a date not
far removed from those of *Macbeth* and *Lear*, a conclusion fairly supported by the
'tests' of versification. No trustworthy external evidence exists as to the date of
Othello, unless importance be attached to the [passage in *The Newe Metamorphosis*,
cited by Halliwell. But Halliwell, as we have seen, subsequently withdrew all belief
in its critical value].

HUDSON, on the strength of the performances before the Duke of Wirtemberg in 1610,
and before Prince Charles in 1613, from Burbadge's Elegy (see *post*), and from the lack

of other authentic contemporary notices, is inclined to give a late date, either 1609 or early in 1610. 'And the internal evidence of style and manner is, I think, in entire 'harmony with that conclusion; the diction, versification, and psychologic inwardness 'being such as to speak it into close chronological neighbourhood with *Cymbeline* and '*Coriolanus.*'

In the *New Shakspere Society's Transactions*, 1874, p. 10, FLEAY, by the application of *Metrical Tests*, puts the date of *Othello* as 1605, and *Ib.*, p. 450, INGRAM, in his tabulation of the Plays according to the *Numbers of Light and Weak Endings*, gives *Othello* the Twenty-first place, between *Julius Cæsar* and *Lear*.

DOWDEN (*Shakspere, His Mind and Art*, p. 223): Around the year 1600 are grouped some of the most mirthful comedies that Shakspere ever wrote. Then a little later, as soon as *Hamlet* is completed, all changes. From 1604 to 1610 a show of tragic figures, like the kings who passed before Macbeth, filled the vision of Shakspere. . . . . During these years the imaginative fervour of Shakspere was at its highest, and sustained itself without abatement. There was no feverish excitement in his energy, and there was no pause. . . . . During a certain brief season it may have been that Shakspere altogether ceased to write for the stage. But now in unbroken series, year by year, one great tragedy succeeds another. Having created *Othello*, surely the eye of a poet's mind would demand quietude, passive acceptance of some calm beauty, a period of restoration. But *Othello* is pursued by *Lear*, *Lear* by *Macbeth*, *Macbeth* by *Antony and Cleopatra*, *Antony and Cleopatra* by *Coriolanus*.

The CAMBRIDGE EDITORS were, I think, the first to call attention to 'many oaths and expletives' in Q_1 (see *Text*, p. 342) which, in all the later editions, are altered or omitted. 'This shows,' they continue, 'that the MS. from which it was printed had 'not been recently used as an acting copy.' (From which I infer that they would throw back the date of composition to the early years of the century.)

KNIGHT had noticed long ago this difference in one particular passage between the Folio and Quarto (see I, i, 4), and had conjectured therefrom that the First Quarto was written before the passage of the Statute 3 Jac., 1605, against profanity on the stage.

FURNIVALL places it in Shakspere's THIRD PERIOD (1601–1608), as a companion to *Macbeth* in *The Tempter-yielding Group*, with the date (? 1604).

ROLFE groups this play with *Lear* and *Macbeth*, 'when Shakespeare was in the full maturity of his powers.'

GRANT WHITE'S latest conclusion is that while the allusion to the 'new heraldry' points to 1611, we have an authentic record of its performance in April, 1610. 'It is 'more than possible, then, that the tragedy was originally written before 1606 (in 1605 'or 1604), and that it afterwards received additions on some special occasions.'

If 'time will unfold what plighted cunning hides,' we need but cross our hands and wait. (Will not a few shreds of Shakespeare's mantle suffice to cover me, if, patterned by his fondness for quibbles, I suggest that 'time will unfold what plighted Cunningham hides'?) Nothing else but time, I fear, will ever solve the mystery of these forged leaves in the Revels Book. That they are forged is a settled fact. But, unlike other forgeries, their substance is genuine. Their items are all authenticated by extrinsic evidence. The rough transcript found by Halliwell-Phillipps among Malone's papers repeats every item, except three, word for word. If this transcript is a true copy from a genuine original, then are Cunningham's pages a true copy from the same; and, as we have seen, in Malone's transcript Halliwell-Phillipps puts entire faith. When a scholar so learned and so cautious leads the way, ought we not to follow? Were we all to trust ourselves unreservedly to his guidance, it is doubtful if Shakespearian literature would ever receive a single harmful bias 'down the ringing grooves of change.' Yet, at the same time, may we not be permitted, just by way of showing off an independence which we do not possess, to scrutinize somewhat closely for a minute or two that same transcript of Malone?

One argument in favour of its being a draft from a genuine original, which has great weight with Halliwell-Phillipps, is that Malone said he *knew Othello* was acted in 1604, which he would not have said without the fullest documentary proof, such proof as an inspection of the original would alone have afforded. We all know how thoroughly trustworthy Malone is, and nothing can be farther from my intention than to impugn his accuracy; and yet, although it is not likely, it is not inconceivable that Malone's knowledge extended no farther than to this rough transcript. Malone had the same confidence in Sir William Musgrave that we all have in Malone, and if Sir William had sent the transcript to him as a memorandum of a document awaiting his inspection, it is perfectly consistent with honesty that Malone should refer to the contents of this transcript as 'known' even before he had examined the original, or even if he had never examined the original. Granting that this transcript came from Somerset House, (and it is not easy to see whence else it could have come,) Malone would not hesitate on the strength of it to believe in the existence of the original document. Indeed my supposition receives some faint colour from a letter of Malone to Sir William Musgrave in my possession. In it Malone says: 'I mean to print Queen Elizabeth's letter to Lady Paget as it stands in *Nichols's Progresses*, copied from a MS of Dr Birch in the Museum; surely there can be no harm in saying that the original *is still extant*.' (The Italics are Malone's.) I also happen to have Sir William Musgrave's reply to this very letter, in which he shows more caution than Malone, for he says: 'I certainly have not any objection against your saying, "That you have been informed that the original is still extant."' Although this correspondence refers to facts which it was necessary to keep secret, and therein is somewhat removed from ordinary cases, yet it is, perhaps, worth citing, as showing that Malone, like all the rest of us, was willing to accept as fact that which was known to be such by one in whom he had an absolute trust. Do we not all accept *The Outlines of the Life of Shakespeare* in the same faith? What the original document could have been from which this rough transcript was taken, it is hard to imagine. I do not see how it could have belonged to the Accounts either of the Treasurer of the Chambers or of the Master of the Revels. The fact that it gives the names of the authors of the plays renders it wholly unlike either; it is anomalous in that regard. Could it have been the hasty memorandum of the Revels accountant, from which he intended afterwards to fill out his books, and for that purpose left the blank pages subsequently utilized by Cunningham; who, having found the memorandum, fulfilled the long-neglected duty, and then destroyed the original? But these imaginings are idle, and particularly idle in one as ignorant in such matters as myself. It was the mistrust in this transcript of Malone, written in an unknown hand, of an unknown date, from an unknown source, save that it was among Malone's papers, and unknown, apparently, even to Boswell, that led me to give as large a space as I did to Halliwell-Phillipps's defence of it, which, be it distinctly remembered, is based mainly on Sir Walter Cope's notice of the revival of *Love's Labour's Lost*.

In dealing with questions like this of the date of the composition of a play, it seems to me that it is of the first moment to keep before us the end and aim which gives the subject its importance; we ought to adjust our lines of perspective and so arrange our objects in view that each shall have its true relative value, and that we be not in danger of confounding nearness with magnitude or importance. Every one has a right to select his vanishing-point, and arrange his lines as suit him best; to me it is a great charm in the study of Shakespeare that the number of points from which that myriad-minded man can be studied are as myriad as his mind. If we are searching for the facts of his outward life, then the days and months and years when he wrote his plays are of essential importance. But if the outward conditions of his muddy vesture of decay do not attract us, and we are straining to catch sound of immortal harmony, what profit to us then is there in tides and times? Would a year or two, one way or the other, in the composition of *Othello*, or a dozen years, for that matter, bring us any nearer to a knowledge of the Moor? Would a single throb be added to Romeo's last farewell to Juliet if we knew the very day, or the very hour of the day, when Shakespeare wrote the scene? We must beware that we do not confound in any question like this, the essential and the accidental. Does the history of the Koh-i-nor add one doit to its value or one tint to its rays? It is not the knowledge that it was written in 1604 or in 1704 that fills our theatres when *Othello* is on the stage.

Accepting the date of 1604, I began with a reliance on time, and a trust in Halli-well-Phillipps; there we may safely remain, 'enshelter'd and embay'd.'

DATE OF THE ACTION

MALONE (Note on II, i, 1): All the modern editors following Rowe have supposed the capital of Cyprus to be the place where the scene of *Othello* lies during the last four Acts, but this could not have been Shakespeare's intention; *Nicosia*, the capital city of Cyprus, being situated nearly in the centre of the island, and thirty miles distant from the sea. The principal sea-port town of Cyprus was *Famagusta*, where there was formerly a strong fort and commodious haven,—the only one of any magnitude in the island; and there undoubtedly the scene should be placed. 'Neere unto the haven (says Knolles), standeth an old *castle*, with four towers after the ancient manner of building.' To this castle we find Othello presently repairs.

It is observable that Cinthio, whose novels were first published in 1565, makes no mention of any attack being made on Cyprus by the Turks. From our poet's having mentioned the preparations against this island, which they first assaulted and took from the Venetians in 1570, we may suppose that he intended that year as the era of his tragedy; but by mentioning Rhodes as also likely to be assaulted by the Turks, he has fallen into an historical inconsistency, for they were then in quiet possession of that island, of which they became masters in December, 1522; and if, to evade this difficulty, we refer *Othello* to an era prior to that year, there will be an equal incongruity; for from 1473, when the Venetians first became possessed of Cyprus, to 1522, they had not been molested by any Turkish armament.

REED: The time of this play may be ascertained from the following circumstances. Selymus the Second formed his design against Cyprus in 1569, and took it in 1571. This was the only attempt the Turks ever made upon that island after it came into the hands of the Venetians (which was in the year 1473), wherefore the time must fall in with some part of that interval. We learn from the play that there was a junction of the Turkish fleet at Rhodes in order for the invasion of Cyprus; that it first came sailing towards Cyprus, then went to Rhodes, there met another squadron, and then resumed its way to Cyprus. These are real historical facts which happened when Mustapha, Selymus's general, attacked Cyprus in May, 1570, which, therefore, is the true period of this performance. (See Knolles's *History of the Turks*, pp. 838, 846, 867.)

KNIGHT: The Republic of Venice became the virtual sovereign of Cyprus in 1471, when it assumed the guardianship of the son of Catharine Cornaro, who, being left a widow, wanted the protection of the Republic to maintain the power which her husband had usurped. The island was then first garrisoned by Venetian troops. Catharine, in 1489, abdicated the sovereignty in favour of the Republic. Cyprus was retained by the Venetians till 1570, when it was invaded by a powerful Turkish force, and was finally subjected to the dominion of Selim II in 1571. From that period it has formed [until it was acquired a few years ago by England] a part of the Turkish Empire. Nicosia, the inland capital of the island, was taken by storm; and Famagusta, the principal sea-port, capitulated after a long and gallant defence. It is evident, therefore, that we must refer the action of *Othello* to a period before the subjugation of Cyprus by the Turks. The locality of the scenes after the First Act must be at Famagusta, which was strongly fortified,—a fact which Shakespeare must have known, when in III, ii, Othello says: ' I will be walking on the *works*.'

STAUNTON gives a long extract from Knolles's *History* narrating the ' circumstances originating the siege of Nicosia, "the chief and richest citie of all the Island," and the ultimate conquest of Cyprus by the Turk, (for there was no "segregation of the Turkish fleet" as the play supposes,) of which the most important, it might be said the only important, items, (and Italicized by Staunton,) are as follows: ' For Mustapha, author of that expedition, had before appointed Piall Bassa at a time prefixed *to meet him at the Rhodes, and that he that came first should tarrie for the other, that so they might together saile into Cyprus*.' And again: ' The whole fleet at that time consisted of *two hundred galleys*, amongst whom were diverse galliots,' &c.

DURATION OF THE ACTION

SHAKESPEARE'S art in dealing with Time was first noticed by HALPIN and Professor WILSON, and was referred to in the Preface of *Hamlet*, where is given a brief exposition of their views. According to Professor Wilson, Shakespeare counts off days and hours, as it were, by two clocks, on one of which the true Historic Time is recorded, and on the other the Dramatic Time, or a false show of time, whereby days, weeks, and months may be to the utmost contracted. It is as though the hour-hand pointed to historic time, while the minute-hand, recording fresh sensations with every swing of the pendulum, tells dramatic time. While the former has traveled from one figure to another, the latter has traversed the whole twelve, and is true to the hour when the hammer falls. We know that but an hour has passed, and yet, following the minute-hand, we have lived through the whole twelve. In no one way, it is submitted, does Shakespeare show more emphatically than in this, that he wrote his plays to be heard and not read. In the theatre no trace is noted of this art, or even trick (be it respectfully termed); while on the printed page it may be detected in almost every Scene. In no play is this glamour carried to greater lengths than in *Othello*. That Desdemona should be murdered within thirty-six hours after landing in Cyprus is what no spectator of the play can readily believe; and yet to the reader of the tragedy this headlong speed is so real that it was proclaimed two hundred years ago by Rymer, who hissed and cackled over what he considered an absurdity so glaring, that he believed the exposure would forever disgrace and dethrone Shakespeare. Perhaps it is well that Professor Wilson did not know in whose footsteps he was unconsciously treading—but to what a different goal!

Whilst this legerdemain in regard to dramatic or llusory time is thus pronounced in *Othello*, in scarcely any other is the historic or real time more clearly noted. We can follow the characters through each day, nay, we can discover even the very days of the week, and that Othello landed in Cyprus on Saturday afternoon.

In the foregoing pages no notes in regard to this question of time have been included, except one or two here and there, enough to recall to the student's memory that such a question exists, and should be borne in mind.

It is but fair to say, at the outset, that there are not wanting good scholars who deny this theory of Double Time, and who variously interpret the allusions which Halpin and Wilson consider indications of it. It will be, of course, my endeavour duly to set forth their opposition; but, for the present, let the correctness of the theory be assumed, and let it be taken for granted that here, in *Othello*, Shakespeare has interwoven two different computations of time, the historical or real, the dramatic or illusory.

I propose first to note the passages which point to *Historic Time*, and as briefly as possible; the whole play is at hand and compression is obligatory.

The drama opens at night. Within an hour after the council is adjourned, Othello and Desdemona start for Cyprus. This night we may fancifully call the *First Day*.

How long the voyage from Venice to Cyprus lasts, we have no means of knowing. The distance was great, thirteen or fourteen hundred miles, and the labouring barks were slow and delayed by a tempest; ten days or a fortnight is none too long. Iago's arrival anticipated Cassio's expectation by a *se'en nights'* *speed*. The desperate tempest had lasted during the night, when the wind-shak'd surge had seemed to cast water on the burning Bear; it had evidently cleared up in the afternoon, and the aërial blue appeared. The afternoon was Saturday. At five o'clock the Herald announced that, upon certain tidings *now arrived* of the perdition of the Turkish fleet, there was to be sport and revels till the bell have tolled eleven. Othello tells Cassio to look to the guard *to-night*, and before ten o'clock Iago has begun his temptation of Cassio, from which hour the action steadily proceeds through the night, until Cassio, after his disgrace, resolves to beseech the virtuous Desdemona to undertake for him betimes in the morning. Although on parting Iago wishes him good-night, yet the day was breaking, and Cassio did not go to bed. As soon as he thinks Emilia is stirring, he appears before Othello's dwelling with some musicians, to give his General the good-morrow customary on the morning after marriage.

This is the beginning of the *Second Day*, and in Cyprus, and Sunday.

Emilia admits Cassio, and promises to bestow him where he should have time to speak his bosom freely to Desdemona. The great Third Scene of the Third Act opens with this interview between Desdemona and Cassio; which is broken off by the return of Othello, with Iago, from an inspection of the works; the gentle lady intercedes for the disgraced Lieutenant, and here we learn the days of the week: '*Des.* Good love, call him 'back. *Oth.* Not now, sweet Desdemona, some other time. *Des.* But shall't be shortly? '*Oth.* The sooner, sweet, for you. *Des.* Shall't be to-night [Sunday], at supper? *Oth.* 'No, not to-night. *Des.* To-morrow [Monday] dinner then? *Oth.* I shall not dine at 'home; I meet the Captains at the citadel. *Des.* Why then to-morrow [Monday] night, 'on Tuesday morn. On Tuesday noon or night, on Wednesday morn. I prithee thee name the time, but let it not exceed three days.'

Before this scene closes Othello has become Iago's victim, and withdraws to furnish nimself with some swift means of death for Desdemona, but first he wishes to discover the truth of Iago's assertion that Cassio has the handkerchief; to Desdemona he therefore goes at once. That Othello goes instantly to Desdemona, I infer not only from the eternal fitness of things, (he never could have been in her company one minute without resolving his doubts), but also from his *Aside* when he first greets her: 'Oh hardness to dissemble!' This is his first attempt at dissembling, therefore the first time that he had seen her. He finds that the handkerchief is gone, and leaves her in fury. Cassio sees Bianca and promises to call on her that evening, which is of course Sunday evening, and with this interview between Cassio and Bianca the Third Act closes.

The only chance thus far, it seems to me, for any time to elapse is between the close of the Third and the beginning of the Fourth Act. I was at one time in great hopes that at least some days could be wedged in here, especially since the conversation, with which the Act opens, between Iago and Othello is not only general in its character, as though they were discussing some abstract question of morality, but Othello had actually forgotten all about the handkerchief. I was the victim of Shakespeare's art, and two little words of Bianca's bind the two Acts together as one in point of time. Bianca asks Cassio what he meant by that same handkerchief which he gave her *even now;* so that we are still in Sunday, in the afternoon, after the generous islanders invited by Othello had had their dinner. Bianca repeats her invitation to Cassio to come to supper *to-night.* To supper likewise Othello invites Lodovico, who arrives from Venice before this Scene closes. Before the next Scene closes the trumpets summon to this very supper. After Bianca's supper Cassio is wounded, and after the supper to the Venetian Ambassadors, Desdemona is smothered,—*on Sunday night, within* thirty-six hours after her arrival in Cyprus.

The indications of *Dramatic Time* are not so easily enumerated; they are often mere hints, vanishing touches, leaving an impression not by their force, but by their frequent and varied repetition.

It is not till the Moor is caught in the whirlwind of passion raised by Iago that any necessity arises for these hints of Protracted Time. But, when once caught up, it is of the utmost necessity that the action should drive ahead in storm; one minute's calm would explain everything; yet the delusion must be complete that Othello's passion is of gradual growth. Before our eyes it must be made to pass through all stages of development. In the First Act, therefore, there are but few indications, that I can detect, of this Dramatic Time. There are one or two towards the close of it, where Iago tells Roderigo that 'It cannot be that Desdemona should long continue her love to the Moor, nor he his to her, it *was* a violent commencement, and thou shalt see an answerable sequestration.' The past tense flits by us, and the marriage of the Moor, within the hour, seems already like an old story. Again, before the Senate, Othello speaks as though this were not the first campaign in which he had been accompanied by his wife. He promises for himself with an assurance, clearly born of experience, when he repels the thought that 'Light-winged toys of feathered Cupid' could 'seel his speculative and officed instruments.' Again, Iago, at the very close, leaves us with the impression that his knavery will be slow in its advances. 'Let's see: *After some time* to abuse Othello's ear.' Trusting in this promise that the process will be slow, we accept the order of the subsequent events as in fulfilment of it.

Of one fact in this First Act it is important to be sure, before we leave it, and this is that Othello's marriage takes place on the very night that it was discovered by Brabantio; the first words that Roderigo utters refer to it as an end of all his hopes, and Iago tells Cassio shortly afterwards that Othello 'is made forever if the land carack prove lawful prize which he has secured *to-night.*' If we may suppose that Othello and Desdemona were married for some time before the night on which the play opens, then many of the difficulties of the Short Time in Cyprus disappear. This theory was started and dis-

proved by Professor Wilson in his *Christopher under Canvas* for April, 1850, p. 510.[*]
Seward, one of the interlocutors, is represented as starting this theory, ' That there was
long time at Venice after marriage, and short time at Cyprus;' and in support urged that
' the pliant hour' which Othello says he *once* took to ask Desdemona to be his wife, cannot refer to the day on which the play commences; also, that much weight should be
given to the calm tone, the husband-like and matron-like demeanor, of Othello and
Desdemona when confronted with the Senate. Professor Wilson thus disposes of it.

' *NORTH.* The thing most preposterous to me in a long marriage at Venice, is the
' continued lying position in which it places Othello and Desdemona towards her father.
' Two months—say—or three or four—of difficult deception! when the uppermost cha-
' racteristic of both is clear-souledness—the most magnanimous sincerity. By that,
' before anything else, are they kindred and fit for one another. On that, before any-
' thing else, is the Tragedy grounded—on his unsuspicious openness, which is drawn,
' against its own nature, to suspect her purity that lies open as earth's bosom to the sun.
' And she is to be killed for a dissembler! In either, immense contrast between the
' person and fate. That These Two should truckle to a domestic lie!

' *SEWARD.* Why should not Othello marry Desdemona, and keep her at her father's
' as theorized?

' *NORTH.* It is out of his character. He has the spirit of command, of lordship, of do-
' minion—an *animus imperiosus.* This element must be granted to fit him for his place;
' and it is intimated, and is consistent with and essential to his whole fabric of mind.
' Then, he would not put that which belonged to him out of his power, in hostile keep-
' ing—his wife and not his wife. It is contrary to his great love, which desires and
' would feed upon her continual presence. And against his discretion, prudence, or
' common sense, to risk that Brabantio, discovering, might in fury take sudden violent
' measures—shut her up in a convent, or turn her into the streets, or who knows what
' —kill her. . . . . The least that can be said is, that it invests the sanctimony of mar-
' riage with the air of an illicit amour.

' *TALBOYS.* Then the high-minded Othello running the perpetual and imminent risk
' of being caught thieving — slipping through loop-holes — mouse-holes — key-holes.
' What in Romeo and Juliet is romance, between Othello and Desdemona is almost
' pollution.

' *NORTH.* What a desolating of the MANNERS of the Play! Will you then, in order
' to evade a difficulty of the mechanical construction, clog and whelm the poetry, and
' moral greatness of the Play, with a preliminary debasement? Introduce your Hero
' and Heroine under a cloud? . . . . My dear Seward—pray, meditate but for a moment
' on these words of Desdemona in the Council Chamber: " My noble Father, I do per-
' ceive here A DIVIDED DUTY."—I, iii, 205–214. These are weighty words—of grave
' and solemn import—and the time has come when Desdemona the Daughter is to be
' Desdemona the Wife. She tells simply and sedately—affectionately and gratefully—
' the great primal Truth of this our human and social life. Hitherto her Father has
' been to her the Lord of Duty—the Lord of Duty henceforth is to be her Husband.
' Othello, up to that night, had been but her Lover; and up to that night—for the hid-
' den wooing was nothing to be ashamed of or repented—there had been to her no

---

* See *Blackwood's Magazine* for November, 1849, April and May, 1850: These articles, having
been, in substance, reprinted in the *Transactions of The New Shakspere Society,* 1875–76 and 1877–
79, are accessible to all. These *Dies Boreales* are brilliant, though lacking somewhat of the charm
of the youth and lustihood and poetry of the *Noctes Ambrosianæ,* with their central figure, that
idealized character,—the Shepherd.—ED.

' ' divided Duty '—to her Father's happiness had been devoted her whole filial heart.
' But had she been a married woman for weeks or months before, how insincere—how
' hypocritical had that appeal been felt by herself to be, as it issued from her lips ! The
' Duty had, in that case, been ' divided ' before—and in a way not pleasant for us to
' think of—to her Father violated or extinct. Grant that Othello and Desdemona must
' be married for two months before he murders her—that our hearts and imaginations
' require it. The resemblance to the ordinary course of human affairs asks it. We
' cannot bear that he shall extinguish her and himself—both having sipped only, and
' not quaffed, from the cup of hymeneal felicity. Your soul is outraged by so harsh and
' malignant a procedure of the Three Sisters. Extended time is required for the prob-
' ability—the steps of change in the heart of Othello require it—the construction and
' accumulation of proofs require it—the wheel of events usually rolls with something
' of leisure and measure. So is it in the real World—so must it seem to be on the
' Stage—else no verisimilitude—no ' veluti in speculum.' ' Two months shall elapse
' between marriage and murder,' says Shakespeare—going to write. They must pass at
' Venice, or they must pass at Cyprus. Place Shakespeare in this position, and which
' will he choose ? If at Venice, a main requiring condition is not satisfied. For in the
' fits and snatches of the clandestine marriage Othello has never possessed with full
' embrace, and heart overflowing, the happiness which he destroys. If an earthquake
' is to ruin a palace, it must be built up to the battlements and pinnacles; furnished,
' occupied, made the seat of Pleasure, Pomp, and Power; and then shaken into heaps
' —or you have but half a story. Only at Cyprus, Othello *possesses* Desdemona. There
' where he is Lord of his Office, Lord over the Allegiance of soldier and civilian—of a
' whole population—Lord of the Island, which, sea-surrounded, is as a world of itself—
' Lord of his will—Lord of his Wife. But if, my dear Seward, Shakespeare elects
' time at Venice, he wilfully clouds his two excellent Persons with many shadows of
' indecorum, and clogs his Action with a procedure and a state of affairs, which your
' Imagination loses itself in attempting to define—with improbabilities—with impracti-
' cabilities—with impossibilities. If he was resolute to have a well-sustained logic of
' Time, I say it was better for him to have his Two Months distinct at Cyprus. I say
' that, with his creative powers, if he was determined to have Two Calendar Months
' from the First of May to the First of July, and then in One Day distinctly the first
' suspicion sown and the murder done, nothing could have been easier to him than to
' have imagined, and indicated, and hurried over the required gap of time; and that he
' would have been bound to prefer this course to that inexplicable marriage and no mar-
' riage at Venice. But Shakespeare, my dear Boys, had a better escape. Wittingly
' or unwittingly, he exempted himself from the obligation of walking by the Calendar.
' He knew, or he felt, that the fair proportionate structure of the Action required liberal
' time at Cyprus. He took it; for there it is, recognized in the consciousness of every
' sitting or standing spectator. He knew, or he felt, that the passionate expectation to
' be sustained in the bosoms of his audience required a rapidity of movement in his
' Murder-Plot, and it moves on feet of fire.

' *Seward*. Venice is beginning to fade from my ken.

' *North*. You must go to the Tremendous Double Time at Cyprus, knowing
' that the solution is to be had there, or nowhere.' *

Daniel (*Time Analysis of the Plots*, &c., *New Shakspere Society Trans.*, 1877–79,
p. 239) fully agrees with Professor Wilson that there is no long time at Venice *after*

---

* These extracts are not literal transcripts ; space obliges me to condense them painfully.—Ed.

marriage, but thinks that the supposition of 'long time at Venice *before* marriage' is necessary, as it is the very foundation whereon Iago subsequently builds up Othello's jealousy by his repeated references to Cassio's former connection with Desdemona, and of his having been from first to last the confidant of Othello's wooing. Wilson having said that there is not the slightest ground for supposing an acquaintance, or, at least, intimacy, between Desdemona and Emilia before they started together from Venice, Daniel controverts it, and asserts that, 'rightly considered there is good ground for supposing a *prior acquaintance* in the very first lines of the play.' Roderigo's first speech, 'Never tell me, &c.' is, says Daniel, 'unintelligible, Roderigo's whole connection with 'Iago impossible, except on the supposition that Iago has for some time previous to the 'commencement of the action been fooling the poor gull on the strength of his acquaint 'ance, therefore probably of Emilia's acquaintance, with Desdemona. It offers the only '*possible* explanation of the reproaches with which Roderigo assails Iago here and in sub- 'sequent scenes in Cyprus, II, iii; IV, ii. The "hundred times" that Iago woo'd his 'wife to steal the handkerchief, Othello's questioning with Emilia (IV, ii), and numer- 'ous incidents of her connection with Desdemona, are only *possible* on the supposition 'of this prior acquaintance for the belief in which Wilson sees not the slightest ground.'

I am afraid that Daniel doth protest a tiny bit too much. When he says that 'it offers the only *possible* explanation of the reproaches with which Roderigo assails Iago,' to what does the 'it' refer? To Iago's acquaintance with Desdemona, or to Emilia's acquaintance with her? If to the former, it is hardly an answer to Wilson; if to the latter, he has just said that Iago's use of that acquaintance was only *probable*, and Wilson would at once deny it altogether, on the ground that the acquaintance did not exist. It seems to me that all of Daniel's difficulties here and in Othello's questioning of Emilia, for which 'long time at Venice before marriage' offers, for him, the only solution, ought to be solved by Wilson's Double Time; but this solution has not proved satisfactory to Daniel, whose opinion on this, as on all Shakespearian topics, is entitled to great weight and great respect. That Roderigo and Iago were acquainted with each other long before Othello was married, it has never, for a minute, occurred to anybody to deny; but to say that the only *possible* way in which Iago could have persuaded Roderigo of his power to help him into Desdemona's graces, was by the nearness in which Emilia stood to her, or by the acquaintance of the two women with each other, or even by his own acquaintance with her, is to put a limit to Iago's fertility of resource in lying and to Roderigo's capacity for being gulled, which I, for one, flatly refuse to set; given great capacity to be deceived on the one hand, and great, almost illimitable, capacity to deceive on the other, and it seems to me that we have all that is needed for an indefinite number of ways in which an explanation can be found of Iago's influence over Roderigo. Have we not a specimen of Iago's lying in that very First Scene? Does not Shakespeare, at the very outset, give us a cue to the way in which Iago has been tolling Roderigo on, by that lying description, every syllable of it false, of Othello, the regal Gentleman, evading three Venetian Noblemen with bombast circumstance! horribly stuffed with epithets of war? When Iago can thus lie about Othello, is it to be supposed that he needs such a trifle as the presence of his wife near Desdemona, in order to induce in Roderigo a belief of his unbounded influence with the Magnifico and his daughter? I am much afraid that if we give ourselves up to this supposition, the Gull will have companions.

Furthermore, Daniel interprets the gift of the handkerchief, not as a *marriage* gift, but as a *betrothal* gift, which Othello might have made long before his marriage, whereby ample opportunity is given for 'the hundred times' that Iago asked Emilia to steal it. 'When n y fate would have me wive,' read the Qq (III, iv, 77), which will fully support Daniel's interpretation, and 'the hundred times' before marriage; but 'When my fate would have me *wived*,' read the Ff, which will not support Daniel's interpretation, and with it will tumble 'the hundred times' before marriage. I prefer the Ff, but Daniel, of course, will elect to follow the Qq, and there is no excellent reason why he should not, only somewhere along the pathway I think it would do no harm to rear a placard, bearing on it, 'Beware of using the word *impossible* in Shakespeare!'

Professor Wilson thus takes up the subject of Protracted Time.*

'*TALBOYS*. Long Time cunningly insinuates itself, serpentwise, throughout Desde-
'mona's first recorded conversation with Cassio, at the beginning of III, iii, 25—the
'"Dreadful Scene.' Thus: 'Assure thee, If I do vow a friendship, I'll perform it,'
'and so on, down to line 33: 'Than give thy cause away.' This points to a protracted
'time in the future—and though announcing an intention merely, yet somehow it leaves
'an impression that Desdemona carries her intention into effect—that she does 'watch
'him tame,' does make his 'bed seem a school'—does 'intermingle everything she
'does with Cassio's suit.' Then Desdemona says: 'I have been talking with a suitor
'here, A man *that languishes in your displeasure.*' I cannot listen to that line, even
'now, without a feeling of the heart-sickness of protracted time—'hope deferred maketh
'the heart sick'—*languishes!* even unto death. I think of that fine line in Wordsworth:
'"So fades—*so languishes*—grows dim, and dies.' Far in this Scene, Othello says to
'Iago: 'If more thou dost perceive, let me know more: Set on thy wife to observe.'
'Iago has not said that he had perceived anything, but Othello, greatly disturbed, speaks
'as if Iago had said that he had perceived a good deal; and we might believe that they
'had been a long time at Cyprus. Othello then says: 'This honest creature, doubtless,
'Sees and knows more, much more, than he unfolds.' In all this, sir, we surely have
'a feeling of longish time. 'O curse of marriage! That we can call those delicate
'creatures ours—And not their appetites.' This is the language of a some-time mar-
'ried man—not of a man the morning after his nuptials.

'*NORTH*. The Handkerchief.

'*TALBOYS*. Ay—Emilia's words, III, iii, 338–344: 'I am glad I have found this
'napkin,' &c. Here we have long time, and no mistake. Iago has wooed her to steal
'it a hundred times! When and where? Since their arrival at Cyprus. The words
'naturally give us the impression of long time. In none of his soliloquies at Venice,
'or at Cyprus on their first arrival, has Iago once mentioned that Handkerchief as the
'chief instrument of his wicked design—and therefore Emilia's words imply weeks at
'Cyprus. Again, line 396: 'I slept the next night well.' Next night—night after
'night—many nights—many *wedded* nights—long time at Cyprus.

'*NORTH*. And then Cassio's dream.

'*TALBOYS*. 'I lay with Cassio—*lately*.' Where, but at Cyprus? 'Cursed fate!
'that *gave thee to the Moor*.' And on Othello going off in a rage about the handker-
'chief—what saith Desdemona? '*I ne'er saw this before*.' These few words are full
'charged with long time.

'*NORTH*. They are. And Emilia's—''Tis not a year or two shows us a man.'
'True, that is a kind of general reflection—but a most foolish general reflection indeed,
'if made to a Wife weeping at her husband's harshness the day after marriage.

'*TALBOYS*. Emilia's 'year or two' cannot mean one day—it implies weeks—or
'months. Desdemona then says,—'Something, sure, of state, *Either from Venice, or*

---

* *Blackwood's Maga.*, April, 1850: Again I wish to say that these are not transcripts, but meagre
abridgements, from which, however, I trust nothing essential is omitted.—ED.

'some unhatch'd practice,' &c. Does not *that* look like long time at Cyprus? Unlike
'the language of one who had herself arrived at Cyprus from Venice but the day before.
'And in continuation, Desdemona's 'such observances *As fit the bridal*,' III, iv, 171.
'And that thought brings sudden comfort to poor Desdemona, who says sweetly:
'"Beshrew me much, Emilia,' &c., down to line 176. That is—why did I, a married
'woman some months old, forget that the honeymoon is gone, and that my Othello,
'hero as he is, is now—not a Bridegroom—but a husband? 'Men are not gods.'

'*North.* And Bianca? She's a puzzler.

'*Talboys.* A puzzler, and something more. (See III, iv, 192–204.) Here the
'reproaches of Bianca to Cassio develop long time. For, besides his week's absence
'from her house, there is implied the preceding time necessary for contracting and
'habitually carrying on the illicit attachment. Bianca is a Cyprus householder; Cassio
'sups at her house; his intimacy, which has various expressions of continuance, has
'been formed with her there; he has found her, and grown acquainted with her there,
'not at Venice. I know it has been suggested that she was his mistress at Venice—
'that she came with the squadron from Venice; but for believing this there is here not
'the slightest ground. 'What! keep a week away?' would be a strange exclamation,
'indeed, from one who knew that he had been but a day on shore—had landed along
'with herself yesterday from the same ship—and had been a week cooped up from her
'in a separate berth. And Bianca, seeing the handkerchief, and being told to 'take
'me this work out,' cries—' *To the felt absence now I feel a cause.*' 'To the felt ab-
'sence,' Eight score eight hours! the cause? Some new mistress at Cyprus—not forced
separation at sea.

'*North.* Then, Talboys, where Othello is listening to the conversation of Iago
'and Cassio, which he believes relates to his wife, Othello says, IV, i, 145. 'Have
'you SCORED ME?' That is, have you marked me for destruction, in order that you
'may marry my wife? Othello believes that Cassio is said to entertain an intention of
'marrying Desdemona, and infers that, as a preliminary, he must be put out of the way.
'This on the first day after marriage? No, surely—long time at Cyprus.

'*Talboys.* Iago says to Cassio: 'This is his second fit: *he had one yesterday.*' This
'is a lie—but Cassio believes it. Cassio could not have believed it, and therefore Iago
'would not have told it, had 'yesterday' been the day of the triumphant, joyful, and
'happy arrival at Cyprus. Assuredly, Cassio knew that Othello had had no fit *that* day;
'that day he was Othello's lieutenant—Iago but his Ancient—and Iago could know
'nothing of any fits that Cassio knew not of—therefore—Long Time.

'*North.* 'For I will make him tell the tale anew, Where, how, how oft, how long
'ago, and when, He hath—and is again to—' He does so—and Othello believes what
'he hears Cassio tell of Bianca to be of Desdemona. Madness any way we take it—
'but madness possible only—on long time at Cyprus.

'*Talboys.* Then, sir, 'They do command him home, Deputing Cassio in his gov-
'ernment.' What are we to make of that?

'*North.* The Recall, except after considerable time, would make the policy of the
'Senate frivolous—a thing Shakespeare never does, for the greatness of political move-
'ments lies everywhere for a support to the strength and power of his tragical fable.
'Half that we know of Othello out of the Scenes is, that he is the trusted General of
'the Senate. What gravity his esteem with you derives hence, and can we bear to
'think of him superseded without cause? Had Lodovico, who brings the new com-
'mission, set off the day after Othello from Venice? No. You imagine an intercourse,
'which has required time, between Othello, since his appointment, and the Senate.

' Why, in all the world, do they thus suddenly depose him, and put Cassio in his place?
' You cannot very well think that the next measure of the Senate, after entrusting the
' command of Cyprus, their principal Island, to their most tried General, in most criti-
' cal and perilous times, was to displace him ere they hear a word from him. They
' have not had time to know that the Turkish Fleet is wrecked and scattered, unless
' they sit behind Scenes in the Green-room.

'*TALBOYS*. We must conclude that the Senate must give weeks or months to this
' New Governor ere interfering with him.—To recall him before they know he has
' reached Cyprus—nay, to send a ship after him next day—or a day or two following
' his departure—would make these ' most potent, grave, and reverend Signors,' enig-
' mas, and the Doge an Idiot. What though a steamer had brought tidings back to
' Venice that the Turks had been ' banged' and ' drowned?' That was not a sufficient
' reason to order Othello back before he could have well set his foot on shore, or taken
' more than a look at the state of the fortifications, in case the Ottoman should fit out
' another fleet.

'*NORTH*. Then mark Lodovico's language. He asks, seeing Othello strike his
' wife—as well he may—' Is it his use?' Or did the letters ' work upon his blood,
' and new-create this fault?' And Iago answers, ' It is not honesty in me to speak
' *what I have seen and known*.' Lodovico says, ' The noble Moor, whom our Senate
' call all in all sufficient.' Then they have not quarrelled with him, at least—nor lost
' their good opinion of him! Iago answers, ' He is much changed?' What, in a day?
' And again—' It is not honesty in me to speak what I have seen and known.' What,
' in a day? Lodovico comes evidently to Othello after a long separation—such as
' affords room for a moral transformation; and Iago's words—lies as they are—and
' seen to be lies by the most unthinking person—yet refer to much that has passed in
' an ample time—to a continued course of procedure. But in all the Play, nothing is
' so conclusive of long time as IV, ii, 3–14. If all this relates to their residence at
' Cyprus, it indicates many weeks. Then a word about Emilia. Now, consider, first,
' her character. She seems not very principled, not very chaste. Yet how strong her
' affection for Desdemona, and her faith in her purity! She witnesses for her, and she
' dies for her! I ask, how long did that affection and that opinion take to grow? a few
' days at Venice, and a week while they were sea-sick aboard ship? No. Weeks—
' months. A gentle lady once made to me that fine remark,—' Emilia has not much
' ' worth in herself, but is raised into worth by her contact with Desdemona—into heroic
' ' worth!' ' I care not for thy sword—I'll make thee known, though I lost twenty
' ' lives.' The impure dying a voluntary martyr for the pure is to the highest degree
' affecting—is the very manner of Shakespeare, to express a principal character by its
' influence on subordinate ones—has its own moral sublimity; but more than all, for
' our purpose, it witnesses time. Love, and Faith, and Fidelity, won from her in whom
' these virtues are to be first created! Othello, in his wrath, calls Emilia ' a closet-lock-
' ' and-key of villainous secrets: and yet she'll kneel and pray; I have seen her do't.'
' Where and when? It could only have been at Cyprus; and such language denotes a
' somewhat long attendance there on Desdemona. ' Some of your function, mistress,'
renewed to Emilia—when, after conversing with Desdemona, Othello is going out—
' is his treatment of one whom he supposes to have been serviceable to his wife's and
' Cassio's amour. Where? There, only there, in Cyprus, by all witnessing, palpably.
She could not before. He speaks to her as *professional* in such services, therefore
' long dealing in them; but this all respects this one intrigue, not her previous life.
' The wicked energy of the forced attribution vanishes, if this respects anything but her

helpfulness to his wife and her paramour, and at Cyprus—there—only there. Nothing
' points to a farther back looking suspicion. Iago's 'thousand times committed' can
' only lengthen out the stay at Cyprus. Othello still believes that she once loved him
' —that she has fallen to corruption. Could he have the most horrible, revolting, and
' loathsome of all thoughts, that he wedded her impure ? and not a hint given of that
' most atrocious pang ? Incredible—impossible ! I can never believe, if Shakespeare
' intended an infidelity taking precedence of the marriage, that he would not by word
' or by hint have said so.' [In answer to this last assertion, Daniel urges, as is men-
' tioned above, that 'the very foundation on which Iago builds up Othello's jealousy' is
the relationship existing before marriage between Cassio, Desdemona, and the Moor
himself; 'surely,' says Daniel (p. 229), 'this is a pretty strong hint, and Othello, in IV,
' ii, 103,' where he first directly accuses Desdemona of unchastity, 'gives another
pretty strong hint too.'] 'Lastly, the wedding sheets were *reserved ;* they had been
' laid by for weeks—months—time long enough to give a saddest character to the
' bringing them out again—a serious, ominous meaning—disturbed from the quietude,
' the sanctity, of their sleep by a wife's mortal presentiment that they may be her shroud.'

In that storehouse of information, *The Shakespeare Key* (p. 217), COWDEN-CLARKE
gives the following references to Long Time, which were not noticed by Wilson : I, iii,
283–328; I, iii, 419; II, i, 32; II, i, 89–91; III, iii, 64–75; *Ib.*, 496; *Ib.*, 537; III,
iv, 130. On this last passage is the following note : ' It is in this brief Scene that so
much lapse of time is *implied ;* for Cassio speaks of his 'former suit,' and Desdemona
sends for him to inform him of the progress she has made in her advocacy on his
behalf, although there is no absolutely-stated interval since she begged Othello to let
Cassio come and plead for recall, and her husband refused to allow this return to be
made either 'to-night,' 'to-morrow,' or within the next 'three days.' So systematically
is Long Time *implied* while Short Time is *preserved*, that it is impossible not to believe
in this having been the author's thorough intention and artistic plan.' Also, III, iv,
145; IV, ii, 163; *Ib.*, 182; *Ib.*, 207–212.

Even in addition to these enumerated by Wilson and Cowden-Clarke, it seems to
me that a few other instances which intimate Long Time may be gleaned. Thus,
II, ii, 345, on the very first evening in Cyprus, after Cassio's disgrace, Iago speaks
of Othello's having given himself up to the contemplation of Desdemona's graces to
such an extent that the general's wife is now the general; such an assertion seems
to require a long course of marked attention, in public and in private, to justify it.
Again, Roderigo was a man of wealth; in the pursuit of his pleasure he could afford
to buy jewels rich enough to half corrupt a votarist; before he left Venice he may be
supposed to have fulfilled his promise to Iago, and to have converted all his land into
money; his last words were, 'I'll go sell all my land.' Iago speaks of the amount
of his gold and jewels as large; and yet he has been in Cyprus but a few hours before
he tells Iago that his money is almost spent, that he has not more than enough to last
him to get back to Venice; and in referring to himself as hunting in a chase we have
visions of a lavish expenditure, day after day, and week after week; nor does Iago
diminish this impression when he speaks of the *dilatory* time and of the *patience* which
their work demands. Again, Cassio expresses to Desdemona a fear that the policy
which obliges Othello to treat him coldly may last *so long* that Othello will *forget* him.

This question of Shakespeare's use of these Two Times is so important (of more
importance in this than in almost any other play) that it is incumbent on us to give
good heed to Wilson's explanation of it, whereof the substance I have here endeavoured to extract ·

'The usefulness of the Two Times is palpable from first to last—of the Short Time 'for maintaining the tension of the passion—of the Long for a thousand general needs. 'Thus Bianca must be used for convincing Othello very potently, positively, unanswer 'ably. But she cannot be used without supposing a protracted intercourse between 'her and Cassio. Iago's dialogue with him falls to the ground if the acquaintance 'began yesterday. But superincumbent over all is the *necessity of our not knowing* 'that Iago begins the Temptation, and that Othello extinguishes the Light of his Life, 'all in one day. And observe how this concatenation of the passionate scenes operates. 'Let the Entrances of Othello be four—A, B, C, D. You feel the close connection of 'A with B, of B with C, of C with D. You feel the coherence, the nextness, and all 'the force of the impetuous Action and Passion resulting. But the logically-consequent 'near connection of A with C, and much more with D, as again of B with D, you *do* '*not feel*. Why? When you are at C, and feeling the pressure of B upon C, you have 'lost sight of the pressure of A upon B. At each entrance you go back one step—you 'do not go back two. The suggested intervals continually keep displacing to distances 'in your memory the formerly felt connections. This could not so well happen in real 'life, where the relations of time are strictly bound upon your memory, though some- 'thing of it happens when passion devours memory. But in fiction, the conception 'being loosely held, and shadowy, the feat becomes easily practicable. Thus the Short 'Time tells for the support of the Passion, along with the Long Time, by means of vir- 'tuous installations from the hand or wing of Oblivion. From one to two you feel no 'intermission—from two to three you feel none—from three to four you feel none; but 'I defy any man to say that from one to four he has felt none. I defy any man to say 'honestly that 'sitting at the Play' he has kept count from one to four. Besides every 'past Scene, constituting a marked moment in the progress of the Play, has the effect for 'the Poet, as well as for you, of protracting the time in retrospect,—throwing everything 'that has passed further back. The goings-out and re-enterings of Othello have a 'strangely deluding effect—they disconnect the time more than you can think—and all 'the changes of persons on the stage, all shiftings of scenes and droppings of curtains, 'break and dislocate and dilate the time to your imagination, till you do not in the least 'know where you are. In this laxity of your conception, all hints of extended time 'sink in and spring up, like that fungus which, on an apt soil, in a night grows to a 'foot diameter. Shakespeare, we have seen, in his calmer constructions, shows, in a 'score of ways, weeks, months; that is therefore the true time, or call it the historical 'time. Hurried himself, and hurrying you on the torrent of passion, he forgets time, 'and a false show of time, to the utmost contracted, arises. I do not know whether 'he did not perceive this false exhibition of time, or perceiving, he did not care. But 'we all must see a reason, and a cogent one, why he should not let in the markings of 'protraction upon his dialogues of the Seduced and the Seducer. If you ask me, How 'stood the time in the mind of Shakespeare? I answer, I do not know. The ques 'tion splits itself into two: first, 'How did he *project* the time?' Second, 'How did '"he conceive it in the progress of the Play?' My impression is, that he projected 'extended time. If so, did he or did he not know that in managing the Seduction he 'departed from that design by contracting it into a Day? Did he deliberately entertain 'a double design? If he did, how did he excuse this to himself? Did he say, 'A '"stage necessity, or a theatrical or dramatic necessity'—namely, that of sustaining at 'the utmost possible reach of altitude the tragical passion and interest—'requires the '"precipitation of the passion from the first breathing of suspicion—the 'Ha! Ha! I '"like not that,' of the suggesting Fiend—to the consecrated 'killing myself, to die upon

" ' a kiss!'—all in the course of fifteen hours—and this tragical vehemency, this impet-
" ' uous energy, this torrent of power I will have; at the same time I have many reasons
" ' —amongst them the general probability of the action—for a dilated time; and I, being
" ' a magician of the first water, will so dazzle, blind, and bewilder my auditors that
" ' they shall accept the double time with a double belief—shall feel the unstayed rush-
" ' ing on of action and passion, from the first suggestion to the cloud of deaths—and
" ' yet shall remain with a conviction that Othello was for months Governor of Cyprus
" ' —they being on the whole unreflective and uncritical persons?'

' *TALBOYS*. And, after all, who willingly criticises his dreams or his pleasures?

' *NORTH*. And the Audience of the Globe Theatre shall not—for ' I hurl my dazzling
" ' spells into the spungy air,' and ' the spell shall sit when the curtain has fallen.' Shake-
' speare might, in the consciousness of power, say this. For this is that which he has—
' knowingly or unknowingly—done. Unknowingly? Perhaps—himself borne on by
' the successively rising waves of his work. For you see, Talboys, with what prolonged
' and severe labour we two have arrived at knowing the reality of the case which now
' lies open to us in broad light. We have needed time and pains, and the slow settling
' of our understandings, to unwind the threads of delusion in which we were encoiled
' and entoiled. If a strange and unexplained power could undeniably so beguile us—a
' possibility of which, previously to this examination, we never have dreamt, how do we
' warrant that the same dark, nameless, mysterious power shall not equally blind the
" ' Artificer of Fraud'? There *are* the Two Times, the Long and the Short; and each
' exerts upon you its especial virtue. I can believe that Shakespeare unconsciously did
' what Necessity claimed,—the impetuous motion on, on, on of the Passion,—the Long
' Time asked by the successive events; the forces that swayed him, each in its turn, its
' own way. And put up with these Two Times we must,—one for our sympathy with
' Othello's tempest of heart,—one for the verisimilitude of the transaction.

' Illusion, a constituent of Poetry, is WHEN THE SAME THING IS, AND IS NOT. Pa—
' God bless him!—makes believe to be a Lion. He roars, and springs upon his prey.
' He at once believes himself to be a Lion, and knows himself to be Pa. Just so with
' the Shakespeare Club—many millions strong. The two times at Cyprus *are there;*
' the reason for the two times—to wit, probability of the Action, storm of the Passion—
' *is there;* and if any wiseacre should ask, ' How do we manage to stand the *known*
' together-proceeding of two times?' the wiseacre is answered—' We don't stand it—
' for we know nothing about it. We are held in a confusion and a delusion about the
' time.' We have effect of both—distinct knowledge of neither. We have suggestions
' to our Understanding of extended time—we have movements of our Will by precipi-
' tated time. Does any man by possibility ask for a scheme and an exposition, by which
' it shall be made luminous to the smallest capacity *how* we are able distinctly all along
' to know, and bear in mind, that the preceding transactions are accomplished in a day,
' and at the same time and therewithal, distinctly all along to know and bear in mind
' that the same transactions proceeding before our eyes take about three months to
' accomplish? Then, I am obliged—like the musicians, when they are told that, if
' they have any music that may not be heard, Othello desires them to play it—to make
' answer, ' Sir, we have none such.' It is to ask that a deception shall be not only
' seemingly but really a truth! If you ask me—which judiciously you may—what or
' how much did the Swan of Avon intend and know of all this astonishing legerdemain,
' when he sang thus astonishingly? Was he, the juggler, juggled by aërial spirits,—
' as Puck or Ariel? I put my finger to my lips, and nod on him to do the same; **and**
if I am asked, ' Shall a modern artificer of the Drama, having the same pressure **from**

'within and from without, adopt this resource of evasion?' I can answer with great
'confidence, 'He had better look before he leap.'

'*TALBOYS*. Assume, sir, that Shakespeare knew what he was doing.

'*NORTH*. Then the Double Time is to be called—an Imposture.

'*TALBOYS*. Oh, my dear sir,—oh, oh!

'*NORTH*. A good-natured Juggler, my dear Talboys, has cheated your eyes. You
'ask him to show you how he did it. He does the trick slowly—and you see. 'Now,
''good Conjurer, *do it slowly, and cheat us*.' 'I can't. I cheat you by doing it quickly.
''To be cheated, you must *not* see what I do; but you must *think* that you see.' When
'we inspect the Play in our closets the Juggler does his trick slowly. We sit at the
'Play, and he does it quick. When you see the trick again done the right way,—that
'is, quick,—you cannot conceive how it is that you no longer see that which you saw
'when it was done slowly! Again the impression returns of a magical feat.

'*TALBOYS*. I doubt, if we saw *Othello* perfectly acted, whether all our study would
'preserve us from the returning imposture.'

For me, after this revelation, 'the rest is silence.' The only time when Wilson does
not take me with him is when he suggests that Shakespeare's use of these Two Times
may have been unconscious. The more I study Shakespeare, the more profoundly do
I become impressed with the evidences on every hand of his consummate art. From
the bias to the world's estimate of him which Milton gave us we have scarcely yet
recovered. There are not wanting those who even at this late day believe that Shakespeare warbled his native wood notes wild with as much unconsciousness as does a song-
sparrow. It will be many a long day yet, I think, before we exhaust the evidences
of his myriad-sided art. There can be no subtle effect produced on us by the interlacing of these Two Times which Shakespeare himself did not feel, and did not fore-
cast.

Daniel, however, does not believe in these Two Times, and is inclined to attribute
the discrepancies, which a disbelief in them detects, to the imperfect state of the text,
an asylum always at hand and wide open as a retreat from any and every Shakespearian
difficulty; lest I do injustice to a scholar whose opinion is entitled to more weight than
mine, let me quote his words:

DANIEL (*New Shakespere Soc. Trans.*, 1877–79, Part ii, p. 231): 'But though I think
'it must be admitted that long time at Venice before marriage is an element worthy of
'consideration as affording some explanation of many otherwise simply impossible inci-
'dents of the play, I am forced to admit that this explanation is far from satisfactory.
'Incidents such as the recall of Othello by the Senate before it could be known that
'he had landed in Cyprus are not affected by it in the least. Long time at Cyprus *after*
'*marriage* is absolutely necessary for the probability of the plot; but before I seek refuge
'in the . . . . inexplicable mystery of 'double time,' I should like to be convinced that
'the author himself did not provide it. I say, with Professor Wilson, that 'with his
'creative powers, if he was determined to have Two Calendar Months from the First
'of May to the First of July, and then in One Day distinctly the first suspicion sown
'and the murder done, nothing could have been easier to him than to have imagined,
'and indicated, and hurried over, the required gap of time.' Long familiarity with
'Shakespeare's work has convinced me, as it must have convinced most students, that
'we cannot with certainty affirm that any of his plays have reached us in the state in
'which they left his hands: in some cases their corruption and mutilation for stage pur-
'poses can be proved to demonstration, and it is quite possible that in *Othello* some
'scenes may have been struck out and others so run together as to confuse the time-

plot originally laid down by the author. The links in the chain of time, the absence
'of which so startles the reader, would not be, and indeed are not, missed in the visible
'action on the stage; but we should not, therefore, rashly jump to the conclusion that they
'never existed, and therefore that the author deliberately designed an impossible plot.'

FLEAY (*Robinson's Epitome of Literature,* 15th June, 1879) proposes a third solution, which partakes somewhat of the nature of Daniel's, in so far as it suggests a division of the Acts different from that in the QqFf. Convertite as I am to Wilson's Double
Time, I find answers therein, in the foregoing pages, to Fleay's arguments. After a rapid
review of the First and Second Acts, and Scenes i, ii, and iii of Act Third, Fleay proceeds : 'So far the commentators and I are agreed, but I do not agree that a consider-
'able time must have elapsed since the landing, to render the dialogue intelligible.
'They allege, for instance, that Roderigo's money could hardly have been spent on the
'first night of his arrival. Why not? The voyage has been tempestuous, and, unless
'I quite misinterpret the allusions to it, has occupied not less than a week. Roderigo
'is just the man to empty his purse in one night's gaming, and Iago would not procras-
'tinate in that matter. Moreover, he may have been spending heavily at Venice before
'the marriage.

'Iago has asked Emilia a hundred times to steal the 'hankercher.' When? says
'Daniel. On the voyage, surely.' [Daniel, in a foot-note, p. 231, says, 'Mr. E. H.
'Pickersgill calls attention to the time occupied by the voyage to Cyprus as suggesting
'a *possible* explanation with reference to Emilia's 'hundred times.']

'Iago says: 'I lay with Cassio lately.' But Cassio has not been abed in Cyprus,
'says Daniel again. And what then? Does this over-careful critic take this statement
'for a narrative of fact? or does he imply that Shakespeare must have made all his
'villains lie so carefully as never to clash with possibility?

'Up to this point the arguments for a long residence in Cyprus seem to me over-
'strained and futile: and at this point comes in the same question I raised as to *A
'Midsummer Night's Dream :* 'are the present divisions into acts to be regarded as
''authentic'? Why should they be, since they can in no instance be traced to Shake-
'speare's lifetime? I would therefore end the Third Act here, and allow a week's
'interval between this Scene and the next. There is no reason for the immediate con-
'secution of the Scenes, except Wilson's opinion, regarded as cogent by Daniel, that
'Othello would not have let an hour elapse before inquiring about the 'hankercher.'
'Perhaps Othello would not: but Othello *under Iago's inspiration* probably would.
'And, besides, we have the positive statement of Bianca that Cassio has been away
'*for a week ;* and, moreover, time is absolutely necessary for the Senate to hear of the
'loss of the Turkish fleet, and to send to recall Othello. These are positive integral
'parts of the plan, not to be neglected in any scheme.

'And why are scholiasts' opinion of what their author should, must, or ought to have
'done, to be preferred to the direct allegations of the text? In IV, i, again, we hear
'that Othello had a fit *yesterday.* This at once disproves Daniel's notion that Acts III,
'IV, V, all take place on one day, and gives us a reason for Othello's delay in inquir-
'ing about the 'hankercher.' Othello, under Iago's guidance, has, it seems to me,
'been waiting (after III, iii) to let Desdemona betray herself: after some days she does
'so by a *repeated* application on Cassio's behalf (III, iv, 18). The first application had
'been utilized by Iago to excite Othello, and so produced the first fit. But this is con-
'jectural. My main object is not to add more guesses to Shakespearian criticism, but
'to submit the following scheme of time for this play,—not founded on my own preju-
'dications, but taken from the text itself :

'*Act I, Sc. i, ii, iii.*—One day. Interval for voyage. *Act II, Sc. i, ii, iii.*—One day.
'*Act III, Sc. i, ii, iii.*—One day (Sunday). Interval of a week, at least. *Act IV,*
'*Sc. i, ii, iii; Act V, Sc. i, ii, iii.*—One day. Where my Act IV begins with what
'is now Act III, Sc. iv, and my Act V with the present Act IV, Sc. iii.'

THE SOURCE OF THE PLOT

POPE: The Story is taken from Cynthio's Novels. THEOBALD: Cinthio Giraldi
seems to have designed his Tale as a Document to young Ladies against dispropor-
tioned Marriages: *di non se accompagnare con huomo, cui la Natura, & il Cielo, &
il modo della Vita disgiunge da noi;* that they should not link themselves to such,
against whom Nature, Providence, and a different way of Living have interposed a
Bar. Our Poet inculcates no such Moral; but rather, that a Woman may fall in Love
with the Virtues and shining Qualities of a Man, and therein overlook the Difference
of Complexion and Colour.

FARMER: I have seen a French translation of Cynthio, by Gabriel Chappuys, Paris,
1584. This is not a faithful one, and I suspect through this medium the work came
into English. [This translation is reprinted by FRANÇOIS-VICTOR HUGO in his edition
of Shakespeare, Paris, 1868, vol. v, pp. 443–458.—ED.]

SIMROCK (*Quellen des Shakespeare*, &c., Berlin, 1831, iii, 181) ridicules the idea that
it is necessary to find a translation into English of Giraldi Cinthio. 'As if,' he says in
scorn, 'it would not have been mere child's play for such a genius as Shakespeare to
have mastered Italian and French! . . . . It is as probable that the story of Cinthio
'was founded in fact as in fiction. Waiblinger, in the *Taschenbuch, Penelope*, 1831,
'asserts that there is an Italian ballad on this subject of Othello, but we have looked
'for it in vain in Wolff's *Egeria*. At all events, the style of the "novel" renders it not
'unlikely that it originated in some popular romance, such as minstrels, who wandered
'around the country with painted placards, were wont to sing. This "novel" belongs
'to the best of Cinthio's, whose skill as a narrator we do not highly prize.' [While
declining to accept Rawdon Brown's hypothesis as set forth in his *Marin Sanuto*
(see *post*), Simrock in his 2d edition in 1870 expressed himself as not doubting but
that] 'the Moor was an historic character, not a negro, whose colour had been miscon-
'ceived through a mistaken interpretation of his name.'

KNIGHT: It is not improbable that [Cinthio's novel] is of Oriental origin; the revenge of the Moor, as there described, is of that fierce and barbarous character which
is akin to the savage manner in which supposed incontinence is revenged amongst the
Arabs. The painfully affecting tale of *The Three Apples*, in *The Thousand and One
Nights*, is an example of this; and, further, there is a similarity between the stolen
apple and the stolen handkerchief. The malignity of the slave in the Arabian tale,
too, is almost as motiveless as that of Iago; [but the Iago of Cinthio was not motiveless.—ED.]

COLLIER: Shakespeare may have read Cinthio's story in the original language; it is
highly probable that he was sufficiently acquainted with Italian for the purpose.

[In 1837, RAWDON BROWN published, at Venice, *Ragguagli sulla Vita e sulle Opere
di Marin Sanuto, &c.*, wherein (i, 226–235) he conjectured that a certain 'Christophal
Moro,' a 'Luogotenente di Cipro,' who returned from Cyprus in 1508 after having
lost his wife, was the original of the Moor of Venice of Giraldi Cinthio. In the incidents of this warrior's life Brown found sufficient similarity to the novel of Cinthio to

lead him to suppose that the story was popular enough to have supplied the details to Shakespeare at the hands of some of the members, high or low, attached to the Italian Embassy in London. In the name Barbarigo, of the Secretaries of the Embassy from 1610 to 1616, Brown discerns the name Brabantio; in Gratiano, a certain Gradenigo; in Montano, a Mocenigo, &c. The theory in this shape depends for its support on a date for the composition of *Othello* quite as late as that assigned to it by Warburton or Chalmers; and as we have relinquished all dates after 1604, this theory, I fear, must be abandoned with them. Its author, however, did not desert it; he subsequently returned to it, and this time with a date as early as 1603; see his letter in *The Academy, post.* One fact, in connection with it, is certainly curious, and that is that in the Barbarigo family, as proved by an Item in a Will, there actually was a slave-girl named Barbara. Brown sums up his theory, which finely witnesses to his knowledge of early Venetian History, as follows (p. 234): 'I suppose that there was a mystery 'connected with the death of Cristofal Moro, the "Luogotenente" of Cyprus, out of 'which was made a romance by mingling fact and fancy. This romance, passed over 'to England years and years afterwards, was translated and read by Shakespeare. *Ven-* '*ice was the fashion;* and from a romance of Venetian history *The Moor of Venice* 'became an English tragedy.'—ED.

KLEIN (*Geschichte des Dramas. Das Italienische Drama,* ii, 384) finds a resemblance which he deems quite striking between several passages in *Othello* and Ludovico Dolce's *Marianna* (first acted in 1565), and suggests that Shakespeare while working on his tragedy may have had the Italian in view.

In *Marianna* there is one situation which resembles *Othello.* Salome, Herod's sister, has secretly accused Marianna, Herod's wife, of having bribed his cup-bearer to poison him. Erode (Herod) cross-questions the cup-bearer, who confirms the charge. Like Othello, Herod demands proofs. 'The Cup-bearer envelops Erode's soul in his 'snaky coils, until, like Iago, he finds the chance to dart his poisonous fang. 'They ''who brood on crime,' he hisses; 'play the game so close that one hand knows not ''what the other does.'' Erode is determined that the cup-bearer shall repeat the accusation in the presence of the Queen, and Marianna is called.

Erode addresses her:

> ' Marianna, io torrei perder il regno,
> E insieme rimaner mendico e nudo
> Prima, ch'aver cagion, come n' ho troppa
> D' imputarti, o crudel, delitto alcuno.'

To which Marianna replies:

> ' Se delitto è d' avervi amato sempre
> Con quello amor, ch' amar si dee consorte,
> Et onorato, come mio Signore,
> Avete alta cagion d' odiarmi ognora.'

('Marianna, I would gladly lose my kingdom, And remain for aye a beggar and unclad, Rather than have cause, as but too much I have, To impute to thee, O cruel one, any crime.' The parallel passage, which will occur to every one, is, of course: 'Had it pleas'd Heaven,' &c., IV, ii, 57. Marianna's reply is in the same scene: 'If it be a crime to have always loved you With that love with which one should love a husband, And to have honoured you as my lord, You have deep cause to hate me always.')

While noting these parallelisms, and suggesting, as I have said, that Shakespeare may have used Marianna as a lay figure in draping his tragedy, Klein acknowledges the grander scale on which Shakespeare worked and the loftier key in which his drama is pitched; whereby 'the wild, gloomy, hellish temperament of a Herod is transfigured into the lofty, noble, clear soul of a grand-hearted, guileless man.' To me it would be impossible in Shakespeare's case to infer any familiarity with Dolce, even were the parallelisms many times more numerous and more exact. But Klein's opinions on dramatic subjects are always to be respectfully heard, and treated with the deference due to an antagonist whose weapon, were he living, would be 'the whole tree of knowledge torn up by the roots.'

In *The Academy* (9th January, 1875) appeared the letter above referred to, written in Venice, from RAWDON BROWN, which gives interesting and fuller details from early Venetian documents concerning the bearers of the name of 'Moro,' in one of whom, Christopher, as we have seen, the writer finds the original Othello. After giving some proofs of credulity, on the part of the Venetian Senate, in stories quite as marvellous as any in Othello's travels' history, Brown proceeds : 'Fronting the summit of the "Giants' 'Stair," where the Doges of Venice were crowned, there are still visible four shields '"spotted with mulberries" ("strawberries" in the description of Desdemona's hand- 'kerchief), indicating that that part of the palace portal on which they are carved was 'terminated in the reign of Christopher Moro, whose insignia are three mulberries sable 'and three bends azure on a field argent; the word "Moro" signifying in Italian either 'mulberry-tree or blackamoor.

'In July, 1469, this Doge .... Christopher Moro effected indirectly the annexation of 'Cyprus to Venice, and in May, 1505, as a reward for military and diplomatic services, 'the Grand Council elected his namesake—Christopher Moro, son of Lorenzo—lord- 'lieutenant of the island, where he remained, after his term of service had expired, and 'by reason of his being thus accidentally on the spot, he was appointed to defend it from 'an hypothetical attack which, according to report, was meditated either by the Soldan, 'the Sofi, or the Turk. This statement exists in the summary of a dispatch from Chris- 'topher Moro's successor, the Lord-Lieutenant Lorenzo Giustinian, who adds that he 'and the counsellors had "elected Christofal Moro captain of the fourteen ships detained 'by them for fear;" and it is a curious coincidence that the tenour of the official advices 'from Cyprus corresponds precisely with the causes assigned for the subsequent dispatch 'of Othello from Venice for the defence of that island, as in Act I, Scene iii, of Shake- 'speare's tragedy. And, finally, the return of Christopher Moro to Venice is recorded in 'Marin Sanuto's Diaries thus : A. D. 1508, October 22. "Item. The ship from Syria 'arrived, having on board Christopher Moro, on his return from the Lord-Lieutenancy 'of Cyprus. 1508, October 26. In the morning there presented himself to the College, 'Christopher Moro, returned Lord-Lieutenant from Cyprus, and elected Captain in Can- 'dia, *wearing his beard for the death of his wife* [Desdemona?] *on her way from Cyprus,* 'as *heard previously, and he made his report.*" .... To return to Christopher Moro. He 'was decidedly a lady's man, as according to Barbaro's genealogies he was married four 'times. Nor should it be forgotten that the tale, whether told by Cinthio or Shake- 'speare, must have its incidents dated between 1486, when Catherine Cornaro abdicated 'in favour of Venice, until the fall of Famagosta, in 1571. Further, Moro's military 'exploits in the Romagna, against Cæsar Borgia, and subsequently during the League of Cambrai, as recorded by the Venetian historians, and by an inscription which once 'existed in the Palazzo Pretorio at Padua, would warrant his saying of himself, 'I have done the State some service, and they know it.'

'Cinthio s novel, it may be added, would never have sufficed Shakespeare for his
Othello. The Italian described Desdemona's handkerchief as a 'nose-napkin' (*pannicello da naso*), and says it was most delicately wrought, but does not give the design,
which reveals the whole thing. Had he called things by their right names, the sale
' of his book in Venice would have been prohibited. . . . . Among the Venetians in Eng-
' land from 1603 to 1615 there were the secretary Scaramelli, and the ambassadors Duodo,
' Correr, Francesco Contarini, and Foscarini, from one or other of them, or from some
' of their attendants, Shakespeare—who may, perhaps, have been struck by some Eng-
' lish translation of Cinthio's tales—might easily have ascertained the true story of *his*
' Othello.'

In *The Academy* of 20 February, 1875, E. H. PICKERSGILL replied to Rawdon
Brown, and among other arguments gives a shrewd reason for Shakespeare's conversion
(if it be a conversion) of the 'three mulberries sable' into 'strawberries.' By the
' assumption that the " strawberries " were Othello's insignia *at all*, we should involve
' Shakespeare in a gross inconsistency. For, of course, in that case, Cassio, when he
' found the handkerchief dropped in his bed-chamber, could not have been in doubt
' respecting its ownership; he would have recognized it, at once, as the property of
' Desdemona. In Cinthio's novel, Cassio actually does recognize it, not by any insig-
' nia upon it, but by the curious inwrought " Moresco work." ' Furthermore, Pickersgill asks : ' If Shakespeare was acquainted with the historical Moro's military exploits
' in the Romagna, why does he prefer to mention Rhodes, Cyprus, and Aleppo as the
' scenes of the exploits of his Othello ?' The most conclusive argument against Brown's
theory Pickersgill finds in the actual date, settled by Reed, of Othello's dispatch to
Cyprus [see p. 357], which was sixty years after Christopher Moro's governorship of
the island.

Lastly, in *The Athenæum*, 18 September, 1875, C. ELLIOT BROWNE asks : ' Was
' Shakespeare indebted for any part of the conception of Othello to the story of Sam-
' piero, the famous Corsican leader ? . . . . The hint was thrown out more than a cen-
' tury ago by the anonymous writer of a paper in Dodsley's *Museum*, when replying to
' some of Rymer's criticisms upon this drama. He said (in substance), why this con-
' tinual cry about the unnaturalness of Othello, when there is evidence from real life
' that a brave soldier, whose character resembled in many points that which Shake-
' speare has given to the Moor, being placed in similar circumstances of terrible per-
' plexity, behaved almost exactly as Othello is represented to have done ?

' There is some resemblance between the careers of Sampiero and Othello. Sam-
' piero, or, as the name is more correctly written, San Pietro di Bastelica, was an Italian
' adventurer in the service of France, who had arrived at high distinction by conduct
' and valour; and he had married, against the wish of all her relatives, the beautiful
' Corsican heiress, Vanina d'Ornano. . . . . In 1563, Sampiero, leaving his wife in France,
' went to Constantinople to beg assistance for the Corsicans from the Turks. During
' this absence his Genoese enemies are said to have tampered with some servants of his
' wife's household, and caused a report to reach Constantinople that she was living on
' too intimate terms with his secretary, Antonio. Immediately returning to France,
' Sampiero came up with his wife at Aix; and after a scene which all accounts agree
' to have been characterized on his part by a strange mixture of passionate tenderness
' and brutal ferocity, and on hers by gentle, uncomplaining submiss on, he asked pardon
' upon his knees for the deed he was about to commit, and deliberately strangled her
' with her handkerchief. It is proper to add, that there is in existence another version
' of the affair, in which the cause of Vanina's fate is attributed to her husband's indig

'nation at some secret advances which she had made to the Genoese government for 'the purpose of obtaining his pardon, thus excluding altogether the motive of jealousy.

'Although wanting in several important points of resemblance, this story comes 'much nearer to the murder-scene of the drama than that of the tale in the "Heca-'tommithi." . . . . This Sampiero tragedy made so great a noise in Europe, that it is 'almost impossible to believe that Shakespeare would be unacquainted with it.'

The Hecatommithi of GIOUANBATTISTA GIRALDI CINTHIO are divided into Ten Decades, each Decade devoted to a particular subject, whereto ten Stories or Novels furnish the appropriate illustrations.

The Third Decade deals with 'The Unfaithfulness of Husbands and of Wives,' and is dedicated, let us hope with permission, to the 'Illvstrissima Signora la Signora Laura Eustochia da Este.'

The Seventh Novel in this Decade is here faithfully reprinted from the original edition, issued 'In Venegia M·D·LXVI.' Here and there the ampersands are changed to *e* and *et;* and *u* is changed to *v.*

A translation of this Novel appeared in MRS LENOX's *Shakespear Illustrated,* 1753, vol. i, p. 101. Again in 1795, it was translated by WOLSTENHOLME PARR; this translation was reprinted by Collier in the first edition of *Shakespeare's Library,* and again by W. C. Hazlitt in the second. Lastly, in 1855, by JOHN EDWARD TAYLOR. This translation is here reprinted on the same page with the Italian.

It was translated into German by WIELAND, and appeared in the *Teutsche Mercur,* Weimar, 1773, p. 63. Again by ECHTERMEYER, HENSCHEL, and SIMROCK in *Quellen der Shakespeare,* Berlin, 1831.

Of the author, Giraldi Cinthio, TAYLOR, in the Introduction to his Translation, says that he 'was a nobleman of Ferrara, and a Professor of Philosophy in that city;' and 'adds that 'it is somewhat amusing to read the terms in which he speaks of the 'composition of his work, in connection with his 'grave studies of philosophy,'—by 'the light of which, the fount and origin of laudable habits, and of all honest disci-'pline, and likewise of every virtue, I have sought to perfect my work, which is wholly 'directed, with much variety of examples, to censure vicious actions and to praise honest 'ones,—to make men fly from vice and embrace virtue.' What could the reader expect 'from this proem (which is found *totidem verbis* in all the books of this school), but a work of untarnished purity and morality?—all I can say is, he would be disappointed '

DECA TERZA

Un Capitano Moro piglia per mogliera una cittadina Venetiana, un suo Alfieri l'accusa di adulterio al Marito; cerca, che l' Alfieri uccida colui, ch' egli credea l'Adultero; il Capitano uccide la Moglie, è accusato dall' Alfieri, non confessa il Moro, ma essendovi chiari inditij, è bandito; Et lo scelerato Alfieri, credendo nuocere ad altri, procaccia a sè la morte miseramente. [*A Moorish Captain takes to wife a Venetian Dame, and his Ancient accuses her of adultery to her husband; it is planned that the Ancient is to kill him whom he believes to be the adulterer; the Captain kills the woman, is accused by the Ancient, the Moor does not confess, but after the infliction of extreme torture, is banished; and the wicked Ancient, thinking to injure other provided for himself a miserable death.*]

NOVELLA VII.

FU già in Venezia un Moro, molto valoroso, il quale, per essere prò della persona, e per haver dato segno, nelle cose della guerra, di gran prudenza, e di vivace ingegno, era molto caro a que' signori, i quali nel dar premio a gli atti vertuosi avanzano quante Republiche fur mai. Avenne, che una virtuosa Donna, di maravigliosa bellezza, Disdemona chiamata, tratta non da appetito donnesco, ma dalla virtù del Moro, s' innamorò di lui: et egli, vinto dalla bellezza, e dal nobile pensiero della Donna, similmente di lei si accese, et hebbero tanto favorevole Amore, che si congiunsero insieme per matrimonio, anchora che i parenti della Donna facessero ciò, che poterono, perche, ella altro marito si prendesse, che lui: e vissero insieme di sì concorde volere, et in tanta tranquillità, mentre furono in Venetia, che mai tra loro non fù non dirò cosa, ma parola men, che amorevole. Occorse, che i Signori Venetiani fecero mutatione delle genti d' arme, ch' essi sogliono tenere in Cipri: et elesseno per Capitano de soldati, che là mandavano, il Moro. Il quale, anchora che molto lieto fosse dell' honore, che gli era offerto (però che tal grado di degnità non si suol dare senon ad huomini, e nobili, e forti, e fedeli, e che habbiano mostrato havere in sé molto valore) si scemava nondimeno la sua allegrezza, qualhora egli si poneva innanzi la lunghezza, e la malagevolezza del viaggio, pensandosi, che Disdemona ne devesse rimanere offesa: la Donna, che altro bene non haveva al mondo, che il Moro, et era molto contenta, del testimonio, c' haveva havuto il Marito della sua virtù da così possente, e nobile Republica non vedea l' hora, che il Marito, colle sue genti, si mettesse in camino, et ella andasse seco in compagnia in così honorato luogo, ma le dava gran noia il vedere il Moro turbato. Et, non ne sapendo la cagione, un giorno mangiando gli disse; Che vuole egli dir, Moro, che poi, che vi è stato dato dalla Signoria così honorato grado, ve ne state tanto maninconico; a Disdemona disse il Moro, Turba la contentezza del ricevuto honore, l'amore, che io ti porto, perche io veggo, di necessità, delle due cose deverne avenir l' una: overo, che io ti meni con esso meco a pericoli del Mare: o vero, che, per non ti dar questo disago, ti

There once lived in Venice a Moor, who was very valiant and of a handsome person; and having given proofs in war of great skill and prudence, he was highly esteemed by the Signoria of the Republic, who in rewarding deeds of valour advanced the interests of the State.

It happened that a virtuous lady of marvellous beauty, named Disdemona, fell in love with the Moor, moved thereto by his valour; and he, vanquished by the beauty and the noble character of Disdemona, returned her love; and their affection was so mutual that, although the parents of the lady strove all they could to induce her to take another husband, she consented to marry the Moor; and they lived in such harmony and peace in Venice that no word ever passed between them that was not affectionate and kind.

Now it happened at this time that the Signoria of Venice made a change in the troops whom they used to maintain in Cyprus, and they appointed the Moor commander of the soldiers whom they dispatched thither. Joyful as was the Moor at the honour proffered him, such dignity being only conferred on men of noble rank and well-tried faith, and who had displayed bravery in arms,—yet his pleasure was lessened when he reflected on the length and dangers of the voyage, fearing that Disdemona would be pained at his absence. But Disdemona, who had no other happiness in the world than the Moor, and who rejoiced to witness the testimony of his valour her husband had received from so powerful and noble a Republic, was all impatient that he should embark with his troops, and longed to accompany him to so honourable a post. And all the more it vexed her to see the Moor so troubled; and not knowing what could be the reason, one day, when they were at dinner, she said to him, 'How is it, O Moor, that when so honourable a post has been conferred on you by the Signoria, you are thus melancholy?'

The Moor answered Disdemona, 'My pleasure at the honour I have received is disturbed by the love I bear you; for I see that of necessity one of two things must happen,—either that I take you with me to encounter the perils of the sea, or, to save

lasci in Venetia. La prima non mi potrebbe essere se non grave, perche ogni fatica, che tu ne sostenessi, et ogni pericolo, che ci sopravenisse, mi recherebbe estrema molestia. La seconda, devendoti lasciare, mi sarebbe odioso a me medesimo; perche, partendomi da te, mi patirei dalla mia vita. Disdemona, ciò inteso; Deh, disse, Marito mio, che pensieri son questi che vi vanno per l' animo? a che lasciate, che cosa tal vi turbi? voglio io venire con voi, ovunque anderete, Se bene così devessi passare in camiscia per lo fuoco, come son per venire per acqua con voi, in sicura, e ben guarnita nave: e, se pure vi saranno pericoli, e fatiche, io con voi ne voglio essere a parte, e mi terrei d'essere poco amata da voi, quando, per non mi havere in compagnia nel mare, pensaste di lasciarmi in Venetia, o vi persuadeste, che più tosto mi volessi star quì sicura, ch' essere con voi in uno istesso pericolo. Però voglio, che vi apparecchiate al viaggio, con tutta quella allegrezza, che merita la qualità del grado, che tenete. Gjttò allhora le braccia al collo tutto lieto il Moro alla Mogliera, e con un affettuoso bacio le disse: Iddio ci conservi lungamente in questa amorevolezza, Moglie mia cara: et, indi a poco, pigliati gli suoi arnesi, e messossi ad ordine per lo camino, entrò, colla sua Donna, e con tutta la compagnia, nella galea: e date le vele al vento, si mise in camino: e con somma tranquillità del Mare, se n'andò in Cipri. Haveva costui nella compagnia un alfiero di bellissima presenza, ma della più scelerata natura, che mai fosse huomo del mondo. Era questi molto caro al Moro, non havendo egli delle sue cattività notitia alcuna. Perche, quantunque egli fosse di vilissimo animo, copriva nondimeno, coll' alte, e superbe parole, e colla sua presenza, di modo la viltà, ch' egli chiudea nel cuore, che si scopriva nella sembianza un' Ettore, od un Achille. Havea similmente menata questo malvagio la sua Moglie in Cipri, la quale era bella, et honesta giovane: e per essere Italiana, era molto amata dalla Moglie del Moro, e si stava la maggior parte del giorno con lei. Nella medesima compagnia era ancho un Capo di squadra, carrissimo al Moro: Andava spessissime volte questi a casa del Moro, e spesso mangiava con lui e

---

you from this danger, I must leave you here in Venice. The first could not be otherwise than serious to me, for all the toil you would have to bear and every danger that might befall you would cause me extreme anxiety and pain, yet, were I to leave you behind me, I should be hateful to myself, since in parting from you I should part from my own life.'

Disdemona, on hearing this, replied: 'My husband, what thoughts are these that wander through your mind? Why let such things disturb you? I will accompany you whithersoe'er you go, were it to pass through fire, as now to cross the water in a safe and well-provided ship; if indeed there are toils and perils to encounter, I will share them with you. And in truth I should think you loved me little were you to leave me here in Venice, denying me to bear you company, or could believe that I would liefer bide in safety here than share the dangers that await you. Prepare then for the voyage with all the readiness which the dignity of the post you hold deserves.'

The Moor, in the fulness of his joy, threw his arms around his wife's neck, and with an affectionate and tender kiss exclaimed, 'God keep you long in such love, dear wife!' Then speedily donning his armour, and having prepared everything for his expedition, he embarked on board the galley with his wife and all his troops, and, setting sail, they pursued their voyage, and with a perfectly tranquil sea arrived safely at Cyprus.

Now amongst the soldiery there was an Ensign, a man of handsome figure, but of the most depraved nature in the world. This man was in great favour with the Moor, who had not the slightest idea of his wickedness; for, despite the malice lurking in his heart, he cloaked with proud and valorous speech and with a specious presence the villainy of his soul with such art that he was to all outward show another Hector or Achilles. This man had likewise taken with him his wife to Cyprus, a young, and fair, and virtuous lady; and being of Italian birth she was much loved by Disdemona, who spent the greater part of every day with her.

In the same Company there was a certain Captain of a troop, to whom the Moor was much affectioned. And Disdemona, for this cause, knowing how much her husband

con la Moglie. La onde la Donna che lo conosceva così grato al suo Marito, gli dava segni di grandissima benivolenza. La qual cosa era molto cara al Moro. Lo scelerato Alfiero, non curando punto la fede data alla sua Moglie, nè amicitia, nè fede, nè obligo, ch' egli havesse al Moro, s' innamorò di Disdemona ardentissimamente; e voltò tutto il suo pensiero a vedere, se gli poteva venir fatto di godersi di lei: ma non ardiva di dimostrarsi, temendo, che, se il Moro se ne avedesse, non gli desse subito morte. Cercò egli con varij modi, quanto più occultamente poteva, di fare accorta la Donna, ch' egli l' amava. Ma ella, c' havea nel Moro ogni suo pensiero, non pensava punto nè allo Alfiero, nè ad altri. Et tutte le cose, ch' egli facea, per accenderla di lui, non più operavano, che se fatte non le havesse. Onde s' imaginò costui, che ciò avenisse, perche ella fosse accesa del Capo di squadra; e pensò volerlosi levar dinanzi agli occhi, e non pure a ciò piegò la mente, Ma mutò l' amore, ch' egli portava alla Donna, in acerbissimo odio; e si die, con ogni studio, a pensare, come gli potesse venir fatto, che ucciso il Capo di squadra, se non potesse goder della Donna, il Moro anco non ne godesse. Et rivolgendosi per l' animo varie cose, tutte scelerate, e malvagie, alla fine, si deliberò di volerla accusare di Adulterio al Marito, e dargli ad intendere, che l' Adultero era il Capo di squadra; Ma sappiendo costui l' amore singolare, che portava il Moro a Disdemona, e l' amicitia, ch' egli havea col Capo di squadra, conosceva apertamente, che, se con astuta froda non faceva inganno al Moro, era impossibile a dargli a vedere nè l' uno, nè l' altro. Per la qual cosa si mise ad aspettare, che 'l tempo, et il luogo gli aprisse la via da entrare a così scelerata impresa. Et non passò molto, che il Moro, per haver messa mano alla spada il Capo di squadra, nella guardia, contra un soldato, e dategli delle ferite, lo privò del grado: la qual cosa fù gravissima a Disdemona. Et molte volte haveva tentato di rappacificare il Marito con lui. Tra questo mezzo disse il Moro allo scelerato Alfieri, che la Moglie gli dava tanta seccagine per lo Capo di squadra, che temea finalmente, di non essere astretto a ripigliarlo. Prese da ciò il mal' huomo argomento di por mano a gli orditi inganni, e disse;

---

valued him, showed him proofs of the greatest kindness, which was all very grateful to the Moor. Now the wicked Ensign, regardless of the faith that he had pledged his wife, no less than of the friendship, fidelity, and obligation which he owed the Moor, fell passionately in love with Disdemona, and bent all his thoughts to achieve his conquest; yet he dared not to declare his passion openly, fearing that, should the Moor perceive it, he would at once kill him. He therefore sought in various ways, and with secret guile, to betray his passion to the lady; but she, whose every wish was centred in the Moor, had no thought for this Ensign more than for any other man; and all the means he tried to gain her love had no more effect than if he had not tried them. But the Ensign imagined that the cause of his ill success was that Disdemona loved the Captain of the troop; and he pondered how to remove him from her sight. The love which he had borne the lady now changed into the bitterest hate, and, having failed in his purposes, he devoted all his thoughts to plot the death of the Captain of the troop and to divert the affection of the Moor from Disdemona. After revolving in his mind various schemes, all alike wicked, he at length resolved to accuse her of unfaithfulness to her husband, and to represent the Captain as her paramour. But knowing the singular love the Moor bore to Disdemona, and the friendship which he had for the Captain, he was well aware that, unless he practised an artful fraud upon the Moor, it were impossible to make him give ear to either accusation; wherefore he resolved to wait until time and circumstance should open a path for him to engage in his foul project.

Not long afterwards it happened that the Captain, having drawn his sword upon a soldier of the guard, and struck him, the Moor deprived him of his rank; whereat Disdemona was deeply grieved, and endeavored again and again to reconcile her husband to the man. This the Moor told to the wicked Ensign, and how his wife importuned him so much about the Captain that he feared he should be forced at last to receive him back to service. Upon this hint the Ensign resolved to act, and began to

Hà forse Disdemona cagione di vederlo volentieri. Et perche? disse il Moro, Io non voglio, rispose l' Alfieri, por mano tra marito, e moglie: ma, se terrete aperti gli occhi, voi stesso lo vi vedrete; Nè per diligenza, che facesse il Moro, volle l' Alfieri più oltre passare: Benchè lasciarono tali parole, così pungente spina nell' animo del Moro, che si diede con sommo studio a pensare ciò, che volessero dire tali parole, e se ne stava tutto maninconioso. La onde, tentando un giorno la Moglie di ammollire l' ira sua verso il Capo di squadra, e pregandolo a non volere mettere in oblio la servitù, e l' amicitia di tanti anni, per un picciolo fallo; essendo massimamente nata pace, fra il Soldato ferito, et il Capo di squadra, venne il Moro in ira, e le disse: Gran cosa è questa, Disdemona, che tu tanta cura ti pigli di costui, Non è però egli nè tuo fratello, nè tuo parente, che tanto ti debba essere a cuore. La Donna, tutta cortese, et humile; non vorrei, disse, che voi vi adiraste con meco, altro non mi muove, che il dolermi di vedervi privato di così caro amico, qual sò, per lo testimonio di voi medesimo, che vi è stato il Capo di squadra: non hà però egli commesso sì grave errore, che gli debbiate portare tanto odio. Ma voi Mori sete di natura tanto caldi, ch' ogni poco di cosa vi muove ad ira, et a vendetta. A queste parole più irato rispose il Moro, tale lo potrebbe provare, che non sel crede: vedrò tal vendetta delle ingiurie, che mi son fatte, che ne resterò satio. Rimase la Donna tutta isbigotita a queste parole: et, veduto fuor del suo costume, il Marito, contra lei riscaldato, humilmente disse; altro, che buon fine, a parlarvi di ciò non mi hà indotta, ma perche più non vi habbiate di adirar meco, non vi dirò più mai di ciò parola. Veduta il Moro la instanza, che di nuovo gli havea fatta la Moglie, in favore del Capo di squadra, s' imaginò che le parole, che gli havea detto l' Alfieri, gli havessero voluto significare, che Disdemona fosse inamorata di lui, et se n' andò a quel ribaldo tutto maninconioso, e cominciò a tentare, che egli più apertamente gli parlasse. L' Alfieri, intento al danno di questa misera Donna, dopo l' havere finto di non voler dir cosa, che fosse per dispiacer-

---

work his web of intrigue. 'Perchance,' said he, 'the lady Disdemona may have good reason to look kindly on him.'

'And wherefore?' said the Moor.

'Nay, I would not step 'twixt man and wife,' replied the Ensign, 'but let your eyes be witness to themselves.'

In vain the Moor went on to question the officer,—he would proceed no further; nevertheless, his words left a sharp, stinging thorn in the Moor's heart, who could think of nothing else, trying to guess their meaning and lost in melancholy. And one day, when his wife had been endeavouring to pacify his anger toward the Captain, and praying him not to be unmindful of ancient services and friendship for one small fault, especially since peace had been made between the Captain and the soldier he had struck, the Moor was angered, and exclaimed, 'Great cause have you, Disdemona, to care so anxiously about this man! Is he a brother, or your kinsman, that he should be so near your heart?'

The lady, with all gentleness and humility, replied, 'Be not angered, my dear lord; I have no other cause to bid me speak than sorrow that I see you lose so dear a friend as, by your own words, this Captain has been to you; nor has he done so grave a fault that you should bear him so much enmity. Nay, but you Moors are of so hot a nature that every little trifle moves you to anger and revenge.'

Still more enraged at these words, the Moor replied, 'I could bring proofs—by heaven it mocks belief! but for the wrongs I have endured revenge must satisfy my wrath.'

Disdemona, in astonishment and fright, seeing her husband's anger kindled against her, so contrary to his wont, said humbly and with timidity, 'None save a good intent has led me thus to speak with you, my lord; but to give cause no longer for offence, I'll never speak a word more on the subject.'

The Moor, observing the earnestness with which his wife again pleaded for the Captain, began to guess the meaning of the Ensign's words; and in deep melancholy he went to seek that villain and induce him to speak more openly of what he knew. Then the Ensign, who was bent upon injuring the unhappy lady, after feigning at first

gli, mostrandosi vinto da preghi del Moro, disse; Io non posso negare, che non m' incresca incredibilmente, di havervi a dir cosa, che sia per esservi più di qualunque altra molesta: ma, poi che pur volete, ch' io la vi dica, e la cura, che io debbo havere dell' honor vostro, come di mio signore, mi sprona anco a dirlovi, non voglio hora mancare nè alla vostra dimanda, nè al debito mio. Devete adunque sapere, che, non per altro, è grave alla Donna vostra il veder il Capo di squadra in disgratia vostra, che per lo piacere, che ella si piglia con lui, qual' hora egli in casa vostra viene: come colei, a cui già è venuta a noia questa vostra nerezza. Queste parole passarono il cuore al Moro insino alle radici: Ma, per saper più oltre (anchora, ch' egli credesse vero quanto havea detto l' Alfieri, per lo sospetto, che già gli era nato nell' animo) disse, con fiero viso; non sò io che mi tenga, che non ti tagli questa lingua, tanto audace, che hà havuto ardire di dar tale infamia alla Donna mia. L' Alfiero allhora, non mi aspettava, disse, Capitano, di questo mio amorevole ufficio, altra mercede; Ma, poi che tanto oltre mi hà portato il debito mio, et il desiderio dell' honor vostro: io vi replico, che così stà la cosa, come intesa l' havete, et se la Donna, col mostrar di amarvi, vi hà così appannati gli occhi, che non habbiate veduto quel, che veder devevate, non è mica per ciò, che io non vi dica il vero. Perche il medesimo Capo di squadra l' hà detto a me, come quegli, cui non pareva la sua felicità compiuta, se non ne faceva alcuno altro consapevole; Et gli soggiunse: e, se io non havessi temuta l' ira vostra, gli havrei dato, quando ciò mi disse, quella mercede, coll' ucciderlo, della quale egli era degno. Ma poscia, che il farvi sapere quello, che più a voi, che a qualunque altro appartiene, me ne fà havere così sconvenevole guiderdone: me ne vorrei essere stato cheto, che non sarei, tacendo, incorso nella disgratia vostra. Il Moro allhora tutto cruccioso, se non mi fai, disse, vedere cogl' occhi quello, che detto mi hai, viviti sicuro, che ti farò conoscere, che meglio per te sarebbe, che tu fossi nato mutolo. Agevol mi sarebbe stato questo, soggiunse il Malvagio, quando egli in casa vostra veniva, ma hora, che, non per quello che bisognava, ma per vie più lieve

---

great reluctance to say aught that might displease the Moor, at length pretended to yield to his entreaties, and said, 'I can't deny it pains me to the soul to be thus forced to say what needs must be more hard to hear than any other grief; but since you will it so, and that the regard I owe your honour compels me to confess the truth, I will no longer refuse to satisfy your questions and my duty. Know, then, that for no other reason is your lady vexed to see the Captain in disfavour than the pleasure that she has in his company whenever he comes to your house, and all the more since she has taken an aversion to your blackness.'

These words went straight to the Moor's heart; but in order to hear more (now that he believed true all that the Ensign had told him) he replied, with a fierce glance, 'By heavens, I scarce can hold this hand from plucking out that tongue of thine, so bold, which dares to speak such slander of my wife!'

'Captain,' replied the Ensign, 'I looked for such reward for these my faithful offices,—none else; but since my duty, and the jealous care I bear your honour, have carried me thus far, I do repeat, so stands the truth, as you have heard it from these lips; and if the lady Disdemona hath, with a false show of love for you, blinded your eyes to what you should have seen, this is no argument but that I speak the truth. Nay, this same Captain told it me himself, like one whose happiness is incomplete until he can declare it to another; and, but that I feared your anger, I should have given him, when he told it me, his merited reward, and slain him. But since informing you of what concerns you more than any other man brings me so undeserved a recompense, would I had held my peace, since silence might have spared me your displeasure.'

Then the Moor, burning with indignation and anguish, said, 'Make thou these eyes self-witnesses of what thou tell'st, or on thy life I'll make thee wish thou hadst been born without a tongue.'

'An easy task it would have been,' replied the villain, 'when he was used to visit at

cagione, l havete scacciato, non mi potrà essere se non malagevole, che anchora che io stimi, ch' egli di Disdemona sı goda, qualhora voi gliene date l' agio, molto più cautamente lo dee fare hora, che si vede esservi venuto in odio, che non facea di prima. Ma anco non perdo la speranza li potervi far vedere quel, che creder non mi volete. Et con queste parole si dipartıono. Il misero Moro, come tocco da pungentissimo strale, se n' andò a casa, attendenċo che venisse il giorno, che l' Alfieri gli facesse veder quello, che lo devea far, per sempre, misero. Ma non minor noia dava al maladetto Alfieri la castità, ch' egli sapeva, che osservava la Donna, perche gli parea non poter ritrovar modo a far credere al Moro quello, che falsamente detto gli haveva : e, voltato in varie parti il pensiero, pensò lo Scelerato a nuova malitia. Andava sovente la Moglie del Moro, come hò detto, a casa della Moglie dell' Alfieri, e se ne stava con lei buona parte del giorno, onde veggendo costui ch' ella talhora portava seco un pannicello da naso, ch' egli sapeva, che le havea donato il Moro, il qual pannicello era lavorato alla moresca sottilissimamente, et era carissimo alla Donna, e parimente al Moro, si pensò di torgliele secretamente, e quindi apparecchiarele l' ultimo danno. Et havendo egli una fanciulla di tre anni, la quale era molto amata da Disdemona, un giorno, che la misera Donna a casa di questo reo si era andata a stare, prese egli la fanciulla in braccio, et alla Donna la porse : La quale la prese, e la si reccò al petto; questo Ingannatore, che eccellentemente giocava di mano, le levò da cintola il pannicello così accortamente, ch' ella punto non se ne avide, e da lei, tutto allegro, si dipartì. Disdemona, ciò non sappiendo, se ne andò a casa : e occupata da altri pensieri, non si avide del pannicello. Ma, indi ad alquanti giorni, cercandone, e nol ritrovando, stava tutta timida, che il Moro con gliele chiedesse, come egli sovente facea. Lo scelerato Alfieri, pigliatosi commodo tempo, se ne andò al Capo di squadra, e con astuta malitia gli lasciò il pannicello a capo del letto, nè se nè avide il Capo di squadra, se non la seguente mattina, che levandosi del letto, essendo il pannicello caduto in terra, vi pose il piede sopra : nè sapendosi imaginare, come in casa

your house; but now that you have banished him, not for just cause, but for mere frivolous pretext, it will be hard to prove the truth. Still, I do not forego the hope to make you witness of that which you will not credit from my lips.'

Thus they parted. The wretched Moor, struck to the heart as by a barbed dart, returned to his home, and awaited the day when the Ensign should disclose to him the truth which was to make him miserable to the end of his days. But the evil-minded Ensign was, on his part, not less troubled by the chastity which he knew the lady Disdemona observed inviolate; and it seemed to him impossible to discover a means of making the Moor believe what he had falsely told him; and, turning the matter over in his thoughts in various ways, the villain resolved on a new deed of guilt.

Disdemona often used to go, as I have already said, to visit the Ensign's wife, and remained with her a good part of the day. Now, the Ensign observed that she carried about with her a handkerchief, which he knew the Moor had given her, finely embroidered in the Moorish fashion, and which was precious to Disdemona, nor less so to the Moor. Then he conceived the plan of taking this kerchief from her secretly, and thus laying the snare for her final ruin. The Ensign had a little daughter, a child three years of age, who was much loved by Disdemona, and one day, when the unhappy lady had gone to pay a visit at the house of this vile man, he took the little child up in his arms and carried her to Disdemona, who took her and pressed her to her bosom; whilst at the same instant this traitor, who had extreme dexterity of hand, drew the kerchief from her sash so cunningly that she did not notice him, and overjoyed he took his leave of her.

Disdemona, ignorant of what had happened, returned home, and, busy with other thoughts, forgot the handkerchief. But a few days afterwards, looking for it and not finding it, she was in alarm, lest the Moor should ask her for it, as he oft was wont to do. Meanwhile, the wicked Ensign, seizing a fit opportunity, went to the Captain of the troop, and with crafty malice left the handkerchief at the head of his bed without his discovering the trick, until the following morning, when, on his getting out of bed,

l' havesse, conoscendolo cosa di Disdemona, deliberò di dargliele : et attendendo che il Moro fosse uscito di casa, se nè andò all' uscio di dietro, et ivi picchiò; volle la Fortuna, che parea, che coll' Alfieri congiurata si fosse alla morte della meschina : che in quell hora appunto, il Moro si venne a casa : et udendo picchiare l' uscio, si fece alla finestra : e tutto cruccioso, disse, chi picchia là? Il Capo di squadra, udita la voce del Moro, temendo, ch' egli non scendesse a danno suo, senza rispondere parola si diede a fuggire. Il Moro, scese le scale : e aperto l' uscio, uscí nella strada, e cercando di lui nol ritrovò. Onde entrato in casa, pieno di mal talento, dimandò alla Moglie, chi fosse colui, che la giù picchiava. La Donna rispose quel, che vero era, che nol sapeva. Ma il Moro disse, mi hà egli paruto il Capo di squadra; Non sò, io disse ella, se sia stato nè egli, nè altri. Rattenne il Moro il furore, quantunque d' ira ardesse, Nè prima volle far cosa alcuna, che parlasse, coll' Alfieri, alquale subitamente se n' andò, e gli disse quanto era occorso, e lo pregò ad intendere dal Capo di squadra tutto quello, ch' egli poteva intorno a ciò. Egli, lieto di così fatto avenimento, gli promise di farlo. Et al Capo di squadra parlò un giorno costui, che il Moro era in luogo, onde gli poteva vedere insieme ragionare. Et parlandogli di ogn' altra cosa, che della Donna, faceva le maggiori risa del mondo : e mostrando di maravigliarsi, facea di molti atti, e col capo, e colle mani, come, che udisse cose maravigliose. Il Moro, tosto che gli vide partiti, andò verso l' Alfieri, per sapere ciò, che colui detto gli havesse. Questi, dopo haversi fatto lungamente pregare, al fin gli disse, non mi hà egli celata cosa alcuna, e mi hà detto, che si hà goduto della Moglie vostra ogni volta, che voi coll' esser fuori, gli ne havete dato tempo : e che l' ultima fiata, ch' egli è stato con lei, gli hà ella donato quel pannicello da naso, che voi, quando la sposaste, le deste in dono. Il Moro ringratiò l' Alfieri, e gli parve, che se ritrovava, che la Donna non havesse il pannicello, potesse essere chiaro, che così fosse, come gli havea detto l' Alfieri. Per la qual cosa un giorno, dopo desinare, entrato

---

the handkerchief fell upon the floor, and he set his foot upon it. And not being able to imagine how it had come into his house, knowing that it belonged to Disdemona, he resolved to give it to her; and waiting until the Moor had gone from home, he went to the back door and knocked. It seemed as if fate conspired with the Ensign to work the death of the unhappy Disdemona. Just at that time the Moor returned home, and hearing a knocking at the back door, he went to the window, and in a rage exclaimed, ' Who knocks there? ' The Captain, hearing the Moor's voice, and fearing lest he should come down stairs and attack him, took to flight without answering a word. The Moor went down, and opening the door hastened into the street and looked about, but in vain. Then, returning into the house in great anger, he demanded of his wife who it was that had knocked at the door. Disdemona replied, as was true, that she did not know; but the Moor said, ' It seemed to me the Captain.'

'I know not,' answered Disdemona, ' whether it was he or another person.'

The Moor restrained his fury, great as it was, wishing to do nothing before consulting the Ensign, to whom he hastened instantly, and told him all that had passed, praying him to gather from the Captain all he could respecting the affair. The Ensign, overjoyed at the occurrence, promised the Moor to do as he requested, and one day he took occasion to speak with the Captain when the Moor was so placed that he could see and hear them as they conversed. And whilst talking to him of every other subject than of Disdemona, he kept laughing all the time aloud, and, feigning astonishment, he made various movements with his head and hands, as if listening to some tale of marvel. As soon as the Moor saw the Captain depart, he went up to the Ensign to hear what he had said to him. And the Ensign, after long entreaty, at length said, ' He has hidden from me nothing, and has told me that he has been used to visit your wife whenever you went from home, and that on the last occasion she gave him this handkerchief which you presented to her when you married her.'

The Moor thanked the Ensign, and it seemed now clear to him that, should he find Disdemona not to have the handkerchief, it was all true that the Ensign had told to him. One day, therefore, after dinner, in conversation with his wife on various sub-

in varij ragionamenti colla Donna, le chiese il pannicello. La infelice che di questo havea molto temuto, a tal dimanda, divenne nel viso tutta fuoco; et per celare il rossore, il quale molto bene notò il Moro, corse alla cassa, e finse di cercarlo. Et dopo molto haverlo cercato; non sò, disse, com' hora non lo ritrovi, l' havreste voi forse havuto? s' havuto lo havessi, disse egli, perche te lo chiederei io? ma ne cercherai più agiatamente un' altra volta. Et partitosi cominciò a pensare, come devesse far morire la Donna, et insieme il Capo di squadra, sì, che a lui non fosse data colpa della sua morte. Et pensando giorno, et notte sopra ciò, non poteva fare, che la Donna non si avedesse, ch' egli non era quegli, che verso lei, per adietro, essere soleva. Et gli disse più volte, che cosa havete voi, che così vi turbi? che ove solevate essere il più festoso huomo del mondo, siete hora il più maninconico, che viva? Trovava il Moro varie cagioni di rispondere alla Donna, ma non ne rimaneva ella punto contenta. Et posto ch' ella sapesse, che per niuno suo misfatto, non devesse essere così turbato il Moro, dubitava nondimeno, che per la troppa copia, ch' egli haveva di lei, non gli fosse venuta a noia. Et talhora diceva colla Moglie dell' Alfieri, Io non sò, che mi dica io del Moro, egli soleva essere verso me tutto amore, hora, da non sò che pochi giorni in qua, è divenuto un' altro: et temo molto di non essere io quella, che dia essempio alle giovani di non maritarsi contra il voler de suoi; et che da me le Donne Italiane imparino, di non si accompagnare con huomo, cui la Natura, et il Cielo, et il modo della vita disgiunge da noi. Ma, perche io sò, ch' egli è molto amico del vostro Marito, et communica con lui le cose sue: vi prego, che se havete intesa cosa alcuna da lui, della quale mi possiate avisare, che non mi manchiate di aiuto, et tutto ciò le diceva dirottamente piangendo; la Moglie dell' Alfieri, che il tutto sapeva, (come colei, cui il Marito haveva voluta usare per mezzana alla morte della Donna) ma non l'haveva ella mai voluto acconsentire, et temendo del Marito, non ardiva di dirle cosa alcuna; Solo le disse, habbiate cura di non dare di voi sospetto al Marito, e cercate con ogni studio, ch' egli in voi conosca amore, et fede; ciò faccio io, disse ella,

---

jects, he asked her for the kerchief. The unhappy lady, who had been in great fear of this, grew red as fire at this demand; and to hide the scarlet of her cheeks, which was closely noted by the Moor, she ran to a chest and pretended to seek the hand-kerchief, and after hunting for it a long time, she said, ' I know not how it is—I cannot find it; can you, perchance, have taken it?'

'If I had taken it,' said the Moor, 'why should I ask it of you? but you will look better another time.'

On leaving the room, the Moor fell to meditating how he should put his wife to death, and likewise the Captain of the troop, so that their death should not be laid to his charge. And as he ruminated over this day and night, he could not prevent his wife's observing that he was not the same towards her as he had been wont; and she said to him again and again, ' What is the matter? What troubles you? How comes it that you, who were the most light-hearted man in the world, are now so melancholy?'

The Moor feigned various reasons in reply to his wife's questioning, but she was not satisfied, and, although conscious that she had given the Moor no cause, by act or deed, to be so troubled, yet she feared that he might have grown wearied of her; and she would say to the Ensign's wife, ' I know not what to say of the Moor; he used to be all love towards me; but within these few days he has become another man; and much I fear that I shall prove a warning to young girls not to marry against the wishes of their parents, and that the Italian ladies may learn from me not to wed a man whom nature and habitude of life estrange from us. But as I know the Moor is on such terms of friendship with your husband, and communicates to him all his affairs, I pray you, if you have heard from him aught that you may tell me of, fail not to befriend me.' And as she said this, she wept bitterly.

The Ensign's wife, who knew the whole truth (her husband wishing to make use of her to compass the death of Disdemona), but could never consent to such a project, dared not, from fear of her husband, disclose a single circumstance: all she said was, ' Beware lest you give any cause of suspicion to your husband, and show to him by

ma nulla mi giova. Il Moro, in questo mezzo tempo, cercava tutta via di più certificarsi di quello, che non havrebbe voluto ritrovare: e pregò l' Alfieri, che operasse di modo, che potesse vedere il pannicello in podestà del Capo di squadra: e benche ciò fosse grave al Malvagio, gli promise nondimeno di usare ogni diligenza, perche egli di ciò si certificasse. Haveva il Capo di squadra una donna in casa, che maravigliosi trapunti faceva sù la tela di rensa, la quale veggendo quel pannicello, et intendendo, ch' era della Donna del Moro, et ch' era per esserle reso, prima ch' ella l' havesse, si mise a farne un simile: e mentre ella ciò faceva, s' avide l' Alfieri, ch' ella appresso uno finestra si stava, e da chi passava per la strada poteva essere veduta, onde fece egli ciò vedere al Moro, Il quale tenne certissimo, che l' honestissima Donna fosse in fatto Adultera; Et conchiuse coll' Alfiero, di uccidere lei, et il Capo di squadra, trattando ambidue tra loro come ciò si devesse fare; lo pregò il Moro, ch' egli volesse essere quegli, che il Capo di squadra uccidesse, promettendo di restargliene obligato eternamente. Et ricusando egli di volere far cosa tale come malagevolissima, e di molto pericolo, per essere il Capo di squadra non meno accorto, che valoroso, dopo molto haverlo pregato, datagli buona quantità di danari, lo indusse a dire, che proverebbe di tentar la fortuna. Fatta questa resolutione, uscendo una sera il Capo di squadra di casa di una meretrice, colla quale egli si sollazzava, essendo la notte buia, gli si accostò l' Alfiero con la spada in mano, et gli dirizzò un colpo alle gambe, per farlo cadere, et avenne, ch' egli gli tagliò la destra coscia a traverso, onde il misero cadde: gli fù addosso l' Alfieri, per finire di ucciderlo. Ma havendo il Capo di squadra, che coraggioso era, et avezzo nel sangue, et nelle morti, tratta la spada; et, così ferito come egli era, dirizzatosi alla difesa, gridò ad alta voce; io sono assassinato. Per la qual cosa, sentendo l' Alfieri correr gente, et alquanti de Soldati, ch' ivi attorno erano alloggiati, si mise a fuggire, per non vi essere colto: e, data una volta, fè vista anch' egli di essere corso a romore. Et ponendosi tra gli altri, vedutagli mozza la gamba, giudicò che se bene non era morto, morirebbe

---

every means your fidelity and love.'—'Indeed I do so,' replied Disdemona, 'but it is all of no avail.'

Meanwhile the Moor sought in every way to convince himself of what he fain would have found untrue, and he prayed the Ensign to contrive that he might see the handkerchief in the possession of the Captain. This was a difficult matter to the wicked Ensign; nevertheless, he promised to use every means to satisfy the Moor of the truth of what he said.

Now, the Captain had a wife at home who worked the most marvellous embroidery upon lawn, and seeing the handkerchief, which belonged to the Moor's wife, she resolved, before it was returned to her, to work one like it. As she was engaged in this task, the Ensign observed her standing at a window, where she could be seen by all the passers-by in the street, and he pointed her out to the Moor, who was now perfectly convinced of his wife's guilt. Then he arranged with the Ensign to slay Disdemona and the Captain of the troop, treating them as it seemed they both deserved. And the Moor prayed the Ensign that he would kill the Captain, promising eternal gratitude to him. But the Ensign at first refused to undertake so dangerous a task, the Captain being a man of equal skill and courage; until at length, after much entreating and being richly paid, the Moor prevailed on him to promise to attempt the deed.

Having formed this resolution, the Ensign, going out one dark night, sword in hand, met the Captain on his way to visit a courtesan, and struck him a blow on his right thigh, which cut off his leg and felled him to the earth. Then the Ensign was on the point of putting an end to his life, when the Captain, who was a courageous man and used to the sight of blood and death, drew his sword, and, wounded as he was, kept on his defence, exclaiming with a loud voice, 'I'm murdered!' Thereupon the Ensign, hearing the people come running up, with some of the soldiers who were lodged thereabouts, took to his heels to escape being caught; then turning about again, he joined the crowd, pretending to have been attracted by the noise. And when he saw the Captain's leg cut off, he judged that, if not already dead, the blow must, at all events,

ad ogni modo di quel colpo; e, quantunque fosse di ciò lietissimo, si dolse nondimeno col Capo di squadra, come s' egli suo fratello fosse stato. La mattina la cosa si sparse per tutta la Città, et andò anco alle orecchie di Disdemona, onde ella, ch' amorevole era, et non pensava ch' indi le devesse avenir male, mostrò di havere grandissimo dolore di così fatto caso; di ciò fece il Moro pessimo concetto. Et andò a ritrovare l' Alfieri, et gli disse; Tu sai bene, che l' Asina di mia Moglie è in tanto affanno, per lo caso del Capo di squadra, ch' ella è per impazzare. Et come potevate, disse egli, pensare altrimente, essendo colui l' anima sua? Anima sua, eh? replicò il Moro, Io le trarrò ben' io l' anima del corpo, che mi terrei non essere huomo, se non togliessi dal mondo questa malvagia. Et discorrendo l' uno con l' altro, se di veleno, o di coltello si devea far morir la Donna, nè accettandosi questo, nè quello da loro, disse l' Alfiero; un modo mi è egli venuto nella mente, che vi sodisfararete, et non se ne havrà sospetto alcuno. Et egli è tale, La casa, ove voi state, è vecchissima, e il palco della camera vostra hà di molte fessure; voglio, che con una calza piena di rena percotiamo Disdemona, tanto ch' ella nè muoia, perche non appaia in lei segno alcuno di battitura: morta, ch' ella sarà, faremo cadere parte del palco, et romperemo il capo alla Donna, fingendo, che una trave nel cadere rotta gliele habbia, et uccisa: et, a questo modo, non sarà persona, che di voi pigli sospetto alcuno, stimando ognuno la sua morte essere venuta a caso. Piacque al Moro, il crudel consiglio: et, aspettato il tempo, che convenevole gli parve, essendo egli una notte con lei nel letto, et havendo già nascoso l' Alfieri in un camerino, che nella camera entrava, l' Alfiero, secondo l' ordine tra lor dato, fè non sò che strepito nel camerino: e, sentitolo, subitamente disse il Moro alla Moglie; hai tu sentito quello strepito? hollo sentito, disse ella; levati soggiunse il Moro, e vedi che cosa è. Levossi la infelice Disdemona: e, tosto ch' ella fù appresso il camerino, n' uscì l' Alfieri, il quale, essendo forte, et di buon nerbo, colla calza, che in punto haveva, le diede una crudel percossa, nel

---

end his life; and whilst in his heart he was rejoiced at this, he yet feigned to compassionate the Captain as he had been his brother.

The next morning the tidings of this affair spread through the whole city, and reached the ears of Disdemona; whereat she, who was kind-hearted and little dreamed that any ill would betide her, evinced the greatest grief at the calamity. This served but to confirm the Moor's suspicions, and he went to seek for the Ensign, and said to him, 'Do you know that my wife is in such grief at the Captain's accident that she is well nigh gone mad.'

'And what could you expect, seeing he is her very soul?' replied the Ensign.

'Ay, soul forsooth!' exclaimed the Moor; 'I'll draw the soul from out her body; call me no man if that I fail to shut the world upon this wretch.'

Then they consulted of one means and another—poison and daggers—to kill poor Disdemona, but could resolve on nothing. At length the Ensign said, 'A plan comes to my mind, which will give you satisfaction and raise cause for no suspicion. It is this: the house in which you live is very old, and the ceiling of your chamber has many cracks; I propose we take a stocking, filled with sand, and beat Disdemona with it till she dies; thus will her body bear no signs of violence. When she is dead we can pull down a portion of the ceiling, and thus make it seem as if a rafter falling on her head had killed the lady. Suspicion cannot rest on you, since all men will impute her death to accident.'

This cruel counsel pleased the Moor, and he only waited for a fitting time to execute the plot. One night, when he and Disdemona had retired to bed, the Ensign, whom the Moor had concealed in a closet which opened into the chamber, raised a noise in the closet, according to a concerted plan; whereat the Moor said to his wife, 'Did you not hear that noise?'

'Indeed I heard it,' she replied.

'Rise,' said the Moor, 'and see what 'tis.'

The unhappy Disdemona rose from bed, and the instant she approached the closet, out rushed the Ensign, and being strong and of stout nerve, he beat her cruelly with

mezzo della schiena, onde la Donna subito cadde, senza poter trarne appena fuori il fiato. Ma con quella poca voce, che potè havere, chiamò il Moro, che l' aiutasse; et egli, uscito del letto, le disse, Sceleratissima Donna, la mercede hai della tua dishonestà, così si trattano quelle, che fingendo di amare i loro Mariti, pongono loro le corna in capo. La misera Donna, ciò udendo, e sentendosi giunta al fine (però che l' Alfiero un' altro colpo dato le havea) disse, che in testimonio della sua fede, ella chiamava la giustitia divina, poi, che, quella del mondo le veniva meno; et chiamando ella Iddio, che l' aiutasse, sopragiungendo la terza percossa, rimase uccisa dall' empio Alfieri. Poscia, messala nel letto, e spezzatale la testa, fecero egli, et il Moro, cadere come haveano ordinato fra loro il palco della camera, e cominciò il Moro a chiamare soccorso, che la casa cadeva, alla voce del quale corsono i vicini, e scoperto il letto, trovarono la Donna sotto le travi morta. La qual cosa, per la buona vita della Donna, increbbe ad ognuno. Il giorno seguente fù Disdemona sepellita, con universal dolore di quel popolo. Ma non volle Iddio, giusto riguardatore de gli animi altrui, che così gran sceleragine se ne rimanesse senza la dicevole pena. Imperò, che il Moro, che la Donna haveva amato più, che gli occhi suoi, veggendosene privo, cominciò ad havere tanto desiderio di lei, che l' andava, come fuori di sè, cercando per tutti i luoghi della casa: et considerando tra sè, che l' Alfieri era stato cagione, ch' egli havesse perduta, colla sua Donna, tutto il dolce della vita, et anco sè medesimo; gli venne lo Scelerato in tanto odio, che non haveva occhio, col quale vedere lo potesse : et, se non havesse havuto timore della inviolabile giustitia de Signori Venetiani, l' havrebbe palesamente ucciso. Ma non potendo far questo, con sua salvezza, gli levò la insegna, e più nol volle nella compagnia, onde nacque tanta aspra nimicitia tra l' uno, e l' altro, che non si potrebbe imaginare la maggiore, nè la più grave. Per la qual cosa l' Alfiero, peggiore di tutti gli scelerati, voltò tutto il pensiero a danni del Moro. Et, ritrovato il Capo di squadra, che già era risanato,

---

the bag of sand across her back; upon which Disdemona fell to the ground, scarce able to draw her breath; but with the little voice she had left, she called upon the Moor for aid. But the Moor, leaping from bed, exclaimed, 'Thou wickedest of women, thus has thy falseness found its just reward, the recompense to wives who, counterfeiting love, place horns upon their husbands' brows.'

The wretched lady, hearing these words, and feeling that she was near her end, (for the Ensign had given her another blow,) appealed to the justice of Heaven, since justice here had failed her, in proof of her fidelity and truth; and as she was thus calling Heaven to witness, the wicked Ensign inflicted a third blow, under which she sank lifeless on the floor.

Then the Ensign and the Moor, laying Disdemona on the bed and wounding her head, pulled down part of the ceiling of the chamber, as they had arranged; whereupon the Moor began to call aloud for help, exclaiming that the house was falling. Hearing this uproar, the neighbours all came running up, and there found Disdemona lying dead beneath a rafter,—a sight which, from the good life of that poor lady, did fill all hearts with sorrow.

On the following day Disdemona was buried, followed to the grave by the universal grief of the people. But Heaven, the just regarder of all hearts, willed not that so wicked a deed should go unpunished. Ere long the Moor, whom Disdemona had loved more than her own life, began to feel such sorrow at her loss that he went wandering about as one bereft of reason, searching in every part of the house. And reflecting in his thoughts that the Ensign had been the cause that he had lost, with Disdemona, all joy in life, he conceived so deep a hatred to that wicked man he could not bear to set eyes on him, and had it not been for his fear of the inviolable justice of the Signoria of Venice, he would have slain him openly. But being unable to do this with safety, he deprived him of his rank, and would not allow him to remain in his Company; whereat such an enmity arose between the two that no greater or more deadly can be imagined.

The Ensign, that wickedest of all bad men, now turned his thoughts to injuring the

et con una gamba di legno se n' andava in vece della tagliata, gli disse; Venuto è il tempo, che tu possi far vendetta della tua tagliata gamba: Et, quando tu voglia venire con esso meco a Venetia, io ti dirò, chi è stato il malfattore, che qui non ardirei di dirloti, per molti rispetti: et io ne farò, per te, testimonio in guidicio. Il Capo di squadra, che si ritrovava fieramente offeso, et non sapeva perche; ringratiò l' Alfieri, e seco a Venetia se ne venne. Ove giunti, che furono, egli gli disse, che il Moro era stato quegli, che gli havea tagliata la gamba, per openione, che gli era nata nella testa, che egli si giacesse con Disdemona: e, che, per questa medesima cagione egli haveva uccisa lei, e poscia data voce, che il palco caduto uccisa l' havesse. Il Capo di squadra, inteso ciò, accusò il Moro alla Signoria, e della gamba a lui tagliata, e della morte della Donna, et indusse per testimonio l' Alfieri, il quale disse; che l' uno, e l' altro era vero, perche il Moro haveva il tutto communicato seco, e l' havea voluto indurre a fare l' uno, e l' altro maleficio: e che, havendo poscia uccisa la Moglie, per bestial gelosia, che gli era nata nel capo, gli havea narrata la maniera, ch' egli havea tenuto in darle morte. I Signori Venetiani, intesa la crudeltà, usata dal Barbaro, in una lor cittadina, fecero dar delle mani addosso al Moro in Cipri, e condurlo a Venetia, e con molti tormenti cercarono di ritrovare il vero. Ma, vincendo egli, col valore dell' animo, ogni martorio, il tutto negò, così constantemente, che non se ne pote mai trarre cosa alcuna. Ma, se bene, per la sua constanza, egli schifò la morte, non fu però, che, dopo lo essere stato molti giorni in prigione, non fosse dannato a perpetuo essilio, nel quale finalmente fù da parenti della Donna, com' egli meritava, ucciso. Andò l' Alfieri alla sua patria: et, non volendo egli mancare del suo costume, accusò un suo compagno, dicendo, ch' egli ricercato l' havea di ammazzare un suo nimico, che gentilhuomo era, per la qual cosa fù preso colui, e messo al martorio: et negando egli esser vero, quanto dicea l' accusatore, fù messo al martorio anco l' Alfieri per paragone. Ove, fù talmente collato, che gli si corropero le interiora: onde, uscito

---

Moor; and seeking out the Captain, whose wound was by this time healed, and who went about with a wooden leg in place of the one that had been cut off, he said to him, ''Tis time you should be avenged for your lost limb; and if you will come with me to Venice, I'll tell you who the malefactor is, whom I dare not mention to you here for many reasons; and I will bring you proofs.'

The Captain of the troop, whose anger returned fiercely, but without knowing why, thanked the Ensign, and went with him to Venice.   On arriving there the Ensign told him that it was the Moor who had cut off his leg, on account of the suspicion he had formed of Disdemona's conduct with him; and for that reason he had slain her, and then spread the report that the ceiling had fallen and killed her.   Upon hearing which, the Captain accused the Moor to the Signoria, both of having cut off his leg and killed his wife, and called the Ensign to witness the truth of what he said.   The Ensign declared both charges to be true, for that the Moor had disclosed to him the whole plot, and had tried to persuade him to perpetrate both crimes; and that, having afterwards killed his wife out of jealousy he had conceived, he had narrated to him the manner in which he had perpetrated her death.

The Signoria of Venice, when they heard of the cruelty inflicted by a barbarian upon a lady of their city, commanded that the Moor's arms should be pinioned in Cyprus, and he be brought to Venice, where, with many tortures, they sought to draw from him the truth.   But the Moor, bearing with unyielding courage all the torment, denied the whole charge so resolutely that no confession could be drawn from him.   But, although by his constancy and firmness he escaped death, he was, after being confined for several days in prison, condemned to perpetual banishment, in which he was eventually slain by the kinsfolk of Disdemona, as he merited.   The Ensign returned to his own country, and, following up his wonted villainy, he accused one of his companions of having sought to persuade him to kill an enemy of his, who was a man of noble rank; whereupon this person was arrested and put to the torture; but when he denied the truth of what his accuser had declared, the Ensign himself was likewise tortured to make him prove the truth of his accusations; and he was tortured so that his body ruptured, upon

di prigione, et condotto a casa, miseramente sè ne morì; tal fece Iddio vendetta della innocenza di Disdemona. Et tutto questo successo narrò la Moglie dell' Alfieri, del fatto consapevole, poi ch' egli fù morto, come io lo vi hò narrato.

---

which he was removed from prison and taken home, where he died a miserable death. Thus did Heaven avenge the innocence of Disdemona; and all these events were narrated by the Ensign's wife, who was privy to the whole, after his death, as I have told them here.

OTHELLO'S COLOUR

GENTLEMAN (*Dram. Censor*, 1770, i, 151): I remember once to see this esteemed performer [Quin] play the Moor in a large powdered major wig, which, with the black face, made such a magpie appearance of his head, as tended greatly to laughter; one stroke, however, was not amiss—coming on in white gloves, by pulling off which the black hands became more realized. [Quin retired from the stage in 1750.—ED.]

Othello's colour, and Desdemona's indifference to it, is intimated and explained by LE TOURNEUR in a note on ' My Mother had a Maid called Barbarie,' IV, iii, 32, which he thus translates: ' Ma mere avoit auprès d'elle une jeune fille, nommée Barbara. C'étoit une Moresse, une pauvre Moresse,' and refers us to Othello's speech before the Senate, I, iii, 151, where, in a note, it is explained that, to Desdemona, Othello's ' couleur noire n'étoit pas non plus pour elle une nouveauté. On verra dans la suite, que sa mere avoit une Moresse à son service. Ainsi son amour pour un brave More n'a rien d'étrange ni d'invraisemblable. Habituée dès l'enfance à la compagnie d'une Moresse, elle a dû être moins révoltée de cette couleur dans un âge plus avancé.'

JOHN GALT (*Lives of the Players*, London, 1831, i, 268): It would be a curious speculation to attempt to determine the cause of Garrick's failure in Othello, for a failure it must be considered, as compared with his transcendency in other parts. In the just and natural inflection of the voice, we have no cause to doubt that he was equally excellent. The probability, therefore, is that he failed in the expression of the countenance alone, and that this default and short-coming to expectation was entirely owing to the black disguise he was obliged to assume.

On the epithet 'thick-lips,' applied, I, i, 72, by Roderigo to Othello, COLERIDGE (p. 249) has the following: Roderigo turns off to Othello; and here comes one, if not the only, seeming justification of our blackamoor or negro Othello. Even if we supposed this an uninterrupted tradition of the theatre, and that Shakespeare himself, from want of scenes, and the experience that nothing could be made too marked for the senses of his audience, had practically sanctioned it,—would this prove aught concerning his own intention as a poet for all ages? Can we imagine him so utterly ignorant as to make a barbarous negro plead royal birth,—at a time, too, when negroes were not known except as slaves? As for Iago's language to Brabantio, it implies merely that Othello was a Moor, that is, black. Though I think the rivalry of Roderigo sufficient to account for his wilful confusion of Moor and Negro, yet, even if compelled to give this up, I should think it only adapted for the acting of the day, and should complain of an enormity built on a single word, in direct contradiction to Iago's ' Barbary horse.' Besides, if we could in good earnest believe Shakespeare ignorant of the distinction, still why should we adopt one disagreeable possibility instead of a ten times greater and more pleasing probability? It is a common error to mistake the epithets applied by the *dramatis personæ* to each other as truly descriptive of what the audience ought to see or know. No doubt Desdemona saw Othello's visage in his mind; yet, as we are con stituted, and most surely as an English audience was disposed in the beginning of th. seventeenth century, it would be something monstrous to conceive this beautiful Vene- tian girl failing in love with a veritable negro. It would argue a disproportionateness, a want of balance, in Desdemona, which Shakespeare does not appear to have in the least contemplated.

HAWKINS (*Life of Edmund Kean*, i, 221): Kean regarded it as a gross error to make Othello either a negro or a black, and accordingly altered the conventional black to the light brown which distinguishes the Moors by virtue of their descent from the Caucasian race. Although in the tragedy Othello is described with a minuteness which leaves no doubt that Shakespeare intended him to be black, there is no reason to sup- pose that the Moors were darker than the generality of Spaniards, who, indeed, are half Moors, and compared with the Venetians he would even then be black. There is some variety in the colour of the Moors, but it never approaches so deep a hue as to conceal all change of colour. Betterton, Quin, Mossop, Barry, Garrick, and John Kemble all played the part with black faces, and it was reserved for Kean to innovate, and Coleridge to justify, the attempt to substitute a light brown for the traditional black. The alteration has been sanctioned by subsequent usage.

HUNTER (*New Illust.*, ii, 280): Shakespeare, in IV, ii, 257, seems to point to Mau- ritania as the native country of Othello, who is hence to be regarded as a Moor in the proper sense of the word, a native of the northern coast of Africa, towards the west; and the expression 'black' is to be interpreted as meaning no more than *very dark*, and this in comparison with the fair European. *Moor*, however, it may be observed, was used by English writers very extensively, and all the dark races seem, by some writers, to be regarded as comprehended under it. Sir Thomas Elyot calls the Ethi- opians, Moors. A distinction was sometimes made between black Moors and white Moors.

KNIGHT (*Note* on I, i, 72): This passage has been received as indicating the inten- tion of Shakespeare to make Othello a Negro. It is very probable that the popular notion of a Moor was somewhat confused in Shakespeare's time, and that the descend- ants of the proud Arabs, who had borne sovereign sway in Europe ('men of royal siege'), and, what is more, had filled an age of comparative darkness with the light of their poetry and their science, were confounded with the uncivilized African, the despised slave. We do not think, however, that Shakespeare had any other intention than to paint Othello as one of the most noble and accomplished of the proud children of the *Ommiades* and *Abbasides*. The expression 'thick-lips,' from the mouth of Rod- erigo, can only be received dramatically, as a nick-name given to Othello by the folly and ill-nature of this coxcomb. Whatever may have been the practice of the stage, even in Shakespeare's time,—and it is by no means improbable that Othello was repre- sented as a Negro,—the whole context of the play is against the notion. [The fol- lowing observations were communicated to Knight by a friend:] In the ages of her splendour, Venice was thronged with foreigners from every climate of the earth; and nowhere else, perhaps, has the prejudice of colour been so feeble. A more important fact, as regards Desdemona's attachment, is that it was the policy of the Republic to employ foreign mercenaries, and especially in offices of command, for the obvious pur- pose of lessening to the utmost the danger of cabal and intrigue at home. The fami- lies of Senators, or other chief citizens, were in the habit of seeing, in their dark-com- plexioned guests, those only who were distinguished by ability and by the official rank thereby gained,—picked men, whose hue might be forgotten in their accomplishments.

IT Hac'xitt's *Notes and Comments on Shakespeare*, pp. 217–249, are certain observations and opinions by JOHN QUINCY ADAMS, which cannot but 'make the judicious
grieve.' So high is my admiration for that great statesman, that it seems almost like
an act of lese-majestie, even to refer to these opinions here. The ex-President out-
Herauds Heraud in his denunciation of Desdemona; not, however, like Heraud, for
her lack of truth, but on the score of her wantonness as shown by her marriage with a
'rude, unbleached African.' It is enough to refer to these Notes; let who will, search
them out. I cannot but think that, by way of palliation, we may therein read between
the lines the public answer, wrung from the depths of vexation, to that inconsequent
question with which the Abolitionists of old were wont constantly to be assailed, and
which that 'old man eloquent' must have had thrust at him a thousand times : 'How
would you like your daughter to marry a nigger ? '—ED.

VERPLANCK : There was nothing in the Moor's descent so to affect his social position
in the eyes of Cinthio's readers or Shakespeare's audience, as to surprise them at his
being received on equal footing in the family of a Venetian noble, or attaining the
highest military rank in the service of the Republic. Yet it is equally clear that, in
regard to Desdemona, his race and colour are not a matter of indifference ; they are
especially dwelt upon as one of the grounds of jealousy ; they place between the Moor
and the Venetian lady a natural barrier, which it requires a 'downright violence and
storm of fortune' to break down. It is the admiration of high intellect, of heroic qualities and achievements,—such as has been sometimes known in real life to overcome
most strange disparities of age, character, and external circumstances,—which gives
the lady to see Othello's visage only 'in his mind.' She does not lose her own social
position by marriage with one under whom Italian and Cypriot nobles (Cassio, Iago,
Montano) are ambitious to serve, and with whom the princes and rulers of the State
associate as companions ; yet her love to him would appear in itself strange and unac-
countable, had not the Poet opened to us 'the pure recesses of her mind,' and showed
us whence it sprung.

WILSON (*Blackwood's Maga.*, April, 1850, p. 484):
' *NORTH*. I cannot but believe that the Othello of Shakespeare is black, and all
' black. I cannot conceive the ethnography of that age drawing, on the stage espe-
' cially, the finer distinction which we know between a Moor and a Blackamoor or
' Negro. The opposition, entertained by Nature, is between White and Black, not
' between White and Brown. You want the opposition to tell with all its power : " I
' saw Othello's visage in his mind " is nothing, unless the visible visage is one to be
' conquered,—to be accepted by losing sight of it. I say again, I cannot imagine the
' contemporary audience of Shakespeare deciding colour between a Moor and a Negro.
' The tradition of the Stage, too, seems to have made Othello jet black. Such, I opine,
' was the notion of the Moor, *then*, to the People, to the Court, to the Stage, to Shake-
' speare.
' *TALBOYS*. Woolly-headed ?
' *NORTH*. Why, yes,—if you choose,—in opposition to the "curled darlings."
' *TALBOYS*. Yet Coleridge said, " it would be something monstrous to conceive this
' beautiful Venetian girl falling in love with a veritable Negro."
' *NORTH*. Coleridge almost always thought, felt, wrote, and spoke finely, as a Critic,
' —but may I venture, in all love and admiration of that name, to suggest that the re-
' moval which the Stage makes of a subject from reality must never be forgotten ? In
' life you cannot bear that the White Woman shall marry the Black Man. You could
' not bear that an English Lady Desdemona,—Lady Blanche Howard,—should, under

'any imaginable greatness, marry General Toussaint or the Duke of Marmalade.
'Your senses revolt with offence and loathing. But on the stage some consciousness
'that everything is not as literally meant as it seems,—that symbols of humanity, and
'not actual men and women, are before you,—saves the Play.

' *TALBOYS*. I believe that Wordsworth's line, "The gentle Lady married to the
'Moor," expresses explicitly the feeling of the general English heart,—pity for the
'contrast, and a thought of the immense love that has overcome it.

' *NORTH*. White and Black is the utter antithesis,—as, at intensity, Night and Day.
'Yes, Talboys,—every jot of soot you take from his complexion, you take an iota from
'the signified power of love.

' *TALBOYS*. As you say, sir, the gap which is between the Stage and Reality must
'prevent, in our hearts, anything like loathing of the conjunction.

' *NORTH*. The touch of such an emotion would annul the whole Tragedy. A dis-
'parity, or a discrepancy, vast as mysterious,—but which love, at the full, is entitled to
'overlook—overstep! Whether Fate dare allow prosperity to a union containing so
'mighty an element of disruption, is another question. It seems like an attempt at
'overruling the "Æterna fœdera rerum.". . . . Talboys, I cannot help thinking that
'Shakespeare shows up in Othello foul passions,—that you see in him two natures con-
'joined,—the moral Caucasian White and animal tropical Black. In the Caucasian,
'the spiritual or angelical in us attains its manifestation. In the offspring of the trop-
'ics, amongst the sands and under the suns of Africa, the animal nature takes domina
'tion. The sands and suns that breed Lions, breed men with Lions' hearts in them.
'The Lion is for himself noble, but blood of the Irrational in the veins of the Rational
'is a contradiction. The noblest moral nature and the hot blind rage of animal blood!

' *TALBOYS*. Ay, the noblest moral nature, and high above every other evidence of it,
'his love of HER,—which, what it was, and what it would have remained, or become,—
'and what he was and would have been, had Iago not been there, we may imagine!
'With all the power of a warrior, and a ruler, he has the sensibility of a Lover,—with
'all spontaneous dignity and nobility, he has the self-mastery of reason,—before his
'overthrow.

' *NORTH*. Wherefore, my dear Sheriff, I prefer Othello as a specimen of the *Ethical
' Marvellous*. Like, as in another kingdom, a Winged Horse, or a Centaur,—the meet-
'ing of two natures which readily hold asunder. All this has under the Æthiop com-
'plexion its full force,—less if you mitigate,—if not mitigate merely, but take away,
'where are we all? The innate repugnance of the White Christian to the Black Moor-
'ish blood, is the ultimate tragic substratum,—the "*must*" of all that follows. Else,—
'*make* Othello White,—and, I say again, *see* where we are!

' *TALBOYS*. Shakespeare, sir, was not one to flinch from the utmost severity of a
'Case.

' *NORTH*. Not he, indeed,—therefore I *swear* Othello is a Blackamoor.

' *TALBOYS*. And I take it, sir, that Othello's natural demeanour is one of great grav-
'ity, to which the passionate moods induced are in extremity of contrast. I conceive
that, by these mixtures and contrasts, he is rendered picturesque and poetical.

' *NORTH*. I swear Othello was a Blackamoor,—and that Desdemona was the Whitest
'Lady in Europe.'

GRANT WHITE (*Shakespeare's Scholar*, 1854, p. 432): Shakespeare nowhere calls
Othello an Ethiopian, and also does not apply the term to Aaron in the horrible *Titus
Andronicus;* but he continually speaks of both as Moors; and as he has used the first
word elsewhere, and certainly had use for it as a reproach in the mouth of Iago, it

seems that he must have been fully aware of the distinction in grade between the two races, although his notion of their distinctive traits was, perhaps, neither very true nor very clear. Indeed, I could never see the least reason for supposing that Shakespeare intended Othello to be represented as a negro. With the negroes the Venetians had nothing to do, that we know of, and could not have, in the natural course of things; whereas, with their over-the-way neighbours, the Moors, they were continually brought in contact. These were a warlike, civilized, and enterprising race, which could furnish an Othello; whereas, the contrary has always been the condition of the negroes. The reasons for supposing Othello to be a negro are few and easily set aside, which is not the case of those which show him to be a Moor. The most conclusive of the former is Roderigo's calling Othello 'thick lips'; but this is the result of Shakespeare's want of exact information. He had, doubtless, never seen either a Moor or a negro, and might very naturally confuse their physiological traits; but a man of his knowledge and penetration could not fail to know the difference between the position and the character of the nation which built the Alhambra and that which furnished their stock in trade to the Englishmen who, when he wrote *Othello*, were supplying the plantations in the West Indies with slaves, and, soon after his death, introduced negro slavery into Virginia. In addition to this epithet 'thick lips,' there are several allusions to Othello as having the visage of the devil, as black, and as being, therefore, the very reverse of attractive to a woman like Desdemona. But this proves nothing; for Shakespeare has applied these identical epithets to so eminent and undeniable a Moor as the Prince of Morocco. In the *Mer. of Ven.* I, ii, Portia says, upon the announcement of the royal Moor, 'if he have the condition of a saint and the complexion of a devil, I had rather he would shrive me than wive me.' He himself prays her, 'Mislike me not for my complexion'; and she, when he has selected the wrong casket, says, 'May all of his complexion choose me so'; and yet he was not jetty black like a negro, but tawny; for the stage direction in II, i, in the Qq is, '*Enter*, Morochus, *a tawny Moor, all in white.*' Plainly, then, the devilish visage attributed to Othello, and the assumed repulsiveness of his colour, makes him out, in Shakespeare's estimation, only a Moor, and not even a very black Moor at that. But there is direct evidence that he was a Mauritanian [from Iago's calling him a 'Barbary horse,' and from his telling Roderigo that Othello was going to Mauritania].

HENRY REED (*Lectures on Tragic Poetry*, p. 268): The repulsive notion that Othello was a black,—a coarse-featured African,—seems to me directly at variance with the requisitions of both poetry and history; and I cannot but think it is an error, which may be traced either to some false critical theory, or else more probably to the too literal interpretation of passages in the play, the unimaginative reading which is fatal so often to the spirit of poetry. The hero is styled 'Othello, *the Moor*;' such is his title and familiar designation throughout. He was one of that adventurous race of men who, striking out from the heart of Arabia, had made conquest of Persia and Syria; and, overturning the ancient sovereignty of Egypt, swept in victory along the whole northern coast of Africa; and, passing thence across the narrow frith of the Mediterranean, scattered the dynasty of the Goths with Roderic at their head. . . . . How true to his nature was it for Othello to stand in conscious pride,—the descendant of a race of kings, the representative of the Arabs who had been sovereigns of Europe,—his spirit glowing with noble ancestral memories! And, on the other hand, how perfectly consistent it was with the debasing malignity of Iago, and with the petulant disappointment of Roderigo, to be blind to all that ennobled and dignified the Moorish name— to see no distinction between the chivalrous Moor, the chieftain of Christian armies, and the barbarous Ethiop,—the despised slave. It was natural that vulgar words should be uttered from the lips of such men, and also that the parental frenzy of Desdemona's father should find relief in the same strain of vituperative misrepresentation, the propensity of a fresh and angry grief to magnify its injury. Such are the authorities that have led to the supposition that Othello was black. In one scene, indeed, he speaks so of himself; but it is when he is in Iago's grasp,—when he is 'changing with the poison.' The agony of doubt has heaved over the lofty complacent bearing of his happier moments, and his speaking of himself as black is,—what is very natural to such condition of mind,—a piece of morbid exaggeration; just as when, in the same scene, he describes himself as 'declined into the vale of years.' On every account, it is better to clear the fancy of this false conception of Othello's colour, most of all for the sake of our sympathies with the gentle Desdemona; for if we are brought to believe that this bright, this fair-faced, Venetian lady was wedded to a black, we should almost be tempted to think that the monstrous alliance was fitly blotted out in its fearful catastrophe. . . . . The Moorish complexion of Othello, not intended to produce in our minds disgust at Desdemona's choice, is made to serve an important dramatic purpose, in that it greatly ministers to his suspicions of his wife's fidelity. It is the first unprompted argument for doubt; the first suggested by Othello's own thoughts, and, of course, quickly seized on and fomented by Iago. It serves, too, to account for the extreme sensitiveness of Othello's sense of honour,—that which is a prime element in his character.

J. E. TAYLOR (*Introduction to Trans. of Cinthio*, p. 13) : We have merely to deal with the poet's own conception of the character, and to take this as the standard by which to judge its delineation : the drama, as a work of art, is simply amenable to the rules of art. And this is an instructive instance of the fact that artistic truth may consist with accidental errors which lie beyond the pale of art ; the character of Othello may be in itself perfect,—faultless ; and yet, when a nationality is affixed to it, it may violate the physical and moral laws of nature displayed in the distinction of races. This is a very minor point of mere speculation, not of criticism ; still it is open to discussion. The novelist speaks of the *blackness* (negrezza) of the Moor, and that Shakespeare had the outward figure of a black present to his thoughts appears more than probable from numerous allusions in the Play. . . . . Nothing can be more conclusive than these expressions, and the tradition of the Stage (there is reason to believe) has uniformly represented Othello as a black from Shakespeare's day to the present. Nevertheless, this in no degree affects the character of the Moor, for the reasons just stated.

HALLIWELL : The reference to 'Mauritania,' IV, ii, 257, surely settles the disputed question, Was Othello a negro ? Certainly not. He was a Moor of lofty lineage, with thick lips and a very dark complexion. 'Black Othello' was the dark-complexioned Othello. So the word 'black' was employed in Shakespeare's time, as in the following extract : ' *Quest.* Why do some women love men that bee blacke, and other, those that be faire and well coloured ? *An.* Women of feeble sight love them that bee blacke, because blacknesse doth joyne and unite the sight too much disparkled, and by this meanes doth comfort the same. Or else we may well say that every thing doth love and desire his like. They therefore which be hote of nature love them that be blacke, because they be more prone to heate. Other which be of colder nature do love them that be white, because they bě of cold complexion, the mother of whitenesse.'—*Delect-*
ble Demaundes and Pleasant Questions, 1596, p. 10.

HUDSON (also in reference to 'Mauritania') : This passage proves, so far as anything said ⟩y Iago may be believed, that Othello was not meant to be a Negro, as has been represented, both on the stage and off, but a veritable Moor. His kindred, the Mauritanians,—from whose 'men of royal siege he fetched his life and being,' and among whom he was about to retire,—though apt enough to be confounded with the negroes, were as different from them externally as brown is from black; internally, in mind and character, the difference was far greater. [In his *Preface*, p. 33, Hudson writes:] The difference of Moors and Negroes was as well known in Shakespeare's time as it is now; and that he thought them the same is no more likely from this play than from *The Merchant of Venice*, where the Prince of Morocco comes as a suitor to Portia, and in a stage direction of the Qto is called 'a *tawny* Moor.'

MARY PRESTON (*Studies in Shakespeare*, 1869, p. 71): In studying the play of *Othello*, I have always *imagined* its hero *a white* man. It is true the dramatist paints him black, but this shade does not suit the man. It is a stage decoration, which *my taste* discards; a fault of colour from an artistic point of view. I have, therefore, as I before stated in *my readings* of this play, dispensed with it. Shakespeare was too correct a delineator of human nature to have coloured Othello *black*, if he had personally acquainted himself with the idiosyncrasies of the African race.

We may regard, then, the daub of black upon Othello's portrait as an *ebullition* of fancy, a *freak* of imagination,—the visionary conception of an ideal figure,—one of the few erroneous strokes of the great master's brush, the *single* blemish on a faultless work.

Othello *was* a *white* man! [The Authoress dates her Preface from 'Oaklands, Harford County, Maryland.'—ED.]

LEWES (*On Actors and the Art of Acting*, p. 145): Othello is black,—the very tragedy lies there; the whole force of the contrast, the whole pathos and extenuation of his doubts of Desdemona, depend on this blackness. Fechter makes him a half-caste, whose mere appearance would excite no repulsion in any woman out of America.

ERL RYGENHOEG (*Am. Bibliopolist*, Dec., 1875): A thousand examples might be quoted to show that in Shakespeare's time a dark or *brunette* complexion was indicated by calling a person 'black.' Thus, in the English Bible, 1611, *Song of Solomon*, i, 6, 7; and in the very play under consideration, II, i, Desdemona asks, 'How if she be *black* and witty?'

SNIDER (i, 105): Othello was not a Hottentot on the one hand, nor was he a Caucasian on the other; he was, however, born in Africa, and his physiognomy is thoroughly African. The point which the Poet emphasizes so often and so strongly is the difference of race between him and Desdemona. He is her equal in rank, for he comes of royal lineage; he is the peer of her family in honor and fame, for he is the most distinguished man in Venice. The sole difference which is selected as the ground of the collision is the difference of race. This fact is sufficient for all dramatic purposes, to ascertain the exact shade of his skin may be left to those who have leisure to play with probabilities.

GRANT WHITE (*Note in 2d Edition on* 'thick lips,' I, i, 72): Shakespeare's notions about Moors and Negroes were, we may be sure, far from being clear and discriminating; and it is to be remarked that even Moors have thicker lips than the white European races.

[That Shakespeare meant to represent Othello as 'black,' I cannot but think, and 'black' in the full meaning of the word, not 'dark-complexioned' as Desdemona uses it in 'How if she be black and witty,' nor 'tawny,' but thoroughly *black*. Disregarding the 'thick lips' of Iago, or the 'sootie bosome' of Brabantio, or any phrase uttered by Othello's enemies in moments of passion, to me, beyond a peradventure, Othello himself supplies the evidence, 'which will not down,' where he says (III, iii, 445): 'My name that was as fresh As Dian's visage, is now *begrim'd and blacke* As mine owne face.' The epithet 'begrim'd' amplifies and confirms the sootie hue. Its æsthetic propriety, I am taught by Wilson; its offencelessness, when I read the play, I learn from Lamb; and since actors now present the tawny hve, I am not offended when 'sitting at the play.'—ED.]

ACTORS

THE first Actor of Othello was RICHARD BURBAGE, at whose death, in 1618, appeared an Elegy, which, 'from a manuscript in the possession of the late Mr Heber,' Collier printed in his *History of Dramatic Poetry* (iii, 299, 2nd ed.). The following are the lines which relate to Othello:

> ' But let me not forget one chiefest part
> ' Wherein, beyond the rest, he mov'd the heart,
> ' The grievèd Moor, made jealous by a slave,
> ' Who sent his wife to fill a timeless grave,
> ' Then slew himself upon the bloody bed.
> ' All these and many more with him are dead.'

Another version is given in Ingleby's *Centurie of Prayse* (p. 131, 2nd ed.) from a MS. in the Huth Library, whereof all that concerns us here is as follows:

> ' hee's gone & wth him what A world are dead.
> ' which he reuiu'd, to be reuiued foe,
> ' no more young Hamlett, ould Heironymoe
> ' kind Leer, the Greued Moore, and more befide,
> ' that liued in him; haue now for euer dy'de.'

The name of NATHAN FIELD appears among the list of Actors, prefixed to the First Folio. Collier in his *Hist. of Dram. Poetry* (iii, 437, 2d ed.) has the following concerning him : ' If we may believe an epigram written about this time and handed down to us in MS, Field was of a jealous turn of mind ; and it leads us to remark upon the probability that Burbage, some time before his death, had relinquished to Field the part of Othello.' [The first two, and last two lines of this epigram, are as follows :] ' Field is, in sooth, an actor—all men know it, And is the true Othello of the poet. . . . . Since, as the Moore is jealous of his wife, Field can display the passion to the life.'

HALLIWELL-PHILLIPS (*Outlines*, 5th ed., p. 177): The Tragedy of *Othello*, originally known under the title of the Moor of Venice, ... was very popular, Leonard Digges speaking of the audiences preferring it to the laboured compositions of Ben Jor3o2. In 1609, a Stage-loving parent, one William Bishop of Shoreditch, who had perhaps been taken with the representation of the tragedy, gave the name of Othello's perfect wife to one of his twin daughters. . . . . These scattered notices, accidentally preserved, doubtlessly out of many others that might have been recorded, are indicative of its continuance as an acting play; a result that may, without disparagement to the author, be attributed in some measure to the leading character having been assigned to the most accomplished tragic actor of the day,—Richard Burbage. The name of the first performer of Iago is not known, but there is a curious tradition, which can be traced as far back as the close of the Seventeenth century, to the effect that the part was originally undertaken by a popular comedian, and that Shakespeare adapted some of the speeches of that character to the peculiar talents of the actor. [Hereupon are given the two following Illustrative Notes:] According to Wright's *Historia Histrionica*, 1699, p. 4, Taylor was distinguished in this part [Iago], but probably not until after the death of Shakespeare. The insertion of Taylor's name in the list of Shakespearian actors in ed. 1623, merely proves that he had been one of them in or before that year. 'I'm assur'd, from very good hands, that the person that acted Iago was in much esteem of a comedian which made Shakespear put several words and expressions into his part, perhaps not so agreeable to his character, to make the audience laugh, who had not yet learnt to endure to be serious a whole play.'—Gildon's *Reflections on Rymer's Short View of Tragedy*, 1694.

MALONE (*Hist. Account of the English Stage*, Var. '21, vol. iii, p. 126): The first woman that appeared in any regular drama on a public stage, performed the part of Desdemona; but who the lady was, I am unable to ascertain. The play of *Othello* is enumerated by Downes as one of the stock-plays of the King's Company on their opening their theatre in Drury Lane in 1663; and it appears from a paper found with Sir Henry Herbert's Office-book, that it was one of the stock-plays of the same company from the time they began to play without a patent at the Red Bull in St. John Street. Mrs Hughs performed the part of Desdemona in 1663, when the company removed to Drury Lane, and obtained the title of the King's Servants; but whether she performed with them while they played at the Red Bull, or in Vere Street, has not been ascertained. Perhaps Mrs Saunderson made her first essay there, though she afterwards was enlisted in D'Avenant's Company. The received tradition is, that she was the first English actress. [Mrs Saunderson afterwards married Betterton. Unmarried women were not called *Miss* 'until after the Revolution,' says Davies in his edition of Downes, p. 28; the first instance of its use which he found was in Flecknoe's Epigrams, 1669.—ED.] The verses which were spoken by way of introducing a female to the audience were written by Thomas Jordan, printed, I believe, in 1662. [Malone here reprints the whole Prologue, but I think a short extract will satisfy all demands of curiosity or of refinement:]

> 'But to the point:—In this reforming age
> 'We have intents to civilize the stage.
> 'Our women are defective, and so siz'd
> 'You'd think they were some of the guard disguis'd:
> 'For to speak truth, men act, that are between
> 'Forty and fifty, wenches of fifteen;
> 'With bone so large, and nerve so incompliant,
> 'When you call Desdemona, enter Giant.—
> 'We shall purge everything that is unclean,
> 'Lascivious, scurrilous, impious, or obscene;
> 'And when we've put all things in this fair way,
> 'Barebones himself may come to see a play.'

The Epilogue is in the same strain of apology [with a side-light thrown on Othello's colour]:

> 'Then he that censures her in such a case,
> 'Hath a soul blacker than Othello's face.
> 'But ladies what think *you?* for if you tax
> 'Her freedom with dishonour to your sex,
> 'She means to act no more, and this shall be
> 'No other play but her own tragedy.'

From a paper in Sir Henry Herbert's handwriting, I find that *Othello* was performed by the Red Bull Company (afterwards his Majesty's Servants) at their new theatre in Vere Street, near Clare Market, on Saturday, December 8, 1660, for the first time that winter. On that day, therefore, it is probable an actress first appeared on the English stage.

COLLIER (*New Facts*, &c., 1835, p. 6) stated that he had been permitted to examine at Bridgewater House the manuscripts of Lord Ellesmere, the Keeper of the Great Seal to Queen Elizabeth and Lord Chancellor to James I; among the papers, there preserved, he found a volume of MS Ballads; collected, as he conjectured, 'about the date of the Protectorate, when old broadsides were becoming scarce, and new ones far from abundant, as the Puritans set their faces against anything like popular amusements. I apprehend that most of those in the volume were copied from printed originals, many of which are now lost.' In the list of these Ballads, as given by Collier (*New Particulars*, &c., 1836, p. 45), there appeared the following: 'Tragedy of *Othello* the Moor. 'Anonymous, but following Shakespeare's Tragedy very closely. Not printed.'

'There can be no doubt,' Collier goes on to say, 'that this Ballad was written subsequently to Shakespeare's tragedy; it was founded upon the play in consequence of its popularity, and not the play upon it. . . . . It varies slightly from the play, and makes Iago a Spaniard, as indeed his name indicates. The change was, perhaps, made in accordance with the prejudice of the time when it was written, possibly about 1625, after the breaking off of the Spanish Match. It is as follows, and here I preserve the spelling of the MS, since it may aid in some degree in fixing the age of the production:

THE TRAGEDIE OF OTHELLO THE MOORE

The foule effects of jealousie,
  Othelloe's deadly hate,
Iagoe's cruell treacherie,
  And Desdemonae's fate,
In this same ballad you may reade,
  If soe you list to bye,
Which tells the blackest, bloodiest **deede**
  Yet ever seen with eye.

In Venice City, long time since,
  A Noble Moore did live,
Who to the daughter of a Prince
  In secrecie did wive.
She was as faire as he was blacke,
  A sunshine and a cloude:
She was as milde as playfull childe,
  But he was fierce and proude.

And lovede he her, as well he **might,**
  For deerlie she lovde him:
She doated on his brow of night,
  And on each swarthie limbe.
Othello was this noble Moore,
  A Souldeir often tride,
Who many victories did procure
  To swell Venetian pride.

Faire Desdemona was the name
  This lovelie ladie bare:
Her father had great wealth and **fame,**
  And she his onelie heire.

Therefore, when he at length found out
   His daughter thus was wed,
To breake their bonds he cast about,
   But onelie firmer made.

And much rejoiced he to know,
   And to that end did worke,
The State his wife would part him fro
   To fight against the Turke.
But she ne would remaine behinde,
   For that she did not wed;
She'd live and die with one so kinde,
   And soe she plainlie said.

The Turkes the while did threat the Isle
   Of Cyprus with a fray,
And thither must Othello speede
   And that without delaye.
To Cyprus steere they both, nor feare
   Could touch the lady's hart;
The Lord she lovde she knew was neare,
   Whom death should not depart.

But when they came to Cyprus Isle
   To her great joye they found,
That heaven had fought the fight the while
   The Turkes were sunk and drownd.
A storme had late assailde their fleete,
   That most of them were lost:
And you will owne it was most meete
   The crescent should be crost.

Now, while upon the Isle they stayde,
   The luckelesse lotte befell,
By a false Spaniard's wicked ayde,
   Which I am now to tell.
He was the Antient to the Moore
   For he so closelie wrought,
He held him honest, trusty, sure,
   Until he found him nought.

Iago was the monster's name,
   Who lovde the lady long;
But she denied his sute and claime,
   Though with a gentle tongue.
For this he silent vengeance vowd
   Upon the happie Moore,
And took a way without delay
   To make his vengeance sure.

There was a Captain of the band,
   And Cassio was his name,
In happie moode by nature pland,
   Of strong and lustie frame:
He was Lieftenant to the Moore,
   A post of trust and weight,
And therefore he must partner bee
   Of the foule traitor's hate.

He whisper'd at Othelloe's backe
   His wife had chaungde her minde,
And did not like his sootie blacke,
   As he full soone would finde;

But much preferrd the ruddie dye
  Of her owne countreymen;
And bade him keepe a warie eye
  On her deportment then.

Tut, tut, then quoth the hastie Moore,
  Deepe as the throat you lye.
I wish I did, quoth he, for sure
  Much liefer would I die,
Then see what I my selfe have seene.
  What have you seene ? he cride—
What onelie would become a queane,
  Not my deare general's bride.

Ile heare no more, Othello said :
  That I am blacke is true,
And she is faire as morning ayre
  But that she always knew.
Well onelie keepe a warie eye
  Upon her actions now :
Cassio's the man, I do not lye,
  As you will soone allowe.

You thought she lovde you, that she came
  With you to this hot Isle :
Cassio was with you, and the dame
  On him did closelie smile.
I needes must grieve to see my Lord
  So wantonly deceived :
Thus far I prithee take my word,
  It is to be believed.

O god, what proofe hast thou of this ,
  What proofe that she is foule ?
Proofe you would have—tis not amis,
  Ile give it on my soule.

Cassio will talke you in his sleepe,
  And speakes then of your wife.
He cannot anie secret keepe
  An it would save his life
This showes that he may love my wife,
  The doubting Moore replied ;
And if tis true she loves him too,
  Better they both had died.

Behold, my Lord, Iago said,
  Know you this token true ?
And then a handkerchief displaid,
  Which well Othello knewe.
Twas one he Desdemona gave
  When they were wedded first,
Wrought with embroiderie so brave :
  With rage he well nie burst.

Whence got you that, whence got you that ?
  Tell me or instant die !
She gave it Cassio, but thereat
  Why roll your yellow eye ?
It is but one of tokens more
  That he, I know, can bost ;
And she has his, no doubt, good store,
  I recke not which has most.

Now, this same well knowne handkerchiefe
  That very morne he stole,
And thus the cruel vengeful theife
  Rackde brave Othelloes soule.
His wife was true, and pure as dewe
  Upon the lillie white.
No bounds his tameless passion knew
  But rushing from the sight,

He sought his lady as she layde
  Within her virgin bed,
And there his hands of blackest shade
  He dyed to gory red :
But first he chargde her with the crime,
  Which ever she denyed,
And askt but for a little time
  To prove the traytor lyed.

O, twas a piteous sight to see
  A thing so meeke and faire,
Torne with such salvage crueltie
  By her long lovelie haire.
Then came the caitiffe to rejoyce
  His blacke hart with the viewe,
But soone twas provde by many a voice
  The Ladie had beene true.

Twas provde the handkerchiefe he stole,
  And then the same he layde
Where Cassio for a suertie came,
  That he might be betrayde.
Othello stood as one distraught
  To heare what thus was showne,
That Desdemona, even in thought,
  To sinne had never knowne.

He fomde, he stampt, he ravde, he tore,
  To thinke upon his deede
Then struck Iago to the floore,
  But onelie made him bleede.
For deadliest tortures he was savde,
  And suffring them he dide :
A lesson milde to traytors vilde,
  May such them still betide.

Upon his Desdemonae's coarse
  Othello cast him than,
In agonie of deepe remorse,
  A broken harted man.
With charitie, he said, relate
  What you this day have seene,
Think once how well I servde the State,
  And what I once have beene.

Then with the dagger, that was wet
  With his dear Ladies bloud,
He stabde him selfe and thus out let
  His soule in gory floud.
This storie true you oft times knew,
  By actors playde for meede ;
But still so well, twas hard to tell
  If twas not truth in deede.

Dicke Burbidge, that most famous man,
   That actor without peere,
With this same part his course began,
   And kept it manie a yeare.
Shakespeare was fortunate, I trow,
   That such an actor had.
If we had but his equall now
   For one I should be glad.

Finis.

[In a foot-note on the fourth line of the last stanza, Collier says :] 'As Burbage "began his course" as an actor many years before *Othello* was written, the meaning of the author of this ballad may be that Burbage played the part of Othello originally, and retained it until his death.   Otherwise, we must take it as a mere guess, and not a happy one, that Burbage commenced as an actor in *Othello*.   The great probability is, that Burbage was upon the stage, as a boy, when Shakespeare first joined the company in 1586 or 1587.'   [Collier reiterates in the text that] 'Burbage was, of course, dead, and it is certainly a mistake to assert that he began his course with Othello.'   [Some of the other ballads in this volume have been held to be spurious, and, I suppose, on the principle of *noscitur ex sociis*, doubts have been cast on the foregoing.   Indeed, INGLEBY publicly challenged its genuineness in *The Academy* in 1876.   The stanza which he selected as proving its 'very modern composition' is the tenth, and the line which he therein italicised is, '*He whisper'd at Othelloe's backe*'; he also italicised, in the same stanza, the words '*much preferrd.*'   He then justifies his challenge and marshals his proof that the whole ballad is a forgery, as follows : ' The first line of this ' stanza [viz. the line just quoted in Italics] might have been suggested by the second ' of Retsch's Outlines to Schiller's *Fridolin*, of which Mr Collier published a transla- ' tion of great merit in 1824.'   This is all the proof, which I can find, that he adduces. That a scholar so eminent and a critic so keen should, with apparent gravity, give us this hypothetical pluperfect subjunctive *might have been*, after whetting our appetites for a downright perfect indicative *was*, lay beyond my comprehension, till my eye caught the date of the Number of *The Academy*—the First of April!—ED.]

SAMUEL PEPYS, 1660, October 11.—Here, in the Park, we met with Mr Salisbury, who took Mr Creed and me to the Cockpit to see 'The Moor of Venice,' which was well done.   Burt acted the Moor; by the same token, a very pretty lady that sat by me, called out, to see Desdemona smothered.

1666, August 20.—To Deptford by water, reading 'Othello, Moor of Venice,' which I ever heretofore esteemed a mighty good play; but having so lately read 'The Adventures of Five Houres,' it seems a mean thing.

1668, February 6.—To the King's playhouse, and there . . . . did see 'The Moor of Venice' but ill acted in most parts; Mohun, which did a little surprise me, not acting Iago's part by much so well as Clun used to do; nor another Hart's, which was Cassio's; nor, indeed, Burt doing the Moor's so well as I once thought he did.*

Hawkins (*Life of Kean*, ii, 379): On the 25th of March, 1833, KEAN made his last appearance, as it proved, in Othello, Charles Kean being the Iago and Ellen Tree the Desdemona.   There had been no rehearsal.   He was assisted from his carriage into the dressing-room, where he sank, drooping and nerveless, into a chair.   'Tell my boy,' he said to Charles Kemble, with whom he had become reconciled, 'that I want

---

* All of Pepys's allusions to Shakespeare's plays are collected in INGLEBY's admirable *Centurie of Prayse*; from which those only which refer to *Othello* are here given.—ED.

to see him.' When Charles entered the dressing-room, he found his father so weak that he deemed it advisable to ask Mr Warde to be in readiness to proceed with the part in case of an emergency. 'I am very ill,' Kean murmured; 'I am afraid I shall not be able to go on.' Cheered up by Charles Kemble, who stood by his side with a glass of very hot brandy-and-water, he dressed himself with difficulty. Charles led his father from the dressing-room to the wing, and as the Scene opened they went on. 'The Scene in which the Moor appeared, followed by mine Ancient,' says a writer in *Fraser's Magazine* three months afterwards, 'can never be forgotten by those who beheld it. The applause was tumultuous,—the spirit of enthusiasm pervaded all,—and never more, perhaps, were the generous sympathies of an audience displayed more vividly than at this moment. It may well be considered an era in the annals of the Stage, for we might vainly trace through those annals for a parallel to that scene. It was not merely the fact of a father and son having attained to such excellence in the histrionic art as to be thus qualified to assume, in the same play and on the same occasion, the two most difficult characters in the whole range of the tragic drama, unprecedented as that fact really is,—it was not the mere novelty of a new Iago; but there stood Edmund Kean, the only Othello of the modern stage, no longer opposing the bent of his son's genius, but sacrificing all his repugnance to that son's adoption of his profession, and entering with him upon a trial of skill in that play in which so many an Iago had proved but a foil. It was a spectacle never to be forgotten, to see the great tragedian leading forward his son,—attesting, with a father's pride, their perfect reconciliation,—enjoying the paternal triumph which his success at so early an age could not fail to excite in such a heart as Kean's.' The performance progressed. Noble as ever was his quiet rebuke of Cassio,—'How comes it, Michael, you are thus forgot?' majestic and portentous as ever was his dismissal of the offender. Before the great Third Act commenced he found that his strength was rapidly sinking, and he anxiously enjoined his son,—'Mind, Charley, that you keep before me; don't get behind me in this Act. I don't know that I shall be able to kneel; but, if I do, be sure that you lift me up.' He went on; his determination seemed more than a match for his weakness; and as Iago distilled the first drops of poison into his ear, the force, beauty, and truth of his acting exhibited the evidence of the unfading charm within. He came off with Desdemona, and as he seated himself in a chair near one of the wings, he said, with obvious gratification, 'Charles is getting on to-night; he's acting very well. I suppose that is because he is playing with me.' When he re-entered with 'What, false to *me!*' &c., it was with difficulty that he succeeded in keeping his footing, but the stillness of the immense auditory in front seemed to make him think that something *must* be done, and he shone out brilliantly in the authoritative repulsion of Iago, 'Avaunt, begone,' and the whirlwind of passion with which he continued to accompany, 'I found not Cassio's kisses on her lips.' This exertion cost him dear, as his increasing feebleness showed; but the 'Farewell' apostrophe was as sweet, as musical, as unutterably pathetic as of old. For the last time the melodiousness of his unexerted tones 'came over the spirit like the desolate moaning of the blast that precedes the thunderstorm,' or like 'the hollow and not unmusical murmur of the midnight sea after the tempest had raved itself to rest'; for the last time those tones 'sank into the heart like the sighing of the gentle breeze among the strings of an aëolian harp, or among the branches of a cypress grove,'—*farewell!* 'Is it possible?—my lord!' and then as he endeavoured to abandon himself to the overwhelming storm of passion which followed this calm,—rage, hatred, intervening doubts,—all the Moorish fire and passionateness which blazed out as he turned upon Iago,—a marked change came over the tragedian,

—he trembled,—stopped,—tottered,—reeled; Charles, fearing the worst, went forward and extended his arms; the father made another effort and advanced towards his son with, ' Villain, be sure,' &c., but it was of no use, and with a whispered moan, ' I am dying,—speak to them for me,' he sank insensible into Charles's arms.' A saddening conviction that the acting of Edmund Kean was at an end impressed itself upon the hearts of all; amidst earnest and sympathizing applause he was gently removed from the sight of those whom he had so often moved to admiration, to terror, to wonder, and to tears; and with a delicacy rarely indeed displayed in a theatre, the major part of the audience, not waiting to see the play finished, went away. [Three weeks later, on the 15th of May, Kean died.]

COSTUME

MURPHY (*Life of Garrick*, i, 105): Garrick's benefit was announced in the month of March, for that night he was prepared to act the *Moor of Venice*. He was aware that his stature was inferior to that of his predecessors, and, to assist his figure, he chose to appear in a Venetian dress.

[It may be rash to say it, but I doubt if this ' Venetian dress' amounted to anything more than a high Oriental turban with a plume on it; my reason for this supposition is, that it was this costume which gave rise to a witticism which has been variously attributed to Quin, to Foote, and to Garrick himself, and which would lose its point if the costume were wholly Venetian or wholly Oriental. Hogarth's series of pictures, with which we are all familiar, ' The Harlot's Progress,' were at that time in the height of their popularity; ladies' fans were decorated with copies of them, and the series had even been put on the stage, I believe, as tableaux. One of the series represents the heroine upsetting the breakfast table, just as a little Negro page is bringing in the tea-kettle. The boy is jet black with rolling white eyes, and dressed in laced coat and knee-breeches, and with a disproportionately large turban on his head surmounted by an aigret. When Garrick, then, appeared on the stage in his novel costume as Othello, it is said that Quin exclaimed to his neighbour, ' Here's Pompey,—but where's the tea-kettle?' Garrick's dress, therefore, must have been the same as Pompey's, or there would have been no laugh. Although both Quin and Foote were fully clever enough, and more than cruel enough, to make the speech, yet I prefer to think that it was Garrick himself, as I have seen it somewhere stated, who said when he was dressing for the stage: ' I suppose Quin will say when he sees me, "Here's Pompey, but where's the tea-kettle?"' To this is sometimes added, ' the tea-kettle *and the lamp*,' which I am afraid reveals an unfamiliarity, on the part of the narrator, with the source of the witticism. Fitzgerald (*Life of Garrick*, i, 153) distinctly says, that on this occasion Garrick was dressed in a ' bright scarlet officer's coat.'—ED.]

RUSSELL (*Representative Actors*, p. 128): In his autobiography, F. Reynolds tells us he remembers seeing Barry act Othello ' in a full suit of gold-laced scarlet, a small cocked hat, knee-breeches, and silk stockings, conspicuously displaying a pair of gouty legs.'

BOADEN (*Life of Kemble*, i, 256): In March, 1785, *Othello* was acted at Drury-Lane Theatre; Othello by Mr Kemble—Desdemona, Mrs Siddons. The dress of the Moor at that time was a British general officer's uniform, equally improper with the Moorish jacket and trousers of modern times. The general of an Italian State would wear its uniform; he would never be indulged with a privilege of strutting about like ' a malignant and a turbaned Turk' at the head of a Christian army. Mr Kemble always played parts of this character very finely. He was grand, and awful, and pathetic. But he was a European; there seemed to be philosophy in his bearing; there was reason in his rage; he acted as if Othello truly described himself when he calls himself 'one not easily jealous.' He had never, I think, so completely worked himself into the character as to be identified with it, as was surely the case in his Hamlet, his Macbeth, his King John.

KNIGHT: It has been maintained that, as General of the Venetian army, Othello should wear a Venetian dress; while, on the other hand, it has been contended that the Moorish garb was the more correct, as well as more effective. That Othello was a Christian may be inferred from his marriage with a Christian, and we have, moreover, Iago's express testimony, where, in II, iii, he speaks of Othello as ready, for Desdemona's sake, to renounce 'his baptism, All seals and symbols of redeemed sin.' There ought, therefore, to be no question as to which habit is more correct; the convert would indubitably put off his turban with his faith, and assume the dress of that Republic whose religion he had adopted and whose officer he had become. Indeed, from the commencement of Act II, there can be neither doubt nor choice allowed on the subject, as the General of the Venetian forces, to whatever nation he might trace his birth (and he was always a *foreigner*) [see I, iii, 61], assumed, on the day of his election, a peculiar habit, consisting of a full gown of crimson velvet, with loose sleeves, over which was worn a mantle of cloth of gold, buttoned upon the right shoulder with massy gold buttons. The cap was of crimson velvet, and the baton of office was of silver, ensigned with the winged lion of St. Mark [Knight gives an engraving of this dress from Vecellio]. Of the 'Italian foot' Vecellio gives us a specimen. His defensive armour consists of a back and breast-plate, mail sleeves, and that peculiar species of head-piece called a morion. The 'lads of Cyprus' may, with great probability, be supposed to have belonged to the body of Greek cavalry, first employed by the Venetians. Vecellio presents us with the costume of a 'soldato disarmato,' which would be that of Cassio and Iago when off guard. Its characteristics are the buff jerkin and the scarf of company. See V, i, 29. The scarf was the only uniform then known amongst officers; it bore the colours of the captain under whom they served, and is the origin of the modern sash.

Coryat, who travelled in 1608, says, in his *Crudities* [ii, 19, ed. 1776]: 'I saw the Duke [i. e., Doge] in some of his richest ornaments. . . . . He wore two very rich robes, or long garments, whereof the vppermost was white, of cloth of silver, with great massy buttons of gold; the other cloth of silver also, but adorned with many curious workes made in colours with needleworke. [His train was then holden up by two Gentlemen.]' Howell, in his *Survey of the Signorie of Venice*, 1651, after telling us that the Duke 'always goes clad in silk and purple,' observes that 'sometimes he shows himself to the public in a robe of cloth of gold, and a white mantle; he hath his head covered with a thin coif, and on his forehead he wears a crimson kind of mitre, with a gold border, and, behind, it turns up in form of a horn; on his shoulders he carries ermine skins to the middle, which is still a badge of the Consuls habit; on his feet he wears embroidered sandals' (Vecellio says 'slippers') 'tied with gold buttons; and about his middle a most rich belt, embroidered with costly jewels.' The chiefs of the Council of Ten wore 'red gowns with long sleeves, either of cloth, camlet, or damask, according to the weather, with a flap of the same colour over their left shoulders, red stockings and slippers.' The rest of 'The Tenne,' according to Coryat [p. 33], wore 'blacke chamlet gownes with maruellous long sleeues, that reach almost downe to the ground.' The 'clarissimoes' generally wore 'gownes of blacke cloth, and ouer their left shoulder they haue a flappe made of the same cloth, and edged with black taffata'; and all these 'gowned men,' says the same author, 'doe weare marueilous little blacke caps of felt, without any brimmes at all, and very diminutiue falling bands, no ruffes at all, which are so shallow, that I haue seene many of them not aboue a little inch deepe.' The colour of their under-garments was also generally black, and consisted of a 'slender doublet made close to the body, without much quilting or bombast, and long hose plaine, without those new fangled curiosities and ridiculovs superfluities of panes, plaites, and other light toyes vsed with vs English men.' 'Young lovers,' says Vecellio, 'wear generally a doublet and breeches of satin, tabby, or other silk, cut or slashed in the form of crosses or stars, through which slashes is seen the lining of coloured taffata; gold buttons, a lace ruff, a bonnet of rich velvet, or silk, with an ornamental band, a silk cloak, and silk stockings, Spanish morocco shoes, a flower in one hand, and their gloves and handkerchief in the other.' Speaking of the ladies of Venice, Coryat [p. 35] says: 'Most of the women, when they walke abroad, especially to Church, are vailed with long vailes, whereof some doe reach almost to the ground behinde. These vailes are eyther blacke, or white, or yellowish. The blacke eyther wiues or widowes do weare; the white, maides, and so the yellowish also; but they weare more white then yellowish. It is the custome of these maydes, when they walke in the streetes, to couer their faces with their vailes, *vere cundiæ causâ*, the stuffe being so thin and slight, that they may easily looke through it. For it is made of a pretty slender silke, and very finely curled. . . . . Now whereas I said before, that only maydes do weare white vailes, and none else, I meane these white silk curled vayles, which (as they tolde me) none doe weare but maydes. But other white vayles wives doe much weare, such as are made of holland, whereas the greatest part is handsomely edged with great and very faire bone lace.' Vecellio states that courtesans wore black veils in imitation of women of character. We must not forget that singular portion of a Venetian lady's costume at this period, 'the Chioppine.' [See notes on *Ham.* II, ii, 407.]

The following costumes are given in BOOTH'S *Prompt Book*, p. 120: OTHELLO,— *First Dress:* A long gown of cashmere, wrought with gold and various colours. This is looped up to the hip, on the left side, with jewels. A Moorish burnoose, striped with purple and gold. Purple velvet shoes, embroidered with gold and pearl. A sash of green and gold. A jewelled chain. *Second Dress:* Steel-plate armour. A white burnoose made of African goat's hair. *Third Dress:* A long, white gown, Moorish, with hood, and with scarlet trimmings. A white sash made of goat's hair. Scarlet velvet shoes. Pearl ear-rings. (These dresses, although conformable to Christian ideas, are devised with a view to express the gorgeous barbaric taste of the Moor.) DESDEMONA,—*First Dress:* White satin train, trimmed with illusion and pearls. High, pointed corsage, with ruff. Long, puffed sleeves; pearls between puffs. Stomacher, elaborately embroidered with pearls. Girdle of the same. Diamond ear-rings, cross, and pin. Mary Stuart cap made of white satin and pearls. *Second Dress:* Drab satin train, embroidered with gold. Blue satin poncha, embroidered with gold. Blue satin Mary Stuart cap, trimmed with gold leaves. *Third Dress:* Rose-coloured satin train; the front breadth of white satin, trimmed with three point-lace flounces, headed by a pearl fringe. High, pointed corsage, with ruff. White, pointed stomacher, embroidered with pearls. Pearl girdle. Sleeves puffed with white satin. Bands of rose and pearls between puffs. Mary Stuart cap of rose satin, trimmed with pearls.

WILHELM OECHELHÄUSER (*Einleitung*, p. 28): There is, strictly speaking, no one scene imaginable upon which Cassio's interview with Desdemona, Othello's great scene with Iago, the loss of the handkerchief, Iago's conversation with Emilia, the second interview of Othello with Iago, Desdemona's with Othello and Emilia, and in addition the appearance of Bianca and her dialogue with Cassio, could be acted one after the other. I suggest a terrace, therefore, connected by a colonnade, with the castle in view, and to be entered thence as from the street. There is, however, no serious objection to use the hall [usually set for II, iii, in ordinary Acting Copies], with perhaps an elevated background and colonnade; so that then half the piece from the Second [Third] Scene of Act II to the last Scene of Act IV, inclusive, might be acted without change.

The costume should be that of the period of the Renaissance, as it was in Venice. The architecture is, for Venice, partly Gothic in its combination with Byzantine motives, and partly of the early Renaissance style; in Cyprus, it has an Oriental character.

E. W. GODWIN contributed to *The Architect* a valuable series of suggestive and instructive papers on *The Architecture and Costume of Shakspere's Plays.* The issue of 15 March, 1875, was devoted to *Othello.*

ENGLISH CRITICISMS

DR JOHNSON: The beauties of this play impress themselves so strongly upon the attention of the reader, that they can draw no aid from critical illustration. The fiery openness of Othello, magnanimous, artless, and credulous, boundless in his confidence, ardent in his affection, inflexible in his resolution, and obdurate in his revenge; the cool malignity of Iago, silent in his resentment, subtle in his designs, and studious at once of his interest and his vengeance; the soft simplicity of Desdemona, confident of merit, and conscious of innocence, her artless perseverance in her suit, and her slowness to suspect that she can be suspected, are such proofs of Shakespeare's skill in human nature as, I suppose, it is in vain to seek in any modern writer. The gradual progress which Iago makes in the Moor's conviction, and the circumstances which he employs to enflame him, are so artfully natural, that, though it will perhaps not be said of him [Othello] as he says of himself, that he is 'a man not easily jealous,' yet we cannot but pity him, when at last we find him 'perplexed in the extreme.'

There is always danger lest wickedness, conjoined with abilities, should steal upon esteem, though it misses of approbation; but the character of Iago is so conducted, that he is from the first Scene to the last hated and despised. Even the inferior characters of this play would be very conspicuous in any other piece, not only for their justness, but their strength. Cassio is brave, benevolent, and honest, ruined only by his want of stubbornness to resist an insidious invitation. Roderigo's suspicious credulity and impatient submission to the cheats which he sees practised upon him, and which by persuasion he suffers to be repeated, exhibit a strong picture of a weak mind betrayed by unlawful desires to a false friend; and the virtue of Emilia is such as we often find, worn loosely, but not cast off, easy to commit small crimes, but quickened and alarmed at atrocious villainies. The Scenes from the beginning to the end are busy, varied by happy interchanges, and regularly promoting the progression of the story; and the narrative in the end, though it tells but what is already known, yet is necessary to produce the death of Othello. Had the scene opened in Cyprus, and the preceding incidents been occasionally related, there had been little wanting to a drama of the most exact and scrupulous regularity.

MALONE: I cannot forbear to conclude our commentaries on this transcendent poet with the fine eulogy which the judicious and learned Lowth has pronounced on him, with a particular reference to this tragedy, perhaps *the most perfect* of all his works:

'In his viris [tragediæ Græcæ scilicet scriptoribus] accessio quædam Philosophiæ erat Poetica facultas: neque sane quisquam adhuc Poesin ad fastigium suum ac culmen evexit, nisi qui prius in intima Philosophia artis suæ fundamenta jecerit.

'Quod si quis objiciat, nonnullos in hoc ipso poeseos genere excelluisse, qui nunquam habiti sunt Philosophi, ac ne literis quidem præter cæteros imbuti; sciat is, me rem ipsam quærere, non de vulgari opinione, aut de verbo laborare: *qui autem tantum ingenio consecutus est, ut naturas hominum, vimque omnem humanitatis, causasque eas, quibus aut incitatur mentis impetus aut retunditur, penitus perspectas habeat, ejusque omnes motus oratione non modo explicet, sed effingat, planeque oculis subjiciat, sed excitet, regat, commoveat, moderetur; eum, etsi disciplinarum instrumento minus adjutum, eximie tamen esse Philosophum arbitrari.* Quo in genere affectum Zelotypiæ, ejusque causas, adjuncta, progressiones, effectus, in una Shakspeari nostri fabula, copiosius, subtilius, accuratius etiam veriusque pertractari existimo, quam ab omnibus omnium Philosophorum scholis in simili argumento est unquam disputatum' (*Prælectio prima*, edit. 1763, p. 8). VERPLANCK: The remarkable criticism of Bishop Lowth, often before quoted in its original exquisite Latinity, deserves to be more familiarly known to the English reader: 'He whose genius has unfolded to him the knowledge of man's nature and the force of his passions; has taught him the causes by which the soul is moved to strong emotions, or calmed to rest; has enabled him not only to explain in words those emotions, but to exhibit them vividly to other eyes; thus ruling, exciting, distracting, soothing our feelings,—this man, however little aided by the discipline of learning, is, in my judgement, a philosopher of the highest rank. In this manner, in a single dramatic fable of our own Shakespeare, the passion of jealousy, its causes, progress, incidents, and effects, have been more truly, more acutely, more copiously, and more impressively delineated than has been done by all the disquisitions of all the philosophers who have treated on this dark argument.'

In 1796, at Exeter, England, appeared a volume of *Essays, by a Society of Gentlemen*, wherein, on pp. 395–409, is found: *An Apology for the Character and Conduct of Iago*. The anonymous writer urges as palliations of Iago's conduct: *first*, his being supplanted, through Othello's insensibility and unkindness, by Cassio, and the writer hereupon 'appeals with safety to the officers of the British army' to know if Iago's hostility were not excusable; *second*, he suspects Othello's relations with Emilia; *third* (and this is quite original), 'Iago having a right to expect promotion, had lived, it may naturally be concluded, more profusely than he would otherwise have done; had involved himself in difficulties, or, as Emilia expresses it, had "scanted his former havings"; another cause for chagrin and anger against Othello, whose cruel neglect had obliged him to stoop to meannesses he would otherwise have detested.' *Fourth*, he suspected Cassio had played him false at home. *Fifth*, he was by no means convinced of Desdemona's virtue and purity; 'his suspicions of his wife had soured his temper and excited in him a general aversion to the female sex.' *Lastly*, the writer, who trusts that 'if he has not wholly washed the blackamoor white, he has at least taken a shade from his colour,' in showing that Iago's conduct admits of much palliation, thus sums up: 'On the whole, his conduct to Roderigo, concerning which no accusation has been preferred, appears to be the least excusable. To him he was indebted for pecuniary obligations, but for none of any kind to either of the other characters. On the contrary, from the first of them he had, most decidedly and incontrovertibly, received injuries of the severest kind. He had no trivial cause for his aversion to Cassio. Desdemona, as being a woman, was not an object of his regard; as the friend of Cassio and Æmilia she appeared to him in a disgusting light, and more so probably considered as the wife of Othello. In order to distress *him*, however, not to gratify any aversion towards Desdemona, he contrives her death: she is merely an instrument to effectuate his vengeance; and if vengeance can be vindicated by an accumulation of injuries, Iago's, though exorbitant, was just.'

COLERIDGE (*Notes*, 252): Dr Johnson has remarked that little or nothing is wanting to render *Othello* a regular tragedy but to have opened the play with the arrival of Othello at Cyprus, and to have thrown the preceding Act into the form of narration. Here, then, is the place to determine whether such a change would or would not be an improvement; nay (to throw down the glove with a full challenge), whether the tragedy would or would not, by such an arrangement, become more regular,—that is, more consonant with the rules dictated by universal reason, on the true common-sense of mankind, in its application to the particular case. For in all acts of judgement, it can never be too often recollected, and scarcely too often repeated, that rules are means to ends, and, consequently, that the end must be determined and understood before it can be known what the rules are or ought to be. Now, from a certain species of drama, proposing to itself the accomplishment of certain ends,—these partly arising from the idea of the species itself, but in part, likewise, forced upon the dramatist by accidental circumstances beyond his power to remove or control,—three rules have been abstracted; in other words, the means most conducive to the attainment of the proposed ends have been generalized, and prescribed under the names of the three Unities,—the unity of time, the unity of place, and the unity of action,—which last would, perhaps, have been as appropriately, as well as more intelligibly, entitled the unity of interest. With this last the present question has no immediate concern; in fact, its conjunction with the former two is a mere delusion of words. It is not properly a rule, but in itself the great end not only of the drama, but of the epic poem, the lyric ode, of all poetry, down to the candle-flame cone of an epigram,—nay, of poesy in general, as the proper generic term inclusive of all the fine arts as its species. But of the unities of time and place, which alone are entitled to the name of rules, the history of their origin will be their best criterion. You might take the Greek chorus to a place, but you could not bring a place to them without as palpable an equivoque as bringing Birnam wood to Macbeth at Dunsinane. It was the same, though in a less degree, with regard to the unity of time; the positive fact, not for a moment removed from the senses, the presence, I mean, of the same identical chorus, was a continued measure of time; and although the imagination may supersede perception, yet it must be granted to be an imperfection, however easily tolerated, to place the two in broad contradiction to each other. In truth, it is a mere accident of terms; for the Trilogy of the Greek theatre was a drama in three Acts, and, notwithstanding this, what strange contrivances as to place there are in the Aristophanic *Frogs*. Besides, if the law of mere actual perception is once violated, as it repeatedly is, even in the Greek tragedies, why is it more difficult to imagine three hours to be three years than to be a whole day and night?

WORDSWORTH : Wings have we,—and as far as we can go
    We may find pleasure; wilderness and wood,
    Blank ocean and mere sky, support that mood
    Which with the lofty sanctifies the low.
    Dreams, Books, are each a world; and books, we know,
    Are a substantial world, both pure and good;
    Round these, with tendrils strong as flesh and blood,
    Our pastime and our happiness will grow.
    There find I personal themes, a plenteous store,
    Matter wherein right voluble I am,
    To which I listen with a ready ear;
    Two shall be named pre-eminently dear,—
    The gentle Lady married to the Moor;
    And heavenly Una, with her milk-white Lamb.
            —*Personal Talk*, III, 1807.
             (Vol. iv, p. 25, ed. Knight, 1883.)

LAMB (*Works*, London, 1870, iii, 102; published originally in Hunt's *Reflector*, circa 1810): How many dramatic personages are there in Shakespeare, which, from some circumstance, some adjunct to their character, are improper to be shown to our bodily eye! Othello, for instance. Nothing can be more soothing, more flattering to the nobler parts of our natures, than to read of a young Venetian lady of highest extraction, through the force of love and from a sense of merit in him whom she loved, laying aside every consideration of kindred, and country, and colour, and wedding with a *coal-black Moor*,—(for such he is represented, in the imperfect state of knowledge respecting foreign countries in those days, compared with our own, or in compliance with popular notions, though the Moors are now well enough known to be many shades less unworthy of a white woman's fancy)—it is the perfect triumph of virtue over accidents, of the imagination over the senses. She sees Othello's colour in his mind. But upon the stage, when the imagination is no longer the ruling faculty, but we are left to our poor, unassisted senses, I appeal to every one that has seen *Othello* played, whether he did not, on the contrary, sink Othello's mind in his colour; whether he did not find something extremely revolting in the courtship and wedded caresses of Othello and Desdemona; and whether the actual sight of the thing did not overweigh all that beautiful compromise which we make in reading. And the reason it should do so is obvious, because there is just so much reality presented to our senses as to give a perception of disagreement, with not enough of belief in the internal motives,—all that which is unseen,—to overpower and reconcile the first and obvious prejudices. What we see upon a stage is body and bodily action; what we are conscious of in reading is almost exclusively the mind, and its movements; and this, I think, may sufficiently account for the very different sort of delight with which the same play so often affects us in the reading and the seeing.

[Foot-note]: The error of supposing that because Othello's colour does not offend us in the reading, it should also not offend us in the seeing, is just such a fallacy as supposing that an Adam and Eve in a picture shall affect us just as they do in the poem. But in the poem we have for a while Paradisaical senses given us, which vanish when we see a man and his wife without clothes in the picture. The painters themselves feel this, as is apparent by the awkward shifts they have recourse to, to make them look not quite naked; by a sort of prophetic anachronism, antedating the invention of fig-leaves. So in the reading of the play, we see with Desdemona's eyes; in the seeing of it, we are forced to look with our own.

HAZLITT (*Characters of Shakespeare's Plays*, London, 1817, p. 54): The character of Iago is one of the supererogations of Shakespeare's genius. Some persons, more nice than wise, have thought this whole character unnatural, because his villainy is *without a sufficient motive*. Shakespeare, who was as good a philosopher as he was a poet, thought otherwise. He knew that the love of power, which is another name for the love of mischief, is natural to man. He would know this as well or better than if it had been demonstrated to him by a logical diagram, merely from seeing children paddle in the dirt or kill flies for sport. Iago, in fact, belongs to a class of characters, common to Shakespeare and at the same time peculiar to him; whose heads are as acute and active as their hearts are hard and callous. Iago is to be sure an extreme instance of the kind; that is to say, of diseased intellectual activity, with an almost perfect indifference to moral good or evil, or rather with a decided preference of the latter, because it falls more readily in with his favourite propensity, gives greater zest to his thoughts and scope to his actions. He is quite or nearly as indifferent to his own fate as to that of others; he runs all risks for a trifling and doubtful advantage; and is himself the dupe and victim of his ruling passion—an insatiable craving after action of the most difficult and dangerous kind. 'Our antient' is a philosopher, who fancies that a lie that kills has more point in it than an alliteration or an antithesis; who thinks a fatal experiment on the peace of a family a better thing than watching the palpitations in the heart of a flea in a microscope; who plots the ruin of his friends as an exercise for his ingenuity, and stabs men in the dark to prevent *ennui*. His gayety, such as it is, arises from the success of his treachery; his ease from the torture he has inflicted on others. He is an amateur of tragedy in real life; and instead of employing his invention on imaginary characters or long-forgotten incidents, he takes the bolder and more desperate course of getting up his plot at home, casts the principal parts among his nearest friends and connections, and rehearses it in downright earnest with steady nerves and unabated resolution. . . . . The habitual licentiousness of Iago's conversation is not to be traced to the pleasure he takes in gross or lascivious images, but to his desire of finding out the worst side of everything, and of proving himself an overmatch for appearances. He has none of 'the milk of human kindness' in his composition. His imagination rejects everything that has not a strong infusion of the most unpalatable ingredients; his mind digests only poisons. Virtue or goodness, or whatever has the least 'relish of salvation in it,' is, to his depraved appetite, sickly and insipid; and he even resents the good opinion entertained of his own integrity, as if it were an affront cast on the masculine sense and spirit of his character. Thus at the meeting between Othello and Desdemona, he exclaims: 'O, you are well tun'd now! But I'll set down the pegs that make this music, *As honest as I am*'—his character of *bonhomie* not sitting at all easily upon him. In the scenes where he tries to work Othello to his purpose he is proportionably guarded, insidious, dark, and deliberate. We believe nothing ever came up to the profound dissimulation and dexterous artifice of the well-known dialogue in the Third Act, where he first enters upon the execution of his design (III, iii, 107–128). The stops and breaks, the deep workings of treachery under the mask of love and honesty, the anxious watchfulness, the cool earnestness, and, if we may so say, the *passion* of hypocrisy marked in every line, receive their last finishing in that inconceivable burst of pretended indignation at Othello's doubts of his sincerity: 'O grace! O Heaven forgive me!' (*Ib.* 430–437.)

If Iago is detestable enough when he has business on his hands and all his engines at work, he is still worse when he has nothing to do, and we only see into the hollowness of his heart. His indifference when Othello falls into a swoon is perfectly diabolical. The part, indeed, would hardly be tolerated, even as a foil to the virtue and generosity of the other characters in the play, but for its indefatigable industry and inexhaustible resources, which divert the attention of the spectator (as well as his own) from the end he has in view to the means by which it must be accomplished.*

MACAULAY in his *Essay on Dante* (*Knight's Quarterly Magazine,* Jan., 1824), alludes to the little impression the forms of the external world appear to have made on Dante's mind. 'The feeling of the present age,' he goes on to say, 'has taken a direction diametrically opposite. The magnificence of the physical world, and its influence on the human mind, have been the favorite themes of our most eminent poets. . . . . The orthodox poetical creed is more catholic. The noblest earthly object of the contemplation of man is man himself. The universe, and all its fair and glorious forms, are indeed included in the wide empire of imagination; but she has placed her home and her sanctuary amidst the inexhaustible varieties and the impenetrable mysteries of the mind. *Othello* is, perhaps, the greatest work in the world. From what does it derive its power? From the clouds? From the ocean? From the mountains? Or from love strong as death, and jealousy cruel as the grave! What is it we go forth to see in *Hamlet?* Is it a reed shaken with the wind? A small celandine? A bed of daffodils? Or is it to contemplate a mighty and wayward mind laid bare before us to the inmost recesses?'

MACAULAY (*Edinburgh Review*, 1827, vol. xlv, p. 272): Othello murders his wife; he gives orders for the murder of his lieutenant; he ends by murdering himself. Yet he never loses the esteem and affection of a Northern reader—his intrepid and ardent spirit redeeming everything. The unsuspecting confidence with which he listens to his adviser, the agony with which he shrinks from the thought of shame, the tempest of passion with which he commits his crimes, and the haughty fearlessness with which he

---

* The criticism from which these extracts have been made originally appeared substantially in *The Examiner*, 23 July, 1814, as we learn from a foot-note by W. C. Hazlitt, p. 20, in *The Round Table*, 1881.—ED.

avows them, give an extraordinary interest to his character. Iago, on the contrary, is the object of universal loathing. Many are inclined to suspect that Shakespeare has been seduced into an exaggeration unusual with him, and has drawn a monster who has no archetype in human nature. Now we suspect that an Italian audience, in the fifteenth century, would have felt very differently. Othello would have inspired nothing but detestation and contempt. The folly with which he trusts to the friendly professions of a man whose promotion he had obstructed,—the credulity with which he takes unsupported assertions and trivial circumstances for unanswerable proofs,—the violence with which he silences the exculpation till the exculpation can only aggravate his misery, would have excited the abhorrence and disgust of the spectators. The conduct of Iago they would assuredly have condemned; but they would have condemned it as we condemn that of his victim. Something of interest and respect would have mingled with their disapprobation. The readiness of his wit, the clearness of his judgement, the skill with which he penetrates the dispositions of others and conceals his own, would have ensured to him a certain portion of their esteem.

MRS JAMESON (*Characteristics of Women*, London, 1833, 2nd ed., ii, 31): The cha racter of Hermione is addressed more to the imagination,—that of Desdemona to the feelings. All that can render sorrow majestic is gathered round Hermione; all that can render misery heart-breaking is assembled round Desdemona. The wronged but self-sustained virtue of Hermione commands our veneration; the injured and defence-ness innocence of Desdemona so wrings the soul 'that all for pity we could die.' Des-demona, as a character, comes nearest to Miranda, both in herself as a woman, and in the perfect simplicity and unity of the delineation; the figures are differently draped,—the proportions are the same. There is the same modesty, tenderness, and grace; the same artless devotion in the affections, the same predisposition to wonder, to pity, to admire; the same almost ethereal refinement and delicacy; but all is pure poetic nature within Miranda and around her; Desdemona is more associated with the palpable real-ities of every-day existence, and we see the forms and habits of society tinting her lan-guage and deportment; no two beings can be more alike in character, nor more distinct as individuals.

(P. 35.) The confession and the excuse for her love are well placed in the mouth of Desdemona, while the history of the rise of that love, and of his course of wooing, is, with the most graceful propriety, as far as she is concerned, spoken by Othello, and in her absence. The last two lines summing up the whole,—' She lov'd me for the dan gers I had pass'd, And I lov'd her that she did pity them '—comprise whole volumes of sentiment and metaphysics.

(P. 39.) With the most perfect artlessness, she has something of the instinctive, unconscious address of her sex; as when she appeals to her father :—' So much duty as my mother show'd To you, preferring you before her father, So much I challenge, that I may profess Due to the Moor, my lord.' And when she is pleading for Cassio :—' What! Michael Cassio! That came a wooing with you; and many a time, When I have spoken of you disparagingly [*sic*] Hath ta'en your part?' In persons who unite great sensibility and lively fancy, I have often observed this particular species of address, which is always unconscious of itself, and consists in the power of placing ourselves in the position of another, and imagining, rather than perceiving, what is in their hearts. We women have this *address* (if so it can be called) naturally, but I have seldom met with it in men. It is not inconsistent with extreme simplicity of character, and quite distinct from that kind of art which is the result of natural acuteness and habits of observation,—quick to perceive the foibles of others, and as quick to turn them to its own purposes; which is always conscious of itself, and if united with strong intellect, seldom perceptible to others. In the mention of her mother, and the appeal to Othello's self-love, Desdemona has no design formed on conclusions previously drawn; but her intuitive quickness of feeling, added to her imagination, leads her more safely to the same results, and the distinction is as truly as it is delicately drawn.

(P. 43.) There is another peculiarity which, in reading the play of *Othello*, we rather feel than perceive: through the whole of the dialogue appropriated to Desdemona there is not one general observation. Words are with her the vehicle of sentiment, and never of reflection; so that I cannot find throughout a sentence of general application. The same remark applies to Miranda; and to no other female character of any importance or interest—not even to Ophelia.

The rest of what I wished to say of Desdemona has been anticipated by an anonymous critic, and so beautifully, so justly, so eloquently expressed, that I with pleasure erase my own page, to make room for his:

' *Othello*,' observes this writer, ' is no love-story; all that is below tragedy in the passion of love, is taken away at once by the awful character of Othello; for such he seems to us to be designed to be. He appears never as a lover, but at once as a husband; and the relation of his love made dignified, as it is a husband's justification of his marriage, is also dignified, as it is a soldier's relation of his stern and perilous life. His love itself, as long as it is happy, is perfectly calm and serene,—the protecting tenderness of a husband. It is not till it is disordered that it appears as a passion: then is shown a power in contention with itself,—a mighty being struck with death, and bringing up from all the depths of life convulsions and agonies. It is no exhibition of the power of the passion of love, but of the passion of life, vitally wounded, and self-overmastering. If Desdemona had been really guilty, the greatness would have been destroyed, because his love would have been unworthy, false. But she is good, and his love is most perfect, just, and good. That a man should place his perfect love on a wretched thing is miserably debasing, and shocking to thought; but that loving perfectly and well, he should by hellish human circumvention be brought to distrust and dread, and abjure his own perfect love, is most mournful indeed,—it is the infirmity of our good nature wrestling in vain with the strong powers of evil. Moreover, he would, had Desdemona been false, have been the mere victim of fate; whereas he is now in a manner his own victim. His happy love was heroic tenderness; his injured love is terrible passion; and disordered power, engendered within itself to its own destruction, is the height of all tragedy.

' The character of Othello is, perhaps, the most greatly drawn, the most heroic, of any of Shakespeare's actors; but it is, perhaps, that one also of which his reader last acquires the intelligence. The intellectual and warlike energy of his mind, his tenderness of affection, his loftiness of spirit, his frank, generous magnanimity, impetuosity like a thunderbolt, and that dark, fierce flood of boiling passion, polluting even his imagination, compose a character entirely original, most difficult to delineate, but perfectly delineated.'

Emilia in this play is a perfect portrait from common life, a masterpiece in the Flemish style; and, though not necessary as a contrast, it cannot be but that the thorough vulgarity, the loose principles of this plebeian woman, united to a high degree of spirit, energetic feeling, strong sense, and low cunning, serve to place in brighter relief the exquisite refinement, the moral grace, the unblemished truth, and the soft submission of Desdemona.

(P. 47.) I will only add that the source of the pathos throughout,—of that pathos which at once softens and deepens the tragic effect,—lies in the character of Desdemona. No woman, differently constituted, could have excited the same intense and painful compassion without losing something of that exalted charm which invests her from beginning to end, which we are apt to impute to the interest of the situation, and to the poetical colouring; but which lies, in fact, in the very essence of the character. Desdemona, with all her timid flexibility and soft acquiescence, is not weak; for the negative alone is weak, and the mere presence of goodness and affection implies in itself a species of power;—power without consciousness, power without effort, power with repose,—that soul of grace!

I know a Desdemona in real life, one in whom the absence of intellectual power is never felt as a deficiency, nor the absence of energy of will as impairing the dignity, nor the most imperturbable serenity as a want of feeling; one in whom thoughts appear mere instincts, the sentiment of rectitude supplies the principle, and virtue itself seems rather a necessary state of being than an imposed law. No shade of sin or vanity has yet stolen over that bright innocence. No discord within has marred the loveliness without, no strife of the factitious world without has disturbed the harmony within. The comprehension of evil appears for ever shut out, as if goodness had converted all things to itself; and all to the pure in heart must necessarily be pure. The impression produced is exactly that of the character of Desdemona; genius is a rare thing, but abstract goodness is rarer. In Desdemona we cannot but feel that the slightest manifestation of intellectual power or active will would have injured the dramatic effect. She is a victim consecrated from the first, 'an offering without blemish,' alone worthy of the grand final sacrifice; all harmony, all grace, all purity, all tenderness, all truth! But, alas! to see her fluttering like a cherub, in the talons of a fiend!——to see her—— O poor Desdemona!

MAGINN (*Shakespeare Papers*, London, 1860, p. 257): What appears to me to be the distinguishing feature of Shakespeare is, that his characters are real men and women, not mere abstractions. In the best of us all there are many blots; in the worst there are many traces of goodness. There is no such thing as angels or devils in the world. We have passions and feelings, hopes and fears, joys and sorrows pretty evenly distributed among us; and that which actuates the highest and the lowest, the most virtuous and the most profligate, the bravest and the meanest, must, in its original elements, be the same. People do not commit wicked actions from the mere love of wickedness; there must always be an incentive of precisely the same kind as that which stimulates to the noblest actions,—ambition, love of adventure, passion, necessity. All our virtues closely border upon vices, and are not unfrequently blended. The robber may be generous,—the miser, just,—the cruel man, conscientious,—the rake, honourable,—the fop, brave. In various relations of life, the same man may play many characters as distinct from one another as day from night. . . . . It is necessary for a critical investigation of character, not to be content with taking things merely as they seem. We must endeavour to strip off the covering with which habit or necessity has enveloped the human mind, and to inquire after motives as well as to look to actions. . . . .

As Shakespeare, therefore, draws men, and not one-sided sketches of character, it is always possible to treat his personages as if they were actually existing people; and there is always some redeeming point. The bloody Macbeth is kind and gentle to his wife; the gore-stained Richard, gallant and daring; Shylock is an affectionate father and a good-natured master; Claudius, in *Hamlet*, is fond of his foully-won queen, and exhibits, at least, remorse for his deed in heart-rending soliloquies; Angelo is upright in public life, though yielding to sore temptation in private; Cloten is brutal and insulting, but brave; the ladies are either wholly without blemishes, or have merits to redeem them. . . . .

But Iago! Ay! there's the rub. Well may poor Othello look down to his feet, and not seeing them different from those of others, feel convinced that it is a fable which attributes a cloven hoof to the devil. Nor is it wonderful that the parting instruction of Lodovico to Cassio [*sic*] should be to enforce the most cunning cruelty of torture on the hellish villain, or that all the party should vie with each other in heaping upon him words of contumely and execration. His determination to keep silence when questioned, was at least judicious; for with his utmost ingenuity he could hardly find anything to say for himself. Is there nothing, then, to be said for him by anybody else?

No more than this. He is the sole exemplar of studied personal revenge in the plays. The philosophical mind of Hamlet ponders too deeply, and sees both sides of the question too clearly, to be able to carry any plan of vengeance into execution. Romeo's revenge on Tybalt for the death of Mercutio is a sudden gust of ungovernable rage. The vengeances in the Historical Plays are those of war or statecraft. In Shylock, the passion is hardly personal against his intended victim. A swaggering Christian is at the mercy of a despised and insulted Jew. The hatred is national and sectarian. Had Bassanio or Gratiano, or any other of their creed, been in his power, he would have been equally relentless. He is only retorting the wrongs and insults of his tribe in demanding full satisfaction, and imitating the hated Christians in their own practices. It is, on the whole, a passion remarkably seldom exhibited in Shakespeare in any form. Iago, as I have said, is its only example as directed against an individual. Iago had been affronted in the tenderest point. He felt that he had strong claims on the office of lieutenant to Othello. The greatest exertion was made to procure it for him, and yet he was refused. What is still worse, the grounds of the refusal are military; Othello assigns to the civilians reasons for passing over Iago, drawn from his own trade, of which they, of course, could not pretend to be adequate judges. And worst of all, when this practised military man is for military reasons set aside, who is appointed? Some man of greater renown and skill in arms? *That* might be borne; but it is no such thing. We will find in many professional periodical works the complaint reiterated that 'Preferment goes by letter and affection, Not by old gradation,' and many a curse, loud and deep, is inflicted on that account upon the Horse Guards and Admiralty, who, fortunately, have no individual responsibilities on which disappointed Ancients can fasten. I am sure no British soldier or sailor would carry his anger farther than a passing growl, but the example of Bellingham shows that even in our assassin-hating nation a feeling of injustice done by a superior will drive a man to satiate his vengeance even upon those who have not done him wrong. In the country of Iago, whether from his name we conclude it to be Spain, or from his service, Italy, none of the scruples, or, rather, principles, which actuate or restrain English gentlemen, existed. Least of all were they to be found in the motley armies of adventurers gathered from all quarters, and Iago could not be expected to be very scrupulous as to his method of compassing his revenge. But how effect it? He is obliged to admit that Othello's standing in the state is too important to render it possible that public injury could be done him. In his unhoused condition no point of vantage presented itself whence harm could be wrought. Just then, when Iago's heart was filled with rage, and his head busily, but vainly, occupied in devising means for avenging himself on the man by whom that rage was excited,—just then *Atè*, the Goddess of Mischief, supplies him with all that deepest malignity could desire, by the hasty, ill-mated, and unlooked-for marriage of Othello. It was a devil-send that the most sanguine spirit could not have anticipated, and Iago clutched it accordingly with passionate eagerness. He was tempted and he fell.

When he first conceived his hatred against Othello, he had no notion that it would be pushed to such dire extremity. Revenge is generally accompanied by vanity, indeed there must be always a spice of vanity in a revengeful disposition. He who so keenly feels and deeply resents personal injury or affront must set no small value upon himself. The proud are seldom revengeful, the great never. We accordingly find that Iago engages in his hostilities against Othello more to show his talents than for any other purpose. He proudly lauds his own powers of dissimulation, which are to be now displayed with so much ability (I, i, 64–68). He fancies himself superior to all around in art and knowledge of the world. Roderigo is a mere gull (I, iii, 409). Cassio he considers to be not merely unskilled in war, but a fool (II, ii, 384). Othello is an ass in his estimation (I, iii, 426). The 'inclining' Desdemona he utterly despises, as one who fell in love with the Moor merely for his bragging and telling fantastical lies. His wife he calls a fool; and with these opinions of his great superiority of wisdom and intellect, he commences operations to enmesh them all, as if they were so many puppets. It would be a strange thing, indeed, he reflects, if I were to permit myself to be insulted and my rights withheld by such a set of idiots, whom I can wind round my finger as I please.

He seated him in the seat of the scorner, a character which he who is accounted the wisest of men continually opposes to that of true wisdom. 'Seest thou,' says Solomon, in the Proverbs copied out by the men of Hezekiah, King of Judah, which, whether they be inspired or not, are aphorisms of profound and concentrated wisdom,—'Seest thou a man wise in his own conceit? there is more hope of a fool than of him.'

And the career of Iago ends with his own destruction, amid the abomination set down in another chapter of Proverbs as the lot of the scorner. The jealousy of Othello is not more gradually and skilfully raised and developed than the vengeance of Iago. At first angry enough, no doubt; but he has no defined project. He follows the Moor to take advantage of circumstances to turn them to his own use. Nothing of peculiar malignity is thought upon: if he can get Cassio's place, he will be satisfied (I, iii, 417). The marriage and the sight of Desdemona point out to him a ready way of accomplishing this object. The thought occurs suddenly, and he is somewhat startled at first. He asks himself with eager repetition, 'How? how?' and pauses to think,—'Let me see—.' It is soon settled. 'After some time, to abuse Othello's ear, That he is too familiar with his wife.' But it still alarms him: 'I have it—It's engendered: Hell and night Must bring this monstrous birth to the world's light.'

The plot is not matured even when they all arrive at Cyprus. ''Tis here, but yet confused—Knavery's plain face is never seen till used.' When once fairly entered upon, however, it progresses with unchecked rapidity. He is himself hurried resistlessly forward by the current of deceit and iniquity in which he has embarked. He is as much a tool or passive instrument as those whom he is using as such.

Some critics pronounce his character unnatural, as not having sufficient motive for the crimes he commits. This is not wise. He could not help committing them. Merely to put money in his purse, he gulled Roderigo into a belief that he could assist the poor dupe in his suit for Desdemona. There is no remarkable crime in this. Nor can we blame him for being angry at being somewhat scornfully passed over; we can, at all events, enter into his feelings when he wishes to undermine one whom he considers to be unworthily preferred to him, and to obtain a place which he thinks should be his own, if patronage had been justly dispensed. It was a base thing, indeed, to malign a lady, and possess her husband with jealousy; but he could not have calculated on the harvest of death and crime which the seed of suspicion that he was sowing was destined to bring up. When he makes Cassio drunk, he only anticipates that he will put him in such action as may offend the isle. When framing the device that is to destroy the lieutenant, no thoughts of murder arise before him.

He has no regard for the feelings of Othello, but dreams not that he will kill Desdemona, whom he says he loves. As for the lady herself, his low estimation of woman would, of course, lead him to think but little about her peace and quiet. He excuses himself, besides, by referring to the rumour that Othello had given him cause to be jealous. It is plain that he does not pretend to lay any great stress upon this; nor can we suppose that, even if it were true, it would deeply affect him; but he thinks lightly of women in general, and has no respect whatever for his wife. Indeed, Othello does not hold Emilia in much esteem; and her own conversation with Desdemona, as she is undressing her for bed (IV, iii), shows that her virtue was not impregnable. The injury, therefore, Iago was about to do Desdemona, in lessening her in the respect of her husband by accusing her of such an ordinary offence as a deviation from chastity, and one which *he* did not visit with any particular severity on his own wife, must have seemed trivial. He could not have been prepared for the dire tempest of fury which his first hint of her unfaithfulness aroused in the bosom of Othello. Up to that moment he had done nothing more than gull a blockhead, and endeavour, by unworthy means, to undermine a rival; trickery and slander, though not very honourable qualities, are not of such rare occurrence in the world as to call for the expression of any peculiar indignation when we find them displayed by a clever and plotting Italian.

They have, however, led him to the plain and wide path of damnation. He cannot retract his insinuations. Even if he desired, Othello will not let him. Iago, therefore, had no choice but to go forward. He was evidently not prepared for this furious outburst; and we may acquit him of hypocrisy when he prays Othello to let her live. But Cassio must die :—' He hath a daily beauty in his life That makes me ugly.' A more urgent reason immediately suggests itself :—' And beside, the Moor May unfold me to him : then stand I in much peril. *No—he must die.*' The death of Desdemona involves that of Roderigo :—' Live Roderigo ? He calls me to a restitution large Of gold and jewels, that I bobb'd from him As gifts to Desdemona. *It must not be.*'

Here is the direct agency of necessity. He *must* remove these men. Shortly after, to silence the clamorous testimony of his wife, he *must* kill her. He is doomed to blood.

EDINBURGH REVIEW (*Recent Shakespearian Literature*, July, 1840, p. 491) : But of all Shakespeare's tragic dramas, that which most closely resembles the classical models in the simplicity and obviously comprehended perfection of its plan, is also that which, in its catastrophe and its general impression on the mind, approaches most nearly to the spirit of heathen classicism. *Othello* has in it, not indeed in reality but in appearance, much of the terrific fatalism which overshadows the beautiful in the Attic tragedy; the idea of power, irresistible, irresponsible, unfathomable, consigning humanity to utter destruction. Almost all votaries of Shakespeare seem to have felt, at one stage or another, in their study of this magnificent and most passionate drama, an abased, passive, hopeless weight, which no other of his works leaves behind. The source of this feeling does not lie in the sad fate of Desdemona; for, though that is one of the elements, it is not the principal; the effect of her touching death-scene is skilfully softened, and kept in strict subordination to the leading purpose; and the eyes that weep for the gentle lady's fate look up through their tears with reviving hope to heaven. But the terrible force lies in the catastrophe which follows. Othello falls by his own hand, a consummation which Shakespeare has nowhere else given to any of his tragic characters, except in *Lear* and in one or two of the Roman plays; all the three having their scene in heathenism. And even the suicide is less harrowing than the prostration of soul which has preceded it; a despair which annihilates every thought and feeling except the consciousness of unendurable misery. Nor does any after-scene alleviate the gloom; 'the object poisons sight,' but it is hid from us only by the dropping of the curtain; and the Moor has scarcely expired when the drama closes. When, again, when we look back on the causes which have produced this profoundly tragic catastrophe, we seem, at the first glance, to discover nothing that can impart a moral justification of its horror. The bower of wedded happiness seemed guarded by love and honour; and its inhabitants, though frail because mortal, seemed to be stained by no such guilt as should have condemned them to an end like this. Yet into such a scene of peace the tempter has crept, seducing the hand of man himself to lay desolate his home. All critics of name have felt, more or less strongly, the perplexity of the moral enigma which lies under this tragic tale; but the character of the Moor, in which the explication must be sought, has been interpreted more contradictorily than any other in the range of the poet's works, *Hamlet* itself not excepted.

In truth this drama, if we were able to penetrate wholly into its mysteries of conception, would not be what it is: the work in which the poet has united more admirably than in any other the two great elements of dramatic art. *Lear* is at once more original in invention, more active in imagination, more softly pathetic in feeling; *Romeo and Juliet* has more of true poetry; *Macbeth*, a closer amalgamation of tragic action with thought properly ethical; and *Hamlet* traverses a world of thought in which all other existing dramas linger at the frontier. But *Othello*, above every other drama, unites vehemence and nature in tragic emotion, with truth and vigour in the delineation of character. This play, above all others, harmonizes those two elements, and makes each the counterpart, the supplement, the condition of the existence, of the other.

And as even those feel who have considered as a defect the unsoftened sternness of the closing impression, that impression is not one which, thus unsoftened and unrelieved, lingers long in the mind. As the closing images fade into distance in the memory, and the earlier groups come successively into the foregrounds, a picture is gradually formed in which we recognize with reverential wonder, though with incapacity to account for all its effects, a solemn representation of human life in its most awful relations. If philosophy, if observation of the world, if reflection on the destiny of man, as that destiny appears to him in his natural blindness, furnish no key-note to harmonize this song of tragic import, religious contemplation opens a view in which all becomes deeply and truly significant. We glance backward upon the mysteriously revealed leaves of the book of Time, in which is written the sin that has made the earth barren. We gaze forward through darkness, yet not without hope, on that great journey of the soul in which mortal life is but a step. We behold the principle of evil walking the earth for a time in human shape, and allowed to convert into agents of destruction all the finest of those qualities whose union makes up the compound nature of man; counting kin alike with angelic fellow-creatures, and with the cold clay which imprisons his immortal spirit. When the tempted has become a murderer, the work of the temptation is but half accomplished. The mind of the victim is not yet wholly poisoned, his heart not yet wholly crushed. He must behold—and how does his very soul recoil from himself at the discovery!—he must behold the unmasked visage of the fiend whom he has served; he must learn that all which he has done has been worse than done in vain. In one deep silent pause the events of a lifetime pass across his mind, and he awakens from the trance a broken-hearted man. Every principle which once made his character strong and lofty is annihilated within him; love, imagination, pride of honour and of intellect, all are wrecked in one tremendous shock. The soldier feels his courage broken like a rush; the man whose better nature passion could not shake, weeps like a child; the last effort of his overthrown will is but sufficient to consummate the triumph of evil · and the noble Moor dies the most awful of deaths.

CAMPBELL (*Remarks on the Life and Writings of Shakespeare*): Some allege that Iago is too villainous to be a natural character, but those allegers are simpleton judges of human nature: Fletcher of Saltoun has said that there is many a brave soldier who never wore a sword; in like manner, there is many an Iago in the world who never committed murder. Iago's 'LEARNED SPIRIT' and exquisite intellect, happily ending in his own destruction, were as requisite for the moral of the piece as for the sustaining of Othello's high character; for we should have despised the Moor if he had been deceived by a less consummate villain than 'honest Iago.' The latter is a true character, and the philosophical truth of this tragedy makes it terrible to peruse, in spite of its beautiful poetry. Why has Aristotle said that tragedy purifies the passions? for our last wish and hope in reading *Othello* is that the villain Iago may be well tortured.

This drama, by itself, would have immortalized any poet; what, then, are we to think of Shakespeare, when we may hesitate to pronounce it the best of his plays! Certainly, however, it has no superior in his own theatre, and no rival in any other. The Moor is at once one of the most complex and astonishing, and yet most intelligible pictures, that fiction ever portrayed of human character. His grandeur of soul is natural, and we admire it; his gentleness is equally natural, and we love him for it; his appearance we cannot but conceive to be majestic, and his physiognomy benevolent. The Indian Prince Ramohun Roy, who delighted all hearts in London a few years ago, and who died to our sorrow, was the only living being I ever saw who came up to my conception of Othello's appearance. But the Moor had been bred a barbarian, and though his bland nature and intercourse with the more civilized world had long warred against and conquered the half-natural habits of barbarism, yet those habits at last broke out, and prevailed in the moments of his jealousy. He is not a jealous man by nature, but, being once made jealous, he reverts to savageness, and becomes as terrible as he had before been tender. This contrast in his conduct, however, is not an Ovidian metamorphosis, but a transition so probably managed as to seem unavoidable; yet, the naturalness of the change prevents neither our terror nor pity; on the contrary, the sweetness of his character before its fall is the smoothness of the stream before its cataract; and his bland dispositions, heretofore displayed, appear, like a rich autumnal day, contrasted with the thunder-storm of its evening.

The terrors of the storm are also made striking to our imagination by the gentleness of the victim on which they fall,—Desdemona. Had one symptom of an angry spirit appeared in that lovely martyr, our sympathy with her would have been endangered; but Shakespeare knew better.

EDINBURGH REVIEW (*Shakespeare's Critics*, &c., July, 1849, p. 43) : An ordinary man can model a rude figure out of clay; but to bend the marble to the slightest caprices of the mind, to make its stubborn material plastic to the most airy and delicate conceptions, is the work only of a great artist. To take an example from the dramatic representation of Character : However much we may delight in delineations of character for their own sake, it must be remembered that *the art of the dramatist* is not shown in the mere portrayal of mental states, but in *the adaptation* of those mental states to *the purposes of the drama.* A character may be drawn with skill, and yet not be dramatic. All the traits which do not assist the fuller comprehension of the story are superfluous and inartistic. Suppose jealousy be the passion of the play, as in *Othello*. For simple theatrical purposes the writer may confine himself almost exclusively to this passion, and only exhibit in Othello the jealous husband. It is obvious, however, that our sympathies will not be greatly stirred, unless in this jealous husband we recognize other passions and other traits of human nature; and the great problem is, so to contrive and combine these additional features as not only to make the character *individual* and engaging, but to help forward the action and interest of the piece. An ordinary Moor, in a paroxysm of jealousy, would be a far less touching sight than that of the high-minded, chivalric, open, affectionate Othello. The art of the *poet* is, therefore, to delineate these other qualities; and the art of the *dramatist* is to make them *dramatic agents* in the development of his story. Accordingly, all that we see and hear of Othello are not simply preparations for the exhibition of his jealousy and wrath, but are circumstances skilfully adapted for bringing out the story. We thus learn both how the gentle Desdemona was justified in her love, and how Iago found him so easy a victim; so that at last we listen not only with patience, but compassion, to the noble speech in which, at the moment of executing his stern sentence on himself, he seeks to show that he was worthy of a better fate. Had Shakespeare introduced traits into this portrait which, though consistent in themselves, yet had no bearing on the general picture, he would have ruined its dramatic interest. People do not go to the theatre to learn Moorish customs or to analyse character, but to see a drama; and a drama is not a mirror of life in all its fulness and in all its details. It is an episode in life, and must be so circumscribed.

EDINBURGH REVIEW (*Thackeray's Works*, Jan., 1854, p. 223) : For the perfection of the inconsistent character (as, indeed, for the perfection of every other) we must go to Shakespeare. One of the finest, among the many that he has drawn, is Othello. He is a union not merely of dissimilar qualities, but of dissimilar natures. He is a civilized barbarian. All that we know of his birth is that it is ' fetched from men of royal siege.' How or when he became a Christian we are not told; but it is certain that he must have passed his childhood in a harem, acquiring with his earliest impressions the jealousy and suspicion respecting women, and the domestic despotism of a Mahometan court. His youth and manhood are military; and we find him, at the opening of the play, somewhat declined into the vale of years, a grave and dignified soldier. All the barbarian is obliterated during the first two Acts. Nothing can be more calm or more polished. He does not resent the contumely or even the violence of Brabantio; he pleads his cause with consummate moderation and skill. The suspicion, aroused on the very morning after the arrival in Cyprus, by Iago's dark hints, acts on Othello like a specific poison. It sets on fire all the old Mahometan tendency to jealousy which a European life seemed to have eradicated. His barbarian nature reappears. At first his habits of civilization combat it. He proposes to act as becomes a great Venetian noble; to inquire into his wife's conduct, and, if Iago's suspicions prove unfounded, to forget them; if they are confirmed, to separate himself from Des-

demona : ' If I *do* prove her haggard, I'll whistle her off,' &c.   [Iago's lying representations of Cassio's guilty revelations when asleep] Othello swallows with savage credulity. He no longer thinks of inquiry or separation. He is again the Arab or the
Bedouin of his youth, and no conduct, except such as might fit a Bedouin or an Arab,
occurs to him. He cries, ' Oh blood, Iago, blood ! Within these three days let me hear
thee say, That Cassio's not alive. . . . . Now art thou my lieutenant.' The last words
are remarkable. Othello has so thoroughly forgotten the habits of civilised life, that
he does not see that, after having murdered his wife, the daughter of a Venetian senator, and assassinated Cassio, a man of high rank in the Republic, he cannot remain
governor of Cyprus. From thence until the very last Scene the savage reigns triumphant. He does not preserve even the outward proprieties of his station, but insults and
strikes his wife in the presence of the envoy from the Senate.

But the instant that he has satiated his revenge, the spirit from the desert seems to be
appeased by the sacrifice and quits him. He now ' knows that his act shows horrible
and grim.'

[In his remarks on ' Now art thou my Lieutenant,' the Reviewer has been anticipated
by Professor WILSON in his *Christopher under Canvas*, for April, 1850, ' What did
' Othello intend to do,' asks North, ' after all was accomplished ? He was stone-blind
' to the future. What does he expect ? that when he has killed his wife, everything is
' to go on as smoothly as before ? That no notice will be taken of it ? or that he will
' have to make another speech to the Senate ? He has told them how he married
' her,—the counterpart will be to relate ' a plain, unvarnished tale of my whole course '
' of smothering and stabbing her with bolster and dagger. ' Now thou art my lieuten-
' ant ' shows—if not stone-blindness,—a singular confidence in the future.'—ED.]

J. A. HERAUD (*Shakspere, His Inner Life*, London, 1865, p. 268) : The credulous
Moor of Cinthio is very unlike the loving Othello of the play, and his tempter is moved
to his infamous course by his illicit love for Desdemona. This weak passion is, in the
play, transferred to Roderigo,—a creation of Shakspere's own, partly as a comic relief
to the tragic action and partly as a link of sympathy with the audience. Iago is the
really jealous person, and, suspecting Othello with his own wife, hates him accordingly
and determines on revenge. . . . . A perfect hero cannot be made interesting, and
Shakespeare gives to all his heroes, whatever may be their abstract qualities, some
human infirmity by which they secure our sympathy. Perfect love, such as would
belong to a perfect soul, would ' cast out all fear,' and that of Othello is so perfect in
its degree that it is ' not easily jealous,' nor is it naturally suspicious. But it can be
' wrought,' and therefore there is in his otherwise perfect character a peccant part.
From his scene with Emilia, when he throws her the purse as the portress of Hell's
gate, he shows that he has ' poured his treasures into foreign laps '; and from the revelation which Emilia makes of her own character to her mistress, it is not impossible
that her husband's ugly suspicions were not ill-founded. Othello had been no celibate,
nor pretended to be such, and previous to his acquaintance with Desdemona had cultivated some experiences by which his virtue had not been strengthened. There was
this flaw in his conduct, and by this inlet both suspicion and jealousy might enter ;
neither could have found a thoroughfare in a perfectly innocent character. Even the
' perfect soul,' living the life of camps, had found the preservation of its innocence
impossible. In proportion that it had sinned it had become weak, and thus Othello
was laid open to the temptation of Iago, and liable to a further fall. All mankind are,

in some respect or other, similarly exposed from similar causes to evil communication; and our conscience, therefore, leads us to pity and forgive the noble Moor for his obvious fault and the fatal consequences. These reasons are philosophical and true; and therefore we must not accept Othello as an absolute and direct affirmation of a perfect loving soul, but as a negative instance approximating perfection as near as possible, yet fallible because it could not be identified with it. This view,—all but the highest,— simply because it is not the highest, makes the character and the tragedy possible. . . . .

The theme of the play is Love. In *Romeo and Juliet,* Love before marriage was the argument, now it is Love after. The common Idea is differently conceived by the persons of the drama. . . . . Othello and Iago divide the moral and intellectual view, and the real debate is between the two principals. The latter is naturally a jealous husband, and the revenge which he seeks is to infect his enemy with the same plague. Unfortunately for his victim, there is a joint in his armour loose, as in that of every man, and there enters the poisoned point of his foeman's spear. The tragedy, however, might not have been possible at all but for a defect in Desdemona's character. Her passion was romantic, and there exists fiction in whatever is romantic. She suffers from illusion and loves to be deluded. If she is self-deceived, she likewise deceives others. It is on this ground that Brabantio warns Othello: 'She has deceived her father, and may thee.' In word, deed, thought, she must have been guilty of falsehood; and, virtuous as she otherwise is, we find in the development of the drama that she has one foible. It is the slightest of foibles, but one frequently fatal,—a habit of fibbing. From a timidity of disposition she frequently evades the truth, when attention to its strict letter would raise a difficulty. Practically, too, she dallies with falsehood: 'I am not merry, but I do beguile The thing I am by seeming otherwise.' To *seem otherwise* than she is, in order to obtain her end, is at all times lawful in her estimation; not meaning ill, but to make matters easy. Reticent as Hero,—perhaps more so, because her conduct suppressed the truth when it did not falsify it,—there was always an amount of 'seeming' in it which misled observers: 'A maiden never bold; Of spirit so still and quiet, that her motion Blushed at herself.' Yet, all the time, she was carrying on a love-intrigue with a man of another race and colour, in which she was 'half the wooer.' When this fact is pointed out to Othello, it naturally raises suspicion. One so accustomed to deport herself gives no certain index in her behaviour by which her mental or her moral state may be judged of. All this proceeds not from criminality of disposition, but indolence or susceptibility of temper. Iago practises on the quality· 'For 'tis most easy The *inclining* Desdemona to subdue In any honest suit.' And, even so, she readily undertakes the cause of Cassio, and assures him of success. With her the end consecrates the means, and she regards nothing but the success of her enterprise. How she pleads with Othello for Cassio we know. With characteristic lenity she makes light of his fault, falsely arguing, not unconsciously: 'Save that they *say,* the wars must make examples,' &c. And immediately gives us an insight into her little foible, and how habitually she was induced to indulge in it: 'What! Michael Cassio, That came a-wooing with you, and *many a time When I have spoke of you dispraisingly* Hath,' &c. So that Desdemona had not only disguised her sentiments from her father, but had idly sought to do the same from Cassio, who was in the secret. Iago might have, indeed, inferred from this conduct that the 'super-supple Venetian,' his mistress, was willing to regard the lieutenant with special favour. As she warms in her advocacy with Othello, she puts a further false colouring on the transaction, pretending to disparage the importance to her of the suit she was promoting: 'Nay, when I have a suit Wherein I mean to touch your love indeed, It shall be full of poise and difficult weight, And fearful to be granted.' No lawyer for a fee pleaded more intrepidly in behalf of a criminal client, whose acquittal he desired in the face of the clearest evidence. And in the affair of the handkerchief we find in her the same indifference to truth. She had dropped it in a moment of excitement, and probably forgot the fact; but she is at no pains to recollect, and finds it easier to feign an excuse for the nonce, than to cast about for the true reason. She had certainly questioned Emilia about it, and recognized its importance, if Othello were a jealous person; but as he is not, she will not think too much about it. When Othello asks for it, she is frightened into a direct lie. If at this critical moment Desdemona had confessed the truth, the tragedy would·have been prevented and Iago's plot nipped in the bud. Even on her deathbed the case is the same. She tells Emilia that she had killed herself. . . . . The truth is, that the lady's faults only render her more womanly. They are mainly those of her sex, ay, and of the most amiable of her sex. Desdemona is not a strong-minded, rationalistic woman; but a tender, loving, and devoted one, brought up in the lap of luxury and swayed by her feelings rather than by her reason. Nevertheless, we should not conceal from ourselves that there is even in this a defect, and that therefrom a number of injurious effects ensue which may end fatally.

[' I should have mentioned the very impolite behaviour of Mr Burchell, who, during this discourse, sate with his face turned to the fire, and at the conclusion of every sentence would cry out " Fudge !" '—*Vicar of Wakefield.*—ED.]

EDWARD DOWDEN (*Shakspere—His Mind and Art*, London, 1875, p. 226): There are certain problems which Shakspere at once pronounces insoluble. He does not, like Milton, propose to give any account of the origin of evil. He does not, like Dante, pursue the soul of man through circles of unending torture, or spheres made radiant with the eternal presence of God. Satan, in Shakspere's poems, does not come voyaging on gigantic vans across Chaos to find the earth. No great deliverer of mankind descends from the heavens. Here, upon the earth, evil *is*,—such was Shakspere's declaration in the most emphatic accent. Iago actually exists. There is also on the earth a sacred passion of deliverance, a pure redeeming ardour. Cordelia exists. This, Shakspere can tell for certain. But how Iago can be, and why Cordelia lies strangled across the breast of Lear—are these questions which you go on to ask? Something has been already said of the severity of Shakspere. It is a portion of his severity to decline all answers to questions such as these. Is ignorance painful? Well, then, it is painful. Little solutions of your large difficulties can readily be obtained from priest or *philosophe*. Shakspere prefers to let you remain in the solemn presence of a mystery. He does not invite you into his little church or his little library brilliantly illuminated by philosophical or theological rushlights. You remain in the darkness. But you remain in the vital air. And the great night is overhead. . . . .

If the same unknowable force which manifests itself through man, manifests itself likewise through the animal world, we might suppose that there were some special affinities between the soul of Othello and the lion of his ancestral desert. Assuredly the same malignant power that lurks in the eye and that fills with venom the fang of the serpent, would seem to have brought into existence Iago. ' It is the strength of the base element that is so dreadful in the serpent; it is the very omnipotence of the earth. . . . . It scarcely breathes with its one lung (the other shrivelled and abortive); it is passive to the sun and shade, and is cold or hot like a stone; yet " it can outclimb the monkey, outswim the fish, outleap the zebra, outwrestle the athlete, and crush the tiger." It is a

divine hieroglyph of the demoniac power of the earth,—of the entire earthly nature.' *
Such is the serpent Iago.

(P. 242.) Of the tragic story, wha. is the final issue ? The central point of its spiritual import lies in the contrast between the two men, Iago and his victim. Iago, with
keen intellectual faculties and manifold culture in Italian vice, lives and thrives after
his fashion in a world from which all virtue and beauty are absent. Othello, with his
barbaric innocence and regal magnificence of soul, must cease to live the moment he
ceases to retain faith in the purity and goodness which were to him the highest and
most real things upon earth. Or, if he live, life must become to him a cruel agony.
Shakspere compels us to acknowledge that self-slaughter is a rapturous energy,—that
such prolonged agony is joy in comparison with the earthy life-in-death of such a sou
as that of Iago. The noble nature is taken in the toils because it is noble. Iago suspects his wife of every baseness, but the suspicion has no other effect than to intensify
his malignity. Iago could not be captured and constrained to heroic suffering and rage.
The shame of every being who bears the name of woman is credible to Iago, and yet
he can grate from his throat the jarring music : ' And let me the canakin clink, clink !
And let me the canakin clink ! ' . There is therefore, Shakspere would have us understand, something more inimical to humanity than suffering,—namely, an incapacity for
noble pain. To die as Othello dies is indeed grievous. But to live as Iago lives, devouring the dust and stinging—this is more appalling.

Such is the spiritual motive that controls the tragedy. And the validity of this truth
is demonstrable to every sound conscience. No supernatural authority needs to be summoned to bear witness to this reality of human life. No pallid flame of hell, no splendour of dawning heaven, needs show itself beyond the verge of earth to illumine this
truth. It is a portion of the ascertained fact of human nature, and of this our mortal
existence. We look upon 'the tragic loading of the bed,' and we see Iago in presence
of the ruin he has wrought. We are not compelled to seek for any resolution of these
apparent discords in any alleged life to come. That may also be; we shall accept it,
if it be. But looking sternly and strictly at what is now actual and present to our
sight, we yet rise above despair. Desdemona's adhesion to her husband and to love
survived the ultimate trial. Othello dies ' upon a kiss.' He perceives his own calam-
itous error, and he recognizes Desdemona pure and loyal as she was. Goodness is justified of her child. It is evil which suffers defeat. It is Iago whose whole existence
has been most blind, purposeless, and miserable—a struggle against the virtuous powers
of the world, by which at last he stands convicted and condemned.

D. J. SNIDER (*System of Shakespeare's Dramas*, St. Louis, 1877, ii, 97) : In *Othello*
there are three essential divisions or movements of the entire action. The First is the
external conflict in the Family. The right of the daughter to choose a Moor for her
husband is asserted against the will of the parent. Both sides appeal to the State,
which decides in favour of the marriage, and Othello carries off his bride in triumph.
The guilt of Desdemona is here indicated. The Second movement shows the internal
conflict in the Family between husband and wife. The married pair, though successful
in their external struggle with the father, are now rent asunder; for between such characters no secure, permanent ethical union is possible. Jealousy must arise. Iago seized
only what was already prepared, and used it for his own purposes. The guilt of Othello

---

* Quoted from Richard Owen by Ruskin, *The Queen of the Air*, p. 83.

and his Ancient is here shown. The Third movement is the retribution, which brings home to every person the consequences of his deed.

[It is in the Second movement that Snider is obliged to put forth his strength, and in order to account for the existence of jealousy in a 'character fundamentally free from jealousy,' or to explain how 'an unsuspicious person becomes filled with the most deadly suspicion,' he follows the line of argument set forth by Heraud, but urges it with an emphasis which no one else has ventured, or been sufficiently skilful, to give. As I differ from him, *toto cœlo*, I shall do my best, by copious extracts, omitting no single essential sentence, to set forth his position with entire fairness. I think no one can read even these extracts, let alone the two volumes from which they are taken, without respect for the earnestness and admiration for the ingenuity with which this Ethical view of Shakespeare's dramas is elaborated,—the subject is evidently in an adept's hand. At the close of these extracts from Snider's volume, I shall not repeat the quotation from Goldsmith which I appended to Heraud, however fitly it may express my feelings; after Snider's more vigorous attack I am afraid it might be construed as a tribute to his force and as the resort of feebleness where sturdy arguments are lacking.—ED.]

(P. III.) The character of the Moor is a contradiction,—and, hence, an impossibility,—without some adequate ground for the great change which it undergoes. If he were naturally jealous, there would be needed no motive for his conduct; but the difficult point lies in the fact that he is naturally without jealousy. His characterization, as well as that of Iago, has been pronounced unnatural; and so it is, unless some adequate impelling principle can be given to account for the total inversion of his nature. (P. 112.) Iago's disbelief in the honour of woman must be regarded as the result of his own experience. Married life has for him brought forth only its bitterest fruits. . . . . That his opinion of Emilia is true is very plainly indicated in the last Scene of Act IV. Othello is also well acquainted with her character. He knows her falsehood and infidelity; he will not believe any of her statements, and loads her with the most opprobrious epithets.

We are now brought face to face with a question which it is by no means pleasant to consider, but which has to be discussed if we wish to comprehend the Poet's work. Must we regard the Moor as guilty of what Iago suspects him? There is nothing in the play which shows that Othello was innocent of the charge, but there is much which shows that he was not innocent. The very fact that this suspicion is cast upon him almost at the beginning, and is nowhere removed, seems sufficient to raise the presumption of guilt. It hangs over him like a cloud which will not pass away. Then Emilia's character, instead of precluding, strengthens the supposition of criminal intercourse, and the notion is still further upheld by the knowledge of her habits which Othello betrays. But the veil is never wholly removed. Why does not the Poet openly state the offence, so as to leave no doubt? It is evident that he does not wish to soil the union with Desdemona by dwelling on Othello's incontinence, nor does he desire to throw into the background the difference of race as the leading motive of the play. Still, he would not have us forget the dark surmise; there it remains suspended over the Moor to the last. Iago, to be sure, is a liar; but his lies are meant for others, and not for himself. Besides, Iago is not more certain at first than we, his readers and hearers, are; but the complete success of his plan, which is based on the Moor's guilt, confirms, both for him and for us, the truth of the suspicion.

So much is indicated in the course of the play; but, if the deeper motives of the various characters are carefully examined, this conclusion would seem to become irresistible. Iago is manifestly assailed with the same burning jealousy which afterwards wrought such terrific effects in Othello. Now, what will be the manner of his revenge? The most logical and adequate would be, 'wife for wife;' hence his first thought is to debauch Desdemona. But nothing more is heard of this plan, for it could not possibly be successful. Then comes his most shrewd and peculiar method of avenging his wrong. If he cannot dishonour Othello in reality, he can do it in appearance, with almost the same results. His purpose is to make Othello believe that Desdemona is untrue. This will be a revenge sufficient for his end. It will destroy Othello's happiness and peace of mind just as well as the truth; it will bring upon Othello that which he has brought upon Iago. Another phase of the question now comes up for solution: How far was it possible to excite such a passion in a character like that of Othello? The free, open, unsuspecting nature of the Moor is noted by Iago himself; his noble and heroic disposition would appear least likely to be subject to jealousy. Yet this is the very form of revenge chosen by Iago with surpassing skill. This is, therefore, just the weak side of Othello's character. Why? The solution of the problem lies in the fact above mentioned,—that Iago's suspicion concerning Emilia is true. Othello has been guilty of adultery; he is, therefore, aware that the infidelity of wives is a fact. Here lies the germ of his belief in the faithlessness of Desdemona. His own act thus comes home to him and renders him accursed; his faith in justice can only make him more ready to think that he will be punished through his wife, since that is the mode which his own guilt suggests. Such is the initial point of the fearful jealousy of the Moor, which Iago knows exactly how to reach, since it is a matter lying wholly within his own experience; and he knows also that Othello, on account of previous criminality, must be as capable of this passion as himself. Both the revenge of Iago and the jealousy of Othello, therefore, can be adequately motived only by the guilty conduct of the Moor towards the Ancient's wife.

Moreover, there is no other ground for the relation of marriage between Iago and Emilia, except as a basis for these two main motives of the drama. Thus, too, we see one of the fundamental rules of Shakespeare vindicated,—that man cannot escape his own deed; hence Othello is the author of his own fate, since by his guilt he has called up the avenger who will destroy him and his family; while, without the view above developed, he must appear as an innocent sufferer deceived by a malicious villain. It will, therefore, be seen that two things of the greatest importance have their sole explanation in this view; namely, the manner of Iago's revenge, and his knowledge of the assailable point in Othello's character. Here, also, we find the solution of the Moor's contradictory nature. He is, in general, unsuspecting; but, on account of his guilt, he is capable of one suspicion; namely, that wives may be faithless. The Poet has thus added to the distinction of race,—for which the Moor could not be blamed,—a second motive, the criminal deed, of which he must take the responsibility. The military life of Othello will furnish the third principle,—that of honour, which will impel him to destroy the wife whom he thinks to have violated it in its deepest and most tender part.

[Iago's plans being thus unfolded, Snider shows that his instruments are: First, Roderigo; Second, Cassio, 'an open and notorious libertine,' whom Iago also suspects of undue familiarity with Emilia,—a suspicion which is not confirmed in the play. But to remove all doubt of Cassio's moral weaknesses, Bianca is introduced by the Poet. 'There is no other ground why such an offensive relation should be dragged into the drama.' Emilia is the Third instrument.]

(P. 118.) Such are the instruments; but Iago himself has to manage the far more difficult case of Othello in his relation to Desdemona. This brings us now to the main development of the drama, and, perhaps, the most complete psychological portraiture in Shakespeare. Iago begins the manipulation of Othello's mind through a series of influences adapted exactly to the shifting phases of the Moor's disposition, and increasing in intensity to the end. Given a noble, unsuspecting character, the design is to portray those causes which not only turn it into the opposite of itself, but make it destroy its most beloved object. The primal basis to work upon lies in Othello's own consciousness of guilt. The first point is to faintly touch his suspicion, which is accomplished most easily, for he readily believes what he himself has done to others may happen in his own case. We see how the slightest hint from Iago casts a shadow over his whole being. '*Iago*. Ha! I like not that. *Othello*. What dost thou say? *Iago*. Nothing, my lord, or if— I know not what. *Othello*. Was not that Cassio parted from my wife?' etc. A word from Desdemona is sufficient, however, to allay his mistrust, but another word from Iago is sufficient to arouse it anew in all its intensity. Can any one doubt that this hasty suspicion, on the part of an unsuspecting character, can have any other ground than the consciousness of the same kind of guilt which he is so ready to suspect in another? Iago's artifices are unquestionably skilful, but he found a most fruitful and well-prepared soil; and, besides, his very skilfulness rests upon his comprehending and utilizing so thoroughly the psychological effects of Othello's crime. It is impossible to think that an honest and innocent man could have been so easily led astray. . . . . [In the dialogue where Iago cautions Othello to beware of jealousy, Iago has a twofold purpose,—viz., to inspire Othello with suspicion, and yet to shun any suspicion directed against himself.] (P. 121.) Othello is caught, the reason is manifest. A universally suspicious nature could not have been thus entrapped; it must have suspected the purpose of Iago also, with all his adroitness. Othello is, however, naturally unsuspecting. But guilt has furnished the most fruitful soil for one kind of suspicion; that soil Iago cultivates. Hence the Moor is afraid of only one thing,—the infidelity of his wife; the tricks of Iago lie outside of the horizon of his suspicion. On the other hand, a completely innocent nature could not have been thus entrapped; the psychological basis would have been wholly wanting. Here is seen the reason for the marked outlines of Othello's character. He is not naturally suspicious, otherwise he must have suspected the purpose of Iago; nor is he guiltless, for, if he were, his jealousy could not have been reached by any such artifice.

EDWARD ROSE (*Sudden Emotion: Its Effect upon Different Characters as Shown by Shakspere*—New Shakspere Society, *Transactions*, 1880–82, p. 1).* [The different characters upon which Rose proposes to note the effect of sudden emotions are 'essentially two: the men who are habitually self-conscious, given to analyse their own minds and deeds, and the men who are not.' After proposing as types of the former some modern poets, such as Tennyson, Browning, and Clough, men who constantly look into their own minds and examine their own motives; and as types of the latter, men like Darwin and the Duke of Wellington, who act from obvious motives and with a minimum of self-consciousness,—Rose proceeds:]

With this prelude, let me state my theory as to the effect of sudden emotion—I mean sudden emotion of the most intense kind—upon characters of these two opposing types,

---

* I cannot refrain from expressing my admiration of this thoughtful Essay, and regret that I cannot reproduce it all here. Had the *New Shakspere Society* done no other sterling work in that year, the appearance of this and a following Essay by Mr Rose would have been sufficient to justify its existence.—ED.

as shown by Shakspere. A man of simple nature sees a fact and realizes it : a man in whom the reflective intellect predominates thinks about it. Therefore, a great sudden emotion stuns the one, makes him helpless for the time : the other does not realize it so intensely,—it is more, as I have said, a great deal of new matter to think about, and his intellect is thus stimulated to think twice as fast as usual. Or I might put it thus : our moral nature takes a thing as a whole, our intellect examines, dissects it ; therefore a great event awes our moral nature, but sets our intellect hard at work, and, therefore, men in whom the moral nature predominates are stunned, while men chiefly intellectual are stimulated, by a sudden occurrence of the highest joy or sorrow.

That Shakspere held this theory was suggested to me by two parallel passages : those in which are shown the effects of the Ghost's revelation upon Hamlet, and of the murder of Duncan upon Macbeth. [Here follows the confirmation of his theory in these passages, and on p. 10 we resume :] I will now take some extreme instances of the opposite type of character—Othello, Desdemona, Macduff—that no intermediate gradations may make the contrast less striking. But first I must point out that the most intense emotion of these simpler characters is not so easily put into words by the dramatist, for the reason that its typical expression is silence, or inarticulate sounds of grief or joy. The poet must either leave these to the actor, or give a verbal picture, not strictly dramatic, of a mind which, in reality, would be stunned and speechless. The former alternative is a dangerous one, which Shakspere has rarely adopted,—perhaps the example most nearly perfect is that of Helena, in the Second Act of *All's Well that Ends Well*, who makes only one speech of a dozen words after Bertram has refused to marry her. In the alternative which he generally chose, of giving to intense emotion words more coherent than those of nature would be, there is, I think, a rule by which we can distinguish these utterances from such perfectly dramatic speeches as those of Hamlet and Macbeth : the latter are rich in intellect, filled with varied thoughts variously expressed ; the former are little more than repetitions of the one crushing conception, in words often curiously monotonous. Thus, Macduff's ' *All* my pretty ones ? Did ' you say *all ?* O hell-kite ! *All ?* What, *all* my pretty chickens and their dam At one ' fell swoop ? ' We see so little of Macduff that it is scarcely possible to sum up his character ; but all his one chief scene,—with Malcolm first, and then with Ross,—indicates a man of strong and simple feelings. The words he forces out are only spoken at the urging of his companion, who, indeed, expresses in one phrase Shakspere's theory as to the crushing effect of emotion on those characters who allow themselves to realize it completely and immediately :—' The grief that does not speak Whispers the o'erfraught heart and bids it break.'

Desdemona, the most lovable, I think, of Shakespeare's women, is, perhaps, the strongest example of the rule I have proposed. Othello's attack at once stuns her ; she is brave, and denies his accusation as soon as he speaks it clearly, but the effort is almost too much for her. When, a moment later, Emilia asks her how she does, she can answer only, ' Faith, half asleep.' [See IV, ii, 113–134.]

And, after she has roused herself to one great protest against her lord's suspicion, her mind relapses into bewildered helplessness for the short remainder of her life. She goes over again and again the one thought that she can take in,—the enormous, utterly impossible crime of which she is accused. She realizes only the accusation ; she cannot even *think* the existence of the sin. An exquisitely subtle touch shows how she tries, with her perfect innocence, to imagine what guilt is. She sees Lodovico, a young and handsome man, and wonders if it could be possible for her, another's wife, to love him. She resolves that she ' could not do such a deed for the whole world.' In the last scene of all there is no spring, no elasticity about her mind; no reflection, one might say no thought. In almost all other cases Shakspere shows how strangely the brain does its work in moments of great emotion. Here, by exception, he shows a perfectly simple nature beaten down by terrible reality. At the end her words have the directness and the oneness of a child's begging helplessly for delay of punishment :—'O banish me, my lord, but kill me not!—Kill me to-morrow: let me live to-night!—But half an hour!—But while I say one prayer!'

Hero, by the way, in *Much Ado About Nothing*, is but an early sketch of Desdemona: when she is similarly accused, after a few sentences of simple answers and ejaculations, she falls in a swoon.

The great character of Othello undoubtedly belongs to this class. He has a strong and healthy mind and a vivid imagination, but they deal entirely with first impressions, with obvious facts. If he trusts a man, he trusts him without the faintest shadow of reserve. Iago's suggestion that Desdemona is false comes upon him like a thunderbolt. He *knows* this man to be honest, his every word the absolute truth. He is stunned, and his mind accepts specious reasonings passively and without examination. Yet his love is so intense that he struggles against his own nature, and for a time *compels* himself to think, though not upon the great question whether she is false. He cannot bring his intellect to attack Iago's conclusions, and only argues the minor point: *Why* is she false? But even this effort is too much for him. It is, I have said, against nature; and nature, after the struggle has been carried on unceasingly for hours, revenges herself—he falls into a fit. That this is the legitimate climax of overpowering emotion on an intensely real and single character is plain. This obstruction and chaos of the faculties is the absolute opposite of the brilliant life into which Hamlet's intellect leaps on its contact with tremendous realities.

The soliloquy at the end of Othello's first scene with Iago may appear to make rather against my theory; it does not merely repeat one thought, it goes from point to point: 'If I do prove her haggard I'll whistle her off. Haply that I am black—or, for I am declined into the vale of years—yet that's not much. My relief must be to loathe her. 'Tis the plague of great ones.' But this contradiction, I fancy, is only apparent. He is trying to force his mind to work, as I have said, and it flutters helplessly from one minor point to another; moreover, jealousy is a mean and worrying passion, attaching itself to details, not grand and broad like the greatest love, hate, or ambition. My theory, by the way, may help to account for what has always troubled critics—the extraordinary quickness with which Othello's faith in Desdemona yields to Iago's insinuations. Sudden and intense emotion stuns his nature, and makes it incapable of resistance.

GERMAN CRITICISMS

JOHANN HEINRICH VOSS (*Shakespeare's Othello, uebersetzt*, Jena, 1806, p. vi): For several years it was the wish of Schiller to see *Othello* put upon our stage, but he was too busy with his own creations to undertake the humbler task of translation. Accordingly, when I became more intimate with him I complied with his proposal, and engaged in the agreeable task of working at a translation of this masterpiece of the Muse of Shakspeare. To it I devoted all my leisure hours, and at the beginning of 1805 handed to Schiller the first draft of a faithful translation. We went through it together, discussing with critical nicety the difficult passages until finally the work received its present form. Schiller proposed in the warmer coming days of Spring to have the piece put upon the stage and to superintend the rehearsal. This he did not live to do; the day of his death came sooner than the first of Spring!

The unusual length of the play, and the changes which the centuries, since Shakspeare's time, had produced not only in the demands of the Stage but of the public rendered certain important modifications necessary, which Schiller effected with as sparing a hand as possible. He regretted the necessity of striking out the beginning of Act II, where Iago gives utterance to that hatred of the other sex which he subsequently puts into practice. Schiller was less sparing in other places, where Shakspeare out of the inexhaustible wealth of his genius lavishes it with full hands more plenteously than was necessary. The character of Bianca,—a rôle indispensable, in order, through the introduction of the handkerchief, to excite the frenzy of Othello to the highest degree,—has been in some respects refined, wherefor there was no essential but only a superficial reason. Act IV Schiller began with the swooning of Othello, which is sufficiently explained by Iago's words: 'Work on! My medicine works.' From a fearful effect a fearful cause might be inferred, and this we decided to be better than to have, as in the original, both the cause and the effect before our eyes. In the undressing scene, the noble Desdemona, while Emilia makes her coarse speech, stands without listening to her, sunk in her misgivings, and strikes in with the last verse of the willow-song.

These are the most important changes made by the immortal man. *It was his last work!*

A. W. SCHLEGEL (*Lectures on Dramatic Art and Literature*. Translated by John Black, London, 1815, vol. ii, p. 189): If *Romeo and Juliet* shines with the colours of the dawn of morning, but a dawn whose purple clouds already announce the thunder of a sultry day, *Othello* is, on the other hand, a strongly-shaded picture; we might call it a tragical *Rembrandt*. What a fortunate mistake that the Moor, under which name a baptized Saracen of the northern coast of Africa was unquestionably meant in the novel, has been made by Shakespeare, in every respect, a negro! We recognize in Othello the wild nature of that glowing zone which generates the most raging beasts of prey and the most deadly poisons, tamed only in appearance by the desire of fame, by foreign laws of honor, and by nobler and milder manners. His jealousy is not the jealousy of the heart, which is incompatible with the tenderest feeling and adoration of the beloved object; it is of that sensual kind from which, in burning climes, has sprung the disgraceful ill-treatment of women and many other unnatural usages. A drop of this poison flows in his veins, and sets his whole blood in the most disorderly fermentation. The Moor seems noble, frank, confiding, grateful for the love shown him; and he *is* all this, and, moreover, a hero that spurns at danger, a worthy leader of an army, a faithful servant of the state; but the mere physical force of passion puts to flight in one moment all his acquired and accustomed virtues, and gives the upper hand to the savage in him over the moral man.   The tyranny of the blood over the will betrays itself even in the expression of his desire of revenge against Cassio.   In his repentance when he views the evidence of the deed, a genuine tenderness for his murdered wife, and the painful feeling of his annihilated honour, at last burst forth; and he every now and then assails himself with the rage a despot shows in punishing a runaway slave.   He suffers as a double man; at once in the higher and lower sphere into which his being was divided.   While the Moor bears only the nightly colour of suspicion and deceit on his visage, Iago is black within.   He pursues Othello like his evil spirit, and with his light, and therefore the more dangerous, insinuations, he leaves him no rest; it is as if by means of an unfortunate affinity, founded, however, in nature, this influence was, by necessity, more powerful over him than the voice of his good angel Desdemona.   A more artful villain than this Iago has never been portrayed; he spreads his net with a skill which nothing can escape.   The repugnance inspired by his aims becomes supportable from the attention of the spectators being directed to his means; they furnish infinite employment to the understanding.   Cool, discontented, and morose, arrogant where he dare be so, but humble and insinuating when it suits his purpose, he is a complete master in the art of dissimulation; accessible only to selfish emotions, he is thoroughly skilled in rousing the passions of others, and of availing himself of every opening which they give him: he is as excellent an observer of men as any one can be who is unacquainted with higher motives of action from his own experience; there is always some truth in his malicious observations on them.   He does not merely pretend to an obdurate incredulity as to the virtue of women, he actually entertains it; and this, too, falls in with his whole way of thinking, and makes him the more fit for the execution of his purposes.   As in everything he sees merely the hateful side, he dissolves in the rudest manner the charm which the imagination casts over the relation between the two sexes; he does so for the purpose of throwing into commotion the senses of Othello, whom his heart might easily have convinced of the innocence of Desdemona.   This must serve as an excuse for the numerous expressions in the speeches of Iago from which modesty shrinks back.   If Shakespeare had written in our days he would not, perhaps, have dared to hazard them; but this must certainly have injured the truth of the picture.   Desdemona is an offering without blemish. She is not, it is true, a high ideal representation of sweetness and enthusiastic passion like Juliet; full of simplicity, softness, and humility, and so innocent that she can hardly form to herself an idea of the possibility of infidelity, she seems calculated to make the most yielding and tender wife.   The female propensity wholly to follow a foreign destiny has led her into the only error she ever committed,—that of marrying without the consent of her father.   Her choice seems wrong; and yet she has been gained over to Othello by that which induces the female to honour in man her protector and guide,—admiration of his determined heroism, and compassion for the sufferings which he had undergone.   With great art it is so contrived that from the very circumstance that the possibility of a suspicion of herself never once enters her mind, she is the less reserved in her solicitation for Cassio, by which she more and more heightens the jealousy of the Moor.   To give still greater effect to the angelic purity of Desdemona, Shakspeare has in Emilia associated with her a companion of doubtful virtue.   From the sinful levity of this woman, it is also conceivable that she should not confess the abstraction of the handkerchief when Othello violently demands it back·

this would otherwise be the circumstance in the whole piece the most difficult to justify. Cassio is portrayed exactly as he ought to be to excite suspicion without actual guilt, amiable and nobly disposed, but easily seduced. The public events of the first two Acts show us Othello in his most glorious aspect, as the support of Venice and the terror of the Turks; they serve to withdraw the story from the mere domestic circle, which is done in *Romeo and Juliet* by the dissensions between the houses of Montague and Capulet. No eloquence is capable of painting the overwhelming force of the catastrophe in *Othello*, the pressure of feelings which measure out in a moment the abysses of eternity.

FRANZ HORN (*Shakespeare's Schauspiele erläutert*, Leipzig, 1823, ii, 336): Nothing in poetry has ever been written more pathetic than the scene preceding Desdemona's death; I confess I almost always turn away my eyes from the poor girl with her infinitely touching song of ' Willow, willow, willow,' and I would fain ask the Poet whether his tragic arrow, which always hits the mark, does not here pierce almost too deeply. I would not call the last word with which she dies a lie, or even a ' noble ' lie; this qualification has been wretchedly misused. The lie with which Desdemona dies is divine truth, too good to come within the compass of an earthy moral code.

As already said, all these scenes reach the supreme degree of the pathetic as no other Poet has ever reached it; and here a question may, perhaps, be permitted that seems almost paradoxical : who is there who could have aided the poor dear child Desdemona? To my thinking, the best and surest would have been Portia of Belmont, who cut short all idea of love for the Prince of Morocco with the bare thought that he was black; but then Desdemona would not have been Desdemona.

ULRICI (*Shakespeare's dramatische Kunst.*, Leipzig, 1847, 2te Aflge, 1ste Abt., p. 379. Translated for Bohn's Library by Miss L. Dora Schmitz, London, 1876, vol. i, p. 418): The main springs of the action consequently lie in the characters of the persons represented, and yet the tragic catastrophe arises only indirectly, *not directly*, out of the disposition and the mode of action of the tragic heroes. The construction of the piece, in this, differs distinctly from that of Shakespeare's other tragedies. In *Romeo and Juliet, Hamlet, King Lear*, and *Macbeth*, nay, even in his Historical Tragedies, the poet, in the first place, exhibits a certain position of affairs; he describes the circumstances, relations, and situations, as well as the characters of the surrounding persons among whom his tragic heroes live; in other words, he first lays the foundation upon which the edifice is to be raised, but whose construction it is directly to affect only in so far as the fortunes of his heroes proceed, it is true, from this foundation, but, in the first place and directly, from their own characters, their own actions, their freedom, and self-determination. Thus, to give an example : in *Romeo and Juliet* the furious hatred between the Capulets and Montagues does, indeed, form the basis of the tragic catastrophe, but this relation is a positive one to the two lovers; they, therefore, are aware of it, and if they nevertheless follow the impulse of their passionate love,—out of which alone their tragic ruin is developed,—then it is their own will or the necessary consequence of their own characters. The relations and circumstances, as well as the secondary persons who surround them, certainly do help on their fate, but the primary cause of it is, nevertheless, the state of their own minds and the manner of their own action. It is different with our present drama. Othello does not know of Iago's hatred, of his revengeful spirit, of his wickedness and cunning; he does not see the cliffs upon which his life is to be wrecked, hence he cannot order his purposes and actions in accordance with them. His mode of action, therefore, does not only not arise from his freedom, but, directly, not even from his character; it is rather caused by an inconceivable imposition practised upon him by another person; without this imposition there is in Othello's whole being not even the smallest corner from which such monstrous deeds could burst forth. It is only this external influence which first, as it were, breaks down his whole character, and turns the lowest portion of it uppermost. That he allows himself to be deceived arises, it is true, from his own individuality, but only partially. For, on the other hand, the deceit is so cunningly contrived, so favored by circumstances, that even the most cautious and most circumspect person would have been deceived by it. In short, the distinguishing peculiarity of our drama consists in its being a tragedy of *intrigue*, whereas all Shakespeare's other tragedies are rather tragedies of *character*.

This distinction, which has long been recognized in the domain of comedy, has hitherto not found place in the æsthetic criticism of tragedy, owing to the very good reason that, in reality, the predominance of intrigue is opposed to the nature of tragedy. Intrigue, because invariably based upon the special objects of a single individual, necessarily has the stamp of accident and caprice. If, therefore, it is made the lever of the action, the primary cause of the tragic catastrophe, the tragedy loses its character of grandeur and sublimity; it is precipitated from the region of a higher necessity, of a fate,—which, indeed, lies in the inmost nature of man himself and proceeds from it, but then overpowers and masters him,—into the lower sphere of every-day life, in which only the limited interests and purposes of single individuals mutually combat and outwit one another. The downfall of human greatness and beauty which is not founded upon its own immediate weakness or one-sidedness, but, though not altogether, yet chiefly, occasioned by the cunning and the power of the evil which opposes it, is something revolting; it offends the human sense of justice, and calls forth a doubt of the divine order in the world. In short, it disturbs the impression of what is tragic, because it places the contradictions of human existence in the sharpest dissonance without indicating their dénoûment, or revealing that reconciling power which lies under all events ordained by God.

From the predominance of intrigue, it follows as a matter of course that chance also plays an important part, and that in a certain sense it assumes the character of intrigue. For chance is, in fact, but *objective* caprice, the caprice of *subjective* chance; both correspond with one another because they are internally of one nature. Now, chance is to be as little excluded from tragedy as intrigue; both are essential elements of human life, and, therefore, have a perfect right to be represented in all human actions and fortunes. And yet it is only in the field of comedy that they have a right to be a *principal* power in the dramatic development; they may *predominate* only in comedy. In tragedy, on the other hand, they must be employed only as an additional means to further the development, or as the echo of the outer world, which merely answers to the hero's disposition and mode of action; whereas the actual cause of the tragic fate must be in the character and actions of the hero himself. Regarded in this light, chance, as we have already seen in *Romeo and Juliet*, represents, so to say, the invisible hand of Providence, which leads the tragic complication to its necessary goal; used in this way, it can produce the greatest tragic effect. In *Othello* the catastrophe is first introduced and occasioned by chance. Othello, 'the noble nature whom passion could not shake,' who, in fact, is vulnerable only in the one point, in his love for Desdemona, is first plunged into the heat of passion by Iago's villainy and by the play of chance which favours it, and is thus thrown out of the centre of his existence and brought to ruin. The first accident is the circumstance of Desdemona's losing her handkerchief,—which is as much accident as carelessness; the second is that Emilia finds the handkerchief; the third, that Cassio gives it to Bianca to have the embroidery copied; the fourth, that Othello sees it in Cassio's hand; the fifth, that Bianca happens to be at hand to help in deceiving Othello by Cassio's conduct in conversation with Iago;—it is all these accidents which help to convince Othello of Desdemona's infidelity, and which thus effect the complete ruin of his character. They are, therefore, pre-eminently the levers of the action. Of course, on the other hand, it is indeed highly tragic that human virtue is not able to hold its own against blind chance and common intrigue; but it is tragic only on condition that it is founded upon the insufficiency of the power of the good itself. If, however, the powers of evil are called forth only by accident and intrigue, if, accordingly, the moral force is broken only so far that it is no longer able to defend itself, then the tragic pathos is carried beyond itself, up to a point where it becomes converted into what is hideous and horrible.

The chief motives of the action—which, accordingly, lie but partly in the characters of the dramatic personages, for the most part in the outward accidental circumstances— in our present drama again naturally determine the *composition* of the piece, and, moreover, in the first place, the external composition; that is, the interdependence of the separate scenes, the development of the characters in a definite succession of actions and situations, and the order in which the incidents of the action are presented to the spectator. Beauty of composition—like every other formal beauty—demands, above all things, harmony, clearness, and design; that is, it demands that the final aim of the action, the point to which the dramatic development finally leads, should, from beginning to end, be perceptible through the separate Scenes, and that the characters, the action, and the plot should be developed as rapidly as clearly. This beauty of arrangement is exhibited in the highest perfection in *Othello*. Even the exposition (the First Scene of the First Act) is a proof of this: Roderigo's conversation with Iago not only makes us acquainted with the characters of both, but Iago's hatred, jealousy, and revenge at once reveal the chief motive of the whole action; whereas Brabantio's appearance, his grief and rage,—representing the right of the family which is violated in him,—throws a dark, tragic shadow over Othello's and Desdemona's love at the very commencement of the piece. The following Scenes show us, partly Othello's heroic figure in the zenith of his fame and renown, and partly describe his relation to Desdemona, the origin, the deep intensity, purity, and truth of their love, and then once more point to the storm which threatens their union. The Second Act shows us the threads out of which the complication of the Third Act is woven; first, Othello's arrival in Cyprus, the description of his position in the still restless and agitated country, which again is the reason of his subsequent severity towards Cassio; then Iago's opinions of the female sex, which throw a significant light upon Emilia's character as well as upon his marriage with her; thereupon we have the announcement of the festival, which forms the basis of the following and closing Scene; lastly, we have Cassio's drunkenness, his quarrel with Roderigo and Montano, his deposition, and Iago's advice to him to entreat Desdemona's intercession. The Third Act then weaves the given threads into the net which Othello, in his vehemence, draws over his own head. It is easily seen that from this point everything runs on in a straight line, without digression, towards the one goal. It is only the Second Scene of the Third Act that seems to be a makeshift, which might well be dispensed with. But to make up for this, the

conclusion of the same Act, as well as of the Fourth and Fifth Acts, are the more masterly in composition. With flash upon flash the tragic thunder-cloud relieves itself of
its lightnings; with every word, with every turn of the representation, the course of the
action makes an important advance; from every quarter we see but the one goal; and
yet everything glides on in a natural flow without disturbance and force. As rapidly
and naturally does the path, in the end, run down from its highest summit; the way in
which Othello is undeceived, Iago unmasked and brought to confession, is a true masterpiece of dramatic development.

And yet the external composition, were it ever so perfect, does not make the work
of art an *organic* whole; it is, rather, only the *mechanical* side, the *external, formal*
beauty of lines and outlines, extremely important for rendering the work intelligible
and as regards effect, but a merit shared by every well-devised piece of machinery.
The drama first becomes a living *organism* by its *internal unity*, from which all its
members and parts grow forth as from a fructified germ and develop in accordance with
their destiny, in which unity life has its inmost source, and necessarily determines the
external form, as well as the internal arrangement and formation, of the whole.

G. G. GERVINUS (*Shakespeare*, Leipzig, 1849. Translated by F. E. Bunnett, Lon
don, 1863, ii, 48): Whoever has had opportunity of drawing frequent experience from
family and married life, will find that no other of Shakespeare's Plays presents such
rich and striking application to the actual, oft-recurring circumstances of life,—to circumstances and experiences which attest that the tragedy brought about by parental
tyranny is often exceeded by that which arises from the wilfulness of the child. With
however good reason we assume to ourselves the freedom of the marriage choice and
the right of the child, yet the counter-claim which Shakespeare makes in the *Winter's
Tale* is the justest and the most natural which can be advanced: in making this choice
the father should be at least heard. However independently the newly-founded family
ought to enter upon life, universal experience tells us that there is no security when it
has forcibly sundered itself from the elder families out of which it arose. Men who
from caprice or wilfulness disturb the peace of a family, are little qualified to maintain
peace in their own. The first transgression makes the way easy for another; the
deceitful act makes even him mistrustful against whom deceit was practised in love;
the passion which once forsakes the path of discretion destroys the belief in self-com-
mand and in the power of virtue. And where doubts of this kind are once planted in
the mind, unhappiness and discord are necessarily the bitter fruit.

(P. 51.) The task lay before the Poet to exhibit the passions of jealousy to that
extent in which the lover can be thought capable of destroying the object of his love.
We think a man of inflamed sensibility, of heated blood, of the most violent irritabil-
ity, especially capable of such a deed; and even him only in the frenzy of intoxication,
in the sudden incentive of opportunity, in the feverish excitement of a fit of rage. But
such a deed would never be a subject for art; such a man, acting in an irresponsible
condition, would never win our sympathy for his tragic fate. But could it be conceivable that such a deed could ever be committed by a man of fixed character and stead-
fast disposition, who, indeed, before the act had captivated our interest? in whom this
passion, one of the lowest which actuate a man, could appear so ennobled that he, even
in spite of and after such a deed, could engage our sympathy, ay, even excite our pity?
It would appear improbable. And yet the poet, in Othello, has made such a man commit such a deed; or, rather, he has made it even there be committed by a man who

united two natures, calmness with ardour, rashness with circumspection, the traits which make the murder possible, and those which allow us to admire and pity the murderer.

(P. 103.) 'I am glad thy father's dead,' says Gratiano; 'this sight would make him do him a desperate turn.' But this sentence is also true in its reverse sense. If Desdemona had lived to know it, not the death of her father, but the cause of his death would have been an experience to her just as fearfully undeceiving as the lost confidence of Othello. For just as she had no foreboding of this, she had none also of the effect which her independent step had had upon her father. The same nature and qualities were at work in her when she gave the fatal blow to the life of her father and when she gave occasion for the suspicion of her husband. The same innocence of heart, the same lack of suspicion, the same inability to intend any harm to any one, allowed no touch of bashfulness to appear in her, in the first instance, before the public council, and placed on her lips, subsequently, the dangerous intercession in behalf of Cassio. In both cases she intended to do right and good, and from the very purity of her consciousness arose her misconstrued actions. Like Othello, like Romeo and Juliet, she falls a sacrifice to her own nature, and not to the law of any arbitrary and unjust moral statute; to a nature which, in the strength of that directness and originality which interests us all, oversteps the limits of social custom, unites guilt and innocence in strange combination, which brings down death upon itself as a punishment, and endures death as a triumph,—a nature which divides our feelings between admiration and pity. It seems as if here perfect satisfaction is afforded to all the demands of tragedy. It seems, also, that this performance is consistent with the freest moral view. For the Poet, by this conclusion, has not once for all condemned *every* unequal marriage, nor *every* secret union, just as little as in *Romeo and Juliet* he has condemned all passionate love. With such partiality Shakespeare has never and nowhere meditated upon moral problems. Otherwise, in *All's Well that Ends Well* he would not have carried an unequal marriage to a prosperous end through so many difficulties; he would not in *Cymbeline* have suffered a secret union to turn out for good; nor in the *Merchant of Venice* would he have justified the abduction of a child and a self-willed marriage. Not the letter of the law, but the circumstances and nature of men, are, in the poet's wise opinion, the spring from which good and evil, happiness and unhappiness, arise. *These* furnish also the line of conduct according to which both must be measured. In proportion to the circumstance and nature of the man, evil often becomes a source of good, and good a source of evil, apparent happiness a misfortune, and misfortune a happiness. And this is with conscious intention observed and carried out in this play, in which the noble Desdemona falls into sin through innocence and goodness, and by a sinful lie commits the most beautiful act of forgiveness.

OTTO LUDWIG (*Shakespeare-Studien*, Leipzig, 1872, p. 116): Strange is it that, at a time when our modern tragedies are no longer tolerated and we hear it said that the age for tragedies is past, the tragedies of Shakespeare still continue popular, and not alone among those who study him or perhaps extol his plays merely on account of his name and in order not to lose their reputation among the leaders of opinion. His tragedies deal with the most frightful subjects, with events terrible beyond our conception, with the most violent passions represented as in the common order of things. What are the reasons that these works give pleasure even to our sophisticated age? I believe

1. That as to their subjects, the reason may be found in Shakespeare's sound moral judgement of men and things.

2. And as concerns the mode of representation, the reason lies in the subdued moderation of great power, the grand repose of great vitality, the avoidance not of the violent, but of violence in the representation thereof. Shakespeare portrays the violent, but not violently. It lies in the breadth with which he sets forth his characters and their manifestations,—the constant keeping in mind that it is not reality but art that we have before us, in the richly picturesque, elevated speech, which always avoids the poor, the hasty, the abrupt, which a direct expression of the matter in hand would have the appearance of in reality; the interlacing of allied devices, the methodical movement.—The thought is with Shakespeare immediate, as well as the feeling and action, but the rhythm, although representative, is always in due artistic moderation.—The correct relation between strength and weakness, where, as with Michael Angelo, even the subordinate figures are still beyond the medium fulness of the real.—Then the shortness of the Scenes, the restrictions set to the different movements, often indeed, in the progress of the action the simple pause and physical relief of the change of Scenes.—The avoidance of all material means of straining the attention; the importance of time and place to the good or bad result is only hinted at, never dwelt upon. Furthermore, the brilliant rôles by which admiration of the art of the great actor helps to act against the involuntary delusion of the spectator; then the wealth of the action, which does not permit us to dwell too long upon any one part; the fulness of poetry; the ideality of the characters; the moral considerations,—all these characteristics of the Poet make him for ever popular.—Desdemona's fault is a negative, unconscious one, a lack of foresight resulting from her character. Why, nevertheless, has her fearful ending nothing of the horrible? Because, I believe, her suffering gives her occasion to show such perfect, spiritual beauty, that one forgets the cause and almost the suffering even; nay, we are even thankful therefor. Then through the sympathetic effect of her ideal repose; because the creature in her, struggles not; she fascinates us with her sweet submission to her suffering, caring more for her murderer than for herself. Then there is the artistic beauty and repose of the representation itself. Then there is the harmony of the deed with the plot,—for Othello is really the one to be most pitied. Here hints may be found for the representation of the ideal,—Othello has declared his murderous resolve. He bids Desdemona to get to bed and to dismiss Emilia. Next the preparation for the deed by the attack on Cassio; a second time Othello's resolve declared. The Scene ends, a change follows; Desdemona asleep alone,—a light,—Othello enters. His solemn, judicial bearing! Thus the murder and its relation to both parties make a much deeper impression because we are not terrified, and for the same reason the effect is much more artistic and softened. And further, there is a retarding, alleviating element in Desdemona's repose of character. Thus we have the deed itself, without any of the repulsive accidents which such a deed would have in reality. The poet who knows how to treat it so humanly may well venture to deal with the most terrible subjects.

(P. 119.) *Fatalism in Tragedy.*—In tragedies of character and of passion there is always something fatalistic. We may always say: To such and such, this or that ought not to have happened. The mingle of freedom and necessity which is in our thinking, in our desires, and in our action, exists also in our fate. The best part of poetic impression, of the tragic, lies in the feeling of this insoluble mixture. We may see the necessity of consequences, but not of causes. That there may be such a man in such circumstances, this we see, but not why he is *such* as he is nor why he is placed in such circumstances.

(P. 121.) In every character of every play of Shakespeare's the punishment is in proportion to the wrong-doing. How mild is the punishment of Desdemona, of Cordelia for a slight wrong; how fearful that of Macbeth,—every moment from the commission of his crime to his death, he suffers more than all the suffering of these two women. His deliberate crime belongs to the cold passions; as the deed is done with forethought and in cold blood, so it is avenged by the long-continued tortures of conscience.

(P. 127.) How wonderfully is the Motive of the play devised in the First Act of *Othello!* The whole movement is so conducted as to show us the fuel which lies in the characters themselves, and in the circumstances of the marriage. And what wealth of causes or motives for jealousy is made to appear in the course of the remaining Acts. True it is that at the first seeing or reading of the play, the corporeal life of the action obscures the force and number of the motives; but the oftener and the more connectedly the tragedy is seen or read, so much the more convincing they become. Herein lies the warrant for the immortality of this work of Shakespeare's. The other plays, the oftener they are read, lose their probability and necessity; but this play gains in these respects upon a more intimate acquaintance. We here may learn, First : The art of devising *motives*. For even from what has happened before the play opens, as well as from what happens in the First Act, we know the reason why, and also the story how. Second : We learn construction of the dialogue, whereby the motives hinted at become possible. The dialogue is natural, unforced; everything tending to betray the intention is avoided.—What completeness ! Through the lively, impressive movement, through the ideality of the characters, through the abounding dicta of experience, through sympathy with Iago's *savoir faire* and superior intellect, through his expectant tone, and through the purposes which he betrays, how perfectly are the senses, the heart, and the understanding engrossed and kept busy ! Into what a free, poetic region is the ordinary stuff for tragedy elevated by the imposing background of Venice ! What a theatre-setting for all the characters ! What sharply-drawn forms, rendered all the sharper by contrast ! How richly is a simple story transfigured ! The whole First Act might have been compressed into one Scene. A few questions and answers might have served to tell the whole story. But if the purpose was to model and mould his characters to render a sufficing motive for the whole, past, present, and future, then three Scenes had to be made out of one. And from the way in which he has carried them out, there is no desire on the part of the spectator to have them compressed. I perceive ever more plainly that Shakespeare's form for the most perfect tragedy is indispensable; that it is no license, but a law. How much of real, corporeal life, how much of the relationship between Othello and Iago Brabantio and Roderigo, would have been lost by the concentration of these three Scenes into one ! What a scenic measure would there have been created thereby, from which the succeeding Acts would have suffered ! By the way, how wise it is in Shakespeare not to let Othello alone go blindly into Iago's snares; that all are equally ready to be deceived by him makes Othello's confidence in him not only probable, but even excusable. Othello thereby loses the look of folly which would otherwise have been the case. Everything here is merely an unfolding of the plot by means of the action. All the distracted life, the rousing of Brabantio, his search for Othello, their meeting,—all these are nothing but helps to give a living exposition of the preface to the story of the character and utter unnaturalness of this mesalliance, and of whatever can serve to awaken jealousy.—The characters and incidents are taken out of the sphere of ordinary reality Whatever in and of them is not exclusively related to the object of the action represented, whatever is not a necessary member thereof, is entirely stripped away. This it is which Lessing terms the simplification of the stuff, by which the dramatic action is made to serve the ideal. Thus the action stands like a group in sculpture, everywhere transparent and rounded, not merely in relief or only half free. In *Othello*, Shakespeare, more than elsewhere, gives us an epitome of Nature, a symbol of the laws that rule the course of the world; the science of jealousy, its natural history illustrated by concrete example. But it is only one kind of jealousy, the noblest, born not of the offended senses, but of wounded honour; so to speak, moral, spiritual jealousy.*

FRIEDERICH BODENSTEDT (*Jahrbuch d. deutschen Sh. Gesellschaft*, 1867, p. 258): ' That Desdemona left her father for the Moor involves no crime,' says Vischer. ' The foolish, irascible man deserves no better. Her love for her father and her love for her husband were not to be reconciled.' This opinion appears to me to be more bold than correct. Let us come to an understanding by taking into consideration this act with its immediate consequences. A tenderly beloved daughter breaks the heart of her father by a secret marriage, without having even made the attempt to obtain his consent. She forsakes the old man, whom she has sorely wounded, without one tender word; deprecates his displeasure without imploring his blessing. She speaks to him not as a child to a father, but like an advocate addressing his reason, not appealing to his heart; or, like a debtor settling with his creditors,—so much is due to one, so much to another, and so much to a third.

If such an attitude of a child to a father, whose whole heart is bound up in that child, involves no fault, then this word has lost its meaning. I am sure that here, as in *Lear*, it was the earnest purpose of Shakespeare to represent a serious wrong done by a child to a father, and that the popular feeling, to which Vischer himself, in another place as well as in this instance, appeals, will find Desdemona guilty. Her sin lies not in the fact that she loves the Moor, and for love of him forsakes her father, but that in this, the most critical step in her life, she has no consideration for her father, but justifies herself in terms as rude as if he were to her the most indifferent person in the world. She insists as coolly upon her right as Shylock upon his bond. We can readily imagine that Desdemona knew that it was impossible to obtain her proud father's consent. We can suppose, also, that Othello, in order to avoid the humiliation of a rejection, encouraged her in secretly consummating her hastily formed determination; but nothing of this kind appears in the text, and it is just the care which the Poet takes to avoid every hint in this direction that shows, in the plainest manner possible, his intention to emphasize in the sharpest way Desdemona's lack of filial affection. . . . . It is this lack of filial piety, as well as the fact that Desdemona, having grown up without a mother's tender care and without brother or sister, had early learned to depend upon herself, that explains her indifference to the opinion of the world, the marked self-dependence of her character, and the unbending determination with which, in the weightiest step of her life, she takes counsel only of her own heart. In a city where wealth and luxury flourished

---

* These notes of LUDWIG are to me always interesting (whether I agree with them or not is another matter), as the memoranda and jottings for his own use of a professional dramatist, who was considered one of the most promising of recent times in Germany. Their occasional obscurity and fragmentary style are doubtless due to the fact that their publication was, unfortunately, posthumous.—ED

in their fullest bloom there is such a lack of able men that the lead in war is given to an adventurer, to a Moor,—this it is that wins her heart. She is light, airy, like a sunny May day; he is black and ugly as an overclouded day in autumn, and, withal, so little blinded to his own repulsive exterior that he never would have ventured to woo Desdemona had not she made advances towards him. She is touched by his lofty, manly qualities, by his frank, noble character. . . . . The noblest impulses have brought together two pure hearts; we feel that they are worthy each of the other, and yet we cannot, from the first, evade the fear, that presses involuntarily upon us, of the consequences of this union. We see before us perfect womanhood in the most graceful shape, and perfect manhood in a form most repulsive; and it is as if day and night came together; the two cannot unite !

This remark seems to lead us away from the tragic motive of the play which we have indicated above; but, in reality, it only results therefrom, pointing back to it as its source. For what else is it than a sorrowful conviction that from such a singular union,—a union so unnatural that in the eyes of Brabantio, no happiness could come to his daughter,— what but this feeling caused his opposition, and broke his heart when the union became unalterable? A large share of wounded pride and indignant pain at the disregard shown for his paternal authority may be taken into account, but the essential thing with him is to be found in his concern for his child. And so long as family ties are held sacred, Desdemona will be held guilty towards her father by every healthy mind. Without keeping in mind this wrong, in which Othello shares, done by the heroine, otherwise so lovely, the drama loses its sacredly tragic character, and degenerates into a mere intrigue. For that such a finished villain as Iago should destroy the happiness of two such excellent persons as Othello and Desdemona, without at the same time, consciously or unconsciously, serving higher purposes, can make an impression which is only sorrowful, not tragic. It is otherwise when we take things as they are and keep strictly to the Poet's own words, putting nothing into the play, but explaining everything by what is in it. Then Desdemona's tragic fate affects us because we see that she is the fate herself which prepares the soil whereon Iago sows the seed of his deadly mischief. She voluntarily exchanges the peace of her father's house for the stormy life which she must see before her as the wife of Othello. She is fully aware of the fatal meaning of the step she takes, and is so little forced to it that she bids defiance to the whole world in taking it. She breaks her father's heart to follow her own heart. She takes upon herself the whole responsibility and all the consequences of her act. After such a beginning no healthy temperament can look for a happy ending.

(P. 264.) It is touching now to see how the love, which brings them together, unfolds ever more nobly the farther apart they are sundered by an unhappy fate. One would suffer like them to be so beloved! A moment of such love outweighs the longest ordinary life. Herein is to be found that inner spiritual compensation for the bitter tragedy of their outward life.

(*Einleitung zu der Uebersetzung des Othello*, p. vii): Commentators have considered it cruel in Shakespeare to permit two such thoroughly noble natures as Othello and Desdemona to be the victims of such a wretch as Iago. Whoever fails to understand in Shakespeare's tragic characters the relation between sin and punishment, may regard the former, in this case, light in comparison with the latter; for with the Poet the wrongdoing is not always a crime, popularly considered, but often a mere lack of prudence or thoughtfulness, or the predominance of feeling over prudence and reason. So also with him death is not always to be taken as a punishment, but often as a release from a blasted life or as a rescue from an unhappy future.

WILHELM OECHELHÄUSER (*Othello, für die deutsche Bühne bearbeitet*, Weimar 1876. Einleitung, p. 13): Othello is above all things hero and warrior. Before Desdemona's charms had kindled the flame of love in his heart, warlike exploits, battles, and adventures, were the element in which he lived. The African retired into the background behind his position in the military service of the Christian Republic of Venice, to which he was devoted body and soul; to have vindicated the honor of which was his last proud recollection before death. When, therefore, actors, as many do, seek to give to the personation a dash of Muli Hassan, and to make the African blood of Othello a prominent quality, it is an error, mere clap-trap. Only in the Third and in the beginning of the Fourth Act, where Iago with cynical calculation speculates upon the warmth of his senses, the southern passion of Othello may be, somewhat beyond our European limits, moderately personated. For the rest, he who forgets his paint represents Othello best. It is not the design of the tragedy to illustrate the Moorish character; every European of like quality would, in like circumstances, do just as Othello did. It is not the peculiar jealousy of a Moor, but jealousy in a character little disposed to it, that the poet depicts. He did not make Othello a Moor (or, as Schlegel thinks, he mistook the Saracen of novels for a Moor) in order to mark the representation of him with the stamp of his race. He had a far deeper ethical aim, namely, to contrast the greatness of Othello's character with the ideal purity of Desdemona's love.

Othello, then, should be personated not with the bizarre hastiness and vivacity of the African, but with the quiet, nay aristocratic bearing of the hero, of the mature man of high position, who has 'declined into the vale of years.' Such is the manner in which he presents himself before us in the beginning of the piece; the dignity and repose with which he confronts the enraged father, the manly self-consciousness, and the noble modesty and simplicity which mark his story of his love, reveal to us the essential qualities of his character. In Othello there is no trace of the *parvenu*, who feels himself uncertain of the high position which he has reached, alternating between bullying and cringing, as is often witnessed in real life. He is conscious of his royal descent and of his services, and with just pride takes for granted their silent recognition, without any thought of forcing it by boasting and importunity.

(P. 20.) The direct opposite to the part of Othello must stand boldly out in the thoroughly *plebeian* bearing of Iago. Othello is an aristocrat and a gentleman; Iago, from crown to sole, a plebeian, no trim, knightly villain like Edmund. His vulgar bearing, with which his dress even should be in accord, must be represented as auxiliary to his cunning. Herein is the point where most personators of Iago entirely fail,—the like is most frequently the case in the personation of Richard III,—namely, in the skilful wearing of the mask of an honest man. . . . . A plebeian, countrified behaviour, a homely, careless dress, a tone, now of broad cynicism and soldierly jest, and then of honesty, of fellow-feeling, of unselfish friendship (a masterpiece in this respect is the great Act III, Scene iii) must illustrate the personation of this rôle. Admirably does he hit the right tone for every person and every situation; the keenest knowledge of men underlies his diabolical speculations on the weakness of every individual. His long and frequent dialogues with Roderigo show us an original *nuance* of his ordinary bearing. To all others he is always on the *qui vive;* only with this gull has he an easier task. He ill-treats and plucks this pigeon with the keenest humour, as if to refresh himself, all in the tone of the consideration of a well-meaning older friend. Humour and sarcasm form the salient qualities of his character; he takes thorough delight in his devil's work, which breaks out in his humour.

(P. 21.) Iago is to be represented as at least of the same age as Othello,—that is, as of ripe manhood.

(P. 26.) Generally speaking, too little attention is paid to the part of Emilia, the wife of the infamous Ensign. Most of the adaptations for the stage omit too large a portion of her rôle; and stage managers assign it to inferior talent, as if any soubrette of the theatre were equal to it. The important part which Emilia takes in the catastrophe, her touching devotion to her mistress, the moral courage with which she confronts the deluded Moor and her guilty husband, should indicate that here is work for a skilful and gifted artist. Emilia, in the drama, is in the position of a servant; in Cinthio's novel she appears more as a friend. On the stage she should be represented in a character between the two, as this finds its justification in Italian manners at that period. Her notions of conjugal fidelity, as she airs them in the last Scene of the Fourth Act, are of no account, and stand in sharpest contrast with the ideal which her infinitely finer natured mistress has of the marital relations. But nowhere is there found any ground for supposing, as Schlegel does, that Emilia's practice was in accordance with her loose talk. Cinthio in the novel calls her 'a beautiful and honourable person.' How often do women talk in a light-minded fashion, which authorizes no unfavourable inferences as to their actual characters.

In her whole conduct Emilia is chargeable with only one fatal weakness: obtaining at her husband's wish the lost handkerchief upon which hangs such a fearful tragedy. She certainly had no suspicion of the evil purpose of Iago, to whom she stands in a relation of cold indifference. Putting this one error out of sight, she is the faithful, devoted servant and friend of Desdemona, the unterrified asserter of her innocence, even when she is threatened with death; first by the Moor, and then by her husband, showing therein great moral courage. Her position in the last Scene can be made of commanding importance.——Emilia is to be represented as young, but certainly older than Desdemona.

HERM. FREIH. VON FRIESEN (*Shakspere-Studien*, Wien, 1876, iii, 132): In connection with the character of Othello, composed as it is of so many elements, there comes the question whether this drama, in opposition to the other works of Shakspere, is to be regarded as illustrative of character or of intrigue. It must be granted that if the fate of Othello and Desdemona is determined by Iago's intrigues, then the essential element of a tragedy,—namely, the tragic fault of the sufferers,—is wanting, and the Poet is exposed to an undeniable reproach. Apparently, the predominance of intrigue over the whole development of the action of the play is not to be questioned. We must, first of all, agree as to what is to be understood by intrigue, if it is to be rejected as a motive power to a tragic result. Under all circumstances it is indispensable that, in a true tragedy, the person in whom the interest centres must be led to his fate without loss of his free will and choice. Certainly, then, the voluntary and deliberate proceedings of one or more persons, by which another individual is deprived of his freedom of thought and action, and is thereby doomed to destruction, excludes the tragic fault. But it does not follow that in tragedy the cunning, lies, and plots of one individual practised upon another are not to be introduced. Only the influence of these must be so related to the character of the person suffering under it that he shall be driven to his fate, not irresistibly, but only through the passion which has already shaken his freedom to the utmost, so that in truth he yields only to the impulse of his own will.

This being premised in regard to Iago's influence upon the fate of Othello, no one will be disposed to deny the power of Iago. Yet there is still the question whether the criminality of the intrigue and its fatal effect rests only upon Iago, or whether the actual ground of this effect lies not in Othello's personal character. (P. 135.) Notwithstanding the righteous indignation with which we regard Iago, upon Othello's head falls the chief fault. The right to lay it to his account begins in the natural qualities of his character, and gains in weight, by the circumstances just mentioned, from the wonderful, or at least unusual, excitement of his mind. As in all Shakspere's creations, we cannot help confessing that such an individuality as Othello's,—not only endowed with the most distinguished gifts, but having qualities and ways of thought even antagonistic,—that such a character, and such a character alone, would lie open to the diabolical influence of Iago. All so happens as to remind us, step by step, that for any other to ward off Iago's assaults would have been easy; and if, full of sympathy for Othello and full of indignation at Iago, we are blind to this possibility, and seem to see Othello helplessly entangled in the net which Iago weaves, the reason of it is in the impression which the finished work of the Poet makes on us, in the brilliancy of Othello's speeches, in the poetic force of the emotions which gush involuntarily from within him, contrasted with the coarse hints of Iago, sounding, as it were, from the nether world. While the former delights us and the latter stirs our indignation, we take sides and pardonably overlook the Poet's hint that, although Othello is caught in an almost inextricable net, he has not lost his freedom. With what skill does the Poet use, among other circumstances, everything which he found in the novel! In the novel, Cassio steals away from Othello's sight when he knocks secretly at the back door of the house to return the handkerchief to Desdemona, which is sufficient to increase the jealousy of Othello after it has already been awakened by Iago. In the drama (III, iii) his withdrawal from Desdemona's presence at the appearance of Othello is suspicious, and only on this account affords Iago a circumstance for the first step in his plot because the mind of the Moor is in a state of intense excitement. Furthermore, how narrowly Othello escaped hearing what Iago and Cassio are talking about (IV, i). A word that he might have caught would have been enough to convince him of Iago's treachery. Even the way in which the fatal handkerchief makes its appearance is, in the drama, with fine poetic instinct, entirely different from that of the novel. In the novel, a counterfeit of it is shown to Othello through a window. Thus, Othello was not at all in a position to penetrate the deception, while here he has only to demand an explanation to rend the whole plot to pieces. Equally ingenious is it that the handkerchief in the drama is lost through Othello's and Desdemona's carelessness; while in the novel, Iago gets possession of it by cunning. The whole development of the tragic result hangs upon the finest threads. And here it is especially that the connection of Iago's relation to Roderigo appears of the greatest significance. That in the first examination of Cassio the inquiry into the disturbance does not extend to the question who the man was whom Cassio had beaten, and what cause he had given therefor, is a circumstance only possible from Othello's unsuspicious disposition; while, had the inquiry been pushed that far, Iago's villainy would have been laid bare at the outset. In what danger Iago was in this respect we can surmise when Roderigo (IV, ii), in his distrust of Iago, threatens to go directly to Desdemona. A spark of this distrust in the soul of Othello would have saved him and Desdemona. The struggle of Othello before the murder is at once most significant and most touching. Throughout, the tragic event tends to a catastrophe which results not from accident or the overpowering force of another person, but only from a destiny originating in the inmost nature of the individual. To the very last moment of this fearful scene the threads are not severed by which Othello and Desdemona might be saved. This possibility, presented before our eyes with masterly power, is what moves us most painfully with mingled emotions of fear and sympathy. Let the calm judgement of the spectator be blinded and over-come by the powerful tones which the Poet draws forth from the instrument of his genius; I yet venture to maintain that the catastrophe finds its necessity in the nature of Othello. Even if the demoniac power of Iago drove him to the fatal act, the ground therefor lies only in Othello's personal nature and disposition. In the freedom with which the Poet changes the catastrophe as it is in the novel, we have an unquestionable proof of his poetic art in this direction.

O. F. GENSICHEN (*Studienblätter*, Berlin, 1881, p. 67): In the last Act, after the heart-breaking scene in which the whole fabric of her happiness falls in ruins before her, Desdemona can with the guileless innocence of a child,—fall asleep.

Wonderful, indeed, appears this sleep. No reconciling word between herself and Othello has been spoken; she knows that Othello will appear again in a moment, that he wishes to speak with her alone, and for that reason Emilia is dismissed. His com-ing must explain the terrible change that came over him,—why his love and reverence have been turned into contempt and rage. Desdemona, whose perfect devotion finds that even the stubbornness, the checks, the frowns of her husband 'have grace and favour,' must await with the most painful impatience this critical interview; what rest could she find before peace was restored between her and Othello? And yet she can fall asleep, and so profound is her slumber that she is disturbed neither by the tumult in the street nor by the entrance of Othello into her chamber. Even his kisses fail to awaken her.

Here we see the contrast between her genuine woman's nature and the full man's nature in Othello. His 'bloody passion shakes his very frame,' his 'eye rolls,' he 'gnaws his nether lip'; Desdemona peacefully sleeps, and awakes to receive him with, 'Will you come to bed, my lord?' instead of seeking to deliver him from his unworthy suspicions. Here, too, we find that lovely freedom from care which, in the conscious-ness of her purity, takes not upon itself the trouble of considering the individual differ-ence of temperament. And it is just this point which renders intelligible the possibility of a rupture of her relation to Othello.

[In their zealous and praiseworthy pursuit of 'the tragic fault' which shall, by refer-ring all our misfortunes to our own misdeeds, harmonize Shakespeare's tragedies with human life, some of our German brothers are inclined to push the search to its remotest bounds. Thus GENSICHEN finds that the tragic termination of Othello's wedded life might have been avoided had he only kept up such observances as fit the bridal. 'Had Othello retained a trace,' he says (p. 83), 'of the gallantry of a lover, he would have picked up the handkerchief which Desdemona let fall when she tenderly wished to bind it round his forehead. It was through this neglect of a courteous act that Othello him-self provided Iago with the weightiest proof of his wife's infidelity.'—ED.]

HEINRICH BULTHAUPT (*Dramaturgie der Classiker*, Oldenburg, 1883, p. 222): A villainous knavery, a combination of accidents, is Desdemona's ruin. Her horrible and unmerited end excites the most painful emotion. Cordelia's moral elevation, her nature,—which, notwithstanding her womanly tenderness, so far from shrinking from the conflict with life.advances to meet it,—stands in a much more intimate relation to the dark powers of Fate than this fine, sensuous character of Desdemona, made, as she is, for the full-est enjoyment of life. Cordelia's death affects us tragically. Desdemona's is simply horrible. Can any one who is not infatuated take, with Otto Ludwig, a different view? Can it be seriously maintained that sin and punishment are, in her case, skilfully propor-tioned, and that her punishment for no heinous fault was 'mild'? Mild,—this horrible death? Granting that mere physical destruction by murder amounts to nothing, but, for this young creature, who is pure love, pure devotion, can anything be more terrible than to find herself treated as a harlot, and to be deliberately strangled by the hands of that man for whom she had sacrificed everything? In her last moments, from her awak-ing to her death, did not a whole hell yawn before her? How is it possible to misunder-stand this awful martyrdom! The very circumstance that there is no proportion be-tween her fate and her fault affects us only the more profoundly. This unmerited suffering ennobles her, creates the deepest sympathy, and wins every heart. We forget every error that, in the thoughtlessness of youth, she may have committed. We can only bend the knee before her. Her loveliness, like a saint's, is transfigured by her tears, by her death. From the same source from which has come all that she has done, or left undone, comes her last word, 'Farewell! Commend me to my kind lord.' Her kind lord! Him who has murdered her! This unconquerable love, to my feeling, is appa-rent in a slight, thoroughly Shakespearian touch, than which nothing can be more beautiful. When the Willow Song of poor Barbara occurs to her, when her heart is full to overflowing of suffering, she suddenly remarks, apparently without connection, 'Lodovico is a proper man.' The whole scene of her ill-treatment at the hand of her husband, the coming of her relative, like a true knight, to her defence,—all is present to her again and to us. But she will not complain of her loved husband, who has done the worst to her, who has *struck* her. She thinks, as the memory of the bitter scene fills her mind with grief and her eyes with tears, only of him who had so kindly taken her part, 'He is a proper man!' 'And he speaks well!' she adds.

FRENCH CRITICISMS.

IN *Zaïre*, VOLTAIRE imitated the ground-plan of *Othello ;* that is, Othello's Oriental blood was repeated in Orosmane, the Soldan of Jerusalem, for the handkerchief was substituted an intercepted letter whose innocent contents were misinterpreted; Zaïre dies by the hands of Orosmane, who in turn kills himself. For a full comparison of these two tragedies, I must refer all who are interested to that admirable *Mémoire*, 'couronné au Concours institué par le Gouvernement Belge entre les Universités du Royaume,' *Histoire de l' Influence de Shakespeare sur le Théâtre Français, par* ALBERT LACROIX, Bruxelles, 1856, pp. 53–70; or to GUIZOT's comparison in the Preface to his translation of *Othello*. See also the Introductions to the admirable editions of *Othello*, edited for schools, by GÉRARD, and D'HUGUES, in 1883, and by MOREL in 1884.—ED.

J. F. DUCIS (*Othello. Représentée pour la première fois en 1792. Avertissement.*) La tragédie d'Othello est une des plus touchantes et des plus terribles productions dramatiques qu'ait enfantée le génie vraiment créateur de ce grand homme. L'exécrable caractère de Jago y est exprimé surtout avec une vigueur de pinceau extraordinaire. Avec quelle souplesse effrayante, sous combien de formes trompeuses, ce serpent caresse et séduit le généreux et trop confiant Othello! Comme il l'infecte de tous ses poisons! comme il l'enveloppe de tous ses replis! enfin, comme il le serre, comme il l'étouffe et le déchire dans sa rage! Je suis bien persuadé que si les Anglais peuvent observer tranquillement les manœuvres d'un pareil monstre sur la scène, les Français ne pourraient jamais un moment y souffrir sa présence, encore moins l'y voir développer toute l'étendue et toute la profondeur de sa scélératesse. C'est ce qui m'a engagé à ne faire connaître le personnage qui le remplace si faiblement dans ma pièce, que tout à la fin du dénoûment, lorsque le malheur d'Othello est consommé par la mort de la plus fidèle, de la plus tendre amante, qu'il vient d'immoler aux aveugles transports de sa jalousie. Je me suis bien gardé de le faire paraître du moment qu'il est connu, du moment que je révélé au public le secret affreux de son caractère. Je n'ai pas manqué non plus, dès que je l'ai pu, dans un court récit, d'instruire ce même public de sa punition, de sa mort cruelle dans les tortures. J'ai pensé même que si le spectateur avait pu, dans le cours de la tragédie, le soupçonner seulement, au travers de son masque, d'être le plus scélérat des hommes, puisqu'il est le plus perfide des amis, c'en était fait du sort de tout l'ouvrage, et que l'impression prédominante d'horreur qu'il eût inspirée aurait certainement amorti l'intérêt et la compassion que je voulais appeler sur l'amante d'Othello et sur ce brave et malheureux Africain. Aussi est-ce avec une intention très-déterminée que j'ai caché soigneusement à mes spectateurs ce caractère atroce, pour ne pas les révolter.

Quant à la couleur d'Othello, j'ai cru pouvoir me dispenser de lui donner un visage noir, en m'écartant sur ce point de l'usage du théâtre de Londres. J'ai pensé que le teint jaune et cuivré, pouvant d'ailleurs convenir aussi à un Africain, aurait l'avantage de ne point révolter l'œil du public, et surtout celui des femmes, et que cette couleur leur permettrait bien mieux de jouir de ce qu'il y a de plus délicieux au théâtre, c'est-à-dire de tout le charme que la force, la variété et le jeu des passions répandent sur le visage mobile et animé d'un jeune acteur, bouillant, sensible et enivré de jalousie et d'amour . . . .

J'ai maintenant à parler de mon dénoûment. Jamais impression ne fut plus terrible. Toute l'assemblée se leva, et ne poussa qu'un cri. Plusieurs femmes s'évanouirent. On eût dit que le poignard dont Othello venait de frapper son amante était entré dans tous les cœurs. Mais aux applaudissemens que l'on continuait de donner à l'ouvrage se mêlaient des improbations, des murmures, et enfin même une espèce de soulèvement. J'ai cru un moment que la toile allait se baisser. D'où pouvait naître une impression si extraordinaire, une agitation si tumultueuse ? Me tromperais-je, en croyant qu'elle venait de l'extrême intérêt que j'avais inspiré pour Hédelmone [Desdemona]; de ce que mon spectateur avait désiré trop passionnément qu'elle pût désabuser Othello de son erreur; de ce que je l'avais tenu trop long-temps dans les angoisses de la terreur et de l'espérance; de ce que son désir, trompé au moment du coup de poignard, s'était tourné en une sorte de désespoir, et avait révolté sa douleur même contre l'auteur de l'ouvrage ?

Comment se fait-il cependant que le public, après avoir eu tant de peine à me pardonner mon dénoûment, soit revenu le voir encore pendant le cours de douze représentations ? Ne serait-ce pas qu'il a été averti par la réflexion qu' Othello n'est point un homme féroce, mais un amant égaré, un Africain jaloux, un More, qui frappe ce qu'il a de plus cher, et qui ne survivra pas à sa victime ? Ne serait-ce pas qu'il a senti par instinct que les naturels les plus tendres et les plus sensibles, une fois poussés dans les excès, sont quelquefois les plus près de la barbarie, par la raison peut-être qu'ils en étaient les plus éloignés ?

Cependant quoique le public ait le droit, sous tous les climats, de tracer aux auteurs les limites de la terreur et de la pitié, ces limites pourtant sont plus ou moins reculées selon le caractère des différentes nations. Mon dénoûment a eu de la peine à passer à Paris; et à Londres, les Anglais soutiennent tres-bien celui de Shakespeare. Ce n'est point avec un poignard qu' Othello, sur leur théâtre, immole son innocente victime; il lui presse, dans son lit, et avec force, un oreiller sur la bouche, il le presse et le represse encore jusqu' à ce qu'elle expire. Voilà ce que des spectateurs français ne pourraient jamais supporter. Un poète tragique est donc obligé de se conformer au caractère de la nation devant laquelle il fait représenter ses ouvrages. C'est une vérité incontestable, puisque son principal but est de lui plaire. Aussi, pour satisfaire plusieurs de mes spectateurs, qui ont trouvé dans mon dénoûment le poids de la pitié et de la terreur excessif et trop pénible, ai-je profité de la disposition de ma pièce, qui me rendait ce changement très-facile, pour substituer un dénoûment heureux à celui qui les avait blessés; quoique le premier me paraisse toujours convenir beaucoup plus à la nature et à la moralité du sujet, et que je l'aie eu sans cesse en vue, comme il est facile de le remarquer dès le commencement et dans le cours de ma tragédie. Mais comme je l'ai fait imprimer avec les deux dénoûmens, les directeurs des théâtres seront les maîtres de choisir celui qu'il leur conviendra d'adopter.

[I think the limit of tolerance is reached in thus listening to Ducis himself. It is easy to be severe, and it is easier still to make fun. But we must remember that he lived in an age when the versions of Shakespeare which held the English stage were more discreditable to the taste of the English public than Ducis's versions to the taste of the admirers of Racine and Corneille. The name of Othello is the only one which Ducis retained among his Dramatis Personæ, which are as follows: Moncénigo, *doge de Venise.* Lorédan, *fils de Moncénigo.* Odalbert, *sénateur vénitien.* Hédelmone, *fille d' Odalbert.* Hermance, *nourrice d'Hédelmone.* Othello, *général des troupes vénitiennes.* Pézare, *Vénitien.* La scène est à Venise.—ED.]

GUIZOT, in the *Notice sur Othello,* which precedes his Translation, after speaking of the vivifying effect of Shakespeare's genius on the dry bones of Cinthio's novel, thus proceeds : Ainsi crée le poëte, et tel est le génie poétique. Les événements, les situa tions même ne sont pas ce qui lui importe, ce qu'il se complaît à inventer : sa puissance veut s'exercer autrement que dans la recherche d'incidents plus ou moins singuliers, d'aventures plus ou moins touchantes ; c'est par la création de l'homme lui-même qu'elle se manifeste ; et quand elle crée l'homme, elle le crée complet, armé de toutes pièces, tel qu'il doit être pour suffire à toutes les vicissitudes de la vie, et offrir en tous sens l'aspect de la réalité. Othello est bien autre chose qu'un mari jaloux et aveuglé, et que la jalousie pousse au meurtre ; ce n'est là que sa situation pendant la pièce, et son caractère va fort au delà de sa situation. Le More brûlé du soleil, au sang ardent, à l'imagination vive et brutale, crédule par la violence de son tempérament aussi bien que par celle de sa passion ; le soldat parvenu, fier de sa fortune, et de sa gloire, respec- tueux et soumis devant le pouvoir de qui il tient son rang, n'oubliant jamais, dans les transport. de l'amour, les devoirs de la guerre, et regrettant avec amertume les joies de la guerre quand il perd tout le bonheur de l'amour ; l'homme dont la vie a été dure, agitée, pour qui des plaisirs doux et tendres sont quelque chose de nouveau qui l'étonne en le charmant, et qui ne lui donne pas le sentiment de la sécurité, bien que son carac- tère soit plein de générosité et de confiance ; Othello enfin, peint non-seulement dans les portions de lui-même qui sont en rapport présent et direct avec la situation acci- dentelle où it est placé, mais dans toute l'étendue de sa nature et tel que l'a fait l'en- semble de sa destinée ; c'est là ce que Shakespeare nous fait voir. De même Iago n'est pas simplement un ennemi irrité et qui veut se venger, ou un scélérat ordinaire qui veut détruire un bonheur dont l'aspect l'importune ; c'est un scélérat cynique et raisonneur, qui de l'egoïsme s'est fait une philosophie, et du crime une science ; qui ne voit dans les hommes que des instruments ou des obstacles à ses intérêts personnels ; qui méprise la vertu comme une absurdité et cependant la hait comme une injure ; qui conserve, dans la conduite la plus servile, toute l'indépendance de sa pensée, et qui, au moment où ses crimes vont lui coûter la vie, jouit encore, avec un orgueil féroce, du mal qu'il a fait, comme d'une preuve de sa supériorité.

Qu'on appelle l'un après l'autre tous les personnages de la tragédie, depuis ses héros jusqu'aux moins considérables, Desdemona, Cassio, Emilia, Bianca ; on les verra par- aître, non sous des apparences vagues, et avec des seuls traits qui correspondent à leur situation dramatique, mais avec des formes précises, complètes, et tout ce qui constitue la personnalité. Cassio n'est point là simplement pour devenir l'object de la jalousie d'Othello, et comme une nécessité du drame, il a son caractère, ses penchants, ses qual- ités, ses défauts ; et de là découle naturellement l'influence qu'il exerce sur ce qui arrive Emilia n'est point une suivante employée par le poëte comme instrument soit du nœud, soit de la découverte des perfidies qui amènent la catastrophe ; elle est la femme de Iago qu'elle n'aime point, et à qui cependant elle obéit parce qu'elle le craint et quoiqu'elle s'en méfie ; elle a même contracté, dans la société de cet homme, quelque chose de l'immoralité de son esprit ; rien n'est pur dans ses pensées ni dans ses paroles : cependant elle est bonne, attachée à sa maîtresse ; elle déteste le mal et la noirceur. Bianca elle-même a sa physionomie tout à fait indépendante du petit rôle qu'elle joue dans l'action. Oubliez les événements, sortez du drame ; tous ces personnages demeur- eront réels, animés, distincts ; ils sont vivants par eux-mêmes ; leur existence ne s'éva- nouira point avec leur situation. C'est en eux que s'est déployé le pouvoir créateur du poëte, et les faits ne sont, pour lui, que le théâtre sur lequel il leur ordonne de monter.'

It was with a translation of *Othello* that, over fifty years ago, in 1829, Le Comte ALFRED DE VIGNY undertook to break the Academic chains which enfettered the French drama. His struggle and final triumph, aided by VICTOR HUGO, ÉMILE DESCHAMPS, LE DUC DE BROGLIE, CHARLES NODIER, BÉRANGER, and others, form an exceedingly instructive and interesting chapter in the History of the French Stage, but which scarcely comes within the scope of the present work. All that I can do here, is again to refer the student to LACROIX's admirable *Mémoire*, p. 292 et seq.; and to quote from De Vigny's Preface the terms of the problem which he submitted to the French public, from which an idea may be formed of the plan of the whole campaign.

' Or, voici le fond de ce que j'avais à dire aux intelligences, le 24 octobre, 1829.

" Une simple question est à résoudre. La voici :

" La scène française s'ouvrira-t-elle, ou non, à une tragédie moderne produisant :— dans sa conception, un tableau large de la vie, au lieu du tableau resserré de la catastrophe d'une intrigue ;—dans sa composition, des caractères, non des rôles, des scènes paisibles sans drame, mêlées à des scènes comiques et tragiques ;—dans son exécution, un style familier, comique, tragique, et parfois épique ?" '

It is not difficult to see what the result must have been when *Othello* was brought forward as an answer to these questions. Our Gallic brothers are not stocks and stones, and the contest was as short as it was sharp. Academic frigidity melted under the rays of a warmth which, springing from Nature, was directed by Art, Shakespeare's art, the finest the world has known.

In the following January, in 1830, an Article appeared in the *Revue française* by M. le duc DE BROGLIE, which I should like to transfer bodily to these pages. I admire it for its style, its boldness, its liberality, its admiration of Shakespeare even while confessing a fidelity to certain convictions which are opposed to Shakespeare. Herewith are passages which we cannot afford to overlook :

Le Théâtre Français s'est rendu, faute d'avoir été secouru à propos et ravitaillé en temps opportun. Dans la soirée du 25 octobre dernier, Attila-Shakespeare en a pris possession avec armes et bagages, enseignes déployées, au fracas de mille fanfares. Pauvres poëtes de la vieille roche, qu'allez-vous devenir ? Il ne reste plus aux âmes faibles qu'à se rendre, à sacrifier sur l'autel des faux dieux, et aux vrais croyants qu'à s'envelopper la tête de leur manteau.

Plaisanterie à part, la révolution qui s'opère depuis quelque temps dans le goût du public est un phénomène curieux et singulièrement digne d'attention. Jamais plus notable changement ne s'est prononcé avec plus d'éclat et de rapidité.

(P. 53.) Que cet homme [Shakespeare] est un étonnant peintre de la nature humaine ! combien il est vrai qu'il a reçu d'en haut quelque chose de cette puissance créatrice qui souffle sur un peu de poussière, et qui l'anime pour la vie et l'éternité !

Dans l'entrevue avec Brabantio, Othello ne prononce pas quinze vers ; devant le sénat, Desdémona n'en profère pas vingt ; et pourtant déjà Othello existe tout entier, Desdémona existe tout entière ; ils sont là, l'un et l'autre, vivant sous nos yeux, se déployant sans contrainte, dans toute la grâce et la singularité de leur caractère, dans toute leur individualité naïve et impérissable. Supprimez le reste de la pièce, vous n'effacerez de notre mémoire ni Desdémona ni Othello ; placez-les à plaisir dans un autre ordre de circonstances ; allez, évertuez-vous : mais ne vous trompez pas, car nous les connaissons, nous savons d'avance ce qu'ils peuvent dire ou faire.

Et pourtant, dans ces caractères, que de complexité, que de contrastes, que de finesse et de nuances !

(P. 57.) Figurez-vous un homme qui n'aurait vécu depuis longtemps qu'à la clarté des bougies, des lampions ou des verres de couleur, qui n'aurait vu que des cascades d'opéra, des montagnes de toile peinte et des guirlandes de fleurs artificielles, et qui se trouverait transporté tout-à-coup, par une magnifique matinée du mois de juillet, au souffle de l'air le plus pur, sous les tranquilles et gracieux noyers d'Interlaken, en face des glaciers d'Oberland; et vous aurez une assez juste idée de la situation morale d'un habitué de nos premières représentations lorsqu'il vient à se trouver, à l'improviste, en présence de ces beautés si simples, si grandes et si naturelles.

Un second point sur lequel le sentiment involontaire du public français s'est trouvé tout-à-fait en désaccord avec les admirateurs de Shakespeare, c'est le rôle d'Iago. Ce rôle, qui est la cheville ouvrière de la pièce, est grandement célèbre en Angleterre et ailleurs; tous les critiques sans exception, anglais, allemands ou français, ne tarissent pas dans leurs éloges. A la scène, il nous a paru déplaire généralement; déplaire d'une manière très-prononcée, et qui allait croissant d'acte en acte, tellement que, s'il eût été joué avec moins d'aplomb et de décision, il lui serait certainement arrivé malheur. Pourquoi a-t-il déplu?

Il était assez curieux, à la fin de chaque acte, d'entendre chaque spectateur donner la raison de sa répugnance, le motif de son aversion. Celui-ci trouvait Iago trop immoral; celui-là, au contraire, ne le trouvait pas assez habile hypocrite: on ne se vante pas ainsi de sa scélératesse, disait-il; un troisième était révolté de voir commettre le crime en plaisantant; ainsi de suite.

Selon nous, le rôle a déplu parce qu'il n'est pas bon; parce qu'il est, non pas inconséquent (quoi de plus naturel à l'homme que l'inconséquence?) mais incohérent, parce que les parties dont il se compose ne tiennent pas ensemble, et qu'à son égard, on ne sait vraiment à quelle idée se prendre. Telle est du moins notre manière de voir. Que les dévots à Shakespeare nous anathématisent, si c'est leur bon plaisir.

Qu'est-ce qu'Iago?

Est-ce le malin esprit, ou du moins son représentant sur la terre? Othello a-t-il raison quand il le regarde aux pieds pour voir s'il ne les aurait pas fourchus? Est-ce un être qui fait le mal pour l'amour du mal, et qui vient souffler des poisons sur l'union d'Othello et de Desdémona, par ce seul motif que Desdémona est une créature angélique et qu'Othello est un homme loyal, brave et généreux?

Alors pourquoi donner à Iago des motifs humains et intéressés? Pourquoi nous montrer en lui une basse cupidité, le ressentiment d'une injure faite à son honneur, l'envie d'un poste plus élevé que le sien? Pourquoi le voyons-nous dévaliser ce pauvre Roderigo, comme Scapin ou Sbrigani escamotent à un imbécile la bourse qu'il a dans son pourpoint? Ces passions de bas aloi détruisent tout le fantastique du rôle; le démon n'a ni humeur ni honneur; il n'a ni rancune, ni colère, ni convoitise; c'est un personnage désintéressé; il fait le mal parce que le mal est le mal, et qu'il est, lui, le malin.

Iago est-il, au contraire, comme il s'en fait gloire, le parfait égoïste, l'homme qui sait, au suprême degré, s'aimer lui-même, l'être qui sait subordonner hiérarchiquement ses désirs, selon leur degré d'importance, et disposer ensuite ses actions de manière à tendre invariablement à sa plus haute satisfaction, coûte que coûte à autrui, sans scrupule, sans remords, et aussi sans se laisser détourner par des velléités d'un ordre inférieur?

Alors pourquoi poursuit-il en même temps trois ou quatre buts distincts, et d'une importance pour lui très-inégale? Pourquoi entreprend-il coup sur coup vingt projets différents qu'il abandonne l'un après l'autre? Pourquoi surtout prodigue-t-il, dans chaque occasion, cent fois plus de méchanceté que le besoin de la circonstance ne le comporte?

(P. 62.) Il [Iago] réussit, dira-t-on.

Il réussit, ainsi le veut l'auteur. Mais le bon sens, qu'en dit-il?

L'auteur lui-même réussit, mais d'où vient? C'est parce que telle est la profondeur et la vivacité de sa conception première que les invraisemblances les plus choquantes, les absurdités les plus inconcevables passent inaperçues; c'est parce que personne n'a l'envie ni le loisir de regarder aux ressorts du drame. Autre chose est pourtant de nous donner ces absurdités pour des mérites.

Oui, cela est très-vrai; depuis le premier moment où la première insinuation s'échappe des lèvres d'Iago pour atteindre l'oreille du More, depuis ces paroles fatales : ' Ah! ceci me déplaît,' jusqu' au moment solennel où le rideau tombe sur les cadavres des deux amants, le spectateur n'a pas la possibilité de respirer. Vous entendriez voler une mouche dans la salle, et bien maladroits sont les amis dont le zèle s'efforce d'interrompre par des applaudissements cette anxiété qui va croissant de minute en minute.

Dès le premier mot, tout est dit, tout est décidé.

Adieu pour jamais, Desdémona, adieu Othello. Desdémona n'apparaît plus que comme l'innocent oiseau qui se débat faiblement sous la serre d'un vautour, mais d'un vautour qui se débat lui-même en furieux sous la serre d'un autre vautour, et se venge, sur la pauvre victime, des effroyables tortures auxquelles il est en proie.

Le spectateur contemple ce tableau, non point avec cette curiosité inquiète qui passe tour à tour de la crainte à l'espoir, mais, s'il est permis de le dire, et en tenant compte de toutes les différences, avec quelque chose de cette angoisse inexprimable qui s'empare de nous lorsque, dans une cour de justice, nous assistons aux vains efforts de malheureux entraînés vers une condamnation fatale et indubitable.

(P. 69.) La scène où Desdémona se déshabille, avant de se mettre au lit, est donc bien véritablement, pour elle, ce quart d'heure de grâce que l'on accorde aux condamnés avant de les conduire au supplice; en vain essaie-t-elle de donner le change à Emilia, de se faire illusion à elle-même, de détourner sa pensée sur quelque sujet frivole; le plus intime de son âme reparaît et surgit à chaque mot. Et telle est aussi cette scène pour le spectateur éperdu; il compte les minutes; il s'attache au moindre incident; il se cramponne à la moindre chose; il demande pourquoi pas encore ce nœud, pourquoi pas encore cette agrafe; il voudrait, en quelque sorte, saisir Desdémona par sa robe et la retenir.

Poëtes tragiques, voilà votre maître; prenez leçon de lui, si vous savez en prendre

Victor Hugo (*William Shakespeare*, Paris, 1864, p. 321): Maintenant qu'est-ce qu'Othello? C'est la nuit. Immense figure fatale. La nuit est amoureuse du jour. La noirceur aime l'aurore. L'africain adore la blanche. Othello a pour clarté et pour folie Desdémona. Aussi comme la jalousie lui est facile! Il est grand, il est auguste, il est majestueux, il est au-dessus de toutes les têtes, il a pour cortège la bravoure, la bataille, la fanfare, la bannière, la renommée, la gloire, il a le rayonnement de vingt victoires, il est plein d'astres, cet Othello, mais il est noir. Aussi comme, jaloux, le héros est vite monstre! le noir devient nègre. Comme la nuit a vite fait signe à la mort!

A côté d'Othello, qui est la nuit, il y a Iago, qui est le mal. Le mal, l'autre forme de l'ombre. La nuit n'est que la nuit du monde; le mal est la nuit de l'âme. Quelle obscurité que la perfidie et le mensonge! avoir dans les veines de l'encre ou la trahison, c'est la même chose. Quiconque a coudoyé l'imposture et le parjure, le sait; on est à tâtons dans un fourbe. Versez l'hypocrisie sur le point du jour, vous éteindrez le soleil. C'est là, grâce aux fausses religions, ce qui arrive à Dieu.

Iago près d'Othello, c'est le précipice près du glissement. Par ici! dit-il tout bas. Le piège conseille la cécité. Le ténébreux guide le noir. La tromperie se charge de l'éclaircissement qu'il faut à la nuit. La jalousie a le mensonge pour chien d'aveugle. Contre la blancheur et la candeur, Othello le nègre, Iago le traître, quoi de plus terrible! ces férocités de l'ombre s'entendent. Ces deux incarnations de l'éclipse conspirent, l'une en rugissant, l'autre en ricanant, le tragique étouffement de la lumière.

Sondez cette chose profonde, Othello est la nuit. Et étant la nuit, et voulant tuer, qu'est-ce qu'il prend pour tuer? le poison? la massue? la hache? le couteau? Non, l'oreiller. Tuer, c'est endormir. Shakespeare lui-même ne s'est peut-être pas rendu compte de ceci. Le créateur, quelquefois presque à son insu, obéit à son type, tant ce type est une puissance. Et c'est ainsi que Desdémona, épouse de l'homme Nuit, meurt étouffée par l'oreiller, qui a eu le premier baiser et qui a le dernier souffle.

H. TAINE (*Histoire de la Littérature Anglaise*, Paris, 1866, ii, 232): Mais le trait qui Iago véritablement achève, et le range à côté de Méphistophélès, c'est la vérité atroce et le vigoureux raisonnement par lequel il égale sa scélératesse à la vertu. . . . . Ajoutez à tous ces traits une verve diabolique, une invention intarissable d'images, de caricatures, de saletés, un ton de corps de garde, des gestes et des goûts brutaux de soldat, des habitudes de dissimulation, de sang-froid et de haine, de patience, contractées dans les périls et dans les ruses de la vie militaire, dans les misères continues d'un long abaissement et d'une espérance frustrée; vous comprendrez comment Shakespeare a pu changer la perfidie abstraite en une figure réelle, et pourquoi l'atroce vengeance d'Iago n'est qu'une suite nécessaire de son naturel, de sa vie et de son éducation.

IN proof of the difficulties attending the translation of Shakespeare into German, I gave in *Macbeth* eighteen or twenty German versions of 'Double, double toil and trouble,' &c.; which was well enough chosen as an instance where foreigners have to contend with a difficulty that might be termed merely technical. The lines, to English ears, convey but little definite meaning; their vagueness, combined with the bubbling sound as of boiling, imparts the Abracadabra suggestion of a witch's charm. I am not sure that some of the versions there given do not fulfil the essential conditions of a translation where, as I have said, the difficulty is technical. A fairer test of translation is to be found in lines where words have a peculiar signification and an inherent charm to English ears, without which the whole passage is naught, and where, if a single word be changed, the spell is snapt, just as the fractured point of a Prince Rupert's tear reduces the crystal globule to sand. For instance, take those lines which Iago utters as he sees Othello approaching, after the first administration of the 'poisonous mineral':

> 'Look where he comes: Not poppy, nor mandragora,
> Nor all the drowsy syrups of the world,
> Shall ever medicine thee to that sweet sleep
> Which thou owd'st yesterday.'

It seems sheer impertinence to attempt to point out to English readers any especial charm where every phrase is full of beauty, but for my present purpose I must be pardoned for calling attention to three words here. Is there any other word in the English tongue that can be substituted for 'drowsy'? *Sleepy* certainly cannot. There is no resistance in *sleepy*. For *sleep* one composes his limbs, and repose is wooed. *Narcotic* is worse, it has a repulsive odor; and *soporific* is pedantic. But in 'drowsy' there is half-wakefulness, utter weariness, and nodding resistance to the potent drug. Thus, also, 'syrup,' which is not *juice*, or *potion*, or *essence*, or *extract*, nor anything but that heavy liquid sweetness whose very sluggishness suggests its power in reserve, whose inertness by contrast renders its essence more quick, and it is redolent of its home in the East. Lastly comes 'medicine,' with its suggestion of illness, and dis-ease, and restoration. Of course all the other words in these lines are exquisitely chosen, but then they are such as can be transferred readily from one language to another. The vague sonorousness of 'mandragora' speaks quite as powerfully, it may be supposed, to French or German or Italian ears as to ours. But the three words which I have specified, 'drowsy,' 'syrup,' and 'medicine,' must be felt, or the translation falls short; it may be through the fault of the translator or through the deficiency of his mother tongue.

Furthermore, in examining the following translations, another question suggests itself,—a question which I have never been able to answer satisfactorily. Should a translation of poetry be in prose or rhythm? A discussion of this far-reaching question is hardly germane here; my present purpose is fulfilled in calling attention to what seems to me to be the fact, that in the prose translations which follow, the suggestions of the original are reproduced somewhat more completely than in those in rhythm. But, alack the day, what does the passage amount to without the exquisite cadence of 'Nor all the drowsy syrups of the world'? which seems, in its undulation merely, to suggest the quiet 'unfurling' of twilight and the solemn tolling of the curfew. 'In every language,' said Southey, 'there is a magic of words as untranslatable as the *Sesame* in the Arabian tale,—you may retain the meaning, but if the words be changed the spell is lost.' Of course, this is true in German. Not while the world lasts will Gretchen's song be translated: 'Meine Ruh ist hin, Mein Herz ist schwer.'

LE TOURNEUR, Paris, 1776: Va, ni l'opium, ni la mandragore, ni toutes les potions assoupissantes de l'univers ne te rendront jamais ce doux sommeil que tu goûtas hier pour la dernière fois.

ALFRED DE VIGNY, Paris, 1829:

> Va, déchire ton cœur ! va, ni le feu, ni l'eau,
> Les boissons de pavot, d'opium, de mandragore,
> Ne pourront te guérir et te donner encore
> Ce paisible sommeil que tu goûtas hier.

BENJAMIN LAROCHE, Paris, 1842: Le voici qui vient !—Ni les pavots, ni la mandragore, ni tous les sirops soporifiques du monde ne te rendront le doux sommeil que tu avais hier.

FRANÇOIS-VICTOR HUGO, Paris, 1862: Tenez, le voici qui vient ! Ni le pavot, ni la mandragore,—ni tous les sirops narcotiques du monde—ne te rendront jamais ce doux sommeil—que tu avais hier.

M ALCIDE CAYROU, Paris, 1876:

> Va! recours au pavot comme à la mandragore,
> Si tu le veux, choisis l'opium, l'ellébore:
> Tu n'auras plus jamais, non, ce sommeil heureux
> Que tu goûtais hier dans ton nid amoureux!

LOUIS DE GRAMMONT, Paris, 1882:

> Othello vient.   Ah! c'en est fait.   Le plus puissant
> Narcotique jamais ne pourra rendre au More
> Le sommeil qu'il goûtait hier.   La mandragore
> Et le pavot seront désormais superflus
> Pour vaincre son angoisse: il ne dormira plus!

JEAN AICARD, Paris, 1882:

> Il vient. . . . . Je disais donc? . . . . Mandragore ou pavots,
> Va, rien ne saura plus te rendre le repos!

WIELAND, Zürich, 1766: Seht, da kommt er! Weder Mohn-Saamen, noch Mandragora, noch alle einschläfernde Säfte in der Welt zusammen genommen werden dir jemals diesen süssen Schlaf wiedergeben, den du gestern noch hattest.

ESCHENBURG, Mannheim, 1779: Sieh, da kömmt er!—Weder Mohnsamen, noch Mandragora, noch alle einschläfernde Säfte auf der Welt werden dir jemals den süssen Schlaf wieder schaffen, den du gestern noch hattest.

LUDEWIG SCHUBART, Leipzig, 1802: Sieh da kommt er wieder.   Weder Mohnsaft, noch Alraun, noch alle einschläfernden Säfte der Welt, werden dir je den süssen Schlaf wieder verschaffen, den du noch gestern genossen.

DR JOHANN HEINRICH VOSS, Jena, 1806:

> Da kommt er her!   Nicht Mohn noch Mandragora
> Noch alle Schlummersäfte der Natur
> Erkünsteln je den süssen Schlaf dir wieder,
> Den du noch gestern hattest.

JOHANN WILHELM OTTO BENDA, Leipzig, 1826:

> Da kommt er! sieh!   Nicht Mohn, Mandragora,
> noch alle andre Säfte für den Schlaf
> stell'n je den süssen Schlummer wieder her,
> den du noch gestern schliefst.

PHILIPP KAUFMANN, Berlin, 1832:

> Da kommt er schon!   Kein Mohnsaft noch **Alraun**,
> Noch alle Schlafgetränke in der Welt
> Stelln je dir wieder her den süssen Schlaf.
> Den du noch gestern hattest.

A. W. VON SCHLEGEL (? BAUDISSIN) Berlin, 1832:

>   Da kommt er.   Nicht Mandragora noch Mohn,
>   Noch alle Schlummersäfte der Natur
>   Verhelfen je dir zu dem süssen Schlaf,
>   Der gestern dich erquickt.

ERNST ORTLEPP, Stuttgart, 1839:

>   Sieh da, er kommt!   Nicht Mohn, nicht Mandragora,
>   Noch alle Schlummersäfte der Natur
>   Sind fähig, dir den süssen Schlaf zurückzuzaubern,
>   Den du noch gestern schliefst.

MORIZ RAPP, Stuttgart, 1843:

>   Nicht Mohnsaft, noch ein Opium, noch was sonst
>   Von Specerei'n wirkt auf den goldnen Schlummer,
>   Nichts soll dir jemals mehr dazu verhelfen,
>   Wie du ihn gestern noch geschlummert hast.

DR F. JENCKEN, Mainz, 1854:

>   Da kommt er her! nicht Mohn noch Mondragora, [*sic*]
>   Nicht irgend sonst ein tüchtig Schlummersäftchen,
>   Wird Deiner Nacht die sanfte Ruh mehr schaffen,
>   Wie sie Dir gestern noch vergönnt.

OSWALD MARBACH, Leipzig, 1864:

>   Da kommt er!   Ha, nimm Opium, mein Freund,
>   Nimm was du willst, für dich giebts keinen Trank,
>   Der den gesunden Schlaf dir wieder giebt
>   Den du bis heut gehabt.

W. JORDAN, Hildburghausen, 1867:

>   Da kommt er.   Mohnsaft nicht, noch Mandragora,
>   Noch alle Schlummertränke der Natur
>   Verhelfen dir zum süssen Schlaf von gestern.

FRIEDERICH BODENSTEDT, Leipzig, 1867:

>   Da kommt er her.   Nicht Mohn, noch Mandragora,
>   Noch alle Schlummersäfte dieser Welt
>   Verschaffen je den süssen Schlaf dir wieder,
>   Der gestern dein war.

L. TIECK (Bearbeitet von DR A. SCHMIDT.   Herausgegeben durch die DEUTSCHE SHAKESPEARE-GESELLSCHAFT), Berlin, 1871:

>   Da kommt er.   Mohnsaft nicht noch Hexenkraut.
>   Noch alle Schlummerkräfte der Natur,
>   Verhelfen je dir zu dem süssen Schlaf,
>   Den du noch gestern hattest.

MAX MOLTKE, Leipzig, n. d. :

> Doch sieh, er kommt !—Nicht Mohn, nicht Mandragora,
> Noch alle Schlummersäfte von der Welt
> Verschaffen je den süssen Schlaf dir wieder
> Den du noch gestern schliefst.

ΙΩΑΝΝΗΣ Δ. ΜΑΝΩΛΗ. ΕΝ ΚΩΝΣΤΑΝΤΙΝΟΥΠΟΛΕΙ. 1873.

Ἰδοὺ ἔρχεται· καὶ οὔτε μήκων, οὔτε μανδραγόρας, καὶ οὐδὲ πάντα τὰ ὑπνωττικὰ ποτὰ τοῦ κόσμου θέλουν δυναθῇ νὰ σοὶ ἐπαναγάγωσι τὸν γλυκὺν ἐκεῖνον ὕπνον, τοῦ ὁποίου ἀπήλαυσες χθὲς διὰ τελευταίαν φοράν.

ΔΗΜΗΤΡΙΟΣ ΒΙΚΕΛΑ. ΕΝ ΑΘΗΝΑΙΣ. 1876.

Ἔρχεται.—Οὔτ' ἡ θερειακή, οὔτε ὁ μανδραγόρας,
οὔτ' ὅλα τὰ ὑπνωτικὰ καὶ ἰατρικὰ τοῦ κόσμου
δὲν ἠμποροῦν πλέον ποτὲ τὸν ὕπνον νὰ σοῦ δώσουν,
ποῦ χθὲς γλυκοκοιμήθηκες.

Shakspeare volgarizzate, &c., Firenze, 1801 : Eccolo, ei viene; Nè il papavero, nè la mandragora, nè qualunque altra pozione sonnifera, potrà ridonarti quel dolce sonno, di cui jeri hai gustato.

IGNAZIO VALLETTA, Firenze, 1830: Guardate come viene! nè papavero, nè mandragola, nè tutti i soporiferi del mondo ti porgeran più quella grata medicina di sonno, che godevi jeri.

GIUNIO BAZZONI e GIACOMO SORMANI, Milano, 1830: Oh! eccolo che giugne. No, nè i papaveri, nè la mandragora, ne tutte le bevande soporifere dell' universo potranno giammai renderti quel dolce sonno di cui godesti la scorsa notte.

CARLO RUSCONI, 1831 : Eccolo ! . . . . Nè i papaveri, nè la mandragola, nè alcun soporifero di questo mondo potrà più renderti il dolce sonno che ieri ancora provasti.

GIULIO CARCANO, Milano, 1843–53 (used by SALVINI and ROSSI):

> —— Ve' ch' egli vien. Giammai
> Papavero o mandragora, nè quante
> Ha il mondo essenze soporose, darti
> Il rimedio potran di quel soave
> Sonno che jer gustasti.

ANDREA MAFFEI, Firenze, 1869 :

> —— È qui! . . . . Non succo d'erbe,
> Non virtù di mandragora, nè d'altra
> Soporosa sostanza a te potranno
> Quel dolce sonno ridonar che gli occhi
> Jeri ancor ti velava.

JAIME CLARK, Madrid, n. d. (? 1873–74):

> —Vedle allí. Ni adormidera
> Beleño, ni mandrágora, ni todos
> Los zumos soporíferos del mundo
> Podrán apropinarte el dulce sueño
> Que disfrutaste ayer.

Let me not be understood as citing these translations in any carping, critical spirit. They are all good, and some of them admirable, as exact and literal as is possible. Where they have failed, they have failed because they *must*.

I add the following, and, did space permit, could continue the series in Russian, in Polish, in Bohemian, and in Hebrew,—not, however, as examples of translation, for my having in these languages is a younger brother's revenue, but as illustrations of the universality of Shakespeare's presence in every land, and in every tongue:—

JURRIAAN MOULIN, Haarlem, 1857:

> Daar komt hij, zie! Geen mankop of alruin,
> Geen sluimerdrank ter wereld die uw oog
> Ooit aan dien zoeten slaap weêr helpen zal,
> Die gister u verkwikte.

DR L. A. J. BURGERSDIJK, Leiden, 1885:

> Daar komt hij, zie! Geen heul- noch alruinsap,
> Noch al der wereld sluimerdranken brengen
> Den zoeten slaap u weder, die nog gist'ren
> U eigen was.

CARL AUGUST HAGBERG, Lund, 1861:

> Der kommer han.
> Nu kan ej opium, mandragora
> Och hela vida verldens slummer-droppar
> Förhjelpa dig till lika ljuflig sömn,
> Som den du sof i går.

EDV LEMBCKE, Kjöbenhavn, 1866:

> —— der er han.
> Nu skal ei Valmu, ei Alrunesaft,
> ei nogen Sovedrik i Verden vide
> dig mere dysse i saa söd en Sövn
> som den, du sov igaar.

LIST OF EDITIONS COLLATED IN THE TEXTUAL NOTES

THE FIRST QUARTO (Ashbee's Facsimile) [Q$_1$]	1622
THE FIRST FOLIO .. .. .. [F$_1$]	1623
THE SECOND QUARTO .. .. .. [Q$_2$]	1630
THE SECOND FOLIO .. .. .. [F$_2$]	1632
THE THIRD QUARTO .. .. .. [Q$_3$]	1655
THE THIRD FOLIO .. .. .. [F$_3$]	1664
THE FOURTH FOLIO .. .. .. [F$_4$]	1685
ROWE (First Edition) .. .. .. [Rowe i]	1709
ROWE (Second Edition) .. .. .. [Rowe ii]	1714
POPE (First Edition) .. .. .. [Pope i]	1723
POPE (Second Edition) .. .. .. [Pope ii]	1728
THEOBALD (First Edition) .. .. [Theob. i]	1733
THEOBALD (Second Edition) .. .. [Theob. ii]	1740
HANMER .. .. [Han.]	1744
WARBURTON .. .. [Warb.]	1747
JOHNSON .. .. [Johns.]	1765
CAPELL .. .. [Cap.]	1768
JENNENS .. .. [Jen.]	1773
JOHNSON and STEEVENS .. .. .. [Steev. '73]	1773
JOHNSON and STEEVENS .. .. .. [Steev. '78]	1778
JOHNSON and STEEVENS .. .. .. [Steev. '85]	1785
MALONE .. .. [Mal.]	1790
STEEVENS .. .. [Steev.]	1793
RANN .. .. [Rann] .. .. .. (?) 1794
REED'S STEEVENS .. .. .. [Var. '03]	1803
REED'S STEEVENS .. .. .. [Var. '13]	1813
BOSWELL'S MALONE .. .. .. [Var.]	1821
KNIGHT .. .. [Knt]	1841
COLLIER (First Edition) .. .. .. [Coll. i]	1843
SINGER (Second Edition) .. .. [Sing. ii]	1856
DYCE (First Edition) .. .. .. [Dyce i]	1857
COLLIER (Second Edition) .. .. [Coll. ii]	1858
STAUNTON .. .. [Sta.]	1860
R. GRANT WHITE (First Edition) .. [Wh. i]	1861
THE GLOBE EDITION (CLARK and WRIGHT) .. .. [Glo.]	1864
KEIGHTLEY .. .. [Ktly]	1864

CHARLES and MARY COWDEN-CLARKE	[Clarke]	..	..	..	(?) 1864
THE CAMBRIDGE EDITION (CLARK and WRIGHT)	[Cam.]	..	..	..	.. 1866
HALLIWELL (Folio Edition) ..	[Hal.]	..	..	..	.. 1865
DYCE (Second Edition)	[Dyce ii]	..	..	..	.. 1866
DELIUS (Third Edition)	[Del.]	..	..	..	.. 1872
DYCE (Third Edition)	[Dyce iii]	..	..	..	.. 1875
COLLIER (Third Edition) ..	[Coll. iii]	..	..	..	.. 1877
ROLFE	[Rlfe]	..	..	..	.. 1879
HUDSON	[Huds.]	..	..	..	.. 1881
R. GRANT WHITE (Second Edition) ..	[Wh. ii]	..	..	..	.. 1883

In the Textual Notes the symbol Ff indicates the agreement of the Second, Third, and Fourth Folios. The agreement of the three Quartos is indicated by Qq.

The frequent omission of the apostrophe in the Second Folio, a peculiarity of that edition, is not generally noted.

The sign + indicates the agreement of ROWE, POPE, THEOBALD, HANMER, WARBURTON, and JOHNSON.

When WARBURTON precedes HANMER in the Textual Notes, it indicates that HANMER has followed a suggestion of WARBURTON'S.

The words *et cet.* after any reading indicate that it is the reading of *all other* editions.

The abbreviation (subs.) indicates that the reading is *substantially* given, and that immaterial variations in spelling, punctuation, or stage directions are disregarded.

Coll. (*MS*) refers to COLLIER'S annotated Second Folio.

Quincy (*MS*) refers to QUINCY'S annotated Fourth Folio.

An Emendation or Conjecture which is discussed in the Commentary is not repeated in the Textual Notes; nor is 'conj.' added to any name in the Textual Notes unless it happens to be that of an editor, in which case its omission would be misleading.

All citations of Acts, Scenes, and Lines in *Romeo and Juliet, Macbeth, Hamlet,* and *Lear* refer to this edition of those plays; in citations from other plays the GLOBE EDITION is followed.

I have not called attention to every little misprint in the Folio. A reference to the Textual Notes will always show them to be misprints by the agreement of all the Editors in their correction.

Nor is notice taken of the first Editor who adopted the modern spelling, or who substituted commas for a parenthesis, or changed ? to !. At the same time some comparatively trifling peculiarities are noted, such as the use of hyphens, to which some Editors, Staunton, for instance, attach value. The variations in the spelling of the word 'murther,' where it occurs so frequently in Act V, is not noted. The spelling is almost uniformly *murder* in the Quartos, but in the Folios it is apparently arbitrary; in V, ii, 145, it is ' Murther,' and in the second line after, we have 'murder'd.'

Otherwise, even the most manifest misspellings in the Quartos and Folios are recorded, to supply what aid they may in estimating the value of the texts or their individuality; for instance, 'Cyprus' and 'Lieutenant' are almost invariably spelled, in the First Quarto, *Cypres* and *Leiutenant.* I have tried always to record every instance in the Quartos, especially in the First, of any really intelligent punctuation.

It may well be conceived that no part of my labours is more onerous than this of collation; for which there is so little to show, and at which I do not suppose that one reader in a hundred, or in five hundred, ever even as much as glances. But the work has to be done, somebody must do it, and I seem to have drawn the unhappy lot. Wherefore let me say that, thus far, I have not flinched, but, to ensure accuracy, I have gone over every syllable of the collation, in these forty, and more, editions, *twice*, several months apart, and have arisen from the task with the conviction that I have, after all, by no means evaded the inexorable law of imperfection.

It once occurred to me that if I ever hereafter edit another play, which is very doubtful, I might abridge the labour by disregarding the successive editions put forth by the same editor, and take only his last edition, in which, presumably, his maturest judgement is to be found. But this attempt, I am afraid, would be vain. Editors have rights which those who collate them are bound to respect, and foremost among these rights is that of credit for precedence in emendation; this can be respected only by noting the first editions. If therefore of a modern Editor his first edition must be recorded, it is equally incumbent to note his last. Nigh twenty years of close study passed between Dyce's First Edition and his latest, over thirty-five between Collier's, and shall we take the sallet days and disregard the ripened judgement? Wherefore I see no chance to ease the task in this direction,—nor in any other. If this burdensome collation is to be done at all, it must be done so thoroughly that future students may begin where we leave off.

In the collation of the Quartos and Folios I have allowed myself no discretion; what has attracted my attention, I infer would attract any one else's. In these days, when Shakespeare's mood is to be detected in the number of syllables in his lines, I shrink from fathoming the issues which may depend on the spelling of a word.

I have taken no notice of the commentaries on the text given by ROBERT DEVERELL in the annotated *Othello* contained in the Third Volume of his *Hieroglyphics;* of course they illustrate nothing but the midsummer madness of the poor fellow whose pure lunacy explains all difficulties by 'appearances in the moon.' For instance, I open the volume at random: 'There has been much question about the manner of pro-'nouncing the line, "If I quench thee," &c.; but if the first part of it be referred to 'the taper only (as formed out of the streaks of light on Cassio's body), and the latter 'part not merely to the death of Desdemona (in character), but to the obscuration, or 'extinction rather, of the part of the moon which forms her prototype, the difficulty will 'be removed.' It is not easy at first to repress a smile,—it is impossible, over some of the many grotesque wood-cuts,—but the pathos of the jangled bells drowns all sense of the ludicrous, and we can only close the book with a sigh.

Although in the Preface I have referred to the notes which my friend EDWIN BOOTH prepared for me, and which enrich the foregoing pages, yet I wish again, for his sake, to emphasise the fact that their informal, off-hand style is due to the circumstances under which they were written, with no thought on his part that they were to be seen by any one but by him at whose request they were made. On the last page of the Prompt Book wherein they were written is the following note, which, I think should be given here, as it explains and justifies what I have just said: 'Some Notes for ye Novice, H. H. F. I have jotted here some of the odd notions that flit through my head while acting. In cold blood 'tis difficult to recall them, but I think I've done pretty well. Much may be stale,—I've often found my 'original' ideas very well moth-eaten and musty with age, and 'tis long since I have overhauled the Commentators. I find that I've repeated myself often, and in my 'fidgets' have left out words in many sentences, while the grammar (which I abhor) will doubtless confuse you. However, I have kept my promise as best I can. I hope when you act Othello or Iago, or any other character in this play, that my suggestions may be of service.'

In the Commentary I have, in many a place, put ED. where I should much prefer to have omitted it. But I beg to have it understood that it is present not as a claimant, but as a safeguard, that upon none of my betters may be fathered my folly. Partly for the same reason, I have in my notes used the First Person Singular, but mainly because if anywhere we are restricted to the expression of our own individual opinions, it is in the interpretation of Shakespeare; there, as in the Republic of Letters, each man can speak but for himself alone, and the monarchical 'we' is an assumption of authority without the substance.

[In this closing hour of my labour, and since the foregoing has been put in type, the mail brings me the Facsimile of the First Quarto, 'publisht' by C. Praetorius in London, with an admirable Introduction by HERBERT A. EVANS, M. A., which gives, clearly and succinctly, all needful information in regard to this particular Text, and a comparison of it and the First Folio. This Facsimile is one of a series of all the Shakespearian Quartos, now issuing in London, whose excellence is to be paralleled but by its cheapness. If any word of mine can extend a knowledge of this most commendable publication, I can only wish that I were 'trumpet-tongued.'—ED.]

LIST OF BOOKS FROM WHICH EXTRACTS
HAVE BEEN MADE

GIRALDI CINTHIO: *Hecatommithi*, Venegia 1566
HOLLAND: *Translation of Plinie* 1635
RYMER: *Short View of Tragedy* 1693
EARL OF SHAFTESBURY: *Characteristics* 1714
PECK: *New Memoirs of Milton* 1740
FIELDING: *A Journey from this World to the Next* 1743
UPTON: *Observations* 1746
WHALLEY: *Enquiry into the Learning of Shakespeare* 1748
GREY: *Critical, Historical, and Explanatory Notes* 1754
EDWARDS: *Canons of Criticism* 1765
PERCY: *Reliques* 1765
HEATH: *Revisal, &c.* 1765
TYRWHITT: *Observations, &c.* 1766
WARNER: *Letter to Garrick* 1768
GENTLEMAN: *Dramatic Censor* 1770
LE TOURNEUR: *Shakespeare, traduit dè l'Anglois*, Paris 1776
WARTON: *History of English Poetry*, vol. iii 1781
RITSON: *Remarks, &c.* 1783
DAVIES: *Dramatic Miscellanies* 1784
M. MASON: *Comments, &c.* 1785
DUCIS: *Œuvres*, Paris (edition 1830) 1792
WHITER: *Specimen of a Commentary, &c.* 1794
PARR: *Story of the Moor of Venice* 1795
Essays by a Society of Gentlemen, Exeter 1796
DU BOIS: *The Wreath* 1799
CHALMERS: *Supplemental Apology* 1799
MURPHY: *Life of Garrick* 1801
WALDRON. *Shakespearian Miscellany* 1802
LORD CHEDWORTH: *Notes, &c.* 1805
VOSS: *Othello, uebersetzt*, Jena 1806
DOUCE: *Illustrations* 1807
PYE: *Comments on the Commentators* 1807
DEVERELL: *Discoveries in Hieroglyphics, &c.* 1813
MARTINUS SCRIBLERUS: *Explanations, &c.*, Edinburgh 1814
BECKET: *Shakespeare's Himself Again* 1815
SCHLEGEL: *Lectures, translated by Black* 1815
DRAKE: *Shakespeare and his Times* 1817
HAZLITT: *Characters, &c.* 1817

NICHOLS: *Literary Illustrations, &c.*, vol. ii 1817
ZACHARY JACKSON: *Shakespeare's Genius Justified* 1818
HORN: *Shakespeare's Schauspiele erläutert*, Leipzig 1823
BOADEN: *Life of J. P. Kemble* 1825
HAZLITT: *Plain Speaker* 1826
DRAKE: *Memorials of Shakespeare* 1828
DE BROGLIE: *Sur Othello*, Paris 1830
SIMROCK: *Quellen des Shakespeare's*, Berlin 1831
COLLIER: *History of English Dramatic Poetry* (ed. ii, 1879) 1831
GALT: *Lives of the Players* 1831
MRS JAMESON: *Characteristics of Women* 1832
COLLIER: *New Facts* 1835
COLLIER: *New Particulars* 1836
RAWDON BROWN: *Ragguagli sulla Vita di Marin Sanuto, &c.*, Venice .. 1837
CAMPBELL: *Dramatic Works of Shakespeare* 1838
GUEST: *History of English Rhythms* 1838
BROWN: *Shakespeare's Autobiographical Poems* 1838
COLLIER: *Further Particulars* 1839
SHAKESPEARE SOCIETY: *The Revels Book* 1842
COLLIER: *Shakespeare's Library* (New Edition by W. C. Hazlitt, 1875) .. 1843
DYCE: *Remarks, &c.* 1844
HUNTER: *New Illustrations, &c.* 1845
VERPLANCK: *Shakespeare's Works*, New York 1847
BRAND: *Popular Antiquities, &c.* (Bohn's edition, 1873) 1848
HALPIN: *Dramatic Unities* 1849
ROFFE: *Ghost Belief of Shakespeare* 1851
COLLIER: *Notes and Emendations* 1852
DYCE: *Few Notes* 1853
SINGER: *Shakespeare's Text Vindicated* 1853
PEPYS: *Diary, &c.* (Fifth Edition, London) 1854
QUINCY: *MS Corrections in F_2*, Boston 1854
WHITE: *Shakespeare's Scholar* 1854
WALKER: *Shakespeare's Versification* 1854
TAYLOR: *The Moor of Venice* 1855
WOOD: *Personal Recollections, &c.*, Philadelphia 1855
COLLIER: *Seven Lectures, &c.* 1856
LLOYD: *Essays* (from Singer's Second Edition) 1858
LORD CAMPBELL: *Shakespeare's Legal Acquirements* 1859
WALKER: *Critical Examination of the Text, &c.* 1859
REED: *Lectures on English History*, London 1859
DYCE: *Strictures, &c.* 1859
BUCKNILL: *Shakespeare's Medical Knowledge* 1859
JERVIS: *Proposed Emendations* 1860
MAGINN: *Shakespeare Papers* 1860
FECHTER: *Acting Edition* 1860
OTTLEY: *Fechter's Othello* 1861
BAILEY: *The Received Text* 1861
GERVINUS: *Commentaries* (trans. by F. E. Bunnett), London 1862
.. 1863

HACKETT: *Notes, &c.*, New York 1863
DEIGHTON: *Notes on Othello*, Allahábád 1864
VICTOR HUGO: *William Shakespeare*, Paris 1864
WORDSWORTH: *Shakespeare and the Bible* 1864
BEISLY: *Shakespeare's Garden* 1864
HERAUD: *Shakespeare. His Inner Life* 1865
ARROWSMITH: *Shakespeare's Editors and Commentators* 1865
CARTWRIGHT: *New Readings* 1866
TAINE: *Littérature Anglaise* (Deuxième Édition), Paris 1866
BODENSTEDT: *Othello, uebersetzt*, Leipzig 1867
FORSYTH: *Some Notes, &c.* 1867
KLEIN: *Geschichte des Dramas. Das Italienische*, Leipzig 1867
KEIGHTLEY: *Shakespeare Expositor* 1867
GOULD: *The Tragedian* 1868
FITZGERALD: *Life of Garrick* 1868
GILES: *Human Life in Shakespeare* 1868
HAWKINS: *Life of Edmund Kean* 1869
MARY PRESTON: *Studies in Shakespeare*, Philadelphia 1869
ABBOTT: *Shakespearian Grammar* 1870
DANIEL: *Notes and Emendations* 1870
LAMB: *Works*, London 1870
HARTING: *Ornithology of Shakespeare* 1871
LUDWIG: *Shakespeare-Studien*, Leipzig 1872
RUSKIN: *Munera Pulveris* 1872
MASSEY: *The Secret Drama, &c.* 1872
JOHN HUNTER: *Othello, with Notes* 1873
REES: *Life of Forrest* 1874
DOWDEN: *Shakspere. His Mind and Art* 1875
LEWES: *On Actors and the Art of Acting* 1875
WARD: *History of English Dramatic Poetry* 1875
EARL OF SOUTHESK: *Saskatchewan* 1875
FRIESEN: *Shakspere-Studien*, Wien 1876
FLEAY: *Shakespeare Manual* 1876
ULRICI: *Shakespeare's Dramatic Art, &c.* (translated by Miss Schmitz) .. 1876
OECHELHÄUSER: *Othello, bearbeitet*, Weimar 1876
SNIDER: *System of Shakespeare's Dramas*, St Louis 1877
ALGER: *Life of Forrest* 1877
BULLOCH: *Studies on the Text of Shakespeare* 1878
EDWIN BOOTH: *Prompt-Book of Othello* 1878
ELLACOMBE: *Plant-Lore of Shakespeare* 1878
HERR: *Scattered Notes, &c.*, Philadelphia 1879
COWDEN-CLARKE: *The Shakespeare Key* 1879
INGLEBY: *Centurie of Prayse* 1879
MOBERLY: *Romeo and Juliet* 1880
SWINBURNE: *A Study of Shakespeare* 1880
GENSICHEN: *Studienblätter*, Berlin 1881
INGLEBY: *Shakespeare. The Man and the Book*, Part ii 1881
ELZE: *Hamlet* 1882
BULTHAUPT: *Dramaturgie der Classiker*, Oldenburg 1883

GÉRARD: *Othello, avec des Notes. Precèdée d'une Étude sur Shakespeare, par* Dr James Darmesteter, Paris 1883

PURNELL: *Othello, with Notes* 1883

D'HUGUES: *Othello, avec des Notes,* Paris 1883

WORDSWORTH: *Works* (ed. Knight) 1883

HEARD: *Shakespeare as a Lawyer* 1883

MRS KEMBLE: *Records of Later Life* 1884

HALES: *Notes and Essays* 1884

ELZE: *Notes on Elizabethan Dramatists,* Halle 1884

MOREL: *Othello, avec des Notes,* Paris 1884

HALLIWELL-PHILLIPPS: *Outlines of the Life of Shakespeare* (Fifth Edition) .. 1885

LEO: *Shakespeare-Notes* 1885

GRANT WHITE: *Studies in Shakespeare* 1886

CHAPPELL'S *Popular Music* .. .. **n. d.**

RUSSELL'S *Representative Actors* .. .. **n. d.**

The Academy
American Bibliopolist
The Athenæum
Bibliotheca Sacra
Blackwood's Magazine
Cornhill Magazine
Edinburgh Review
The Galaxy
New Shakspere Society
Notes and Queries
Philological Society's Transactions
Robinson's Epitome of Literature
Shakespeariana
Temple Bar

INDEX

A = before verbal nouns	IV, i, 195
A = one	II, ii, 342
Abhor	IV, ii, 191
Absorption of *it*	I, iii, 220
Absorption of personal pronoun	II, i, 79
Absorption of *t* final ..	II, ii, 214
Absorption of *the*	I, ii, 4
Absorption of *you*	I, ii, 12
Acknown	III, iii, 372
Action, Date of	357
Action, Duration of ..	359
Active sense of adjectives in *-able* or *-ible*	I, iii, 356
Actors	396
Actress, the first	397
Adams, J. Q., Notes ..	391
Addition	II, ii, 8
Adjectives in *-able* or *-ible* used actively	I, iii, 356
Advised = cautious	I, ii, 69
Affects, the young	I, iii, 291
Affin'd	I, i, 42
Affin'd	II, ii, 243
Aim = guess	I, iii, 10
Akes	IV, ii, 79
And-a	II, ii, 106
Anthropophague	I, iii, 167
Apology for Iago	408
Arrivancie	II, i, 40
As (omitted)	II, i, 180
As = that, after *such* ..	I, i, 80
As = that	V, ii, 203
Assay	I, iii, 26
Auntient	I, i, 35
Ballad of *Othello*	398
Beam	I, iii, 357
Beard	I, iii, 371
Before me	IV, i, 162
Begrimed	III, iii, 445
Besort	I, iii, 264
Bodenstedt, Remarks ..	440
Bombast	I, i, 17
Booth's Reprint, Variations in	I, ii, 74
Booth's Reprint " "	I, iii, 399
Brace	I, iii, 32
Brown, Rawdon, Source of Plot	372
Browne, E. Elliot, Source of Plot	375
Bulthaupt, Remarks ..	445
But = except	I, i, 138
But = prevention	IV, iii, 38
By = about	I, iii, 24
Campbell, Remarks ..	420
Carve	II, ii, 197
Cast	I, i, 164
Cast	II, ii, 31
Cast	II, ii, 202
Cast	V, ii, 400
Certes	I, i, 19
Chamberers	III, iii, 309
Chances	I, i, 79
Charter	I, iii, 273
Cherubin	IV, ii, 73
Chidden	II, i, 14
Chrysolite	V, ii, 179
Cinthio, Giraldi	376
Circumstance	I, i, 17
Coat (secret armour) ..	V, i, 29
Coleridge on Othello's Colour	389
Coleridge on the Unities ..	409
Collied	II, ii, 231
Committed	IV, ii, 83
Companions	IV, ii, 168
Composition, Date of ..	344
Composition	I, iii, 3
Condition	II, i, 282

Condition	IV, i, 210	
Consequence (omission of plural *s*)	II, ii, 81	
Construe	IV, i, 118	
Consuls	I, i, 27	
Consuls	I, ii, 51	
Contraction in participles ..	I, i, 56	
Convinc'd	IV, i, 33	
Costume	404	
Counter-caster	I, i, 33	
Countryman (Iago a Venetian)	V, i, 112	
Courtesy	II, i, 118	
Court of Guard	II, i, 251	
Craftily qualified ..	II, ii, 56	
Creature = trisyllable ..	III, iii, 482	
Crie	II, ii, 398	
Cries on	V, i, 62	
Criticall	II, i, 142	
Cue	I, ii, 101	
Cunning	III, iii, 57	
Curled darlings	I, ii, 85	
Damn'd in a faire wife ..	I, i, 22	
Daniel, Duration of Action	370	
Dearest	I, iii, 102	
De Broglie, Remarks ..	450	
Defeat	I, iii, 371	
Defunct	I, iii, 291	
Delighted	I, iii, 320	
Demerits = merits ..	I, ii, 25	
Desdemon	III, i, 58	
Desdemona, the meaning of	I, iii, 168	
Desdemona " "	336	
Desdemona	V, ii, 85	
Despised	I, i, 177	
De Vigny's *Othello* ..	450	
Dilations	III, iii, 144	
Direct session	I, ii, 105	
Discourse of thought ..	IV, ii, 182	
Dispose	I, iii, 421	
Dote	II, i, 239	
Double comparative ..	I, iii, 127	
Double comparatives ..	I, i, 105	
Double negatives	I, iii, 25	
Double of the duke's ..	I, ii, 16	
Doubt = suspicion	III, iii, 217	
Doubt = suspicion	III, iii, 490	
Dowden, Remarks	424	
Dreadful bell .. .	II, ii, 199	
Ducis's Version .. .	447	
Edinburgh Review	418	
Edinburgh Review	421	
Enchafed	II, i, 19	
Engines	IV, ii, 250	
Ensteeped	II, i, 82	
Enwheele	II, i, 102	
Erring	I, iii, 385	
Escape = escapade	I, iii, 223	
Essentiall vesture	II, i, 74	
Eternal = infernal	IV, ii, 154	
Ethical dative	I, i, 53	
Exclusion of native officers	I, iii, 61	
Exhibition	I, iii, 263	
Exhibition	IV, iii, 83	
Extravagant	I, i, 149	
Exufflicate	III, iii, 211	
Fadome	I, i, 167	
Faire wife	I, i, 22	
Falls, used transitively ..	IV, i, 273	
Favour	I, iii, 371	
Fear, active use of	I, ii, 88	
Fife	III, iii, 408	
First Quarto	339	
Florentine	III, i, 44	
Folio printed from a theatre transcript	II, ii, 231	
Folly = wantonness	V, ii, 165	
Fond	II, i, 163	
For, confused with *or* ..	I, ii, 75	
Forehead	III, iii, 331	
Fortitude	I, iii, 248	
Forty = indefinite number ..	III, iii, 505	
Free	II, ii, 367	
Free	III, iii, 150	
Friesen, Remarks	443	
From = away from	I, i, 144	
Fruitfull	II, ii, 372	
Function	II, ii, 379	
Garbe	II, i, 339	
Genischen, Remarks ..	445	
Gervinus, Remarks ..	436	
Gloss	I, iii, 252	
Go = come	I, i, 197	
God be with you	I, iii, 214	

God buy you	.. ..	III, iii, 433
Grace	.. ..	IV, iii, 101
Gratify	.. ..	V, ii, 265
Graze	.. ..	IV, i, 299
Green-ey'd	.. ..	III, iii, 194
Grise	.. ..	I, iii, 227
Guards of the Pole	..	II, i, 17
Guizot, Remarks	..	449
Gundelier	.. ..	I, i, 138
Habits	.. ..	I, iii, 128
Halliwell, Othello's Colour		394
Handkerchief, description of		III, iv, 68
Hands, not hearts	..	III, iv, 56
Hardness	.. ..	I, iii, 259
Hazlitt, Remarks	..	411
Heaven, a plural	..	IV, ii, 58
Heraud, Remarks,	..	422
Hip, on the	..	II, i, 338
His = its	.. ..	I, ii, 15
Honor...Honesty	..	V, ii, 306
Hope's (not surfetted to death)		II, i, 58
Horn, Remarks	..	433
Hudson, Othello's Colour	..	394
Huswiues	.. ..	II, i, 132
I in -*ity*, dropped	..	III, iii, 295
Iago, apology for	..	408
Iago's age	..	I, iii, 343
Iago's jealousy	..	I, iii, 414
Iago, the name	..	335
Idle	.. ..	I, iii, 163
Incontinently	..	I, iii, 336
Index	.. ..	II, i, 289
In = during	..	I, ii, 116
Ingeniuer	..	II, i, 75
Ingredient	..	II, ii, 335
In happy time	..	III, i, 33
In = into	..	V, ii, 358
Injointed	..	I, iii, 44
In = on	.. ..	I, iii, 85
Insertion in Acting Copies	..	I, iii, 161
In spleen	..	IV, i, 102
Instruction	..	IV, i, 50
Intentively	..	I, iii, 178
Interpolated *a*	..	III, iii, 92
Interpolated *s*	..	III, iv, 136
Interpolation of *s*	..	I, i, 31
Interpolation of *s*	..	IV, i, 54
Inversion of adjectives and nouns	.. ..	II, i, 57
Is, with plural subject	..	I, i, 188
I was = a monosyllable	..	III, iv, 195
Jameson, Mrs, Remarks	..	413
Jealous	.. ..	III, iii, 212
Jealous	.. ..	III, iv, 179
Jealousy (Leontes's and Othello's)	..	III, iii, 126
Johnson, Dr, Criticism	..	407
Jove substituted for God	..	II, i, 91
Justly = truthfully	..	I, iii, 147
Kean's last appearance	..	402
Klein, Source of Plot	..	373
Knave	.. ..	I, i, 49
Lamb, Charles, Remarks	..	410
Learn = teach	..	I, iii, 208
Liberall	..	II, i, 188
Lookes (for lookst)	..	II, ii, 201
Lowth, Remarks	..	408
Ludwig, Remarks	..	437
Lust's Dominion	..	I, iii, 172
Lust's Dominion	..	II, i, 229
Macaulay, Remarks	..	412
Maginn, Remarks	..	415
Maine	..	II, i, 15
Mandragora	..	III, iii, 384
Marble	..	III, iii, 523
Marke, bless the	..	I, i, 35
Mauritania	..	IV, ii, 259
Meere	..	II, ii, 5
Might, Officers of	..	I, i, 200
Mineral	..	II, i, 330
Minerals	..	I, ii, 91
Mistress = trisyllable	..	IV, ii, 104
Modern	..	I, iii, 129
Mocke	..	III, iii, 194
Mocks	..	V, ii, 189
Moe	..	IV, iii, 62
Monstrous = trisyllable	..	II, ii, 242
Moraller	..	II, ii, 327
Mortal	..	II, i, 84
Most (*the* omitted)	..	II, i, 28
Motion	..	I, ii, 92
Motion	..	I, iii, 114
Mummey	..	III, iv, 88

Napkin .. .. .. III, iii, 335
Negatives, double .. .. I, iii, 125
Nephewes .. .. .. I, i, 124
News .. .. .. I, iii, 3
Non-suites .. .. .. I, i, 19
North .. .. .. V, ii, 273
Not almost .. .. .. III, iii, 78
Notorious .. .. .. V, ii, 299
Nuptiall .. .. .. II, ii, 9

Oake .. .. .. III, iii, 242
Obsequious .. .. .. I, i, 50
Odd even .. .. .. I, i, 136
Oechelhäuser, Remarks .. 442
Of = concerning .. .. III, iii, 245
Off-capt .. .. .. I, i, 14
Officers of might .. .. I, i, 200
Of hers .. .. .. V, ii, 6
Omission of plural *s* .. II, ii, 81
Or confused with *for* .. I, ii, 75
Othello's Colour 389
Othello, the name 335
Other = otherwise .. .. IV, ii, 16

Pagans .. .. .. I, ii, 121
Parts (Voltaire) .. .. III, iii, 308
Passage .. .. .. V, i, 47
Passion .. .. .. III, iii, 145
Pattent .. .. .. IV, i, 216
Pepys, Diary 402
Perplexed .. .. .. V, ii, 420
Pickersgill, Source of Plot .. 375
Pierced .. .. .. I, iii, 245
Plot, Source of 372
Ponticke Sea .. .. III, iii, 516
Portance .. .. .. I, iii, 162
Portents (accent) .. .. V, ii, 54
Practised = plotted .. .. I, ii, 90
Prefixes dropped .. .. I, iii, 217
Pregnant .. .. .. II, i, 268
Presentiment .. .. IV, iii, 29
Presently .. .. .. V, ii, 66
Preston, Othello's Colour .. 395
Proball .. .. .. II, ii, 368
Prophane .. .. .. I, i, 127
Prophane .. .. .. II, i, 188
Profanity, Statute against .. I, i, 7
Proper = very .. .. I, iii, 84
Put or .. .. .. II, i, 171
Put on .. .. .. II, ii, 382

Pye's remark on Desdemona III, iii, 28
Pyoners .. .. .. III, iii, 402

Qualification .. .. II, i, 307
Quality .. .. .. I, iii, 279
Quarter .. .. .. II, ii, 204
Quartos, The 339
Question .. .. .. I, iii, 31
Question = conversation .. I, iii, 133
Quests .. .. .. I, ii, 54

Raven .. .. .. IV, i, 25
Reed, Othello's Colour .. 393
Remorse .. .. .. III, iii, 426
Repeals .. .. .. II, ii, 388
Reprobance .. .. .. V, ii, 261
Resolu'd .. .. .. III, iii, 209
Revolt = inconstancy .. III, iii, 217
Riches (sing.) .. .. II, i, 98
Right garbe .. .. II, i, 339
Ripe .. .. .. II, ii, 410
Rose, on Sudden Emotion .. 428
Rymer, General estimate of IV, i, 10

S interpolated .. .. I, i, 31
S interpolated .. .. III, iv, 136
S interpolated .. .. IV, i, 54
S for *st* .. .. IV, ii, 207
Sagitary .. .. .. I, i, 173
Sagitary .. .. .. I, iii, 136
Salvini's omission .. .. IV, i, 57
Satiety .. .. .. II, i, 261
Saucie .. .. .. I, i, 141
Save you .. .. .. IV, i, 237
Schlegel, Remarks 431
Scorn, time of .. .. IV, ii, 64
Second Quarto 341
Secure .. .. .. I, iii, 14
Seele .. .. .. III, iii, 242
Seele .. .. .. I, iii, 297
Seige .. .. .. I, ii, 25
Seize upon .. .. V, ii, 443
Segregation .. .. II, i, 12
Selfe-Bounty .. .. III, iii, 220
Selfe-charitie .. .. II, ii, 226
Sense .. .. .. IV, iii, 103
Sequestration .. .. I, iii, 375
Set down .. .. .. II, i, 231
Shaftesbury, derivation of
  Desdemona .. .. I, iii, 168

She = her	.. .. ..	IV, ii, 5
She that	.. .. ..	II, i, 173
Should I lose	.. ..	III, iv, 25
Simrock, Source of Plot	..	372
Singular verbs with plural antecedents	.. ..	I, iii, 312
Sir, the	.. .. ..	II, i, 199
Sith ..	.. .. ..	III, iii, 438
Skillet	.. .. ..	I, iii, 300
Slave ..	.. .. ..	IV, ii, 156
Sleepes	.. .. ..	III, iii, 477
Slipper	.. .. ..	II, i, 274
Slubber	.. .. ..	I, iii, 252
Snider, Remarks	.. ..	425
So = such	.. .. ..	I, iii, 68
Solicit	.. .. ..	V, ii, 33
Soon at night	.. ..	III, iv, 229
Speculative instrument	..	I, iii, 297
Spells	.. .. ..	I, iii, 76
Splinter	.. .. ..	II, ii, 352
Stage directions	.. ..	III, iii, 335
Stage directions not to be taken literally	.. ..	III, iii, 383
Stage transcript the source of F₁	.. .. ..	II, ii, 231
Still = constantly	.. ..	I, iii, 170
Stope	.. .. ..	II, ii, 46
Strange	.. .. ..	V, ii, 256
Stuff ..	.. .. ..	I, ii, 4
Subjunctive indicated by position of the verb	..	V, i, 17
Substitution of *s* for *st*	..	II, ii, 201
Success	.. ..	III, iii, 259
Superfluous *s*	.. ..	I, i, 31
Superfluous *s*	.. ..	III, iii, 78
Swore	.. .. ..	I, iii, 183
Talk	.. .. ..	IV, iii, 31
Tame (Pye's Remark)	..	III, iii, 28
Tane out	.. ..	III, iii, 344
Text, Discussion of ..	..	341
Thick-lips	.. ..	I, i, 72
Third Quarto	..	341
Thou art = monosyllable	..	V, ii, 168
Thou (where used)	..	II, ii, 275
Three fingers	.. ..	II, i, 197
Time of scorn	.. ..	IV, ii, 64
To, omitted before infinitive	IV, ii, 15
To do = ado	.. ..	IV, iii, 37

Tongued	.. .. ..	I, i, 27
Too blame ..	.. ..	III, iii, 244
To who	.. ..	I, ii, 64
Trash...trace	.. ..	II, i, 336
Traverse	.. ..	I, iii, 399
Trym'd	.. ..	I, i, 54
Uds pitty	.. ..	IV, iii, 84
Ulrici, Remarks	.. ..	433
Unbonnetted	.. ..	I, ii, 26
Unbookish	.. ..	IV, i, 118
Unhoused	.. ..	I, ii, 29
Unproper	.. ..	IV, i, 81
Uses ..	.. ..	IV, iii, 114
Usurp'd	.. ..	I, iii, 371
Vanity	.. ..	IV, ii, 193
Verennessa ..	.. ..	II, i, 30
Vertuous	.. ..	III, iv, 131
Villaine	.. ..	V, ii, 213
Visage	.. ..	I, iii, 280
Voltaire's *Zaïre*	.. ..	447
Voluble	.. ..	II, i, 270
Voss, Schiller's version	..	431
Walk = withdraw	.. ..	IV, iii, 9
Wanting = missing ..	..	III, iii, 398
Warrant = monosyllable	..	IV, i, 233
Waste	.. ..	IV, ii, 276
Well desired	.. ..	II, i, 237
Well said ..	.. ..	IV, i, 133
Wench	.. ..	V, ii, 355
Were...beer (rhyme)	..	II, i, 183
Wheeling ..	.. ..	I, i, 149
Whether = monosyllable	..	I, ii, 102
Who (uninflected) ..	..	I, ii, 64
Will = wish ..	.. ..	V, ii, 246
Wilson's *Rhetorique*	..	III, iii, 188
Wilson, Othello's Colour	..	391
With, omission of ..	..	I, iii, 109
Wordsworth's Sonnet	..	410
Would = liked	..	I, iii, 170
Wracke	.. ..	II, i, 27
Wretch	.. ..	III, iii, 104
Y'are	.. ..	III, iii, 253
Y'are	.. ..	III, iii, 450
Yerk'd	.. ..	I, ii, 7
You (where used) ..	..	II, ii, 275
You were (monosyllabic) ..		I, ii, 34

Catalog
of
DOVER BOOKS

BOOKS EXPLAINING SCIENCE

(Note: The books listed under this category are general introductions, surveys, reviews, and non-technical expositions of science for the interested layman or scientist who wishes to brush up. Dover also publishes the largest list of inexpensive reprints of books on intermediate and higher mathematics, mathematical physics, engineering, chemistry, astronomy, etc., for the professional mathematician or scientist. For our complete Science Catalog, write Dept. catrr., Dover Publications, Inc., 180 Varick Street, New York 14, N. Y.)

CONCERNING THE NATURE OF THINGS, Sir William· Bragg. Royal Institute Christmas Lectures by Nobel Laureate. Excellent plain-language introduction to gases, molecules, crystal structure, etc. explains "building blocks" of universe, basic properties of matter, with simplest, clearest examples, demonstrations. 32pp. of photos; 57ᵛ figures. 244pp. 5⅜ x 8.
T31 Paperbound **$1.35**

MATTER AND LIGHT, THE NEW PHYSICS, Louis de Broglie. Non-technical explanations by a Nobel Laureate of electro-magnetic theory, relativity, wave mechanics, quantum physics, philosophies of science, etc. Simple, yet accurate introduction to work of Planck, Bohr, Einstein, other modern physicists. Only 2 of 12 chapters require mathematics. 300pp. 5⅜ x 8.
T35 Paperbound **$1.60**

THE COMMON ·SENSE OF THE EXACT SCIENCES, W. K. Clifford. For 70 years, Clifford's work has been acclaimed as one of the clearest, yet most precise introductions to mathematical symbolism, measurement, surface boundaries, position, space, motion, mass and force, etc. Prefaces by Bertrand Russell and Karl Pearson. Introduction by James Newman. 130 figures. 249pp. 5⅜ x 8.
T61 Paperbound **$1.60**

THE NATURE OF LIGHT AND COLOUR IN THE OPEN AIR, M. Minnaert. What causes mirages? haloes? "multiple" suns and moons? Professor Minnaert explains these and hundreds of other fascinating natural optical phenomena in simple terms, tells how to observe them, suggests hundreds of experiments. 200 illus; 42 photos. xvi + 362pp.
T196 Paperbound **$1ᵣ95**

SPINNING TOPS AND GYROSCOPIC MOTION, John Perry. Classic elementary text on dynamics of rotation treats gyroscopes, tops, how quasi-rigidity is induced in paper disks, smoke rings, chains, etc, by rapid motion, precession, earth's motion, etc. Contains many easy-to-perform experiments. Appendix on practical uses of gyroscopes. 62 figures. 128pp.
T416 Paperbound **$1.00**

A CONCISE HISTORY OF MATHEMATICS, D. Struik. This lucid, easily followed history of mathematics from the Ancient Near East to modern times requires no mathematical background itself, yet introduces both mathematicians and laymen to basic concepts and discoveries and the men who made them. Contains a collection of 31 portraits of eminent mathematicians. Bibliography. xix + 299pp. 5⅜ x 8.
T255 Paperbound **$1.75**

THE RESTLESS UNIVERSE, Max Born. A remarkably clear, thorough exposition of gases, electrons, ions, waves and particles, electronic structure of the atom, nuclear physics, written for the layman by a Nobel Laureate. "Much ·more thorough and deep than most attempts . . . easy and delightful," CHEMICAL AND ENGINEERING NEWS. Includes 7 animated sequences showing motion of molecules, alpha particles, etc. 11 full-page plates of photographs. Total of nearly 600 illus. 315pp. 6⅛ x 9¼.
T412 Paperbound **$2.00**

WHAT IS SCIENCE?, N. Campbell. The role of experiment, the function of mathematics, the nature of scientific laws, the limitations of science, and many other provocative topics are explored without technicalities by an eminent scientist. "Still an excellent introduction to scientific philosophy," H. Margenau in PHYSICS TODAY. 192ₚp. 5⅜ x 8.
S43 Paperbound **$1.25**

FADS AND FALLACIES IN THE NAME OF SCIENCE, Martin Gardner. The standard account of the various cults, quack systems and delusions which have recently masqueraded as science: hollow earth theory, Atlantis, dianetics, Reich's orgone theory, flying saucers, Bridey Murphy, psionics, irridiagnosis, many other fascinating fallacies that deluded tens of thousands. "Should be read by everyone, scientist and non-scientist alike," R. T. Birge, Prof. Emeritus, Univ. of California; Former President, American Physical Society. Formerly titled, "In the Name of Science." Revised and enlarged edition. x + 365pp. 5⅜ x 8.
T394 Paperbound **$1.50**

THE STUDY OF THE HISTORY OF MATHEMATICS, THE STUDY OF THE HISTORY OF SCIENCE, G. Sarton. Two books bound as one. Both volumes are standard introductions to their fields by an eminent science historian. They discuss problems of historical research, teaching, pitfalls, other matters of interest to the historically oriented writer, teacher, or student. Both have extensive bibliographies. 10 illustrations. 188pp. 5⅜ x 8.   T240 Paperbound **$1.25**

THE PRINCIPLES OF SCIENCE, W. S. Jevons. Unabridged reprinting of a milestone in the development of symbolic logic and other subjects concerning scientific methodology, probability, inferential validity, etc. Also describes Jevons' "logic machine," an early precursor of modern electronic calculators. Preface by E. Nagel. 839pp. 5⅜ x 8. S446 Paperbound **$2.98**

SCIENCE THEORY AND MAN, Erwin Schroedinger. Complete, unabridged reprinting of "Science and the Human Temperament" plus an additional essay "What is an Elementary Particle?" Nobel Laureate Schroedinger discusses many aspects of modern physics from novel points of view which provide unusual insights for both laymen and physicists. 192 pp. 5⅜ x 8.
T428 Paperbound **$1.35**

BRIDGES AND THEIR BUILDERS, D. B. Steinman & S. R. Watson. Information about ancient, medieval, modern bridges; how they were built; who built them; the structural principles employed; the materials they are built of; etc. Written by one of the world's leading authorities on bridge design and construction. New, revised, expanded edition. 23 photos; 26 line drawings, xvii + 401pp. 5⅜ x 8.   T431 Paperbound **$1.95**

HISTORY OF MATHEMATICS, D. E. Smith. Most comprehensive non-technical history of math in English. In two volumes. Vol. I: A chronological examination of the growth of mathematics from primitive concepts up to 1900. Vol. II: The development of ideas in specific fields and areas, up through elementary calculus. The lives and works of over a thousand mathematicians are covered; thousands of specific historical problems and their solutions are clearly explained. Total of 510 illustrations, 1355pp. 5⅜ x 8. Set boxed in attractive container.   T429, T430 Paperbound, the set **$5.00**

PHILOSOPHY AND THE PHYSICISTS, L. S. Stebbing. A philosopher examines the philosophical implications of modern science by posing a lively critical attack on the popular science expositions of Sir James Jeans and Arthur Eddington. xvi + 295pp. 5⅜ x 8.
T480 Paperbound **$1.65**

ON MATHEMATICS AND MATHEMATICIANS, R. E. Moritz. The first collection of quotations by and about mathematicians in English. 1140 anecdotes, aphorisms, definitions, speculations, etc. give both mathematicians and layman stimulating new insights into what mathematics is, and into the personalities of the great mathematicians from Archimedes to Euler, Gauss, Klein, Weierstrass. Invaluable to teachers, writers. Extensive cross index. 410pp. 5⅜ x 8.
T489 Paperbound **$1.95**

NATURAL SCIENCE, BIOLOGY, GEOLOGY, TRAVEL

A SHORT HISTORY OF ANATOMY AND PHYSIOLOGY FROM THE GREEKS TO HARVEY, C. Singer. A great medical historian's fascinating intermediate account of the slow advance of anatomical and physiological knowledge from pre-scientific times to Vesalius, Harvey. 139 unusually interesting illustrations. 221pp. 5⅜ x 8.   T389 Paperbound **$1.75**

THE BEHAVIOUR AND SOCIAL LIFE OF HONEYBEES, Ronald Ribbands. The most comprehensive, lucid and authoritative book on bee habits, communication, duties, cell life, motivations, etc. "A MUST for every scientist, experimenter, and educator, and a happy and valuable selection for all interested in the honeybee," AMERICAN BEE JOURNAL. 690-item bibliography. 127 illus.; 11 photographic plates. 352pp. 5⅜ x 8⅜.   S410 Clothbound **$4.50**

TRAVELS OF WILLIAM BARTRAM, edited by **Mark Van Doren.** One of the 18th century's most delightful books, and one of the few first-hand sources of information about American geography, natural history, and anthropology of American Indian tribes of the time. "The mind of a scientist with the soul of a poet," John Livingston Lowes. 13 original illustrations, maps. Introduction by Mark Van Doren. 448pp. 5⅜ x 8.   T326 Paperbound **$2.00**

STUDIES ON THE STRUCTURE AND DEVELOPMENT OF VERTEBRATES, Edwin Goodrich. The definitive study of the skeleton, fins and limbs, head region, divisions of the body cavity, vascular, respiratory, excretory systems, etc., of vertebrates from fish to higher mammals, by the greatest comparative anatomist of recent times. "The standard textbook," JOURNAL OF ANATOMY. 754 illus. 69-page biographical study. 1186-item bibliography. 2 vols. Total of 906pp. 5⅜ x 8.   Vol. I: S449 Paperbound **$2.50**
Vol. II: S450 Paperbound **$2.50**

THE BIRTH AND DEVELOPMENT OF THE GEOLOGICAL SCIENCES, F. D. Adams. The most complete and thorough history of the earth sciences in print. Covers over 300 geological thinkers and systems; treats fossils, theories of stone growth, paleontology, earthquakes, vulcanists vs. neptunists, odd theories, etc. 91 illustrations, including medieval, Renaissance wood cuts, etc. 632 footnotes and bibliographic notes. 511pp. 308pp. 5⅜ x 8.   T5 Paperbound **$2.00**

FROM MAGIC TO SCIENCE, Charles Singer. A close study of aspects of medical science from the Roman Empire through the Renaissance. The sections on early herbals, and "The Visions of Hildegarde of Bingen," are probably the best studies of these subjects available. 158 unusual classic and medieval illustrations. xxvii + 365pp. 5⅜ x 8.   T390 Paperbound **$2.00**

SAILING ALONE AROUND THE WORLD, Captain Joshua Slocum. Captain Slocum's personal account of his single-handed voyage around the world in a 34-foot boat he rebuilt himself. A classic of both seamanship and descriptive writing. "A nautical equivalent of Thoreau's account," Van Wyck Brooks. 67 illus. 308pp. 5⅜ x 8.   T326 Paperbound **$1.00**

TREES OF THE EASTERN AND CENTRAL UNITED STATES AND CANADA, W. M. Harlow. Standard middle-level guide designed to help you know the characteristics of Eastern trees and identify them at sight by means of an 8-page synoptic key. More than 600 drawings and photographs of twigs, leaves, fruit, other features. xiii + 288pp. 4⅝ x 6½.
                                                                    T395 Paperbound **$1.35**

FRUIT KEY AND TWIG KEY ("Fruit Key to Northeastern Trees," "Twig Key to Deciduous Woody Plants of Eastern North America"), **W. M. Harlow.** Identify trees in fall, winter, spring. Easy-to-use, synoptic keys, with photographs of every twig and fruit identified. Covers 120 different fruits, 160 different twigs. Over 350 photos. Bibliographies. Glossaries. Total of 143pp. 5⅝ x 8⅜.   T511 Paperbound **$1.25**

INTRODUCTION TO THE STUDY OF EXPERIMENTAL MEDICINE, Claude Bernard. This classic records Bernard's far-reaching efforts to transform physiology into an exact science. It covers problems of vivisection, the limits of physiological experiment, hypotheses in medical experimentation, hundreds of others. Many of his own famous experiments on the liver, the pancreas, etc., are used as examples. Foreword by I. B. Cohen. xxv + 266pp. 5⅜ x 8.
                                                                    T400 Paperbound **$1.50**

THE ORIGIN OF LIFE, A. I. Oparin. The first modern statement that life evolved from complex nitro-carbon compounds, carefully presented according to modern biochemical knowledge of primary colloids, organic molecules, etc. Begins with historical introduction to the problem of the origin of life. Bibliography. xxv + 270pp. 5⅜ x 8.   S213 Paperbound **$1.75**

A HISTORY OF ASTRONOMY FROM THALES TO KEPLER, J. L. E. Dreyer. The only work in English which provides a detailed picture of man's cosmological views from Egypt, Babylonia, Greece, and Alexandria to Copernicus, Tycho Brahe and Kepler. "Standard reference on Greek astronomy and the Copernican revolution," SKY AND TELESCOPE. Formerly called "A History of Planetary Systems From Thales to Kepler." Bibliography. 21 diagrams. xvii + 430pp. 5⅜ x 8.
                                                                    S79 Paperbound **$1.98**

URANIUM PROSPECTING, H. L. Barnes. A professional geologist tells you what you need to know. Hundreds of facts about minerals, tests, detectors, sampling, assays, claiming, developing, government regulations, etc. Glossary of technical terms. Annotated bibliography. x + 117pp. 5⅜ x 8.   T309 Paperbound **$1.00**

DE RE METALLICA, Georgius Agricola. All 12 books of this 400 year old classic on metals and metal production, fully annotated, and containing all 289 of the 16th century woodcuts which made the original an artistic masterpiece. A superb gift for geologists, engineers, libraries, artists, historians. Translated by Herbert Hoover & L. H. Hoover. Bibliography, survey of ancient authors. 289 illustrations of the excavating, assaying, smelting, refining, and countless other metal production operations described in the text. 672pp. 6¾ x 10¾. Deluxe library edition.   S6 Clothbound **$10.00**

DE MAGNETE, William Gilbert. A landmark of science by the man who first used the word "electricity," distinguished between static electricity and magnetism, and founded a new science. P. F. Mottelay translation. 90 figures. lix + 368pp. 5⅜ x 8. S470 Paperbound **$2.00**

THE AUTOBIOGRAPHY OF CHARLES DARWIN AND SELECTED LETTERS, Francis Darwin, ed. Fascinating documents on Darwin's early life, the voyage of the "Beagle," the discovery of evolution, Darwin's thought on mimicry, plant development, vivisection, evolution, many other subjects Letters to Henslow, Lyell, Hooker, Wallace, Kingsley, etc. Appendix. 365pp. 5⅜ x 8.   T479 Paperbound **$1.65**

A WAY OF LIFE AND OTHER SELECTED WRITINGS OF SIR WILLIAM OSLER. 16 of the great physician, teacher and humanist's most inspiring writings on a practical philosophy of life, science and the humanities, and the history of medicine. 5 photographs. Introduction by G. L. Keynes, M.D., F.R.C.S. xx + 278pp. 5⅜ x 8.   T488 Paperbound **$1.50**

LITERATURE

WORLD DRAMA, B. H. Clark. 46 plays from Ancient Greece, Rome, to India, China, Japan. Plays by Aeschylus, Sophocles, Euripides, Aristophanes, Plautus, Marlowe, Jonson, Farquhar, Goldsmith, Cervantes, Molière, Dumas, Goethe, Schiller, Ibsen, many others. One of the most comprehensive collections of important plays from all literature available in English. Over ⅓ of this material is unavailable in any other current edition. Reading lists. 2 volumes. Total of 1364pp. 5⅜ x 8.
Vol. I, T57 Paperbound **$2.00**
Vol. II, T59 Paperbound **$2.00**

MASTERS OF THE DRAMA, John Gassner. The most comprehensive history of the drama in print. Covers more than 800 dramatists and over 2000 plays from the Greeks to modern Western, Near Eastern, Oriental drama. Plot summaries, theatre history, etc. "Best of its kind in English," NEW REPUBLIC. 35 pages of bibliography. 77 photos and drawings. Deluxe edition. xxii + 890pp. 5⅜ x 8.
T100 Clothbound **$5.95**

THE DRAMA OF LUIGI PIRANDELLO, D. Vittorini. All 38 of Pirandello's plays (to 1935) summarized and analyzed in terms of symbolic techniques, plot structure, etc. The only authorized work. Foreword by Pirandello. Biography. Bibliography. xiii + 350pp. 5⅜ x 8.
T435 Paperbound **$1.98**

ARISTOTLE'S THEORY OF POETRY AND THE FINE ARTS, S. H. Butcher, ed. The celebrated "Butcher translation" faced page by page with the Greek text; Butcher's 300-page introduction to Greek poetic, dramatic thought. Modern Aristotelian criticism discussed by John Gassner. lxxvi + 421pp. 5⅜ x 8.
T42 Paperbound **$2.00**

EUGENE O'NEILL: THE MAN AND HIS PLAYS, B. H. Clark. The first published source-book on O'Neill's life and work. Analyzes each play from the early THE WEB up to THE ICEMAN COMETH. Supplies much information about environmental and dramatic influences. ix + 182pp. 5⅜ x 8.
T379 Paperbound **$1.25**

INTRODUCTION TO ENGLISH LITERATURE, B. Dobrée, ed. Most compendious literary aid in its price range. Extensive, categorized bibliography (with entries up to 1949) of more than 5,000 poets, dramatists, novelists, as well as historians, philosophers, economists, religious writers, travellers, and scientists of literary stature. Information about manuscripts, important biographical data. Critical, historical, background works not simply listed, but evaluated. Each volume also contains a long introduction to the period it covers.

Vol. I: **THE BEGINNINGS OF ENGLISH LITERATURE TO SKELTON, 1509, W. L. Renwick. H. Orton.** 450pp. 5⅛ x 7⅛.
T75 Clothbound **$3.50**

Vol. II: **THE ENGLISH RENAISSANCE, 1510-1688, V. de Sola Pinto.** 381pp. 5⅛ x 7⅛.
T76 Clothbound **$3.50**

Vol. III: **THE AUGUSTANS AND ROMANTICS, 1689-1830, H. Dyson, J. Butt.** 320pp. 5⅛ x 7⅛.
T77 Clothbound **$3.50**

Vol. IV: **THE VICTORIANS AND AFTER, 1830-1914, E. Batho, B. Dobrée.** 360pp. 5⅛ x 7⅛.
T78 Clothbound **$3.50**

EPIC AND ROMANCE, W. P. Ker. The standard survey of Medieval epic and romance by a foremost authority on Medieval literature. Covers historical background, plot, literary analysis, significance of Teutonic epics, Icelandic sagas, Beowulf, French chansons de geste, the Niebelungenlied, Arthurian romances, much more. 422pp. 5⅜ x 8.
T355 Paperbound **$1.95**

THE HEART OF EMERSON'S JOURNALS, Bliss Perry, ed. Emerson's most intimate thoughts, impressions, records of conversations with Channing, Hawthorne, Thoreau, etc., carefully chosen from the 10 volumes of The Journals. "The essays do not reveal the power of Emerson's mind . . .as do these hasty and informal writings," N. Y. TIMES. Preface by B. Perry. 370pp. 5⅜ x 8.
T447 Paperbound **$1.85**

A SOURCE BOOK IN THEATRICAL HISTORY, A. M. Nagler. (Formerly, "Sources of Theatrical History.") Over 300 selected passages by contemporary observers tell about styles of acting, direction, make-up, scene designing, etc., in the theatre's great periods from ancient Greece to the Théâtre Libre. "Indispensable complement to the study of drama," EDUCATIONAL THEATRE JOURNAL. Prof. Nagler, Yale Univ. School of Drama, also supplies notes, references. 85 illustrations. 611pp. 5⅜ x 8.
T515 Paperbound **$2.75**

THE ART OF THE STORY-TELLER, M. L. Shedlock. Regarded as the finest, most helpful book on telling stories to children, by a great story-teller. How to catch, hold, recapture attention; how to choose material; many other aspects. Also includes: a 99-page selection of Miss Shedlock's most successful stories; extensive bibliography of other stories. xxi + 320pp. 5⅜ x 8.
T245 Clothbound **$3.50**

THE DEVIL'S DICTIONARY, Ambrose Bierce. Over 1000 short, ironic definitions in alphabetical order, by America's greatest satirist in the classical tradition. "Some of the most gorgeous witticisms in the English language," H. L. Mencken. 144pp. 5⅜ x 8.
T487 Paperbound **$1.00**

MUSIC

A DICTIONARY OF HYMNOLOGY, John Julian. More than 30,000 entries on individual hymns, their authorship, textual variations, location of texts, dates and circumstances of composition, denominational and ritual usages, the biographies of more than 9,000 hymn writers, essays on important topics such as children's hymns and Christmas carols, and hundreds of thousands of other important facts about hymns which are virtually impossible to find anywhere else. Convenient alphabetical listing, and a 200-page double-columned index of first lines enable you to track down virtually any hymn ever written. Total of 1786pp. 6¼ x 9¼. 2 volumes. T133. The Set, Clothbound **$15.00**

STRUCTURAL HEARING, TONAL COHERENCE IN MUSIC, Felix Salzer. Extends the well-known Schenker approach to include modern music, music of the middle ages, and Renaissance music. Explores the phenomenon of tonal organization by discussing more than 500 compositions, and offers unusual new insights into the theory of composition and musical relationships. "The foundation on which all teaching in music theory has been based at this college," Leopold Mannes, President, The Mannes College of Music. Total of 658pp. 6½ x 9¼. 2 volumes. S418 The set, Clothbound **$8.00**

A GENERAL HISTORY OF MUSIC, Charles Burney. The complete history of music from the Greeks up to 1789 by the 18th century musical historian who personally knew the great Baroque composers. Covers sacred and secular, vocal and instrumental, operatic and symphonic music; treats theory, notation, forms, instruments; discusses composers, performers, important works. Invaluable as a source of information on the period for students, historians, musicians. "Surprisingly few of Burney's statements have been invalidated by modern research . . . still of great value," NEW YORK TIMES. Edited and corrected by Frank Mercer. 35 figures. 1915pp. 5½ x 8½. T36 The set, Clothbound **$12.50**

JOHANN SEBASTIAN BACH, Phillip Spitta. Recognized as one of the greatest accomplishments of musical scholarship and far and away the definitive coverage of Bach's works. Hundreds of individual pieces are analyzed. Major works, such as the B Minor Mass and the St. Matthew Passion are examined in minute detail. Spitta also deals with the works of Buxtehude, Pachelbel, and others of the period. Can be read with profit even by those without a knowledge of the technicalities of musical composition. "Unchallenged as the last word on one of the supreme geniuses of music," John Barkham, SATURDAY REVIEW SYNDICATE. Total of 1819pp. 5⅜ x 8. 2 volumes. T252 The set, Clothbound **$10.00**

HISTORY

THE IDEA OF PROGRESS, J. B. Bury. Prof. Bury traces the evolution of a central concept of Western civilization in Greek, Roman, Medieval, and Renaissance thought to its flowering in the 17th and 18th centuries. Introduction by Charles Beard. xl + 357pp. 5⅜ x 8.
T39 Clothbound **$3.95**
T40 Paperbound **$1.95**

THE ANCIENT GREEK HISTORIANS, J. B. Bury. Greek historians such as Herodotus, Thucydides, Xenophon; Roman historians such as Tacitus, Caesar, Livy; scores of others fully analyzed in terms of sources, concepts, influences, etc., by a great scholar and historian. 291pp. 5⅜ x 8. T397 Paperbound **$1.50**

HISTORY OF THE LATER ROMAN EMPIRE, J. B. Bury. The standard work on the Byzantine Empire from 395 A.D. to the death of Justinian in 565 A.D., by the leading Byzantine scholar of our time. Covers political, social, cultural, theological, military history. Quotes contemporary documents extensively. "Most unlikely that it will ever be superseded," Glanville Downey, Dumbarton Oaks Research Library. Genealogical tables. 5 maps. Bibliography. 2 vols. Total of 965pp. 5⅜ x 8. T398, T399 Paperbound, the set **$4.00**

GARDNER'S PHOTOGRAPHIC SKETCH BOOK OF THE CIVIL WAR, Alexander Gardner. One of the rarest and most valuable Civil War photographic collections exactly reproduced for the first time since 1866. Scenes of Manassas, Bull Run, Harper's Ferry, Appomattox, Mechanicsville, Fredericksburg, Gettysburg, etc.; battle ruins, prisons, arsenals, a slave pen, fortifications; Lincoln on the field, officers, men, corpses. By one of the most famous pioneers in documentary photography. Original copies of the "Sketch Book" sold for $425 in 1952. Introduction by E. Bleiler. 100 full-page 7 x 10 photographs (original size). 244pp. 10¾ x 8½ T476 Clothbound **$6.00**

THE WORLD'S GREAT SPEECHES, L. Copeland and L. Lamm, eds. 255 speeches from Pericles to Churchill, Dylan Thomas. Invaluable as a guide to speakers; fascinating as history past and present; a source of much difficult-to-find material. Includes an extensive section of informal and humorous speeches. 3 indices: Topic, Author, Nation. xx + 745pp. 5⅜ x 8.
T468 Paperbound **$2.49**

FOUNDERS OF THE MIDDLE AGES, E. K. Rand. The best non-technical discussion of the transformation of Latin paganism into medieval civilization. Tertullian, Gregory, Jerome, Boethius, Augustine, the Neoplatonists, other crucial figures, philosophies examined. Excellent for the intelligent non-specialist. "Extraordinarily accurate," Richard McKeon, THE NATION. ix + 365pp. 5⅜ x 8. T369 Paperbound **$1.85**

THE POLITICAL THOUGHT OF PLATO AND ARISTOTLE, Ernest Barker. The standard, comprehensive exposition of Greek political thought. Covers every aspect of the "Republic" and the "Politics" as well as minor writings, other philosophers, theorists of the period, and the later history of Greek political thought. Unabridged edition. 584pp. 5⅜ x 8.
T521 Paperbound **$1.85**

PHILOSOPHY

THE GIFT OF LANGUAGE, M. Schlauch. (Formerly, "The Gift of Tongues.") A sound, middle-level treatment of linguistic families, word histories, grammatical processes, semantics, language taboos, word-coining of Joyce, Cummings, Stein, etc. 232 bibliographical notes. 350pp. 5⅜ x 8.
T243 Paperbound **$1.85**

THE PHILOSOPHY OF HEGEL, W. T. Stace. The first work in English to give a complete and connected view of Hegel's entire system. Especially valuable to those who do not have time to study the highly complicated original texts, yet want an accurate presentation by a most reputable scholar of one of the most influential 19th century thinkers. Includes a 14 x 20 fold-out chart of Hegelian system. 536pp. 5⅜ x 8.
T254 Paperbound **$2.00**

ARISTOTLE, A. E. Taylor. A lucid, non-technical account of Aristotle written by a foremost Platonist. Covers life and works; thought on matter, form, causes, logic, God, physics, metaphysics, etc. Bibliography. New index compiled for this edition. 128pp. 5⅜ x 8.
T280 Paperbound **$1.00**

GUIDE TO PHILOSOPHY, C. E. M. Joad. This basic work describes the major philosophic problems and evaluates the answers propounded by great philosophers from the Greeks to Whitehead, Russell. "The finest introduction," BOSTON TRANSCRIPT. Bibliography, 592pp. 5⅜ x 8.
T297 Paperbound **$2.00**

LANGUAGE AND MYTH, E. Cassirer. Cassirer's brilliant demonstration that beneath both language and myth lies an unconscious "grammar" of experience whose categories and canons are not those of logical thought. Introduction and translation by Susanne Langer. Index. x + 103pp. 5⅜ x 8.
T51 Paperbound **$1.25**

SUBSTANCE AND FUNCTION, EINSTEIN'S THEORY OF RELATIVITY, E. Cassirer. This double volume contains the German philosopher's profound philosophical formulation of the differences between traditional logic and the new logic of science. Number, space, energy, relativity, many other topics are treated in detail. Authorized translation by W. C. and M. C. Swabey. xii + 465pp. 5⅜ x 8.
T50 Paperbound **$2.00**

THE PHILOSOPHICAL WORKS OF DESCARTES. The definitive English edition, in two volumes, of all major philosophical works and letters of René Descartes, father of modern philosophy of knowledge and science. Translated by E. S. Haldane and G. Ross. Introductory notes. Total of 842pp. 5⅜ x 8.
T71 Vol. 1, Paperbound **$2.00**
T72 Vol. 2, Paperbound **$2.00**

ESSAYS IN EXPERIMENTAL LOGIC, J. Dewey. Based upon Dewey's theory that knowledge implies a judgment which in turn implies an inquiry, these papers consider such topics as the thought of Bertrand Russell, pragmatism, the logic of values, antecedents of thought, data and meanings. 452pp. 5⅜ x 8.
T73 Paperbound **$1.95**

THE PHILOSOPHY OF HISTORY, G. W. F. Hegel. This classic of Western thought is Hegel's detailed formulation of the thesis that history is not chance but a rational process, the realization of the Spirit of Freedom. Translated and introduced by J. Sibree. Introduction by C. Hegel. Special introduction for this edition by Prof. Carl Friedrich, Harvard University. xxxix + 447pp. 5⅜ x 8.
T112 Paperbound **$1.85**

THE WILL TO BELIEVE and HUMAN IMMORTALITY, W. James. Two of James's most profound investigations of human belief in God and immortality, bound as one volume. Both are powerful expressions of James's views on chance vs. determinism, pluralism vs. monism, will and intellect, arguments for survival after death, etc. Two prefaces. 429pp. 5⅜ x 8.
T294 Clothbound **$3.75**
T291 Paperbound **$1.65**

INTRODUCTION TO SYMBOLIC LOGIC, S. Langer. A lucid, general introduction to modern logic, covering forms, classes, the use of symbols, the calculus of propositions, the Boole-Schroeder and the Russell-Whitehead systems, etc. "One of the clearest and simplest introductions," MATHEMATICS GAZETTE. Second, enlarged, revised edition. 368pp. 5⅜ x 8.
S164 Paperbound **$1.75**

MIND AND THE WORLD-ORDER, C. I. Lewis. Building upon the work of Peirce, James, and Dewey, Professor Lewis outlines a theory of knowledge in terms of "conceptual pragmatism," and demonstrates why the traditional understanding of the a priori must be abandoned. Appendices. xiv + 446pp. 5⅜ x 8.
T359 Paperbound **$1.95**

THE GUIDE FOR THE PERPLEXED, M. Maimonides One of the great philosophical works of all time, Maimonides' formulation of the meeting-ground between Old Testament and Aristotelian thought is essential to anyone interested in Jewish, Christian, and Moslem thought in the Middle Ages. 2nd revised edition of the Friedlander translation. Extensive introduction. lix + 414pp. 5⅜ x 8.
T351 Paperbound **$1.85**

DOVER BOOKS

THE PHILOSOPHICAL WRITINGS OF PEIRCE, J. Buchler, ed. (Formerly, "The Philosophy of Peirce.") This carefully integrated selection of Peirce's papers is considered the best coverage of the complete thought of one of the greatest philosophers of modern times. Covers Peirce's work on the theory of signs, pragmatism, epistemology, symbolic logic, the scientific method, chance, etc. xvi + 386pp. 5 ⅜ x 8.
T216 Clothbound **$5.00**
T217 Paperbound **$1.95**

HISTORY OF ANCIENT PHILOSOPHY, W. Windelband. Considered the clearest survey of Greek and Roman philosophy. Examines Thales, Anaximander, Anaximenes, Heraclitus, the Eleatics, Empedocles, the Pythagoreans, the Sophists, Socrates, Democritus, Stoics, Epicureans, Sceptics, Neo-platonists, etc. 50 pages on Plato; 70 on Aristotle. 2nd German edition tr. by H. E. Cushman. xv + 393pp. 5⅜ x 8.
T357 Paperbound **$1.75**

INTRODUCTION TO SYMBOLIC LOGIC AND ITS APPLICATIONS, R. Carnap. A comprehensive, rigorous introduction to modern logic by perhaps its greatest living master. Includes demonstrations of applications in mathematics, physics, biology. "Of the rank of a masterpiece," Z. für Mathematik und ihre Grenzgebiete. Over 300 exercises. xvi + 241pp. 5⅜ x 8.
Clothbound **$4.00**
S453 Paperbound **$1.85**

SCEPTICISM AND ANIMAL FAITH, G. Santayana. Santayana's unusually lucid exposition of the difference between the independent existence of objects and the essence our mind attributes to them, and of the necessity of scepticism as a form of belief and animal faith as a necessary condition of knowledge. Discusses belief, memory, intuition, symbols, etc. xii + 314pp. 5⅜ x 8.
T235 Clothbound **$3.50**
T236 Paperbound **$1.50**

THE ANALYSIS OF MATTER, B. Russell. With his usual brilliance, Russell analyzes physics, causality, scientific inference, Weyl's theory, tensors, invariants, periodicity, etc. in order to discover the basic concepts of scientific thought about matter. "Most thorough treatment of the subject," THE NATION. Introduction. 8 figures. viii + 408pp. 5⅜ x 8.
T231 Paperbound **$1.95**

THE SENSE OF BEAUTY, G. Santayana. This important philosophical study of why, when, and how beauty appears, and what conditions must be fulfilled, is in itself a revelation of the beauty of language. "It is doubtful if a better treatment of the subject has since appeared," PEABODY JOURNAL. ix + 275pp. 5⅜ x 8.
T238 Paperbound **$1.00**

THE CHIEF WORKS OF SPINOZA. In two volumes. Vol. I: The Theologico-Political Treatise and the Political Treatise. Vol. II: On the Improvement of Understanding, The Ethics, and Selected Letters. The permanent and enduring ideas in these works on God, the universe, religion, society, etc., have had tremendous impact on later philosophical works. Introduction. Total of 862pp. 5⅜ x 8.
T249 Vol. I, Paperbound **$1.50**
T250 Vol. II, Paperbound **$1.50**

TRAGIC SENSE OF LIFE, M. de Unamuno. The acknowledged masterpiece of one of Spain's most influential thinkers. Between the despair at the inevitable death of man and all his works, and the desire for immortality, Unamuno finds a "saving incertitude." Called "a masterpiece," by the ENCYCLOPAEDIA BRITANNICA. xxx + 332pp. 5⅜ x 8.
T257 Paperbound **$1.95**

EXPERIENCE AND NATURE, John Dewey. The enlarged, revised edition of the Paul Carus lectures (1925). One of Dewey's clearest presentations of the philosophy of empirical naturalism which reestablishes the continuity between "inner" experience and "outer" nature. These lectures are among the most significant ever delivered by an American philosopher. 457pp. 5⅜ x 8.
T471 Paperbound **$1.85**

PHILOSOPHY AND CIVILIZATION IN THE MIDDLE AGES, M. de Wulf. A semi-popular survey of medieval intellectual life, religion, philosophy, science, the arts, etc. that covers feudalism vs. Catholicism, rise of the universities, mendicant orders, and similar topics. Bibliography. viii + 320pp. 5⅜ x 8.
T284 Paperbound **$1.75**

AN INTRODUCTION TO SCHOLASTIC PHILOSOPHY, M. de Wulf. (Formerly, "Scholasticism Old and New.") Prof. de Wulf covers the central scholastic tradition from St. Anselm, Albertus Magnus, Thomas Aquinas, up to Suarez in the 17th century; and then treats the modern revival of scholasticism, the Louvain position, relations with Kantianism and positivism, etc. xvi + 271pp. 5⅜ x 8.
T296 Clothbound **$3.50**
T283 Paperbound **$1.75**

A HISTORY OF MODERN PHILOSOPHY, H. Höffding. An exceptionally clear and detailed coverage of Western philosophy from the Renaissance to the end of the 19th century. Both major and minor figures are examined in terms of theory of knowledge, logic, cosmology, psychology. Covers Pomponazzi, Bodin, Boehme, Telesius, Bruno, Copernicus, Descartes, Spinoza, Hobbes, Locke, Hume, Kant, Fichte, Schopenhauer, Mill, Spencer, Langer, scores of others. A standard reference work. 2 volumes. Total of 1159pp. 5⅜ x 8.
T117 Vol. 1, Paperbound **$2.00**
T118 Vol. 2, Paperbound **$2.00**

LANGUAGE, TRUTH AND LOGIC, A. J. Ayer. The first full-length development of Logical Positivism in English. Building on the work of Schlick, Russell, Carnap, and the Vienna school, Ayer presents the tenets of one of the most important systems of modern philosophical thought. 160pp. 5⅜ x 8.
T10 Paperbound **$1.25**

ORIENTALIA AND RELIGION

THE MYSTERIES OF MITHRA, F. Cumont. The great Belgian scholar's definitive study of the Persian mystery religion that almost vanquished Christianity in the ideological struggle for the Roman Empire. A masterpiece of scholarly detection that reconstructs secret doctrines, organization, rites. Mithraic art is discussed and analyzed. 70 illus. 239pp. 5⅜ x 8.
T323 Paperbound **$1.85**

CHRISTIAN AND ORIENTAL PHILOSOPHY OF ART. A. K. Coomaraswamy. The late art historian and orientalist discusses artistic symbolism, the role of traditional culture in enriching art, medieval art, folklore, philosophy of art, other similar topics. Bibliography. 148pp. 5⅜ x 8.
T378 Paperbound **$1.25**

TRANSFORMATION OF NATURE IN ART, A. K. Coomaraswamy. A basic work on Asiatic religious art. Includes discussions of religious art in Asia and Medieval Europe (exemplified by Meister Eckhart), the origin and use of images in Indian art, Indian Medieval aesthetic manuals, and other fascinating, little known topics. Glossaries of Sanskrit and Chinese terms. Bibliography. 41pp. of notes. 245pp. 5⅜ x 8.
T368 Paperbound **$1.75**

ORIENTAL RELIGIONS IN ROMAN PAGANISM, F. Cumont. This well-known study treats the ecstatic cults of Syria and Phrygia (Cybele, Attis, Adonis, their orgies and mutilatory rites); the mysteries of Egypt (Serapis, Isis, Osiris); Persian dualism; Mithraic cults; Hermes Trismegistus, Ishtar, Astarte, etc. and their influence on the religious thought of the Roman Empire. Introduction. 55pp. of notes; extensive bibliography. xxiv + 298pp. 5⅜ x 8.
T321 Paperbound **$1.75**

ANTHROPOLOGY, SOCIOLOGY, AND PSYCHOLOGY

PRIMITIVE MAN AS PHILOSOPHER, P. Radin. A standard anthropological work based on Radin's investigations of the Winnebago, Maori, Batak, Zuni, other primitive tribes. Describes primitive thought on the purpose of life, marital relations, death, personality, gods, etc. Extensive selections of original primitive documents. Bibliography. xviii + 420pp. 5⅜ x 8.
T392 Paperbound **$2.00**

PRIMITIVE RELIGION, P. Radin. Radin's thoroughgoing treatment of supernatural beliefs, shamanism, initiations, religious expression, etc. in primitive societies. Arunta, Ashanti, Aztec, Bushman, Crow, Fijian, many other tribes examined. "Excellent," NATURE. New preface by the author. Bibliographic notes. x + 322pp. 5⅜ x 8.   T393 Paperbound **$1.85**

SEX IN PSYCHO-ANALYSIS, S. Ferenczi. (Formerly, "Contributions to Psycho-analysis.") 14 selected papers on impotence, transference, analysis and children, dreams, obscene words, homosexuality, paranoia, etc. by an associate of Freud. Also included: THE DEVELOPMENT OF PSYCHO-ANALYSIS, by Ferenczi and Otto Rank. Two books bound as one. Total of 406pp. 5⅜ x 8.
T324 Paperbound **$1.85**

THE PRINCIPLES OF PSYCHOLOGY, William James. The complete text of the famous "long course," one of the great books of Western thought. An almost incredible amount of information about psychological processes, the stream of consciousness, habit, time perception, memory, emotions, reason, consciousness of self, abnormal phenomena, and similar topics. Based on James's own discoveries integrated with the work of Descartes, Locke, Hume, Royce, Wundt, Berkeley, Lotse, Herbart, scores of others. "A classic of interpretation," PSYCHIATRIC QUARTERLY. 94 illus. 1408pp. 2 volumes. 5⅜ x 8.
T381 Vol. 1, Paperbound **$2.50**
T382 Vol. 2, Paperbound **$2.50**

THE POLISH PEASANT IN EUROPE AND AMERICA, W. I. Thomas, F. Znaniecki. Monumental sociological study of peasant primary groups (family and community) and the disruptions produced by a new industrial system and emigration to America, by two of the foremost sociologists of recent times. One of the most important works in sociological thought. Includes hundreds of pages of primary documentation; point by point analysis of causes of social decay, breakdown of morality, crime, drunkenness, prostitution, etc. 2nd revised edition. 2 volumes. Total of 2250pp. 6 x 9.   T478 2 volume set, Clothbound **$12.50**

FOLKWAYS, W. G. Sumner. The great Yale sociologist's detailed exposition of thousands of social, sexual, and religious customs in hundreds of cultures from ancient Greece to Modern Western societies. Preface by A. G. Keller. Introduction by William Lyon Phelps. 705pp. 5⅜ x 8.
S508 Paperbound **$2.49**

BEYOND PSYCHOLOGY, Otto Rank. The author, an early associate of Freud, uses psychoanalytic techniques of myth-analysis to explore ultimates of human existence. Treats love, immortality, the soul, sexual identity, kingship, sources of state power, many other topics which illuminate the irrational basis of human existence. 291pp. 5⅜ x 8.   T485 Paperbound **$1.75**

ILLUSIONS AND DELUSIONS OF THE SUPERNATURAL AND THE OCCULT, D. H. Rawcliffe. A rational, scientific examination of crystal gazing, automatic writing, table turning, stigmata, the Indian rope trick, dowsing, telepathy, clairvoyance, ghosts, ESP, PK, thousands of other supposedly occult phenomena. Originally titled "The Psychology of the Occult." 14 illustrations. 551pp. 5⅜ x 8.
T503 Paperbound **$2.00**

DOVER BOOKS

YOGA: A SCIENTIFIC EVALUATION, Kovoor T. Behanan. A scientific study of the physiological and psychological effects of Yoga discipline, written under the auspices of the Yale University Institute of Human Relations. Foreword by W. A. Miles, Yale Univ. 17 photographs. 290pp. 5⅜ x 8.   T505 Paperbound **$1.65**

HOAXES, C. D. MacDougall. Delightful, entertaining, yet scholarly exposition of how hoaxes start, why they succeed, documented with stories of hundreds of the most famous hoaxes. "A stupendous collection . . . and shrewd analysis, "NEW YORKER. New, revised edition. 54 photographs. 320pp. 5⅜ x 8.   T465 Paperbound **$1.75**

CREATIVE POWER: THE EDUCATION OF YOUTH IN THE CREATIVE ARTS, Hughes Mearns. Named by the National Education Association as one of the 20 foremost books on education in recent times. Tells how to help children express themselves in drama, poetry, music, art, develop latent creative power. Should be read by every parent, teacher. New, enlarged, revised edition. Introduction. 272pp. 5⅜ x 8.   T490 Paperbound **$1.50**

LANGUAGES

NEW RUSSIAN-ENGLISH, ENGLISH-RUSSIAN DICTIONARY, M. A. O'Brien. Over 70,000 entries in new orthography! Idiomatic usages, colloquialisms. One of the few dictionaries that indicate accent changes in conjugation and declension. "One of the best," Prof. E. J. Simmons, Cornell. First names, geographical terms, bibliography, many other features. 738pp. 4½ x 6¼.
T208 Paperbound **$2.00**

MONEY CONVERTER AND TIPPING GUIDE FOR EUROPEAN TRAVEL, C. Vomacka. Invaluable, handy source of currency regulations, conversion tables, tipping rules, postal rates, much other travel information for every European country plus Israel, Egypt and Turkey. 128pp. 3½ x 5¼.
T260 Paperbound **60¢**

MONEY CONVERTER AND TIPPING GUIDE FOR TRAVEL IN THE AMERICAS (including the United States and Canada), **C. Vomacka.** The information you need for informed and confident travel in the Americas: money conversion tables, tipping guide, postal, telephone rates, etc. 128pp. 3½ x 5¼.   T261 Paperbound **65¢**

DUTCH-ENGLISH, ENGLISH-DUTCH DICTIONARY, F. G. Renier. The most convenient, practical Dutch-English dictionary on the market. New orthography. More than 60,000 entries: idioms, compounds, technical terms, etc. Gender of nouns indicated. xviii + 571pp. 5½ x 6¼.
T224 Clothbound **$2.50**

LEARN DUTCH!, F. G. Renier. The most satisfactory and easily-used grammar of modern Dutch. Used and recommended by the Fulbright Committee in the Netherlands. Over 1200 simple exercises lead to mastery of spoken and written Dutch. Dutch-English, English-Dutch vocabularies. 181pp. 4¼ x 7¼.   T441 Clothbound **$1.75**

PHRASE AND SENTENCE DICTIONARY OF SPOKEN RUSSIAN, English-Russian, Russian-English. Based on phrases and complete sentences, rather than isolated words; recognized as one of the best methods of learning the idiomatic speech of a country. Over 11,500 entries, indexed by single words, with more than 32,000 English and Russian sentences and phrases, in immediately usable form. Probably the largest list ever published. Shows accent changes in conjugation and declension; irregular forms listed in both alphabetical place and under main form of word. 15,000 word introduction covering Russian sounds, writing, grammar, syntax. 15-page appendix of geographical names, money, important signs, given names, foods, special Soviet terms, etc. Travellers, businessmen, students, government employees have found this their best source for Russian expressions. Originally published as U.S. Government Technical Manual TM 30-944. iv + 573pp. 5⅝ x 8⅜.   T496 Paperbound **$2.75**

PHRASE AND SENTENCE DICTIONARY OF SPOKEN SPANISH, Spanish-English, English-Spanish. Compiled from spoken Spanish, emphasizing idiom and colloquial usage in both Castilian and Latin-American. More than 16,000 entries containing over 25,000 idioms—the largest list of idiomatic constructions ever published. Complete sentences given, indexed under single words —language in immediately usable form, for travellers, businessmen, students, etc. 25-page introduction provides rapid survey of sounds, grammar, syntax, with full consideration of irregular verbs. Especially apt in modern treatment of phrases and structure. 17-page glossary gives translations of geographical names, money values, numbers, national holidays, important street signs, useful expressions of high frequency, plus unique 7-page glossary of Spanish and Spanish-American foods and dishes. Originally published as U.S. Government Technical Manual TM 30-900. iv + 513pp. 5⅝ x 8⅜.   T495 Paperbound **$1.75**

SAY IT language phrase books

"SAY IT" in the foreign language of your choice! We have sold over ½ million copies of these popular, useful language books. They will not make you an expert linguist overnight, but they do cover most practical matters of everyday life abroad.

Over 1000 useful phrases, expressions, with additional variants, substitutions.

Modern! Useful! Hundreds of phrases not available in other texts: "Nylon," "air-conditioned," etc.

The ONLY inexpensive phrase book **completely indexed.** Everything is available at a flip of your finger, ready for use.

Prepared by native linguists, travel experts.

Based on years of travel experience abroad.

This handy phrase book may be used by itself, or it may supplement any other text or course; it provides a living element. Used by many colleges and institutions: Hunter College; Barnard College; Army Ordnance School, Aberdeen; and many others.

Available, 1 book per language:

Danish (T818) 75¢
Dutch T(817) 75¢
English (for German-speaking people) (T801) 60¢
English (for Italian-speaking people) (T816) 60¢
English (for Spanish-speaking people) (T802) 60¢
Esperanto (T820) 75¢
French (T803) 60¢
German (T804) 60¢
Modern Greek (T813) 75¢
Hebrew (T805) 60¢

Italian (T806) 60¢
Japanese (T807) 60¢
Norwegian (T814) 75¢
Russian (T810) 75¢
Spanish (T811) 60¢
Turkish (T821) 75¢
Yiddish (T815) 75¢
Swedish (T812) 75¢
Polish (T808) 75¢
Portuguese (T809) 75¢

LISTEN & LEARN language record sets

LISTEN & LEARN is the only language record course designed especially to meet your travel needs, or help you learn essential foreign language quickly by yourself, or in conjunction with any school course, by means of the automatic association method. Each set contains three 33⅓ rpm long- playing records — 1½ hours of recorded speech by eminent native speakers who are professors at Columbia, N.Y.U., Queens College and other leading universities. The sets are priced far below other sets of similar quality, yet they contain many special features not found in other record sets:

* Over 800 selected phrases and sentences, a basic vocabulary of over 3200 words.
* Both English and foreign language recorded; with a pause for your repetition.
* Designed for persons with limited time; no time wasted on material you cannot use immediately.
* Living, modern expressions that answer modern needs: drugstore items, "air-conditioned," etc.
* 128-196 page manuals contain everything on the records, plus simple pronunciation guides.
* Manual is fully indexed; find the phrase you want instantly.
* High fidelity recording—equal to any records costing up to $6 each.

The phrases on these records cover 41 different categories useful to the traveller or student interested in learning the living, spoken language: greetings, introductions, making yourself understood, passing customs, planes, trains, boats, buses, taxis, nightclubs, restaurants, menu items, sports, concerts, cameras, automobile travel, repairs, drugstores, doctors, dentists, medicines, barber shops, beauty parlors, laundries, many, many more.

"Excellent . . . among the very best on the market," Prof. Mario Pei, Dept. of Romance Languages, Columbia University. "Inexpensive and well-done . . . an ideal present," CHICAGO SUNDAY TRIBUNE. "More genuinely helpful than anything of its kind which I have previously encountered," Sidney Clark, well-known author of "ALL THE BEST" travel books. Each set contains 3 33⅓ rpm pure vinyl records, 128- 196 page   with full record text, and album. One language per set. LISTEN & LEARN record sets are now available in—

FRENCH	the set $4.95	**GERMAN**	the set $4.95
ITALIAN	the set $4.95	**SPANISH**	the set $4.95
RUSSIAN	the set $5.95	**JAPANESE** *	the set $5.95

* Available Sept. 1, 1959

UNCONDITIONAL GUARANTEE: Dover Publications stands behind every Listen and Learn record set. If you are dissatisfied with these sets for any reason whatever, return them within 10 days and your money will be refunded in full.

DOVER BOOKS

ART HISTORY

STICKS AND STONES, Lewis Mumford. An examination of forces influencing American architecture: the medieval tradition in early New England, the classical influence in Jefferson's time, the Brown Decades, the imperial facade, the machine age, etc. "A truly remarkable book," SAT. REV. OF LITERATURE. 2nd revised edition. 21 illus. xvii + 228pp. 5⅜ x 8.
T202 Paperbound **$1.60**

THE AUTOBIOGRAPHY OF AN IDEA, Louis Sullivan. The architect whom Frank Lloyd Wright called "the master," records the development of the theories that revolutionized America's skyline. 34 full-page plates of Sullivan's finest work. New introduction by R. M. Line. xiv + 335pp. 5⅜ x 8.
T281 Paperbound **$1.85**

THE MATERIALS AND TECHNIQUES OF MEDIEVAL PAINTING, D. V. Thompson. An invaluable study of carriers and grounds, binding media, pigments, metals used in painting, al fresco and al secco techniques, burnishing, etc. used by the medieval masters. Preface by Bernard Berenson. 239pp. 5⅜ x 8.
T327 Paperbound **$1.85**

PRINCIPLES OF ART HISTORY, H. Wölfflin. This remarkably instructive work demonstrates the tremendous change in artistic conception from the 14th to the 18th centuries, by analyzing 164 works by Botticelli, Dürer, Hobbema, Holbein, Hals, Titian, Rembrandt, Vermeer, etc., and pointing out exactly what is meant by "baroque," "classic," "primitive," "picturesque," and other basic terms of art history and criticism. "A remarkable lesson in the art of seeing," SAT. REV. OF LITERATURE. Translated from the 7th German edition. 150 illus. 254pp. 6⅛ x 9¼.
T276 Paperbound **$2.00**

FOUNDATIONS OF MODERN ART, A. Ozenfant. Stimulating discussion of human creativity from paleolithic cave painting to modern painting, architecture, decorative arts. Fully illustrated with works of Gris, Lipchitz, Léger, Picasso, primitive, modern artifacts, architecture, industrial art, much more. 226 illustrations. 368pp. 6⅛ x 9¼.
T215 Paperbound **$1.95**

HANDICRAFTS, APPLIED ART, ART SOURCES, ETC.

WILD FOWL DECOYS, J. Barber. The standard work on this fascinating branch of folk art, ranging from Indian mud and grass devices to realistic wooden decoys. Discusses styles, types, periods; gives full information on how to make decoys. 140 illustrations (including 14 new plates) show decoys and provide full sets of plans for handicrafters, artists, hunters, and students of folk art. 281pp. 7⅞ x 10¾. Deluxe edition.
T11 Clothbound **$8.50**

METALWORK AND ENAMELLING, H. Maryon. Probably the best book ever written on the subject. Tells everything necessary for the home manufacture of jewelry, rings, ear pendants, bowls, etc. Covers materials, tools, soldering, filigree, setting stones, raising patterns, repoussé work, damascening, niello, cloisonné, polishing, assaying, casting, and dozens of other techniques. The best substitute for apprenticeship to a master metalworker. 363 photos and figures. 374pp. 5½ x 8½.
T183 Clothbound **$7.50**

SHAKER FURNITURE, E. D. and F. Andrews. The most illuminating study of Shaker furniture ever written. Covers chronology, craftsmanship, houses, shops, etc. Includes over 200 photographs of chairs, tables, clocks, beds, benches, etc. "Mr. & Mrs. Andrews know all there is to know about Shaker furniture," Mark Van Doren, NATION. 48 full-page plates. 192pp. Deluxe cloth binding. 7⅞ x 10¾.
T7 Clothbound **$6.00**

PRIMITIVE ART, Franz Boas. A great American anthropologist covers theory, technical virtuosity, styles, symbolism, patterns, etc. of primitive art. The more than 900 illustrations will interest artists, designers, craftworkers. Over 900 illustrations. 376pp. 5⅜ x 8.
T25 Paperbound **$1.95**

ON THE LAWS OF JAPANESE PAINTING, H. Bowie. The best possible substitute for lessons from an oriental master. Treats both spirit and technique; exercises for control of the brush; inks, brushes, colors; use of dots, lines to express whole moods, etc. 220 illus. 132pp. 6⅛ x 9¼.
T30 Paperbound **$1.95**

HANDBOOK OF ORNAMENT, F. S. Meyer. One of the largest collections of copyright-free traditional art: over 3300 line cuts of Greek, Roman, Medieval, Renaissance, Baroque, 18th and 19th century art motifs (tracery, geometric elements, flower and animal motifs, etc.) and decorated objects (chairs, thrones, weapons, vases, jewelry, armor, etc.). Full text. 3300 illustrations. 562pp. 5⅜ x 8.
T302 Paperbound **$2.00**

THREE CLASSICS OF ITALIAN CALLIGRAPHY. Oscar Ogg, ed. Exact reproductions of three famous Renaissance calligraphic works: Arrighi's OPERINA and IL MODO, Tagliente's LO PRESENTE LIBRO, and Palatino's LIBRO NUOVO. More than 200 complete alphabets, thousands of lettered specimens, in Papal Chancery and other beautiful, ornate handwriting. Introduction. 245 plates. 282pp. 6⅛ x 9¼.
T212 Paperbound **$1.95**

THE HISTORY AND TECHNIQUES OF LETTERING, A. Nesbitt. A thorough history of lettering from the ancient Egyptians to the present, and a 65-page course in lettering for artists. Every major development in lettering history is illustrated by a complete alphabet. Fully analyzes such masters as Caslon, Koch, Garamont, Jenson, and many more. 89 alphabets, 165 other specimens. 317pp. 5⅜ x 8.
T427 Paperbound **$2.00**

LETTERING AND ALPHABETS, J. A. Cavanagh. An unabridged reissue of "Lettering," containing the full discussion, analysis, illustration of 89 basic hand lettering tyles based on Caslon, Bodoni, Gothic, many other types. Hundreds of technical hints on construction, strokes, pens, brushes, etc. 89 alphabets, 72 lettered specimens, which may be reproduced permission-free. 121pp. 9¾ x 8. **T53 Paperbound $1.25**

THE HUMAN FIGURÉ IN MOTION, Eadweard Muybridge. The largest collection in print of Muybridge's famous high-speed action photos. 4789 photographs in more than 500 action-strip-sequences (at shutter speeds up to 1/6000th of a second) illustrate men, women, children—mostly undraped—performing such actions as walking, running, getting up, lying down, carrying objects, throwing, etc. "An unparalleled dictionary of action for all artists," AMERICAN ARTIST. 390 full-page plates, with 4789 photographs. Heavy glossy stock, reinforced binding with headbands. 7⅞ x 10¾. **T204 Clothbound $10.00**

ANIMALS IN MOTION, Eadweard Muybridge. The largest collection of animal action photos in print. 34 different animals (horses, mules, oxen, goats, camels, pigs, cats, lions, gnus, deer, monkeys, eagles—and 22 others) in 132 characteristic actions. All 3919 photographs are taken in series at speeds up to 1/1600th of a second, offering artists, biologists, car-toonists a remarkable opportunity to see exactly how an ostrich's head bobs when running, how a lion puts his foot down, how an elephant's knee bends, how a bird flaps his wings, thousands of other hard-to-catch details. "A really marvelous series of plates," NATURE. 380 full-pages of plates. Heavy glossy stock, reinforced binding with headbands. 7⅞ x 10¾. **T203 Clothbound $10.00**

THE BOOK OF SIGNS, R. Koch. 493 symbols—crosses, monograms, astrological, biological symbols, runes, etc.—from ancient manuscripts, cathedrals, coins, catacombs, pottery. May be reproduced permission-free. 493 illustrations by Fritz Kredel. 104pp. 6⅛ x 9¼. **T162 Paperbound $1.00**

A HANDBOOK OF EARLY ADVERTISING ART, C. P. Hornung. The largest collection of copyright-free early advertising art ever compiled. Vol. I: 2,000 illustrations of animals, old automo-biles, buildings, allegorical figures, fire engines, Indians, ships, trains, more than 33 other categories! Vol II: Over 4,000 typographical specimens; 600 Roman, Gothic, Barnum, Old English faces; 630 ornamental type faces; hundreds of scrolls, initials, flourishes, etc. "A remarkable collection," PRINTERS' INK.

Vol. I: Pictorial Volume. Over 2000 illustrations. 256pp. 9 x 12. **T122 Clothbound $10.00**
Vol. II: Typographical Volume. Over 4000 speciments. 319pp. 9 x 12. **T123 Clothbound $10.00**
Two volume set, Clothbound, only **$18.50**

DESIGN FOR ARTISTS AND CRAFTSMEN, L. Wolchonok. The most thorough course on the creation of art motifs and designs. Shows you step-by-step, with hundreds of examples and 113 detailed exercises, how to create original designs from geometric patterns, plants, birds, animals, humans, and man-made objects. "A great contribution to the field of design and crafts," N. Y. SOCIETY OF CRAFTSMEN. More than 1300 entirely new illustrations. xv + 207pp. 7⅞ x 10¾. **T274 Clothbound $4.95**

HANDBOOK OF DESIGNS AND DEVICES, C. P. Hornung. A remarkable working collection of 1836 basic designs and variations, all copyright-free. Variations of circle, line, cross, diamond, swastika, star, scroll, shield, many more. Notes on symbolism. "A necessity to every designer who would be original without having to labor heavily," ARTIST and ADVERTISER. 204 plates. 240pp. 5⅜ x 8.
T125 Paperbound $1.90

THE UNIVERSAL PENMAN, George Bickham. Exact reproduction of beautiful 18th century book of handwriting. 22 complete alphabets in finest English roundhand, other scripts, over 2000 elaborate flourishes, 122 calligraphic illustrations, etc. Material is copyright-free. "An essential part of any art library, and a book of permanent value," AMERICAN ARTIST. 212 plates. 224pp. 9 x 13¾. **T20 Clothbound $10.00**

AN ATLAS OF ANATOMY FOR ARTISTS, F. Schider. This standard work contains 189 full-page plates, more than 647 illustrations of all aspects of the human skeleton, musculature, cutaway portions of the body, each part of the anatomy, hand forms, eyelids, breasts, location of muscles under the flesh, etc. 59 plates illustrate how Michelangelo, da Vinci, Goya, 15 others, drew human anatomy. New 3rd edition enlarged by 52 new illustrations by Cloquet, Barcsay. "The standard reference tool," AMERICAN LIBRARY ASSOCIATION. "Excellent," AMERICAN ARTIST. 189 plates, 647 illustrations. xxvi + 192pp. 7⅞ x 10⅝. **T241 Clothbound $6.00**

AN ATLAS OF ANIMAL ANATOMY FOR ARTISTS, W. Ellenberger, H. Baum, H. Dittrich. The largest, richest animal anatomy for artists in English. Form, musculature, tendons, bone structure, expression, detailed cross sections of head, other features, of the horse, lion, dog, cat, deer, seal, kangaroo, cow, bull, goat, monkey, hare, many other animals. "Highly recommended," DESIGN. Second, revised, enlarged edition with new plates from Cuvier, Stubbs, etc. 288 illustrations. 153pp. 11⅜ x 9. **T82 Clothbound $6.00**

ANIMAL DRAWING: ANATOMY AND ACTION FOR ARTISTS, C. R. Knight. 158 studies, with full accompanying text, of such animals as the gorilla, bear, bison, dromedary, camel, vulture, pelican, iguana, shark, etc., by one of the greatest modern masters of animal drawing. Innumerable tips on how to get life expression into your work. "An excellent reference work,' SAN FRANCISCO CHRONICLE. 158 illustrations. 156pp. 10½ x 8½. **T426 Paperbound $2.00**

DOVER BOOKS

THE CRAFTSMAN'S HANDBOOK, Cennino Cennini. The finest English translation of IL LIBRO DELL' ARTE, the 15th century introduction to art technique that is both a mirror of Quatrocento life and a source of many useful but nearly forgotten facets of the painter's art. 4 illustrations. xxvii + 142pp. D. V. Thompson, translator. 6⅛ x 9¼. T54 Paperbound **$1.50**

THE BROWN DECADES, Lewis Mumford. A picture of the "buried renaissance" of the post-Civil War period, and the founding of modern architecture (Sullivan, Richardson, Root, Roebling), landscape development (Marsh, Olmstead, Eliot), and the graphic arts (Homer, Eakins, Ryder). 2nd revised, enlarged edition. Bibliography. 12 illustrations. xiv + 266 pp. 5⅜ x 8. T200 Paperbound **$1.65**

STIEGEL GLASS, F. W. Hunter. The story of the most highly esteemed early American glassware, fully illustrated. How a German adventurer, "Baron" Stiegel, founded a glass empire; detailed accounts of individual glasswork. "This pioneer work is reprinted in an edition even more beautiful than the original," ANTIQUES DEALER. New introduction by Helen McKearin. 171 illustrations, 12 in full color. xxii + 338pp. 7⅞ x 10¾. T128 Clothbound **$10.00**

THE HUMAN FIGURE, J. H. Vanderpoel. Not just a picture book, but a complete course by a famous figure artist. Extensive text, illustrated by 430 pencil and charcoal drawings of both male and female anatomy. 2nd enlarged edition. Foreword. 430 illus. 143pp. 6⅛ x 9¼. T432 Paperbound **$1.45**

PINE FURNITURE OF EARLY NEW ENGLAND, R. H. Kettell. Over 400 illustrations, over 50 working drawings of early New England chairs, benches, beds cupboards, mirrors, shelves, tables, other furniture esteemed for simple beauty and character. "Rich store of illustrations . . . emphasizes the individuality and varied design," ANTIQUES. 413 illustrations, 55 working drawings. 475pp. 8 x 10¾. T145 Clothbound **$10.00**

BASIC BOOKBINDING, A. W. Lewis. Enables both beginners and experts to rebind old books or bind paperbacks in hard covers. Treats materials, tools; gives step-by-step instruction in how to collate a book, sew it, back it, make boards, etc. 261 illus. Appendices. 155pp. 5⅜ x 8. T169 Paperbound **$1.35**

DESIGN MOTIFS OF ANCIENT MEXICO, J. Enciso. Nearly 90% of these 766 superb designs from Aztec, Olmec, Totonac, Maya, and Toltec origins are unobtainable elsewhere! Contains plumed serpents, wind gods, animals, demons, dancers, monsters, etc. Excellent applied design source. Originally $17.50. 766 illustrations, thousands of motifs. 192pp. 6⅛ x 9¼. T84 Paperbound **$1.85**

AFRICAN SCULPTURE, Ladislas Segy. 163 full-page plates illustrating masks, fertility figures, ceremonial objects, etc., of 50 West and Central African tribes—95% never before illustrated. 34-page introduction to African sculpture. "Mr. Segy is one of its top authorities," NEW YORKER. 164 full-page photographic plates. Introduction. Bibliography. 244pp. 6⅛ x 9¼. T396 Paperbound **$2.00**

THE PROCESSES OF GRAPHIC REPRODUCTION IN PRINTING, H. Curwen. A thorough and practical survey of wood, linoleum, and rubber engraving; copper engraving; drypoint, mezzotint, etching, aquatint, steel engraving, die sinking, stenciling, lithography (extensively); photographic reproduction utilizing line, continuous tone, photoengravure, collotype; every other process in general use. Note on color reproduction. Section on bookbinding. Over 200 illustrations, 25 in color. 143pp. 5½ x 8½. T512 Clothbound **$4.00**

CALLIGRAPHY, J. G. Schwandner. First reprinting in 200 years of this legendary book of beautiful handwriting. Over 300 ornamental initials, 12 complete calligraphic alphabets, over 150 ornate frames and panels, 75 calligraphic pictures of cherubs, stags, lions, etc., thousands of flourishes, scrolls, etc., by the greatest 18th century masters. All material can be copied or adapted without permission. Historical introduction. 158 full-page plates. 368pp. 9 x 13. T475 Clothbound **$10.00**

* * *

A DIDEROT PICTORIAL ENCYCLOPEDIA OF TRADES AND INDUSTRY, Manufacturing and the Technical Arts in Plates Selected from "L'Encyclopédie ou Dictionnaire Raisonné des Sciences, des Arts, et des Métiers," of Denis Diderot, edited with text by C. Gillispie. Over 2000 illustrations on 485 full-page plates. Magnificent 18th century engravings of men, women, and children working at such trades as milling flour, cheesemaking, charcoal burning, mining, silverplating, shoeing horses, making fine glass, printing, hundreds more, showing details of machinery, different steps in sequence, etc. A remarkable art work, but also the largest collection of working figures in print, copyright-free, for art directors, designers, etc. Two vols. 920pp. 9 x 12. Heavy library cloth. T421 Two volume set **$18.50**

* * *

SILK SCREEN TECHNIQUES, J. Biegeleisen, M. Cohn. A practical step-by-step home course in one of the most versatile, least expensive graphic arts processes. How to build an inexpensive silk screen, prepare stencils, print, achieve special textures, use color, etc. Every step explained, diagrammed. 149 illustrations, 8 in color. 201pp. 6⅛ x 9¼. T433 Paperbound **$1.45**

MATHEMATICS, MAGIC AND MYSTERY, Martin Gardner. Astonishing feats of mind reading, mystifying "magic" tricks, are often based on mathematical principles anyone can learn. This book shows you how to perform scores of tricks with cards, dice, coins, knots, numbers, etc., by using simple principles from set theory, theory of numbers, topology, other areas of mathematics, fascinating in themselves. No special knowledge required. 135 illus. 186pp. 5⅜ x 8.
T335 Paperbound **$1.00**

MATHEMATICAL PUZZLES FOR BEGINNERS AND ENTHUSIASTS, G. Mott-Smoth. Test your problem-solving techniques and powers of inference on 188 challenging, amusing puzzles based on algebra, dissection of plane figures, permutations, probabilities, etc. Appendix of primes, square roots, etc. 135 illus. 2nd revised edition. 248pp. 5⅜ x 8.
T198 Paperbound **$1.00**

LEARN CHESS FROM THE MASTERS, F. Reinfeld. Play 10 games against Marshall, Bronstein, Najdorf, other masters, and grade yourself on each move. Detailed annotations reveal principles of play, strategy, etc. as you proceed. An excellent way to get a real insight into the game. Formerly titled, "Chess by Yourself." 91 diagrams. vii + 144pp. 5⅜ x 8.
T362 Paperbound **$1.00**

REINFELD ON THE END GAME IN CHESS, F. Reinfeld. 62 end games of Alekhine, Tarrasch, Morphy, other masters, are carefully analyzed with emphasis on transition from middle game to end play. Tempo moves, queen endings, weak squares, other basic principles clearly illustrated. Excellent for understanding why some moves are weak or incorrect, how to avoid errors. Formerly titled, "Practical End-game Play." 62 diagrams. vi + 177pp. 5⅜ x 8.
T417 Paperbound **$1.25**

101 PUZZLES IN THOUGHT AND LOGIC, C. R. Wylie, Jr. Brand new puzzles you need no special knowledge to solve! Each one is a gem of ingenuity that will really challenge your problem-solving technique. Introduction with simplified explanation of scientic puzzle solving. 128pp. 5⅜ x 8.
T167 Paperbound **$1.00**

THE COMPLETE NONSENSE OF EDWARD LEAR. The only complete edition of this master of gentle madness at a popular price. The Dong with the Luminous Nose, The Jumblies, The Owl and the Pussycat, hundreds of other bits of wonderful nonsense. 214 limericks, 3 sets of Nonsense Botany, 5 Nonsense Alphabets, 546 fantastic drawings, much more. 320pp. 5⅜ x 8.
T167 Paperbound **$1.00**

28 SCIENCE FICTION STORIES OF H. G. WELLS. Two complete novels, "Men Like Gods" and "Star Begotten," plus 26 short stories by the master science-fiction writer of all time. Stories of space, time, future adventure that are among the all-time classics of science fiction. 928pp. 5⅜ x 8.
T265 Clothbound **$3.95**

SEVEN SCIENCE FICTION NOVELS, H. G. Wells. Unabridged texts of "The Time Machine," "The Island of Dr. Moreau," "First Men in the Moon," "The Invisible Man," "The War of the Worlds," "The Food of the Gods," "In the Days of the Comet." "One will have to go far to match this for entertainment, excitement, and sheer pleasure," N. Y. TIMES. 1015pp. 5⅜ x 8.
T264 Clothbound **$3.95**

MATHEMAGIC, MAGIC PUZZLES, AND GAMES WITH NUMBERS, R. V. Heath. More than 60 new puzzles and stunts based on number properties: multiplying large numbers mentally, finding the date of any day in the year, etc. Edited by J. S. Meyer. 76 illus. 129pp. 5⅜ x 8.
T110 Paperbound **$1.00**

FIVE ADVENTURE NOVELS OF H. RIDER HAGGARD. The master story-teller's five best tales of mystery and adventure set against authentic African backgrounds: "She," "King Solomon's Mines," "Allan Quatermain," "Allan's Wife," "Maiwa's Revenge." 821pp. 5⅜ x 8.
T108 Clothbound **$3.95**

WIN AT CHECKERS, M. Hopper. (Formerly "Checkers.") The former World's Unrestricted Checker Champion gives you valuable lessons in openings, traps, end games, ways to draw when you are behind, etc. More than 100 questions and answers anticipate your problems. Appendix. 75 problems diagrammed, solved. 79 figures. xi + 107pp. 5⅜ x 8.
T363 Paperbound **$1.00**

CRYPTOGRAPHY, L. D. Smith. Excellent introductory work on ciphers and their solution, history of secret writing, techniques, etc. Appendices on Japanese methods, the Baconian cipher, frequency tables. Bibliography. Over 150 problems, solutions. 160pp. 5⅜ x 8.
T247 Paperbound **$1.00**

CRYPTANALYSIS, H. F. Gaines. (Formerly, "Elementary Cryptanalysis.") The best book available on cryptograms and how to solve them. Contains all major techniques: substitution, transposition, mixed alphabets, multafid, Kasiski and Vignere methods, etc. Word frequency appendix. 167 problems, solutions. 173 figures. 236pp. 5⅜ x 8.
T97 Paperbound **$1.95**

FLATLAND, E. A. Abbot. The science-fiction classic of life in a 2-dimensional world that is considered a first-rate introduction to relativity and hyperspace, as well as a scathing satire on society, politics and religion. 7th edition. 16 illus. 128pp. 5⅜ x 8.
T1 Paperbound **$1.00**

DOVER BOOKS

HOW TO FORCE CHECKMATE, F. Reinfeld. (Formerly "Challenge to Chessplayers.") No board needed to sharpen your checkmate skill on 300 checkmate situations. Learn to plan up to 3 moves ahead and play a superior end game. 300 situations diagrammed; notes and full solutions. 111pp. 5⅜ x 8.   T439 Paperbound **$1.25**

MORPHY'S GAMES OF CHESS, P. W. Sergeant, ed. Play forcefully by following the techniques used by one of the greatest chess champions. 300 of Morphy's games carefully annotated to reveal principles. Bibliography. New introduction by F. Reinfeld. 235 diagrams. x + 352pp. 5⅜ x 8.   T386 Paperbound **$1.75**

MATHEMATICAL RECREATIONS, M. Kraitchik. Hundreds of unusual mathematical puzzlers and odd bypaths of math, elementary and advanced. Greek, Medieval, Arabic, Hindu problems; figurate numbers, Fermat numbers, primes; magic, Euler, Latin squares; fairy chess, latruncles, reversi, jinx, ruma, tetrachrome other positional and permutational games. Rigorous solutions. Revised second edition. 181 illus. 330pp. 5⅜ x 8.   T163 Paperbound **$1.75**

MATHEMATICAL EXCURSIONS, H. A. Merrill. Revealing stimulating insights into elementary math, not usually taught in school. 90 problems demonstrate Russian peasant multiplication, memory systems for pi, magic squares, dyadic systems, division by inspection, many more. Solutions to difficult problems. 50 illus. 5⅜ x 8.   T350 Paperbound **$1.00**

MAGIC TRICKS & CARD TRICKS, W. Jonson. Best introduction to tricks with coins, bills, eggs, ribbons, slates, cards, easily performed without elaborate equipment. Professional routines, tips on presentation, misdirection, etc. Two books bound as one: 52 tricks with cards, 37 tricks with common objects. 106 figures. 224pp. 5⅜ x 8.   T909 Paperbound **$1.00**

MATHEMATICAL PUZZLES OF SAM LOYD, selected and edited by M. Gardner. 177 most ingenious mathematical puzzles of America's greatest puzzle originator, based on arithmetic, algebra, game theory, dissection, route tracing, operations research, probability, etc. 120 drawings, diagrams. Solutions. 187pp. 5⅜ x 8.   T498 Paperbound **$1.00**

THE ART OF CHESS, J. Mason. The most famous general study of chess ever written. More than 90 openings, middle game, end game, how to attack, sacrifice, defend, exchange, form general strategy. Supplement on "How Do You Play Chess?" by F. Reinfeld. 448 diagrams. 356pp. 5⅜ x 8.   T463 Paperbound **$1.85**

HYPERMODERN CHESS as Developed in the Games of its Greatest Exponent, ARON NIMZOVICH, F. Reinfeld, ed. Learn how the game's greatest innovator defeated Alekhine, Lasker, and many others; and use these methods in your own game. 180 diagrams. 228pp. 5⅜ x 8.   T448 Paperbound **$1.35**

A TREASURY OF CHESS LORE, F. Reinfeld, ed. Hundreds of fascinating stories by and about the masters, accounts of tournaments and famous games, aphorisms, word portraits, little known incidents, photographs, etc., that will delight the chess enthusiast, captivate the beginner. 49 photographs (14 full-page plates), 12 diagrams. 315pp. 5⅜ x 8.   T458 Paperbound **$1.75**

A NONSENSE ANTHOLOGY, collected by Carolyn Wells. 245 of the best nonsense verses ever written: nonsense puns, absurd arguments, mock epics, nonsense ballads, "sick" verses, dog-Latin verses, French nonsense verses, limericks. Lear, Carroll, Belloc, Burgess, nearly 100 other writers. Introduction by Carolyn Wells. 3 indices: Title, Author, First Lines. xxxiii + 279pp. 5⅜ x 8.   T499 Paperbound **$1.25**

SYMBOLIC LOGIC and THE GAME OF LOGIC, Lewis Carroll. Two delightful puzzle books by the author of "Alice," bound as one. Both works concern the symbolic representation of traditional logic and together contain more than 500 ingenious, amusing and instructive syllogistic puzzlers. Total of 326pp. 5⅜ x 8.   T492 Paperbound **$1.50**

PILLOW PROBLEMS and A TANGLED TALE, Lewis Carroll. Two of Carroll's rare puzzle works bound as one. "Pillow Problems" contain 72 original math puzzles. The puzzles in "A Tangled Tale" are given in delightful story form. Total of 291pp. 5⅜ x 8.   T493 Paperbound **$1.50**

PECK'S BAD BOY AND HIS PA, G. W. Peck. Both volumes of one of the most widely read of all American humor books. A classic of American folk humor, also invaluable as a portrait of an age. 100 original illustrations. Introduction by E. Bleiler. 347pp. 5⅜ x 8.   T497 Paperbound **$1.35**

Dover publishes books on art, music, philosophy, literature, languages, history, social sciences, psychology, handcrafts, orientalia, puzzles and entertainments, chess, pets and gardens, books explaining science, intermediate and higher mathematics mathematical physics, engineering, biological sciences, earth sciences, classics of science, etc.
Write to:

Dept. catrr.
Dover Publications, Inc.
180 Varick Street, N. Y. 14, N. Y.